D0197148

Making Waves

A History

of Feminism

in Western

Society

NATIONAL UNIVERSITY
LIBRARY   SAN DIEGO

Making Waves

A History of Feminism in Western Society

Marlene LeGates

Capilano College

COPP CLARK LTD.
Toronto

© Copp Clark Ltd., 1996

No part of this publication may be reproduced, stored in a retrieval system or transmitted, in any form or by any means, without the prior written permission of the publisher or, in the case of photocopying or other reprographic copying, a licence from CANCOPY (Canadian Copyright Licensing Agency), 6 Adelaide Street East, Suite 900, Toronto, Ontario, M5C 1H6.

An honest attempt has been made to secure permission for the material contained herein. Any errors or omissions are wholly unintentional, and the Publisher will be grateful to learn of them.

ISBN: 0-7330-5483-9

Publisher: Jeff Miller
Managing editor: Barbara Tessman
Editor: Camilla Jenkins
Developmental editor: Bay Ryley
Designer: Kyle Gell
Cover design: Mary Opper
Cover photo: © Michael Gosbee/The Image Bank
Typesetter: Carol Magee
Printing and binding: Metrolitho

Canadian Cataloguing in Publication Data

LeGates, Marlene
Making waves: a history of feminism in Western society
Includes bibliographical references and index.
ISBN 0-7730-5483-9
1. Feminism - History.   I. Title.
HQ1121.L44 1996   305.42'09   C95-932728-2

Copp Clark Ltd.
2775 Matheson Blvd. East
Mississauga, Ontario
L4W 4P7

Printed and bound in Canada

1   2   3   4   5   5483-9   00 99 98 97 96

Contents

To Al Dreher and Rebecca LeGates

Preface

The last twenty years have witnessed a veritable explosion in the writing of women's history. This book is an attempt to explain one part of it, the history of feminism, based on the best of modern scholarship.

Although I began writing this book in the summer of 1992, in a sense I have been working on it throughout those twenty years, actually twenty-four. The year 1972 marked a beginning in two ways: I became a mother and also a teacher of women's history. My daughter became a feminist and a women's studies graduate, and my work in women's history has resulted in this book. My daughter and my students have together been sources of inspiration. I began to write in order to explain to them their place and mine, as feminists, in history. The brief history of the second women's movement that resulted, designed as a supplementary reading for my women's history class, would become Chapter 10 of this book. Before I could explain it to others. I needed to understand as a historian what I had experienced as a participant.

At the same time, I was exploring the history of feminism from the other end of the time frame, in my persona as a historian of early modern Europe. The result was a lecture that I gave in 1989 on feminism in historical perspective for the Women's Studies Lecture Series at Capilano College, the first in a series of public lectures designed for colleges, high schools, and other groups. I found that there was a general audience as well as an academic one interested in the topic. I owe a great deal to Sandra Moe and my other colleagues who initiated the lecture series and kept our Women's Studies Program alive through hard times and to Karin Lind, who first suggested that I write down some of the wonderful stories I had collected.

This book is intended, then, as an historical introduction for students and non-students to what has become arguably the most important social movement of our time. It is also an exploration, a critical study of individuals and issues placed within the social context of their times. It will have succeeded if it gives food for thought, stimulating readers to read more or even to find answers of their own.

I owe a great debt to those who encouraged me in my writing, Karen Ewing and Cam Sylvester, as well as those who read and commented on individual chapters: Robert Campbell, Sheila Delany, Margot Dreher, Graham Forst, Rhoda Friedrichs, Brenda Ireland, Sandra Moe, and Patricia Singer. I owe special thanks to Mary Lynn Stewart, who read the entire manuscript; Karen Offen, who read the later chapters as well as making available the first three chapters of her book-in-progress on the history of European feminism; Monica Sandor, who corrected many points in Chapter 2; and the anonymous reviewer who read Chapter 10 and suggested helpful additions. Camilla Jenkins provided skilful and diligent copy editing; my editors, Jeffrey Miller and Barbara Tessman, were invaluably supportive. Joan Hollman, Laraine Hamilton, and Katrina Watts showed remarkable patience; Capilano College library staff David Lambert and James Kwok and the Interlibrary Loan office at the University of British Columbia assisted greatly; and the Capilano Professional Development Committee generously provided a one-term paid leave and a small grant to work on the project.

For me this book has been a delight to write, but my friends and family may not have experienced it in the same way. Although my dedication to this project meant that my partner had to take over full responsibility for home and garden, cope with the financial loss from the reduced teaching loads and unpaid leave necessary to complete it, and accept the redefinition of shared activities as footnote checking and proofreading instead of kayaking and backpacking, he never once complained. Nor did he ever waver in his support and conviction of its worth. To him and to my daughter, who also devoted many hours to helping with it and countless more to listening about it, I dedicate this book.

I

Feminism and Patriarchy: An Introduction

While I was writing this book, my daughter presented me with the latest copy of *Ms.* magazine, featuring the lead article, "50 Ways to Be a Feminist." With photos and descriptions of fifty individuals the feature reported, "The beauty of this movement of ours is that it's so fluid—ever moving, evolving, growing. . . . If we devoted every page of every issue for the next 22 years to describing the many ways you are putting feminism into practice, we still wouldn't come close to covering it all."[1]

How to harness that approach for my history of feminism, I wondered. Could I write about the fifty ways, or five hundred ways for that matter, of "having been" a feminist? The grammatical difficulties aside, the idea of capturing the fluidity of feminism over time was what I hoped this book would do. I wanted to catalogue and evaluate all the diverse strategies that women have developed to challenge patriarchal control, whether in thought or action.

Two problems demanded some resolution, however, before I could define the parameters of my topic. The first was how to deal with current issues debated by feminist scholars, such as the relative importance of differences or similarities among women or the need to evaluate different theoretical perspectives. The second was the problem of looking at the past through the concerns of the present. How could I define feminism in a way that was meaningful over time and yet do justice to the specific contexts that constrained the choices open to individuals?

I found no easy or conclusive way of resolving either of those problems and decided that to do so at the start of my research would in fact be unwise and arbitrary. I therefore resolved to consider all possibilities as defined by other historians, including those who employed the adjective *feminist* to immensely diverse individuals and time periods. Their judgments, as well as primary sources from the periods under consideration, constituted the raw material for my analysis. The result is intended to be both an analysis of key thinkers and activists and a synthesis of a new and exciting tradition of historical scholarship.

FINDING FEMINISM

> *Every feminist has their own private feminism.*

MADELEINE PELLETIER, 1908

> *I myself have never been able to find out precisely what feminism is, I only know that people call me a feminist whenever I express sentiments that differentiate me from a doormat or a prostitute.*

REBECCA WEST, 1913

One of the major issues in contemporary feminism is the debate over difference. This concern has been raised in part by women of colour, who have objected to the inclination of white, middle-class feminists to assume they include all women when they speak of "we." The challenge is to acknowledge women's diversity while simultaneously describing their oppression as a group. How does one give adequate weight to the experiences that women have in common while respecting those that divide them? Is gender a stronger bond than class or race? Is it true, as a contemporary feminist claims, that "any woman in the world has more in common with any other woman—regardless of class, race, age, ethnic group, nationality—than any woman has with any man"?[2]

White, middle-class feminists, who have predominated in organized feminist movements, have tended to think so. In fact, many scholars agree that the recognition of women as an oppressed social group was a precondition for the development of feminist theory. In her analysis of the women's movement in the United States in the 1970s, Joan Cassell wrote, "When a woman's consciousness is raised, she perceives herself and other women as members of a degraded group and is committed to altering this state." To come to this perception, women had to disassociate themselves, Cassell believed, from their primary ties to men, that is, ties of family, class, race, or culture. Rather than looking down on or up to other women, they had to perceive themselves "as part of a group composed of women."[3] Cassell's view, reasonable as it seems, assumes that gender can be isolated from other parts of a woman's identity. This assumption reflects the perspective of one whose class and ethnic identity are not problematic because they are privileged.

This kind of thinking characterized much of first-wave feminism, the organized women's movements of the late nineteenth and early twentieth centuries. The French activist Nelly Roussel, for example, assumed that all women had interests in common. "Among us there are no 'ruling classes,' no 'privileged classes,'" she wrote in 1904. "*All of us* can declare war on today's society, for all of us are more or less ruined, our bodies, our hearts, our consciences brutalized by its laws. Great ladies are mistreated by princely brutes; *bourgeoises* dispossessed of their property; working women frustrated by their meager salaries."[4]

Some feminists today continue this "essentialist" view. What unites women, they argue—what is essentially common to all women—is their experience of male oppression. As a result of their social conditioning, women emphasize relationships and responsibilities to others; they learn to value sharing and nurture, co-operation, and connection. These values may translate into women's greater support for political candidates who promote peace or ecology. They can also have repercussions for science and medicine, which have traditionally been male defined. For Barbara McClintock, a biologist who won the 1983 Nobel Prize, scientific investigation assumes a complex relation between the self and the object studied, between mind and nature. An holistic outlook may be more natural to women because of the importance they give to relationships. Note that these values are not necessarily linked to a female *nature*—although some contemporary feminists will so argue—but can be accepted as the result of a gendered social *experience*, in which girls learn to be person oriented and boys are encouraged to manipulate objects, distancing themselves from them in order to analyze or control them.

Other feminists disagree with this emphasis on commonality, insisting instead that any generalization of women's experiences does an injustice to their diversity. Two historians conclude from their research into early nineteenth-century French feminism, "We have had to acknowledge that we cannot truly know how women who are different from ourselves—women of other races, ethnicities, religions, classes, sexual orientations—experience oppression; nor can we know this for women of the past."[5] It is easy to point out that Nelly Roussel is simply wrong in her denial that "privileged classes" exist among women. In the early twentieth century, when Roussel was writing, most upper- and middle-class women had, and assumed they would always have, female servants. Few feminists of Roussel's time would have recognized themselves as oppressors of other women.

This issue has significant implications for how one goes about writing a history of feminism. Because women of colour or working-class women experience multiple oppressions, gender oppression may not stand out for them in the way it does for other women. Chicana, black, and Asian-American feminists have in fact explicitly repudiated a feminism that does not go beyond gender issues. May it not be the case that only the most advantaged women have had the privilege of focusing on gender oppression and thus of defining themselves historically as feminists? Is a history of Western feminism, then, inherently an elitist exercise? How can such a project be compatible with an understanding of feminism as a movement that challenges all injustices? What, then, would not be a feminist issue?

I believe it is too simplistic to define feminism historically as an exclusively middle-class movement. It is true that most activists were relatively privileged. In fact it was often awareness of the privileges of the men closest to them—for example, the education available to their brothers and not to themselves—that sparked their sense of gender injustice. At the same time, their own economic dependency left them vulnerable. Many personally experienced the fineness of the line between middle and lower class and even poverty or destitution.

In certain countries, such as the United States and England, feminist movements developed a relatively heterogeneous membership. It is nonetheless true that the women who were most aware of class divisions usually chose not to identify themselves as feminists. This was so even when they consciously struggled against gender oppression. These women thought of themselves as socialists and often identified feminists as their chief enemy because they believed that feminism detracted from the class struggle of workers against capitalists. Should they be included in a history of feminism? What about working women who fought to improve their material situation and that of their families? Their lack of property or higher education made any protest against unjust property laws or professional barriers, both traditional feminist concerns, irrelevant, but they organized around economic issues just the same. Were seventeenth-century French women who attacked and mutilated tax collectors feminists? Barcelona housewives and women textile workers who demonstrated against high prices in 1918? African-American and African-Canadian women who organized services for their communities? Jewish women in Toronto during the Great Depression who boycotted kosher butchers because of high prices? Is a history of feminism simply a history of women's activism?

Other historians have suggested a way to resolve these difficulties by distinguishing between different kinds of women's activism. Temma Kaplan, for example, describes the actions of the Barcelona housewives as rooted in a *female* rather than a feminist consciousness because they were acting in accordance with traditional gender roles. As wives and mothers, they were motivated by their concern for the well-being of their families. Nancy Cott adds another category of communal or group consciousness to distinguish women's actions that come from a sense of belonging to a community, defined perhaps by race or class. Black women's activism within their communities could fall into this category, as could the actions of working women supporting their husbands' union activities. What is interesting, however, is that women motivated by a female or communal consciousness could act in ways inconsistent with gender roles or community expectations. Distinguishing women's activism from feminism, Cott argues, "Feminism should designate something more specific than women's entrance into public life . . . [namely] an [expressed] intention to alter gender hierarchy."[6] In conservative societies such as France or Germany in the late nineteenth century, however, women's demands to enter public life were undeniably feminist. It is crucial therefore to analyze specific contexts. If feminism is one strategy for social change, it is important to explore just why and under what conditions women's activism becomes feminism.

Theoretical Approaches

Another major issue in contemporary feminism, alongside the debate over differences among women, is how to evaluate different varieties of feminism. The list of feminisms today is bewildering: liberal, equity, equal or natural rights feminism, Marxist feminism, socialist feminism (further divisible into dual or unified systems theory feminism), radical feminism, revolutionary feminism, reform feminism, cultural feminism, existential feminism, psycho-analytic feminism (with a split between object-relations and Lacanian theory feminists), postmodern feminism, black feminism, Jewish feminism, Asian feminism, Chicana feminism (with possible subdivisions of Chicana liberal, Chicana cultural nationalist, and Chicana insurgent feminism), and status-oriented or survival-oriented feminism, to suggest only some possibilities! The past had its feminisms also. Writing in 1915 Katharine Anthony identified the following divisions within the women's movement in Germany alone: socialist feminism and bourgeois feminism; conservative, moderate, and radical feminism; Christian and neutral feminism; old feminism and young feminism; suffrage feminism and feminist feminism. Can we be as positive as she was that those divisions were "only the growing pains of a healthy coalescence"?[7]

Perhaps the most important theoretical distinction today with antecedents in the past is the distinction between liberal, equity, or equal rights feminism on the one hand and cultural feminism on the other. Liberal or equal rights feminism originated during the eighteenth-century Enlightenment. Cultural feminism is similar to what in the late nineteenth and early twentieth centuries was called social or maternal feminism. Some claim, not without justification, that feminism has always oscillated between these two poles. What is this difference and why is it important?

Whereas liberal or equal rights feminism stresses the similarity of women and men, cultural feminism emphasizes their differences. The former has as its goal the creation of a society free of gender distinctions. As Judith Lorber puts it, "The long-term goal of feminism must be no less than the eradication of gender as an organizing principle of postindustrial society."[8]

Cultural feminists, on the other hand, adopt what can be called a woman-centred perspective, one that values the female values and culture arising from women's unique experiences. To surrender this uniqueness, cultural feminists maintain, is to capitulate to male norms of equality as sameness. Defining feminism as the pursuit of equality with men fails to challenge male values just as it fails to ask, to which men do women want to be equal? Cultural feminists would not agree with a definition of feminism as the pursuit of political, economic, or legal equality. Their alternative is to define feminism in terms of women's growing autonomy, judging their success by the extent to which women have imposed their values on society. Note, by the way, that this alternative rules out the possibility that men can be feminists.

While liberal feminism looks to women's gain of legal and political rights, one of the most forceful contemporary applications of cultural feminism has been to question whether women have really progressed by gaining these rights historically. In her study of American legal history, Joan Hoff analyzes the "enormous time-lags" between what women demand and what they finally achieve. Because women have wanted only what men have been prepared to give them, it has always been "too little, too late." By the time of women's so-called victory, economic and social developments had already left them behind, and "almost without exception each legal change or improvement . . . has reflected the American past, not its future."[9] Hoff calls for a radical or cultural feminist vision based on women's standards of justice and progress, inspiring change rather than reflecting it.

But varieties of cultural feminism in the past have not necessarily always had radical implications. Take, for example, the issue of motherhood in first-wave feminism. Because so many of women's experiences have been linked with motherhood, many feminists have tried to redefine its social importance, as opposed to rejecting it. Hence the term *maternal feminism*. Was this a subversion or a surrender? Was maternal feminism inherently radical in taking women's experience as its standard? Or did it represent an accommodation to gendered assumptions about women as mothers? Were maternal feminists reaching out to ordinary women, women who found their self-worth in mothering, in a laudable attempt to radicalize them? Or were they using the lowest common denominator as an expedient move to gain broader support?

To put these questions another way, what is the difference between a female consciousness and a feminist one? Women's reaction to denigration can be—and has often been—the celebration of values that the dominant culture disparages. Were the women poets and writers who helped to create and celebrate a female literary tradition from the Middle Ages on feminists even if they did not mention women's oppression in their writings? Is any strategy that circumvents or subtly challenges traditional gender expectations necessarily a feminist one? Is the recognition of a female culture a precondition for feminism? Or does feminism arise rather as a reaction *against* a female culture?

Again, the answers lie in analyzing specific historical contexts. Women's culture had different implications when it was represented by, for example, nuns in the late Middle Ages, suffragists in the late nineteenth century, or fascist women in Nazi Germany. My focus in any case has not been to provide answers so much as to illustrate issues. I would much rather open possibilities, so that we can appreciate the breadth of women's concerns and strategies, than eliminate them by imposing an arbitrary definition of feminism on the past.

In indicating my intent to relate feminism to historical contexts, however, I am taking a position with which many cultural feminists would disagree. My use in this book of traditional historical terms and chronology can be criticized by cultural feminists as the adoption of "male-derived" categories. There is truth in their objection, which I override partly in the interests of simplicity and partly in the belief that it is useful to know just how exclusive or inclusive traditional categories are when applied to women's issues and experiences. I am not a determinist in the sense of believing that a situation determines how individuals and groups will operate, but I do believe that it determines the choices open to them.

Feminists before Feminism?

All historians run the risk of inadvertently reading their own values into the past. The word *feminism,* for example, is of surprisingly recent origin, arising barely one hundred years ago. To use the word in relation to anything before the late nineteenth century is anachronistic. Some historians have therefore scrupulously avoided doing so. Others speak of prefeminism, protofeminism, or primitive feminism. What is the truth behind these qualifications? Did the phenomenon exist before the word? Were there feminists before feminism?

If we define feminism as an *organized* movement for women's rights and interests, we can find it in the mid-nineteenth century, when women's movements first arose in North America and Europe, but we are still faced with the problem of finding an adequate term for earlier advocates for women. Nonetheless, as historians have recognized, neither women's consciousness of their own oppression nor the determination of individuals and groups to combat it was dependent on the birth of modern terminology. This consciousness is what I have looked for in early feminism. Further, one has to ask what form feminism could take in traditional European society before the English, American, and French revolutions of the late seventeenth and eighteenth centuries created a vocabulary of liberation.

This problem has not hindered historians from considering such early historical figures as Jesus or Queen Elizabeth I as feminists. The early fifteenth-century writer Christine de Pizan is commonly regarded as a feminist, the first to be recorded. Yet what do we make of her defence of the traditional subordination of woman to man, "God has . . . ordained man and woman to serve Him in different offices . . . each in their ordained task"? Or of her advice to women to "be humble and patient"?[10] Here was no demand for equal rights or shared political power.

Just as women experience their oppression differently in different times, places, and social situations, so they express their protests differently as well. Christine de Pizan did not use the term *patriarchy,* nor did she question male dominance. She did object to the way women as a group were treated, however, and she was concerned to rectify it. I recognize her objection and concern, within that context, as feminist. We cannot expect her and her contemporaries to embrace our critique of their society, but we can appreciate her contribution to the process of questioning traditions that subordinated women.

In the pages that follow, we meet a wide variety of women and of protests. The first part of the book, covering the period from late antiquity to the French Revolution, explores the difficulty of finding feminism in the absence of theories of social change. Individuals did protest against patriarchy. Rebellious women disguised themselves as men, escaped from fiancés or parents, defied priests, beat or poisoned husbands or masters, became vagabonds, or took to their beds. The observation of Charlotte Woodward, a nineteenth-century American working woman who believed that in her time there was no community "in which the souls of some women were not beating their wings in rebellion,"[11] is surely applicable to periods before the nineteenth century as well. Whether this beating of wings became public depended on the context. Religious women in the Middle Ages, for example, had to find sympathetic male scribes to record their visions.

Historian Lyle Koehler has summarized the limitations of seventeenth-century New England women who rebelled against the church: "Not always aware of the causes of their rebelliousness, [women heretics] had no social formula for restructuring the world in which they lived. As women hungry for freedom but restricted by seventeenth-century awarenesses, they could do little more than adapt their religious beliefs into a vehicle for protest." Only when tools of change were available, whether in the form of new ideas or economic options, could feminism become such a formula for restructuring society. Until then how many were there like the Puritan Elizabeth White, who described herself as outwardly "somewhat more Mild" than other women but inwardly "like a Wolf chained up"?[12] As with so many other women, her inner turmoil brought her only depression and illness.

In this early stage of feminism, before the late eighteenth century, women were attempting to find a voice in a predominantly male culture. They tended to find their motivation in religion, education or the lack of it, or the literary debate known as the *querelle des femmes*. These subjects are explored in Chapters 2, 3, and 4. The querelle des femmes, or the woman question, prompted women's recognition of themselves as a social group and thus bridged the gap between individual protest and feminist theory. Though it inspired women to speak out against discrimination and disparagement, however, they did not yet attempt to effect change in institutions. Women could only plead for better treatment or, like Christine de Pizan, counsel resignation and accommodation. The insight that women should act on their sense of grievance is historically the culmination of a long process.

Demands for institutional change became possible only when institutions were seen to be of human rather than of divine origin. This realization, which triggered a second stage of feminism, came from developments in the late seventeenth and eighteenth centuries, documented in Chapters 5 and 6. This second stage forms a transition to the study of organized feminist movements, described in Chapters 7 to 10. Within this third stage, organized movements have commonly been divided into first-wave feminism (nineteenth and early twentieth centuries) and second-wave feminism (beginning in the mid- or late 1960s).

The Complexity of Causes

Like early feminism, the organized feminism of the nineteenth and twentieth centuries poses challenges to the historian. Take the question of causes. Is it possible to generalize about what caused feminist movements? First-wave feminism has been linked to nineteenth-century intellectual, religious, and economic developments, specifically liberalism, Protestantism, and the Industrial Revolution. Many studies agree that liberalism and Protestantism generated the idea of feminism; the Industrial Revolution, by taking work out of the home and giving middle-class women leisure, created the opportunity to put the idea into action.

The reality is more complex. The liberal emphasis on individualism and equality that justified the American and French revolutions in the late eighteenth century inspired women to apply the language of "the rights of man" to themselves. But inspiration also came from the early or utopian socialists, who opposed the liberal ideology of equal rights as abstract and selfishly individualist. Feminism was also associated closely but not exclusively with Protestantism. Protestantism, or any religion for that matter, could as easily inspire a defence of the status quo as a challenge to it. Nor was feminism exclusively middle-class. The relation between intellectual, political, and economic developments and feminist thought is too complex to be limited to any one formula.

That said, I must admit that I find the theory of relative status deprivation an intriguing explanation for the rise of feminism. It has been suggested as a cause of feminism in the Renaissance and in the seventeenth century as well as of first- and second-wave feminist movements. Status deprivation in this context means that women experienced fewer opportunities while groups with which they were associated—their brothers or husbands for example—found greater opportunities. Women could also experience the discrepancy between traditional expectations, usually centred around domesticity, and new ones, such as the need to increase the family's income through paid employment. Alternatively, consider the tension between the ideals of individualism and self-fulfilment, so important in modern society, and women's continued dependence on fathers or husbands. All of these contributed to women's awareness of gender grievance. Yet I prefer to see the result not as a linear progression but as a series of fluctuating discrepancies between possibilities and realities.

The problem of identifying the causes of feminism raises the problem of isolating, and thus categorizing, its different branches. A distinction is commonly made between moderate, radical, and socialist feminism, but the attempt to codify different branches of feminism also founders on the messiness of the past. Recall Katharine Anthony's long list of varieties of German feminism that she found in 1915. What seems moderate in one context is radical in another. The demand for women's suffrage was very radical initially, yet is often considered characteristic of moderate feminism. By the late nineteenth century it was moderate in North America but remained radical in Germany. Thus I have tried to do justice to the complexities of particular contexts.

We can draw two different "lessons" from the history of feminism. One is the depressing awareness that little has changed for women over so many years, that many people have expended their time and energy in the same causes. When Margaret Haig, Lady Rhondda, wrote that she founded the feminist weekly *Time and Tide* in the 1920s because she wanted "passionately, urgently, to change customs and influence ideas,"[13] her words seem pathetic given the forces of conservatism that swamped feminism in the interwar years. Why did so little come of her efforts and those of all the other women who laboured so hard for so many decades?

There is, however, another lesson of the past, and that is to appreciate just how radical feminism is. The strength of resistance that feminists have aroused is the measure of the revolutionary nature of their demands. Elizabeth Cady Stanton, one of the founders of the nineteenth-century American women's movement in 1848, recognized this when she recorded the response to the meeting that initiated the movement: "No words could express our astonishment on finding, a few days afterward, that what seemed to us so timely, so rational, and so sacred, should be a subject for sarcasm and ridicule." She quoted a senator who understood feminism's revolutionary message:

> If there is any revolutionary claim in this country, it is that of woman suffrage. [Laughter.] It revolutionizes society; it revolutionizes religion; it revolutionizes the Constitution and laws; and it revolutionizes the opinions of those so old-fashioned among us as to believe that the legitimate and proper sphere of woman is the family circle, as wife and mother, and not as politician and voter.[14]

Rather than conservative hyperbole, these sentiments express precisely the implications of feminism. Should we wonder why progress at times was so slow? Perhaps we can appreciate the obstacles more when we begin with a look at the nature of patriarchy in Western society for, illogical as it may seem, antifeminism preceded feminism.

DESCRIBING PATRIARCHY

I am independent, king, lord of all!

GEORGE HAM, a farmer in Upper Canada,
responding to his abused wife Esther,
who asked to reconcile with him, 1825

What are the traditions and practices that have subordinated women and where did they come from? What assumptions have feminists had to battle? What obstacles have they encountered in forming and expressing their views?

Unlike the word *feminism,* which is just over a hundred years old, *patriarchy* is an ancient word, meaning in Greek, "the rule of the father" and originally used to describe the herding societies of the Old Testament, in which the authority of the father over family members was practically absolute. It acquired its feminist meaning relatively recently when Kate Millett, in *Sexual Politics* (1969), used it to describe male domination over women. While feminists may dispute the origins of patriarchy, most will confidently assert that patriarchy is as old as civilization itself. Why was this the case? Why do we have to wait until the fifteenth or seventeenth century to find the beginnings of feminist theory or until the mid-nineteenth century to find organized feminist movements? Why did the demand for equality take as long as it did to develop if the oppression of women is so ancient?

Generalizations about patriarchy are risky because of the ways in which its impact on individuals varies, and not only by class, culture, or race. Within the same generation, the same town or village, the same neighbourhood, manor, or tenement, individual circumstance and personality dilute or strengthen what society accepts as legal and traditional. Within everyone's experience are examples of women who benefit from and help to perpetuate patriarchal attitudes and men who do not. The English author Carolyn Steedman, recounting her 1950s childhood, writes, "A father like mine dictated each day's existence; our lives would have been quite different had he not been there. But he didn't *matter*, and his singular unimportance needs explaining. His not mattering has an effect like this: I don't quite believe in male power; somehow the iron of patriarchy didn't enter into my soul."[15] Her father's authority was blunted not only by his frequent absences but also by his vulnerability in the outside world. Steedman describes how an outing with her father ended in a confrontation with a forestkeeper, which revealed to her her father's powerlessness.

But patriarchy is not so much about individual men or women and their personal and familial relationships as it is about institutions and values, politics and culture, and concepts of authority and order. Feminist theorist Juliet Mitchell puts it this way:

> A patriarchal society bequeaths its structure to each of us (with important variations according to the material conditions of class and race), [and] gives us . . . the cultural air we breathe. . . . Whether or not the actual father is there does not affect the perpetration of the patriarchal culture within the psychology of the individual; present or absent "the father" always has his place. His actual absence may cause confusion, or on another level, relief, but the only difference it makes is within the terms of the overall patriarchal assumption of his presence. In our culture he is just as present in his absence.[16]

Kate Millett defined patriarchy in terms of its public dimension: "The military, industry, technology, universities, science, political office, and finance—in short, every avenue of power within the society, including the coercive force of the police . . . [rests] in male hands."[17] Patriarchy shapes institutions primarily and individuals secondarily. The twentieth-century English novelist Virginia Woolf movingly described this effect:

> The very word "society" sets tolling in memory the dismal bells of a harsh music: shall not, shall not, shall not. You shall not learn; you shall not earn; you shall not own, you shall not—such was the society relationship of brother to sister for many centuries. . . . Inevitably we look upon societies as conspiracies that sink the private brother, whom many of us have reason to respect, and inflate in his stead a monstrous male, loud of voice, hard of fist, childishly intent upon scoring the floor of the earth with chalk marks, within whose mystic boundaries human beings are penned, rigidly, separately, artificially.[18]

While we must be sensitive to the variations occasioned by time, place, situation, and personality, a reading of European and North American history supports a description of four kinds of constraints that most women would have experienced in some degree during their lives: exclusion from political authority; exclusion from cultural authority, including formal education; economic exploitation; and vulnerability to sexual exploitation. Let us consider each in turn.

Characteristics of Western Patriarchy

History has traditionally been written as the record of political events, but women were customarily prohibited from formal participation in politics. In ancient Athens the acropolis, the political heart of the city and today the main attraction for most tourists, was closed to respectable women except during certain public festivals. Democracy, or the "rule of the people," as practised by the ancient Greeks, was in reality an exclusive men's club, closed to the three-quarters of the population that was not of legal age, male, free, and, in the case of Athens, of Athenian parentage. The Greek dramatist Sophocles could imagine an Antigone, a young woman challenging a tyrant, but there is no evidence that she or the other strong women of Greek drama were anything but literary fantasies. When the Greek philosopher Aristotle defined man as "a political animal," he intended "man" to signify males and not to be used as a generic term for humans.

There were, as we shall see below, notable exceptions. Women fought wars, led military campaigns, inherited or seized office, issued and enforced edicts. Cleopatra, Boudicca, Joan of Arc, Elizabeth I, Mary Tudor, Catherine the Great—these are the names that may come to mind when one thinks of important women in the past. These were women who wielded political or military authority. But they were women in what were regarded as masculine positions, unusual women in unusual circumstances. They were women temporarily participating in masculine pursuits.

Women were trained from birth to be subservient to male authority. During the French Revolution in the late eighteenth century, a revolution that justified itself by the ideology that all *men* are created equal, a male participant asked, without sarcasm, "Is it a daughter to which you have given birth? Instruct her early to make a sacrifice of her will; you will ensure the tranquility of her life."[19] At the end of the nineteenth century, the German philosopher Heinrich von Treitschke summarized the wisdom of centuries when he pronounced, "Authority is male, that is a statement which is self-evident."[20] Treitschke did not consider that authority could also be female when women gave orders to servants or farmhands, or disciplined employees or slaves. Black slaves had to subordinate themselves not only to their white masters but to white women and children. Women, then, could be accomplices in patriarchal oppression as well as its victims.

Authority should not be confused with power, the unofficial influence or control that potentially anyone can exercise. Women have exercised power in a variety of ways, through speech or silence, through co-operation, or through the lack of it. Still, the benefits of authority or *legitimized* power, such as social prestige and profit, were usually available only to select white men.

Some feminist scholars have universalized women's exclusion from public authority to argue that in all known societies men have been associated with public activities and women with the private and domestic sphere, a difference assumed to relate to nature as opposed to culture. The dichotomy of private roles for women and public roles for men was already firmly entrenched in the ancient world. The Greek author Xenophon in the fourth century BC justified a gender-based division of labour: "For [God] made the man's body and mind more capable of enduring cold and heat, and journeys and campaigns; and therefore imposed on him the outdoor tasks. To the woman, since he has made her body less capable of such endurance, I take it that God has assigned the indoor tasks. . . . [Her] duty will be to remain indoors."[21] Over two thousand years later the French writer Restif de la Bretonne wrote much the same thing:

> The cares of a household divide naturally into two sorts: those of the exterior and those of the interior of the home. It is in the order of things that the Man, who is the most vigorous, the most free, be charged with the rough work, the affairs that require travel, a long application, etc.; and that the woman, more delicate, encumbered by pregnancies and by children, be domestic, and have only the little details.[22]

Restif even suggested that upper-class women be kept from learning to read or write in order to better confine them within the home. That idea was attractive enough to be repeated in the early nineteenth century.

The assignment of women to the home has been, then, a long-standing Western tradition. What has fluctuated is how the home has been perceived. Before the nineteenth century, the household was often seen as an extension of public authority rather than as its antithesis. The housewife was responsible for its moral functioning; she acted as a representative of public order, not as the representative of her husband. Management of household affairs could include relations with family and neighbours. Indeed, one historian says of seventeenth- and eighteenth-century Holland that "neighborhood and village life was determined by women."[23] Thus it is crucial to distinguish between theory and reality. The social geography of Western society vitiates the theory reserving public space to men. Women and men mixed in the fields, markets, taverns, and church, on docks and in stagecoaches, when they rode horses, peddled goods, or walked the highways. Women's occupation of public space depended, like everything else, upon ethnicity and social class. Female slaves in ancient Greece had access to public spaces that was denied their mistresses. Black female slaves in the American south were expected to do field work alongside men. Working-class women combined marriage and paid employment long before it became acceptable for middle-class women to work outside the home.

Also included in the public realm are cultural and political authority. Men have monopolized philosophy, literature, and language. The result has been to constitute men as the norm and to marginalize women. To the extent that women were considered at all, they were added on, as deviants or subjects deserving special consideration. As a male student asked in annoyance when I brought up the subject of women in class, "Why can't you talk about something all of us can relate to?"

Men have typically been equated with reason and intellect, order and self-control, activity and strength. Women have been considered as inferior in all those categories. They have represented emotion and madness, disorder and passion, passivity and weakness. Not only are these "feminine" characteristics contradictory. They have never been consistently applied. Physical weakness may have been appropriate for a white, southern Victorian woman, but it was scarcely acceptable for the black female slave whose work made possible her mistress's leisure. Conversely, what was regarded as moral weakness was expected in the slave but intolerable in her mistress.

Women's exclusion from cultural authority went along with their lack of access to formal education. At times in the Middle Ages women were associated with learning—learning thrived in the early female religious houses, and literacy was an advantage for noblewomen—but from the twelfth century on higher education became a male monopoly, broken scarcely a hundred years ago when women were admitted to universities. Before then, learned women were dependent upon supportive male relatives, and female literacy lagged behind male literacy. Virginia Woolf refers to this cultural gap and its class and gender assumptions when she describes her surprise upon being asked by a man for her ideas on how to prevent war: "Suppose that the Duke of Devonshire, in his star and garter, stepped down into the kitchen and said to the maid who was peeling potatoes with a smudge on her cheek: 'Stop your potato peeling, Mary, and help me to construe this rather difficult passage in Pindar,' would not Mary be surprised and run screaming to Louisa the cook, 'Lawks, Louie, Master must be mad!'"[24]

This exclusion created a gap not only between men and women but also among women. Because of it women were unable to sustain a tradition of feminist thinking and criticism. In *The Creation of Feminist Consciousness,* Gerda Lerner describes women thinkers across the centuries who were unable to build on the writings of their foremothers. Each one, working alone, not only had to reformulate the answers to questions that others had asked, and answered, but had to defend her ability to do so. The result was an enormous waste of time and energy as well as a barrier to women's "coming into consciousness as a collective entity."[25] What one scholar eloquently says of women in ancient Greece holds true for most of Western history. Women's speech "was severed from the name of action: it filled the air, echoed for a time, and faded from official memory with none to record it or to embody it in public forms."[26]

While public space included culture, private space has always included the primary responsibility for children. When farms and shops were places where both spouses worked together, fathers may have been closer to their children than when factory bells beckoned them off to work, and in poor rural settings child care might not have involved much more than swaddling the baby and hanging it up on the wall out of harm's way. Nonetheless, women in those settings still experienced a "double burden." They were expected to contribute to the family's material well-being—bringing in wages if necessity demanded and producing at home such essentials as clothing, medicine, food, soap, and candles—as well as caring for children. In 1762 Mary Collier, an English washerwoman, described the double burden of a female agricultural worker in terms that will sound familiar to women today:

We must make haste, for when we home are come,
We find again our Work but just begun;
So many Things for our Attendance call,
Had we ten Hands, we could employ them all.
Our Children put to Bed, with greatest Care
We all Things for your coming home prepare:
You sup, and go to Bed without Delay,
And rest yourselves till the ensuing Day;
While we, alas! but little Sleep can have,
Because our froward Children cry and rave;
Yet, without fail, soon as Day-light doth spring,
We in the Field again our work begin.[27]

Again, this responsibility meant different things to women in different situations. Female servants or slaves would have mitigated much of this burden for their mistresses while adding to their own.

Was the theory of patriarchy muted by the fact of economic partnership? Women's productive and reproductive capacities could be sources of strength and power for themselves and their families, but their greater responsibilities and work burden were rarely appreciated. An exception is the nineteenth-century Sicilian proverb that acknowledged, "If the father is dead, the family suffers. If the mother dies, the family cannot exist."[28] Even when acknowledged, the fact that women spent their lives serving others meant that much less time and support for themselves.

To put it simply, women have lacked economic options. Although they have worked harder than men, they have always been paid one-third to one-half less. This has been true no matter what the historical period, the country, or the type of work; yet few recognize it as an historical constant. Sometimes women were lucky. In response to the labour shortage caused by the Black Death in the fourteenth century, women grape harvesters in southern France were paid four-fifths of what their male counterparts earned. By the end of the sixteenth century, however, female farm workers were getting only 37 percent of what men were earning.

In general, white men have been, and still are, favoured with the ownership and control of property. Where unmarried women enjoyed property rights, such as under English common law, these were surrendered upon marriage. Well into the twentieth century, even after British married women gained the right of ownership over the wages they received from paid employment, income saved by them out of their household budgets or earned by taking in boarders was still considered their husbands' property. Although the absence of property did not reduce women to passivity—they could still provoke respect for their productive and reproductive contributions—property was the basis for both social status and political rights, such as the right to vote.

Control of women's sexuality and fertility has also been fundamental to patriarchy and has been expressed through a double standard traceable to the earliest historical records. Under ancient Germanic law a man was not legally

> *In 1854 the English feminist Barbara Leigh Smith Bodichon sum-marized the legal position of married women in her pamphlet* Married Women and the Law.
>
> A man and wife are one person in law; the wife loses all her rights as a single woman, and her existence is entirely absorbed in that of her husband. He is civilly responsible for her acts; she lives under his protection or cover, and her condition is called coverture.
>
>   A woman's body belongs to her husband; she is in his custody, and he can enforce his right by a writ of *habeas corpus.*
>
>   What was her personal property before marriage, such as money in hand, money at the bank, jewels, household goods, clothes, &c., becomes absolutely her husband's, and he may assign or dispose of them at his pleasure whether he and his wife live together or not. . . .
>
>   Neither the Courts of Common Law nor Equity have any direct power to oblige a man to support his wife. . . .
>
>   Money earned by a married woman belongs absolutely to her husband; that and all sources of income, excepting those mentioned above, are included in the term personal property. . . .
>
>   The legal custody of children belongs to the father. During the life-time of a sane father, the mother has no rights over her children, except a limited power over infants, and the father may take them from her and dispose of them as he thinks fit.

capable of committing adultery against his wife. He could only be punished for violating the property of another man, but his wife could be put to death for the same offence. A medieval Spanish law code proclaimed what everyone assumed, "Adultery is exclusively a female crime."[29] The Spanish Civil Code of 1881 still did not permit the wife to lay adultery charges against her husband as grounds for separation.

    Part of this control of sexuality is women's vulnerability to male violence, which ranges from sexual abuse, wife beating, and rape to culturally enforced heterosexuality. In her study of the history of rape Susan Brownmiller observes, "'Thou shalt not rape' was conspicuously missing from the Ten Commandments."[30] Wife-killing became a theme of English ballads in the late seventeenth century; its absence before then indicates only that the crime was not yet considered abhorrent enough to merit attention, except for cases of unusual brutality. In nineteenth-century Canada George Ham, quoted at the beginning of this section, went on to admonish Esther Ham, "I have the whip in my own hand, and I shall use it as I shall think proper." The courts completely supported him, for in spite of testimony that he had indeed whipped his wife, this action apparently did not satisfy the legal requirement that a woman's life must be put in jeopardy before she was allowed to leave her husband. Nineteenth-century Canadian court records reveal "case after case" of "women brutalized by vicious husbands. They were strangled, beaten with the handles of brooms, scalded with boiling water, threatened with loaded revolvers, kicked, bloodied, bruised, blackened, and blistered." Nonetheless, only when the wife could prove "danger to life, limb or health"[31] was she entitled to some legal relief. Fearful of curbing the husband's authority, the judges were loath to find in her favour. Counteracting this, there is evidence that women in the past had greater recourse to female networks, and the fact that family violence was more public than it is today worked in their favour.

Men acquired perhaps their most systematic power over women's bodies in the institution of slavery. Female slaves were not only commodities for reproduction but vehicles for their owners' sexual enjoyment. All married women were legally bound to submit to their husbands' sexual demands, but slaves were vulnerable to both owners and husbands, the demands of owners overriding those of husbands. Even after the emancipation of slaves in the United States, white men continued to assume the sexual availability of black women.

At the same time women fought back to control their bodies and reproduction. They opted for celibacy or for living with other women; they exploited the popular image of the henpecked or cuckolded husband; they passed on contraceptive knowledge and resorted to abortion or even infanticide. Far from moulding women into passive victims, patriarchal restrictions framed a dynamic ranging from resignation to resistance.

Justifications of Patriarchy

Even as they found ways around them, why did most women (and men) put up with these restrictions? The answer is that until relatively recently patriarchy was seen as natural and divinely ordained. The justifications for women's subordination come from the two roots of Western civilization, the Greco-Roman heritage and the Judaeo-Christian tradition.

For the ancient Greeks women's inferiority was expressed through an understanding of biology that pictured women's bodies as similar but inferior to men's. According to the Greeks, men had the advantage of excess heat, which not only caused their genitals to descend but nourished their reasoning abilities. Reason was the foundation of public, that is, intellectual and political, life. Women's colder and wetter humours, which kept their genitals inside the body and the blood from rising to their brains, explained their intellectual inferiority. Unlike the inferiority of slaves, who were seen to lack judgment because of their unfree status, or of children, who lacked it because of their age, female inferiority was inherent.

The theme of a physiologically based inferiority echoes throughout the centuries. The medieval theologian Thomas Aquinas paraphrased Aristotle in saying that women were "naturally subject to man, because in man the discernment of reason predominates."[32] In the late nineteenth century women's purportedly smaller brains were said to determine their lesser intellectual abilities. Dr Edward Clarke, an American educator, warned in 1873 of the dangers of education for girls because they would use their blood to nourish their brains rather than to menstruate. He cited the case of a young student who not only studied but exercised during menstruation and became an invalid at the age of eighteen as a result. In the early twentieth century authorities in the United States considered grounding female pilots during their menstrual periods. Even more recently, premenstrual hormones have been blamed for decreased intellectual capacity.

Sometimes these assumptions benefited women. In traditional Europe, for example, the law at times treated women more leniently because they were not considered to be as responsible for their actions as were men. The seventeenth-century English Puritan Richard Baxter advised husbands to be patient towards wives who might be willful by reason of "a natural passionate weakness, or by melancholy, or crazedness." The husbands' lack of restraint he judged a "more inexcusable fault and folly than hers, who hath not the power of reason as you have."[33]

The Judaeo-Christian tradition reinforced physiological assumptions with religion. The fundamental text was the Genesis account of Eve's creation after Adam and from his rib and of her role in the fall from grace in the garden of Eden. But Genesis has two accounts of woman's creation. The first account, Genesis 1:27, which was actually written later, reads: "So God created man in his own image, in the image of God created he him; male and female created he them." This version of the simultaneous creation of male and female was overlooked by most male commentators. Instead, the story of woman's secondary creation, in Genesis 2:22–23, justified her subordination: "And the Lord God caused a deep sleep to fall upon Adam, and he slept: and he took one of his ribs, and closed up the flesh instead thereof; And the rib, which the Lord God had taken from man, made he a woman, and brought her unto the man."

Also important in this selective reading of Genesis was the description of Eve as created not only after Adam but from him. This was usually interpreted to mean that only man reflected the purely spiritual. According to the fourth-century Christian apologist John Chrysostom, "Formed first, man has the right to greater honor."[34] Hildegard of Bingen, a spirited and independent-minded twelfth-century nun who did not readily acknowledge subjection to any man, including pope or emperor, nonetheless affirmed that "man was made in [God's] image and likeness . . . [and] therefore presides over the tribunal of the world, ruling all creatures, while the woman is under his mastery, and subject to him."[35] The phrase *the second sex* refers to the order of creation as well as to status. Man is the model, woman the deviation.

Eve's responsibility for the fall became a commonplace in moral literature. As she was seduced through the serpent's speech, so she in turn seduced Adam. Rabbinical law forbade women to read or sing before men on the grounds that their voices were sexually provocative. In view of women's public silence, it is ironic that classical, Jewish, and Christian authors all associated woman with dangerous speech. The sirens in Homer's *The Odyssey* lure men to their death. The shrew, whose power lies in her tongue, was a staple

▷ *The views of the Greek philosopher Aristotle (384–322 BC) would dominate Western thought for almost fifteen hundred years.*

... The female, in fact, is female on account of inability of a sort, viz it lacks the power to concoct semen. ...

Now of course [in conceiving] the female, qua female is passive, and the male, qua male is active. ...

... Wherever possible and so far as possible the male is separate from the female, since it is something *better* and more divine in that it is the principle of movement for generated things, while the female serves as their matter.

Some offspring take after their parents. ... Males take after their father more than their mother. ... Others do not take after a human being at all in their appearance, but have gone so far that they resemble a monstrosity. ... The first beginning of this deviation is when a female is formed instead of a male, though (a) this indeed is a necessity required by Nature, since the race of creatures which are separated into male and female has got to be kept in being; and (b) since it is possible for the male sometimes not to gain the mastery either on account of youth or age or some such cause, female offspring must of necessity be produced by animals.

... While still within the mother the female takes longer to develop than the male does; though once birth has taken place everything reaches its perfection sooner in females than in males—e.g., puberty, maturity, old age—because females are weaker and colder in their nature; and we should look upon the female state as being as it were a deformity, though one which occurs in the ordinary course of nature.

Source: Aristotle, *Generation of Animals,* trans. A.L. Peck, Loeb Classical Library (Cambridge, MA: Harvard University Press, 1943). Reprinted with permission.

of Greek and Roman misogyny. Christian apologists used the danger of women's speech as a rationale for placing restrictions on them. St Paul, for example, drew on Hebrew law and custom to enjoin women to silence in church. Almost two thousand years later, allied propaganda in World War II drew on fears of women as spies or traitors who reveal their countries' secrets through irresponsible chatter: a Finnish war poster depicted a giant padlock securing a woman's lips.

Both natural and divine law thus justified the exclusion of women from the public realm and their placement under male authority. Divine law was still called upon throughout the nineteenth century to keep women in place. A conservative contributor to the debate over female suffrage in Britain observed, "The real fact is that man in the beginning was ordained to rule over the woman, and this is an Eternal decree which we have no right and no power to alter."[36] His fellow countryman, Thomas Carlyle, called the principle that men should rule in the house "an eternal axiom, the Law of Nature . . . which no mortal departs from unpunished."[37] Nor was this belief confined to men. "There does not exist a reasonable woman, however superior that she might be to her husband," affirmed an eighteenth-century French woman, "who aspires to shaking off a yoke imposed by divine law."[38]

The emphasis on the authority of men over women served a broader function than just to keep women in line. It reflected the structure of society as a whole. Traditional Europe—Europe before the political and economic revolutions of the late eighteenth and nineteenth centuries—was hierarchical as well as patriarchal. The monarch was the apex of society, mirroring the authority of God, which was further modelled in the authority of every husband and father as head of his family, no matter how low in the social hierarchy he was. Preachers, philosophers, and jurists commonly described husbands as kings or gods. In 1616, for example, the English preacher William Whately referred to the husband as "a little God in the family,"[39] appropriately enough in a marriage sermon. In medieval marriage ceremonies the bride symbolized her submission by prostrating herself at her husband's feet. Husband killing in preindustrial England was categorized as petit treason rather than homicide; the act was judged comparable to but lesser than high treason, defined as disloyalty to the monarch. In the eighteenth century, the Age of Enlightenment, a subscriber to the English journal *The Spectator* renewed the theme: "You must have observed . . . that nothing is more gratifying to the Mind of Man than Power or Dominion, and this I think my self amply possessed of, as I am the Father of a Family."[40] Even after the French Revolution destroyed the ancien régime, a legislator commented, "Marriage prepares the government of the family and brings about the social order; it establishes the primary degrees of subordination necessary for its formation."[41] Feminists and antifeminists could agree that gender roles maintained social order and that the social relation of the sexes was inherently political. (The exception in this hierarchy was the slave family, where the wife owed obedience to her master rather than to her husband. For this reason, white theorists did not consider them to be "proper" families.)

Although this way of describing the family was dominant, men and women of letters could draw on other traditions, which at times contradicted the prevailing discourse. For example, Neoplatonists described feminine and masculine as complementary forces throughout the universe. This way of thinking was reflected in a sixteenth-century German poem, which proposed marriage as a model of "heavenly harmony":

The man should be like the sun
And the woman should be like the moon,
The sun's light is indeed clear,
Yet the moon's is just as dear.[42]

This version of marriage would offer small comfort to single women, who because they were not living under direct male authority were considered to be a major social problem. Sixteenth- and seventeenth-century German and French towns enacted legislation intended to prevent unmarried women from taking up residence, and there is good evidence to suggest that these masterless women were the main victims of the witch hunt that gripped Europe in the same period. While older, often widowed, women were condemned as witches, young, unmarried mothers were convicted of infanticide in campaigns inspired by savage misogyny.

Yet even the witch hunt can illustrate that patriarchal control was far from absolute. It illustrates patriarchy at a time of crisis, when rulers worried about their ability to maintain social order. Women have generally made gains in times of disorder, at least until action provokes reaction. It is possible to read women's history in the West as running parallel but in counterpoint to men's history. Periods of general gain for "man" exhibit, upon analysis, restricted opportunities for women. Such was true for the classical age of ancient Greece, the central Middle Ages, the Renaissance, the seventeenth century, and the eighteenth-century Enlightenment. Conversely, women have gained opportunities in times of general social upheaval, for example, the early Middle Ages, the early nineteenth century, and during the two world wars.

Two insights from modern feminism have implications for the historian of feminism: first, the awareness of differences among women; and second, the validation of female experiences and female culture. The problem is how to apply these insights not only to the history of women's movements but also to the time before the term *feminism* entered our vocabulary. The approach adopted here is to examine broad possibilities within particular historical contexts.

Older than feminism and indeed inspiring it, patriarchy has been a prime characteristic of Western civilization. Political and cultural invisibility, intellectual restrictions, sexual vulnerability, and economic exploitation, all justified in the name of nature and of God, have shaped women's lives, both stimulating and hindering the development of feminism and feminist thought.

Neither patriarchy nor feminism, nor their interaction, has been simple or straightforward. To adopt the description of Jean Elshtain, used in a different context, where we expect a "superhighway, straight and smooth," we find instead "twists and unexpected turns, retracings of earlier steps, wild, even dangerous bumps, dead ends, detours and destinations uncertain."[43] Developments that inspired feminists also inspired their opponents. Actions brought reactions. The following chapters attempt to make sense of these starts and stops and to evaluate their cumulative effect.

NOTES

1 "The Many Faces of Feminism," *Ms.* 5, 1 (July–August 1994): 33.

2 Sonia Johnson, 1984 candidate for the United States presidency, as quoted by Robyn Rowland and Renate D. Klein, "Radical Feminism: Critique and Construct," in *Feminist Knowledge: Critique and Construct,* ed. Sneja Gunew (Routledge: London, 1990), 281.

3 Joan Cassell, *A Group Called Women: Sisterhood and Symbolism in the Feminist Movement* (New York: Donald McKay, 1977), 17, 31.

4 "Nelly Roussel, 1904," in *Women, the Family, and Freedom: The Debate in Documents,* ed. Susan Groag Bell and Karen M. Offen, vol. 2, *1880–1950* (Stanford: Stanford University Press, 1983), 134.

5 Claire Goldberg Moses and Leslie Wahl Rabine, eds., *Feminism, Socialism, and French Romanticism* (Bloomington: Indiana University Press, 1993), 3.

6 Nancy F. Cott, "What's in a Name? The Limits of 'Social Feminism': or, Expanding the Vocabulary of Women's History," *Journal of American History* 76 (1988): 820, 826.

7 Katharine Anthony, *Feminism in Germany and Scandinavia* (New York: Henry Holt, 1915), 15. Anthony actually spoke of feminists, not feminisms.

8 Judith Lorber, "Dismantling Noah's Arc," in *Gender in Intimate Relationships: A Microstructural Approach,* ed. Barbara J. Risman and Pepper Schwartz (Belmont, CA: Wadsworth Publishing, 1989), 58.

9 Joan Hoff, *Law, Gender and Injustice: A Legal History of U.S. Women* (New York: New York University Press, 1991), 6, 3.

10 Quoted in Beatrice Gottlieb, "The Problem of Feminism in the Fifteenth Century," in *Women of the Medieval World: Essays in Honor of John H. Mundy,* ed. Julius Kirshner and Suzanne F. Wemple (Oxford: Basil Blackwell, 1985), 354.

11 Quoted in Angela Y. Davis, *Women, Race & Class* (New York: Random House, 1981), 56.

12 Lyle Koehler, *A Search for Power: The "Weaker Sex" in Seventeenth-Century New England* (Urbana: University of Illinois Press, 1980), 259, 167.

13 Quoted in Johanna Alberti, *Beyond Suffrage: Feminists in War and Peace, 1914–28* (New York: St Martin's Press, 1989), 137.

14 Elizabeth Cady Stanton, *Eighty Years and More: Reminiscences 1815–1897* (1898; reprint, New York: Schocken, 1971), 319–20.

15 Carolyn Steedman, *Landscape for a Good Woman: A Story of Two Lives* (London: Virago Press, 1986), 19.

16 Juliet Mitchell, *Women, The Longest Revolution: Essays on Feminism, Literature and Psychoanalysis* (London: Virago Press, 1984), 231–32.

17 Kate Millett, *Sexual Politics* (New York: Avon, 1969), 25.

18 Virginia Woolf, *Three Guineas* (1938; reprint, San Diego: Harcourt Brace Jovanovich, 1966), 105.

19 Jean-François Saint-Lambert, quoted in Candice E. Proctor, *Women, Equality, and the French Revolution* (New York: Greenwood Press, 1990), 9.

20 Quoted in Bärbel Clemens, *"Menschenrechte haben kein Geschlecht!" Zum Politikverständnis der bürgerlichen Frauenbewegung* (Pfaffenweiler: Centaurus-Verlagsgesellschaft, 1988), 52 (my translation).

21 Xenophon, *Memorabilia and Oeconomicus*, trans. E.C. Marchant (London: William Heinemann, 1959), 421, 425.

22 Quoted in Proctor, *Women, Equality, and the French Revolution*, 5.

23 Rudolf M. Dekker, "Women in Revolt: Popular Protest and Its Social Basis in Holland in the Seventeenth and Eighteenth Centuries," *Theory and Society* 16 (1987): 349.

24 Woolf, *Three Guineas*, 85

25 Gerda Lerner, *The Creation of Feminist Consciousness: From the Middle Ages to Eighteen-seventy* (New York: Oxford University Press, 1993), 10.

26 Jean Bethke Elshtain, *Public Man, Private Woman: Women in Social and Political Thought* (Princeton: Princeton University Press, 1981), 14.

27 Mary Collier, *The Woman's Labour* (1739), in *First Feminists: British Women Writers 1578–1799*, ed. Moira Ferguson (Bloomington: Indiana University Press, 1985), 260.

28 Quoted in Bonnie S. Anderson and Judith P. Zinsser, *A History of Their Own: Women in Europe from Prehistory to the Present*, vol. 1 (New York: Harper and Row, 1988), 88.

29 Cristina Segura Grafino, "Situacion juridica y realidad social de casadas y viudas en el medievo hispano (Andalucia)," in *La Condicion de la mujer en la Edad Media: Actas del coloquio celebrado en la Casa de Velazquez, del 5 al 7 de noviembre de 1984*, ed. Yves-Rene Fonquerne and Alfonso Esteban (Madrid: Casa de Velazquez, 1986), 127 (my translation).

30 Susan Brownmiller, *Against Our Will: Men, Women and Rape* (New York: Simon and Schuster, 1975), 9.

31 Constance Backhouse, *Petticoats and Prejudice: Women and Law in Nineteenth-Century Canada* (Toronto: Women's Press, 1991), 171, 175, 176.

32 Thomas Aquinas, *Basic Writings of Saint Thomas Aquinas*, vol. 1, *God and the Order of Creation: Summa theologica, part i*, ed. Anton C. Pegis (New York: Random House, 1945), 880–81.

33 Quoted in Phyllis Mack, *Visionary Women: Ecstatic Prophecy in Seventeenth-Century England* (Berkeley: University of California Press, 1992), 26.

34 Quoted in R. Howard Bloch, *Medieval Misogyny and the Invention of Western Romantic Love* (Chicago: University of Chicago Press, 1991), 24.

35 Quoted in Carolly Erickson, *The Medieval Vision: Essays in History and Perception* (New York: Oxford University Press, 1976), 211.

36 Earl Percy (1873), quoted in Brian Harrison, *Separate Spheres: The Opposition to Women's Suffrage in Britain* (London: Croom Helm, 1978), 58.

37 Quoted in Lee Holcombe, *Wives and Property: Reform of the Married Women's Property Law in Nineteenth-Century England* (Toronto: University of Toronto Press, 1983), 78.

38 Mlle Archambault (1750), quoted in Proctor, *Women, Equality, and the French Revolution*, 31.

39   Quoted in Linda Woodbridge, *Women and the English Renaissance: Literature and the Nature of Womankind, 1540–1620* (Urbana: University of Illinois Press, 1984), 130.

40   Donald F. Bond, ed., *The Spectator* (Oxford: Clarendon Press, 1965), 273.

41   Quoted in Proctor, *Women, Equality, and the French Revolution,* 174. As late as the 1960s French politicians still regarded the family as hierarchal and resisted fundamental reform of the 1804 Napoleonic law code, which enshrined the father as the head of the family.

42   Quoted in Heide Wunder, *"Er ist die Sonn', sie ist der Mond": Frauen in der Frühen Neuzeit* (Munich: C.H. Beck, 1992), 266 (my translation).

43   Elshtain, *Public Man, Private Woman,* xii.

2

From Jesus
to
Joan of Arc

*I*n spite of the durability and pervasiveness of patriarchy, women protested their oppression. Not until the late seventeenth and eighteenth centuries did an ideology of social change develop that would enable women and men to imagine alternative social and gender relations. And not until the mid-nineteenth century would women begin to form organized feminist movements. In more subtle ways, however, using the cultural symbols and avenues available to them, individual women in preindustrial society sought to be heard and to liberate themselves from patriarchal authority.

Christianity, although absorbing earlier and contemporary misogyny, was a potent force for liberation. It revolutionized relations between the sexes and contributed the idea of moral equality among human beings, which was to help justify the political revolutions of the eighteenth century. Its more immediate effect, in the words of a medieval historian, was to initiate "a new era . . . in the history of feminism."[1] This chapter looks at restrictions on and opportunities for women in the contexts of the early Christian church and medieval Europe. It describes the actions of women determined to exploit or ignore the limitations imposed on their sex and asks whether these actions can be interpreted as feminist.

EARLY CHRISTIAN ERA, CA. 4–500

The early Christian church provided a receptive environment for women. Jesus was remarkably open to women in his teachings and actions, welcoming them equally with men to the community of believers. Women were

Early Christian Era, CA. 4 BC–AD 500

4 BC–AD 29-30	Jesus
ca. 67	St Paul
ca. 313	Christianity legalized
360	Separation of Eastern and Western empires
378–532	Germanic invasions
390	Christianity instituted as the state religion of the Roman empire
476	Fall of Rome

Early Middle Ages, CA. 500–1000

529	Emergence of monasticism in the West
ca. 850	Emergence of feudalism

High Middle Ages, CA. 1000–1300

11th century	Revival of trade
1075	Beginning of Gregorian reform movement
1098–1179	Hildegard of Bingen

Late Middle Ages, CA. 1300–1500

1337–1453	Hundred Years War between England and France
1340–1400	Geoffrey Chaucer
1347–80	Catherine of Siena
1348–50	Black Death
ca. 1373–1440	Margery Kempe
1412–31	Joan of Arc

prominent as his friends and disciples, in his parables, and at his death. A woman, Mary Magdalene, was the first witness to the resurrection. Women appeared as both leaders and followers in the early Christian communities. Before the line was clearly drawn between clergy and laity, they led house churches by virtue of their position as managers of the household and may even have presided over the service. By the third century women may have made up the majority of church members. Pagan detractors saw this association of women with Christianity as a liability and vilified the movement as composed of "the foolish, dishonourable and stupid . . . only slaves, women and little children."[2] The sexual promiscuity traditionally ascribed to women spilled over to taint the early church as well.

Much of Christianity's appeal to women lay, perhaps surprisingly to modern readers, in the idea of sexual abstinence. Contrary to our popular image of uninhibited Greeks and Romans indulging in wanton behaviour, ancient writers praised the mental and physical virtues of chastity. They directed their advice to practise moderation to adult men, whom they believed had the will-power to control their bodies. Women were not thought capable of such self-control. In contrast to the Greeks and Romans, Christians posited an ideal of virginity instead of simply continence and promoted it for both women and men.

In early Christian communities, social differences were considered irrelevant. Individuals who felt the need to distinguish themselves could choose martyrdom: a martyr was regarded as an exemplary Christian, assured of salvation through an act of ultimate renunciation. When Rome legalized the new religion and the possibility of martyrdom receded, renunciation came to be understood primarily as sexual renunciation, another form of redemption through denial of the physical body. In this spiritual environment, men and women found asceticism, or the practice of self-denial, appealing. Unlike other religions such as Buddhism, where heroic asceticism was largely confined to men, Christianity offered women equal opportunity for sexual abstinence.

We can understand the attraction of such an option in a demographically fragile society where marriage and childbirth were every woman's unquestioned destiny. In the world of late Antiquity, the time of the early church, each woman needed to produce five offspring just to maintain the population. In this context sexual abstinence was subversive. Although some women in the ancient world could be religious celibates, as were the vestal virgins, they were dedicated by others and would marry after a certain age, thus suspending rather than subverting their normal life course. In Christianity, the alternative of *permanent* virginity was popularized by women themselves; an influential lobby of widows and single women revolted against conventional social expectations and influenced Christian theologians to override their own preferences in order to accommodate this revolutionary desire.

The story of Thecla dramatizes the life of a Christian heroine of the second century. It belongs to the collection of so-called apocryphal gospels, early Christian writings that were not included in the New Testament. In the story, Thecla of Iconium, a young woman on the eve of marriage, is so captivated by the idea of the virgin life as preached by the apostle Paul that she rejects the entreaties of parents and her betrothed to marry. Thecla runs away from home, at one point cutting her hair and dressing like a man and enduring many ordeals. Paul demurs when Thecla catches up with him and asks to be baptized. Undeterred, Thecla baptizes herself. In the end, she achieves not martyrdom, but fame, wealth—to be dispensed as charity—and independence, bringing the word of God to many.

It has been suggested that Thecla's story was written by a woman. Whether or not this is true, the story may well be the product of an oral literary tradition extending back to ancient Greece. An historical Thecla may never have existed, but for the first thousand years of Christian history no

> ▶ *In addition to the threat of being burned alive, Thecla of Iconium had to fight off sexual advances and wild beasts. Note how women rally to Thecla's side.*
>
> And Paul . . . taking Thecla came into Antioch. But immediately as they entered a Syrian by the name of Alexander, one of the first of the Antiochenes, seeing Thecla fell in love with her, and sought to win over Paul with money and gifts. But Paul said: "I do not know the woman of whom thou dost speak, nor is she mine." But he, being a powerful man, embraced her on the open street; she however would not endure it, but looked about for Paul and cried out bitterly, saying: "Force not the stranger, force not the handmaid of God! Among the Iconians I am one of the first, and because I did not wish to marry Thamyris I have been cast out of the city." And taking hold of Alexander she ripped his cloak, took off the crown from his head, and made him a laughing-stock. But he, partly out of love for her and partly in shame at what had befallen him, brought her before the governor; and when she confessed that she had done these things, he condemned her to the beasts [since Alexander was arranging games]. But the women were panic-stricken, and cried out before the judgment-seat: "An evil judgment! A godless judgment!" But Thecla asked of the governor that she might remain pure until she was to fight with the beasts. And a rich woman named Tryphaena, whose daughter had died, took her under her protection and found comfort in her. When the beasts were led in procession, they bound her to a fierce lioness, and the queen Tryphaena followed her. And as Thecla sat upon her back, the lioness licked her feet, and all the crowd was amazed.
>
> *Source:* "The Acts of Paul and Thecla," in Edgar Hennecke, *New Testament Apocrypha*, ed. Wilhelm Schneemelcher, vol. 2, *Writings Relating to the Apostles, Apocalypses and Related Subjects* (Philadelphia: Westminster Press, 1964). Reprinted with permission.

one doubted her authenticity. She was revered as a saint and sometimes even called an apostle. Her cult was widespread throughout Asia Minor and seems to have appealed particularly to women. It is not hard to see why, since she was a rather feisty role model. The church father Tertullian complained at the end of the second century that some women were using Thecla's example to justify their own teaching and baptizing. The association of the story with Paul is provocative since in the legend he commissions Thecla to teach but in his epistles he commands women to silence. Even if the story belongs to the realm of folklore, its message to girls was very different from, say, that of Cinderella in later times.

Although not many women could hope to achieve Thecla's fame, consecrated virgins were regarded with awe. Within villages their presence was welcomed as a sign of divine protection and mercy for the entire community. Widows who refused remarriage likewise won status: "Mature, financially independent, and already influential, the Christian widow had made a decision to embrace continence that was as formal and as heroic as that of . . . the average members of the clergy." Rather than limiting women's options, the commitment to abstinence opened up a variety of lifestyles. Peter Brown calls attention to "the sheer diversity of female ascetic experience and practice." Some women lived in the seclusion of their homes, either with their families or heading their own households. Many of the latter attracted other women, to whom they read scripture and dispensed spiritual advice. Others shunned company altogether to practise rigorously ascetic lives of self-denial focused on prayer and fasting. Pilgrimages and missionary work offered opportunities for travel to those who had the means. Melania the Elder, a wealthy Roman heir who was left widowed at the age of twenty-two after suffering many miscarriages and the deaths of two children, travelled to the East, visiting hermits in the Nitrian desert before settling in Jerusalem. There she used her wealth to endow two monasteries, one for men and one for women, and used the shelter of the latter to indulge her desire for learning. "The world of female piety represented . . . a zone of exceptional fluidity and free choice."[3]

The communities that composed the early Christian church were extremely diverse. In particular, the groups that would later be denounced as heretical were open to women. In the second century Irenaeus, Bishop of Lyon, complained that "groups of women from every walk of life were leaving homes, parents, and husbands to follow [false] prophetic teachers."[4] In these sects women often became the teachers: the Manichees had women among their elect, and men and women travelled together; in the Marcionite sect women worked as priests and bishops; the Montanists honoured two women, Prisca and Maximilla, as founders of their movement; and the Gnostics not only honoured women as teachers and priests but also promoted an androgynous image of God. In many of these sects women and men enjoyed not only spiritual but intellectual companionship, in effect forming co-educational study groups.

Finally, among both the orthodox and the heretics, women were influential patrons. Their wealth and prestige enabled them to make a permanent impact on the church. The house churches they founded and supported were decisive in providing leadership for early Christian communities, and the women who hosted them may have presided over the eucharistic rite before it became formally separated from the fraternal meal. No wonder that women took advantage of the options that Christianity offered in comparison to the limitations of their roles in Roman society as wives and mothers.

Unfortunately, this openness to women was short-lived. Already in the second century, an alternative current existed within the early church that strove to establish a hierarchical line of authority. The bishops, who represented this direction, feared ascetic individuals as potential interlopers who could command respect based on their achievements rather than on their position within the community. Hopeful of appealing to a broad following, the bishops were also sensitive to traditional social values. They therefore condemned the groups that idealized asceticism and that encouraged women to practise ascetic equality. By the fifth century if not earlier, they had succeeded in establishing a patriarchal church structure. Strict regulations were imposed on religious women and they were excluded from positions of influence. Deaconesses, highly regarded in the third century and at times recognized as full members of the clergy, were now condemned. The asceticism that had opened options to women by allowing them to reject sexuality and the tyranny of the womb was now monopolized by men who saw sexuality as symbolized by a seductive woman. When in the fourth century the old monk Apa Sisoes was urged to live closer to civilization, he replied, "Where there is no woman, that is where we should go."[5]

THE MIDDLE AGES, 500—1500

The impact of the Germanic migrations in the late fourth and fifth centuries completed the growing divergence of the eastern and western halves of the Roman empire. At the beginning of the fifth century the formality of Roman rule was maintained in the West; by the end of the century the map of Europe was a mosaic of separate Germanic kingdoms. Under the rule of bishops, the church provided the rudiments of welfare and instruction. Periods of political consolidation, in which church and state worked together, meant setbacks for women. The variety of religious lifestyles that women had formerly enjoyed was curtailed, and by the seventh century all religious women were ordered confined to monasteries (a generic name for all religious houses). In practice, however, decentralized conditions set limitations to the control of church and state. The monasteries achieved a high degree of autonomy, which women were able to exploit.

Early Monasticism

The monastic life offered enormous benefits to upper-class women whose families could afford the dowry required for admittance. It provided a refuge from the violence of secular life, the only practical alternative to marriage or remarriage, the comfort and support of female companionship, the possibility of literary or scientific pursuits, and, not least, spiritual fulfilment. Reading was prescribed for nuns as well as monks, and some women achieved Europe-wide reputations for scholarship. The seventh-century English abbess Hilda of Whitby, for example, was famous for her learning. Many saints' lives assumed to have been written by men are now thought to be the work of women, given the high intellectual standards of women's monasteries.

Above all, monasticism gave expression to female piety. The female monasteries of the early medieval period were the result of a spontaneous religious expression, initiated by women, who turned to monasticism as other avenues were closed to them. Women were among the most enthusiastic followers of the Irish monks, such as Columbanus, who travelled to Europe in the sixth century. Their harsh monasticism appealed to the nobility, and noblewomen used their resources to endow religious houses for themselves and their female relatives, creating islands of female society and culture.

Paradoxically, monasticism also offered scope to the politically ambitious. As important landowners, monasteries were economic, administrative, and political centres. Abbesses often had much the same power as abbots to hear confession, appoint their successors, govern villages, coin money, collect revenues, and raise armies. The double monasteries of the seventh and eighth centuries consisted of separate communities of women and men, usually presided over by an abbess. The male workforce and clergy associated with the double monasteries provided the practical assistance and male protection that female monastic houses established in remote areas would need. Individual nuns—such as Lioba, who accompanied the monk Boniface on his mission to Germany in the mid-eighth century—could still carry out missionary work. Like monks they could travel throughout Europe, carrying precious manuscripts, teaching, and founding religious houses.

Monastic women kept alive the inspiring traditions of the early church. Hrotsvit, a tenth-century German canon and the first known Christian dramatist, filled her plays with the praiseworthy deeds of virgin martyrs. At a time when the classical authors still set literary standards, Hrotsvit criticized the Roman dramatist Terence for choosing to depict "the shameless acts of lascivious women." In their place she substituted "the laudable chastity of sacred virgins."[6] In her vision of the mother church, twelfth-century Hildegard of Bingen placed virgins and virgin martyrs after the apostles as the second order of the church, celebrating the maiden as "the noble daughter of the celestial Jerusalem."[7]

Two Twelfth-Century Women

Another early tradition inspired not only the art but the lives of medieval women. The gift of prophecy was seen as particularly female since it was appropriate that God should choose to speak through the weak and despised. Medieval men and women commonly prefaced their writing with admissions of humility, but women could better exploit the dramatic paradox of God speaking through "a wretched woman," as the thirteenth-century mystic Mechthild of Magdeburg put it.[8] Thomas Aquinas, the great male theologian of the Middle Ages, associated prophecy with women, ranking it as a higher source of spiritual authority than the all-male priesthood.

How far this tradition could be carried can be seen in the life of Hildegard of Bingen (1098–1179). Hildegard was the tenth child of a German noble family. Perhaps for this reason, as a tithe offering, her parents dedicated her to the church when she was eight years old. Rather than selecting an established monastery, they sent her to join Jutta of Sponheim, a young noblewoman who had decided to become an anchorite, that is, to live out her life in a small cell, or enclosure, attached to a Benedictine monastery. Hildegard thus had to make the transition from being part of a large, busy family to living in seclusion with Jutta and one servant. Appropriately, her enclosure was celebrated by a rite that approximated a burial service since she and Jutta, as was true of all nuns, were to live as if dead to the world.

Logically, we should thus have heard no more of Hildegard. Yet she and Jutta were soon joined by other women, and by the time Hildegard was a teenager, the cell had become a small Benedictine convent. When Jutta died in 1136, the sisters unanimously chose Hildegard as their abbess. The real turning point in her life came a few years later when she received the latest in a series of visions she had been having since she was a small child. At forty-two she was told to "say and write what you see and hear."[9] She proceeded cautiously, first informing her secretary, who informed the abbot, who informed the archbishop, who informed the pope. In due course a commission investigated, and Hildegard was given papal approval to record what the Holy Spirit transmitted through her.

Hildegard had proceeded with the blessings of the authorities, but the Benedictine monks were not so eager to endorse the command God next sent her, to move her convent. An independent religious house would deprive them not only of the benefits of administering the convent's wealth but also of other material and spiritual advantages derived from association with a newly famous seer. Hildegard recorded the opposition: "My abbot, and the monks and the populace in that province . . . were determined to oppose us."[10] In response she took to her bed with an illness that left her motionless and speechless. Unable to rouse her, the abbot became convinced that Hildegard was merely relaying God's command, and he no longer stood in her way. Perhaps as a form of insurance the ever astute Hildegard had also taken the precaution of lining up influential supporters.

Successful in this enterprise, Hildegard went on to accomplishments that seem truly spectacular coming from one who was intended to live in seclusion. She wrote complex theological and medical works, composed music and poetry, practised medicine, corresponded with emperors, popes, and other illustrious persons who wrote to her for advice, and even preached in public, undertaking the last in a series of preaching tours when she was in her seventies. She also became known as a miracle worker and an exorcist when she freed a woman from an evil spirit.

Hildegard's biographer asks:

> How are we to account for such prodigious activity in areas where women, if not actually forbidden to participate, were at least not actively encouraged? How many other women of the time do we find preaching with official approval, exorcizing, founding their own convents, and above all composing works which have given them a place among the "fathers, doctors and writers of the Church"?[11]

The answer lies in Hildegard's conviction that she was "the mouthpiece of the lord" and her success in convincing others of her mission. Her activities were justified on the basis of her "privileged access to the *'secreta Dei'*—'the secrets of God.'"[12] St Bernard, one of the greatest churchmen of his day, wrote to her,

We bless the divine grace which resides in you. . . . How can I aspire to instruct and advise you, who have attained hidden knowledge and in whom the influence of Christ's anointing still lives. There is no longer any need to instruct you, since it has been said of you that you are capable of examining the secrets of the heavens and discerning, by the light of the Holy Spirit, that which is beyond the knowledge of man. I have the task of asking you not to forget me and those united with me in spiritual fraternity before God.[13]

The final honour came in the sixteenth century when her name was included in an official list of saints of the Catholic Church.

We can better appreciate Hildegard's accomplishments when we compare her to another famous woman of this time, Heloïse (1101–64), whose story has been better known because it was linked to that of her lover and husband, the famous scholar Peter Abelard. Unlike Hildegard, the young Heloïse participated in the heady intellectual climate of Paris and by the age of seventeen, as Abelard himself noted, was distinguished throughout France for her learning. Her attractions were such that Abelard decided "she was the one to bring to my bed."[14] Notwithstanding this cool seduction, the two fell in love and married when Heloïse became pregnant. In order not to jeopardize Abelard's career they kept their marriage a secret but thereby angered Heloïse's uncle Fulbert, fearful of scandal. When Abelard moved Heloïse to a convent to protect her from Fulbert's abuse, Fulbert retaliated by having Abelard castrated. Subsequently, Abelard withdrew to a monastery and ordered Heloïse to do likewise, even though by her own admission she had no inclination for a religious life.

Although Heloïse came to terms with her vocation and became a strong-minded and efficient administrator, her intellectual potential remained unfulfilled. She never produced a major work and has been remembered more for her tragic romance with Abelard than for any achievement of her own. Perhaps this contrast with Hildegard reflects the different milieu of the two women. Hildegard, while somewhat insecure about her lack of formal learning, was in fact well educated. Her works testify to her familiarity with the major Christian thinkers. Although this knowledge was part of her background, it did not constrain her originality. Aware of traditional arguments about woman's inferiority, she proceeded as if these did not matter.

Heloïse, on the other hand, was educated in the world rather than within a cloister. When Abelard first proposed marriage to her, she rejected the idea as harmful to his career and, as reported by Abelard, quoted standard misogynist and antimatrimonial passages from biblical and ancient sources to support her argument. She thus inadvertently became "the first woman to argue for the devaluation of women in western thought."[15] Although her other writings and her actions imply a more complex view of woman, it may be that Heloïse internalized this misogyny because she lacked the support system available to Hildegard. Women raised in monasteries, Caroline Bynum tells us, were more sheltered from contemporary notions of women as morally and intellectually inferior and thus less likely to be affected by them.[16]

Alternatives

Both Hildegard and Heloïse lived in the shadow of the Gregorian reform movement, which began in the late eleventh century. It was an ascetic movement aimed at removing secular influences from the church. Monastic in origin, it fed on the fear of female sexuality and reiterated the ideal of strict enclosure—confinement within the monastery—for nuns. The renewed fear of sexual temptation, along with the burden of providing financial and spiritual support for female dependent houses, led monks to disavow responsibility for religious women. In the early twelfth century Abbot Conrad of Marchtal warned,

> Recognizing that the wickedness of women is greater than all the other wickedness of the world, and that there is no anger like that of women, and that the poison of asps and dragons is more curable and less dangerous to men than the familiarity of women, [we] have unanimously decreed for the safety of our souls, no less than for that of our bodies and goods, that we will on no account receive any more sisters to the increase of our perdition, but will avoid them like poisonous animals.[17]

The High Middle Ages also saw demographic and economic changes that were disadvantageous for women. A population increase resulted in more noble families adopting the principle of primogeniture, according to which the eldest son inherited the estate. Daughters no longer enjoyed inheritances that they could use to found or enrich religious houses. Inflation also put a strain on fixed revenues. Female monasteries thus faced a desperate loss of material and spiritual resources.

Women's piety did not falter in the face of such restraints. Rather, religious women created new varieties of spiritual expression and displayed a willingness to explore non-institutionalized options. As the double monasteries and powerful abbesses of the earlier period faded from memory, a rich variety of alternative lifestyles appeared, testifying to the resourcefulness and creativity of female religiosity.

One example is the solitary life chosen by Christina of Markyate (ca. 1097–1160), an English woman from a noble family who pledged herself to virginity as a child in spite of her parents' wish for an advantageous marriage. When defied, her mother not only beat her but encouraged Christina's fiancé to seduce her. In desperation Christina dressed as a man and, like Thecla, ran away, to spend four years hiding in a space so cramped she could not even turn around or stand up.

Other women who sought alternatives include a thirteenth-century saint, Juliana of Cornillon, who lived in a variety of settings ranging from a leper hospital to a Cistercian convent, and the late-fourteenth-century recluse, Julian of Norwich. Although Julian may have at one time belonged to a religious community, she apparently chose to live alone in order to concentrate on her visions, perhaps to finish the task of writing them down. Yet her choice did not preclude human contact. Another visionary, Margery Kempe, sought her out for advice and enjoyed their "holy conversation . . . for the many days that they were together."[18] In thirteenth-century

Italy and Flanders women and men thronged to hear the teachings of widows who had gained reputations as holy women; one of them, Margaret of Cortona, had at one time been a prostitute.

Women participated fully in the emotionally intense piety and mysticism that were the typical forms of religious expression in the thirteenth and fourteenth centuries. In fact, almost all the female saints of those centuries were mystics, in comparison to only a small percentage of male saints. Unlike clerical office and formal theological education, from which women were excluded, mysticism, defined as a direct and individual communication with God, was accessible to women. Further, the emergence of written vernacular languages gave women uneducated in Latin a vehicle through which to express themselves. Although most clerics were still apt to envision the ideal religious woman as enclosed, quiet, and humble, a very different tradition of outspoken holy women was becoming evident to contemporaries.

One of the most famous female mystics of the Middle Ages was Catherine of Siena (1347–80). Like Hildegard, Catherine came from a large family. Her mother had twenty-five children, though fewer than half survived infancy. Like Christina of Markyate, Catherine was destined by her family for a prestigious marriage, but this was not what Catherine had in mind for herself. When still a child she vowed herself to a life of virginity, which she carried through despite intense parental resistance. Catherine's confessor quotes her parents as saying, "You wretched girl! . . . Take a husband you must. You will never get a moment's peace until you give in."[19] To enforce her submission, Catherine was assigned a heavy regime of domestic tasks for the family.

But Catherine rejected her parents' plans with the assurance of one who saw herself as chosen by God. Later, her self-confidence led her to challenge God himself when he seemed to renege on a promise that the members of her family would die only with the assurance of salvation:

> O my Lord and my God, is this how you fulfil your promise to me that no member of this household should be lost? . . . Now I see [my mother] lying dead before me, without having received the Sacraments of the Church! I implore you, in the name of all your deeds of mercy, not to let me be mocked like this. While I live I will not move an inch from this spot until you give me back my mother alive.[20]

Which God apparently did, since Catherine's mother, it turned out, had only appeared to be dead. Later, lying ill with a high fever and boils all over her body, Catherine persuaded her mother to secure her admission into a community of Dominican laywomen. Both in her refusal to yield and in her willingness to exploit sickness Catherine reminds one of Hildegard.

Catherine's communication with God and her interpretation of what God wanted her to do allowed her to defy familial authority and social convention. She became outspoken on political matters as well, engaging in a drawn-out correspondence with the pope and serving as special envoy both for the pope and for the city of Florence. She reportedly preached to the pope "with such a wonderful grace, eloquence, and authority, that the Pope himself and all that were about him were astonished to hear her."[21]

Catherine of Siena's confessor, Raymond of Capua, recorded her defiance of her parents.

On that very day . . . she plucked up courage, and putting all her trust in the Lord gathered round her her parents and her brothers, and spoke out boldly in these words: "It is now a long time since you first took counsel, and began negotiations, as you said, to have me married off as the bride of some mere mortal man. The very thought of this filled me with loathing, as I made plain to you in many silent ways, whose meaning, however was unmistakable. But God has commanded us to honour our father and our mother, and for the reverence due to them I have never bluntly spoken out my mind until now. But the time has come when I can be silent no longer. I will lay bare my heart to you and say out plain and straight what I am resolved to do. It is no new-found purpose that I speak of, but one that has been clearly known to me, and firmly willed, from childhood. Already, when I was still a child in years I made a vow of virginity, not, however, in the way a child would do, but after long consideration and acting on solid grounds. I made this vow to my Lord and Saviour Jesus Christ, and to his glorious Mother. I promised them that never would I take another spouse but him alone. And now in course of time, as the Lord himself has willed it, I have arrived at mature age and mature knowledge. Take notice, then, that my resolution is so firm in this regard that it would be easier to soften the very rock than to move my heart a hairsbreadth from its holy purpose. The more you try to do so, the more you will discover that you are only wasting your time. Be advised by me, and put a stop once and for all to any matchmaking in my regard. This is a matter in which I have not the slightest intention of yielding to your will. I must obey God rather than man. If you are willing to keep me in your house on this condition—even as a servant-maid if you so desire—I for my part am willing to serve you with pleasure, to the best of my knowledge and ability. But if you decide that I must, because of my resolve, be banished from your home, then rest assured that my heart will not deviate one jot from its resolution."

Source: Conleth Kearns, O.P., trans. and ed., *The Life of Catherine of Siena, by Raymond of Capua,* preface by Vincent de Couesnongle, O.P., Master of the Dominican Order (Wilmington, DE: Michael Glazier, 1980). Reprinted with permission.

Catherine of Siena, Christina of Markyate, Thecla, these women drew on their virginity as the main source of their power. In the thirteenth and fourteenth centuries, however, it became possible for married women to aspire to holiness. The most famous was Catherine's contemporary, Birgitta of Sweden (1302?–73), later St Birgitta. Born into a high-ranking noble family, Birgitta married at thirteen despite an early inclination for a religious life. She persuaded her husband to live with her chastely until they were old enough to conceive children and thereafter strictly regulated their sexual intercourse. In spite of her marital and maternal obligations—she had eight children—Birgitta became more and more ascetic. Her husband's death in 1343 freed her to become a prophet and pilgrim. At age forty-seven she journeyed to Rome and called on the church to reform itself. This was a time of division in the papacy, and Birgitta joined the party calling for the return of the pope from Avignon to Rome. She spoke with an assurance bolstered by her visions and undoubtedly by her high social standing as well. The order of nuns that she founded was dedicated to the Virgin Mary and gave an authority to the abbess reminiscent of the earlier double monasteries. Although the Birgittine Order provoked criticism for that reason, its monastery in England, Syon Abbey, became an influential centre and example of women living under female leadership.

A last example of an independent-minded woman is Margery Kempe (ca. 1373–1440), a married woman who defied social convention without either the advantage of nobility or the convenience of widowhood. Although one biographer describes Margery as a "middle-class housewife,"[22] her family was of the English urban upper middle class, "of worthy kindred,"[23] as Margery herself put it. Although not noble, Margery owed much of her self-assurance and probably the tolerance of the authorities as well to her respectable family background.

Unlike the other women mentioned, Margery received her religious calling only after marriage and childbirth. Christ first appeared to her as she lay ill after the birth of her first child. Later, like Hildegard, she became privy to "many secret things . . . by inspiration of the Holy Ghost."[24] Not until twenty years and thirteen children later did she reach a compromise with her husband, whom she generally describes as affectionate and supportive. He agreed to renounce sex in return for her recognition of her social and financial obligation to him, namely, to eat with him on Fridays instead of fasting and to pay his debts. Their agreement freed her from any further marital obligation, although Margery did nurse her husband in his final illness. Interestingly, Margery never mentions her children except for one wayward son whom she successfully brought to mend his ways.

Margery used her freedom to travel, meeting various clergymen and anchorites to discuss her revelations, and to go on pilgrimages, first to Jerusalem and Rome, later to Spain and Germany. Although pilgrims necessarily travelled in groups or with escorts, Margery's uncontrolled fits of weeping and constant talk of God made her a difficult travelling companion. More than once she was abandoned to her own resources but remained undaunted.

Even without her eccentricities, Margery was unusual in that she aspired to a religious life in the world rather than in a monastery or cell. She was denounced as a hypocrite by contemporaries who found her conduct bewildering or offensive, but her conviction of Christ's guidance sustained her in her dealings with her husband, the public, and the authorities. Few middle-class housewives in subsequent centuries would have the courage or inclination to gain freedom and autonomy by breaking with convention as Margery did.

Although Margery found support in meeting Julian of Norwich and in her knowledge of contemporary and earlier saintly women, she made her way essentially alone in a male world. In contrast, most religiously inclined women chose to live collectively, although not always in ways welcomed by the church. The beguines, who begin to appear in historical records after 1200, were townswomen from various social classes who lived together in chastity and poverty, earning a modest living by washing wool, teaching, or nursing. Yet they were not nuns, for they took no vows and could leave their communities at any time. Historian Joan Kelly called them undeniably feminist in their "will to independence from male authority."[25] This statement is difficult to support because the beguines were under the supervision of a parish priest, a male spiritual director, and legal and financial guardians chosen from the municipal aldermen.

It is difficult to generalize about the beguines since they followed no collective rule or practice. Some lived at home but most lived in separate communities, mainly in the towns of the Low Countries and along the Rhine. Their uniqueness came from their attempt to find a middle path, to live apart from the world yet within it. They were self-supporting but earned only enough to support their austere lifestyle, often owning nothing but their clothing and beds. Their highest priority was their spiritual life. At one community in Ghent, for example, two women would take turns reading devotional passages to the others, who worked in silence. It is also difficult to speculate about the beguines' motives. Many commentators, then and now, have pointed out the surplus of poor, single women in these urban centres and the practicality of giving them an alternative to marriage. The lack of a dowry requirement doubtless explains the large numbers of women involved, as well as their varied social backgrounds. In other areas of Europe, for example, in Italy, unattached women also came together to lead a religious life without formal vows.

Although some communities of beguines continued to exist even until the early twentieth century, from 1240 on they were the subject of repeated condemnations by church councils and popes. The diversity of their practices, the lack of regulation and hierarchy among them, their spiritual autonomy, even their economic activities—which appeared to threaten the guilds—all made them suspect. In particular, their attempt to create their own place in society without the conventional anchors of family or monastery vexed the authorities. It did not help that some individuals became associated with heresies. Most of the beguine communities, however, were allowed to fade peacefully away, victims of the economic decline of the late Middle Ages.

MEDIEVAL FEMINISM?

Was there feminism in any of this, in the alternatives created by the virgins and martyrs of the early church, by the powerful and learned nuns of the early Middle Ages, by the prophets, mystics, and beguines of the later centuries? Is any of it related to nineteenth- and twentieth-century feminism?

The most obvious difference between these early examples and later feminists was that the latter explicitly recognized and condemned women's oppression. They were aware of themselves as feminists. One can compare, for example, Catherine of Siena's revolt against parents and culture with the much later revolt of the Frenchwoman Madeleine Pelletier (1874–1939). Pelletier, who claimed to have been born a feminist, was judged the most radical feminist of her generation. Like the earlier woman, Pelletier rebelled against her mother's hopes for an advantageous marriage. "For an intelligent woman," Pelletier announced, "marriage is moral suicide."[26] Like Christina of Markyate, she cut her hair and donned masculine clothing in response to her mother's pressure to dress and behave as a marriageable young lady. More significantly for our comparison, she also vowed herself to chastity. But Pelletier's vow was fundamentally political since she interpreted sexual relations as harmful to women within the context of male dominance. She consciously understood her society to be an oppressive patriarchy and related her motives and actions to it.

Did Christina or Catherine have the understanding that Gerda Lerner calls the first stage of feminist consciousness: "the awareness of a wrong"?[27] Clearly they knew that the conventional life of a married woman was not for them. Additionally, Catherine attempted to end the corruption she perceived in the church and in her country. Yet both thought in terms of spirit versus flesh or holiness versus sinfulness rather than in terms of male dominance and oppression of women. The wrong they targeted was the obstinacy of those who failed to recognize God's plan and, presumably, themselves as agents of it. The obstinacy of the world was, however, something that any Christian had to accept. Their goal was intimacy with God rather than empowerment of either themselves or women as a group. They thus fail the litmus test suggested by Joan Kinnaird, who defines a "true feminist" as distinguished by her "identification with her sex as a whole and a personal commitment to the advancement of women."[28]

It is hard to fault the Middle Ages for lacking feminist theory when the idea of a social order alterable by human action for human benefit lay several centuries in the future. The world medieval people knew, complete with hierarchy and patriarchy, was a world ordained by God. Even Hildegard of Bingen accepted the dominant ideology:

> For when God looked upon man he was well pleased, for man was made in his image and likeness. . . . But at her creation woman partook of a mixture of the two [man and God]; she is a different creature, created through another than God. . . . The man therefore presides over the tribunal of the world, ruling all creatures, while the woman is under his mastery, and subject to him.[29]

Hildegard's acceptance of this theory does not seem to have limited either her actions or her thoughts. She wrote, for example, of woman and man as complementary in their natures and in their reproductive roles. As well, she viewed the divine and the soul as both feminine and masculine in nature. Unlike many of her contemporaries she characterized women as less sexual than men and minimized Eve's guilt in original sin while emphasizing Satan's role. Although Hildegard saved her highest appreciation for sexual purity and renunciation, she was able to write about sexual activity with erotic overtones and express a frank appreciation of nature. Although she employed an abundance of rich and complex feminine symbolism in her theology, she drew no conclusions from it that would empower either herself, whom she saw as an exception, or other women. Hildegard supported the eleventh-century Gregorian reform movement that had such disastrous consequences for convents and staunchly defended clerical hierarchy and privilege. In two other ways she supported the status quo: she refused to admit non-nobles to her cloister and she rejected homosexuality as contrary to nature.

Lay Noblewomen

We can appreciate the practical impact of women using religion to create a sphere of autonomy for themselves when we look at the lives of secular women. At times during the Middle Ages lay noblewomen enjoyed significant power and influence. In the sixth through eleventh centuries the absence of centralized states in Europe meant that political power became localized and based on land ownership. This situation gave considerable opportunity to propertied women. Bridal gifts, favourable inheritance laws, early widowhood, all placed material resources in women's hands. One tenth-century Italian noblewoman accumulated more than thirty-seven large royal manors through grants from her family and husband.

Queens were able to exploit court politics and the uncertainties of royal succession to wield power. Some used military prowess. Aethelflaed of Mercia ruled independently in the tenth century, building and defending a line of fortresses against the Vikings and the Welsh. She led an alliance of kings and rulers of northern Britain. Upon her death her supporters chose her only daughter to rule. Historian Pauline Stafford calls the tenth century "a century of women."[30] Queen-regents occupied thrones in England, the Ottoman empire, Italy, France, and Lorraine for a short period in the 980s.

These women were the beneficiaries of favourable circumstances. They knew how to exploit opportunities, but they had no control over them. Legal changes that allowed daughters to inherit belonged to a period of great land acquisitions in which there was wealth enough for both daughters and sons. When conditions changed, women lost. In the eleventh century, the adoption of primogeniture stabilized succession and deprived later queens of a major sphere of activity.

Even while the question of succession was still open, royal women were dependent upon male support and could be suddenly left friendless and vulnerable. Emma, widowed by the death of the West Frankish king Lothar and abandoned by her son, wrote, "I am that Emma, once queen of the Franks, who commanded such armies, now without even domestic companions to accompany me." Pauline Stafford summarizes, "The queen's position, power and status derived almost entirely from husband and marriage. Deprived of these the range of options was limited."[31]

Circumstances could benefit women, but they could also victimize them. The ninth-century Frankish noblewoman Dhuoda lived in this "age of opportunity." After her marriage she was virtually abandoned by her husband. Her husband sent their first son away at the age of fifteen and had their second son taken away from Dhuoda before his baptism, so that she did not even know his name two years later. Her husband's embroilment in royal politics led to rumours that he was having an affair with the emperor's wife, Judith, and he was later beheaded by Judith's son. Dhuoda's sister-in-law was drowned as a witch, one brother-in-law was beheaded, another was blinded, and there is evidence that both her sons were later beheaded as well. Although Dhuoda found solace in her spiritual meditations and writings, perhaps the saddest fact is that if it were not for the manuscript she wrote, a treatise addressed to her son, we would never know of her existence, for she is mentioned nowhere else. The experience of laywomen might explain in fact why the religious option was so appealing and why the numbers of religious women grew steadily throughout the Middle Ages.

The few successful laywomen bequeathed no feminist consciousness to their daughters. If they were aware that they lived in a patriarchal society, they were largely willing to play by the rules men had made. Women acted as men did to gain power and ruled as men did when they got it.

Women and Clerical Authority

Did religious women escape male dominance? Although they may have evaded the control of their families, did they not transfer that control to the church? Were they not still dependent on male authority and goodwill?

All the women mentioned so far accepted the authority of the clergy. God told Margery Kempe how pleased he was "because you are obedient to Holy Church, and you obey your confessor and follow his counsel."[32] Although arrested at times by suspicious authorities and threatened with burning as a heretic, she remained steadfastly orthodox. However reluctant, Catherine of Siena obeyed her confessor's orders to eat at least once a day, even though it caused her painful vomiting. What we know about the relationship of these women to their confessors and advisers suggests complementarity and mutuality; after all, it is thanks to these men for the most part that we even know about the women whose visions they recorded and whose lives they described. Even when the relationship was troubled, most visionaries, with the exception of heretics, wanted to die with the blessing of the clergy as good, orthodox believers.

Just as happened in the early centuries of Christianity, heresy was attractive to some. Women may even have been preponderant in the heretical groups of the twelfth to fourteenth centuries. David Herlihy points out that women appeared more frequently in heretical sects than in any other forum in medieval culture.[33] Georges Duby has described medieval heresy as seen by its contemporaries as "a kind of feminist movement." The tendency in most heretical sects to treat men and women as equals went "completely counter to the fundamental structure of society."[34] Some groups, such as the Lollards, accepted women as priests or preachers. Among the Cathars of southern France women could attain the highest status of *perfecti.*

Others went further. One thirteenth-century sect in Italy believed they could be saved only through a woman, namely, their leader Guglielma of Milan, whose life supposedly paralleled the life of Jesus. Guglielma stipulated that her helpmate Manfreda would become pope and appoint women cardinals. The followers of Bloemardine in the Low Countries likewise tried to set up a church with a female clergy. Prous Boneta in fourteenth-century southern France considered herself the redeemer of humanity whom God had sent to preach his word throughout the world.

Without resorting to heresy, there were other, more subtle ways in which women could defy the authority of the church. The women who claimed authority as visionaries were aware that they could be seen as usurping male authority. For that reason, they were careful to emphasize that it was God who spoke, not they themselves. Reluctant to credit or record their visions, they did so only by divine command, like Hildegard at the age of forty-two or Margery Kempe in her sixties. God's command to Hildegard was explicit, designed to overcome her anxiety: "But because you are timid in speaking and simple in expounding and unlearned in writing these things, tell and write them not in accord with human speech, or the understanding of human invention, or the will of human composition, but in accord with what you see and hear in the heavens above, in the marvels of God."[35]

God's call to women to speak was, of course, a defiance of the biblical command for women to be silent. The resulting anxiety may have prompted the ill-health that so many of them experienced. Hildegard suffered from chronic illness, which seemed to flare up just before she undertook major projects. She raised herself "up from sickness"[36] in order to write her first work and received the strength to persevere in writing it for ten years. Margery Kempe reported that "she was many times ill while this treatise was being written." Yet as soon as she began dictating, she would suddenly become "hale and healthy."[37] The one mystic who spoke in her own rather than God's voice, Marguerite Porète, was burned as a heretic in 1310 even though her ideas were not so different from those of other mystics and were widely diffused among her contemporaries.

Sometimes God commanded these women to speak out or act in ways that more directly infringed on priestly prerogatives or church tradition. Gertrude the Great, a thirteenth-century German nun, reported that Christ had given her powers of forgiveness and ordination. Other women similarly claimed that God had directly contravened St Paul's injunction against women speaking in church. Margery Kempe defended herself against this same injunction by pointing out that she never spoke *from the pulpit:* "I use only conversation and good words, and that I will do while I live." Later Paul himself appeared in a vision to Margery and seemed to commiserate with her for suffering "much tribulation because of his writing"[38] in as close to an apology as one can imagine coming from the saint.

The fate of Joan of Arc (1412–31) illustrates the fine line between mysticism and heresy, between behaviour the authorities were willing to tolerate and behaviour they were not. Of all the women mentioned so far Joan was the only one of truly humble origins. She was a peasant; a neighbour testified to her family's poverty. From the age of thirteen she heard voices, which directed her to fight for the king of France against the English invaders. Out of the rich folkloric and religious tradition that was part of French rural culture came many female visionaries who could have served as role models for Joan, but Joan's voices led her to an act quite remarkable for a young girl—leading an army into battle. Her common background may have made it easier for the court and nobles to desert her when her string of victories ended.

Although politics played a large role in Joan's capture and trial, the church had no trouble finding her guilty of witchcraft and heresy. Joan's crime was her refusal to accept clerical authority. When asked, "If the Church Militant tells you that your revelations are illusions, or diabolical things, will you defer to the Church?" she declared, "I will defer to God. . . . I have acted by the order of God: it is impossible for me to say otherwise. In case the Church should prescribe the contrary, I should not defer to any one in the world, but to God alone."[39]

The other mystics discussed here also felt that they owed their highest obedience to God's command as spoken directly to them, but they proceeded by first securing the approval of the clergy for their visions and usually for their actions. Joan, in contrast, neither worked closely with a confessor nor sought clerical approval or guidance. She attempted to operate autonomously from her own religious experience, as had Marguerite Porète, also burned at the stake. Church approval depended, therefore, on the perceived readiness of women to submit to clerical authority. One wonders how much another charge weighed additionally against Joan; the charge was pride, or defying the norms for womanly behaviour by disobeying her parents, dressing like a man, and living like a soldier.

Considering Joan of Arc's fate, it is remarkable that some women were motivated by their prophetic voice to criticize the clergy directly. Margery Kempe rebuked anyone who swore regardless of whether the sinner was a lay person or a cleric. Although otherwise obedient and deferential to clerics she respected, she responded tartly to the Archbishop of York, who accused her of being "a very wicked woman": "Sir, I also hear it said that you are a wicked man. And if you are as wicked as people say, you will never get to heaven, unless you amend while you are here."[40] Mechthild of Magdeburg had been even less tactful: "God calls the canons goats because their flesh stinks of lasciviousness in the eternal truth before the Holy Trinity."[41] Catherine of Siena denounced cardinals as "ingrates, boors, and hirelings . . . fools, worthy of a thousand deaths!"[42]

Strange as it may seem, these women were not truly defiant. They were exploiting the tradition that assumed female inferiority and equated women with weakness and humility. These were the very qualities that made women appropriate channels for the divine. God told Mechthild of Magdeburg,

Whenever I bestowed a special grace
I always sought for the lowest,
The least, the best concealed place.[43]

In other words, the woman who became a prophet underscored her own inferiority rather than denying it. Prophecy could thus function as a safety valve
that allowed women to bypass authority in special situations while reinforcing it at all other times. The idea of the female prophet was a subtle form of
social control. The more women spoke out, the more they supported patriarchal assumptions about their second-class status.

A more basic challenge to clerical authority may have come from the
characteristic extremism of women's devotional practices. Was this a reaction
against the clergy's plea for moderation? The more the church strove to
accommodate the laity, by recognizing marriage as a sacrament, for example,
or by discouraging strict asceticism, the more women refused to be accom-
modated. The clergy's efforts to create a secondary place for women in the
church did not satisfy "pious women [who] elaborated a religiosity that was
in no way moderate, a sense of self that was in no way secondary." This
amounted to "a rejection of a successful and moderate church, with its cosy
domestication of women."[44]

In her book *Holy Feast and Holy Fast* Caroline Bynum analyzes the practice of food renunciation, which was one form of devotional extremism.
Food, its preparation, its consumption, its donation to the poor, but above
all its renunciation in the form of extreme fasting, was a dominant theme in
the lives of female saints and mystics in the late Middle Ages. To fast was to
suffer, and to suffer was to identify with Christ on the cross. Pain was holy.
Bynum describes the visions of late medieval women as streaming with
blood. One contemporary account describes how nuns "in Advent and
Lent . . . hack at themselves cruelly, hostilely lacerating their bodies until the
blood flows, with all kinds of whips, so that the sound reverberates all over
the monastery and rises to the ears of the Lord of hosts sweeter than all
melody."[45]

Suffering was a means of redemption, for oneself and for others.
Catherine of Siena was the extreme example. As a teenager she wore an iron
chain bound tightly around her body, beat herself severely three times a day
for one and one-half hours on each occasion, and at one time kept silent,
except for confession, for three years. Above all, she refused to eat. After the
age of fifteen she began restricting her diet to bread, raw vegetables, and cold
water. Later, she only chewed on herbs. Although she didn't swallow them,
she vomited the juices since her stomach could no longer digest anything.
Most times she gave up food altogether except for the consecrated host at
communion. She died at the age of thirty-three, presumably from starvation
but secure in her conviction that the souls of her family would thereby be
saved.

Fasting had practical as well as spiritual benefits, argues Bynum. It
enabled women "to control their bodies and their world." Food preparation

was closely associated with women; food was the one resource women could control. Whereas men gave up property, women gave up food:

> Women's food practices frequently enabled them to determine the shape of their lives—to reject unwanted marriages, to substitute religious activities for more menial duties within the family, to redirect the use of fathers' or husbands' resources, to change or convert family members, to criticize powerful secular or religious authorities, and to claim for themselves teaching, counselling, and reforming roles for which the religious tradition provided, at best, ambivalent support.[46]

Some women would forget to cook and shop while in mystical trances. Others gave away the family's food. Like Catherine of Siena, in the fifteenth century Lidwina of Schiedham used fasting to get her parents to back away from an unwanted marriage, thus avoiding the flight from home that Christina of Markyate had found necessary.

The observations that historian Nancy Cott makes about American Protestant women in the late eighteenth and early nineteenth centuries who practised what Cott calls "a sort of holy selfishness" apply to medieval women as well. Like the Protestant missionaries Cott describes, medieval religious women practised "a submission of self that was simultaneously a pronounced form of self-assertion."[47] Its attraction may be gauged by the incidence of imposters. We hear, for example, of a thirteenth-century woman who pretended to need no nourishment other than what angels and other heavenly creatures provided. Another one in the early sixteenth century reportedly ate only the eucharist. Both women were discovered to supply themselves with substantial earthly nourishment at night when they thought themselves alone. As punishment, both were executed.

For all that, food renunciation seems a long way from feminism. Its similarity to anorexia has not escaped the attention of historians. William Davis has commented sympathetically on the modern anorexic's desire to connect only to herself, to deny the needs that would make her dependent on men. Believing that medieval religious women also struggled "to free themselves of the shackles of male authority," Davis finds the result paradoxical:

> In doing so, they may have unwittingly colluded with the very forces they were attempting to bypass. The holy anorectic's resolve to be absolutely free of bodily desires so as to unite with God seems to underscore the idea that femininity, in its natural or perhaps instinctive state, is dangerous and potentially sinful. . . . From this perspective the church fathers would have done well to remain awestruck by the religiosity of the holy anorectics in their charge. They did not have to enforce their domination via suspicions of demonic possession or complicated formulas for beatification. The saints themselves were unknowingly supporting their cultural values by equating bodily purity with essential holiness. Or, to put it another way, the women who struggled to express their sense of self by becoming holy did so in a way that reinforced a male interpretation of female psychology.[48]

Just as contemporary women aspire to cultural standards of thinness, so medieval women aspired to specific models of holiness. Even this form of extremism ultimately confirmed medieval patriarchal values.

The same paradox seems to apply to women's renunciation of sex, which was in line with Christian misogyny. As discussed in Chapter 1, the ancient Greeks equated man with reason and woman with sensuality. The Christian emphasis on Eve as seducer added a moral dimension to the physiological definition of the female as characterized by sexual lust. A life of continence was the only way, therefore, for women to redeem themselves in the eyes of the clergy. Devotion to God necessitated the renunciation of femaleness. The sentiment of Philo Judeus in the first century was common among the church fathers: "Progress is nothing else than the giving up of the female gender by changing into the male."[49] It is difficult to see any connection between self-abnegation, in whatever form, and feminism. How can such a thorough-going denial of the physical person be construed as personally liberating?

The Meaning of Symbols

William Davis assumes that the holy anorexics were accepting "a male interpretation of female psychology," but did women necessarily understand and use symbols in the same way as men? It may be true that female prophets reinforced the notion of female inferiority, but to whom and for whom? When the heretic Marguerite Porète claimed, "I—*because* I am lowly—am the exemplar of salvation,"[50] it is difficult to see this statement as a confirmation of her inferiority.

Caroline Bynum rejects the idea that female piety was primarily a reflection or even a reversal of male symbols. Although women drew on dominant images such as the suffering Christ, they did not interpret them the same way or assign to them the same importance that men did. Religious men sought to embrace the central paradox in Christianity, that God suffered by taking on human form, by inverting the stereotype of powerful men and weak women. When they opposed flesh to spirit, they meant female flesh, which more than male flesh symbolized the weakness and physicality of humanity. They called themselves women to express their humility. In these ways they were exploiting the contrast of male and female. Women, however, did not resort to paradox, contrasts, or inversion of symbols. They also understood human flesh as female, but unlike men they did not have to deny their gender to do so. Their symbolism embraced and enhanced the ordinary experiences of women's social and biological lives: eating, nurturing, and suffering. Women's symbols, according to Bynum, expressed not a denial of the flesh but a "deepening of ordinary human experience that came when God impinged upon it."[51] Thus medieval women's religiosity, understood on its own terms, does not necessarily convey the negativity that modern historians associate with renunciation and asceticism.

Debate over the significance of the cult of the Virgin Mary further illustrates this problem of the meaning of symbols. Marina Warner, in her study of the cult of the Virgin, warns that "in the very celebration of the perfect human woman, both humanity and women were subtly denigrated." "Every facet of the Virgin had been systematically developed to diminish, not increase, her likeness to the female condition. Her freedom from sex, painful delivery, age, death, and all sin exalted her *ipso facto* above ordinary women and showed them up as inferior." The Virgin was thus an unlikely role model. Warner quotes Simone de Beauvoir, the twentieth-century French feminist: "For the first time in human history the mother kneels before her son; she freely accepts her inferiority. This is the supreme masculine victory."[52]

Others have argued as well that the cult of the Virgin was designed to channel and control lay piety, to defuse the attraction of heresies. Devotion to the Virgin was associated with twelfth-century monastic culture, with monks rather than with female mystics. Additional evidence suggests that the cult of the Virgin attracted more men than women whereas women's devotion tended to be more Christocentric. Certainly feminine language and symbolism were common among monks and in no way implied increased respect for women. Conversely, it was a female mystic, Julian of Norwich, who elevated the notion of Jesus as mother to the central image of her theology. Julian has been described as "supreme among those Christian thinkers who have perceived God (and God's relationship to the soul) unrestricted by patriarchal language and masculine imagery."[53]

The women mystics who did refer to Mary saw her as an inspiration and a source of empowerment. Birgitta of Sweden was certain that Mary had chosen her to be the special representative of God on earth, in keeping with a tradition that because the world had been lost through a woman, it would be saved through one. Other women saw in Mary the channel through which Christ became human. For Hildegard of Bingen it was Mary's body that formed Christ's body. Thus Hildegard could declare that "it is exactly *female* flesh—the very weakness of woman—that restores the world."[54] Christina of Markyate found more comfort and instruction in Mary than in Jesus. It was possible for female mystics, when they pictured Mary in heaven, to see her role as confirming the absolute heavenly equality of male and female.

It is therefore difficult to know how much to make of female symbols. Although Hildegard used female symbolism to convey the mystery of Christ uniting divinity and humanity, she also described the times in which she lived as "effeminate," meaning weak and corrupt. For Catherine of Siena, *virile* was a positive quality and a favourite adjective, which she did not hesitate to apply to herself. Had these women internalized gendered stereotypes? Do either of them fit the description Elizabeth Petroff gives of the female mystic as "a female subject, living autonomously in a world she defines, speaking a language she invents and controls"?[55] And if so, were they thereby feminists?

Female Culture or Feminist Culture?

When we speak of a feminine piety or religious practice self-consciously adopted by women, we are describing a female culture. Such a culture, independent of male norms, seems to have been the product of the networks formed by religious women. Whereas male mystics were often isolated, women tended to cluster in religious houses that achieved a reputation for mysticism. Even non-cloistered women could find role models and cultivate their sense of belonging to a tradition of heroic women. We have seen that women were inspired by Thecla's story to teach and baptize, much to the consternation of church authorities. Margery Kempe was familiar with past and contemporary holy women who provided her with role models. She found reassurance when God told her, "Just as I spoke to St Bridget [Birgitta], just so I speak to you, daughter."[56]

Although a medieval female culture existed, it was not a feminist one. In the nineteenth and twentieth centuries, feminists exploited the radical potential of a female culture to assert values fundamentally different from those of the dominant culture. In the Middle Ages, the only tangible result of female culture was to accommodate a small number of individuals, none of whom identified with women as a group subordinated because of gender. If they identified with a group, it was with their religious community. Where they were exceptional, their exceptionality served to reinforce the idea of the subordination of woman as a whole. If anything, the female mystics of the later Middle Ages tended to be less conscious of gender than were their male counterparts.

Useful in this context is Linda Gordon's distinction between feminist and non-feminist traditions in women's thought and culture. In discussing the methodological problems of writing feminist history, Gordon affirms that feminism is based on a "controversial political interpretation and struggle."[57] It is not just the result of a socially constructed experience but entails criticizing and rejecting part of what society considers female. In the latter category we can put the assumptions of woman's inferiority, however empowering they were to some medieval women.

The evidence we have of medieval women forming strong networks, creating their own pattern of religious experience, appropriating traditional symbols, escaping directly from one kind of patriarchal control while indirectly undermining another does not constitute feminism or a feminist tradition. The fact that women could envision themselves or other women as "saviors or messiahs, as advisors to kings and popes, even as priests and cardinals, or as the holder of the papal office itself"[58] demands our respect, but the struggle of these exceptional women took place within a larger context of subordination that went unchallenged. Although they and their early Christian predecessors managed to carve out a sphere of limited autonomy for themselves, they left no foundation for the future. Ultimately they were as dependent upon circumstance as were secular women.

Individual women throughout the centuries would continue to find in religion an inspiration that would give them self-confidence and self-respect. But when the opportunities afforded by tolerant clergymen began to disappear, as was already happening in the fifteenth century, only the truly exceptional could find an audience and then only with the most cautious and clever use of language. While we can admire the subversive protest of medieval women and appreciate their tenacity and courage in the face of hostility and disparagement, the theoretical basis for feminist politics still lay in the future.

NOTES

1   Suzanne Fonay Wemple, *Women in Frankish Society: Marriage and the Cloister 500 to 900* (Philadelphia: University of Pennsylvania Press, 1981), 149. R.A. Nisbit, in 1973, described first-century Christianity as "a kind of women's liberation" (quoted in Elisabeth Schussler Fiorenza, *In Memory of Her: A Feminist Theological Reconstruction of Christian Origins* [New York: Crossroad, 1986], 263).

2   Celsus, second century, quoted in Ramsay MacMullen, *Christianizing the Roman Empire A.D. 100–400* (New Haven: Yale University Press, 1984), 37.

3   Peter Brown, *The Body and Society: Men, Women, and Sexual Renunciation in Early Christianity* (New York: Columbia University Press, 1988), 150, 284, 266.

4   Paraphrased in Jo Ann McNamara, *A New Song: Celibate Women in the First Three Christian Centuries* (New York: Harrington Park Press, 1985), 67.

5   Quoted in Brown, *The Body and Society,* 242.

6   Quoted in Katharina M. Wilson, "The Saxon Canoness: Hrotsvit of Gandersheim," in *Medieval Women Writers*, ed. Katharina M. Wilson (Athens: University of Georgia Press, 1984), 38.

7   Hildegard of Bingen, *Scivias,* trans. Mother Columba Hart and Jane Bishop (New York: Paulist Press, 1990), 205.

8   Mechthild von Magdeburg, *Flowing Light of the Divinity,* ed. Susan Clark, trans. Christiane Mesch Galvani (New York: Garland Publishing, 1991), 100.

9   Quoted in Sabina Flanagan, *Hildegard of Bingen, 1098–1179: A Visionary Life* (London: Routledge, 1989), 4.

10 Fiona Bowie and Oliver Davies, eds., *Hildegard of Bingen: An Anthology* (New York: Crossroad, 1990), 65.

11 Flanagan, *Hildegard of Bingen, 1098–1179,* 13.

12 Ibid., 15.

13 Quoted in Shulamith Shahar, *The Fourth Estate: A History of Women in the Middle Ages* (London: Routledge, 1983), 56.

14 Betty Radice, trans., *The Letters of Heloïse and Abelard* (Harmondsworth: Penguin Books, 1974), 66.

15 Sister Prudence Allen, *The Concept of Woman: The Aristotelian Revolution 750 BC–AD 1250* (Montreal: Eden Press, 1985), 292.

16 Caroline Walker Bynum, *Jesus as Mother: Studies in the Spirituality of the High Middle Ages* (Berkeley: University of California Press, 1982), 185. Prudence Allen argues just the opposite with regard to Hildegard, that her theories of sex complementarity, or equality, arose from her experience of "women and men jointly participating in the practice of philosophy" (p. 408). Although Disibodenberg, the site of Hildegard's first convent, was a double monastery, there is no evidence to conclude that the women and men studied together.

17 Quoted in R.W. Southern, *Western Society and the Church in the Middle Ages* (London: Penguin Books, 1970), 314.

18 Margery Kempe, *The Book of Margery Kempe*, trans. B.A. Windeatt (London: Penguin Books, 1985), 78–79.

19 Raymond of Capua, *The Life of Catherine of Siena*, trans. Conleth Kearns (Wilmington, DE: Michael Glazier, 1980), 46.

20 Ibid., 230–31.

21 Quoted in Margaret M. Miles, *Image as Insight: Visual Understanding in Western Christianity and Secular Culture* (Boston: Beacon Press, 1985), 87.

22 Clarissa W. Atkinson, *Mystic and Pilgrim: The Book and the World of Margery Kempe* (Ithaca, NY: Cornell University Press, 1983), 13.

23 Kempe, *Book of Margery Kempe*, 44.

24 Ibid., 34.

25 Joan Kelly, "Early Feminist Theory and the *Querelle des Femmes,* 1400–1789," in *Women, History and Theory: The Essays of Joan Kelly* (Chicago: University of Chicago Press, 1984), 68. Similarly, Carolyn Walker Bynum writes in *Holy Feast and Holy Fast: The Religious Significance of Food to Medieval Women* (Berkeley: University of California Press, 1987), 14, "Indeed, for the first time in Christian history, we can identify a women's movement (the beguines)." German historians have commonly used the term women's movement to describe the beguines and other groups of religious women.

26 Quoted in Karen Offen, "New Documents for the History of French Feminism During the Early Third Republic," *History of European Ideas* 8, 4–5 (1987): 623.

27 Gerda Lerner, *The Creation of Patriarchy* (New York: Oxford University Press, 1986), 242.

28 Joan Kinnaird, "Mary Astell and the Conservative Contribution to English Feminism," *Journal of British Studies* 19 (1979): 58.

29 Quoted in Carolly Erickson, *The Medieval Vision: Essays in History and Perception* (New York: Oxford University Press, 1976), 211.

30 Pauline Stafford, *Queens, Concubines, and Dowagers: The King's Wife in the Early Middle Ages* (Athens: University of Georgia Press, 1983), 141.

31 Ibid., 175, 174.

32 Kempe, *Book of Margery Kempe*, 108.

33 David Herlihy, *Opera Muliebria: Women and Work in Medieval Europe* (New York: McGraw-Hill, 1990), 121. Bynum, however, regards this thesis as unproven (*Jesus as Mother*, 249 n).

34 Georges Duby, *The Knight, the Lady and the Priest: The Making of Modern Marriage in Medieval France* (New York: Random House, 1983), 109.

35 Quoted in Barbara Newman, *Sister of Wisdom: St. Hildegard's Theology of the Feminine* (Berkeley: University of California Press, 1987), 26.

36 Bowie and Davis, eds., *Hildegard of Bingen*, 70.

37 Kempe, *Book of Margery Kempe*, 260.

38 Ibid., 164, 199.

39 Quoted in Anne Llewellyn Barstow, *Joan of Arc: Heretic, Mystic, Shaman* (Lewiston: Ewin Mellen Press, 1986), 94.

40 Kempe, *Book of Margery Kempe,* 163.

41 Mechthild von Magdeburg, *Flowing Light of the Divinity,* 173.

42 Catherine of Siena, "To Three Italian Cardinals," in *Medieval Women Writers,* ed. Wilson, 261, 262. This document is not listed in the table of contents but is included as part of a chapter by Joseph Berrigan entitled "The Tuscan Visionary: Saint Catherine of Siena."

43 Mechthild von Magdeburg, *Flowing Light of the Divinity,* 56.

44 Bynum, *Holy Feast,* 240.

45 Quoted in ibid., 210.

46 Ibid., 189, 220.

47 Nancy F. Cott, *The Bonds of Womanhood: "Woman's Sphere" in New England, 1780–1835* (New Haven, CT: Yale University Press, 1977), 140–41.

48 William N. Davis, "Epilogue," in Rudolph M. Bell, *Holy Anorexia* (Chicago: University of Chicago Press, 1985), 185.

49 Quoted in R. Howard Bloch, *Medieval Misogyny and the Invention of Western Romantic Love* (Chicago: University of Chicago Press, 1991), 107.

50 Quoted in Bynum, *Holy Feast,* 279.

51 Ibid., 295. Jo Ann McNamara suggests another interpretation, that women's self-imposed suffering may have been an alternative way to continue a tradition of giving at a time when they no longer controlled much material wealth. See her article "The Need to Give: Suffering and Female Sanctity in the Middle Ages," in *Images of Sainthood in Medieval Europe,* ed. Renate Blumenfeld-Kosinski and Timea Szell (Ithaca, NY: Cornell University Press, 1991), 199–221.

52 Marina Warner, *Alone of All Her Sex: The Myth and the Cult of the Virgin Mary* (New York: Alfred A. Knopf, 1976), xxi, 153, 183.

53 Atkinson, *Mystic and Pilgrim,* 192.

54 Bynum, *Holy Feast,* 265.

55 Elizabeth Alvilda Petroff, *Body and Soul: Essays on Medieval Women and Mysticism* (New York: Oxford University Press, 1994), 21.

56 Kempe, *Book of Margery Kempe,* 83.

57 Linda Gordon, "What's New in Women's History," in *Feminist Studies/Critical Studies,* ed. T. de Lauretis (Bloomington: Indiana University Press, 1986), 30.

58 Barstow, *Joan of Arc,* 42.

3

The Impact of the Renaissance: Women, Learning, and the Creative Arts

No one who has studied women in the past can help but be impressed by the frequency and intensity of their desire for learning, a desire that usually went unfulfilled. In her recent study of the rise of feminist consciousness, Gerda Lerner begins with the systematic disadvantage that women suffered in education. Women's exclusion from the opportunities given their brothers not only prevented individuals from engaging in satisfying and creative work but also deprived society as a whole of the contributions of one-half of its members. In addition, women intellectuals expended inordinate energy in proving their worth, trying to counter the assumption of their inherent mental inferiority. "Women, for far longer than any other structured group in society," asserts Lerner, "have lived in a condition of trained ignorance."[1]

The Renaissance of the fifteenth and sixteenth centuries had the potential to alter that situation; for the first time in centuries influential men in intellectual circles aired the idea that women and men could benefit from the same education. Education ranked alongside religion in motivating women to express themselves publicly and thereby challenge the male monopoly on culture and men's ideas of women's proper role.

Nevertheless, the promise of the Renaissance was not realized for more than a handful of women privileged by high class standing. Even then, social endorsement of their achievements was grudging and qualified. Those women who were able to study and express themselves intellectually did so in the face of overwhelming odds. Not surprisingly, most of them internalized society's ambivalence about their achievements. Religious faith sustained medieval women against the opposition and ridicule of contemporaries and

1267–1337	Giotto di Bondone
1312–21	Dante Alighieri writes *The Divine Comedy*
1341	Francesco Petrarch crowned poet laureate in Italy
ca. 1385–1400	Geoffrey Chaucer writes *Canterbury Tales*
1455	Gutenberg bible printed
1465–1558	Cassandra Fedele
1475–1564	Michelangelo
1505–44	Margaret More Roper
1513	Niccolò Machiavelli writes *The Prince*
1532–1625	Sofonisba Anguissola
1543	Nicolas Copernicus writes *On the Revolutions of the Heavenly Spheres*
1564–1616	William Shakespeare
1564–1642	Galileo Galilei
1565–1645	Marie de Gournay
1593–1652?	Artemisia Gentileschi
ca. 1640–89	Aphra Behn
1651–95	Sor Juana Inés de la Cruz
1685–1750	Johann Sebastian Bach

would continue to sustain women in the sixteenth and seventeenth centuries, as we shall see in Chapter 4. But the learned and creative women of the Renaissance and later who were not directly inspired by religion could make no equivalent claim for a holy mission. Occasionally they found female role models but they were primarily aware of their uniqueness and their isolation. This exceptionality impeded them in identifying with and promoting women's interests as a group.

Knowing the difficulties faced by intellectually ambitious women, we can appreciate why feminist movements developed relatively late in history. What is striking is how little the restrictions and opportunities for female learning changed over five hundred years. The pattern of self-doubt and apology that emerged during the Renaissance continued to hold for most intellectually and creatively ambitious women through the nineteenth century. This chapter looks at women with generally secular interests who tried to express themselves through learning or through their talents as writers and painters. The first part examines the theoretical and practical obstacles to women's higher education. It explores the manner in which women confronted barriers and the influence that this experience had on the formation of a feminist consciousness. To show continuity, the text draws on examples from the late fifteenth century to the mid-nineteenth. The second part of the chapter, which reflects the results of the abundant recent scholarship on women writers and painters, analyzes examples of such women from the six-teenth century to the end of the eighteenth.

WOMEN AND LEARNING

A learned Woman is thought to be a Comet, that bodes
Mischief, when ever it appears.

BATHSUA MAKIN, 1673

The rise of universities, open only to men, in the twelfth and thirteenth cen-turies was a setback for women. The prominence of the nuns who had been educational and literary pioneers was eclipsed by the authority of male uni-versity graduates. Although women were formally barred from universities, a handful, supported by influential men, managed to get degrees from German and Italian institutions over the centuries. Anna Maria van Schurman in the seventeenth century was allowed to attend university lectures in Utrecht, hid-den in a cubicle. Other women disguised themselves as men. When a woman student attending the university in Kraków in the early fifteenth century was detected and asked the reasons for her disguise, she answered simply, "For the love of learning."[2]

By reviving the literature and values of ancient Greece and republican Rome, the Renaissance challenged medieval educational theory and practice, which was based on the philosophy of scholasticism and the university study of theology, medicine, and law. In contrast, Renaissance scholars, or human-ists, posited the ideal of learning grounded in a study of the humanities: moral philosophy, history, and literature. Much of this learning took place outside the university, in private homes through tutors or in small academies. Alongside the medieval goal of contemplating and glorifying God came the desire to inspire and guide an active life in the service of family and state.

What did this mean for women? A learned woman of high rank was not only a testimony to the humanists' faith in the benefits of education but also an ornament to her family in a society that valued culture. The immediate beneficiaries were the daughters of aristocratic families in fifteenth- and sixteenth-century Italy, who were either taught by their fathers or encouraged to study alongside their brothers with tutors. Many of these young women became renowned for their learning. In the late fifteenth century, Cassandra Fedele won honour for her family and community by delivering public addresses at the University of Padua, to the people of Venice, and before the Venetian government. A century later, Sara Coppio Sulam, born in the Jewish ghetto of Venice in 1590, mastered Latin, Greek, Italian, Spanish, and Hebrew. Sulam hosted a literary salon, where women and men could meet for stimulating conversation, and she also carried on a debate with Catholic philosophers and clerics through her letters.

In the sixteenth century poets and writers sought the support of such *grandes dames* as Vittoria Colonna and Veronica Gambara, both widely praised by contemporaries for their poetry as well as their patronage. In 1516 a male writer paid tribute to the famous women of his age, "who abandoned the needle and cloth and joined the Muses on Mount Helicon to quench their thirst at the sacred fountain."[3] Writing was not only compatible with womanly duties; it crowned them, at least for aristocratic women. The ideal lady of the Italian Renaissance was exemplary in her roles not only as wife and mother but also as patron and poet.

As the Renaissance spread north, upper-class women hosted literary salons in France. Catherine of Aragon, assiduously educated by her mother, Queen Isabella of Castile, brought the new learning with her to England when she came to marry the brother of Henry VIII. Throughout the sixteenth century women associated with the English court such as Elizabeth I, Lady Jane Grey, Mary Sidney Wroth, and Margaret More Roper were honoured by their contemporaries for their erudition. Elsewhere, Queen Katerina Jagellonica of Sweden, Margaret of Austria, and Louise of Savoy won renown for both statecraft and learning. A French woman writing in the late sixteenth century was able to assure her daughter that she was "living at a propitious time for learning."[4]

Outside these circles, the influence of Renaissance ideas on education for women was circumscribed. Not even many noble families in England outside the royal court educated their daughters along with their sons, and everywhere, women scholars and writers outside the most elevated circles were regarded with ambivalence, either as geniuses or as monsters. A French humanist cautioned, "I would be most reluctant to encourage girls to pursue book learning unless they were princesses, obliged by their rank to assume the responsibilities, knowledge, competence, administration, and authority of men. Then doubtless, as in the case of Queen Elizabeth, an education can stand girls in good stead."[5] In other words, only when a woman might have to stand in for a man was it feasible that she be given an education that was designed to train men for leadership roles in society.

Thus, although many humanists approved of women's education, their endorsement was not unconditional. The more open-minded of them urged that women be educated in order to compensate for their inherently weaker nature, but the whole question of girls' education was surrounded, as Ruth Kelso tells us, by an atmosphere of "doubt, timidity, fear" in contrast to the "free, bright world" of the discussion on educating boys.[6] Let us look more closely at the reasons why.

The Sexual Politics of Learning

Educators' reluctance stemmed first from the potential subversiveness of educating women. It challenged the basic definition of the differences between the sexes as established in the ancient world: man alone was defined as having the rational faculties that equipped one for an intellectual and public life. Bathsua Makin, a seventeenth-century English educator who ran a girls' school, understood this when she wrote, "To offer to the World the liberal Education of Women is to deface the Image of God in Man." Like many others before and after, she tried to reassure her readers, "My intention is not to equalize Women to Men."[7]

A woman with an aptitude for learning was likely to be seen as a contradiction in terms, an intellectual transvestite. Cassandra Fedele, the Venetian prodigy mentioned above, was called "'the miracle of the age'; for a male soul had been born in one of female sex."[8] This idea of the exceptional woman as manly would have a long subsequent history and helps explain the application of the term *feminism* to movements for women's emancipation. The term was first coined in the late nineteenth century to describe a medical condition of men with supposedly feminine characteristics. It did not require much imagination to apply the term to women who were seen as masculine, that is, advocates for women's rights. Fear of the confusion of sexual identity has a long history and helps to explain the depth of resistance both to learned women and to feminism.

The Judaeo-Christian tradition was not any more encouraging to women's learning than was the classical tradition. Jewish law explicitly commanded men, not women, to study, in order to teach their sons the scriptures. In fact, Jewish men were admonished not to teach their daughters for fear that the latter's intellectual limitations would lead them to trivialize the Torah. Christians, for their part, invoked the command of St Paul, "Let the woman learn in silence with all subjection. But I suffer not a woman to teach nor to usurp authority over the man, but to be in silence" (1 Tim. 2:11–12).

A second difficulty was that women's speech was connected to sexual desire because the serpent had spoken to Eve in the Garden of Eden in order to seduce her and she in turn had spoken to Adam. The result of all this wanton conversation was original sin. Thus knowledge had a sexual connotation: to *know* a woman meant to know her sexually. In *The Book of the Courtier* (1528), an influential description of Italian court society written by Baldesar Castiglione in the form of conversations between women and men, the word *conversatione* conveys both social and sexual connotations, much as *intercourse* does in English. Women who spoke in public or engaged in public discourse through writing threatened to transgress the norms for their sex of chastity and silence. Understood as public was any activity that took women out of the realm of the family. Women who were actors and musicians, for example, were often accused of being courtesans, and while the phrase *public man* referred to a citizen, *public woman* meant prostitute.

An Italian male author summarized the climate in the fifteenth century when he warned, "It is proper . . . that not only [their] arms but indeed also the speech of women never be made public; for the speech of a noble woman can be no less dangerous than the nakedness of her limbs." Thus, he urged that "women should believe that they have achieved the glory of eloquence if they honor themselves with the outstanding ornament of silence. . . . All that is desired of them is eloquent, well-considered and dignified silence."[9] As a result, most women writers took great pains to assure their readers that their boldness in writing did not in any way imply a transgression of sexual propriety. Anna Maria van Schurman announced on the title page of her book advocating female education (1638) that the author was a virgin. Later in the century Margaret Cavendish, Duchess of Newcastle, reassured her readers, "I am chaste, both by nature, and education."[10]

Critics of women's education thus had a ready and predictable line of attack against women who transgressed, seeing them as morally and intellectually deviant. While one male humanist praised a female contemporary for having overcome her nature, another warned, "An eloquent woman is never chaste."[11] A seventeenth-century male writer chided, "It is a miracle if a woman in wishing to overcome her sex and in giving herself to learning and the languages, does not stain her soul with vice and filthy abominations."[12]

Perhaps because of this association with sexuality, learning was better tolerated for girls, who were assumed to be sexually immature, than it was for mature women. The sixteenth-century French poet Madeleine des Roches understood this when she lamented, "But when I lost the freedom of my youth, / My feathered pen was broken 'ere I flew."[13] But even young women felt the pressure of public censure. Elena Cornaro mastered six languages and received a degree in philosophy from the University at Padua in the late seventeenth century, no small feat considering that women were still officially barred from universities. Huge crowds, curious at such a freak of nature, turned out to see the degree-granting ceremony. Cornaro's reaction to all the fuss was to avow silence as woman's highest ornament; and she retired from public view, to work in private until she died from a debilitating illness six years later.

The orientation of humanist education posed a third obstacle to women's learning. Its goal was to prepare men for their roles as citizens, but with the exception of a few stateswomen such as Elizabeth I in England women were barred from politics. Why should other women be educated? Humanists generally took a utilitarian tack, arguing that education would better enable women to carry out their roles in the private sphere, as subordinates, as wives and mothers. The sixteenth-century English educator Richard Hryde wrote, characteristically, "She that will be good, learning shall cause her to be much the better."[14] Bathsua Makin, in *An Essay to Revive the Antient Education of Gentlewomen* (1673), agreed: "Do not deny Women their due, which is to be as well instructed as they can; but let Men do their duty, to be wiser than they are."[15] One hundred and fifty years later women were still offering reassurance. Eliza Southgate, who graduated from an American female academy at the beginning of the nineteenth century, observed that "far from destroying the harmony [between the sexes] that ought to subsist," women's education "would fix it on a foundation that would not totter at every jar. Women would be under the same degree of subordination that they now are; enlighten and expand their minds, and they would perceive the necessity of such a regulation to preserve the order and happiness of society."[16]

The traditionalists were not so easily convinced. One sixteenth-century Italian author rejected learning for women not because of their incapacity—that would be to belittle the influence he ascribed to education—but because of its unsuitability. Educated women would become proud and want to rule the house. He understood the dangers only too well: "Open the door of the cage and the bird is almost certain to fly out."[17] The result was the consensus of educators that women must not be encouraged or allowed to compete with men in any way. This hazard in fact lessened as many cultural activities, such as science, became more professionalized, accessible only to male elites, from the seventeenth century on. Even then, as we shall see, women both resisted their exclusion and found alternative fields of expertise.

Last but far from least were the practical obstacles. A woman who wanted an education had to have high social standing, wealth and leisure, a supportive male relative, thick skin, and, in addition, enormous perseverance. Elizabeth Cary, in the late sixteenth century, ran up substantial debts bribing servants to bring her candles in defiance of her mother's orders not to read at night. Marie de Gournay, a seventeenth-century French woman whose father died when she was still a child, studied and read in secret, teaching herself Latin by comparing Latin texts with French translations. Although Anna Maria van Schurman, commonly regarded as the most learned woman of the seventeenth century, had a supportive father, she realistically observed that few women had parents "who want or are able to teach them themselves; and without the best of tutors, work in this area cannot be conducted."[18] Like Bathsua Makin, she suggested that learning be reserved for women with leisure.

Lifestyles for Learned Women

A look at women's strategies for learning over several centuries reveals the continuity of the obstacles they faced even though environments could range from receptive to chilly. It might seem at first glance that the cultural climate of the Italian Renaissance was relatively encouraging to learned women, but authors Margaret King and Albert Rabil have eloquently described the tensions experienced by the thirty or so known women humanists of that time. Celebrated as girl prodigies, most renounced their intellectual activities when they matured.

Three exceptions stand out. Isotta Nogarola (1418–66) turned from secular to sacred studies in her early twenties but continued to live with her mother, devoting herself to her books. King and Rabil speculate that her chronic illness may have been the result of the high price she had to pay for an intellectual life: "perpetual chastity and isolation from other learned people."[19]

Cassandra Fedele (1465–1558), the Venetian prodigy, married but continued her studies only after a gap of seventeen years. Even with a long widowhood—her husband died seven years after their marriage but she lived to be ninety-three—she never fulfilled the potential her early achievements suggested. She replied to a female colleague's dilemma over whether to marry or study by advising her to "choose that to which nature more inclines you,"[20] never doubting that such a choice had to be made. Like Nogarola, and like many of the medieval mystics described in Chapter 2, Fedele suffered a chronic, perhaps psychosomatic, illness.

The third example, Laura Cereta (1469–99), was unique in studying more intensely after marriage, especially as the death of her husband after only eighteen months caused her to seek consolation in her studies. She found no welcome in the world of letters, however, her only male correspondent urging her to retire to a religious life. Without support and besieged by critics, "her pen fell silent." Although all these women had enjoyed the support of their fathers, they found they could not continue their studies as adults: "There was simply no place for the learned woman in the social environment of Renaissance Italy. What was a young girl to do who had been encouraged, had excelled, and had grown to love studies enough to dream of a humanist vocation?"[21]

English court and aristocratic circles in the early sixteenth century duplicated the relatively receptive climate of Renaissance Italy. For one woman, at least, it had happier consequences. Margaret More Roper (1505–44) enjoyed the support of her father, Sir Thomas More, and his humanist friends. More, enormously proud of his daughter's accomplishments, encouraged her to continue her studies even after her marriage. Still, it was within fixed limits, as he indicated: "Content with the profit and pleasure of your conscience, in your modesty you do not seek for the praise of the public, nor value it overmuch even if you receive it, but because of the great love you bear us, you regard us—your husband and myself—as a sufficiently large circle of readers for all that you write."[22]

It may be that Thomas More regarded a quiet, private life as the ideal one for both women and men, allowing each to pursue spiritual contemplation without distraction. One wonders, though, to what extent Margaret More Roper's family responsibilities were compatible with focused contemplation. As an English woman in the following century would remark, "We are willing to acknowledge all time borrowed from family duties is misspent: the care of children's education, observing a husband's commands, assisting the sick, relieving the poor and being serviceable to our friends."[23] In any case, in the eyes of contemporaries More Roper was the paragon of a dutiful daughter and self-effacing wife, a testimony to the successful internalization of (male) humanists' expectations for learning in support of traditional female virtues. In keeping with her father's expectations, More Roper never published any of her writings.

A striking contrast to More Roper was Marie de Gournay (1565–1645) in France. Contrary to the norm, Gournay was eager to display her learning and, as a result, earned the vilification of her peers. Her father's death left her family in difficult financial straits; when her mother died Gournay took it upon herself to pay the family's debts and provide for her five siblings. Lacking a supportive relative, she studied in secret. When she was twenty-six, she made the decision to remain single, which meant living from her writings. As a result of this decision as well as her determination to speak out on topics forbidden to women, such as theology, she was a favourite target for detractors, who criticized her unconventional lifestyle, learning, and outspokenness. She yearned to be invited to the all-male meetings of the Parisian academies. In *The Ladies' Grievance* (1626), she expressed a frustration that probably came from personal experience: "Happy are you, therefore, for whom it is no crime to be intelligent and learned, since the mere fact that you are a man allows you to think and do as you please and makes whatever you say right, and other people will believe you or at any rate listen to you." Men thought they were always right: "That man who pronounces thirty stupidities will nonetheless win the prize on account of his beard."[24]

Gournay went on to describe "the insolent manner in which we [women] are ordinarily treated in conversation, to the extent that we participate in conversation at all," how women are patronized with "a smile or a nod," and how they are dismissed with the thought, "It is only a woman speaking."[25] In her recital of famous women she valorized women who wrote or spoke in public, characterizing, for example, Mary Magdalene as a preacher rather than as a reformed prostitute. Born two generations after Margaret More Roper, Gournay suffered keenly from the lack of a supportive circle of family and friends.

Anna van Schurman (1607–78), who mastered Hebrew, Arabic, Chaldee, Syriac, Greek, Turkish, Latin, French, Italian, Spanish, English, German, and Flemish and who also wrote an Ethiopian grammar, ultimately abandoned her studies in order to live as a member of a radical religious sect. While van Schurman's choice reflects the heightened religious values of the seventeenth century and the decline of the humanist tradition that had so cautiously encouraged women's learning, her withdrawal may also have been an escape from the tensions a woman intellectual faced, analogous to the illnesses suffered by female mystics in the Middle Ages and female humanists in Renaissance Italy.

The traditional alternative to marriage was the convent. But the monastic life, which had nourished so many learned women in the Middle Ages, was not necessarily ideal for all intellectually ambitious women. The seventeenth-century Mexican nun Sor Juana Inés de la Cruz (1651–95), called "America's first feminist,"[26] complained of the inconveniences of her convent, such as nuns singing and playing music in an adjoining cell, which intruded upon her studies. When at eighteen she decided to become a nun she confessed that "the spiritual exercises and company of a community were repugnant to the freedom and quiet I desired for my studious endeavors."[27] Nor did the convent furnish either teacher or colleagues with whom she could discuss her reading, but her admitted distaste for marriage may have been founded on the realization that a religious life was the only option for a woman with intellectual interests.

Sor Juana left a moving account of her passion for learning in a letter she wrote to her bishop in 1691 that included her intellectual autobiography. She described how, when she was not yet three years old, she followed her older sister to school and became "inflamed with the desire to know how to read." She even refused to eat cheese because of its rumoured effect in dulling the brain, "for in me the desire for learning was stronger than the desire for eating."[28] When she was six or seven she begged her mother to let her dress as a boy in order to be tutored in Mexico City. When her mother refused, she consoled herself with books from her grandfather's extensive library. Later, living in Mexico City with relatives, when she felt she was not learning fast enough she would cut her hair short to give herself a goal, so much to learn before it grew back to its previous length.

A brief biography published just after Sor Juana's death tells how well the sixteen-year-old acquitted herself when interrogated by a council of forty learned men. Although that account may be legendary, the novelty of a girl prodigy led the city's governing elite to overlook the fact that Juana came from a family of small landholders and that her mother never married. The ruling couple took her under their wing and for a time Juana was a maid-in-waiting at court. When a benefactor supplied her with a dowry that enabled her to enter the convent, she became a nun but continued to have an active

▶ *In this passage from the intellectual autobiography she wrote in 1691, Sor Juana Inés de la Cruz describes her unquenchable passion for learning.*

At one time . . . a very saintly and ingenuous Abbess who believed that study was a thing of the Inquisition, commanded me not to study. I obeyed her (the three some months her power to command endured) in that I did not take up a book; but that I study not at all is not within my power to achieve, and this I could not obey, for though I did not study in books, I studied all the things that God had wrought, reading in them, as in writing and in books, all the workings of the universe. . . .

And what shall I tell you, lady, of the natural secrets I have discovered while cooking? I see that an egg holds together and fries in butter or in oil, but, on the contrary, in syrup shrivels into shreds; observe that to keep sugar in a liquid state one need only add a drop or two of water in which a quince or other bitter fruit has been soaked; observe that the yolk and the white of one egg are so dissimilar that each with sugar produces a result not obtainable with both together. I do not wish to weary you with such inconsequential matters, and make mention of them only to give you full notice of my nature, for I believe they will be occasion for laughter. But, lady, as women, what wisdom may be ours if not the philosophies of the kitchen? Lupercio Leonardo spoke well when he said: how well one may philosophize when preparing dinner. And I often say, when observing these trivial details: had Aristotle prepared victuals, he would have written more.

Source: Margaret Sayers Peden, trans. and intro., *A Woman of Genius: The Intellectual Autobiography of Sor Juana Inés de la Cruz*, 2nd ed. (Salisbury, CT: Lime Rock Press, 1987). Lime Rock Press is an independent small press located in Connecticut, and initiated the first English-language translation of this major early declaration of women's intellectual freedom. Reprinted by permission.

social life, receiving visitors and writing poems at their request much as she had before her enclosure. Rebuked by her confessor for her worldliness, she responded hotly, asking "What direct authority . . . did you have to dispose of my person and my God-given free will?" She admitted, in words that sound impudent compared to those of medieval religious women, "I am not as submissive as others of your daughters in whom you might better employ your doctrine."[29]

To her confessor she presented a spirited defence of women's right to study: "Who has forbidden women to engage in private and individual studies? Have they not a rational soul as men do? . . . . Well, then, why cannot a woman profit by the privilege of enlightenment as they do? Is her soul not as able to receive the grace and glory of God as that of a man?" Later, in her letter to the bishop she would add other arguments, including examples of biblical, classical, and contemporary women noted for their learning. As for herself, she contended that she had no choice. God had so endowed her: "I have this inclination and if it is evil I am not the one who formed me thus—I was born with it and with it shall I die."[30] In fact, however, her situation changed after 1688 due to less supportive rulers and a hostile archbishop. By 1693, perhaps under orders, she had stopped writing and given away her books. Two years later she succumbed to an epidemic while nursing her sister nuns.

Sor Juana may have found convent life inconvenient, but her support at court allowed her unusual freedom to pursue her interests. Anna van Schurman and Marie de Gournay were able to remain single and pursue their studies, but other women were not so fortunate. No man had to make a similar choice or to defend his right to study as did an intellectually minded woman.

Some women, however, were able to use their social status to good advantage. Upper-class women in seventeenth- and eighteenth-century France and England, where the new science had taken hold, were able to exploit their position as patrons, much as Italian noblewomen had in the fifteenth century. They used their social prestige to gain access to the new knowledge, offering male intellectuals public recognition in return for tutoring. In time, male-only universities and professional academies replaced these networks of nobility, but for a brief period women participated enthusiastically in the creation of a new discipline. In addition to reading, translating, and popularizing scientific works, some women carried out research. Maria Cunitz (1610–64) in Germany published a series of astronomical tables. Because she tired herself from observing the stars at night, however, she was criticized for neglecting her household.

Although some of these women maintained contacts with each other through correspondence, more typically the learned woman was aware of her isolation. An exception to this state of affairs was provided by the salon. Begun in France in the seventeenth century, salons survived into the eighteenth and early nineteenth centuries as the only secular institutions to offer support to learned women. In the eighteenth century, the French salons created a structured working space for women and men of letters who were critical of frivolity. The women who hosted them prepared for their role seriously, learning as apprentices at the salons of older women and thoroughly planning the weekly sessions. Similar gatherings appeared in England and Germany, but members of the English Bluestockings circle still encountered the ambivalence surrounding learned women.

One hundred and fifty years after Marie de Gournay, the English scholar and Bluestocking Elizabeth Carter (1717–1806) echoed the earlier woman's complaint that men engaged in conversation would dismiss or ignore the women who were present. Carter knew Latin, French, German, Italian, Spanish, Portuguese, Arabic, and Hebrew; she also wrote poems and translated the Greek philosopher Epictetus. Like so many other learned women, she had depended on male support for her education, in this case, her father, a clergyman who gave all his children the same classical education. She expressed her gratitude in a poem in 1762:

> Ne'er did thy Voice assume a Master's Pow'r,
> Nor force Assent to what thy Precepts taught;
> But bid my independent Spirit soar,
> In all the Freedom of unfetter'd Thought.[31]

Even this was not enough to overcome Carter's fear of ridicule, and she undertook her translation of Epictetus only at the urging of female friends who begged her for appropriate reading material. Her nephew noted that her work, which was financially successful, "made a great noise all over Europe." Yet her contemporary Samuel Johnson found reassurance in the fact that Carter "could make a pudding . . . and work a handkerchief as well as compose a poem." Each period of activity for Carter was followed by a time of withdrawal, and her biographer surmises that she lacked "consistent confidence and determination" to put herself in the public eye.[32] One is reminded of Heloïse some seven hundred years earlier and the effect that an internalized misogyny may have had on women's scholarship.

Other members of the Bluestocking group showed the same hesitation. Elizabeth Montagu, who authored a work on Shakespeare, wrote to a male friend, "Extraordinary talents may make a Woman admired, but they will never make her happy. . . . A Woman that possesses them must be always courting the World, and asking pardon, as it were, for uncommon excellence."[33] That these women went as far as they did testifies to the effectiveness of the supportive network that they created in their immediate environment. When Elizabeth Carter was forced to take up sewing to support herself, Elizabeth Montagu rallied her friends to pay for the publication of Carter's translation and herself endowed Carter with an annual pension.

Although the Bluestockings embodied conservative values and rejected outright the arguments of contemporary feminists such as Mary Wollstonecraft, their emphasis on virtue prepared the way for other women by making learning more acceptable. By 1779 a male writer could dismiss the old views that learning was unsuitable for women as "narrow and unphilosophical prejudices." He guardedly asserted, "Learning is equally attainable, and, I think, equally valuable, to the woman as the man."[34] This was not the last word to be heard on the subject. In the early nineteenth century French conservatives toyed with the idea of forbidding women to learn to read or write, and the learned woman has still had to fight for acceptance down to the present day. As a modern feminist has reported, her father's advice to her was, "You're far too attractive, Sally, to let on to men how clever you are."[35]

The difficulties faced by women intellectuals continued in much the same vein for at least four hundred years after the Renaissance, as we can see in the life of Margaret Fuller (1810–50). Fuller might have had an easier time had she lived in Europe, but there were few role models for her in the United States. Born to one of New England's oldest families, she was a close associate of Ralph Waldo Emerson. But though her male acquaintances went on to Harvard University and careers as lawyers or ministers, she had to defy contemporary social norms if she wanted a life of letters.

Rigorously educated by her father, she was a social misfit by the age of ten, absorbed in books, with no childhood friends and few social graces. Her love of learning stayed with her throughout her life as did a reputation for eccentricity and arrogance, for what her biographer describes as "queenly self-assurance." The latter was most likely the thick skin needed to deflect criticism, since her private letters reveal frequent despondency and self-doubt. As a young woman she wrote, "I felt within myself great power, and generosity, and tenderness; but it seemed to me as if they were all unrecognized, and as if it was impossible that they should be used in life. I was only one-and-twenty; the past was worthless, the future hopeless."[36] Later she complained, "Womanhood is at present too closely bounded to give me scope."[37] A brilliant conversationalist and correspondent, Fuller successfully cultivated a wide network of intense friendships despite her reputation for arrogance. It is hard to know how much of the initial unfavourable reactions to her came from the all too familiar repugnance towards any gifted woman. People's opinion invariably changed from dislike to esteem when they got to know Fuller better.

By Fuller's time a feminist tradition of demanding equal education for women existed, and Fuller spoke to this demand in her book *Woman in the Nineteenth Century* (1845). She insisted that women must develop their mental independence. Her argument owed as much to contemporary Romantic literature and the Transcendentalist philosophy of her circle as it did to feminism. Although she wrote, "We would have every arbitrary barrier thrown down. We would have every path laid open to woman as freely as to man," she equivocated about giving women political rights. She also tended to question whether women could make the same intellectual contributions as men, although this doubt may be part of the long tradition of female self-deprecation. She repeated the centuries-old platitude, "It is well known that of every strong woman they say she has a masculine mind" and reported that a male friend of hers said she "deserved in some star to be a man."[38] In a now familiar pattern Fuller suffered throughout her life from debilitating headaches.

Fuller also faced the same tension between sexuality and learning as did earlier women. Although romantically inclined and deeply passionate, she resigned herself to a life of celibacy, assuming that her intellectual independence was incompatible with marriage. Her resolution wavered, however, when on a long-awaited trip to Europe in 1847, she met and fell in love with an Italian aristocrat. The meeting was accidental; he knew nothing of Fuller's reputation and shared few of her literary interests but offered a stable, supportive relationship. Because of his family's standing, marriage was impossible. When Fuller became pregnant, she went into seclusion, confiding her predicament to only one close friend. Dependent upon her literary connections for the sale of her writings and fearful of reaction in puritanical America, she left her baby with a nurse. When the revolution of 1848 in Italy made her lover an exile, Fuller resolved to return to the United States with her family. The couple married and in 1850 boarded a ship for New York, which sank in a storm off the New Jersey coast in which Fuller and her family perished.

Does Education Make a Feminist?

Although a woman's determination to get an education could be a feminist act, the learned or professional woman was not necessarily, or even usually, a feminist. Much was written from the fifteenth to the nineteenth century asserting women's capacity for learning, but it was usually placed in the theoretical context of a debate known as the woman question, or the querelle des femmes (see Chapter 4). The writing of Mary Astell in the early eighteenth and Mary Wollstonecraft in the later eighteenth century was exceptional, as we shall see.

Bathsua Makin (ca. 1608–75) was also an unusual participant in the debate because she was an educator herself. Perhaps her reassurances about the secondary role of education in women's lives should be seen as strategic, designed to win over prospective clients. Makin repeated the platitude that education would uplift women, thereby improving the moral tone of society, yet she also insisted that women had an innate love of learning and refused to limit her school's curriculum: "I cannot tell where to begin to admit women, nor from what part of Learning to exclude them in regard of their capacities. The whole *Encyclopedia* of Learning may be useful some way or another to them."[39] In spite of this bravado, Makin concealed her name, passing herself off to her readers as a male author.

The Bluestockings were too timid to become professional writers, but many other learned women, such as Christine de Pizan, Madeleine Neveu and her daughter Catherine des Roches, Marie de Gournay, and Makin did write for money. Christine de Pizan and the two des Roches women were quite successful, de Gournay less so. Makin died in poverty. The eighteenth-century Anglo-Saxon scholar Elizabeth Elstob failed to support herself by her writings and ended up as a governess. She described her dilemma poignantly: "When my School is done, my little ones leave me incapable of either reading, writing, or thinking, for their noise is not out of my head until I fall asleep, which is often late."[40]

The main obstacle to financial independence was that women could not get access to the concrete professional rewards and patronage that awaited learned men. This disadvantage, already severe in the Renaissance, became more acute in the seventeenth century as the expansion of the state and the establishment of scientific academies created opportunities for educated men, whose status thereby rose.

Lacking external support, women found their rewards within themselves. As with Sor Juana Inés de la Cruz, moving testimonies document their love of learning. The seventeenth-century Spanish playwright Maria de Zayas confessed, "The moment I see a book, new or old, I drop my sewing and can't rest until I've read it."[41] In a poem written by Catherine des Roches in 1579, Envy threatens,

> I will incite
> Husbands to become tyrants of their wives
> By prohibiting them books and learning
> Thus depriving them of the desire even to live.[42]

Contesting the humanist assumption that learning had to have a practical application, Cassandra Fedele ardently asserted, "I march forth [to defend] the belief that even though the study of letters promises and offers no reward for women and no dignity, every woman ought to seek and embrace these studies for that pleasure and delight alone that [comes] from them."[43] Even Anna van Schurman, who warned against idle curiosity in women, herself admitted to wanting to learn everything that could be known.

From our perspective, these women could have put their talents to better use had they become more defiant. Literary historian Lisa Jardine argues that the classical education of the Renaissance was for women a red herring, diverting them from more useful activity, such as involvement in politics. But women were no different in this respect than men; classical education was not designed to foster critical thinking in either women or men. One studied the classical authors in order to appreciate and imitate them, not to criticize. Knowledge came from referring to and building upon the accomplishments of scholars of the past. Even when debate and criticism were encouraged, they never extended to the foundations of society. Then too, learned women, like men, were protective of their status as members of the elite. As participants in their society and culture, they accepted its values. Thus while they might be bitter, they would not become rebellious.

Nonetheless, their love of learning and the obstacles they faced in pursuing it deserve our respect. They put all their efforts into becoming accepted, or, failing that, into coping with their critics. While not feminists, they testify to the need of women to be taken seriously and to their courage in challenging the male monopoly on learning and culture.

WOMEN IN THE CREATIVE ARTS

Besides satisfying a love of learning, education also enabled women to express themselves creatively. Although historians tend to conclude that women's social and political position declined during the Renaissance, literary and artistic critics take a more optimistic view, citing women's contributions to and subversions of such genres as lyrical poetry, novellas, and pastoral romances in literature or family portraiture in painting. Urban centres throughout Europe—such as Seville, Venice, Poitiers, Lyon, and Amsterdam—replaced court circles in creating a stimulating environment supportive of writers and artists. The growing custom of writing in vernacular languages rather than in Latin was encouraging to women who lacked formal study. The number of women writers and visual artists increased greatly from the mid-seventeenth century on and they achieved some acceptance. The result has been described as "a legacy of feminist aesthetics"[44] although these women, like the learned women already discussed, did not usually become feminists. Let us look more closely at some examples from literature and painting.

Women Writers

> *Alas! a woman that attempts the pen,*
> *Such an intruder on the rights of men,*
> *Such presumptuous Creature, is esteem'd,*
> *The fault, can by no vertue be redeem'd.*

> ANNE KINGSMILL FINCH,
> COUNTESS OF WINCHILSEA, 1713

In the fifteenth and sixteenth centuries, women writers proceeded cautiously. Many preferred translations to original compositions since translation was judged to be less assertive and thus a less masculine activity. Translators could disclaim responsibility for the ideas expressed in the work, as did Margaret Tyler in the preface to her English translation of a Spanish romance in 1578: "The invention, disposition, trimming, & what els in this story, is wholly an other mans, my part none therein but the translation."[45] Her disclaimer aside, translators did edit their works through additions, omissions, and adaptations. In fact, Tyler not only advocated women's right to translate both secular and religious works but also contended that if women could translate romances, they could as well write them.

Women who composed their own works used various strategies to defuse their impact: the self-deprecating remarks that were common in the writings of medieval women; the claim that publication was made under pressure from friends or perhaps even without the author's knowledge; dedication to a female patron; or anonymous publication. In seventeenth-century England Rachel Jevon claimed that she was helpless to resist the inspiration that led her to celebrate the king's return in verse:

> Before your sacred feet these lines I lay
> . . . .
> Though for my sex's sake I should deny,
> Yet exultation makes the verse, not I.[46]

Not all women authors were cautious or modest about their literary efforts. The sixteenth-century French poet Louise Labé defiantly declared, "If anyone reaches the stage at which she is able to put her ideas into writing, she should do it with much thought and should not scorn the glory, but adorn herself with this rather than with chains, rings, and sumptuous clothes."[47] Labé's contemporary, Hélisenne de Crenne, author of a semi-autobiographical romance of passionate love, unabashedly confessed, "What a boundless pleasure it is for me to think that my books are being published in this great city of Paris."[48] And whereas Thomas More had counselled his daughter to write only for her immediate family, Madeleine Neveu gave very different parental advice when she told her daughter to "seek out fame and immortality through her writings."[49]

These women were the exceptions, however. Most female authors were content to be quietly subversive, infusing traditional genres with a feminine, if not feminist, voice. One example is the love lyric, as studied by Ann Jones. As a form of private expression the love lyric was considered more suitable for women than, say, epic poetry, but in view of the link between speech and sexuality, its subject matter made it a "transgressive genre." Jones describes with sympathy the deft manoeuvring of the sixteenth-century French poet Catherine des Roches (1542–87). In the environment in which des Roches wrote, men could engage in risqué, sometimes obscene conversations and compositions that would be considered offensive coming from a respectable woman. She managed to combine wit and modesty, however, and thereby both preserved her reputation and supported herself and her mother after the latter's second husband died and left them in debt. Jones characterizes her strategies as "a quiet revolution," "a radical revision of the speaking position" in lyric poetry.[50]

More daring were two other sixteenth-century writers, Louise Labé and Veronica Franco, who developed more directly oppositional voices. Labé (1520?–66), the only daughter of a prosperous artisan in Lyon, France, learned fencing and equestrian skills as a young woman. She reportedly wore male clothes and may have participated in a jousting tournament, which along with her success in attracting the company of men of high social standing provoked envy and gossip. Her poems expressed a female point of view on love and human relations and dealt frankly with sexuality:

> Kiss me again, again, kiss me again!
> Give me one of the luscious ones you have,
> Give me one of the loving ones I crave:
> Four hotter than burning coals I shall return.[51]

Not surprisingly, the Protestant reformer John Calvin denounced Labé as a prostitute although "the jewel of Lyon" enjoyed the support of her husband and her city. Two hundred years later, during the French Revolution, the National Guard of Lyon produced an emblem in her honour with the motto, "you predicted our destiny, / For to break our chains you first flew free."[52]

Unlike Labé, Veronica Franco (1546–91) was an upper-class prostitute, or courtesan. Her home, Venice, was famous for its beautiful and talented courtesans as well as being a centre of letters and book publishing. Her family was of fairly high social standing, from the class of professionals and bureaucrats, although her mother, also a courtesan, had become impoverished. Franco herself experienced a period of luxurious living followed by poverty when her wealthy patron died. She had married when young but left her husband shortly thereafter, when pregnant. She had six children, according to her testimony, all by different men.

Franco aspired to be an "honest" courtesan, that is, to win fame and respect in the public sphere of letters. Since she was already a "public" woman, having defied the ideal of female chastity, she dared to defy the taboo of silence as well, something no respectable Venetian woman could do. Although Franco had access to one of Venice's most prestigious literary salons and the support of influential patrons, she still had to cope with the envy and competition of male writers who vied with her for public acknowledgment and patronage. As well, courtesans were looked upon as scapegoats for the city's disasters, symbols of the crass materialism of a commercial economy or of the disorder that accompanied outbreaks of bubonic plague.

For these reasons Franco was the object of scurrilous poems and was even denounced to the Inquisition and subjected to an interrogation. Through each trial she acquitted herself well, responding to her anonymous accuser with composure and verve:

> When we women, too, are armed and trained,
> we'll be able to stand up to any man,
> for we have hands and feet and hearts like yours;
> and although we may be soft and delicate,
> some men who are delicate are also strong;
> and others, though rude and rough, are cowards.
> Women have not yet realized this,
> for if they once resolved to do it,
> they could fight to the death with any of you.

Although Franco celebrated sexual pleasure, she could also downplay sexuality in order to present herself and all courtesans as capable of moral and intellectual integrity. Her writings, like those of Louise Labé, have been credited with "a protofeminist identification with women as a group."[53] Franco's concern for other women manifested itself concretely in her will, which after providing for her immediate and extended family stipulated that the balance of her estate should help provide dowries for poor women. She additionally petitioned the government to establish a home for poor married women or unmarried mothers, which it did in the late 1570s.

Louise Labé and Veronica Franco were poets, but the literary form that came to be most closely associated with women writers was the novel. In France the modern novel was the product of seventeenth-century salons, the unique social and cultural space created by aristocratic women. Under the direction of their hosts the salons nourished a female culture, encouraging women to speak and to write by favouring conversation rather than lectures and encouraging improvisations or dramatic readings. These helped to neutralize the advantage that men enjoyed by virtue of their formal education. Out of these conversations came the novel, beginning with Madeleine de

Scudéry's *Artamène, ou Le Grand Cyrus* (1649–53). In place of the heroic and fantastic adventures of the romance, the novel featured dialogue and the exploration of human relations, buttressed by historical and psychological realism. The themes were what we would today call women's issues: marriage, separation, mother–daughter bonds, female friendship. In dramatizing them, the salon writers revealed the political implications of family matters in the ancien régime and thus challenged the divorce between public and personal. They also indirectly contested the traditional idea of authorship, for these novels seem to have been a collaborative effort, the result of group readings and circulated rewritings. The name attached to the finished product may have indicated the woman who led the salon or the man who assisted with the final version or publication rather than a sole author.

There was no comparable social situation in England at that time, and perhaps for that reason the rise of the English novel is associated with the eighteenth rather than the seventeenth century and with the middle classes rather than the nobility. An English woman with unusual literary ambitions in the seventeenth century was unlikely to find much support among her female peers, as we know from the example of Margaret Cavendish, Duchess of Newcastle (1623–73). Cavendish enjoyed the generous support of her husband and the natural attributes of a lively and curious mind bolstered by an unflinching egotism. Her works include six scientific treatises, five collections of poems and fantasies, two volumes of plays, as well as essays and letters.

She also wanted to be famous: "Though I cannot be Henry the Fifth, or Charles the 2nd; yet, I will endeavour to be, Margaret the First."[54] She demanded, "Shall only men live by Fame, and women dy in Oblivion?"[55] This sentiment, which may charm us today, deeply offended her contemporaries, who thought her "bold even to madness." A female friend wrote, "Sure the poor woman is a little distracted, she could never be so ridiculous else as to venture at writing books. . . . If I could not sleep this fortnight I should not come to that."[56] Cavendish was one of the very few female authors of this period to sign her name to her works.

The lesson was not lost on other writers. Her younger contemporary, Katherine Philips (1632?–64), was the model of everything Cavendish was not: modest, retiring, the writer of graceful lyrics. She allowed her translation of a French play to be published but drew the line at a volume of poetry. When it was published without her knowledge, she refused to acknowledge her authorship: "But should I once own it publicly, I think I should never be able to show my face again."[57] She claimed she would prefer to burn her papers than make them known. She succeeded in having the edition suppressed and an apology from the printer advertised. It may be that Philips was only exploiting the conventional stereotype of female modesty; in reality she did not hesitate to make her writings known in royal and aristocratic circles. She did not want them printed, to be sure, but neither did she shy away from more traditional forms of recognition.

An even more flamboyant example of an unconventional female writer than the Duchess of Newcastle was Aphra Behn (ca. 1640–89), whose life was as interesting as her writings. Behn became involved in a slave rebellion in the West Indies, where she also hunted large game and was the first European to visit a Native tribe. Later she became a spy for King Charles II and, when her royal remuneration was slow in coming, was imprisoned for debt. She has been described as an abolitionist, England's first novelist, and a sexual pioneer. A successful dramatist, she had seventeen plays produced in as many years, thus managing to make a comfortable living. Aided by the bold climate of Restoration theatre, she tackled the same racy topics as male playwrights and was as willing to use sexy female characters and scenes to titillate the audience and thus secure her popularity. Of her Virginia Woolf said, "All women together ought to let flowers fall upon the tomb of Aphra Behn . . . for it was she who earned them the right to speak their minds."[58] A late eighteenth-century edition of the *Dictionary of National Biography* promoted a very different point of view, denouncing Behn as one whose wit "ought to be . . . consigned if possible to eternal oblivion."[59]

Behn made her most radical attack against the double standard. She insisted on the same sexual freedom for women as for men and reversed sexual stereotypes. The character Hellena, in Behn's play *The Rover*, reveals a lively interest in men in spite of being destined for a nunnery. Her sister asks in horror, "Who will like thee well enough to have thee, that hears what a mad wench thou art?" "Like me!," Hellena answers saucily, "I don't intend every he that likes me shall have me, but he that I like."[60]

Behn also attacked the hypocrisy of arranged marriages. In her poem "On Desire," she wrote,

> She's only infamous, who to her bed
> For interest takes some nauseous clown she hates;
> . . . .
> All the desires of mutual love are virtuous.

Is it a coincidence that Behn, along with the two other poets who celebrated female heterosexual love, Louise Labé and Veronica Franco, was not of high social standing? In fact, Behn may have been illegitimate, further underlining her outsider status. Predictably, Behn's contemporaries saw her as abnormal, a "thing out of nature."[61]

Well into the nineteenth century women authors continued to be aware on some level of the discomfort caused by their gender. Literary historians Sandra M. Gilbert and Susan Gubar have persuasively described the "anxiety of authorship" that women writers experienced because of the assumption that such activity was inappropriate for their sex. Women continued to apologize for their work, fear publication, adopt male pseudonyms, or, as in the case of George Sand, flaunt their sex, much as Aphra Behn had done earlier. In the writings of such accomplished authors as the Brontë sisters, George Eliot, or the American poet Emily Dickinson, Gilbert and Gubar detect a suppressed anger at patriarchal values and self-loathing at their own connivance and identification with them. Even Marmee, the exemplification of selfless motherhood in Louisa May Alcott's *Little Women* (1869), admitted, "I am angry nearly every day of my life."[62]

In the Epilogue to her play, Sir Patient Fancy *(1677–78), quoted here, Aphra Behn responded to critics who complained about her immodesty.*

I here and there o'erheard a Coxcomb cry,
Ah, Rot it—'tis a Woman's Comedy,
One, who because she lately chanc'd to please us,
With her damn'd Stuff, will never cease to teeze us.
What has poor Woman done, that she must be
Debar'd from Sense, and sacred Poetry?
Why in this Age has Heaven allow'd you more,
And Women less of Wit than heretofore?
We once were fam'd in story, and could write
Equal to Men; cou'd govern, nay, cou'd fight.
We still have passive Valour, and can show,
Wou'd Custom give us leave, the active too,
Since we no Provocations want from you.
. . . .
That we have nobler Souls than you, we prove,
By how much more we're sensible of Love;
Quickest in finding all the subtlest ways
To make your Joys, why not to make you Plays?
We best can find your Foibles, know our own,
And Jilts and Cuckolds now best please the Town;
Your way of Writing's out of fashion grown.
Method, and Rule—you only understand;
Pursue that way of Fooling, and be damn'd.
Your learned Cant of Action, Time and Place,
Must all give way to the unlabour'd Farce.
To all the Men of Wit we will subscribe:
But for your half Wits, you unthinking Tribe,
We'll let you see, whate'er besides we do,
How artfully we copy some of you:
And if you're drawn to th' Life, pray tell me then,
Why Women should not write as well as Men.

Yet this anger did not lead, at least not directly, to feminism. Alcott did gain some satisfaction from the Gothic novels she published pseudonymously, novels with delightfully wicked and assertive heroines, in contrast to the "moral pap" she so disdained in *Little Women*. Yet for the most part, her anger and that of her female contemporaries remained repressed, visible only to modern feminist critics who look for images of female powerlessness and sublimated rage. Rather than openly confront patriarchal values, authors such as George Eliot and Colette invented heroines who were ultimately less independent and assertive than their creators. Was this their way of asking forgiveness for female transgression? If so, we can sympathize with this tendency of women writers to redeem themselves through the self-denial of their heroines.

Women Painters

Many of the patterns that surface in the lives of women intellectuals and writers also characterize those of women painters. If anything, self-expression was more difficult for women painters during the Italian Renaissance because painting was still regarded as a craft, carried on in workshops to which they had no formal admittance. Exclusion from workshops was not universal. In seventeenth-century Germany, for example, the unexpectedly high percentage of women astronomers can be explained by their participation in family observatories. Even there, however, the family rather than the individual was the determining factor. In any family enterprise some daughters or wives would be expected to contribute. Unlike daughters in the noble families of the Italian Renaissance whose fathers gave them a humanist education, daughters in artisan families participated in a practical rather than a decorative sense. There was presumably little scope for their own preferences or self-expression. In any case, guild records from Renaissance Italy indicate an almost complete absence of women.

Of positive value, on the other hand, was the fact that families and cities took the same pride in art prodigies as they did in the oddity of a learned woman. Such was the case with Marietta Robusti (1560–90), the daughter of the Italian painter Tintoretto. Dressed as a boy, she accompanied her father in public and worked alongside her brothers in his workshop. Although her father was proud of her, he spurned invitations from the Holy Roman Emperor and the Spanish king to bring her to their courts. Instead, Marietta was married off to a silversmith, who promised to obey Tintoretto's conditions that Marietta should not leave her father's household during his lifetime. Four years after her marriage, she died in childbirth.

A very different and unprecedented parental encouragement came from the father of Sofonisba Anguissola (1532–1625) of Cremona, Italy. Not only did her father give his six daughters an education usually reserved for boys but he also encouraged Sofonisba to study art, perhaps because he had so many daughters to provide for and hoped that she could make her own living. When just fourteen, she and a younger sister were sent to study with a local artist. After a trip to Rome, where she came into contact with Michelangelo and received his encouragement, she began to win renown as a portrait painter. Commissioned to paint the Duke of Alba's portrait, she was subsequently invited to Spain to serve as court painter and lady-in-waiting to the young queen. After the queen's death, the king of Spain arranged a marriage for the thirty-nine-year-old Anguissola with a Sicilian nobleman. Their marriage was cut short by his death nine years later, but on the voyage home from Sicily the ship's captain fell in love with Anguissola and they were married in 1580. Relocating to Genoa, Anguissola hosted a salon for artists and nobles. The Dutch artist Anthony Van Dyck painted her portrait one year before her death in 1625 at the age of ninety-two. The epitaph erected by her husband honoured her "who is recorded among the illustrious women of the world, outstanding in portraying the images of man, so excellent that there was no equal in her age. Orazio Lomellino, in sorrow for the loss of his great love, in 1632, dedicated this little tribute to such a great woman."[63] Although there is no reason to doubt her husband's sincerity, gifted women were often described with exaggerated praise. It underlined their separateness from other women and focused attention on their freakishness rather than on their art.

Anguissola seems to have had it all—fame, wealth, marriage, and love. It is noteworthy, however, that as the first famous woman artist of the Renaissance, she came from sixteenth-century Cremona rather than fifteenth-century Florence, much more a centre of artistic development. Anguissola was tolerated as a prodigy, as were Marietta Robusti, Cassandra Fedele, and Sor Juana. She also redeemed her oddity by her reputation as an accomplished gentlewoman; she was known for her humility and piety, and in her own self-portraits she celebrates her modesty and deportment. It is also important to note that Anguissola was primarily a portrait painter. It was impossible for women to study nude male models, and they were thus excluded from the most prestigious genre, that of historical painting. Anguissola was nonetheless capable of turning a limitation into an artistic asset, painting family groups with warmth and giving close attention to needlework and costume details. She inspired other women portrait painters.

Because women supposedly lacked men's powers of reason, contemporaries thought women artists capable of diligence but not invention. Artistic genius was considered to be beyond them. In contrast to Anguissola and to other women who strove for acceptance, the early Baroque artist Artemisia Gentileschi (1593–1652?) was determined to compete with the best male artists and to take risks in expressing her artistic individuality. Her biographer describes her as "the first documented woman in Western history to fulfil our concept of artistic genius."[64]

Like most other women artists Gentileschi was fortunate in enjoying the support of her painter-father and in finding patrons who appreciated her work. She shunned conventional depictions of female heroines and nudes, preferring to portray women as more physical than erotic, as energetic and powerful rather than passive and sexual. She depicted the biblical heroine Judith as intense and coldly determined as she decapitated the tyrant Holofernes, thereby rejecting the traditional portrayals of Judith as youthful, beautiful, virginal or, alternatively, seductive. Her Judith symbolizes "female defiance of male power," becoming a "fully antipatriarchal female character."[65]

Although she had no close female friends, Gentileschi portrayed women's solidarity in her paintings. Her biographer suggests that this was perhaps a way of compensating for the betrayal of an early female friend who may have connived in Gentileschi's rape at the hands of a fellow artist. Although her father forced the rapist to stand trial and Gentileschi not only testified that she had struggled against him but withstood the torture of the thumb screws to prove she was not lying, her rapist spent only eight months in prison before winning a delayed acquittal. Gentileschi went on to marry, but we know little of her marriage. Her notoriety as a result of the rape trial evidently freed her to pursue her art although she found the self-promotion needed to win patrons exhausting work.

Still, Gentileschi was relatively successful. If she had a "powerful feminist message,"[66] her contemporaries did not seem to have been aware of it; they were not offended by her images of powerful and active women. She was the only woman artist to rival the fame of the great male painters of her day, but although she taught a daughter to paint she was more intent on finding her a good husband. As Marie de Gournay and so many others had found, attaining financial independence was indeed a difficult enterprise.

One last female painter in traditional European society deserves mention, the Dutch artist Judith Leyster (1609–60). By Leyster's time, the Netherlands offered a receptive environment for women painters. Historical paintings celebrating male figures had waned in favour of small-scale paintings that could be hung in private homes. Their subjects—flowers, still lifes, landscapes—could be painted from close observation. The existence of an open market allowed painters the freedom to paint first, then sell, rather than having to find a patron first.

Leyster did in her painting what Louise Labé and Veronica Franco did in their verse, recasting a traditional genre or subject from a female perspective. Her famous painting, *The Proposition* (1631), portrays a man offering money for sexual favours to a woman who is bent over her sewing. Absent are the lightheartedness and prurience of seduction scenes as traditionally painted. Instead, the scene evokes the woman's embarrassment and her dignity. We do not know if Leyster's achievement was appreciated by her contemporaries, but we do know that after her marriage in 1636 her output declined dramatically.

Although the learned and creative women of the Renaissance and subsequent centuries found support, it was ambivalent and always within strictly defined limits. Learned women were oddities, alternately welcomed and vilified. Lacking access to the opportunities and rewards enjoyed by their male peers, they put all their energies into finding some acceptance. Their yearning to be accepted precluded a feminist rebellion.

Women writers and painters tended to express themselves in subtle ways, taking refuge in acceptable subject matter or manipulating traditional genres. Even the boldest of them had to find the support necessary to make a living. Most achieved the means for self-expression by sacrificing or disguising any radical content. Their printed apologies, modest self-portrayals, and virtuous living reassured men that they need not feel threatened. As long as women scholars and artists had to fight for acceptance, studying, writing, and painting could be described as feminist acts but they did not necessarily lead to feminist consciousness.

NOTES

1 Gerda Lerner, *The Creation of Feminist Consciousness: From the Middle Ages to Eighteen-seventy* (New York: Oxford University Press, 1993), 10.

2 Quoted in Michael H. Shank, "A Female University Student in Late Medieval Kraków," in *Sisters and Workers in the Middle Ages,* ed. Judith M. Bennett, Elizabeth A. Clark, Jean F. O'Barr, B. Anne Vilen, and Sarah Westphal-Wihl (Chicago: University of Chicago Press, 1989), 192.

3 Ludovico Ariosto, paraphrased in Joseph Gibaldi, "Child, Woman, and Poet: Vittoria Colonna," in *Women Writers of the Renaissance and Reformation,* ed. Katharina M. Wilson (Athens: University of Georgia Press, 1987), 22.

4 Madeleine Neveu (des Roches), quoted in Katharina M. Wilson, "Introduction," in *Women Writers of the Renaissance and Reformation,* ed. Wilson, ix.

5 Agrippa d'Aubigné (1552–1630), in *Not in God's Image: Women in History from the Greeks to the Victorians,* ed. Julia O'Faolain and Lauro Martines (New York: Harper and Row, 1973), 186.

6 Ruth Kelso, *Doctrine for the Lady of the Renaissance* (Urbana: University of Illinois Press, 1956), 58.

7 Bathsua Makin, *An Essay to Revive the Antient Education of Gentlewomen* (1673), in *First Feminists: British Women Writers 1578–1799,* ed. Moira Ferguson (Bloomington: Indiana University Press, 1985), 129, 139.

8 Margaret King, "Book-Lined Cells: Women and Humanism in the Early Italian Renaissance," in *Beyond Their Sex: Learned Women of the European Past,* ed. Patricia Labalme (New York: New York University Press, 1980), 76. In the 1920s in France female students like Simone de Beauvoir were still being exhorted to cultivate the man within them (see Chapter 10).

9 Francesco Barbero, quoted in Peter Stallbrass, "Patriarchal Territories: The Body Enclosed," in *Rewriting the Renaissance: The Discourses of Sexual Difference in Early Modern Europe,* ed. Margaret W. Ferguson, Maureen Quilligan, and Nancy J. Vickers (Chicago: University of Chicago Press, 1986), 127.

10 Quoted in Angeline Goreau, "Aphra Behn: A Scandal to Modesty (c. 1640–1689)," in *Feminist Theorists: Three Centuries of Key Women Thinkers,* ed. Dale Spender (New York: Pantheon Books, 1983), 17.

11 Quoted in King, "Book-Lined Cells," 77.

12 Quoted in Patricia Labalme, "Women's Roles in Early Modern Venice: An Exceptional Case," in *Beyond Their Sex,* ed. Labalme, 139.

13 Madeleine des Roches, "First Ode," in *The Defiant Muse: French Feminist Poems from the Middle Ages to the Present,* ed. Domna C. Stanton (N.p., 1986), 45.

14 Richard Hryde, "A Devout Treatise upon the 'Pater Noster,'" in Elizabeth McCutcheon, "The Learned Woman in Tudor England: Margaret More Roper," in *Women Writers of the Renaissance and Reformation,* ed. Wilson, 466.

[15] Bathsua Makin, *An Essay to Revive the Antient Education of Gentlewomen* (1673), in *Women Writers of the Seventeenth Century,* ed. Katharina M. Wilson and Frank J. Warnke (Athens: University of Georgia Press, 1989), 297.

[16] Quoted in Nancy F. Cott, *The Bonds of Womanhood: "Woman's Sphere" in New England, 1780–1835* (New Haven, CT: Yale University Press, 1977), 107.

[17] Giovanni Bruto (1555), paraphrased in Kelso, *Doctrine for the Lady of the Renaissance,* 61.

[18] Anna Maria van Schurman, *Whether the Study of Letters Is Fitting for a Christian Woman?* in *Women Writers of the Seventeenth Century,* ed. Wilson and Warnke, 175.

[19] Margaret L. King and Albert Rabil, Jr., eds., *Her Immaculate Hand: Selected Works by and about the Women Humanists of Quattrocento Italy* (Binghamton, NY: Medieval and Renaissance Texts and Studies, 1983), 18.

[20] "An Exchange of Letters between Cassandra Fedele and Alesandra Scala," in ibid., 87.

[21] King and Rabil, eds., *Her Immaculate Hand,* 24, 25.

[22] Quoted in McCutcheon, "The Learned Woman in Tudor England," 460.

[23] Mary Evelyn, quoted in Angeline Goreau, *Reconstructing Aphra: A Social Biography of Aphra Behn* (New York: The Dial Press, 1980), 34–35.

[24] Marie de Gournay, *The Ladies' Grievance,* in *Women Writers of the Seventeenth Century,* ed. Wilson and Warnke, 23, 24.

[25] Ibid., 23.

[26] Rosario Hiriart, "America's First Feminist," *Americas* 25 (May 1973): 2.

[27] Margaret Sayers Peden, ed. and trans., *A Woman of Genius: The Intellectual Autobiography of Sor Juana Inés de la Cruz* (Salisbury, CT: Lime Rock Press, 1982, 1987), 26.

[28] Ibid., 28.

[29] Nina M. Scott, "'If You Are Not Pleased to Favor Me, Put Me out of Your Mind . . .': Gender and Authority in Sor Juana Inés de la Cruz and the Translation of Her Letter to the Reverend Father Maestro Antonio Núñez of the Society of Jesus," *Women's Studies International Forum* 11, 5 (1988): 436, 437. According to Scott, this letter may have never been sent, although some copies did circulate.

[30] Ibid., 435, 436.

[31] Sylvia Harcstark Myers, *The Bluestocking Circle: Women, Friendship, and the Life of the Mind in Eighteenth-Century England* (Oxford: Clarendon Press, 1990), 172.

[32] Ibid., 171, 158, 176.

[33] Quoted in ibid., 183.

[34] Quoted in ibid., 285.

[35] Sally Alexander, quoted in Michelene Wandor, *Once a Feminist: Stories of a Generation* (London: Virago, 1990), 91.

[36] Paula Blanchard, *Margaret Fuller: From Transcendentalism to Revolution* (Reading, MA: Addison-Wesley, 1987, 1978), 40, 86.

[37] Quoted in Alice S. Rossi, ed., *The Feminist Papers: From Adams to de Beauvoir* (New York: Columbia University Press, 1973), 152.

38 Margaret Fuller, *The Great Lawsuit. Man versus Men. Woman versus Women* (1843), in *The Feminist Papers,* ed. Rossi, 164, 166.

39 Quoted in Mitzi Myers, "Domesticating Minerva: Bathsua Makin's 'Curious' Argument for Women's Eduction," in *Studies in Eighteenth-Century Culture,* vol. 14, ed. O.M. Brack, Jr. (Madison: University of Wisconsin Press, 1985), 186.

40 Quoted in Mary Elizabeth Green, "Elizabeth Elstob: 'The Saxon Nymph' (1683–1736)," in *Female Scholars: A Tradition of Learned Women Before 1800,* ed. J.R. Brink (Montreal: Eden Press Women's Publications, 1980), 154.

41 Maria de Zayas, "To the Reader," in *The Enchantments of Love: Amorous and Exemplary Novels,* trans. and intro. H. Patsy Boyer (Berkeley: University of California Press, 1990), 2.

42 Catherine des Roches, "The Works of M. Des Roches of Poitiers the Daughter (1597)," in Anne R. Larsen, "The French Humanist Scholars: Les Dames de Roches," in *Women Writers of the Renaissance and Reformation,* ed. Wilson, 250.

43 Cassandra Fedele, "Oration in Praise of Letters," in *Her Immaculate Hand,* ed. King and Rabil, 77.

44 Wilson and Warnke, "Introduction," in *Women Writers of the Seventeenth Century,* ed. Wilson and Warnke, xii.

45 Quoted in Tina Krontiris, *Oppositional Voices: Women as Writers and Translators of Literature in the English Renaissance* (London: Routledge, 1992), 46.

46 Quoted in Elaine Hobby, *Virtue of Necessity: English Women's Writing 1649–88* (London: Virago, 1988), 19.

47 Louise Labé, "To Mademoiselle Clémence de Bourges of Lyon," in Jeanne Prine, "Poet of Lyon: Louise Labé," in *Women Writers of the Renaissance and Reformation,* ed. Wilson, 149.

48 Hélisenne de Crenne, "Fourth Invective Letter" (1551), in *A Renaissance Woman: Hélisenne's Personal and Invective Letters,* ed. and trans. Marianna M. Mustacchi and Paul J. Archambault (Syracuse, NY: Syracuse University Press, 1986), 102.

49 Quoted in Larsen, "The French Humanist Scholars," in *Women Writers of the Renaissance and Reformation,* ed. Wilson, 234.

50 Ann Rosalind Jones, *The Currency of Eros: Women's Love Lyric in Europe, 1540–1620* (Bloomington: Indiana University Press, 1990), 75.

51 Quoted in Margaret L. King, *Women of the Renaissance* (Chicago: University of Chicago Press, 1991), 215. While Keith Cameron, *Louise Labé: Renaissance Poet and Feminist* (New York: Berg, 1990), labels Labé a feminist (p. ix), Domna C. Stanton excluded her from her collection, *The Defiant Muse,* because Labé's verse was "not 'feminist'" (p. xxv).

52 Quoted in Jones, *The Currency of Eros,* 31, 177.

53 Ibid., 196, 6.

54 Quoted in Hilda L. Smith, *Reason's Disciples: Seventeenth-Century English Feminists* (Urbana: University of Illinois Press, 1982), 81.

55 Quoted in Jane Spencer, *The Rise of the Woman Novelist: From Aphra Behn to Jane Austen* (Oxford: Basil Blackwell, 1986), 24.

56 Quoted in Goreau, "Aphra Behn," 18.

57 Quoted in Goreau, *Reconstructing Aphra,* 144.

58 Virginia Woolf, *A Room of One's Own* (1928; reprint, Harmondsworth: Penguin Books, 1970), 66.

59 Quoted in Margaret W. Ferguson, "A Room Not Their Own: Renaissance Women as Readers and Writers," in *The Comparative Perspective on Literature: Approaches to Theory and Practice,* ed. Clayton Koelb and Susan Noakes (Ithaca, NY: Cornell University Press, 1988), 112.

60 Aphra Behn, *The Rover,* in *Oroonoko, The Rover and Other Works,* ed. Janet Todd (London: Penguin Books, 1992), 189.

61 Quoted in Goreau, *Reconstructing Aphra,* 230, 268.

62 Sandra M. Gilbert and Susan Gubar, *The Madwoman in the Attic: The Woman Writer and the Nineteenth-Century Literary Imagination* (New Haven and London: Yale University Press, 1979), 51, 483. As late as 1959 a literary critic, in his introduction to the *Selected Poems of Emily Dickinson,* suggested that "woman poet" was "a contradiction in terms" (p. 541).

63 Quoted in Ilya Sandra Perlingieri, *Sofonisba Anguissola: The First Great Woman Artist of the Renaissance* (New York: Rizzoli, 1992), 210.

64 Mary D. Garrard, *Artemisia Gentileschi: The Image of the Female Hero in Italian Baroque Art* (Princeton, NJ: Princeton University Press, 1989), 137.

65 Ibid., 280.

66 Ibid., 8.

4

Religion, Politics, and Literature in Early Modern Europe

The period of the Protestant Reformation and the resulting religious wars in Europe was one of political disorder. States responded by attempting to consolidate their political authority, using the absolute monarchy of Louis XIV of France (1661–1715) as a model. Governments extended their concern to matters of marriage and sexuality and stressed their subjects' obedience and subordination, values to be learned within the family. At the same time, European economic expansion brought colonization and cultural conflict, including the enslavement of indigenous peoples, to other parts of the world. Increased economic competition and specialization reduced economic options for women and devalued both their wages and their status. Although initially beneficial in offering women opportunities for religious activism, the Protestant Reformation and Catholic Counter-Reformation ultimately strengthened the forces of repression and conservatism. The European witch persecution, which stretched from the mid-sixteenth to the mid-seventeenth century, is a dramatic symbol of this period in women's history.

Despite these setbacks, however, or perhaps as a result of them, individual women continued to protest. As before, some used religion to assert their spiritual independence, now additionally encouraged by the religious fluidity of the Reformation period. Others took up the promise of Renaissance humanism to express themselves as scholars and authors. Now we can trace a third source of inspiration. Misogynist tracts, although age old in their sentiments, flourished in number and vitriol in the seventeenth century. They met their match in women who attacked this literary tradition with a new-found self-confidence. Most female authors of defences of women led or tried to lead conventional lives while rejecting the ancient justifications for women's

1492	Jews expelled from Spain
1517	Martin Luther writes Ninety-five Theses
ca. 1520–50	Spain gains control of Central and South America
1529–34	Henry VIII of England breaks with the papacy
1545–63	Counter-Reformation begins with the Council of Trent
1558–1603	Elizabeth I reigns in England
1560s–1650s	Height of the European witch persecutions
1608	France establishes a settlement at Quebec
1642–49	English Civil War
1648–53	La Fronde
1653–58	Oliver Cromwell's Protectorate in England
1661–1715	Louis XIV of France

oppression. (In this they were unlike the medieval dissidents, who had used traditional justifications for living unconventional lives, but like the learned and creative women described in the previous chapter, who for the most part strove for acceptance.) In their protest against literary misogyny they and their male co-defenders created the beginnings of feminist theory. This chapter explores, first, the opportunities and restrictions posed by religion in the sixteenth and seventeenth centuries; second, the scope for women in politics; third, the relationship between literature and life; and finally, the literary debate on woman known as the *querelle des femmes.*

WOMEN AND RELIGION

> *Women as prophets enjoyed virtually the only taste of public authority they would ever know.*
>
> PHYLLIS MACK, 1992

> *If any [women] have a moving to speak the truth, obey; and then when you have done return to your places again with speed.*
>
> GEORGE FOX, 1624–91,
> Founder of the Quakers

Women and Catholicism

Even before the start of the Protestant Reformation in 1517, the opportunities that religious women had seized in the Middle Ages narrowed. The mid-fifteenth-century theologian Jean Gerson foreshadowed the reaction against female visionaries when he denounced women's enthusiasm as "extravagant, changeable, uninhibited, and therefore not to be considered trustworthy."[1] Women's purported weakness and vulnerability had previously qualified them to be the mouthpiece of God, but in the sixteenth and seventeenth centuries they were more likely to be seen as instruments of the devil. Although some women still insisted on speaking out as prophets, many more came under attack as witches for what was essentially the same activity. According to one study, the proportion of female saints fell from a peak of almost 28 percent in the fifteenth century to 18 percent in the sixteenth century and 14.4 percent in the seventeenth.

The Roman Catholic Church was willing to recognize some holy women in Spain and Italy as exceptional. One was the sixteenth-century nun and saint Teresa of Avila (1515–82). Teresa underwent intense mystical experiences and under their inspiration sought to establish a reformed, austere community that would accept women without dowries, a radical act in Spain, a nation obsessed with lineage. She also fought to allow her nuns silent, contemplative prayer rather than the public prayers normally chanted by monks or nuns for the souls of benefactors. She was successful, but at the cost of exhausting battles with hostile authorities and endless compromises. The following passage was struck out in her writings, censured by the church or perhaps by herself, and only recently deciphered: "Lord of my soul, you did not hate women when You walked in the world; rather you favored them always with much pity and found in them as much love and more faith than in men." One detects bitterness in the lines she addressed to God, "You are a righteous Judge and not like the judges of the world, who are sons of Adam, and, after all, men, so there is no virtue in a woman that they do not consider suspect."[2]

One hundred years later the English nun Mary Ward (1585–1645) set out to foster Catholic renewal by establishing girls' schools throughout Europe that would provide instruction not only in religion and morality but also in the liberal arts. The goal was to prepare girls for either a secular or a religious life. In either case, Ward considered the study of Latin essential. She planned to model her teaching institute on the Jesuits, a monastic order directly under the pope. Ward and her companions also set forth to engage in missionary work in Protestant England, again in imitation of the Jesuits. While of great practical value, the enterprise threatened church tradition, which stipulated enclosure for nuns and reserved apostolic work to men. Ward revealed her confidence in a tart response to a comment on women's weakness: "There is no such difference between men and women that women may not do great things," she declared. "For what think you of this word, 'but women'? As if we were in all things inferior to some other creature which I suppose to be man!"[3] Ward's initiative, as well as her travels, leading to arrest in England and imprisonment in Germany, brought criticism down on the "runaway nun" and her "galloping girls." In 1631 the pope dissolved her institute, thereby confirming the decision of the Council of Trent that nuns could not leave their cloister except in case of fire, leprosy, or contagious disease.

The influence of the Catholic Church was not wholly negative. Protestantism abolished monasticism, but Catholicism continued to offer upper-class women the option of an institutionalized religious life. A seventeenth-century French observer testified to the enduring popularity of this choice:

> Among the virgins consecrated to God, how many decided to dedicate their lives to the state of virginity only after consideration of unhappy marriages? Thus, strangely enough, marriages in some way promote virginity, and the uglier they are, the more they serve to produce the beauty of virgins. If all marriages were happy, the millions of holy women who serve God in purity in the cloisters, would perhaps never have entered [religion].[4]

Catholicism offered women other benefits, as we shall see below, but only grudgingly and in the face of persistent pressure from religious women.

Women and Protestantism

The Protestant Reformation was also ambivalent in its effects on women. In addition to abolishing monasteries, Protestantism emphasized the Bible, with the effect of buttressing the father's position within the family by the authority of the Old Testament. At the same time, Protestants argued for religious freedom of conscience within marriage as well as within the state. Protestant moralists simultaneously encouraged the ideal of companionate marriage and of the submissive, obedient wife.

Even the encouragement of female literacy was ambivalent. The Protestant reformer Martin Luther urged that girls attend school at least one hour a day in order to learn scripture, but although Protestant authorities in Europe and the colonies proposed schools for girls, few were established. Where they were, education was usually confined to religious instruction and domestic skills. Historian Margaret King describes the "little schools" as so named because "little was taught."[5] As well, Protestants scorned Latin, the language of intellectuals, as "popish." The classical education of the Renaissance was no longer fashionable. As we saw in the previous chapter, Anna Maria van Schurman renounced her studies when she joined a religious sect and withdrew from the world, an action consistent with the climate of the times.

Nonetheless, literacy among women increased substantially. The number of published books addressed to female readers rose although a nervous government in England in 1543 forbade all women except those from the upper class to read the Bible. Pious women like Elizabeth Bury—who resolved "*to keep a daily Memorial of what she did; which should be a Witness betwixt God and her own Soul*"[6]—were encouraged to scrutinize their experiences in search of evidence of God's grace. Sometimes the results made their way into print. About 20 percent of English women's published writing from the seventeenth century comes from Quakers, a remarkably high proportion when one considers that Quakers numbered only about 1 percent of the population. The activism of Quaker women extended well beyond writing, as we shall see.

All told, the Reformation had a dramatic influence on women writers by making religion an appropriate subject for them. They no longer had to get individual permission to write, as had been true of medieval religious women. Already in the second half of the sixteenth century we can identify a number of English women who wrote books of prayers and meditations for private devotion and who translated sermons and religious treatises. They recognized themselves as pious authors, signing their names to their works and taking part in religious debate. Some, like Isabella Whitney, who wrote in the 1560s and 1570s, went on to other genres. Whitney felt emboldened enough to turn to poetry, her piety overcoming her doubts about such an audacious undertaking.

Religion could also isolate women writers in a separate female culture, however. Women writers who limited themselves to subjects considered appropriate condemned themselves to literary and social conservatism. While religion continued to have a subversive potential, the equation of the church with the status quo made most religious women reluctant to challenge contemporary social norms. Although women in subsequent centuries would be inspired by religious faith to become feminists, they were many times outnumbered by those whose religion led only to acceptance or resignation.

Religious Activism

Religious dissent did inspire some sixteenth- and seventeenth-century women to combine writing with heroic action. Anne Askew (1521–46), an English woman who converted to Protestantism during the reign of the Catholic queen Mary I, defied state, church, and husband to do so. She was turned out of her home and possibly denounced by her husband, then tortured and burned for heresy at the age of twenty-five. Her martyrdom was not unique but her account of her examination—in which she portrayed herself as clever, self-assured, and purposeful—was. Whereas a contemporary male admirer saw Askew as a passive instrument of God, her own account lacked self-effacement. She described with confidence, if not with pride, how she outfoxed her questioners, turning their questions back on them and meeting their accusations with calm courage, wit, and irony. Anne Askew was humble before God but not before her enemies.

Argula von Grumbach, in sixteenth-century Germany, was luckier. She familiarized herself with Protestant teachings and intervened with the authorities on behalf of a persecuted theologian. The only response she got was a lampoon written by an anonymous university student, whom von Grumbach then challenged to a public debate:

Christ Himself has let me know
That I should not be afraid to go
Since I will represent Him well
. . . .

> Although I am not educated
> I am not afraid to say it.
> I will come and without fear
> To honor God, whom I revere.[7]

Ordered by her husband to stop writing, she obeyed, although she called him tyrannical and continued to express her religious sentiments in her private correspondence.

In Catholic France, which was caught up in religious and civil wars, Protestant women acted as pillars of resistance, opposing conversion, organizing escape routes, and suffering torture and execution. Catholic women also staunchly defended their faith. Elizabeth Cary (1585–1639) in England converted to Catholicism and as a result was separated from her husband and children and reduced to poverty. Like Anne Askew, she wrote about her situation, although indirectly. In *Mariam, Faire Queene of Jewry,* the first original drama by an English woman, she created a sympathetic portrait of a young married woman facing the question of obedience to a husband's despotic authority. Cary ended her play with Mariam's death and heroic self-denial, an allusion to the Christian reliance on a spiritual reward for earthly suffering in which she found personal comfort.

In seventeenth-century France, Catholic women persuaded the church to revise its position on the rule of strict enclosure for nuns. In a wave of religious enthusiasm, women perceived the need for an active stance in order to combat Protestantism. They fought for the right to live as unmarried women in the world, with the flexibility and mobility needed to pursue their teaching mission. In stages, these women and their supporters forced a number of small victories, in effect overriding the Council of Trent. Pious women of all social classes—this democratization was itself an innovation—formed small communities to undertake parish responsibilities, in particular the education of girls, who were excluded from boys' classrooms. Sometimes these were formal monastic orders, like the Ursulines, which had won special permission to take in day students. Other groups created an intermediary role for women, an alternative to both marriage and convent, much like the beguines of the Middle Ages. Also like the beguines, they encountered hostility from social and clerical conservatives but were ultimately successful, forcing the church to accommodate them in a manner reminiscent of women in the early years of Christianity.

Besides promoting the model of an active life for religious women, these groups incalculably benefited girls throughout the country and French Canada, teaching them to read. Almost unheard of at the beginning of the century, at its end education for girls had become accepted and respectable, along with women teachers. Promotion of education continued into the eighteenth century with the religious group known as the Jansenists championing learning for women. Eager to extend the role of the laity in religion in general, the Jansenists supported women's right to read the Bible and participate in church services.

European Jews were not spared the effects of intolerance. In Portugal and Spain at the end of the fifteenth century they were forced to convert to Catholicism or flee. Dona Gracia Nasi, born in Portugal in 1510, was one of those who converted but still considered herself a Jew. Widowed at twenty-six with a young daughter, she went to Antwerp to run the family business with her brother-in-law. After his death she fled Antwerp rather than see her daughter married to a Catholic nobleman. After a sojourn in Venice she settled in Ferrara, where she finally felt secure enough to practise Judaism openly. As she had done previously, she used her wealth to help other Jews escape persecution.

Protestant Prophets

A very different kind of religious activism, the prophetic tradition used to such effect by medieval women, lived on in the radical Protestant sects, in many of which women were dominant. Although women's works account for less than 1 percent of all published texts in seventeenth-century England, half of them were prophecies. In Germany and the Low Countries the religious movement known as Pietism supported women's preaching and teaching in the home as well as their prophesying. The German sectarian Anna Owena Hoyers (1584–1655) echoed her medieval predecessors when she wrote the poem, "For the Christian Reader." Unlike the medieval prophets, the women in these radical sects represented all social classes. Hoyers came from a well-to-do peasant family. She began writing when she was almost forty years old, widowed, and with six children to support.

Historian Joan Kelly called such women "feminists in action," who "actively liberated themselves from male clerical rule and their husbands as well."[8] A study of thirty-eight well-known English women visionaries in the mid-seventeenth century confirms that those who became prominent were either single or widowed. Anna Trapnel, admitting to a magistrate that she was unmarried, asked him, "Then having no hindrance, why may not I go where I please, if the Lord so will?"[9] Those who were married had to overcome their husbands' opposition, but not all were as resourceful as Elinor Channel, who was struck dumb until her husband allowed her to travel to London to deliver her prophecy. The noblewoman Lady Eleanor Davies Douglas, whose husband had burned her book, foretold his death and even took to wearing mourning in anticipation of the happy event. He died the year after. It undoubtedly helped that most of these women were economically independent, as seamstresses, businesswomen, or landholders.

Although generally more moderate and restrained than contemporary male prophets, some women give us glimpses of bold alternatives. Davies Douglas foresaw a female deity, herself in fact, who would bring peace to the world. Many shared her vision of a world marked by religious toleration, an unusual goal in such a sectarian age. All prophets in the utopia imagined by Mary Cary, a poor London woman, would be women, infant mortality would be eliminated, and women would be able to own property. "The

> *Although Anna Owena Hoyers gained recognition through her writings, some of them published in 1650 were declared heretical.*

This book, by a woman writ,
Is the better because of it,
Because its like has ne'er been seen:
Wit and sense from woman's pen.
Just consider what you read
And to the scoffers pay no heed,
Who say it isn't right.
For Mary Christ his special praise reserved,
Even though Martha cooked and served,
Because she chose the better role
In that she chose to save the soul.
So does the present woman too
As this book will prove to you
That wisdom is not to be found
In colleges and learnèd rounds,
But from the Holy Ghost alone
Can the highest things be known.
God would have you feel no shame
If He speaks in woman's name.
And should you, readers, peruse this work
And thereupon decide its worth,
The Holy Spirit will illuminate
And Lead you to the Pearly Gate.
Amen.

Source: Anna Owena Hoyers, "For the Christian Reader," in *The Defiant Muse: German Feminist Poems from the Middle Ages to the Present, A Bilingual Anthology,* ed., intro., and trans. Susan L. Cocalis (New York: Feminist Press at the City University of New York, 1986). Reprinted with permission.

streets shall be full of boys and girls playing," she wrote, "and old men and old women shall live till they come to a good old age, till they walk with a staff in their hand for age."[10]

These visionaries walked a fine line between the divine and the diabolical. Although often coming to their conclusions from their own study of scripture, female prophets had to present themselves as filled with a power beyond them. How were contemporaries to judge whether this power came from God or the devil? The authorities revealed their perplexity in their treatment of Lady Eleanor Davies Douglas, who was alternately praised as a national prophet, imprisoned, or institutionalized in a mental asylum. Her daughter, who was also her closest and most enduring supporter, summarized the age-old ambiguity accorded to public women by engraving on her mother's tombstone, "In a woman's body, a man's spirit."[11]

Historians face similar difficulties in interpreting this phenomenon, as Phyllis Mack has described in her study of women visionaries in England, in particular the Quakers. The Quakers first appeared in the late 1640s and early 1650s and generally supported sexual egalitarianism in spiritual matters. Out of about three hundred known female visionaries active around that time, more than 220 were Quakers. In public, they engaged in provocative and audacious behaviour, hurling insults at their audiences. Margaret Fell, the mother of Quakerism, denounced an Anglican priest as a child of "the whore of Babylon . . . the mother of harlots." "Thou drinks deep of her abomination and filthiness and fornication," she accused. In 1666, Fell would publish an assertive defence of female preaching, *Women's Speaking Justified*, based on her reading of biblical history. Another woman, Elizabeth Stirredge, personally presented her message to the king, warning him to "hear and fear the Lord God of heaven and earth."[12] Quaker women of all ages, from eleven to sixty, travelled widely as itinerant preachers, not only in England but also in Europe, the North American colonies, and even the Middle East. Unlike the visionary women of the previous decade, the Quakers tended to be married and mothers. Those who travelled did so at great cost to their private lives although they did not hesitate to follow their call even if their husbands disapproved.

Did these women thereby achieve some kind of personal liberation? Phyllis Mack warns us against such an assumption. In their own and contemporaries' understanding, these women were assertive precisely because they did not make an issue of their gender. Note that Margaret Fell, in the above quotation, used a traditional negative image of woman as whore. Like their medieval predecessors, seventeenth-century female visionaries spoke as prophets, not as women. Thus, one Quaker woman explained, "They say Paul would not permit of a woman to speak in the church; it is true . . . no more do not the Quakers; neither do they permit a woman to speak in the church, nor a man that is born of a woman; but he that is born of God, whether in male or in female, let him speak freely."[13] In most sects a woman who was allowed to shout prophecies was not allowed to ask a question in church or address the congregation. Even the Quakers assumed the subjection of women in marriage and their exclusion from secular public authority. In spite of their travels, Quaker women did not seek to escape domestic responsibilities, as many of the medieval mystics did, but remained closely tied to their families and communities.

Herein lay the innovation of Quakerism, allowing women both spiritual authority and a role in society rather than in the cloister. This authority was formally institutionalized in separate women's meetings, which Margaret Fell organized. The meetings exercised jurisdiction over economic matters, such as charity disbursements and the business affairs of widows, and family matters, such as marriage and sexual morality. Their influence over family matters was a unique example of women exercising public authority over men, a fact not missed by critics both within the movement and without. Hence the reaction of one contemporary that such female government was "a thing never heard of . . . except the government of the *Amazons*."[14] Their unique collective authority perhaps explains why Quaker women would be disproportionately represented in nineteenth-century British and American feminism.

At the time, however, Quakers and other religiously active women ultimately stressed their own passivity and lack of self-control, reinforcing the stereotype of female inferiority. They would have agreed with the sixteenth-century reformer Katharina Zell, who asked that she be judged "not according to the standards of a woman, but according to the standards of one whom God has filled with the Holy Spirit."[15] Even the Puritan Anne Hutchinson, who defied ministerial authority by commenting upon sermons in seventeenth-century Massachusetts, defended herself much as Margery Kempe had done in the fifteenth century, by arguing that she was exercising "a gift of Prophecy," not "a publick Ministery."[16]

Hutchinson (1591–1643) and Anne Bradstreet (1612–72) illustrate the different paths open to Protestant women in the seventeenth century. The two were neighbours and near contemporaries yet had dramatically different experiences. Both were Puritans, educated, married, and mothers of large families. Both emigrated with their families from England to colonial Massachusetts in the 1630s. Hutchinson was the daughter of a clergyman, whereas Bradstreet was born to gentry and had a more encompassing education at home from her brothers' tutors in the Renaissance tradition still viable among some families.

Hutchinson is remembered primarily for her role in the antinomian controversy, a theological disagreement over the respective roles of God's grace and human good works in salvation. She took the position that God's grace alone was sufficient, thereby reducing the role of the clergy and traditional standards of morality. Her views came to light during the biweekly meetings that she held for women in her home to discuss sermons. "But when that was done," her prosecutor reported, "shee would comment upon the Doctrines, and interpret all passages at her pleasure."[17] Charismatic and eloquent, she attracted large numbers of women, so that a contemporary described antinomianism as a delusion peculiar to women. In 1637–38 she was tried for defying ministerial authority and for claiming direct communication with God. Hutchinson was subsequently excommunicated and banished from the colony. Not surprisingly, this mother of fifteen children was also accused of sexual misconduct, still expected from any woman who intruded into the public sphere. She went to Rhode Island, where her husband and sons had prepared a home, and then to New York, where she and most of her family perished in an Indian attack a few years later.

Hutchinson exemplified the importance that Puritans placed on reading the Bible although she was not content to accept others' interpretation of it. At her trial she, like Joan of Arc almost two hundred years earlier, was accused of role reversal: "You have stept out of your place, *you have rather bine a Husband than a Wife and a preacher than a Hearer; and a Magistrate than a Subject.*" When told, "We must . . . restrain you from maintaining this course,"

Hutchinson replied archly, "If you have a rule for it from God's word you may."[18] Hutchinson's sin was her intellectual defiance of church authority.

Anne Bradstreet also read the Bible and agonized over religion, but her expression was private rather than public, taking the form of personal meditations and poetry. When her brother-in-law published a volume of her poems in England in 1650, reportedly without her knowledge, he introduced it with the reassurance that the book "is the work of a woman, honoured, and esteemed where she lives, for her gracious demeanour, her eminent parts, her pious conversation, her courteous disposition, her exact diligence in her place, and discrete managing of her family occasions, and more than so, these poems are the fruit but of some few hours, curtailed from her sleep and other refreshments."[19] Although the disclaimer that the writer had not been distracted from domestic responsibilities was common, was he perhaps also thinking of Anne Hutchinson's infamy when he wrote those lines?

Yet Bradstreet has been acknowledged as a feminist in her own quiet way. Writing poetry was still an unusual activity for a woman, especially for a married woman with other obligations, living in an environment that did not encourage open self-expression. Bradstreet's most productive period coincided with the births of her eight children and was hardly "the fruit but of some few hours." Although she wrote about familiar subjects—her children, her frequent illnesses, and her love for her husband—she also used poetry to express her spiritual crises and her thoughts on cosmology and history. A poem with the descriptive title "Before the Birth of One of Her Children" deals with the possibility of her death and records the message she wished to leave for her husband. On another occasion, when her house burned down, Bradstreet reported her sorrow but also found in her distress an opportunity to meditate on the vanity of earthly possessions: "I blest His name that gave and took, / That laid my goods now in the dust."[20]

One critic sees in Bradstreet the same emphasis on the feminine as found in Hildegard of Bingen's theology. Another describes Bradstreet's emphasis upon unity rather than hierarchy, co-operation rather than competition. Although her poems were first published without her knowledge, she immediately corrected them in anticipation of a subsequent printing. More pertinent than her brother-in-law's reassurance is Bradstreet's own prologue in which she revealed her sensitivity to the reception a woman writer could expect:

> Men can do best, and women know it well.
> Preeminence in all and each is yours;
> Yet grant some small acknowledgement of ours.[21]

Her life and ideas were very different from Hutchinson's, yet both women transcended the conventional role prescribed for their sex.

The phenomenon of women preachers and prophets would resurface, or continue, through the nineteenth century, but each period of such activity was invariably followed by a reaction. Anne Hutchinson has been described as embodying a "kind of primitive feminism" that "consisted essentially of the recognition of her own strength and gifts, and the apparent belief that other women could come to the same recognition."[22] She and the heroic Quaker women provided role models of female assertiveness and courage. Although not many women would openly follow these examples, periods of heretical conflict in Massachusetts also witnessed increased female criminality and deviance, perhaps testifying to greater stress over sex roles.

Ultimately, in Massachusetts and elsewhere the old order was reimposed. The restoration of the English monarchy in 1660 coincided with a wave of renewed misogyny. Faced with external pressure, sectarians began to put their house in order. By the end of the seventeenth century Quaker women, in spite of their formal jurisdiction over some matters, were admonished not to interfere with their brethren in mixed meetings. Those who continued to preach in the eighteenth century were praised for their modesty, charity, discipline, and motherhood. Their continued jurisdiction over charity and family matters was justified as being in keeping with the notion of women's sphere. Methodist women were allowed to preach in the eighteenth century but only if they felt an extraordinary call and then only to other women. Even this privilege was rescinded in 1803. The overall legacy of the religious controversies was a perceived need for order, which invariably meant repression. As with the Renaissance, the Reformation did not directly inspire an explicit feminism.

WOMEN AND POLITICS

The ultimate beneficiary of the years of disorders and wars unleashed in the name of religion from the 1520s to 1648 was the state, welcomed by many as the only means to re-establish order. Monarchy, authority, hierarchy, patriarchy—each reinforced the other. The family functioned as a microcosm of society; the relationship between ruler and subject was mirrored in that between parents and children or between husband and wife. A French royal declaration on marriage, issued in 1639, announced, "Marriages are the schools of states, the source and the origin of civil society, and the foundation of the families which make up republics, which serve as sources forming their administration and in which the natural reverence of children for their parents is the bond of legitimate obedience of subjects for their sovereigns."[23]

Paradoxically, this period also witnessed the rise of powerful queens: Mary Tudor, Elizabeth I of England, Christina of Sweden, and Catherine the Great of Russia. Elizabeth (1533–1603) was young and isolated when she came to power in England, in a court consisting mostly of men. She dealt inventively with the anomaly of a woman ruler by exploiting traditional symbols, presenting herself both as a Protestant virgin and as mother of England. Was her reputed virginity a refusal to accept a husband's authority? It proved to be very useful diplomatically, allowing her to explore possible marital alliances for years and years, entertaining proposals from representatives of various European countries until well into her forties and playing them off against one another. A recent biographer describes Elizabeth's deliberate exploitation of her virginity, an anachronistic symbol in a Protestant society, as "a feminist attitude,"[24] but literary historian Lisa Jardine argues instead that the use of traditional images gave Elizabeth an "abstract and generalised authority," acting to remove the taint of her sex: "Positively buried under the accumulated weight of all this reassuringly affirmative symbolism, Elizabeth's femaleness fades into insignificance."[25]

Indeed, Elizabeth defended her magistracy in masculine terms: "I know I have the body of a weak and feeble woman, but I have the heart and stomach of a king, and a king of England too." A contemporary complimented her by affirming that "the constitution of her mind is exempt from female weakness."[26] Elizabeth's reign saw the distribution of the "Homily on Matrimony" throughout England for the official use of preachers performing marriage ceremonies. It exhorted women to obey their husbands. Every married man upon hearing it read in church would be assured that he could command his wife's obedience.

A seventeenth-century French queen, Marie de Medici, who governed for her minor son when her husband was assassinated in 1610, exhibits a similar ambiguity as a female role model. She encouraged the portrayal of women as saviours and heroes, insisting on her own inclusion in representations of famous women and appropriating female allegorical figures such as Justice and classical goddesses like Minerva. This "assertively feminist queen"[27] may have inspired the artist Artemisia Gentileschi, who developed the same theme of the heroic woman in her painting. On the other hand, Marie also had herself depicted as the Virgin Mary, a more ambiguous symbol.

Some learned women looked to queens for inspiration. Both seventeenth-century German scholar Anna Maria van Schurman and eighteenth-century English scholar Elizabeth Elstob cited Elizabeth I as an example of an accomplished woman. Anne Bradstreet wrote an elegy in honour of Elizabeth, celebrating her reign as an example of female power. During the reign of Queen Anne in eighteenth-century England more plays written by women were produced than in any other time up to the present. Her subject Mary Astell asked, "May we not hope that She will not do less for Her own Sex than She has already done for the other?"[28] Nonetheless, as Lisa Jardine points out, no stateswoman ever appointed or even considered appointing a woman to any position at court other than the expected one of lady-in-waiting. A decidedly misogynist queen was Christina of Sweden (1626–89), whose father raised her as a boy, suiting her own inclinations completely. Christina refused to tolerate the idea of marriage, which "appeared to her an unbearable subordination." Rather than marry, she abdicated her throne. Instead of criticizing restrictive gender roles, however, Christina disparaged her gender, describing it as "my greatest defect." "My feeling is," she confessed, "that women should never reign; and I am so convinced of this that I would have, without a doubt, taken away all right of succession from my daughters, had I married."[29]

Were the women who took part in the Fronde, the civil revolts in mid-seventeenth-century France, any more forward looking? Officers, nobles, townspeople, and peasants all joined in this insurrection against the crown, but historians are divided over the role that women played. One describes these years as notorious for the meddling and intrigue of aristocratic women and judges their motives as essentially selfish and petty. Women connived in order to join their lovers, to negotiate special favours, to satisfy "personal vengeances and grievances,"[30] or simply to escape from the tedium of their daily lives into something more akin to the fantasy world they read about in romances. One wonders whether historians who take this view have been influenced by contemporary accounts that vehemently condemned women in the public sphere. Already in 1634, Richelieu, the first minister of the kingdom, had written, "A woman caused the world's fall; nothing is more capable of harming the State than this sex." The male leaders of the Fronde were not necessarily any more disinterested than the women who were involved. Other historians have hailed the Fronde as the beginning of French feminism, at least a feminism of action. It was remarkable for the extent of female participation, both politically and militarily, and has even been described as a "woman's war."[31] After the war women chose to exercise their influence through literature rather than politics, but the literature that emerged from salon writing carried political implications, which will be explored in Chapter 5.

As for lower-class women, when their families' welfare was threatened they became the key instigators of and participants in the protests typical of preindustrial society, namely riots over food shortages and high prices. In France, women terrorized and mutilated tax collectors. In 1648–49 they menaced members of the Parlement—the highest judicial court—with pistols and daggers, pointing out that they were dying of hunger while the officials were amusing themselves and earning money at the people's expense. In New France, women enjoyed a reputation for insubordination vis-à-vis the authorities. In one instance an officer sent to calm women who were infuriated by the bishop's decision to transfer them to another parish reported that they were waiting "with rocks and sticks in their hands to kill me" and that they chased him, yelling "stop, thief, we want to kill you and throw you in the swamp."[32] Dutch women appear frequently as inciters of political and religious riots. In one episode in 1621 women walked through the streets of Rotterdam shouting, according to a bystander, "Women can do nothing wrong."[33]

Less visibly defiant but no less effective, slave women in the New World resisted their enslavement with a wide range of tactics, from truancy, disobedience, or feigned illness or idiocy to more violent responses, such as murder or arson. But success was difficult in the face of a master's pressure; in vain did Rose Williams, a slave in the American South, resist living with a man her owner had selected for her. Although she gave in ultimately, her resentment remained: "After what I does for the master, I never wants no truck with any man. The Lord forgive this coloured woman, but he have to excuse me and look for some others for to 'plenish the earth."[34]

Did the New World offer white women more freedom and opportunity than they had in Europe? Historians have made that claim for both the Thirteen Colonies and New France, pointing out that demographic imbalance between the sexes made women more valued. Both areas were frontier societies, where white women could take on unusual responsibilities, such as military defence or trading with Natives. Already in the seventeenth century the colonies had a reputation for greater gender parity; the governor of Massachusetts Bay Colony wrote home to deny the rumour that women could vote in Plymouth. Though unfeminine behaviour was more tolerated than in Europe, it did not necessarily lead to feminism. In fact, toleration may have pre-empted feminist resistance by allowing women greater latitude in expressing frustration. Even when imported to the frontiers of the New World, women's roles were restricted. Like medieval women, women in both colonial North America and early modern Europe may have dealt with the tension and conflict of restrictive sex roles by experiencing hysterical fits and illness. They also engaged in verbal and physical abuse of husbands and neighbours. Society was relatively tolerant of this kind of female insubordination, as demonstrated by the popularity of the sex role reversal theme in literature and popular culture, as we will see below.

In troubled times women were more apt to exploit the image of the insubordinate female. The unusual and chaotic conditions surrounding the Civil War in England in the 1640s encouraged "great multitudes of women" to petition the House of Commons, complaining of economic suffering. They justified their daring action "because Christ hath purchased us at as deare a rate as He hath done Men" and "because women are sharers in the common calamities that accompany both Church and Commonwealth." They hastened to reassure, however, "We doe it not of any selfe-conceit or pride of heart, as seeking to equall ourselves with men, either in Authority or wisdome; But according to our places to discharge that duty we owe to God." A more explicitly political action was associated with the radicals known as the Levellers, whose leader John Liliburne was in and out of prison during the late 1630s and 1640s. In 1649, women petitioners demanded his release but were told by parliament that "the matter . . . was of a higher concernment than they understood, that the House gave an answer to their husbands, and therefore desired them to go home and look after their own business and meddle with their housewifery."[35] Alerted to the danger of female assertiveness, parliament additionally took the measure of changing the language of a bill authorizing a loyalty oath, specifying that it would apply to "men" rather than to "persons."

Although many radical groups thrived in the politically volatile climate of mid-seventeenth-century England, none of them proposed any political rights for women. The most radical talked of dispensing with property qualifications for male suffrage but never considered extending the vote to women. Gerrard Winstanley, leader of the Diggers movement, proposed that women and men should be free to marry whom they loved, endowing themselves with portions from the common lands, "for we are all of one blood, mankind, and for portion, the Common Storehouses are every man and maid's portion, as free to one as to another." He even protested rape as "robbery of a woman's bodily freedom."[36] The effect of these views was insubstantial. Neither direct action by women themselves nor the radical political opinions of their male contemporaries resulted in any feminist claims. Not until the next century would the equal rights language of liberal individualism inspire some to broaden the attack upon aristocratic privilege to one against male privilege.

LITERATURE AND LIFE

I live as well contented as any Maid can,
What need I entangle my self with a Man?
I walk where I please at my own command,
I need not say 'Shall I, pray shall I, husband?'

SEVENTEENTH-CENTURY ENGLISH BALLAD

Although not welcomed in political life, assertive women, to an extraordinary degree, were a dominant literary and artistic theme in early modern Europe. Seventeenth-century English, French, and Spanish drama is rich in examples of powerful and influential women. Their sphere of influence ranged from the household, dominated by the shrewish wife, to the nation, led by a warrior or Amazonian queen. These heroines escaped from unwanted marriages, lived as outlaws, fought or hunted in male disguise, and led independent lives. In Spanish drama from the 1570s on, the "masculine woman" was one of the most popular character types. At least one new play of this sort appeared every year from 1590 to 1660. The Spanish stage took assertive women for granted.

Of particular appeal was the woman dressed in male clothing. In Spain the theme became a common, almost tedious, convention. It was popular in England also, appearing in almost one-quarter of the plays written between 1660 and 1700. Whereas Shakespeare had earlier used it as a dramatic device to give his heroines more freedom, the transvestite heroines who appeared in the 1610s and 1620s were more assertive, giving no excuses for their apparel. French novels also sported an enormous number of heroines who rode, hunted, and fought like men, and the femme forte, the woman of strength and heroism, became a common icon in the visual arts.

It is tempting to interpret this female assertiveness as a reflection of social reality. In both France and Spain, some real-life examples might have inspired contemporary artists. The popularity of the theme in France may have also reflected the involvement of women in the Fronde. The vogue of female heroes in England coincided with a spate of sermons denouncing women who wore male doublets and jerkins, a pamphlet war on the subject of masculine women and feminine men, and a directive of King James I to the clergy in 1620, ordering them to preach "against the insolencie of our women." Linda Woodbridge suggests the existence of a female transvestite movement in London,[37] which reflected the greater mobility of women in an urban setting. At the very least, she believes, playwrights were responding to pressure from more vocal audiences, specifically, from female play-goers.

As with political women, however, we should not overestimate the feminist component here. There are other ways to explain the literary fashion. In the aftermath of the religious wars, the Spanish theatre adopted a pessimistic tone. Perhaps this mood encouraged playwrights to deal with the depressing subject of women's dependency and to sympathize with imaginary female rebels. The subject may have also served to deflect attention away from the reality of pressing economic and political problems. In France the popularity of strong heroines may have reflected no more than the preference of Baroque writers for the unusual and the extraordinary. They stand out because they are exceptional, not because they are typical. Renaissance and Baroque writers were fascinated with the devices of inversion and paradox.

What turns these women into heroines is always some unusual circumstance, such as a unique education, a concealed high birth, or, as in the case of Joan of Arc, divine assistance. In other words, it is always something other than their innate capacity. Exceptionality reinforces rather than negates the general assumption about the inferiority of women. If such powerful women represent the exceptional, what lesson do they convey? Here the critics are unanimous. The moral lies in their ultimate submission. Lisa Jardine, who warns against the tendency to interpret these heroines too literally, notes that they may be strong but they are also "morally reprehensible." The Spanish heroines who opt for independence are shown as motivated by vanity, pride, or some other moral flaw. The playwrights' sympathy for women who become outlaws to escape forced marriages is limited to letting them repent at the end. Women's ultimate submission symbolizes a restored social order. As Jardine summarizes, the shrew's victory is always short-lived: "Misrule is [always] set to rights."[38] Even Amazons ultimately fall in love with men. The images of powerful women thus ironically reinforce patriarchy. The shrew's power to exploit female weapons of gossiping and scolding is illusory: "It is only 'telling tales' and 'calling names,'" nothing more than "a semblance of power, which threatens disorder without actually freeing [woman] from her multiple obligations and constraints." Similar to the convention that allowed women prophets to speak when divinely inspired, women in literature during this period spoke not as women but as literary stereotypes.

The men in the audiences would have been pleased with these examples of ultimate female submission, as well as titillated by the sight of female curves revealed in men's more form-fitting clothing, but what did women think? A modern critic of the Spanish theatre suggests that it may have inspired some real women, citing the example of Catalina de Erauso, who disguised herself as a man to escape from a convent in the early seventeenth century and serve as a conquistador in the New World for eighteen years. At the very least, women would have vicariously enjoyed the heroine's freedom and adventures and perhaps identified with the spirited women on stage. John Fletcher's play, "The Woman's Prize; or, The Tamer Tamed" (ca. 1611), for example, stars a disobedient wife reinforced by an army of cheering women who come to join her in her "bold stand for marital freedom." They all shout in an inspiring chorus, "The woman shall wear the breeches!" Linda Woodbridge is hopeful about the play's effect: "a real world whose literature admits to [the insubordinate wife's] celebration as an imaginative possibility is capable of celebrating her in the flesh eventually."[39]

We can test this hypothesis against the fate of non-fictional "masculine women." From the sixteenth to eighteenth centuries there are many accounts of women adopting men's dress. One study includes 119 women who lived as men in the Netherlands between 1550 and 1839 and who presumably constituted only the tip of the iceberg. They testify to the existence of a thriving tradition of female cross-dressing. Many of these women, in fact most, were either soldiers or sailors. Historian Lillian Faderman calls such women "in a sense, among the first feminists. Mute as they were, without a formulated ideology to express their convictions, they saw the role of women to be dull and limiting."[40] Not all cross-dressers, however, had feminist motives. The women included in the Dutch study cross-dressed for a variety of reasons. Those in the military or merchant marine were sometimes following a loved one or looking for an alternative to prostitution. In fact, the employment opportunities in the seafaring countries, England and Holland, probably prompted female cross-dressing to flourish in this corner of Europe. Other women were trying to escape unwanted marriages, like Thecla fifteen centuries earlier or Christina of Markyate in the Middle Ages. Some were patriots who wanted to take up arms in defence of their country; others were simply hiding from the law.

Were some of these women lesbians? The records reveal that some cross-dressers wooed other women. Catharine Margaretha Linck in eighteenth-century Germany entered into an official marriage with another woman. Her use of a stuffed-leather penis, which fooled her partner according to the latter's testimony, reinforces the belief of historians that Europeans before the end of the eighteenth century were unable to conceive of amorous relationships between women other than in the familiar pattern of heterosexual marriage. Women had to present themselves as men in order to express their love of other women. The same conclusion emerges from a study of a lesbian nun in seventeenth-century Italy. Benedetta Carlini was a visionary who took on the guise of a male guardian angel named Splenditello in order to have sex with another nun. Both Carlini and her partner were apparently convinced by this role-playing, at least until the latter's doubts surfaced during a papal investigation of Carlini's visions. While we do not know the investigators' conclusion, we do know that a few years later Carlini went to prison, where she spent thirty-five years before her death. Still, she was treated more leniently than Linck, who was beheaded for sodomy.

Since cross-dressers were often involved in and punished for other criminal activities, it is difficult to generalize about how their contemporaries judged them. Much depended on the circumstances and the motive. Some were praised for their military exploits. Catalina de Erauso received a royal pension as well as an official privilege, confirmed by the pope, to dress as a man. Deborah Sampson received a pension for her soldiery during the American Revolution. The most serious disapproval was reserved for those, like Linck, who dressed as men in order to court or marry other women. Still, Dutch judges were reluctant to impose the stipulated death penalty, perhaps because they had difficulty imagining an intimate relationship between women or taking it seriously. Even in Linck's case the court expressed doubts about whether two women could in fact commit sodomy. A more usual penalty was exile or a few years imprisonment, whereas male homosexuals were generally executed. The most severe penalties were reserved for women who impersonated men sexually, by using false genitalia, for example. Like male homosexuals, they would usually be executed. Curiously, the common people seem to have reacted more negatively to female cross-dressers than the elite did, at least to judge from popular songs. Significantly, de Erauso maintained that she was a virtuous woman and, confirmed by matrons who examined her, as virginal as the day she was born.

Most female cross-dressers were probably unacquainted with theatrical conventions, but some may have been inspired to cross-dress after playing men's roles on the stage. The English actor Charlotte Cibber Charke (?–1760) dressed as a man both on the stage and off. Since Charke ran afoul of the theatrical establishment, her male disguise had the concrete benefits of hiding her from her creditors and widening her employment opportunities. At one time she became a gentleman servant; another time she won the affections of an unsuspecting young, wealthy heiress. Was Charke one of those "first feminists" who found the role of women to be dull and limiting? In her autobiography, published in 1755, Charke describes her early penchant for dressing up and her disinclination for learning "housewifery perfections." She learned to ride and shoot instead. Only when a neighbour complained that it was "inconsistent with the character of a young gentlewoman to follow such diversions" did her parents take away her gun. Charke had such a "veneration for Cattle and Husbandry"[41] that when the family's groom was fired, she stood watch at the gate for a week to turn away any applicants, so she could take on the job. Fired up by her experience of helping her uncle in his medical practice, she set up a dispensary for her neighbours, turning to herbs when her father withdrew her credit at the local pharmacy. For one client who complained of rheumatism and an upset stomach she imaginatively concocted a syrup of garden snails and brown sugar. To her surprise, the mixture worked, but a subsequent drought dried up her supply of snails. Charke married and had a daughter but the marriage was not a success. She left her husband and went on the stage but jeopardized her career by speaking out against the theatrical establishment, including her father. She then formed a puppet theatre and also tried her hand at managing an oil shop and a tavern before becoming a strolling player. By this time male dress had become a habit although she does not explain why. Charke's many talents were never fully realized; she died in obscurity and poverty. Judging from her autobiography, it seems that her irrepressible personality would have resisted conventional female behaviour even if literary or theatrical models had been absent.

The difficulties of relating literature to life are perceptively explored in Joy Wiltenburg's study of popular literature in Germany and England. Ballads and broadsides depicted powerful and subversive women escaping or defying male control. Wives engaged in a battle for marital dominance employed a range of weapons, from wiles and flattery, passive resistance, adultery, gossip, and scolding to the threat of violence or actual husband beating. In seventeenth-century English sources especially, the number and intensity of violent wives increased, with the women winning three times as often as their husbands. At the very least, the tales of marital discord "show recognition that the realities of human interaction contradict the dogma of male supremacy." Thus, a cuckolded husband complained in a 1638 English ballad:

be we great or small,
we must be at their call;
How e're the cards doe fall,
we men must suffer all.[42]

How should we interpret this literature? These stories were first of all meant as entertainment; their purpose was to amuse. The reversal of sexual roles was funny, but the joke depended on the cultural assumption that the man should be in charge. Authority was thus both comically debunked and subtly reinforced. Because the joke was at the expense of the henpecked and cuckolded husband, it served as a warning to men, threatening them with shame and ridicule for failing to control their wives. Similarly, outspoken women would presumably have had qualms about being depicted as shrews. A model of female deviance might also have encouraged women, however, operating as a two-edged sword by "offering women the satisfaction of feeling in control—and of exercising some control at the level of individual interaction—and discouraging them from seeking to disturb the hierarchy itself." Such an outlet would help explain the longevity of male dominance:

> For the women of early modern Europe, at any rate, life within patriarchy need not have implied adoption of a slave mentality. . . . Rather, women could have been encouraged to see themselves as mistresses of an alternative, if socially inferior, order, even as they could undermine male rule on a personal level by the use of their personal strengths of intelligence and courage.[43]

This is reminiscent of the effect of the holy anorexics discussed in Chapter 2, who may have unwittingly reinforced male notions of female psychology. Rather than encouraging the development of feminism, the popular literature of early modern Europe obstructed it.

Is it possible that the literature reflected a change in women's social or economic position? Most historians agree that there was no improvement in women's economic situation to justify a new image. Whereas the preindustrial period was once seen as a golden age where women and men worked together as equal partners in their own establishments, more recent studies have shown that women's work in European rural and urban settings has always been low in status, low skilled, and low paying. Although this was once thought to result from changes in the late Middle Ages, it now seems to describe accurately women's work from the earliest records available to European historians. The situation may in fact have worsened as the growth of a market economy began to affect household production and the family became more dependent on piecework that women did at home. Specialization and greater competition increased the advantage of men who had access to university education or formal training. At times women protested their declining position in crafts and certain occupations. In 1671, for example, Jane Sharp tried to defend women's monopoly of midwifery, which was being invaded by "male midwives." These attempts were rarely successful. In contrast to Linda Woodbridge's claim that the economic situation had improved for London women, Joy Wiltenburg finds that English women "were effectively excluded from positions of economic power by the mid-sixteenth century." Perhaps, paradoxically, women were allowed to be assertive in literature because they were no longer seen as threatening or competitive. "The street literature does not prove that English women enjoyed more power than their German counterparts; in economic terms it may even be that the opposite was true."[44]

Economic change was accompanied by the attempt of the state to extend control over its subjects. For women this meant an upsurge in prosecutions for witchcraft, infanticide, and sexual offences. The brunt fell on young single women and widows, women not under male control. Legislation in French and German towns targeted "masterless" women, forbidding them residency unless they moved in with a male relative or employer. Ballad and theatre audiences could enjoy the fantasy of assertive women making choices, but it was unrelated to women's real options.

THE QUERELLE DES FEMMES

Feminism is learning where to put the blame.

ETHEL KLEIN, 1984

The genre for a discussion of "the woman question" from the fifteenth to the end of the seventeenth century was the *querelle des femmes,* a literary debate about the vices and virtues of woman. In one form or another it extended from the ancient world to the end of the eighteenth century. In the late Middle Ages, the debate came to involve full-scale attacks and defences. Renaissance humanists added non-Christian examples and amplified the issue with discussions of marriage and the family in relation to the state. These matters became especially compelling to Protestant writers during the Reformation. By the late sixteenth and seventeenth centuries the printing press enabled the debate to reach a wider audience, and in Spain, England, and France, themes associated with the querelle spilled over to drama and other literature. An early eighteenth-century German catalogue listed more than five hundred works on the subject. Its themes echoed in almost all writing about women.

Characterized as a debate between feminism and antifeminism, the querelle has been described as the venue for the origins of feminist thought. Although earlier historians called attention to the feminism of individual participants, such as Christine de Pizan in the early fifteenth century or Poullain de la Barre in the seventeenth century, Joan Kelly in a 1982 essay hailed the debate itself as "the vehicle through which most early feminist thinking evolved." She saw it as inspiring "a solid, four-hundred-year-old tradition of women thinking about women and sexual politics in European society before the French Revolution." In contrast to historians who see it as an indication of women's gain in status, Kelly perceives the querelle as a response to the losses women were experiencing, a form of "intellectual resistance."[45] According to her, this tradition would later join with the parallel one of feminist activism to create the women's movement.

Christine de Pizan

The first woman known to participate in the querelle was Christine de Pizan (1365–1430?), who has been often described as the first feminist. She was a Venetian-born noblewoman whose father and husband had both been employed at the French court. She made use of her court connections when, at the age of twenty-five, she became a widow and had to support herself, three small children, her mother, and a niece. She became a successful writer of poems and prose works, which won the commissions she needed to provide an income for herself and her family.

Christine de Pizan's best known work, *The Book of the City of Ladies* (1404–5), opens with a description of her response to an earlier misogynist work by Mathéolus. Her aversion to the book led her to speculate on the tradition of misogyny, to wonder why "so many different men—and learned men among them—have been and are so inclined to express both in speaking and in their treatises and writings so many wicked insults about women and their behavior." Although she could counter their opinions with her own and other women's experiences, the weight of authority was persuasive: "Yet I still argued vehemently against women, saying that it would be impossible that so many famous men . . . could have spoken falsely on so many occasions." Christine then describes her subsequent depression: "As I was thinking this, a great unhappiness and sadness welled up in my heart, for I detested myself and the entire feminine sex, as though we were monstrosities in nature." She deplores her fate in having been born female and beseeches, "Alas, God, why did You not let me be born in the world as a man?" In response appear three female figures, Reason, Rectitude, and Justice. They tell Christine de Pizan to trust her instincts, to articulate consciously "what you know for a certainty."[46] In answer to her questions, they furnish the proof she needs to counter misogyny. Together they build a symbolic city to celebrate the virtues of women.

Reason first dispels Christine de Pizan's deference to authority: "It also seems that you think that all the words of the philosophers are articles of faith, that they could never be wrong." Thus encouraged, she challenges the classical justification, based on biology, for woman's inferiority. She appeals on Christian grounds: woman could not be an imperfection of nature since God could not have created anything imperfect. Christianity also inspires Christine de Pizan to argue for the equality of souls: "God created the soul and placed wholly similar souls, equally good and noble in the feminine and in the masculine bodies." Her contention that "there is not the slightest doubt that women belong to the people of God and the human race as much as men, and are not another species or dissimilar race, for which they should be excluded from moral teachings"[47] will echo in Mary Wollstonecraft's plea for moral equality three centuries later.

Having dissected classical authority, Christine turns to Christian sources of misogyny. Like Hildegard of Bingen (see Chapter 2) but without any knowledge of her famous predecessor, she argues that the virtue of the Virgin Mary redeemed the sin of Eve. Drawing on the high respect the Virgin

▶ *In her* Book of the City of Ladies, *three allegorical figures appear before Christine de Pizan, representing Reason, Rectitude, and Justice. Here, Lady Reason explains why they have come.*

There is another greater and even more special reason for our coming which you will learn from our speeches: in fact we have come to vanquish from the world the same error into which you had fallen, so that from now on, ladies and all valiant women may have a refuge and defense against the various assailants, those ladies who have been abandoned for so long, exposed like a field without a surrounding hedge, without finding a champion to afford them an adequate defense, notwithstanding those noble men who are required by order of law to protect them, who by negligence and apathy have allowed them to be mistreated. It is no wonder then that their jealous enemies, those outrageous villains who have assailed them with various weapons, have been victorious in a war in which women have had no defense. Where is there a city so strong which could not be taken immediately if no resistance were forthcoming, or the law case, no matter how unjust, which was not won through the obstinance of someone pleading without opposition? And the simple, noble ladies, following the example of suffering which God commands, have cheerfully suffered the great attacks which, both in the spoken and the written word, have been wrongfully and sinfully perpetrated against women by men who all the while appealed to God for the right to do so. Now it is time for their just cause to be taken from Pharaoh's hands, and for this reason, we three ladies whom you see here, moved by pity, have come to you to announce a particular edifice built like a city wall, strongly constructed and well founded, which has been predestined and established by our aid and counsel for you to build, where no one will reside except all ladies of fame and women worthy of praise, for the walls of the city will be closed to those women who lack virtue.

Source: Selections from *The Book of the City of Ladies* by Christine de Pizan, translated by Earl Jeffrey Richards, copyright © 1982 by Persea Books, Inc. Reprinted by permission of Persea Books, Inc.

enjoyed in the late Middle Ages, she names Mary ruler of her city and addresses her, "Since God chose His spouse from among women, most excellent Lady, because of your honor, not only should men refrain from reproaching women but should also hold them in great reverence."[48] In her poem, "The Epistle to the God of Love," she depicts Mary as an empowering symbol for women: "Joyful and proud women should truly be, / Since they have the same form as she."[49] In the same poem she adds other arguments: Jesus' example of showing esteem for women, the fact that the women never abandoned him, and, again echoing Hildegard of Bingen, Eve's creation from Adam's rib, a finer substance than the earth from which Adam was created.

But Christine de Pizan's main refutation of misogyny rests on her historical list of women worthies. Referring to Boccaccio's *Concerning Famous Women* (ca. 1380), she reworked his classical examples and added Christian ones, focusing on women famous for their virtue rather than merely infamous. Although modern readers may wince at the indiscriminate mixing of mythical, literary, and historical sources and question her at times quixotic interpretations, her work has been hailed as the first challenge to history written from a male point of view. She calls up an impressive parade of women to prove the importance of their contributions as rulers, warriors, artists, scientists, and inventors. Her discussion of the role of women in early Christianity reappears in subsequent defences of women and even in modern feminist biblical criticism.

In the course of her defence, Christine de Pizan touches on many feminist issues: married women's vulnerability to physical and emotional abuse; sexual coercion (she condemns the unwillingness of men to realize that no means no); the injustice of a double standard that allows men to sin but not women; and the effects of social conditioning (women "know less" because they "stay at home"). She argues for women's education: "If it were customary to send daughters to school like sons, and if they were then taught the natural sciences, they would learn as thoroughly . . . as sons." Although her references are largely to other women of her rank, she specifically includes in her city "women from all classes."[50]

Although much of Christine de Pizan's argument rings true almost six hundred years later, the virtues she extols in women are primarily the ones of humility, obedience, and passivity. Her examples of suffering women, most of whom are "of great beauty," are not what we would celebrate as examples of female heroism. She dwells on the sufferings of fourteen-year-old Fausta, whose tormentors attempted to saw her in two with an iron saw, hammer a thousand nails into her head, and cook her in a cauldron of boiling water. St Christine has her breasts ripped off, is hanged by her hair, and survives showers of boiling oil. Trying to silence her, the judge cuts out her tongue, not once but twice. Not only does St Christine continue to speak, but in sweet revenge the spat-out portion of her tongue hits the judge's eye, blinding him. Husbands equal God in sending torments. Christine de Pizan repeats the story of Griselda, who endured without complaint her husband's repudiation of her and the supposed murder of their two children, all as a test of her virtue. Her advice to women with "husbands who are cruel, mean, and savage" is to be patient and humble. Even if attempts to reform their husbands fail, these wives will at least "acquire great merit for their souls through the virtue of patience."[51]

Christine de Pizan tackles the causes of misogyny, but she tends to see it as an individual and psychological problem rather than as social and institutional. Men malign women out of jealousy or envy; resentment of their own impotence leads them to warn other men away from what they themselves cannot have. However, in "The Epistle to the God of Love," she acknowledges the link between misogyny and the monastic education of clerics, which

> . . . is designed
> To keep them from loving a woman.
> . . . .
> But if women had produced the books,
> I know the product would be different.[52]

What is the solution? Christine draws back from any call for social change. Her claim for spiritual equality entails nothing further: "God has similarly ordained man and woman to serve Him in different offices and also to aid and comfort one another, each in their ordained task."[53] Her stated goal is to change attitudes, to replace scorn for women who fall short of the ideal with honour and praise for women who live up to it. The ideal remains the same, but Christine de Pizan offers positive rather than negative reinforcement.

The Querelle as Debate

The problem of assessing the importance of Christine de Pizan's feminism is the larger one of interpreting the meaning and importance of the querelle itself. The primarily literary nature of the debate complicates matters; it belongs to a context that is first of all about rhetoric rather than about women. Evidence suggests that already in the Middle Ages the querelle des femmes was a required exercise for university students, and in the seventeenth century pedagogical works on rhetoric still used the topic of woman to illustrate methodology. As late as 1772, the Enlightenment author Antoine-Léonard Thomas favoured the classical rhetorical form of thesis, antithesis, and synthesis for his treatise, *Qu'est-ce qu'une femme?* (What is a Woman?), earning the scorn of critics for his inability to reconcile contradictory positions. Literary historian Linda Woodbridge suggests that the youthfulness of many of the writers is reflected in "the textbook quality" of their formal defences. What she says of one work could be applied to most: it "exists not in a world where real women demand rights but in a world where books answer books."[54] This context clarifies many curious features of the debate. Most defences of women were written *before* attacks, or else appeared simultaneously, frequently written by the same author. Often the opponent is imaginary. Such manoeuvring makes sense if we are talking about a literary exercise. The model of debate necessitated two sides, even if one was hypothetical.

But why was the debate about woman? Historian Ian Maclean sees it as part of a timeless tradition, a subject that would attract lively discussion in any age. The assumption that men and women are radically different, indeed that one is superior to the other, heightens the discussion. The more dramatic the contrast, the more interesting the debate. Maclean's characterization of a specific phase of the debate in France can in fact apply to it in its entirety:

> An aesthetic which is characterized by a delight in metamorphosis, paradox, and the mixing of opposites is certain to exploit one of the fundamental distinctions in life as in literature, that between the sexes; but the contradictory nature of woman herself—both angelic and demonic, beautiful and ugly, pure and unclean, compassionate and vengeful, gentle and cruel—is itself eminently attractive to such an artistic vision.

But few will take comfort in his insight that this feminism was so appealing because "of the ease with which it [might] be manipulated to evoke horror or surprise."[55] Why did no one ever debate the virtues or vices of men?

Another odd feature is the contradiction within many of the works, which describe marriage as a society of equals, for example, while also insisting that women are naturally subordinate to men. An Italian author in 1545 declared that woman was as intelligent as man but then advocated an education based on the assumption that she was "feeble, weak-willed, and hence incapable of learning."[56] It is refreshing if sobering to read a French author's frank admission in 1647 that his intention was "not to call women to school": "I do not wish to make graduates of them: nor change their needles and wool into Astrolabes and spheres. I respect too much the boundaries which separate us: and my question concerns only what they are capable of, and not what they should do."[57]

Most of these arguments were completely divorced from the realities of family and political life. Participants would write of the equality of husband and wife as if they considered marriage an abstract relationship, but it was meaningless to discuss the family in isolation from society and the state. In the larger context, the family as a symbol reflected the values of an authoritarian and hierarchical society. The result was that "feminist positions theoretically endorsed were practically dismissed."[58] A modern critic suggests that the debate may even have retarded feminism by giving the impression of serious discussion. Antifeminists' "alleged slander" was in fact a red herring.[59]

Much depends on the context. The seventeenth-century French querelle was part of a broader debate in French society over social mobility. The real question was whether the nobility should maintain its closed ranks or admit new members. Its members could be ennobled on the basis of merit, advantageous marriages, or social and cultural assimilation. The last process was carried out in the salons, where new and old nobility mixed under the leadership of upper-class women. To argue on behalf of woman meant to take a modernist position that endorsed social change. In this context the debate was really about the role of an elite group in modifying the traditional social structure.

A reading of the debate out of context can thus be very misleading. French writers who promoted the idea of love as an integral part of marriage, for example, were actually taking an antifeminist position because they concluded that such a relationship would bind women through ties of affection. The prowoman advocates argued instead for either no marriage or for marriages of economic interest, which would leave women free to bestow their affections elsewhere, as men had been traditionally free to do.

When we see the debate as symbolic or abstract, we can understand other singular features, such as the tendency of prowoman writers to argue that woman was superior rather than equal. This may be the obvious consequence of a society that thought in terms of hierarchy rather than equality, but it may also be a rhetorical device. The opposite of inferiority is superiority, and if the purpose of debate is to heighten contrasts the argument for superiority would be a logical choice. That all this is far removed from any practical attempt to improve women's situation goes without saying.

Prowoman Arguments

An example of an argument for woman's superiority is *Female Pre-eminence* (1529), written by the humanist and reputed feminist Henricus Cornelius Agrippa and dedicated to Margaret of Austria, governor of Franche-Comté. Agrippa's arguments, like those of Christine de Pizan, were widely copied by subsequent writers. While his attempt to secure Margaret's patronage no doubt indicates a practical motive, the form he chose, that of a rhetorical paradox, might also account for his decision to argue for woman's superiority. Agrippa's evidence ranges from the esoteric (based on the cabala, an occult tradition that intrigued him) to the bizarre (maintaining that dead women float belly down while men float belly up, immodestly exposing their genitals). He also draws on medieval arguments (that Adam was created of vile mud but Eve out of his rib, a purer substance) and Neoplatonism (the oft-to-be repeated claim that woman, created last, reflects perfection). Where Agrippa appears more genuinely feminist is in his realization that woman's subordination is culturally determined:

> From what hath been said, appears conspicuously, as if written with *Sunbeams* on a Wall of Chrystal, That this Sex are not *incapable* of, nor were in the primitive and more innocent Ages of the World, *debarr'd* from managing the most arduous or difficult affairs, till the *tyranny* of Men usurpt the dispose of all business, and *unjust Laws*, *foolish Custommes*, and an *ill mode* of education, *retrencht* their liberties. For now a Woman (as if she were only the *pastime* of Mens idle hours, or a thing made meerly for *trifling* Courtiers to throw away their *non*-sensical Complements on) is from her *Cradle* kept at home; and as incapable of any nobler imployment, suffered only to *knit, spin*, or practise the little curiosities of the *Needle*.

He prefers to explain woman's subordination by reference to "the prevalency of *Custome, Education, Chance,* or some *tyrannical* occasion" than to nature or God. Yet this feminist insight fades somewhat against Agrippa's lengthy examples of woman's "incomparable *Neatness*, and *charming Beauty*," which qualities, alas, seem to be inherent. His ultimate goal is mired in chivalry:

"Let us regard [women] with that *Reverence* that is due; pay them that *Devotion* that becomes us; and treat them with all that *respect and veneration* which belongs to such *Terrestrial Angels.*"[60]

Other prowoman writers were only slightly less ingenious than Agrippa. The Renaissance encouraged scrutiny of ancient authorities, who proved encouragingly co-operative in contradicting each other—as Reason had pointed out to Christine de Pizan—on such basic issues as the nature of women, traditionally held to be cold and wet whereas men were defined as hot and dry. Aristotle was discredited by reference to Plato, who in the *Republic* permitted women to share command with men, or by looking at his private life. Lucrezia Marinelli, for example, suggested in 1601 that Aristotle's envy and dislike of his wife was responsible for his misogyny. Baldesar Castiglione's prowoman speaker, Giuliano, in *The Book of the Courtier* (1528), turns the whole argument of woman's biological inferiority around by claiming that "being weaker in body women are abler in mind and more capable of speculative thought than men."[61]

More interesting was the evidence that attempted to discredit biblical authority for woman's inferiority. English writers repeated the interpretation of Eve's creation put forth by Agrippa and Hildegard of Bingen, and the author or authors of one pamphlet restated the adage that woman was not created to be man's slave since she was not created from his foot but from his side, to be his "fellow-feeler, his equal and companion."[62] Others, like Castiglione, argued from the Genesis account of the simultaneous creation of male and female in God's image. One anonymous author in 1516 used the idea of equal creation to counter the classical assumption that woman lacked reason, concluding boldly "that woman is a rational creature who uses understanding, common sense, and reason." A later tract argued that God was androgynous, endowing both men and women with his spirituality and with the "same"[63] understanding and reason.

Historical or anthropological contexts were also employed to explain away traditional assumptions. The young Rachel Speght insisted in 1617, as Quaker leader Margaret Fell later would, that Paul's injunction to women to keep silent referred only to a particular congregation. Marie de Gournay argued ingeniously in 1622 that Jesus was male simply because of historical convenience: a woman of that time lacked the freedom to move about as publicly as a man. She also claimed that all ancient religions had accepted women as priests. Writers drew on anthropology to describe how marriage laws varied in different societies. An Italian writer in 1621 used the example of childbirth practices among the Tartars, where the men took to bed after their wives had given birth, to suggest that many roles assigned to men and women were not attributable to natural or divine law.

Most defenders seem to have had the insight that women and men were different because of social conditioning. If women were ignorant and weak, it was because men had made them so. Castiglione's Giuliano refutes his opponent's contention that every woman wants to be a man because she desires her own perfection by pointing out that "the poor creatures do not wish to become men in order to make themselves more perfect but to gain their freedom and shake off the tyranny that men have imposed on them by their one-sided authority."[64] It became a commonplace to argue that if women received the same education as men, they would be their intellectual equals. Lucrezia Marinelli wrote in 1601, "I wish that these [detractors of women] would make this experiment: that they raise a boy and a girl of the same age, and both of sound mind and body, in letters and in arms. They would see in a short time how the girl would be more perfectly instructed than the boy and would soon surpass him."[65] Using an argument that Mary Wollstonecraft would repeat in 1792, an English tract of 1640 maintained that woman's physical inferiority was not decisive: "And thus, if we be weak by nature, they strive to make us more weak by our nurture: and, if in degree of place low, they strive by their policy to keep us more under."[66]

While most authors based their argument for equality on the similarity of men and women, some argued from difference in ways that anticipated nineteenth-century maternal feminism or twentieth-century cultural feminism. Women were closer to perfection than men in their disposition to peace and concord, asserted an Italian author in 1622. English writers argued that women were more sympathetic, more helpful, and more comforting than men. Although the English writers argued from nature rather than nurture, Charlotte de Brachart suggested in 1604 that women's marginality within society made them more prudent than men, "a little more clear-sighted in the affairs of the world."[67]

In the querelle, then, one can find strikingly modern arguments for woman's moral, intellectual, and even political equality; a recognition that gender is socially constructed; and a plea for change. These basic positions are still argued by modern feminists. Nevertheless, we are still left with the puzzle of how to interpret it. Was it all for the sake of literary disputation? Did anyone take it seriously?

The Debate as Feminist

Most feminist historians of the debate acknowledge its abstract and literary quality while insisting that real emotions lie beneath its surface. Ruth Kelso, while citing an Italian author's admission in 1545 that "many take up the subject merely to make known to the world the acuteness of their wit," maintains even so that some also wrote out of "sincere belief in women's essential goodness."[68] Ian Maclean believes that the sincerity of Christine de Pizan and most women defenders is not in doubt. Katherine Henderson and Barbara McManus describe the female authors in England as more zealous and outraged than their male counterparts and thus, presumably, more sincere. For Joan Kelly, the personal involvement of women authors was evident. In confirmation, she points out that women, unlike men, rarely if ever wrote on both sides of the querelle .

Kelly is wrong, however, in thinking that the women always wrote in response to a specific attack. The first formal defence written by an

Englishwoman, Jane Anger, *Jane Anger Her Protection for Women* (1589) was spurred by no traceable preceding attack. Anger's outburst, seemingly seething with moral indignation, has been described as a typically "circumspect rhetorical strategy" based on "aesthetic detachment."[69] Indignation at misogyny was a conventional pose. Even Christine de Pizan's moving account of her distress has been described, in its "staginess" and "irony," as "of course, nothing but a set-up."[70] Does this mean that women participants were no more sincere than the men?

It is impossible for us from such a distance to judge these writers' motives although it is certainly significant that women never wrote antifeminist pieces. Conservative writers such as Jacqueline Pascal and Madame de Maintenon in France assumed woman's inferiority, but no woman wrote a misogynist tract and it is admittedly difficult to imagine one doing so. When Rachel Speght repeated misogynist libels in her response to an attack, two subsequent defenders criticized her for it.

Perhaps the answer is "and also" rather than "either/or." While women may have enjoyed participating in an accepted genre, there is every reason to assume that for them it meant something more as well. When the French Renaissance writer Hélisenne de Crenne presented both the anti- and prowoman arguments in her *Invective Letters,* using a husband's antiwoman ravings as a foil for her prowoman case, it is helpful to know that she had personally experienced an abusive husband. Similarly, we can assume the Italian poet Petronilla Paolini Massimi (1663–1726), forced into an unhappy marriage at the age of ten, knew what she was talking about when she wrote,

> I well know the fates war not with us,
> nor does Nature to us deny her gifts:
> the sole oppressor of our worth is man.[71]

Even when there is no evidence of authors having a personal stake in the debate, we can still assume it had more meaning for women than for men. Many modern writers have made the point that misogyny is never just literary. To describe it as a joke obscures the harm jokes cause and how they can be used to evade serious discussion. Did two thousand years of insults have no effect on women's self-respect? Joan Kelly is surely justified in asking how men would react "if women turned out a corpus of literature expressing disgust for men and marriage for a couple of centuries, then modified it to a generalized expression of contempt for men for four centuries more. Would that be a 'merely literary' matter?"[72]

Women's responses seem particularly significant when measured against the traditional injunction to silence. Christine de Pizan thought herself unique in being the first woman to defend her sex although five hundred years earlier Hrotsvit, a nun and playwright, had protested the misogyny that she found in classical authors. The greatest impediment to the development of feminist consciousness was that women lacked the means to transmit their ideas from one generation to another. Their participation in the querelle illustrates both their need for role models and their handicap in being unable to base their ideas upon the contributions of their foremothers.

Women used the debate as an opportunity not only to speak out but to talk back. Mary Tattle-well and Joan Hit-him-home, the pseudonymous authors of *The Women's Sharpe Revenge* (1640), made the connection between the male monopoly on literary culture and women's silence: women are forbidden a liberal education "lest we should be made able to vindicate our own injuries."[73] It seems reasonable to assume that, at least for some, breaking silence was an act of consciousness raising. The pseudonymous English author Constantia Munda's castigation of her opponent's "incredible impudence" and his "scurrilous and depraving tongue" may be within conventional Renaissance use of invective and attacks on person and on style, but it must also have been very satisfying to women accustomed to putting up with misogyny. Munda's threat is a long way from the humility of Christine de Pizan more than two hundred years earlier. "I'll take the pains to worm the tongue of your madness," Munda wrote gleefully, "and dash your rankling teeth down your throat . . . our pens shall throttle you."[74] Even if these women were adopting commonplace rhetorical strategies, they were learning to be confrontational. The result, at the very least, was a new literary role for women.

Saints and martyrs, polemicists and prophets, powerful queens and subversive transvestites—European history from the sixteenth through eighteenth centuries provides suggestive material for those in search of feminism. The overwhelming impression from these centuries, however, is one of increasing restraints for women. Measured against this context of repression, the small gains that individual women won appear to be nothing more than pyrrhic victories. Religious, political, and social rebellion was defused by alternative models that allowed women to express frustration and opposition without challenging institutions or fundamental values. Yet women gained undeniably in achieving and defending their right to speak for themselves and on behalf of all women. Thinkers such as Christine de Pizan perceived the injustice in the way women were viewed and treated. This perception was a stage in the history of feminism, as women began to articulate their own experiences and to generalize from them to those of all women.

While many of the arguments women used in the querelle des femmes sound quite exciting to modern feminist ears, it is important to interpret the debate with caution. It was about rhetoric rather than rights, and even the most radical participants did not expect social change. Women writers' attack on traditional misogyny defines the strengths and limits of their feminism. Across the distance that separates us from these theorists we are disappointed by their solutions, which relied on good will, literary persuasion, and circumstances created by wealth and leisure. A modern writer accurately describes their concern as "regenerating the image of women in the familiar terms of their own culture, not . . . imagining or advocating a different society in which all women might change their ordained feminine nature for equality with men or public power."[75] Joan Kelly reminds us that none of these female authors noticed the most horrendous expression of misogyny in early modern Europe, the witch persecutions. Limited as they were by culture and class, however, these women nonetheless deserve to be recognized as feminists. As a modern author has said in a slightly different context, "It's not the feminism of 1980, but neither should it remain . . . nameless."[76]

NOTES

[1] Quoted in Richard Kagan, *Lucrecia's Dreams: Politics and Prophecy in Sixteenth-Century Spain* (Berkeley: University of California Press, 1990), 114.

[2] Quoted in ibid., 41, 82.

[3] Quoted in Mary Daly, *The Church and the Second Sex* (New York: Harper and Row, 1975), 104.

[4] Quoted in Elizabeth Rapley, *The Dévotes: Women and Church in Seventeenth-Century France* (Montreal: McGill-Queen's University Press, 1990), 19.

[5] Margaret L. King, *Women of the Renaissance* (Chicago: University of Chicago Press, 1991), 172.

[6] Quoted in Sara Heller Mendelson, "Stuart Women's Diaries and Occasional Memoirs," in *Women in English Society 1500–1800,* ed. Mary Prior (London: Methuen, 1985), 185.

[7] Argula von Grumbach, "An Answer in Verse for Someone Studying in Ingolstadt in Answer to Some Verses That He Wrote Recently: Which Transgressions He Lists There," in *The Defiant Muse: German Feminist Poems from the Middle Ages to the Present: A Bilingual Anthology,* ed. Susan L. Cocalis (New York: Feminist Press, 1986), 7.

[8] Joan Kelly, "Early Feminist Theory and the *Querelle des Femmes,* 1400–1789," in *Women, History and Theory: The Essays of Joan Kelly* (Chicago: University of Chicago Press, 1984), 68.

[9] Quoted in Phyllis Mack, *Visionary Women: Ecstatic Prophecy in Seventeenth-Century England* (Berkeley: University of California Press, 1992), 94–95.

[10] Quoted in ibid., 103.

[11] Quoted in ibid., 120.

[12] Quoted in ibid., 176, 181.

[13] Quoted in ibid., 176.

[14] Quoted in ibid., 296.

[15] Quoted in Merry E. Wiesner, "Women's Defense of Their Public Role," in *Women in the Middle Ages and the Renaissance: Literary and Historical Perspectives,* ed. Mary Beth Rose (Syracuse, NY: Syracuse University Press, 1986), 19.

[16] Anne Hutchinson, "The Trial of a Heretic: *Anne Hutchinson* (1637)" in *The Female Experience: An American Documentary,* ed. Gerda Lerner (Indianapolis: Bobbs-Merrill, 1977), 469.

[17] Ibid., 467.

[18] Quoted in Lyle Koehler, *A Search for Power: The "Weaker Sex" in Seventeenth-Century New England* (Urbana: University of Illinois Press, 1980), 222, 223.

19 John Woodbridge, "Epistle to the Reader," in *The Works of Anne Bradstreet,* ed. Jeannine Hensley (Cambridge, MA: Belknap Press of Harvard University, 1967), 3.

20 Anne Bradstreet, quoted in *Works of Anne Bradstreet,* ed. Hensley, 292.

21 Ibid., 16.

22 Koehler, *A Search for Power,* 223, 224.

23 Quoted in David Hunt, *Parents and Children in History: The Psychology of Family Life in Early Modern France* (New York: Harper and Row, 1970), 150.

24 Susan Bassnett, *Elizabeth I: A Feminist Perspective* (Berg: Oxford, 1988), 125.

25 Lisa Jardine, *Still Harping on Daughters: Women and Drama in the Age of Shakespeare,* 2nd ed. (New York: Columbia University Press, 1989), 173, 178.

26 Quoted in Bassnett, *Elizabeth I,* 73–74, 23.

27 Mary Garrard, *Artemisia Gentileschi: The Image of the Female Hero in Italian Baroque Art* (Princeton, NJ: Princeton University Press, 1989), 160.

28 Quoted in Ruth Perry, *The Celebrated Mary Astell: An Early English Feminist* (Chicago: University of Chicago Press, 1986), 188.

29 Jeanette Lee Atkinson, "Sovereign Between Throne and Altar: Queen Christina of Sweden," 409, and Christina, "The Life of Queen Christina, Written by Herself, Dedicated to God" (ca. 1681), 416, 423, in *Women Writers of the Seventeenth Century,* ed. Katharina M. Wilson and Frank J. Warnke (Athens: University of Georgia Press, 1989).

30 Wendy Gibson, *Women in Seventeenth-Century France* (New York: St Martin's Press, 1989), 167.

31 Joan DeJean, *Tender Geographics: Women and the Origins of the Novel in France* (New York: Columbia University Press, 1991), 68, 37.

32 Quoted in Jan Noel, "New France: Les Femmes Favorisées," in *Rethinking Canada: The Promise of Women's History,* 2nd ed., ed. Veronica Strong-Boag and Anita Clair Fellman (Toronto: Copp Clark Pitman, 1991), 40.

33 Quoted in Rudolf M. Dekker, "Women in Revolt: Popular Protest and Its Social Basis in Holland in the Seventeenth and Eighteenth Centuries," *Theory and Society* 16 (1987): 344. The women were probably referring to the popular assumption that the authorities would not punish women as severely as men.

34 Quoted in Jacqueline Jones, *Labor of Love, Labor of Sorrow: Black Women, Work and the Family from Slavery to the Present* (New York: Basic Books, 1985), 35.

35 Quoted in Ellen A. McArthur, "Women Petitioners and the Long Parliament," *English Historical Review* 24 (1909): 698, 700, 707.

36 Quoted in Antonia Fraser, *The Weaker Vessel: Woman's Lot in Seventeenth-Century England* (London: Methuen, 1984), 261, 262.

37 Linda Woodbridge, *Women and the English Renaissance: Literature and the Nature of Womankind, 1540–1620* (Urbana: University of Illinois Press, 1984), 143, 224.

38 Jardine, *Still Harping on Daughters,* 69, 113, 107.

39 Woodbridge, *Women and the English Renaissance,* 198, 267.

40 Lillian Faderman, *Surpassing the Love of Men: Romantic Friendship and Love Between Women from the Renaissance to the Present* (New York: William Morrow, 1981), 61.

41 Fidelis Morgan, *The Well-Known Troublemaker: A Life of Charlotte Charke / Fidelis Morgan with Charlotte Charke* (London: Faber and Faber, 1988), 13, 11, 13.

42 Quoted in Joy Wiltenburg, *Disorderly Women and Female Power in the Street Literature of Early Modern England and Germany* (Charlottesville: University Press of Virginia, 1992), 99, 153.

43 Ibid., 101, 254.

44 Ibid., 256, 265.

45 Kelly, "Early Feminist Theory," 66, 69. Marjorie Henry Ilsley, *A Daughter of the Renaissance: Marie le Jars de Gournay, Her Life and Works* (The Hague: Mouton, 1963), argued before Kelly that the *querelle* gave birth to modern feminism (p. 201).

46 Christine de Pizan, *The Book of the City of Ladies*, trans. Earl Jeffrey Richards (New York: Persea Books, 1982), 3–4, 5, 6.

47 Ibid., 7, 23, 187.

48 Ibid., 218.

49 Christine de Pizan, "The Epistle to the God of Love," in *The Defiant Muse: French Feminist Poems from the Middle Ages to the Present*, ed. Domna C. Stanton (New York: Feminist Press, 1986), 25.

50 Pizan, *City of Ladies*, 165, 63, 214.

51 Ibid., 255.

52 Pizan, "Epistle to the God of Love," 15, 21.

53 Pizan, *City of Ladies*, 31.

54 Woodbridge, *Women and the English Renaissance*, 50, 52.

55 Maclean, *Woman Triumphant*, 264, 232.

56 Ludovico Dolce, quoted in Constance Jordan, *Renaissance Feminism: Literary Texts and Political Models* (Ithaca, NY: Cornell University Press, 1990), 69.

57 Pierre Le Moyne, quoted in Garrard, *Artemisia Gentileschi*, 168–69.

58 Jordan, *Renaissance Feminism*, 248.

59 Woodbridge, *Women and the English Renaissance*, 133.

60 Henricus Cornelius Agrippa, *Female Pre-eminence* (1670), in *The Feminist Controversy of the Renaissance*, ed. Diane Bornstein (Delmar, NY: Scholars' Facsimiles and Reprints, 1980), 76, 77, 14, 82.

61 Baldesar Castiglione, *The Book of the Courtier*, trans. and intro. George Bull (Baltimore: Penguin, 1967), 218.

62 Mary Tattlewell and Joan Hit-him-home, *The Women's Sharpe Revenge: or, An Answer to Sir Seldom Sober That Writ Those Railing Pamphlets Called the Juniper and Crabtree Lectures, etc.* (1640), in *The Women's Sharp Revenge: Five Women's Pamphlets from the Renaissance*, ed. Simon Shepherd (London: Fourth Estate, 1985), 176.

63 Anonymous (1516) and François Billon (1555), quoted in Jordan, *Renaissance Feminism*, 89, 200.

64 Castiglione, *The Book of the Courtier*, 221.

65 Quoted in Kelly, "Early Feminist Theory," 84.

66 Tattlewell and Hit-him-home, *The Women's Sharpe Revenge*, 170.

[67] Quoted in Jordan, *Renaissance Feminism,* 277.

[68] Ruth Kelso, *Doctrine for the Lady of the Renaissance* (Urbana: University of Illinois Press, 1956), 7.

[69] Woodbridge, *Women and the English Renaissance,* 66. Jane Anger pointed out the dangers of obsession with style over substance, criticizing writers whose "mindes are so carried away with the manner, as no care at all is had of the matter: they run so into Rethorick, as often times they overrun the boundes of their own wits, and goe they knowe not whether" (quoted on p. 63).

[70] Christine Reno, quoted in Thelma Fenster, "Did Christine Have a Sense of Humor? The Evidence of the *Epistre au dieu d'amours,*" in *Reinterpreting Christine de Pizan,* ed. Earl Jeffrey Richards (Athens: University of Georgia Press, 1992), 23. This is in striking contrast to Kelly's view of it as "a passage to feminist consciousness" (Kelly, "Early Feminist Theory," 103 n. 49).

[71] Petronilla Paolini Massimi, "To Female Duties Clorinda Scorned," in *The Defiant Muse: Italian Feminist Poems from the Middle Ages to the Present,* ed. Beverly Allen, Muriel Kittel, and Keala Jane Jewell (New York: Feminist Press, 1986), 27.

[72] Kelly, "Early Feminist Theory," 101 n. 24.

[73] Tattlewell and Hit-him-home, *The Women's Sharpe Revenge,* 170. Shepherd makes a persuasive argument that the author was in fact John Taylor.

[74] Constantia Munda, *The Worming of a Mad Dogge: or, A Soppe for Cerberus the Jaylor of Hell. No Confutation but a Sharp Redargution of the Bayter of Women* (1617), in *The Women's Sharp Revenge,* ed. Shepherd, 137, 143, 138.

[75] Elaine V. Beilin, *Redeeming Eve: Women Writers of the English Renaissance* (Princeton, NJ: Princeton University Press, 1987), xvii.

[76] Simon Shepherd, *Amazons and Warrior Women: Varieties of Feminism in Seventeenth-Century Drama* (Brighton: Harvester Press, 1981), 1.

5

Revolutions in Philosophy and Politics

Woman, wake up; the tocsin of reason is being heard throughout the whole universe; discover your rights.

OLYMPE DE GOUGES, 1791

*T*he querelle des femmes provided the only forum in which women in early modern Europe could directly express criticism of traditional views. They were not held back by fear of legal reprisals but rather by the values that they shared with the men of their culture: the assumption that the social order was unchanging and divinely ordained. A society that left unquestioned the hierarchical relations among men would not question those between men and women.

All this changed with the intellectual and political revolutions of the seventeenth and eighteenth centuries. In the seventeenth century, men such as Galileo Galilei and Isaac Newton directly challenged ideas of the natural order that had been accepted for centuries and were buttressed by the authority of Aristotle and the church. In England, where the Glorious Revolution of 1689 established the supremacy of parliament, political thinkers such as John Locke attacked the concept of divinely instituted, absolute monarchy, arguing instead that civil society was a collective human creation, a social contract. Carrying these ideas further, the *philosophes* of the eighteenth-century Enlightenment were determined to shed light on the prejudices of the past and sweep them away, a goal that the French Revolution at the end of the century seemed to achieve, if only temporarily. Women contributed to and shared these new ideas and, in these exciting times, applied them to themselves, challenging the traditions that had justified their subordination. Ironically, the complete failure of their efforts was to inspire in the nineteenth century the first organized feminist movements.

1632	Galileo Galilei writes *Dialogues on the Two Chief Systems of the World*
1637	René Descartes writes *Discourse on Method*
1648	Treaty of Westphalia ends the religious wars
1687	Isaac Newton writes *Principia Mathematica*
1689	Glorious Revolution in England
ca. 1690–1790	The Enlightenment
1694	Mary Astell writes *Serious Proposal to the Ladies*
1762	Jean-Jacques Rousseau writes *Emile*
1776–83	American Revolution
1789	French Revolution begins
1792	Mary Wollstonecraft writes *A Vindication of the Rights of Woman*
1799	Napoleon Bonaparte seizes power

NEW DIRECTIONS IN PHILOSOPHY AND LITERATURE

In 1648 the Treaty of Westphalia ended more than a hundred years of religious wars in Europe that had followed from the Protestant Reformation. Even before then two books appeared that indicated new directions in European thought, Galileo Galilei's *Dialogues on the Two Chief Systems of the World* (1632) and René Descartes' *Discourse on Method* (1637). In each, a rational, mathematical model of reality replaced the traditional reliance on ancient authorities and signalled new trends in science and philosophy.

The Influence of Descartes

Descartes drew on Galileo's conclusions about the natural universe to develop a revolutionary philosophical methodology based on the freedom to question and to doubt. His method implied a spirit of intellectual enquiry irrespective of gender, and he consciously wrote in French rather than in Latin to make his work accessible to women. His disciples included Princess Elizabeth of Bohemia, who applied Descartes' principles to the master himself, pushing him in her letters to defend and clarify his ideas. From the 1640s to the 1660s Cartesianism was the craze in French salons and certain learned women became known as *Cartésiennes*. Although these women left no scholarly works, Cartesianism gave them a tool to use against the traditions that deprived them of recognition.

François Poullain de la Barre (1647?–1723), a free-thinking French priest who eventually converted to Protestantism, illustrates the dramatic effects of Cartesianism applied to the querelle des femmes. While other prowoman writers supported their arguments by quoting rival authorities or mustering the standard examples of famous women, Poullain treated the very idea of woman's inferiority as "nothing but a pure prejudice that we acquire from the appearance of things when we fail to examine them closely." As it was not based on reason, which was Descartes' criterion, such an idea deserved to be rejected. While those sentiments would have warmed the heart of Christine de Pizan, the first woman known to have defended women in the querelle des femmes, Poullain went further and analyzed the historical origins of male supremacy, which he derived from the militarization of early societies. He warned against letting historical accident become prescription, rejecting the idea that "women must [continue to] be in the subservient state in which we see them." The only differences between the sexes were reproductive: the mind itself was "sexless" and "the domain of reason has no boundary." The implications were enormous. Poullain believed that all fields of study should be opened up to women: physics, medicine, physiology, mathematics, law and politics, geography, ecclesiastical history, even theology and canon law. He saw no reason why women could not become rulers, lawyers, judges, even soldiers, if they could overcome the effects of social conditioning. Poullain even valued women's unique work, reproduction: "Thus women seem to be the most valuable members of society, for the service they render is incomparably greater than the contributions of all others."[1]

In one important respect, however, Poullain de la Barre was wholly conventional: his tract is more about philosophy than about women. His stated intent was to illustrate the Cartesian method. To that end, Poullain admitted he looked for "a specific, striking subject (in which everyone takes an interest)," an opinion "as ancient as the world, as widespread as the earth and as universal as the human species itself."[2] The debate on woman conveniently fit the bill. The reader is left with the impression that Poullain de la Barre was no more a sincere feminist than were any of the others who wrote to illustrate the art of argument. His feminism is reduced to an example of the power of rational deduction. Thus Poullain was in some ways very conservative. Although claiming that women were as capable as men, he spent a disproportionate amount of time describing their "unique aptitudes," which turn out to be disappointingly traditional. Girls are, among other things, more gentle, diligent, and patient at work, more obedient, modest, and self-controlled. Women are naturally more reserved and decorous, more pious and sweet than men; their natural compassion, not surprisingly expressed in their greater affection for infants, makes them good at caring for the poor or sick. They are better suited for marriage than are men, making patient wives and devoted mothers. Although Poullain enlivened an old genre with new arguments, his commitment to feminism is dubious.

The same was not true of his spiritual successor in England, Mary Astell (1688–1731), who linked a prowoman position to a concrete proposal to improve women's situation. Astell was one of a number of English women in the late seventeenth and early eighteenth centuries who wrote on women's issues and who have been described as the first group of modern feminists. Although their politics were generally conservative, they reaped[3] the benefits of the intellectual and political ferment of late seventeenth-century England that called into question traditional relationships. Angered by the widening educational gap between women and men they articulated an independent criticism of women's situation. These women, among them Bathsua Makin and Margaret Cavendish, were distinguished from earlier ones by their understanding of women as a social collectivity. That they referred only to women of the propertied classes should not surprise us. It was no more or less than their male counterparts were doing in addressing "man." More important was their assumption that women and men had the same rational capabilities and that social conditioning alone accounted for the differences between them. Abandoning earlier writers' lists of women worthies, they shifted the argument to a common human nature. Of this group Mary Astell stands out as "arguably the first systematic feminist theoretician in the West."[4]

At first glance, Astell seems a very unlikely person to be called a feminist as she was politically ultraconservative. She defended the old order, buttressed by an official church and absolute monarchy, and believed in cultivating "*a Reverence for Authority.*"[5] She saw order as sacred and subordination as its necessary consequence. While some of her male contemporaries would be inspired by the development of liberal thought, she opposed individual rights, religious toleration, and republicanism.

Astell came from a prosperous mercantile family, but her father's death when she was twelve left her dowryless and thus jeopardized her chances for marriage. In any case, it is difficult to imagine her married. Her condemnation of men as sensualists reminds one of the later Victorians. Her biographer describes her as a natural ascetic who, like other women, unconsciously cultivated a blameless lifestyle as a strategy to neutralize her handicap as a woman in the public sphere. Enforcing her asceticism was her sense of independence. Growing up in an all-female household after her father's death had reduced the impact of patriarchy: "Only let me beg to be inform'd, to whom we poor Fatherless Maids, and Widows who have lost their Masters, owe Subjection?"[6] she asked with her typically mild sarcasm. She moved to London and made a successful if modest life for herself by finding patrons, both male and female, to support her writing. Although she never signed her works, which were widely read and discussed, she teased her readers about their authorship. Until her death from cancer, following a mastectomy without anaesthetic, she maintained a quiet and contemplative life in association with other pious and philanthropic women.

Although seemingly very different from the radical Poullain de la Barre, she shared his enthusiasm for the implications of Cartesian ideas. Descartes's postulate that rationality is natural and equally available to women and men gave her self-confidence. As Astell herself noted, "since GOD has given Women as well as Men intelligent Souls, why should they be forbidden to improve them?"[7] Philosophy enabled her to take herself seriously as a thinking woman capable of analyzing her world.

She also concerned herself with the realities of woman's situation, specifically marriage. Aware of the high incidence of unhappy marriages, she wanted women to realize how difficult married life could be and how complete and enforceable were their subservience and dependency. Like other moralists, Astell warned women against generalizing from courtship to marriage: "She must be a Fool with a witness, who can believe a Man, Proud and Vain as he is, will lay his boasted Authority, the Dignity and Prerogative of his Sex, one Moment at her Feet, but in prospect of taking it up again to more advantage; he may call himself her Slave a few days, but it is only in order to make her his all the rest of his Life." Rightly suspicious, she advised women to "Preserve your distance then, keep out of the reach of Danger . . . your Caution cannot be too great."[8] Her solution was traditionally modest: women should choose their husbands wisely. For the unhappy wife, she could only suggest, as had Christine de Pizan three centuries earlier, that she learn from her suffering: "Thus the Husband's Vices may become an occasion of the Wife's Vertues." She observed, again with sarcasm, that "Women are not so well united as to form an Insurrection. They are for the most part Wise enough to Love their Chains, and to discern how very becomingly they set."[9]

Cartesian philosophy had convinced Astell that women were cut out for higher things: "We value [men] too much and our *selves* too little, if we place any part of our desert in their Opinion; and don't think our selves capable of Nobler Things than the pitiful Conquest of some worthless heart."[10] Inspired by both contemporary philosophy and the Christian tradition of the contemplative life, she aspired to restore to Protestant women the option of a single life. To that end, in her *Serious Proposal to the Ladies,* she proposed endowing a college for women, a "*Religious Retirement,*" where women could withdraw from the world to live in the select company of other women. Her scheme reportedly won the interest of Queen Anne but was ultimately condemned as too Catholic for Protestant England.

Although other women had chafed under and protested against the restrictions of patriarchy, Astell is the first who proposed to do something about it. Her proposal came from her commitment to women, an important part of her feminism. She wrote for women, loved them, kept company with them, and inspired them. The title page of her first book announced her as "a Lover of her SEX." Involved with a charity school movement designed to provide education for indigent girls, she stipulated that the school she organized in Chelsea was "always to be under y͏ᵉ Direction of Women." She inspired younger women, and stories about her circulated among the eighteenth-century Bluestockings. Elizabeth Thomas, her contemporary, hailed her enthusiastically as a champion of her sex:

> Too long! indeed, has been our Sex decryed
> . . . .
> Redeem the coming Age! and set us free!
> From the false Brand of *Incapacity*.[11]

We must, however, keep in mind Mary Astell's conservatism. While commenting on political issues of her day, an unusual activity for a woman,

Astell never related them to her feminism. As well, her interest in poor girls notwithstanding, she assumed the wealth and leisure of her readers. Finally, her ultimate goal was religious: to encourage women to prepare not so much for this world as for the next.

The radical tendency of Cartesianism to support open-ended intellectual enquiry and mental equality did not last. Advocacy of systematic doubt gave way to a principle of abstract, universal objectivity. Feminists would use the belief in the objectivity of knowledge to combat prejudice and tradition, but the male bias of the new world view associated with the Scientific Revolution was evident in its image of nature as a malleable and exploitable female, expressed in metaphors of slavery: nature "bound into service," made a "slave," put "in constraint."[12] While women pursued science visibly and enthusiastically in informal academies and networks, the eventual establishment of professional societies ensured that this new knowledge would be monopolized by a small, elite group of professional men.

Nor did Descartes' assumption of reason as gender neutral extend to the other main innovation in intellectual thought of the late seventeenth century, political liberalism. Although a character in an English play written in 1697 applied the idea of the social contract to the family, asking, "The argument's good between king and people, why not between husband and wife?"[13] no feminist or liberal thinker followed it up. When the English political philosopher John Locke described man in the state of nature as a being who lived according to the law of reason, it was obvious to himself and his readers that "man" was gender and class specific. Although Locke did suggest similar education for girls and boys, he also assumed, with his contemporaries, that both women and the working classes lacked the reasoning ability of upper-class men. He explained, "The greatest part of mankind have not leisure for learning and logic, and superfine distinctions of the Schools. . . . It is well if men of that rank (to say nothing of the other sex) can comprehend plain propositions, and a short reasoning about things familiar to their minds."[14] In their attacks upon authority neither the liberating potential of the Scientific Revolution nor that of liberalism was realized when applied to women.

Critiques of Marriage

Although no one followed through on Mary Astell's specific suggestion, literary women in both England and France continued and sharpened her critique of marriage. This was true of many English poets of her generation. Anne Finch, Countess of Winchilsea (1661–1720), happily married herself, wrote in a poem tellingly titled, "The Unequal Fetters," that "Marriage does but slightly tie men / Whilst close prisoners we remain."[15] These women celebrated female friendships in their verse. In fact, they rarely wrote about men. As one scholar comments, "Feminists have rarely developed their ideas without being drawn further from men and closer to women, and the seventeenth-century feminist poets were no exception." In their critique of marriage and celebration of female friendships these poets were as committed as Astell to the idea of women's independence outside marriage. Their success in addressing the public resulted in the editor of the *Athenian Mercury* journal agreeing in 1691 to set aside one issue per month for women's interests since he realized that women "have a very *strong* party in the World."[16]

Salon circles in seventeenth-century France also made critiques of marriage and celebrated female friendship. According to Joan DeJean, the literary gatherings of the 1650s and 1660s continued women's involvement in politics, which had marked the Fronde, the civil war that had recently ended. The new venue was no less subversive. The participants or "literary amazons" simply transferred their influence from the battlefield to the salon. The result was the novel as a feminist creation.[17] Authors explored the sexual politics of marriage and the family from the viewpoint of the individual, with little sympathy for the larger context in which church and state contended for control over marriage and the privileged classes used it for social and economic gain. Characteristic was Madeleine de Scudéry's attitude, as revealed through a character in her novel, *Artamène, ou Le Grand Cyrus* (1649–53): "I am well

---

Mary Lee, Lady Chudleigh (1656–1710), was typical of the English poets who wrote critically of marriage, as we can see in her poem "To The Ladies," from Poems upon Several Occasions *(London, 1703).*

Wife and servant are the same,
But only differ in the name:
For when that fatal knot is tied,
Which nothing, nothing can divide.
When the word *obey* has said,
And man by law supreme has made,
Then all that's kind is laid aside,
And nothing left but state and pride:
Fierce as an eastern prince he grows,
And all his innate rigour shows:
Then but to look, to laugh, or speak,
Will the nuptial contract break.
Like mutes she signs alone must make,
And never any freedom take:
But still be governed by a nod,
And fear her husband as her God:
Him still must serve, him still obey,
And nothing act, and nothing say,
But what her haughty Lord thinks fit,
Who with the power, has all the wit.
Then shun, oh! shun that wretched state,
And all the fawning flatterers hate.
Value yourselves, and men despise,
You must be proud, if you'll be wise.

aware that there are many fine men, but when I consider them as husbands, I think of them in the role of masters, and because masters tend to become tyrants, from that instant I hate them. Then I thank God for the strong inclination against marriage he has given me."[18] Her heroines either reject marriage altogether or accept it only on their own terms.

The novel can be seen as another stage in the querelle des femmes, in which women took the offensive in presenting the prowoman side. Going back to the early seventeenth century, we find Spanish writer Maria de Zayas dramatizing querelle feminism in stories and novellas, forms from which the novel developed. The century had brought a new wave of misogyny in Spain, against which Zayas perhaps reacted. She made the tension between the sexes the main theme of her stories and the men, rather than the women, responsible for evil. Zayas illustrated male brutality and viciousness with dramatic examples; six out of ten stories in her first collection end with wife murder, and the other four include torture and persecution. Her parade of brutalized women reminds one of Christine de Pizan's Christian martyrs, but the ending is different. While Christine could only counsel suffering wives to patience, Zayas sent a clear message to women to avoid marriage and thereby take responsibility for their fate. The purpose of her stories of "disillusionment" was "to enlighten, or disenchant, women about men's deceptions." When her heroine Lysis entered a convent, she did it not so much to escape the world as to escape men. This is one step beyond Christine de Pizan's patient suffering, although there is no attempt to reform the institution of marriage. Although Zayas may have had "a coherent feminist message,"[19] her solution was still individual rather than institutional.

Later French novelists expanded the genre and developed Zayas's themes, strengthening their attack so much that by the 1690s critics damned them as "brazen adventuresses" whose lives were as scandalous as their fiction.[20] Unflinchingly they addressed adultery, illegitimate pregnancies, and sexual passion. Themes of forced or unhappy marriages, cruel husbands, and the lack of economic alternatives for women continued to characterize French women's fiction in the eighteenth century. In 1765, almost 150 years after Maria de Zayas, Jeanne Marie le Prince de Beaumont wrote, "I advise any woman who wants to enjoy life, as they say in society, I advise her, I say, to make a vow of celibacy, it's the only condition that will suit her."[21] Although the solution here seems similar to that adopted by women in the early church and the Middle Ages, these fictional heroines self-consciously chose the single life as an alternative to suffering in a patriarchal institution that was now portrayed as a brutal abuse of power. Marie Jeanne Riccoboni (1713–92), one of the most renowned writers of her time, more than others described the horrors of bad marriages and insisted on addressing issues of gender inequity.

In the hands of these writers, the novel reflected a growing feminist consciousness, reinforcing the idea that marriage ought to promote self-fulfilment rather than the family's property interests. Although some male critics praised these authors, most condemned their writings as a social and political threat and strove to eliminate them from the canon of accepted and admired texts.

The literary anthologies that circulated until the late eighteenth century were made up in large part of women's fiction, but by the early nineteenth century women's writings had been effectively eliminated in favour of texts that affirmed society's rules and established gender roles.

Ambivalence towards or distaste for marriage and the social segregation of young women and men help to explain the popularity of same-sex relationships, which blossomed in the late seventeenth and eighteenth centuries both in literature and in life. These "romantic friendships" among women were characterized by flirting and gift giving, the writing of passionate letters, kissing and fondling, expressions of jealousy or fear of rivals, and vows of eternal love. Historian Lillian Faderman suspects that most of the relationships did not involve genital sex: contemporaries admired their purity, their attainment of spiritualized friendship not possible between women and men as long as women were considered inferior. Enjoying "a phallocentric confidence which ceased to be possible in the twentieth century,"[22] men approved of relationships between women, seeing them as a prelude to marriage that taught potential brides loyalty and devotion. The friendships were also accepted as an approved escape from unhappy marriages. In either case, the outcome of an illegitimate child was not to be feared.

Katherine Philips (1631?–64), discussed in Chapter 3, was famous for her poetic expressions of romantic female friendships. She also detailed her commitment to women in her correspondence, writing that they "set her 'heart on fire.'"[23] Her contemporaries found no scandal in this intensely physical expression of idealized love, seeing it as ennobling. Besides, Philips's decorum in all other aspects of her life prevented any suspicion. Women loving other women, whether physically or not, transgressed only when they defied gender boundaries, by disguising themselves as men, for example. The sexual possibilities of lesbianism were unfathomable to men, who saw themselves as indispensable for women's satisfaction.

Eighteenth-century English novelists continued the theme of love between women. Sarah Robinson Scott portrayed the ideal life of a rural, utopian female community in her novel, *A Description of Millennium Hall* (1762). Less austere than Mary Astell's Protestant nunnery, her heroines' version of the good life included a lush landscape with a vegetable garden and farm that gave them self-sufficiency and an ethic of caring that opened their community to the poor and disabled. The founding residents had a history of unfortunate heterosexual relationships, but their homosocial bonds gave them happiness and security.

Two women who managed to lead that life were Eleanor Butler and Sarah Ponsonby, known as the Ladies of Llangollen. When they eloped in 1778, Ponsonby's family responded with relief that she had not run off with a man. A relative explained that Sarah's conduct, "though it has an appearance of imprudence, is I am sure void of serious impropriety. There were no gentlemen concerned, nor does it appear to be anything more than a scheme of Romantic Friendship."[24] The determination of the pair was revealed by a second, successful elopement when the first was foiled. They ultimately won their families' approval, in the form of a stipend that gave them the financial means to realize the ideal about which other women could only fantasize. Although they shared the same bed for over fifty years, no one doubted their absolute moral rectitude. Their acceptability was aided by their political and social conservatism, reminiscent of Mary Astell's. Rejecting republican ideas, they retained staunchly royalist and aristocratic sympathies. They even dismissed an unmarried servant who had worked for them for three years when she became pregnant. There is no reason to doubt the sincerity of Sarah Ponsonby's denunciation of Eros as "vulgar" in contrast to what she considered the propriety of romantic friendship.

Their exceptional lifestyle did not make Eleanor Butler and Sarah Ponsonby feminists. Protests against marriage and escapes from it remained individual or fictional, and only at the end of the eighteenth century would the feminist critique of the previous century be picked up and carried further. Most women continued to marry and even to welcome marriage as less tyrannical than parental authority. They looked for ways to cope rather than demanding social change. Any substantial challenge to their subordination would have to wait for a general challenge to the political order and social structure of traditional Europe.

The Enlightenment

The eighteenth-century Enlightenment inherited the critical stance of both Cartesianism and the Scientific Revolution, along with a distaste for religious fanaticism that came with the end of the religious wars. Its representatives, the *philosophes,* prided themselves on subjecting everything to questioning and engaged in a wide-ranging discussion on society and morals. The result was a two-pronged attack on Aristotelian and religious authority, which one could reasonably expect to result in a critique of male dominance when applied to women. As French feminist Olympe de Gouges later exulted, "All is possible in this century of light and philosophers."[25]

Such a critique did not materialize, at least not with any consistency or forcefulness. Some philosophes did acknowledge the injustice of women's subordination, others were frankly misogynist, but most displayed a stunning unwillingness to consider the subject seriously. The great work of the French philosophes, the *Encyclopédie* (1751–65), presented a confusing variety of viewpoints. Four articles by four different authors under the heading "Woman" ranged from defamatory to sympathetic. The subject was also undoubtedly raised in salons, which were another venue of philosophe opinion. Although hosted by women, salons of the mid- to late eighteenth century catered more to men than did earlier salons; often the women present were in the minority.

The philosophes and salons did not, however, represent the most radical thinking of the day. That is perhaps best captured by the French oppositional press, disdained by the philosophes as pandering to low taste. Oppositional newspapers existed without official privilege, subject to the whim of government censors. In them bold journalists united women's cause with that of other oppressed groups such as Protestants and Jews. They called for freedom of the press, social action, and even political reform. For a brief period, one of these papers, the *Journal des dames,* provided a sounding board for an energetic and militant feminist, Madame de Beaumer. Begun in 1759 by a male editor desirous of amusing women, whom he imagined to be bored and not very intelligent, the paper came into Beaumer's hands in 1761. As "the first outspoken female journalist," Beaumer embraced a program of radical causes: religious toleration, pacifism, freemasonry, and social justice. But her special cause was feminism. "My only merit," she announced in her first issue, "is to know the full worth of my sex." She challenged women to open their minds, to study, to speak out, to criticize. The pages of her paper were filled with stories about exceptional women in public life, such as Marie de Gournay or Queen Christina of Sweden, as well as examples of working-class women in non-traditional occupations, among them sculptors, clockmakers, chemists, and singers. These Beaumer held up as examples of what women could accomplish. The censors were not impressed; in 1762 they suspended the journal. Beaumer fled to Holland, but in her brief reign as editor she had helped transform the journal's content from the "delicious nothings"[26] intended by its founder into serious issues that were widely debated. In doing so, she furthered the association of feminism with a perspective critical of the status quo rather than supportive of it.

Madame de Beaumer was most certainly a Protestant and may have also been a Mason. The Freemasons were a secret society that promoted the ideals of the Enlightenment. Although most masonic lodges were closed to women, both mixed and women's lodges existed in France and a mixed lodge was established in The Hague in 1751. The initiation ceremonies, which inducted members into different degrees, were powerful rituals. One degree in the French lodges was known as the Order of the Amazons. According to it, "Women were to throw off the yoke of the men and regard as tyrants those who refused to submit to the female order. . . . The creator . . . gave equal intelligence to men and women and it was not too late for women to catch up in the fields of science and statecraft. . . . In marriage, the woman should dominate."[27] It is difficult to know what this meant to the participants, but it seems reasonable to assume that the lodges encouraged women's independence, openness to new ideas, and sense of sisterhood. The number of women affected, however, would have been very small.

Beaumer's *Journal* certainly reached a wider circle than the Freemasons, but it was probably not very representative. The first two editors, both male, had been mortified to discover that female readers responded to their call for contributions with submissions far more radical than either had imagined. However, the woman who took over the journal in 1763, and who was prepared to push a moderate feminism, found out that it simply was not marketable. Readers of both sexes were affronted by any semblance of stridency. She had to face the fact, as Madame de Beaumer had not, that there was no broad-based support for feminism.

What about the novels by Marie Jeanne Riccoboni and others who frankly exposed the sufferings of women in marriage? They must have had a substantial audience, but then so did the popular literature of the *Bibliothèque bleue,* the little blue books peddled throughout France that displayed a harsh misogyny. And what is one to make of the proliferation of libertine novels with their depiction of coldly manipulative women? In opposition to the suffering wife of the feminist novels they presented the evil mother who corrupts her children.

May it not be the case, in fact, that the greater visibility of women in print and their partial championing of feminist issues occasioned a backlash? Coupled with a rise in infant mortality, illegitimate births, prostitution, and libertinism in the second half of the century, the backlash re-energized a long tradition of blaming women for any unfortunate event or development. The philosophes themselves, while enthusiastic about the application of reason to all aspects of humanity, were intensely concerned with moral issues. As reformers, they attacked contemporary society as ignorant, intolerant, and corrupt. Many of them put the blame on women, specifically the intellectual upper-class women who hosted salons, ironically the same women who gave the male philosophes the support and opportunity they needed to air their ideas. Such criticism had begun in the seventeenth century when the salons had promoted the assimilation of new members into the nobility. Conservatives had denounced the process as undermining the social order and held women responsible for it. They urged that women be confined to the home in order to limit their corrupting influence, thus attacking their only acceptable public role. Although by the eighteenth century the salon had begun to be replaced by the world of print as the main forum for discussion of political issues, it still represented access to the elite and women were its gatekeepers. In this context, reformers added their criticism to that of conservatives and denounced salons as despised relics of privilege. Both groups agreed that upper-class women were responsible for the frivolity, extravagance, artificiality, in short, the corruption, of contemporary society.

The solution seemed obvious. Women must reform or be reformed. In 1753 Pierre-Joseph Boudier de Villemert, a widely read moralist, argued that women must be educated to civilize the nation. He was confident of their intellectual capacity and virtue, which, if nurtured by the appropriate education, would become an instrument for moral reform. Education and virtue had long been linked; the novelty in the current of thought that Boudier represented lay in the idea that women's education and virtue could be turned to a public end. The bridge between the individual and society was the family, and thus woman's maternal qualities, Boudier was convinced, could and should be developed: "Nature calls them to the government of their families," he wrote. "Women, learn to know the source of your pleasures and the foundation of your glory. You are mothers and mistresses of the family or you are destined to be; there is your empire."[28]

No representative of this line of thinking was more influential than Jean-Jacques Rousseau (1712–78), who scorned Parisian society because it was under the sway of women. There women usurped men's public role, and where women became men, men became women: "This weaker sex, not in the position to take on our way of life, which is too hard for it, forces us to take on its way, too soft for us; and, no longer wishing to tolerate separation, unable to make us into men, the women make us into women."[29] Perversion of the social and moral order resulted. As a corrective Rousseau used the idea of nature to reaffirm what classical and Christian authorities had always insisted on, that women should be confined to the family and domesticity. Unlike Boudier, he was not convinced of their intellectual parity; they should have a specialized education, directed solely towards their role in the family.

His double moral standard became obvious in *Émile* (1762), Rousseau's popular book on education. Émile, Rousseau's ideal man, is trained to be self-reliant. Émile's judgments will be based on his own needs rather than on those of society. His education will free him from "the crushing force of social conventions." Émile's ideal mate, Sophy, however, is taught to subordinate herself to others. Rousseau wrote, "Nature herself has decreed that woman, both for herself and her children, should be at the mercy of man's judgment," and "woman is made to submit to man and to endure even injustice at his hands." In Sophy, frankness is replaced by guile and freedom by submission. When Émile himself puzzles about Sophy's deference to convention, his tutor explains that the sexes are not meant to be compared: "That same virtue which makes you scorn what men say about yourself, binds you to respect what they say of her you love." Man is defined in terms of his moral and intellectual faculties; woman is defined in terms of her role in reproduction. Nothing must compromise her respectability since she has the potential to cause men to doubt the legitimacy of their heirs. Rousseau affirmed, "The male is only a male now and again, the female is always a female."[30]

Strangely enough, although some women criticized Rousseau's sexism, others were among his most enthusiastic followers, and not only conservative women. Although Mary Wollstonecraft targeted Rousseau as an enemy, most female reformers of the late eighteenth century endorsed his views, as did many nineteenth-century feminists. How can we explain this? At the same time that Rousseau denounced the influence of public women, he glorified woman as wife and mother: "Is there a sight in the world so touching, so respectable as that of a mother surrounded by her children, directing the work of her domestics, procuring a happy life for her husband and prudently governing the home?"[31] Boudier's and Rousseau's homage fit the tendency in eighteenth-century literature and letters to popularize an image of woman as naturally chaste and virtuous in contrast to the traditional view of female nature as sexual and dangerous, of woman as shrew, adulterer, or witch.

This change was part of the philosophes' attack on such traditional Christian concepts as original sin, which Adam and Eve bequeathed to all of their descendants and which justified the role of the church in guiding sinners to salvation. Philosophes' belief in the benefits of education required a more positive view of human nature, although they were too aware of the injustice and intolerance of their age to be overly optimistic about any inherent human propensity to do good. Their view of woman as naturally virtuous was, I suggest, an unconscious reconciliation of these contradictory positions. The interesting aspect of the "new" woman was that her "natural" virtue was not really all that natural. Woman was naturally good because, paradoxically, she was brought up to be, that is, she was socially conditioned to her role. Rousseau was in fact aware of the social origins of woman's nature but unbothered by this contradiction. As he explained, "If the timidity, chasteness, and modesty which are proper to [women] are social inventions, it is in society's interest that women acquire these qualities; they must be cultivated in women."[32] In short, the new woman was a testimony to the success of traditional social controls. She satisfied the desire of the men of the Enlightenment to entertain the possibility of a secular foundation for morality that did not threaten their own male privilege. As a participant would observe at the beginning of the French Revolution in 1789, "In the National Assembly, the majority of the Deputies are fathers, and however virtuous a father might be, it is rare that while wanting to destroy political despotism, he does not wish to conserve domestic despotism."[33] Equality among men could co-exist with hierarchy in the home.

The appeal to men is obvious, but how to explain the appeal of this kind of thinking to women? Although the image of this new woman glorified traditional female virtues, it did so by giving them a new justification: Boudier and Rousseau gave women a political role to play in their capacity as mothers. As moral guardians, women would train their sons to be virtuous citizens and thus contribute to the reform of corrupt society. In Rousseau's ideal republic, which would replace the ancien régime, private women would redeem the destruction wrought formerly by public women. His female readers responded enthusiastically, attracted to the "seductive lure" of promised respect. Although some zealous women would argue during the French Revolution that woman's moral superiority should be graced by political rights, most readers of Rousseau were content to ask for less. As the author of a 1750 tract entitled *La Femme n'est pas inférieure a l'homme* (Woman Not Inferior to Man) poignantly explained, her purpose "was not to incite women to revolt or to change the existing order; she only wanted to end men's contempt for her sex."[34] This was the same goal that Christine de Pizan had held more than three centuries earlier.

We can see the development of maternalism by looking at the third, and last, woman to own and edit the *Journal des dames*. Madame de Montanclos, who took over the journal in 1774, was a social critic *and* a Rousseauist. Calling herself the "Jean-Jacques Rousseau of the female sex," Montanclos was a self-proclaimed proud and privileged mother of several small children. Unlike Rousseau, however, she felt women could have the best of both worlds, and she used herself as proof of the successful combination of motherhood and a career. Like many of Rousseau's readers, she took from him what she wanted, ignoring the curbs placed on Sophy's development. Montanclos did add, reassuringly, that the ultimate beneficiaries of "intelligent motherhood" would be enlightened and patriotic children. She liked to think that "most women these days are devoting themselves to the formation of the hearts and minds of their children." Yet Montanclos found it difficult to reconcile her public and private duties and later confessed that her children were "'distractions' and 'emotional obstacles' to creativity."[35]

Maternalism could be adapted to liberal causes. As in France, the state in the German territories was increasingly concerned to promote child and maternal welfare, but German governments still assumed the authority of the father as head of the family. Towards the end of the century Johann Heinrich Pestalozzi began popularizing his idea of child education under maternal guidance, which he saw as the basis of social and moral development. Following the French Revolution, when reformers were searching for an alternative to traditional community bonds based on deference, Pestalozzi and Friedrich Froebel, founder of the kindergarten concept, would inspire German feminists to interpret motherhood as the crucial link between the family and the state and between the individual and the community. Motherhood for them would mean not confinement to the private sphere but an entry point into public life.

Although embraced by progressives, maternalist thinking was decidedly ambiguous. It advocated a domestic role for women justified in the name of nature rather than religion. In spite of Madame de Montanclos' push for "intelligent motherhood," maternalism more often confirmed the traditional dichotomy of man and woman mirrored in reason and emotion. After 1760 the debate on women in France became less intense, apparently muted by the acceptance of maternalism. In this climate, the intellectual potential of Cartesianism was forgotten, as was the appeal of Mary Astell to women to develop their minds rather than their hearts. Considered emotional beings, women could not fully participate in the Enlightenment, which was defined as an age of reason, nor could they justifiably demand the same rights granted to man on the basis of his rational nature.

The new view of woman as naturally good was popularized in the senti-mental novel, which became as acceptable a genre for women writers in the eighteenth century as devotional literature had been earlier. As in the six-teenth century with respect to religious topics, finding a permissible form of expression tended to discourage writers from taking risks. An explosion of printed materials and the popularity of reading among the growing middle class created for writers an alternative to dependence on aristocratic patron-age. Many women took advantage of this situation, becoming journalists or novelists. The English author Eliza Haywood in the 1720s, for example, was enabled by her writing career to leave an unhappy marriage. As Mary Wollstonecraft would note from her own experience, however, "Few are the modes of earning a subsistence, and those very humiliating."[36] Authors were caught between the desire to depict woman's situation realistically and the need to conform to the romantic expectations of their readers. One who suc-cessfully used the new genre as a form of self-expression was the German writer Sophie von La Roche. Her novel, *The Story of Miss Van Sternheim* (1771), celebrated an intelligent and resourceful heroine. Her fictional Sophie, bearing the same name as Rousseau's ideal wife but a very different personality, triumphs over adversity by acquiring knowledge and developing her character. This new Sophie was far removed from a destiny reduced to pleasing men.

While satisfying middle-class readers, the new image of woman assumed the sexual licentiousness of both aristocratic and working-class white women and all black women, whether enslaved or free. In counterpoint to that, the African-American poet Phillis Wheatley (1735?–84) linked Enlightenment ideals to human beings irrespective of class, race, or gender. Brought to Boston as a slave in 1761, Wheatley became the second woman to publish poetry in America. Educated by her mistress, who realized her unique talents, Wheatley learned to read English easily in just sixteen months and even started learning Latin. While still a teenager she began writing poems on religious and patriotic themes. In one poem she described her "love of Freedom" and her "cruel fate" in being "snatched from Afric's fancied happy seat." "Can I then but pray," she asked, that "others may never feel tyrannic sway?"[37] Wheatley was proof of the potential of both women and blacks for intellectual and creative achievement.

NEW DIRECTIONS IN POLITICS

At this time few women in British North America felt competent to comment on slavery or any other political issue as there was no tradition of upper-class women involving themselves in politics as there was in contemporary France. This was to change as a result of the American Revolution (1776–83), when the Thirteen Colonies won their independence from Great Britain.

The American Revolution

Women began to become involved as the prewar tension intensified. In 1774 fifty-one women in Edenton, North Carolina, signed a petition to support the "publick good," a modest action that nonetheless was the first time that American women had made a formal claim for public responsibility. Many more participated in spinning bees, designed to replace foreign with home-spun goods, and in the accompanying boycott of imported consumer goods. Women who had previously acquiesced in the notion that they should leave politics to the men began reading newspapers and harassing neighbours whose political loyalties were suspect or merchants who monopolized supplies. As hostilities became formalized, some women participated in the conflict as messengers, spies, and even soldiers. Slave women deserted their plantations, fleeing with their children to the British, who had promised them freedom. In 1780 white women in Philadelphia organized a door-to-door fundraising drive for the troops, inspiring women in other states by their example, in spite of the response of one loyalist woman, who reported with distaste that "the ladies going about for money exceeded everything."[38]

Men responded to these gestures with ridicule and condescension. Typical was the reply of John Adams to his wife Abigail Adams, who revealed her avid interest in political issues only in her private writings. In 1776 Abigail asked John to "Remember the Ladies" when considering laws for the new republic. "Do not put such unlimited power into the hands of the Husbands," she urged. "Remember, all Men would be tyrants if they could." If reform were not forthcoming, she suggested, tongue in cheek, that women might "foment a Rebellion, and will not hold ourselves bound by any Laws in which we have no voice, or Representation." In reply John wrote, "As to your extraordinary Code of Laws, I cannot but laugh." He commented upon her sauciness and added, "Depend upon it, We know better than to repeal our Masculine systems. Altho they are in full Force, you know they are little more than Theory. . . . In Practice you know We are the subjects. We have only the Name of Masters."[39]

An interesting but short-lived experiment was the recognition of the voting rights of women and black men in the state of New Jersey. In 1776, the state constitution, perhaps due to Quaker influence, referred to voters simply as "all free inhabitants" who met the requirements of property and residence. A 1790 electoral law that referred to voters as "he or she" acknowledged the practice of the last decade. By 1807, however, the legislators, in a dispute over fraudulent voting, explicitly limited the franchise to free white men. Other areas in which a few women had occasionally voted by virtue of their property and status—for example, France, Britain, Quebec, Nova Scotia, and New Brunswick—also adopted explicit disenfranchisement language in the early or mid-nineteenth century. Thanks to new emphasis on citizenship and its connection to property, a traditional indifference to gender gave way to explicit, legal discrimination.

More significant was the challenge that Elizabeth Freeman made to the legality of slavery in Massachusetts. Legend has it that Freeman overheard a reading of the Declaration of Independence in her master's home and as a result decided to sue the courts for her freedom. We do know that a lawsuit was launched on behalf of Brom, a male slave, along with "Bett" (Elizabeth) and that it resulted in the formal abolition of slavery in Massachusetts in 1781. Elsewhere slavery continued intact; the liberalism of both the Enlightenment and the American Revolution failed to include slaves under "man."

Some women hoped for changes in their private lives. A white woman who took on important responsibilities when her husband was away fighting wanted to continue her contributions after the war. "I hope you will not consider yourself as commander in chief of your own house," she wrote to him, "but be convinced . . . that there is such a thing as equal command."[40] But while American women became politicized as a result of the revolution, many also experienced economic and legal decline in the postwar era as a new industrial order began to take shape. For a variety of complex reasons, including a trend towards legal conservatism, new law codes barred women from previously acceptable economic activities, and in some areas widows lost their automatic entitlement to one-third of their husbands' estates.

The rhetoric of republican motherhood did not compensate for these losses. The revolution strengthened the Rousseauist vision of the home as the training ground for citizenship, according free women a political role defined only in terms of domesticity and motherhood. For American women,

> privatization and patriotic feminization of virtue came at the very moment when postrevolutionary leaders were getting on with the business of carving out political privileges and economic opportunities for themselves and for

many succeeding generations of white males. Just as the most self-sacrificing, community-oriented male revolutionary symbols of virtue and morality were turned over to the care of females, women were being systematically relegated by the new laws of the land to peripheral positions outside the political and economic developments that were shaping the country's destiny.

Future generations of American women were thereby relegated to a "political and legal time-lag behind all white men."[41]

Still, republican motherhood did provide a rationale for women's education, and academies for women blossomed in the 1780s and 1790s. Among educators there was no consensus about what republican women should be taught, whether their instruction should be wholly domestic or, as Judith Sargent Murray, author of an article entitled "On the Equality of the Sexes" (1779), hoped, unconfined and suitable for "a rational being." That this expansion of education would not apply to southern black women was clear from the attempt of an English missionary organization to open schools for black children in Virginia and North Carolina. Very few girls were allowed to attend because, as the organization reported, slave owners would "rather their Slaves shou'd remain Ignorant as brutes."[42]

The French Revolution

The French Revolution at the end of the eighteenth century symbolized the end of the ancien régime in Europe. It had been based on absolute monarchy, a privileged aristocracy, and an official church. When delegates met to draw up a constitution for the country, they referred to the political ideology of liberalism. Their language mirrored that of the American Declaration of Independence of 1776, according to which "all men are created equal with certain inalienable rights." The French counterpart, "The Declaration of the Rights of Man and the Citizen" (1789), articulated the principles of the new order: the arbitrary nature of government under an absolute monarch would be replaced by a government of law decided by the "representatives of the French people," and the injustice of a society honouring the privilege of birth would yield to the principle of equality before the law.

The initial flush of excitement that had greeted the calling of the Estates General generated a surge of petitions and pamphlets from women as well as men, asking the assembly or the king to address their interests. Some dared to hope that the natural rights of man would extend to woman. Etta Palm d'Aelders, a Dutch woman who championed the rights of woman throughout the early years of the revolution, spoke to the delegates: "The glory was reserved for you, Sirs. To be the first to overcome the odious ramparts with which prejudices oppose the recognition of those imprescriptible rights of nature, of which the weakest but most precious half of humanity has been defrauded for so many centuries."[43] But most revolutionaries were neither democrats nor feminists. The Declaration did not include any working-class men, servants, blacks, people of mixed race, or women among "the representatives of the French people." Although there had been some discussion about the first four categories, no one questioned the last one. In 1794 the delegates abolished slavery and granted universal male suffrage—both measures later annulled by Napoleon—but the revolution never seriously challenged women's political and legal inferiority. The handful of feminists who dared to speak out were hounded and ridiculed. The gap between the potential of the revolution and its outcome reveals just how deeply rooted the patriarchal assumptions of society were.

The feminist to make perhaps the most uncompromising demand for women's equality was the aristocrat and philosophe, the Marquis de Condorcet (1743–94). A mathematician and social reformer, Condorcet was confident that scientific principles could be applied successfully to the study of society. Although shy and retiring, as a young man he enjoyed the company of intellectual women in salon society, and he and his wife, Sophy de Grouchy, later established a salon of their own. Although de Grouchy did not leave any writings that would indicate her feminist views, it seems obvious from the nature of their relationship that she encouraged her husband's feminism. Ignoring Rousseau, Condorcet reached back to Poullain de la Barre, like him arguing from Cartesian principles for the similarity of the sexes: "Now the rights of men result simply from the fact that they are sentient beings, capable of acquiring moral ideas and of reasoning concerning these ideas. Women, having these same qualities, must necessarily possess equal rights. Either no individual of the human species has any true rights, or all have the same."[44] Unlike Poullain de la Barre's abstract exercise, however, Condorcet's arguments for equality were given applicability by the immediacy of political events.

During the discussions leading up to the calling of the Estates General, Condorcet had advocated giving women the right to vote on the same grounds as men, that is, with a property qualification. He then radicalized his views in response to the unfolding of events, calling for full suffrage and denouncing the exclusion of women from the rights of citizenship as "an act of tyranny."[45] His reassurance that the exercise of political rights would not take women away from their domestic duties any more than it would take peasants away from their ploughs was most likely an attempt to deflect anticipated opposition. In fact, he worried that his views would offend women, realizing that "Rousseau earned their approbation by saying that they were made only to care for us and are fit only to torment us."[46]

In a 1791 proposal for educational reform presented to the Assembly, the body that superseded the Estates General, Condorcet prescribed full elementary education for girls and boys, adding that women so inclined should be allowed to study as far as they wanted to go. Here also he attempted to disarm his critics. Of four reasons he gave why women should be educated, only the fourth relates to their right to an education; the rest extol the beneficial results for the family. In other ways, Condorcet was uncompromisingly radical. While some of his ideas, such as freeing slaves and instituting divorce, were not unusual for reformers, others, such as legalizing birth control and homosexuality, were.

His strategic concessions notwithstanding, Condorcet was not taken seriously. Tactlessly critical of the government, he was ordered arrested and went into hiding, disguised as a woman. Eventually apprehended, he died in prison in 1794. He had taken the precaution to divorce his adored wife in order to protect his property for their daughter. Sophy de Grouchy enterprisingly turned to painting portraits—a very useful way to immortalize people fearful of imminent death—and later opened a lingerie shop. She revealed her quick wit and courage in a later meeting with Napoleon, replying to his arrogant statement, "I don't like women who meddle in politics," with "You are right, general; but in a country where their heads are cut off, it is natural that they would like to know why."[47]

Although a number of men and women echoed Condorcet's views in a flurry of pamphlets, the other prominent feminists of the revolution were women. The best known is Olympe de Gouges (1748–93), who at times sounds very much like Condorcet although she may not have been familiar with his works. Outraged at women's exclusion from the "Declaration of the Rights of Man and the Citizen," Gouges wrote the "Declaration of the Rights of Woman and the Female Citizen." Unlike Condorcet, she addressed herself to women, and she appended to her declaration a model contract to replace traditional marriage. In it both parties would pledge to unite themselves "for the remainder of our lives and for the duration of our mutual inclinations," with a separation procedure spelled out that would guarantee the rights and interests of any children as well as those of both partners. In a similar vein, Etta Palm d'Aelders spoke before the Assembly, demanding "the equality of rights, without discrimination of sex."[48] Specifically, she criticized a new law on adultery that still discriminated in favour of the husband. Palm d'Aelders wrote, petitioned, organized delegations, and founded one of the first women's clubs of the revolution, campaigning specifically for equal divorce laws. Another outspoken woman, Théroigne de Méricourt, advocated the formation of "legions of amazons," armed women who could help to defend the republic that was established in 1792. In a bellicose speech, she urged women to "compare what we are in the social order with what we should be. . . . Let us break our chains."[49]

What inspired these women to become feminists? Although differing widely in their politics, they shared disreputable backgrounds and led decidedly unconventional lives. Olympe de Gouges, born Marie Gouzes, was the possibly illegitimate daughter of an ex-servant. Forced at sixteen or seventeen into a marriage of convenience, she had a child, and shortly thereafter the marriage ended, either through separation or her husband's death. She created a new name for herself and vowed never to remarry, becoming a playwright and actor. Her play on the abolition of slavery was pulled after only three performances, the mayor of Paris fearing it would promote insurrection in the colonies. Gouges' determination to express herself in writing overcame her poor education; her writing was barely legible and she used phonetic spelling. Etta Palm d'Aelders, who passed herself off as a Dutch baroness, had a long history of political activities in the Netherlands and may have been a spy. Théroigne de Méricourt, of peasant origins, had been mistress to a military officer and attempted a career as a singer. Humiliated and betrayed by the men in her life, she claimed that she had "always been offended by the tyranny which men exercise over my own sex." She wore a riding habit, as she said, "in order to seem to be a man, and thereby to avoid the humiliation of being a woman."[50] Two other women were presidents of the Society of Revolutionary Republican Women, both lower-class but literate, both young, single, and sexually involved with revolutionary men.

In addition to their marginal position in society, which perhaps made it easier for them to take up unfashionable views, these women shared a devotion to the revolution that they placed above their feminism. Historian Candice Proctor emphasizes that "they did not see themselves as women's rights advocates." Only when "their eager contributions had been ridiculed and rebuffed"[51] did they begin to analyze their situation as women and demand the application of equal rights to both sexes. One might compare them to later American feminists in both the first- and second-wave women's movements who came to women's issues after encountering discrimination from their male associates in the antislavery and civil rights movements respectively. The possibility remains, however, that these women were initially attracted to radical ideas by their unhappy experiences as women rather than the other way around.

Unlike later feminists, those of the French Revolution never came together to organize a movement. They were too eccentric, too much "political oddities."[52] Their fate was dismal, if not tragic. Olympe de Gouges was guillotined for her royalist sympathies; Etta Palm d'Aelders fled to Holland; and Théroigne de Méricourt ended up in a lunatic asylum. The others ceased political activism when women were banned in 1793 from participating in politics. Their arguments for political equality ran up against and were absorbed by the competing ideology based on sexual difference, that of Rousseauist republicanism.

French revolutionaries inherited the philosophes' concern for the moral regeneration of society. They found inspiration in Rousseau's vision of a republican government in which women confined their influence to the family in accordance with "nature." One spokesman in 1792 expressed the wishes of his contemporaries: "If one could hope for a happy revolution in the patrie, it would only be one that recalled women to domestic morality."[53] Whereas women had previously been thought incapable of patriotism because their minds could not grasp so abstract a concept, now the dutiful wife and mother was viewed as eminently patriotic. Republicanism depended on the silencing of women. The Republic "was constructed against women, not just without them."[54]

Even many women activists succumbed to this view. Etta Palm d'Aelders wrote, "To give to the future generation healthy and robust men; oh! is that not the field of honor where we must gather our laurels?"[55] Ironically, Olympe de Gouges, herself condemned as a "virago, this woman-man . . . who neglected her household duties in order to meddle in the

▶ *Olympe de Gouges'* Declaration of the Rights of Woman and Female Citizen *(1791) parallels point by point the* Declaration of the Rights of Man and the Citizen *(1789).*

Declaration of the Rights of Woman and Female Citizen,
To be decreed by the National Assembly in its last meetings or in those of the next legislature.

Preamble

The mothers, daughters, and sisters, representatives of the nation, demand to be constituted a national assembly. Considering that ignorance, disregard of or contempt for the rights of women are the only causes of public misfortune and of governmental corruption, they have resolved to set forth in a solemn declaration, the natural, inalienable and sacred rights of woman; to the end that this declaration, constantly held up to all members of society, may always remind them of their rights and duties; to the end that the acts based on women's power and those based on the power of men, being constantly measured against the goal of all political institutions, may be more respected; and so that the demands of female citizens, henceforth founded on simple and indisputable principles, may ever uphold the constitution and good morals, and may contribute to the happiness of all.

Consequently, the sex that is superior in beauty as well as in courage of maternal suffering, recognizes and declares, in the presence and under the auspices of the Supreme Being, the following rights of woman and citizen.

Article One. Woman is born free and remains equal in rights to man. Social distinctions can be founded only on general utility.

II. The goal of every political association is the preservation of the natural and irrevocable rights of Woman and Man. These rights are liberty, property, security, and especially resistance to oppression.

III. The principle of all sovereignty resides essentially in the Nation, which is none other than the union of Woman and Man; no group, no individual can exercise any authority that is not derived expressly from it. . . .

VI. The law should be the expression of the general will: all female and male citizens must participate in its elaboration personally or through their representatives. It should be the same for all; all female and male citizens, being equal in the eyes of the law, should be equally admissible to all public offices, places, and employments, according to their capacities and with no distinctions other than those of their virtues and talents.

Source: Olympe de Gouges, *Les Droits de la femme* (Paris, 1791), trans. Nupur Chaudhuri with SGB and KMO, in *Women, the Family, and Freedom: The Debate in Documents,* ed. Susan Groag Bell and Karen M. Offen, vol. 1, *1750–1880* (Stanford, CA: Stanford University Press). Reprinted with permission of the publisher.

Republic's affairs,"[56] reprimanded women who neglected their domestic responsibilities. In effect urging women to do as she said, not as she did, she lamented, "Women today are mixing in the public assemblies and clubs; they are deserting their homes, it is necessary to lead them back there."[57]

The instrumental role played by working-class women in the early days of the revolution was accepted as long as they claimed to be acting in their traditional role as providers for their families. The women who marched on Versailles in October 1789, bringing the king back with them to Paris, went looking for bread, although they appeared threatening enough. Witnesses described them as armed with broomsticks, lances, pitchforks, swords, pistols, and muskets. Although the men were grateful for the women's help, such a sight unnerved at least one, who feared that women had "made themselves men to fight for the Revolution."[58]

Women's own notion of their patriotic role did not end with securing either bread or the king. The threat of war turned them into defenders of their country, and some dozens fought alongside men. Many more concentrated their energies on fighting internal enemies. They demanded an equal voice in political clubs or founded their own. The Society of Revolutionary Republican Women, comprising several hundred militant women, was the "first political interest group for common women known in western history."[59] It discomforted many revolutionaries, both women and men, with its radical demands for price controls and for a crackdown on enemies of the revolution, as well as its insistence on women's right to arm themselves to defend the *patrie*. Facing the threat of foreign invasion and domestic chaos, the revolutionary government was not inclined to be tolerant. When club members adopted the red cap worn by revolutionary men and tried to impose it forcibly on other women, they went too far. Other women objected and called for the clubs to be closed. In October 1793, after only six months, the government disbanded the Society and all women's clubs and went further to deprive all women of the right to assembly and to petition and to exclude them formally from the army. Later they were forbidden to attend political meetings or to gather in public in groups of more than five.

The National Convention, successor to the Legislative Assembly, was adamant in finding that political activism was incompatible with women's nature. Women lacked physical and moral strength and were therefore not capable of exercising political judgment. Their "natural timidity and modesty," the "softness and moderation which are the charm of their sex" were held incompatible with "elevated thoughts and serious meditations." Marie Antoinette, the former queen of France, was the hated symbol of the ancien régime, combining in her gender and class the aspects blamed for its moral and financial bankruptcy. Although she had been an attentive mother, she became the subject of vicious and obscene insults. The delegates' conclusion, that women should not meddle in public affairs, was foregone. In vain was the objection raised, "Unless you are going to question whether women are part of the human species, can you take away from them this right which is common to every thinking being?"[60]

Women themselves argued their case from traditional grounds. Members of the Cordeliers Club, formed in 1791, explained apologetically that they had temporarily left their domestic duties only because men were not carrying out their public ones. Pauline Léon, an associate of the club who had presented a petition to the Assembly for the right of women to arm themselves and who herself had carried a pike, explained, "I devoted myself altogether to the care of my household, and I set an example of the conjugal love and domestic virtues which are the foundation for love of the Fatherland." These reassurances did not comfort members of the National Convention, who learned from the experience only "how deadly [women] are to the public peace."[61]

In the end, French women were worse off than before the revolution. Divorce and modified adultery laws were eliminated by the Napoleonic Civil Code of 1804, which has been accurately described as "an instrument of revenge."[62] It deprived married women of control over property and compelled them to acquire their husbands' citizenship, thus eliminating the basis for an independent public life. Whereas some women in the ancien régime had enjoyed certain privileges, such as voting, by virtue of their class position, now all women were categorically distinguished from men and discriminated against on that basis. French women would have to wait almost 150 years for the right to vote.

Nevertheless, French women also created a legacy of political action and thought that would be rekindled during the subsequent revolutionary movements of 1848 and 1871. One historian calls their achievement "a consciousness-raising exercise—*we did this.*"[63] At every stage, women had demanded to be heard. They inspired women throughout the European countries affected by the revolution. Women in the Netherlands, Germany, and Italy wrote and demonstrated in favour of revolutionary ideals. Feminist theory, although not consistently using equal rights as a rationale, had at least moved beyond the defensive assertion of relative ability. The definition of a new public sphere combined with women's exclusion from it would inspire first-wave feminist movements.

Mary Wollstonecraft

The writing to come out of the French Revolution that would most influence English-speaking feminists was authored not by a French woman but by Mary Wollstonecraft (1759–97), who travelled to France from England to experience the revolution firsthand. Her major work and a key text in the history of feminism, *A Vindication of the Rights of Woman* (1792), reveals how far feminists had come from Christine de Pizan's *Book of the City of Ladies* (1405) and yet how far they would still have to go to free themselves from traditional expectations.

In spite of the almost four hundred years that separated Christine de Pizan and Wollstonecraft, each was motivated by moral indignation in response to misogynist literature. Each used her own experiences to challenge accepted wisdom. Each saw herself as a unique defender of her sex. Each claimed the spiritual equality of the sexes. Each assumed class and gender distinctions that later feminists would challenge. The differences between Wollstonecraft and Christine de Pizan, however, are greater than the similarities. Wollstonecraft would airily dismiss Christine de Pizan's "women worthies" as only "exceptions to general rules. . . . I wish to see women neither heroines nor brutes; but reasonable creatures."[64] The phrase "reasonable creatures," based on principles of Cartesian rationalism and the language of political liberalism, signals Wollstonecraft's distance from Christine de Pizan's Christian martyrs as well as from the fawning Sophys of Rousseau's inspiration.

Rousseau was Wollstonecraft's irritant, inspiring her by his misogyny just as Mathéolus had inspired Christine de Pizan. Wollstonecraft agreed with him in condemning the superficiality of society women: "Confined then in cages like the feathered race, they have nothing to do but to plume themselves, and stalk with mock majesty from perch to perch. It is true they are provided with food and raiment, for which they neither toil nor spin; but health, liberty, and virtue, are given [up] in exchange."[65] The natural analogy for such women according to Wollstonecraft, who enthusiastically embraced the ideals of the French Revolution, was to a useless and decadent aristocracy. In contrast to Rousseau, however, she did not think that women should be confined to the home. Wollstonecraft found the cause of corruption not in female power but in the lack of it, in women's inability to resist men who taught them to cultivate the most superficial of characteristics—their appearance—in order to satisfy male sensuality and pride. The cunning, deceit, and manipulation that women practised were not evidence of but compensation for their lack of authority. Such deception was unworthy of human beings: "It is this system of dissimulation . . . that I despise. Women are always to *seem* to be this and that—yet virtue might apostrophize them, in the words of Hamlet—Seems! I know not seems!—Have that within that passeth show!"[66]

Like Rousseau, Wollstonecraft wanted to replace degradation with respect, but unlike him she wanted to replace women's servility with independence. By respect she meant self-respect and by independence, independence of mind. A Sophy who was taught to please others only perpetuated women's oppression: "How grossly do they insult us who thus advise us only to render ourselves gentle, domestic brutes!" As for Rousseau's justification—"an undoubted indication of nature"—Wollstonecraft dismissed it as "crude inferences" from habit. She shared the distrust of other liberals for arguments based on tradition as opposed to reason: "It cannot be demonstrated that woman is essentially inferior to man because she has always been subjugated."[67]

Wollstonecraft would replace Rousseau's double moral standard with a single standard of virtue extended equally to women and men. The tendency of "considering females rather as women than human creatures" she considered harmful as well as hypocritical. Her argument was a moral one, in contrast to that of Condorcet. In her conviction that women were meant for higher things, Wollstonecraft reminds one of Mary Astell. "The end, the grand end of [women's] exertions," Wollstonecraft urged, "should be to unfold their own faculties and acquire the dignity of conscious virtue." Whereas Astell had promoted a religious retirement, however, the intervening hundred years had given Wollstonecraft an alternative. Astell had counselled retreat from the world, but Wollstonecraft demanded its reform through a "revolution in female manners."[68]

How did she believe this change could be effected? Although she made tentative suggestions in the *Vindication* about civil equality, political representation, and financial independence, her early death did not allow her to develop these ideas. The major proposal she made was strikingly similar to Condorcet's but more specific: co-educational, public day schools for all children up to age nine. Whereas most children after that age would pursue separate domestic or technical training, those of "superior abilities, or fortune," male or female, would continue the study of science, history, politics, literature, and languages. By providing that "mankind [*sic*] should all be educated after the same model,"[69] Wollstonecraft was confident that women's oppression from arbitrary sexual distinctions would end and the greater happiness and virtue of "mankind" would result.

Even Wollstonecraft was not free from the ambivalence we saw in the feminists of the French Revolution. Like Condorcet, she reassured her readers that she had no wish to take women out of their families, and like him she pointed out the social benefits of reform: only women who were "in some degree independent of men" would make good wives and mothers. She insisted that women's "first duty is to themselves as rational creatures,"[70] but their civic duty was to manage their families, educate their children, and assist their neighbours. Her hope that full-time mothers, if managing their household well (assisted by reliable servants), would still find time for literary or scientific pursuits reminds one of Madame de Montanclos's earlier proposal for "intelligent motherhood."

In contrast to Condorcet, Wollstonecraft was not simply being diplomatic. Although she bravely attempted to live her ideals, her turbulent life left her with a yearning for domestic security. To her American lover, Gilbert Imlay, she described a picture of domestic bliss: "The books sent to me are such as we may read together; so I shall not look into them till you return, when you shall read, whilst I mend my stockings."[71] Like Astell, Wollstonecraft had left home as a young woman to make her way independently; unlike Astell, she had known neither economic nor emotional stability as a child. Her father tried unsuccessfully to establish himself as a gentleman farmer and took out his frustrations on his wife, at times violently. Wollstonecraft's subsequent relationships with women and men reveal a sense of desperation. After Imlay left her, she tried twice to commit suicide. Her life, like her unfinished novel, *Maria; or the Wrongs of Woman* (1798), testifies to the importance love and sexual passion had for her, emotions that in the *Vindication* she tried to suppress under the control of reason. She did eventually achieve a satisfying relationship with the radical author William Godwin, who respected her intellect and independence. They maintained separate households, marrying only when Wollstonecraft became pregnant. Tragically, their life together was cut short when she died in childbirth at the age of thirty-eight.

Wollstonecraft's assumption that women's child-bearing role necessarily entails child rearing compromises her argument that gender equality is based on similarity. Of the feminists of the time, only the German author Theodor Gottlieb von Hippel advocated that fathers as well as mothers should be responsible for raising children, but he did not reveal his authorship of the 1792 essay, *On Improving the Status of Women*. Wollstonecraft was more typical in giving women a private role not economically acknowledged, which thus limited their access to the public sphere. She thereby consigned women to the economic dependence from which she had tried to free them. As historian Joan Landes so aptly put it in her book on women and the French Revolution, "How difficult it is to uncouple women from domestic life."[72]

The seventeenth and eighteenth centuries witnessed an important shift in Western values. References to reason, nature, and equality began to replace reliance on Christian and classical authorities. The Scientific Revolution challenged the static hierarchy of the heavens, and liberalism and the Enlightenment offered the possibility of change in politics and society. The American and French revolutions exploded the old order, and although gains made for women were temporary, the call for liberty and equality set the agenda for the future.

The subordination of women survived all these revolutions. The tendency to base morals on secular rather than spiritual guidelines meant simply substituting nature for God or Aristotle. The idea of woman's moral and intellectual similarity to men competed poorly with the concept of sexual difference based on reproductive roles. Almost none of the feminists of this period challenged women's responsibility for domestic life. Nonetheless, the battle lines for the future were set. The discussion of women's nature and role was no longer an abstract exercise. Around its concrete ramifications women would organize to create feminist movements.

NOTES

1   François Poullain de La Barre, *The Equality of the Two Sexes*, trans. and intro. A. Daniel Frankforter and Paul J. Morman (Lewiston, NY: Edwin Mellen Press, 1989), 21, 15, 85, 117, 69.

2   Ibid., 5.

3   Hilda L. Smith, *Reason's Disciples: Seventeenth-Century English Feminists* (Urbana: University of Illinois Press, 1982), 4.

4   Catherine R. Stimpson, "Foreword," in Ruth Perry, *The Celebrated Mary Astell: An Early English Feminist* (Chicago: University of Chicago Press, 1986), xi.

5   Perry, *The Celebrated Mary Astell*, 166.

6   Mary Astell, *Reflections upon Marriage* (1706), in *The First English Feminist: Reflections upon Marriage and Other Writings by Mary Astell*, ed. Bridget Hill (Aldershot: Gower Publishing, 1986), 85.

7   Quoted in Perry, *The Celebrated Mary Astell*, 79.

8   Mary Astell, *Reflections upon Marriage*, 100, 126–27.

9   Ibid., 97, 86.

10 Mary Astell, *A Serious Proposal to the Ladies, Part 1* (1696), in *The First English Feminist,* ed. Hill, 141.

11 Quoted in Perry, *The Celebrated Mary Astell,* 18, 242, 111.

12 Carolyn Merchant, *The Death of Nature: Women, Ecology, and the Scientific Revolution* (London: Wildwood House, 1982), 169.

13 Quoted in Alice Browne, *The Eighteenth Century Feminist Mind* (Brighton: Harvester Press, 1987), 93.

14 John Locke, *The Reasonableness of Christianity,* in *Locke on Politics, Religion, and Education,* ed. Maurice Cranston (New York: Collier Books, 1965), 230–31.

15 Anne Finch, Countess of Winchilsea, "The Unequal Fetters" (1813), in *The Whole Duty of a Woman: Female Writers in Seventeenth Century England,* ed. Angeline Goreau (New York: Doubleday, 1984), 280.

16 Smith, *Reason's Disciples,* 157, 194.

17 Joan DeJean, *Tender Geographics: Women and the Origins of the Novel in France* (New York: Columbia University Press, 1991), 104, 5.

18 Quoted in Lillian Faderman, *Surpassing the Love of Men: Romantic Friendship and Love Between Women from the Renaissance to the Present* (New York: William Morrow, 1981), 89.

19 H. Patsy Boyer, "Introduction," in Maria de Zayas, *The Enchantments of Love: Amorous and Exemplary Novels,* trans. H. Patsy Boyer (Berkeley: University of California Press, 1990), xvii, xviii.

20 Quoted in DeJean, *Tender Geographics,* 128.

21 Quoted in Joan Hinde Stewart, *Gynographes: French Novels by Women of the Late Eighteenth Century* (Lincoln: University of Nebraska Press, 1993), 35.

22 Faderman, *Surpassing the Love of Men,* 29.

23 Quoted in ibid., 69.

24 Quoted in ibid., 75.

25 Quoted in Candice E. Proctor, *Women, Equality, and the French Revolution* (New York: Greenwood Press, 1990), 43.

26 Nina Rattner Gelbart, *Feminine and Opposition Journalism in Old Regime France: Le Journal des Dames* (Berkeley: University of California Press, 1987), 119, 105, 42.

27 Janet M. Burke, "Freemasonry, Friendship and Noblewomen: The Role of the Secret Society in Bringing Enlightenment Thought to Pre-Revolutionary Women Elites," *History of European Ideas* 10, 3 (1989): 291 n. 12.

28 Quoted in David Williams, "The Fate of French Feminism: Boudier de Villemert's *Ami des femmes,*" *Eighteenth-Century Studies* 14 (Fall 1980): 53.

29 Jean-Jacques Rousseau, *Politics and the Arts: Letter to M. D'Alembert on the Theatre,* trans. Allan Bloom (Ithaca, NY: Cornell University Press, 1960), 100.

30 Jean-Jacques Rousseau, *Émile,* trans. Barbara Foxley (New York: Dutton, 1969), 5–6, 328, 359, 380, 324.

31 Rousseau, *Politics and the Arts,* 87–88.

32 Ibid., 87.

33 Comte d'Antraigues, quoted in Proctor, *Women, Equality, and the French Revolution*, 103.

34 Ibid., 33, 28. As Proctor observes, "It would take a long time to realize that true respect without equality was impossible" (*Women, Equality, and the French Revolution*, 179).

35 Nina Rattner Gelbart, "The *Journal des dames* and Its Female Editors: Politics, Censorship, and Feminism in the Old Regime Press," in *Press and Politics in Pre-Revolutionary France*, ed. Jack R. Censer and Jeremy D. Popkin (Berkeley: University of California Press, 1987), 72, 70, 62.

36 Quoted in Jane Spencer, *The Rise of the Woman Novelist: From Aphra Behn to Jane Austen* (Oxford: Basil Blackwell, 1986), 13.

37 Quoted in Glenna Matthews, *The Rise of Public Woman: Woman's Power and Woman's Place in the United States, 1630–1970* (New York: Oxford University Press, 1992), 50.

38 Quoted in Linda K. Kerber, *Women of the Republic: Intellect and Ideology in Revolutionary America* (Chapel Hill: University of North Carolina Press, 1980), 102.

39 "'Remember the Ladies': Abigail Adams vs. John Adams," in *The Feminist Papers: From Adams to de Beauvoir*, ed. Alice S. Rossi (New York: Bantam Books, 1973), 10–11.

40 Quoted in Mary Beth Norton, *Liberty's Daughters: The Revolutionary Experience of American Women, 1750–1800* (Boston: Little, Brown, 1980), 223–24.

41 Joan Hoff, *Law, Gender and Injustice: A Legal History of U.S. Women* (New York and London: New York University Press, 1991), 38, 54.

42 Quoted in Norton, *Liberty's Daughters*, 254, 259.

43 Quoted in Proctor, *Women, Equality, and the French Revolution*, 44.

44 Marquis de Condorcet, "On the Admission of Women to the Rights of Citizenship (1790)," in *Condorcet: Selected Writings*, ed. Keith Michael Baker (Indianapolis: Bobbs-Merrill, 1976), 98.

45 Quoted in ibid.

46 Quoted in Proctor, *Women, Equality, and the French Revolution*, 113.

47 Quoted in Barbara Brookes, "The Feminism of Condorcet and Sophie de Grouchy," in *Studies on Voltaire and the Eighteenth Century*, ed. Haydn Mason, vol. 189 (Oxford: Voltaire Foundation, 1980), 358 (my translation).

48 Olympe de Gouges, "Declaration of the Rights of Woman" and Etta Palm d'Aelders, "A Call for an End to Sexual Discrimination," in *Women in Revolutionary Paris, 1789–1795: Selected Documents Translated with Notes and Commentary*, ed. Darline Gay Levy, Harriet Branson Applewhite, and Mary Durham Johnson (Urbana: University of Illinois Press, 1979), 94 and 76.

49 Quoted in Elisabeth Roudinesco, *Théroigne de Méricourt: A Melancholic Woman during the French Revolution*, trans. Martin Thom (London: Verso, 1991), 96–97.

50 Quoted in ibid., 71, 98.

51 Proctor, *Women, Equality, and the French Revolution*, 48, 46.

52 Levy, Applewhite, and Johnson, eds., *Women in Revolutionary Paris*, 310.

53 Jacques-Henri-Bernadin de Saint-Pierre, quoted in Proctor, *Women, Equality, and the French Revolution,* 55.

54 Joan B. Landes, *Women and the Public Sphere in the Age of the French Revolution* (Ithaca, NY: Cornell University Press, 1988), 2, 171. Proctor adds, "It is important to realize that the French Revolutionaries did not fail to grant women equal rights merely because it never occurred to them to do so. They were perfectly aware of the female sex's claims to equality, and they did not simply ignore those claims: they categorically rejected them" (*Women, Equality, and the French Revolution,* 144–45).

55 Quoted in Proctor, *Women, Equality, and the French Revolution,* 59.

56 Quoted in Roudinesco, *Théroigne de Méricourt,* 143.

57 Quoted in Proctor, *Women, Equality, and the French Revolution,* 61.

58 Quoted in ibid., 52.

59 Levy, Applewhite, and Johnson, eds., *Women in Revolutionary Paris,* 5.

60 "The National Convention Outlaws Clubs and Popular Societies of Women," in ibid., 216, 217.

61 "Anne Pauline Léon, Femme Leclerc, Reconciles Her Political Behavior with Radical Revolutionary Principles and Policies" and "The National Convention Outlaws Clubs," in ibid., 160, 217.

62 Christine Fauré, *Democracy Without Women: Feminism and the Rise of Liberal Individualism in France,* trans. Claudia Gorbman and John Berks (Bloomington: Indiana University Press, 1991), 129.

63 Olwen H. Hufton, *Women and the Limits of Citizenship in the French Revolution,* The Donald G. Creighton Lectures 1989 (Toronto: University of Toronto Press, 1992), 18.

64 Mary Wollstonecraft, *A Vindication of the Rights of Woman* (New York: W.W. Norton, 1967), 127 n.

65 Ibid., 98.

66 Ibid., 156.

67 Ibid., 50, 133, 73.

68 Ibid., 31, 58, 84.

69 Ibid., 251, 247.

70 Ibid., 213, 218.

71 Quoted in Eleanor Flexner, *Mary Wollstonecraft: A Biography* (Baltimore: Penguin Books, 1972), 192.

72 Landes, *Women and the Public Sphere,* 1.

6

Radicals and Reformers

Feminism, like other reform movements, has emerged during periods in which society tolerates searching self-criticism. . . . Invariably in such cases, some people take the questioning further than anyone had initially intended.

SYLVIA B. BASHEVKIN, 1991

By the first half of the nineteenth century, advocates for women were no longer satisfied simply to appeal for better treatment. For more than four hundred years, learned women had contributed to the debate in the world of letters over woman's role. From the 1820s on, a few women dared to address audiences in person, defying the convention against women speaking in public. They bucked tradition in other ways, by retaining their own names when they married or refusing to vow obedience to their husbands, by demanding the right to divorce or to choose single motherhood, or by proposing that women and men dress alike and share responsibility for housework and child care. Women wrote petitions, held demonstrations, edited feminist newspapers, organized strikes, tried to vote, and even ran for public office. Perhaps most significantly, contending that women constituted a separate, oppressed group, activists took the first steps towards creating autonomous women's movements.

Although they came from very different backgrounds, all these advocates shared the idealism and fervour of their age. Dramatic political and economic changes convinced many that human action could shape the world. Radicals and reformers embraced a variety of causes, of which feminism was only one, and found inspiration from many, often contradictory, sources. They were republicans or socialists, evangelical Christians or free thinkers, philanthropists or labour organizers. Ideological, racial, and class barriers did not yet seem insurmountable. Whether workers or housewives, radicals or conservatives, religious or agnostic, many believed in the possibility of a shared female consciousness.

1780s	Steam engine developed in England
ca. 1790–1850	Romanticism in the arts
1799–1815	Napoleonic era
1825	William Thompson and Anna Wheeler write *Appeal of One Half the Human Race, Women, Against the Pretensions of the Other Half, Men*
	Frances Wright founds community at Nashoba, Tennessee
1830	July Revolution in France
1833	Slavery abolished in British empire
1830s–40s	French utopian socialism flourishes
1832	Reform Bill passed in Britain
	La femme libre published
1837	Victoria becomes queen in Britain
1838-48	Chartist movement
1843	Flora Tristan begins her tour of France
1848	Revolutions in Europe
	Voix des femmes paper formed in Paris
	Karl Marx and Friedrich Engels write *Communist Manifesto*
	Seneca Falls Convention

Unfortunately, the women and men who spoke out on behalf of women were a small minority. Enthusiastic crowds listened raptly to Fanny Wright in America, Emma Martin in Britain, and Flora Tristan in France, but none of these women had much impact during their lives. Only in the United States and Great Britain was an early generation able to lay the basis for an organized movement. Because of political turmoil in continental Europe, feminists there had to begin again later on. Yet the boldness of these pioneers jolted a complacent public, just as their successors were to do in the 1960s. Their actions "represented the symbolic breaking of a long silence,"[1] and their words inspired women in the audiences to take their cause to heart. To understand what motivated these activists and enabled them to speak out, let us look first at the political, religious, and economic background of the time and then at the radical and reform manifestations of its feminism.

BACKGROUND

For centuries women had indignantly protested insults and injustices but had lacked the means to translate grievances into demands for institutional change. The most they could do was appeal for better conduct from both women and men. Now, the fluid situation created by the aftermath of the American and French revolutions and the beginnings of the Industrial Revolution in Britain appeared as a world in the making, a world of potential into which ordinary people could have some input. After centuries of accepting hierarchal relationships as God given and unalterable, radicals and reformers found it possible to imagine a future of human design, based on human needs and desires. The dual revolution in politics and economics generated expectations that encouraged women to demand changes for themselves. Few if any of them began as advocates for women, but as the German reformer Louise Otto exhorted in 1849, "In the midst of the great revolutions in which we find ourselves, women will find themselves forgotten, if they forget to think of themselves!"[2]

Political Ideologies

The political climate of Europe in the early nineteenth century was polarized by the opposing ideologies of liberalism and conservatism, the former represented by the ideas of the French Revolution of 1789, the latter by a European-wide counter-offensive following the defeat of Napoleon in 1815. On the one side, the revolution left a commitment to the ideal of equality before the law, representative government, and secularism. On the other, its opponents defended loyalty to the crown, the aristocracy, and the church. Any debate over the position of women would take place within this context.

Neither side disputed the importance of the patriarchal family. Napoleon, who both ended the French Revolution and defended many of its principles, reaffirmed patriarchy in his law code of 1804. Under it, a married woman needed her husband's permission to attend university, to live apart from him, to buy or sell property, or even to work outside the home. The husband had sole authority over their children, even the right to imprison them. According to the regulations punishing adultery, a wife could be imprisoned for more than two years, or killed by her husband if caught in the act. The husband was punishable only by a fine and then only under certain conditions, such as bringing his mistress into the family home. Not until 1939 was the portion of the code concerning marriage substantially changed, and vestiges remained in France until 1975.

Both liberals and conservatives saw the family as a microcosm of society, the model and basis for other social institutions. To conservatives, it represented hierarchy and order, the last safeguard against social change. It represented order for liberals as well, but they liked to think of the roles within the family as complementary rather than hierarchical. Liberals saw the family as the foundation of the republic; they interpreted women's role of bearing and rearing future citizens as complementary to men's public role as citizens. Superimposed on this division was the ideology of separate spheres, the result of the rapid social changes accompanying the Industrial Revolution and the growth of the middle classes. The public sphere now encompassed business as well as politics, but the private sphere, women's sphere, remained confined to marriage and motherhood.

Liberalism and conservatism thus each assumed women's responsibility for domestic life, and so did most of the activists discussed in this chapter. Even those who argued from the principles of the French Revolution wished to extend equal rights to women as persons while retaining the notion of their social function as wives and mothers. The roles of individuals, citizens, and family members were seen as interlocking rather than contradictory. This framework was consistent with the idea of a uniquely female moral contribution to society, articulated in the 1830s and 1840s in the form of the cult of true womanhood.

The United States provides one example of the link between the political ideology of liberalism and the belief in woman's special role. The American Revolution of 1776, which won the Thirteen Colonies their independence from Britain, established a nation that saw itself as a land of political and economic progress. A climate of optimism promised both individual self-fulfilment and the creation of a more perfect society. For all that, the United States was also rapidly changing, and by the 1840s industrialization, urbanization, and immigration were intensifying the anxiety of those who feared that the lack of monarchy and aristocracy would result in moral anarchy. The traditional bulwark, the clergy, seemed increasingly irrelevant as commercial values replaced religious ones. In this context, Catharine Beecher (1800–78) built on and extended the idea of woman in the home as the moral guardian of society, an updated version of the eighteenth-century notion of republican motherhood.

Beecher, who came from a strict religious background, found herself unable to conform to the spiritual expectations of her father. For her, social issues were more compelling than religious ones, but instead of rejecting the traditional godly virtue of self-denial she associated it with woman's nature, thus secularizing and feminizing it at the same time. She replaced piety with morality and substituted the moral authority of women for that of the clergy. Her biographer explains that Beecher thereby "turned self-sacrifice and submission—traditional values associated with women—into signs of moral superiority and leadership."[3]

These values were ideally suited for reconciling the individual and the community and for smoothing over the class tensions of an emerging industrial society. Thus, Beecher found woman's submission within the family essential as the model for the social harmony a republic needed. She vehemently and explicitly opposed women's political rights: "Woman is to win everything by peace and love . . . but this is all to be accomplished in the domestic circle . . . [by] woman's retaining her place as dependent and defenceless and making no claims and maintaining no rights."[4] Nonetheless, her biographer calls her a feminist because of her efforts to make American society more responsive to women's needs and talents. Beecher herself claimed that although woman held "a subordinate relation in society to the other sex, it is not because it was designed that her duties or her influence should be any the less important, or all-pervading."[5] One might think of this as a "separate and special" version of a "separate but equal" argument.

The class bias of Beecher's thinking is evident in her assumption that men would provide the necessary material security to allow their wives to cultivate selflessness. Although middle-class black women would find the idea of woman's moral virtue a liberating alternative to the racial stereotypes of female immorality bred by slavery, it would have little application to the lives of working women of whatever colour. In fact, by assuming that respectable women did not work outside the home, it degraded the economic contributions of those who did.

Ironically, not only did Beecher's own active single life of teaching and fundraising contradict her notion of woman's domesticity but also she was the first to promote teaching as a quintessentially female profession in the hopes that female values would permeate society. Almira Phelps, teacher and author, repeated a familiar theme when she asked rhetorically, "Is not the character of the future men of our republic, to depend on the mothers we are now educating?"[6] Already in the late eighteenth century, the United States had taken a lead in establishing women's academies. Beecher put most of her energies into training future teachers. The mother-teacher ideal was to be a popular image in North America and in Europe throughout the nineteenth century.

Religion

Catharine Beecher's struggle with orthodox religion is part of a familiar and intriguing pattern of close connection between religion and feminism. Women of very different persuasions—New England Calvinists, Quebec Catholics, English Unitarians—saw their feminist commitment as a calling from God. Others began as members of traditional religious groups but struggled through spiritual crises to arrive at non-sectarian or even secular beliefs while retaining a fervent moral idealism.

The nineteenth century was both increasingly secular and intensely religious. Many found in religious revivalism an antidote to a threatening materialism or disquieting political change. Both before and after the turn of the century, Protestant evangelical movements gripped Britain and North America: "Everywhere, saints and their followers were on the march, and no aspect of . . . social life remained unaffected by their passage."[7] As in earlier centuries, women were prominent among the followers of these sects. In the second Great Awakening, a revivalist movement that swept the eastern United States from the 1790s to the 1830s, women outnumbered male converts three to two. Women predominated as well in the Protestant sect known, somewhat surprisingly, as German Catholicism—actually an ecumenical religious movement—which spread throughout Germany in the 1830s and 1840s.

Some women became leaders. In England in 1770, Ann Lee (1736–84), a blacksmith's daughter, joined a small group that had split from the Quakers and called themselves Shakers because of their exuberant style of worship. Lee, called Mother Ann, became leader of the group and brought them to North America to escape religious persecution. Another Englishwoman,

Joanna Southcott (1750–1814), a former domestic servant, was the most prominent of a number of contemporary female visionaries. She attracted more than a hundred thousand converts to her chiliastic sect, most of them women, with the message that her arrival freed woman from the curse of the Fall and raised her to full spiritual equality. Southcott fiercely denounced male villainy and celebrated female defiance, becoming "a living symbol of what a touch of God's Hand can do for even a humble working woman."[8] Women also emerged as leaders and preachers in Methodist sects, travelling from village to village and preaching in private homes, fields, and outbuildings. In their unconventional lifestyle and emphasis on family ties and the equal economic contributions of all family members, they represented resistance both to middle-class ideals of womanhood and to the growing division between work and home that was transforming the English countryside.

In the United States some of the "saints on the march" were women who became itinerant preachers, working the camp meetings held along the eastern seaboard. A number of them were black, such as Jarena Lee, the first black woman to take up preaching as a career. More famous was the ex-slave Sojourner Truth (ca. 1797–1883). Born Isabella, she worked as a domestic servant in New York City after gaining her freedom in 1827. Deeply religious, she had a vision that commanded her to sojourn the land and declare God's truth to the people. Taking on her new name, she became a preacher, travelling throughout the northeast and later linking her religious convictions with a commitment to the abolition of slavery and to women's rights.

The feminist impulse in religious movements, especially Protestant sects, would continue throughout the nineteenth century. Quakers were disproportionately represented among the early American advocates for women's rights. As well, from 1848 a striking association existed between the most radical of these advocates and those active in the Spiritualist movement, which believed in the ability to communicate with spirits. Later, in the 1870s, Mary Baker Eddy would found Christian Science on the image of "Father Mother God," and Catherine Booth would co-found the Salvation Army, committed to sexual equality within its ranks and adopting military titles rather than "Miss" or "Mrs."

In a very different context, the mid-nineteenth-century Catholic Church in Quebec sponsored Marian devotions, based on the cult of the Virgin and addressed specifically to women to encourage them to strive for purity and perfection. Some Protestant women, like the British feminist Bessie Raynor Parkes, admired the religious networks of the Catholic Church because they allowed women an alternative to marriage and the opportunity to pursue vocations in social welfare and education. Ironically, the slower development of a women's movement in Quebec may have been in part because the religious life offered a partial solution to the lack of educational and economic opportunities that women faced elsewhere. The absence of such outlets outside Catholicism may account for the connection historians have noted between feminism and Protestantism.

Protestantism could also forestall feminism. In the aftermath of the failed revolution of 1848 German state churches cracked down on independent congregations, depriving a developing feminism of its only institutional ally.

In all countries, clerics continued to stress the traditional female virtues of humility and submissiveness, and feminists would find organized religion their most vehement enemy. American and British evangelism exhibited contradictory impulses: American preachers emphasized the ability of individuals to avoid sin; British evangelists dwelt on original sin and Eve's role in the fall from paradise. At the same time, evangelists in both countries were influenced by the eighteenth-century suggestion that women were "naturally" virtuous. As a corrective to what they saw as the moral anarchy of the French Revolution, evangelists took Rousseau's idea of woman's virtue one step further, explicitly equating female virtue with lack of sexual passion. Although it promoted sexual conservatism, the idea of woman's moral influence would also inspire feminists. That development, however, was in the future. When William Godwin published his biography of Mary Wollstonecraft in 1798 and revealed her common-law relationship with Gilbert Imlay, the illegitimacy of her first daughter, and the conception of her second before her marriage to Godwin, the resulting scandal encouraged the association of women's rights with immoral behaviour.

As in the religious sects of the sixteenth and seventeenth centuries, women eventually moved from public preaching into other, less threatening activities, this time into missionary work and bible promotion societies. Tens of thousands of women in Britain and North America taught Sunday school, distributed bibles, and engaged in fundraising. The resulting female networks provided opportunities to develop skills and form close friendships. Justified by religion, these activities could provide a bridge from women's domestic duties to the wider community. They could also confine women's activities to traditional, clerically defined tasks and deflect women from more radical questioning.

One can see this dual potential of religion in the life of Florence Nightingale (1820–1910). Four divine revelations clarified her religious calling and stiffened her rebellion against her family's traditional expectations, but a life within the church did not appeal to her. "I would have given her [the church] my head, my heart, my hand," confessed Nightingale. "She would not have them. She did not know what to do with them. She told me to go back and do crochet in my mother's sewing room; or, if I were tired of that, to marry and look well at the head of my husband's table."[9] Instead, Nightingale channelled her desire for service into the then unconventional profession of nursing, creating her own alternative to a traditional life as wife and mother. Few women would or could follow Nightingale's initiative. As in earlier centuries, the connection between religion and feminism was complex.

The Industrial Revolution

More decisive than either political ideology or religious idealism was the economic transformation associated with the Industrial Revolution, which began in Britain in the 1780s. The Industrial Revolution replaced human and animal muscle power with machines, making the steam engine the symbol of an age. Work that had previously centred around the family unit, either on the farm or in the shop, became centralized in factories. From being owners of their own economic enterprises, men and women more and more often found themselves in the position of dependent wage workers. Landowning and mercantile elites were joined by industrial capitalists, who increasingly insisted that political decisions and economic policy reflect their interests.

Most working families found the transition disruptive and difficult. Mechanization meant unemployment for many skilled artisans and the need for retraining, relocation, or both. Some families found employment together in the factories; many others were thrown back on the piecework traditionally done by women in the home. Indeed, domestic or cottage industries expanded in rural Britain along with agricultural capitalism and often represented the family's only secure source of income in the face of widespread and unpredictable male unemployment. An unexpected result of the expansion of the British cotton textile industry was the revitalization of slavery in the southern United States.

In the long run, certain traditional features of women's work persisted in spite of the Industrial Revolution. Although some young, single white women found independence and new opportunities in factory work, many more pursued the more stable and familiar female livelihood of domestic service. Most women continued to work in traditionally female occupations for wages traditionally lower than men's, and many would-be rebels found their options limited by lack of economic independence. Working-class daughters either helped parents and siblings or saved to marry and begin families of their own. Daughters of business or professional families chafed at their lack of opportunities while watching them widen for their male counterparts.

The revolution had more of an effect, although short-lived from our vantage point in the late twentieth century, on married women's lives. By severing the unity of work and home while leaving intact the presumption that women should care for the family, the Industrial Revolution made it difficult for married women to continue in productive labour. Working-class women, who had always been partners in the family economy, scrambled to find ways to continue contributing to their family's survival. In preindustrial Europe, upper- and middle-class women had provisioned and managed complex households, often working alongside their husbands or substituting for them when the need arose. Now, when goods were increasingly produced outside the home, they had to meet higher standards of housekeeping and become knowledgeable consumers. Although middle-class women supposedly benefited from an increase in domestic servants and a falling birth rate, the lives of many of them still testified to a numbing routine of domestic drudgery. The ideology of domesticity, which celebrated the home as a cherished refuge from a male world of economic and political competition, failed to compensate women for their loss of a contributing economic role. On the other hand, given women's lower wages and limited job opportunities, many appreciated the security of a wage-earning husband who could support his family. Historians who view the ideology of domesticity as a doctrine imposed upon women fail to consider how oppressive the double burden of wage work and housework could be. Still, most families continued to require multiple incomes, and working-class women felt the onus of failing to live up to the ideal of Victorian womanhood.

One consequence of the divorce between home and work for middle-class women was a greater sex role segregation and participation in a more exclusively female culture. They were thus enabled to cultivate female relationships and form life-long supportive and emotional ties that offered a sense of identity and purpose denied them in the public world. These ties, according to historian Nancy Cott, created a context for the development of feminism: "From the sense among women that they shared a collective destiny it was but another step (though a steep one) to sense that they might shape that destiny with their own minds and hands."[10] By assigning a positive value to women's domestic duties and encouraging women's collective identity through sex-specific activities, the ideology of domesticity had the potential, like religion, either to liberate or to confine.

The assumption of many historians that feminism was a movement of leisured middle- and upper-class women does not hold true for the early nineteenth century. Most white and many black American feminists did enjoy a background of economic security, but most European feminists did not. They tended to come from lower middle- or upper working-class families whose income was derived from diverse though usually inadequate sources, such as shopkeeping, a skilled craft, or factory work. Their struggles to make a living gave what historian Barbara Taylor calls a "displaced, ambiguous quality" to their lives,[11] perhaps blurring their sense of class division. Although these women were quite aware of the gap between themselves and more privileged women, they believed that they could bridge it. They spoke on behalf of all women, asserting a common identity as a distinct, oppressed social group. Their appeals, while moving, minimized cultural, racial, and class divisions.

The changes associated with the political and industrial revolutions were most pronounced in Britain, France, and the United States. These countries are the focus for the history of feminism from the 1820s to the end of the 1840s, although change proceeded at a different pace in each one. Industrialization and urbanization developed more quickly in Great Britain and so did the protest raised by working people. In the United States, feminism had a strong republican and rural base. Economic change took hold slowly in France and the small middle class remained socially conservative, but unfulfilled aspirations raised by the French Revolution nourished new ideas that inspired the most radical expression of feminism at this time. In central and southern Europe, as later in the Scandinavian countries and Ireland, men and women with radical or liberal sympathies made their primary commitment to movements for national liberation rather than to those for the emancipation of individuals or social groups. From these general considerations, let us now look at individual movements and the feminists who were active within them, first examining the radical protest that led to feminism in Great Britain and France and then the reform tradition that led to feminism in the United States, with a comparative look at developments in Germany.

THE RADICALS

In spite of, or perhaps in reaction to, a growing conservatism in the aftermath of the French Revolution, radical ideas in Great Britain and France continued to attract support. Protest spread beyond intellectuals as workers in both countries became determined to resist a deteriorating economic situation. Moving beyond the liberal critique of the political power of the monarch and the social prerogatives of the aristocracy, radicals attacked economic and sexual privilege to create movements that were both socialist and feminist. Women were prominent among the small business owners and families of skilled artisans that constituted the bulk of the membership.

Robert Owen (1771–1858) in England and Claude Henri, Comte de Saint-Simon (1760–1825) and Charles Fourier (1772–1837) in France were the founders of what became known as utopian or communitarian socialism, in contrast to the later "scientific" socialism of Karl Marx and Friedrich Engels. Utopian socialists criticized capitalism as responsible for the fragmentation and alienation of society. They proposed co-operative associations and central planning to replace economic competition, but they also had a sweeping social vision that extended beyond economics.

Robert Owen indicted not only private property but also marriage and religion for fostering social disharmony. He described marriage as men's ownership of women, a form of private property, and viewed the family as a unit of exclusivity and self-love that inhibited social ties. He castigated proponents of religion for preaching original sin and other "ignorant superstitions"[12] and for opposing the idea of social progress, which Owen inherited from the Enlightenment and upon which his blueprint for a new moral world was based.

Like Owen, Charles Fourier criticized both the economic system and family life. He condemned them as inefficient and corrupt, producing unwarranted material and emotional suffering. Monogamous marriage was unnatural and unhealthy. Although sympathetic to the plight of husbands—with a customary obsession for mathematical analysis and categorization, he described seventy-two different types of cuckoldry—he regarded women as the chief victims; a bride was simply "a piece of merchandise offered to the highest bidder."[13] In a passage often quoted, he linked the emancipation of women to social progress: "The best nations are always those that accord women the greatest amount of liberty. . . . *The extension of women's privileges is the general principle for all social progress.*"[14]

Owenite Feminism

Marriage, a popular target for feminist critics, became the object of a passionate attack by Owenites William Thompson (1775–1833) and Anna Wheeler (1785–1848). Unlike most of the others in their movement, both were of privileged backgrounds. In 1825, Thompson, described as "in his day by far the most forthright protagonist of women's emancipation,"[15] published the impressively titled *Appeal of One Half the Human Race, Women, Against the Pretensions of the Other Half, Men, to Retain Them in Political, and thence in Civil and Domestic Slavery.* Although his name alone appeared as author, he claimed that the "feeling, sentiments, and reasonings" expressed in the book were in fact Anna Wheeler's. Unsuccessful in his efforts to persuade her to write on her own behalf, he resolved to take on the role of "your interpreter and the scribe of your sentiments." Underneath the denunciation of the marriage code as "that disgrace of civilization" runs the anguish of Wheeler's personal experience. Married at fifteen to an alcoholic, bearing six children, only two of whom survived infancy, she managed to escape being an "involuntary breeding machine and household slave"[16] through an intensive reading program. Historian Barbara Taylor asks us to imagine her, "buried in books and nappies," reading Mary Wollstonecraft's *Vindication of the Rights of Woman* while pregnant for the fifth or sixth time.[17]

Although the *Appeal* is at times reminiscent of the bitterness of Marie de Gournay or Mary Astell, it is much more direct in perceiving and denouncing woman's inequality. Of marriage vows, Thompson, or Wheeler, writes, "To erect uninquiring obedience into a duty, to weave it into a pretended code of morals, to degrade the mind into an acquiescence in injustice, is the last triumph of unrelenting despotism, rarely exacted from ordinary slaves, and reserved without any sort of necessity, for the degradation of the domestic female slave in marriage."[18] The author even claims that married white women are worse off than female slaves, since the latter supposedly share equal status with enslaved men. By the early 1830s British feminists commonly referred to married women as living in domestic slavery; but they adopted the metaphor of slavery from anthropological studies of non-European societies rather than from any knowledge of contemporary black slavery. Slave narratives published in the following years would alert readers to the unique vulnerability of enslaved women. As Harriet Jacobs would write in her autobiographical narrative, *Incidents in the Life of a Slave Girl* (1861), "Slavery is terrible for men; but it is far more terrible for women."[19] Although proposing Owenite co-operatives as the ultimate solution to all oppression, the *Appeal* called for the immediate grant of full equality to (free) women, including political and civil rights, economic and educational opportunities, and the same moral and sexual standards. This amounted to a sweeping program, against which Mary Wollstonecraft's earlier views seemed to William Thompson admittedly "narrow."[20]

Owenites had other quite advanced ideas on female equality, which the resulting British workers' movement attempted to put into practice. Their social activities were deliberately centred on the family, with dances, picnics, concerts, and tea parties replacing the male-frequented pubs. Mixed seating arrangements at dinners horrified opponents. "The consequence was that a common intimacy arose between all parties, and . . . a number of illegitimate children were begotten,"[21] imagined one appalled contemporary. A ban on alcohol and obscene language and an exhortation to men to practise "courteous treatment" were designed to encourage women's participation in social events. Women were urged to attend evening classes, day schools, and Sunday schools and to speak up during discussions. The leadership of the movement remained male dominated, however, although some concern was expressed over the lack of women delegates at the annual congresses.

One way Owenite women could show their initiative was in public speaking. While Owenism was far removed from traditional religion, its religious roots are not difficult to spot. Owenites not only believed in their cause as a mission, but they fought contemporary evangelical movements with the latter's own tools: inspired preaching, language that suggested the coming of the millennium, and calls for conversion. The battle unfolded on the lecture circuit, where families journeyed long miles to be entertained and where millions were exposed to new ideas.

Emma Martin (1812–51), one of the few women among the regular lecturers, came to socialism through membership in a Baptist sect, which she joined at age seventeen. Although attracted to socialist ideas of helping women through education and employment, she was a strict Christian and joined the lecture circuit to argue the divine origins of the Bible against the socialists. In 1837, however, she became convinced by her opponents' arguments and simply switched sides. The fact of a woman addressing an audience in public, coupled with Martin's vehemence and fearlessness, sparked heated and at times violent confrontations among the large crowds that came to hear her. The title alone of one of her lectures enticed and provoked: "The Holy Ghost: HER Nature, Offices and Laws." At another time Martin taunted her audience with a description of woman's character as "the football of society thankful for its kicking. You know it is! Is it not dreadful when one of the sex begins to think for herself? Why others will follow the horrible example! and where will it end?"[22] Martin was either heckled or cheered by her audience depending on their sympathies, and on one occasion she and her small daughter narrowly escaped serious injury from a stone-throwing mob. Her vehemence eventually alienated her associates; exhausted, ill, and poor, she turned to midwifery and devoted her efforts to opposing the male domination of obstetrics.

Martin was typical of the many women attracted to communitarian socialism. She had lower middle-class origins, some education, an unhappy and financially disastrous failed marriage that left her with three small children to support, and had made an unsuccessful attempt to set up a business. Barbara Taylor speculates, "Had she been born forty years earlier the combination of all these factors might have made her one of Wollstonecraft's associates; forty years later and she would probably have been a suffragette."[23] Instead she became an Owenite socialist.

Sexual Reform and Communal Living

In contrast to Robert Owen, the French utopian socialist Charles Fourier worked in virtual isolation but with the benefit of an apparently uninhibited imagination. The result was an elaborate design for a utopian society, or Phalanx, with a richly varied but rigidly organized routine of work and play. Fourier tried scrupulously to treat the sexes as equals and even prescribed that girls and boys dress alike to help prevent sex-role stereotyping. He did assume that boys would predominate in the Little Hordes, groups of children aged nine to fifteen who were naturally attracted to filth and who would be responsible for the dirty work of the commune, such as cleaning the latrines. A traditional division of labour also surfaces in Fourier's plan to have house-keeping and child care done by women, but he softened it by proposing to draw these women from the "small number—certainly . . . no more than a tenth of the women" who would find such work "congenial."[24] Elsewhere, he stipulated that each sex was guaranteed a minimum of one-eighth represen-tation in all of the commune's functions and that women would serve in the highest corps in equal numbers with men. Equally radical was Fourier's assumption that men and women had the same sexual needs. Rejecting Enlightenment rationalism, Fourier declared all the passions good and designed his utopia to guarantee to each person sexual as well as material sat-isfaction. Not surprisingly, he refrained from publishing his more extreme writings on erotic life in the Phalanx during his lifetime, and his disciples concentrated virtuously on the economic aspects.

How did women respond to these new ideas? While many shared Anna Wheeler's enthusiasm, many others seem to have found some aspects disqui-eting. Owenite ideas on marriage reform ranged from the introduction of civil ceremonies and divorce to communal child rearing and contraception but avoided condoning sex outside of marriage. Although there was a long tradition of flexible sexual relations within the working class, such as consen-sual unions, premarital sex leading to marriage, and separation by mutual consent, the economic changes associated with the Industrial Revolution were creating greater instability in family life. Illegitimate children and deser-tions were the result for many women. As well, single women were finding it more difficult to survive economically. In this context, it seems understand-able that safer rather than freer relationships would appear more attractive. Marriage was appealing, *if* founded upon fidelity, monogamous affection, and mutual respect. As an English needlewoman explained, the "only foun-dation" for a happy marriage is "esteem and respect" rather than a temporary "state of excitement quite unfavourable to moral observation and reflec-tion."[25] A sexual revolution held no appeal for her.

Nor did communal living arrangements have much appeal, to judge from the reactions of married women who, with their families, formed the bulk of the membership in the experimental Owenite and Fourierist com-munities established in the United States, Britain, and France in the 1820s and 1840s. According to contemporary accounts, women joined reluctantly and at the behest of their husbands, all the while longing for their "separate fire-side."[26] Younger, single women enjoyed the more relaxed social atmos-phere and tended to adopt the unisex dress of pants and tunic. The married women for their part were reluctant to relinquish the one area that in the out-side world guaranteed their status and sense of worth: their role as domestic managers and as mothers. Most Fourierist communities compromised by offering the option of separate cottages for married couples.

If women lost control of family life, all they gained was more work. Historian Carol Kolmerten summarizes: "The very term everyone was using—'equality'—signified to the reformers that women would be 'allowed' to work full-time in community industries *as well as* be responsible for their families' domestic services." This meant that "being a 'wife' meant serving everyone, not just one's individual family."[27] As one Fourierist complained, "There are so many, and so few women to do the work that we have to be nearly all the time about it."[28] Although women expressed their unfavourable reactions indirectly, through illness and complaints addressed to non-members, the resulting tensions contributed to the breakup of the communities.

Even the work women did for the community was gender specific. The Owenite model community at New Harmony, Indiana, established in 1826, specified as its first principle an "Equality of Rights, uninfluenced by sex or condition, in all adults." The second principle, however, called for "Equality of Duties, modified by physical and mental conformation."[29] This had the effect of nullifying the first principle since the Owenites, like most others of their day, both consciously and unconsciously assumed that women and men were different. In practice women were assigned the community's domestic work: cooking, sewing, laundry, and child care. Even in the schools, which promised equal education to all children, girls were taught "female employments" separately.

Nonetheless, some women were thrilled with what was allowed them. One member of Brook Farm, an American community, described voting as her "first delightful experience of 'Woman's Rights.'. . . This new sense of power and responsibility widened my horizons."[30] Similarly, although the wages they received for their work were typically half of what the men earned—since the men did not consider domestic work as productive as farm work or manufacturing—many women were exhilarated to be paid at all for domestic work. Although few communities survived for long, novelists at the turn of the century would look back to them for inspiration when they set their hand to writing feminist utopias.

Working-Class Politics

Preindustrial Europe had a long tradition of female activism in the form of food riots and strikes, all justified by the responsibilities that women had as family caretakers. This tradition continued during the French Revolution, when working-class women organized in their capacities as wives and mothers in order to contribute to the goals of the revolution. Similarly, in nineteenth-century Britain, when men began organizing around national political issues to protest the lack of representation of urban areas in parliament, artificially high grain prices, and restricted voting rights, their wives and daughters formed female societies to "assist the male population of this country to obtain their rights and liberties,"[31] as the Blackburn Female Reform Society of 1819 put it.

In the British People's Charter movement of 1838–48, tens of thousands of women organized in more than eighty associations throughout the country to raise money, sign petitions, and demonstrate—in the name of "universal" suffrage—for full adult male suffrage. A few Chartist men supported female suffrage, and Chartist women helped found the first recorded female suffrage society in Britain in 1851, the Sheffield Women's Political Association. Nevertheless, most failed to criticize the hypocrisy latent in the concept of universal suffrage restricted to men. Atypical was the author of a letter to a newspaper in 1838 who called herself "A Real Democrat" and demanded "the right of every woman to have a vote in the legislation of her country." More usual was the hope of a woman known only as M.A.B., that "men of sense will not love us less for having talent, provided we use it right and for their benefit."[32] The Chartists, in contrast to Owenites, sought to defend the traditional family structure in order to protect the working class against the adverse effects of industrialization. For them female dignity meant the protection of women's place in the family supported by a male bread-winner. Revealingly, Chartism became a mass movement; Owenism did not.

Criticism of the Chartist stand on gender issues came from an unexpected quarter, a network of writers, journalists, politicians, and lawyers with a common background in radical Unitarianism. Unitarianism was a loose, non-Christian denomination, inspired by the Enlightenment faith in reason, self-fulfilment, and scientific and technological progress. The radicals, mostly men, allied themselves with progressive causes, such as the rights of Jews, Catholics, and women. They believed that female emancipation was necessary for the general cultural revolution they anticipated. Not as radical as the Owenites, they hoped to gain a larger audience by appealing for the reform, not the abolition, of capitalism, marriage, and the family. Their agenda was nonetheless bold and multifaceted. It included female suffrage, sex education, co-operative housing, increased employment opportunities for women, and married women's right to own property. Many of them dropped the word "obey" from their marriage vows; some advocated easier divorce. Mary Leman Grimstone proposed that men assume domestic responsibilities. Grimstone also wrote feminist novels; Anna Jameson engaged in feminist literary criticism. Others translated the novels of George Sand and the Swedish author Frederika Bremer. Although they targeted the lower middle and upper working classes, their real success was in broadening the debate over women's position in intellectual and political circles, thus laying the groundwork for the specific campaigns that subsequent reformers such as Barbara Smith Bodichon would undertake in the 1850s and 1860s. At this stage, however, the women tended to defer to the men in the movement, apparently agreeing that in their present state of bondage they were unable to liberate themselves and, more practically, fearing to antagonize audiences unnecessarily by public speaking.

Even in the Owenist movement, few women aside from a handful of feminists recognized their interests as separate from those of the men. Thousands responded to the campaign that Owenites organized in the late 1820s and early 1830s to form worker-owned shops and workshops. Working women had angrily and stubbornly defended their jobs on several occasions in the first two decades of the nineteenth century but had rarely found support from skilled male workers. Owenism seemed to be different, welcoming women in the struggle for a fair wage. It inspired women to form trade associations—one of the largest was a union of a thousand stocking workers—and co-operative workshops. Like the Chartists, however, these women were usually not feminists. It was rare to see a feminist analysis applied to women workers such as the one that appeared on the women's page of *The Pioneer,* the Owenite newspaper: "It is time the working females of England began to demand their long-suppressed rights. In manufacturing towns, look at the value that is set on woman's labour. . . . Why, I ask, should woman's labour be thus undervalued? . . . Sisters, let us submit to it no longer. . . . Unite and assert your just rights!"[33] One would like to know more as well about the organizer of English bonnet makers in 1834 who urged, "Come to the Union sisters, old and young, rich and poor. . . . Children as yet unborn must have to remember that there was woman as well as men in the Union."[34]

In spite of Owenite commitment to the organization of all workers, Owenites did not always welcome the unionization of women. Employers' increasing reliance on cheap female labour made men doubly defensive. To their traditional reluctance to countenance a public role for their wives, which would threaten their authority within the home, men now added a fear that their status in the workplace would be eroded. One woman tailor lamented "that the men are as bad as their masters." She excepted the few who "would gladly join in raising the price of [the female labourer] to the male standard."[35] The suggestion that equal wages would end competition between workers was ineffective against the economic compulsions that drove many women to accept rock-bottom wages and to replace male strikers as scab labour.

In 1833 a group of Owenite women organized the Practical Moral Union of Women of Great Britain and London. Their purpose was to unite women from all social classes so that "the broad line of demarcation which has been drawn between different classes of women, will be effaced." Historian Barbara Taylor calls this "the first separatist feminist organization established in Britain." It lasted only six or seven months, perhaps succumbing to male opposition. At least one male Owenite protested the idea of women forming "an exclusive union."[36] Anticipating later socialists, he argued that men and women should remain united in order to pursue their common interests. Both Owenism and Chartism failed; subsequently, men turned to trade unions, but women disappeared from working-class politics in Britain for three decades.

In the United States, a unique situation in Lowell, Massachusetts, provoked a predominantly female labour force to organize a series of strikes in the 1830s and 1840s. Building on their common New England background and on a female culture nurtured in the mandatory boarding houses set up by the textile company, women workers translated their solidarity into political activism to oppose wage reductions and to demand a ten-hour work day. The employer's reliance on Irish immigrant workers and refusal to build new boarding houses when the old ones deteriorated brought Lowell militancy to an end in the 1840s but not without leaving some mark. A Boston newspaper in 1834 reported "a flaming Mary Woolstonecroft [*sic*] speech" that one speaker made "on the rights of women and the iniquities of the '*monied* aristocracy,' which produced a powerful effect on her auditors, and they determined 'to have their own way if they died for it.'"[37] Elsewhere, working women used their shared experiences to form mutual aid societies or to protest together against oppressive conditions, but without more resources these efforts were inevitably short-lived.

Saint-Simonian Socialism

The third current of utopian socialism after that of Robert Owen and Charles Fourier was inspired by Saint-Simon in France and formed a bridge from working-class radicalism to feminism. Like Owen and Fourier, Saint-Simon and, after his death in 1825, Barthélemy Prosper Enfantin (1796–1864) criticized competition and selfish individualism as the results of economic progress. Unlike the Owenites or Fourierists, however, the Saint-Simonians saw both gender difference and religious hierarchy as essential to social harmony. Inspired by literary romanticism and a revulsion against the violence and liberal individualism of the French Revolution, they seized on the familiar notion of woman as more sentimental than man and endowed her with a special role in establishing a new reign of peace and love. Men and women were complementary halves, an idea exemplified by Enfantin's choice of a couple-pope to head their church and by his vision of God as androgynous, both "Father and Mother."

In a series of debates from 1829 to 1831 on woman's character and role, Enfantin routed those within the movement who disagreed with his emphasis on gender distinction and especially with his call for the "rehabilitation of the flesh." By this he meant a positive evaluation of the material world, specifically sexuality, in contrast to the Christian preference for spirit over matter. Enfantin rejected the idea of original sin and transformed the old view of woman as sexual into an affirmative force for sexual liberation. In particular, he suggested that his couple-pope could enjoy a variety of sexual partners. This proposal did not go over well with most of his followers, who denounced it as condoning promiscuity, nor with the authorities, who charged him with the "corruption of public morals." Enfantin backed down, admitting that the present male vision of a new morality was necessarily incomplete and proclaiming a search for the "Woman Messiah," who would somehow complete the doctrine. Missionaries dispersed throughout France and to England, Germany, the United States, and ultimately Egypt, where, in the words of historian Claire Moses, "under the Egyptian sun, mystical feminism burned itself out."[38]

Les Femmes Nouvelles

The most self-conscious effort at feminist activity and the first to combine action with feminist theory came from working-class women in France, who combined the inspiring vision of social change suggested by the Saint-Simonians with an analysis of their own experiences as women and workers. The Saint-Simonians had endowed woman with a complementary role in establishing the new age, but it was the women in the group who in the 1830s translated Saint-Simon's abstract, romanticized notion into collective feminist action.

The first female members of the movement had been close relatives and friends of the men in the movement and had obligingly formed a hierarchy, parallel to the men's, in obedience to Enfantin's wishes. People flocked to hear about this new religion as it expanded in the aftermath of the July Revolution of 1830, an insurrection against the government that disappointed workers' hopes. Reportedly, up to half of audience members were women. One listener, Suzanne Voilquin, a seamstress, described herself as thrilled to hear women's issues discussed and to see a woman seated on the dais, among the leaders. What she did not know is that Claire Bazard, the "mother" of the movement as Enfantin was the "father," had to demand the right to be seated there. In spite of a theoretical commitment to full female emancipation, Enfantin was ambivalent on the issue of women's equality. Although he chose two women to represent him at his trial for corrupting public morals, in protest against the all-male jury and women's lack of civil rights, women were at first underrepresented in the movement's leadership and then excluded from it altogether. For Suzanne Voilquin, this exclusion turned out to be a blessing, freeing women from the constant bickering over positions. Perhaps it also freed them from the hypnotic force of Enfantin's personality. In spite of her early enthusiasm, Voilquin had felt stifled in the movement. She complained that the men "think they see a tendency toward usurpation on our part when we dare to demonstrate our *will.*"[39] Cécile Fournel wrote in exasperation, "Again, it's the men who will act, the men, the men!"[40]

The exposure to an ideology of social change with an explicit call for women's participation was empowering, and the women in the movement always remained appreciative. Nonetheless, they were prepared to act on that call in ways that the men had not expected. In contrast to women in the United States and Britain, who came to feminism through their participation in a women's culture, Saint-Simonian women created a separatist culture as a result of their experience in a mixed-sex setting. Confiding their mutual disillusionment and calling themselves *les femmes nouvelles,* or new women, they resolved to organize what was probably "the first consciously separatist women's movement in history." "Men have advised, directed, and dominated us long enough," wrote Joséphine-Félicité Milizet. "It is now up to us to advance along the path of progress without tutelage. It is up to us to work for our liberty by ourselves."[41]

The format they chose was a newspaper run exclusively by and for women, published from 1832 to 1834. Daringly calling it *La femme libre* (The Free Woman) but eventually changing it to *La Tribune des femmes* (The Women's Newspaper), the paper's founders invited "all women, whatever their status, religion, or, views, as long as they feel the sorrows of woman and the people, to come and join us, associate with our work, and share our labors." Voilquin promised contributors a supportive environment, encouraging a free exchange of opinions and rejecting any attempt at censorship. Concerned to establish a forum for women's voices, she avowed, "The *femme nouvelle* does not make herself into a judge of her companions; it is not for us to praise or blame."[42]

As a symbolic gesture of their independence from male control, the contributors used only their first names. As Jeanne-Désirée Veret explained, "We . . . give birth to men. We should give them our names and take our own only from our mothers and God. . . . If we continue to take the names of men . . . we will be slaves without knowing it."[43] They also expressed their autonomy in practical ways, appealing, for example, for co-operation between bourgeois and working-class women. The Saint-Simonians, while actively recruiting workers, had left control of the movement firmly in the hands of the male elite. In contrast, the femmes nouvelles tried to create an egalitarian, inclusive movement of real co-operation across class lines based on women's shared experience of sexual exploitation. The issue of race, however, merited no mention, nor did they take any position on slavery, which continued in French territories until 1848.

It is notable that the femmes nouvelles chose the language of gender difference, symbolized by the term *motherhood*, to express their feminism. Motherhood was to them what sisterhood would be to later feminists, a unity of interests rather than a biological role, a way to validate women's experiences. They found the language of the French Revolution, which spoke of equal rights, inadequate. "Whoever says 'code of laws' speaks of the social regulations made in *everyone's* interest and approved and consented to by *everyone;* but who in truth are *we?*" asked Suzanne Voilquin. "Humanity is not composed only of men."[44] Gender difference for her was a way to affirm woman's importance in order to assert her equality. In Germany as well, feminists used motherhood to affirm women's importance in the family and thus in society, justifying their entry into the public sphere as professionally trained teachers in private kindergartens. This was a very different perspective from that of Catharine Beecher, who had used gender difference to affirm the conservative implications of a doctrine of separate spheres of activity for women and men.

Further indicative of the French women's autonomy was their reaction to Enfantin's suggestions for freer sexual relationships. Some responded with initial enthusiasm. Claire Démar, for example, proposed women's full sexual freedom, without any restraints. Most of the others, however, were ambivalent, if not outright disapproving. Against sexual pleasure they had to balance the physical costs of pregnancy and childbirth, not to mention the possibility of venereal disease—Voilquin's husband infected her—and the emotional and material burden of child rearing. Although some Saint-Simonian men went into retreat in 1832 hoping to gain "insight into women's lot"[45] by doing housework, few women expected them to participate in child rearing. Pauline Roland (1805–52), when she began a relationship, resolved to bring up any children alone. She carried out her pledge, giving her four children from two fathers her name. She would have taken pleasure in the wording of the arrest order issued for her participation in the revolution of 1848, which read, "An unmarried mother, she is the enemy of marriage, maintaining that subjecting the woman to the control of the husband sanctifies inequality."[46]

Pauline Roland and Claire Démar found little emotional or financial support among the Saint-Simonian "family." The persistence of the double standard and the difficulty of earning an adequate living weakened their sexual radicalism. Under these pressures, Démar committed suicide at age thirty-three, and Roland was reduced to writing begging letters to an ex-lover. The lesson was clear, Reine Guindorf explained: "As long as we cannot [own property], we will always be the slaves of men. . . . It is very difficult to speak freely when a woman does not have the means to live independently."[47] The means continued to escape them. A proposal for a communal house for unmarried women and widows was never realized, and under the pressures of earning their livelihoods the femmes nouvelles dispersed.

Flora Tristan

Flora Tristan (1803–44), the most famous of the early French feminists, represents the culmination of utopian socialism and feminism. She seems to have been the only woman during this time whose interest in social reform came from her commitment to feminism rather than the other way around. Was this a result of the sufferings she endured as a child and young woman? Her early life was a series of tragedies: the sudden death of her aristocratic Peruvian father when she was four and the subsequent impoverishment of her family, along with the taint of illegitimacy when French authorities refused to recognize her parents' wedding as valid; the purported suicide of a fiancé whose father disapproved of Tristan; then marriage at eighteen to an employer who allegedly tried to force Tristan into prostitution to pay his gambling debts. In defiance of the Napoleonic Code she walked out on her husband, taking her two small children and pregnant with a third, but her troubles with him were not over. Only after accusing him of incest was Tristan able to win custody of their daughter, whom her husband had taken away from her out of revenge. And only after he shot and almost killed Tristan was she able to get a legal separation, although not the right to remarry. Like the Owenite Anna Wheeler, whom she later met, Tristan became a fierce critic of women's dependence in marriage: "The most oppressed man can oppress another, who is his wife. She is the proletariat of the proletariat itself."[48]

Tristan's travels to England, where she observed the dislocation and poverty caused by industrialization, made her aware of the common exploitation that workers and women suffered under capitalism. Her language was strikingly anticipatory of Karl Marx when she denounced the alienation and fragmentation of workers' lives and called on them to emancipate themselves through union. But unlike Marx, Tristan preferred reform to revolution and believed the emancipation of women to be the key to the emancipation of the working classes. Women, she believed, were "that part of humanity whose mission is to bring peace and love to mankind." In her novel, *Méphis* (1838), she described woman's mission as "to *inspire* man . . . to compel him, through her persistent efforts, to make himself capable of great things."[49] True social harmony would result only when the possibility of divorce and women's economic independence would permit both partners to enter freely and equally into a marriage of love and when women would be educated enough to raise enlightened children.

Impatient of theories without results, Tristan decided to approach workers directly in order to raise their consciousness and make them aware of the need to organize. In 1843, she began a tour of France, meeting with workers, priests, factory owners, and journalists in order to promote her idea of association. She dreamed of workers' halls established in every town, open to women and men equally and guaranteeing them work and education.

▶ *Her book,* Workers' Union *(1843), contained Flora Tristan's message, which she took to the workers of France on her speaking tour.*

Up to the present time, woman has counted for nothing in human societies. What has been the result?—That the priest, the legislator, and the philosopher have treated her as a *real pariah*. Woman (half of humanity) has been *left outside of the church*, outside of the *law*, outside of *society*. . . . For her, no offices in the church, no representation before the law, no offices in the state. The priest said to her: "Woman, you are temptation, sin, evil; you represent the flesh, that is, corruption and rottenness. Weep over your condition, throw ashes on your head, shut yourself in a convent, and there, mortify your heart, which is made for love, and your womb of a woman, which is made for maternity; and when you have thus mutilated your heart and your body, offer them all bloodstained and withered to your God for remission of the original sin committed by your mother Eve." Then the legislator said to her: "Woman, by yourself you are nothing as an active member of humanity; you cannot hope to find a place at the banquet of society. You must, if you want to live, serve as an *appendage* to your lord and master, man. Therefore, young girl, you will obey your father; married woman, you will obey your husband; when you are widowed and old, little value will be set on you." Next the learned philosopher said to her: "Woman, it has been scientifically established that, because of your structure, you are *inferior* to man. . . . You have no intelligence, no understanding of weighty questions, no consistency in your ideas, no capacity for the so-called exact sciences, nor any aptitude for serious projects; finally, you are a creature feeble in body and spirit, faint-hearted and superstitious; in a word, you are only a capricious child, self-willed and frivolous; for ten or fifteen years of your life you are a pretty *little doll*, but full of faults and vices. That is why, woman, man must be *your master* and have complete authority over you". . . .

That is how, for the 6,000 years of the world's existence, the wisest of wise men have judged the *female race*.

Source: Flora Tristan, *Workers' Union* (1843), in *Flora Tristan, Utopian Feminist: Her Travel Diaries and Personal Crusade*, trans., ed., and intro., Doris and Paul Beik (Bloomington: Indiana University Press, 1993). Reprinted with the permission of the publisher.

In many ways Tristan resembled her contemporary, the Scottish radical Fanny Wright, discussed below. Both women were arresting public speakers, both travelled widely and valued their independence, and both were interested in workers' associations. Unlike Wright, however, Tristan believed in an

idealized family, religion, and the Saint-Simonian romanticization of
woman's moral mission. Because the interests of women and men were so
closely related, Tristan appealed to the men she addressed "to demand rights
for women, and, while waiting, to acknowledge them at least *in principle.*"
Thus men were to emancipate women, but Tristan was convinced that in the
end she would emancipate everyone herself. Somewhat paradoxically, given
her call to workers' self-emancipation, she saw herself as a messiah called by
God, who would lead workers to union and enlightenment: "Why shouldn't
I, a woman sensing her own faith and strength, go as the apostles did from
town to town announcing to the workers the GOOD NEWS and preaching
to them *fraternity in humanity, union in humanity.*"[50] She was a martyr, on a
mission of love; her sufferings would redeem others. Hence her impatience
with those who missed the point, the "stupid, bestial, crude, vain" workers
who had not taken her "good and useful" book *Workers' Union* (1843) seriously.[51] Bitterly disappointed at the hostility she encountered, she vowed,
"Poor creatures, I will serve you, in spite of yourselves."[52]

What effect did she have? Contemporaries describe her magnetism and
beauty, her passionate and persuasive words. But French male workers, like
the British, felt threatened by women who would work for cheaper wages.
Their goal was to raise men's wages to allow husbands to support their wives.
Perhaps the resistance she encountered led Tristan to waver in giving women
equal power: in her plan women would hold only two out of seven seats on
the local governing committees, and only ten out of fifty on the central committee. These concessions made no impact. The workers in Bordeaux who
raised a monument to her four years after her death at the age of forty-one
from typhoid fever honoured her as the author of the *Workers' Union* but
ignored her feminism.

1848

Further efforts on behalf of both feminism and socialism were cut short by
the failure of the revolutions of 1848. Repressive policies of conservative
monarchs and years of economic depression triggered revolts throughout
Europe. Women were active participants, demonstrating and fighting alongside the men. In Austria, Italy, and the German states the cause of liberalism
was joined to that of nationalism. Italian women responded enthusiastically
to the nationalist Giuseppe Mazzini and joined revolutionary armies fighting
for a united republican Italy.

In France, republicans and socialists united to topple the monarchy and
establish a republic with adult male suffrage. Women who had edited *La
Tribune des femmes* joined forces with former contributors to the *Gazette des
femmes,* a republican newspaper published in the mid-1830s by bourgeois
ex–Saint-Simonian women. The *Gazette* had demanded a wide range of
political and civil liberties for women, including the right to vote and the re-
establishment of divorce. Meetings held for subscribers and contributors to
the paper had attracted a number of feminists, including Tristan. The result
of the collaboration of the two groups in 1848 was *Voix des femmes,* a "social-

ist and political journal, organ of the interests of all women,"[53] the first daily feminist newspaper.

Women also joined and formed political clubs, just as they had in 1789, but this time the clubs—such as the Club for the Emancipation of Women and the Committee for the Rights of Women—were avowedly feminist. The most radical was the Vesuvians, whose title suggested "lava, so long held back, that must at last pour out around us."[54] Its members, mostly young unmarried working women, organized street demonstrations and demanded female military service. Adopting the bloomer costume worn by some Saint-Simonian and Fourierist women, they proposed that women and men dress alike. Although their constitution specified that all women marry by age twenty-one and men by twenty-six, they called on husbands to share housework, threatening them with perpetual military service if they resisted.

Whereas socialist women had earlier shunned politics, now they lobbied for the right to vote. Pauline Roland tried to vote in a municipal election but was refused admission to the voting hall. *Voix des femmes* women, insisting on the right to run for office, nominated the famous novelist, George Sand (Aurore Dupin Dudevant), to the new legislature. After Sand rudely rebuffed their invitation, Jeanne Deroin (ca. 1810–94), a former Saint-Simonian, tried to run for office herself. In words that twentieth-century radical feminists would echo, Deroin insisted on the primacy of patriarchy: "We must make it absolutely clear that the abolition of the privileges of race, birth, caste, and fortune cannot be complete and radical unless the privilege of sex is totally abolished. It is the source of all the others, the last head of the hydra."[55] Although she campaigned for weeks, attempting to find supporters, no group dared to support her candidacy. When one delegate finally put a proposal for female suffrage before the Constituent Assembly, the other 899 delegates united to vote against it.

In this context the appeal to motherhood became more pronounced. There may have been practical reasons for this, such as the desire to offset the earlier sexual radicalism. As well, by the late 1840s the economic situation had deteriorated for single women, and the lack of any practical alternative to marriage was even more painfully obvious than before. *Tribune des femmes* women were now older, and many of them were mothers. A celebration of motherhood was something that could justify their life choices. Then, too, traditional misogyny remained strong in France. Jeanne Deroin and others still found it necessary to argue for the rehabilitation of woman's image, for seeing her as a force for good rather than evil, replacing a sexual influence with a moral one. When Eugénie Niboyet defended the nomination of George Sand, she did so "in the name of the holy obligations of the family, in the name of the tender labours of the Mother."[56] The reference is ironic given Sand's reputation for wearing trousers, smoking in public, and enjoying a string of lovers.

George Sand (1804–76) was the model of the emancipated woman, symbolizing a disreputable feminism in the popular imagination. Her novels portray strong and independent female characters who make their own decisions. *Indiana* (1832) was hailed as "an open declaration of war on the Napoleonic Code."[57] The French Senate was sufficiently impressed by her writings to ban all but two of her sixty-odd novels from public libraries. Yet Sand remained aloof from any feminist activity. With her escape from an unsatisfactory marriage and her sympathy for workers she could have been another Flora Tristan. But her liberated lifestyle appears to have been a combination of aristocratic eccentricity and artistic licence. Perhaps her privileged background kept her from a sense of solidarity with other women. The rights she championed were ones personally important to her—namely, divorce and separation—but she rejected political rights for women and found the invitation to run for public office a "ridiculous pretension."[58]

George Sand's liberated lifestyle gave feminism a bad name. Although Louise Otto, who founded a newspaper during the revolutions in Germany in 1848, defended women's right to act for their own and for the common good, she deplored the so-called emancipated women who wanted "to educate woman according to a manly model and to imitate man." It is not hard to see Sand in Otto's reference to "caricatures who have adopted the cruder customs and practices of men as their right, and who have even preferred to see themselves in male attire." For her part, Otto took pride in a critic's rebuke that she was too sentimental, speaking more "from the heart than from the head." She retorted that such was "the essence of woman."[59]

Even with their appeal to motherhood and the family, feminists were no more successful in 1848 than they had been in 1789. By early June the government ordered the club organized by *Voix des femmes* women shut down and, a few weeks later, forbade "women and minor children" from participating in any political clubs. Some *Voix des femmes* diehards fell back on Flora Tristan's strategy of association, successfully organizing groups of women workers. When they attempted to organize four hundred workers' associations into a federation, the government had them arrested on charges of "conspiracy to overthrow the government by violence." Historian Claire Moses describes the results as "devastating." By 1852, all the leaders of French feminism were exiled or dead: "In 1848–49, the French feminist movement was the most advanced and the most experienced of all Western feminist movements. Yet for the next twenty years, feminists would be unable to move forward."[60]

From their prison cells, Jeanne Deroin and Pauline Roland sent greetings in 1851 to the Sheffield Women's Political Association in Britain and to the American women who were organizing a women's rights convention. "Sisters of America!" they wrote, "Your socialist sisters of France are united with you in the vindication of the right of woman to civil and political equality."[61] Now only in Britain and in North America were feminists free to organize; in France and throughout Europe, they would have to wait for a more liberal environment.

Fanny Wright and Radicalism in the United States

Under the influence of republicanism, middle-class Americans were also developing an idealistic vision of a new order. While aware of the social tensions developing from urbanization and industrialization, they did not wish to assist the emancipation of the working classes. Rather, they desired to create a more perfect society through a wide variety of reforms focusing on the perfection of

the individual and the nation. Although indebted to Enlightenment optimism, American reform zeal owed more to the evangelical faith of the revivalist movements. Evangelism was a double-edged sword, however. Essentially
conservative and puritanical, it could create an atmosphere highly
unfavourable to feminism. In the life of Frances (Fanny) Wright (1795–1852),
European radicalism clashed with American religious conservatism.

Robert Dale Owen, son of Robert Owen and a close friend of Wright,
thought her parents' early death and her subsequently "unhappy infancy and
childhood" may have "soured" her. Whatever the reason, although Wright
came from a privileged Scottish background, she saw herself as a born advocate for social justice. As an adolescent she vowed "to wear ever in her heart
the cause of the poor and the helpless; and to aid in all that she could in
redressing the grievous wrongs which seemed to prevail in society." Born
three years after the publication of Mary Wollstonecraft's *Vindication of the
Rights of Woman,* Wright was Wollstonecraft's spiritual successor. Attracted to
the ideas of the French Revolution, she abruptly left the aunt who had raised
her and went to visit the United States, the promised land of freedom. The
self-confidence and assurance of her upper-class background allowed her an
indifference to social convention; she travelled extensively, usually by horse-
back and often without the appropriate male escort. Her biographer suggests
that she may have travelled further than any other woman of her time.
Although enamoured of the United States, she came to detest the slavery,
social distinctions, and gender inequality that she found contrary to republican ideals. Americans were not ready for her ideas on race relations. When
she wrote approvingly of interracial marriage, her views were described by
former president James Madison as "universally obnoxious."[62]

The Owenites at New Harmony gave Wright the inspiration for her own
social experiment: a community that would allow slaves to work for their
freedom while giving them the necessary training. At the same time Wright
specified that "no woman can forfeit her individual rights or independent
existence, and no man assert over her any rights or power whatsoever."[63] The
resulting venture, set up at Nashoba, Tennessee, in 1825, was short-lived, the
victim not only of poor planning and lack of funds but also of allegations of
sexual impropriety when one of the resident trustees admitted to living with
a mulatto woman.

Wright herself was beginning to chafe at the hypocrisy and narrowness
of contemporary ideas on sexuality. She was running headlong into the current religious revival sweeping the eastern states. Determined to resist the
influence of "priestcraft," she began giving public lectures, reportedly the first
woman to do so regularly in the United States. Tall and imposing, she
shocked audiences by condoning sexual passion as "the best source of human
happiness" and repudiating formal marriage ties as meaningless. A contemporary described "her extraordinary gift of eloquence," which along with her
notoriety explained the large crowds that came to hear her.[64]

Wright shared Mary Wollstonecraft's faith in reason and education and
Robert Owen's hope for greater economic equality. Oblivious to the family-
centred values of many who heard her, she advocated state-run boarding
schools as an essential way to minimize the social distinctions between families.

Her vision of a society of educational and economic equality led her to champion the interests of both women and workers. She drew the same parallel between women's emancipation and social progress as did Fourier: "Until women assume the place in society which good sense and good feeling alike assign to them, human improvement must advance but feebly."[65]

Not even Wright's assurance allowed her to face public censure when she found herself pregnant. She retreated into a largely self-imposed isolation, marrying her daughter's father in 1831 although unable to maintain a satisfying relationship with him. Demoralized and increasingly out of touch with American politics, she failed to make a comeback in public life. Although living in France, she made no attempt to establish contact with the French feminists of the 1830s and 1840s whose aspirations she shared.

One of the most contentious figures of her time, Wright was dubbed "The Red Harlot of Infidelity." A journalist captured her impact: "With a brain from Heaven and a heart from Hell, she has employed all the powers of her intellect, to removing the ancient land-marks of morality and social order, and in diffusing the worst principles of the French revolution through this land of the Puritan Fathers." Catharine Beecher, her contemporary, who opposed women's political rights and urged their submission within the family as a model for social harmony, did not spare her contempt: "I cannot conceive any thing in the shape of a woman, more intolerably offensive and disgusting." Although Wright was read and admired by Elizabeth Cady Stanton and Susan B. Anthony, leaders of the later American women's suffrage movement, her daughter vehemently turned against all her mother stood for. Sylva d'Arusmont embraced Christianity and testified in 1874 before an American congressional committee that female suffrage would "wreck human happiness in America!" She condemned "the present woman's movement [for] tempting my sex to man's province to the neglect of its home duties & joys [and] of the rising generation."[66]

THE REFORMERS

In the United States and Britain, feminism was most closely associated with a reform tradition. Most American feminists, in distinction to Fanny Wright, shared the religious piety of their contemporaries. They were demure where Wright was flamboyant, prudish where she was uninhibited, and, at least until the late 1840s, as committed to the bonds of marriage and family as she was opposed. What in Wright was arrogance was in them a collective self-righteousness and faith in a divine mission, which perhaps shielded them more effectively from the criticism of their contemporaries. In Germany also, religion inspired feminists; but in a different context it left them vulnerable to the forces of reaction.

Religion, Feminism, and American Reform

Feminism with religious roots was not new in the nineteenth century, as we have seen. One thinks of Mary Astell, the seventeenth-century Anglican described in Chapter 5, who proposed semi-religious retirement as an alternative to marriage for single women. Whereas Astell was protective of social institutions sanctioned by God, however, American women felt called to reform them. Like the Saint-Simonians, they were convinced of woman's special mission. At a time when men's religious commitment seemed to be weakening, preachers put greater stress on woman's religious sensitivity, thus contributing to the idea of her greater potential for moral influence. Sarah Grimké, who came to women's rights from her work in the antislavery movement, avowed, "I feel deeply that the regeneration of this world is to be achieved through the instrumentality of Woman."[67] God called woman now to act in the world rather than to withdraw from it; any woman, married or single, black or white, would be failing in her moral duty and social responsibility if she did not respond.

The passion for reform was epidemic in the American middle class, and the early nineteenth century witnessed an outburst of philanthropic associations aimed at relieving victims of misfortune, illness, or poverty, or helping fugitive slaves in their transition to freedom. Although reform work followed naturally from the republican and religious encouragement of woman's mission, early activists approached the challenge of forming, staffing, and funding their own organizations with considerable trepidation. At best the clergy gave grudging approval. It was not long before such organizations as the American Female Moral Reform Society, first established in 1834 as the New York Female Moral Reform Society (FMRS), revealed an unwillingness to work within the prescribed limits of female propriety and demanded the right to define their own sphere of action. In conforming to the notion of woman's moral superiority, they were also using it to justify a public role for women.

The FMRS and a similar group, the Female Benevolent Reform Society (FBRS), both dedicated to rescuing prostitutes, provide examples of how reform activity could slide over into feminism. Prostitution confronted reformers with the consequences of the sexual double standard, lower wages, and limited job opportunities for women. In contrast to those who tended to blame "depraved women," the FBRS pointed out how "the treachery of man" contributed to vice and illustrated their argument with examples of male abuse. The FMRS was even more indignant. Its semi-monthly paper, the *Advocate of Moral Reform*, published by an all-women staff and distributed nationally, defiantly printed the names of brothel patrons. Condemned as "outspoken females,"[68] the members refused to compromise and insisted that they would never relinquish their paper.

Their concern with prostitution brought these reformers to criticize women's economic dependency as well as the double standard. They condemned lower wages for women as "unjust and oppressive." An 1846 article in the *Advocate* pointed out how men monopolized most occupations and called for more jobs to be open to women: "Does anyone ask 'Would you have them plead at the bar, or follow the plough?' I frankly answer 'Yes.'" They urged that women view marriage as only one of many alternatives and protested the popular interpretation, promoted by Catharine Beecher, of woman's sphere as limited to her home. A book excerpted in the *Advocate* warned, "If women knew their rights . . . we would never hear of men [dominating them]."[69]

The FBRS, FMRS, and other groups set up an employment bureau, settlement house, daycare centres, industrial schools, women's shelters, and hospitals, including an infirmary run entirely by women. They advocated publicly supported colleges for women, circulated petitions demanding the punishment of men's sexual abuse of women, namely adultery and seduction, and agitated for prison reform and for laws giving married women control over their property. They even wrote women's history. The *Ladies' Wreath*, published by Sarah Martyn, former manager of the Female Guardian Society, published regular features on famous women in history and presented the "Pilgrim Mothers" as role models for readers. Similarly, the *Advocate* claimed that "we hear enough about our forefathers" and wished "to speak a word . . . for our . . . foremothers lest time and the one-sided page of history shall blot them forever from our memories." They also believed that women could unite across class lines. Members of the Seamen's Aid Society of Boston proposed, "Let us pray not each one for herself, but for our sex . . . till the oppressions . . . are removed."[70]

As outspoken and daring as they were in tackling difficult issues, many of these white reformers ignored the issue of race. For black women, race, poverty, and feminism were inextricably linked. Maria W. Miller Stewart (1803–79), a free black and perhaps the first American-born woman to address an audience of women and men in the United States, found the courage to speak in public from her commitment to her race. "Methinks I hear [the question] 'Who shall go forward, and take off the reproach that is cast upon the people of color? Shall it be a woman?'" she asked. "And my heart made this reply—'If it is thy will, be it even so, Lord Jesus!'"[71] Determined to be of service to their communities, black women organized benevolent organizations, among the first formed by any group of women, which commonly blurred the lines between mutual aid, community service, and self-improvement.

Although sensitive to slavery, Maria Stewart worried primarily that free blacks lived "lives of continual drudgery and toil" in spite of their desire to improve their situation. She feared that black women were doomed to work as domestic servants and reproached her "fairer sisters, whose hands are never soiled" by pointing out that most black women had not had the same opportunities for intellectual development. When she had asked these same sisters to practise "equal opportunity"[72] by hiring young black women as shop clerks, they had refused, fearing that they would thereby lose their customers. The solution, Stewart told her audience, was that blacks should rely on themselves: "Possess the spirit of independence. . . . Sue for your rights and privileges."[73] In her speeches Stewart anticipated many of the points that black feminists were to make at the end of the century.

The feminist consciousness of many of the American reformers is impressive, but as an historian reminds us, "The leap from moral reform to feminism was considerable, and most women could not and did not make it."[74] Many volunteers were content to limit their activities to those compatible with woman's role as homemaker and mother. Most members of the reform societies never linked up with the abolitionists who went on to organize feminist movements. Nonetheless, their bridge to public activities is impressive when compared to the difficulty German women had in trying to create something similar.

Religion and Reform in Germany

Since the Reformation, German religious life had been closely tied to the state churches, and state control over welfare precluded any autonomous role for women as agents of charity. When Amalie Sieveking (1794–1859) created a female benevolent society in Hamburg in 1832, a male critic complained that the work was incompatible with women's roles as wives and mothers and "suitable only to persons who are completely alone in the world and can devote themselves exclusively to their calling."[75] Unlike her American counterparts, Sieveking made no claim for women's autonomy either inside or outside the home; an invocation of separate spheres—men dominating the public world of business and economics and women ruling over the home— would have been unacceptably radical.

By the 1840s, a more independent spirit was developing within the Protestant sect known as German Catholicism, its name meaning catholic in the sense of "universal." The sect was ecumenical and encouraged a progressive outlook critical of the power and parochialism of the established churches. Women seem to have predominated throughout the movement, and most congregations allowed women to vote. The Women's Club of 1847, formed in Hamburg to help raise funds for the new congregation, included Jewish women and liberal Protestants. Along with other women's clubs stimulated by the revolutionary developments of 1848, it unabashedly claimed a program of charitable and educational activities to develop women's potential. As members of the Women's Club recalled in 1851, "The more clearly and self-consciously we came to an appreciation of the significance of our own spiritual lives, the more we felt called upon with joy and commitment to work for the intellectual and material well-being of our own sex."[76]

The most daring feminist venture was the Hamburg Academy for Women, established in 1850 and the only institution of its kind in nineteenth-century Germany. Directed mainly by women and supported by an informal national network of women from all religious backgrounds, it was designed to create the possibility of economic independence by training women as teachers. Because public schools did not hire women, the academy developed an associated project to sponsor private kindergartens and primary schools. In taking women out of the home for teacher training and in creating schools that not only enrolled children from various social backgrounds but also refused to provide formal religious instruction for them, the academy was daringly ahead of its time. The unco-operative brother of one student decried the "useless and destructive vanity on the side of women" that allowed them to step "outside of the territory to which God and female humility assigns them."[77] The authorities apparently agreed, singling women out as a special target in the conservative reaction to the political movements of 1848. The Prussian Law of Association of 1850 put political parties off limits to women, ordered the private kindergartens disbanded, and banned German Catholicism. In 1852 the Hamburg academy gave in to pressure and closed. Paternal authority over private as well as public life was reaffirmed, and charities remained firmly under male control. As in France, feminism could not survive in a climate so hostile to reform.

The Antislavery Movement and Feminism

Considering the situation in Europe, we can appreciate all the more the receptive environment for American feminism and the stimulus given by the reform movements most closely linked with it, temperance and antislavery. The temperance movement is considered in a later context, although we may note here that the discrimination experienced by women in the movement prompted some of them to form all-women organizations. The same thing happened in the antislavery movement; black women in Massachusetts and New York were the first to organize separately from men, in 1832. All-female groups mushroomed, and by 1837 the president of the national organization, the Anti-Slavery Convention of American Women, advised in a circular sent to all member societies that women should follow their own consciences rather than bow to their husbands' wills.

A bolder stand came from an unlikely source, two sisters from a respectable, well-to-do, slave-owning southern family. Sarah (1792–1873) and Angelina (1805–79) Grimké both recalled finding slavery morally reprehensible from an early age; Sarah taught her maid to read, secretly, at night, in defiance of the law. Sarah also felt the injustice of a patriarchal society, which stifled her passion for learning while encouraging the studies of her brothers. She managed for a time to submerge her restlessness into the only acceptable outlet for women: religion. She joined a Quaker congregation and followed her "call" to move north, to Philadelphia, where she led a life of self-renunciation and withdrawal in Quaker circles. Angelina, the youngest and most indulged child in the family, was more self-confident than Sarah; after disastrous attempts to reform her family and friends, she left to join her sister, thus publicly taking a stand against slavery.

In the North, the sisters were gradually drawn into the growing debate over slavery. Angelina after much hesitation wrote a letter of support for the antislavery cause, which was published in an antislavery newspaper and won her immediate acclaim. Invited to speak to female audiences, the Grimkés became the first and only women among the forty trained agents in the antislavery movement. In spite of the worries of one adviser that it would become a "Fanny Wright affair,"[78] their "parlour talks" were so popular that they were moved into churches and meeting halls to accommodate the audiences. To oblige interested men, the meetings were opened to mixed audiences.

Such defiance of convention was not completely unprecedented and certainly not unchallenged. In the 1820s, Elizabeth Chandler had written for the antislavery cause but had not dared to sign her work. When Angelina wrote to her countrywomen in the South, calling on them to influence their male relatives against slavery, the authorities in her home town burned her appeal in public and forbade her to return. Yet the greatest storm arose over the phenomenon of women speaking in public. Maria Stewart had to end her speaking career, at least in part due to the opposition she encountered. Even after the pioneering efforts of Stewart and the Grimkés, Abby Kelley, who succeeded the Grimké sisters in the antislavery movement, was described as "that monstrosity, a public speaking woman." As a result of the harassment Kelley received, she was called "our Joan of Arc"[79] by her co-workers. Catharine Beecher exemplified proper female conduct by having her brother read her speech while she sat demurely near him on the stage. A poem by Maria Weston Chapman mockingly describes the controversy:

> Confusion has seized us, and all things go wrong,
> The women have leaped from "their spheres,"
> And, instead of fixed stars, shoot as comets along,
> And are setting the world by the ears!
>
> . . . .
>
> They've taken a notion to speak for themselves,
> And are wielding the tongue and the pen;
> They've mounted the rostrum; the termagant elves!
> And—oh horrid!—are talking to men![80]

Black men often proved to be more receptive both to women's public speaking and to their demand for equal representation in antislavery organizations. Many black men warmed to black women's activism, seeing it as a useful refutation of the supposed intellectual inferiority and docility that whites assumed to be racial characteristics. The all-black American Moral Reform Society in 1839 welcomed women as full members by resolving "that what is morally right for a man to do, is morally right for women." At the same time, however, women in public life threatened those blacks for whom respectability was bound up with the adoption of the ideology of separate spheres. Black women abolitionists had to satisfy those who expected from them both ladylike behaviour and tireless activism on behalf of the race. William Lloyd Garrison, the noted abolitionist, wrote in 1832 to Sarah Douglass, "My hopes for the elevation of your race are mainly centered upon you and others of your sex."[81]

The issue of women's participation proved to be more contentious among white abolitionists and split the movement in 1840. Only the radical wing allowed women to take part alongside men; the more conservative branch restricted them to the female societies. When the British and Foreign Anti-Slavery Society issued invitations for a world conference in London in 1840 and discovered that American delegations might include women, it hurriedly specified that the invitations were only for gentlemen. The women arrived anyway, but a narrow vote forced their exclusion and they had to sit behind a curtain in the gallery. There, Elizabeth Cady Stanton, as a new bride accompanying her husband to the conference, joined them. With a shared sense of outrage, she and the Quaker minister and abolitionist Lucretia Mott vowed to call a convention of American women when they returned home.

Although delayed eight years, the resulting Seneca Falls meeting of 1848 commonly marks the beginning of the organized American women's rights movement. The "Declaration of Sentiments" adopted by the participants was modelled on the Declaration of Independence, just as Olympe de Gouges in 1791 had based her Declaration of the Rights of Woman on the model of the Declaration of the Rights of Man and the Citizen. While drawing attention to the inequality of the franchise, civil rights, divorce and child custody laws, and moral standards, however, the Declaration, like the one on which it was modelled, failed to include even a mention of slavery or racism.

The failure was ominous but not unprecedented. Black women had welcomed white women in their antislavery organizations but the reverse was not always true, although white women may have had a better record than white men did. Nevertheless, racism and racial inequality were acceptable to some white women even as they condemned slavery. Black women's agenda, which targeted both racism and sexism, was thus, according to one scholar, "the most dangerous and radical that this generation of reformers could formulate, for it represented the possibility of overturning two of the most firmly entrenched forms of oppression."[82] Sadly, most white feminists failed to follow their lead.

Both black and white abolitionists commonly referred to female slaves as their sisters. Sarah Douglass appealed to other free women to "bear in our hearts the sorrows, the ignorance, the degradation of our captive sisters." Her heart, she wrote, was "filled with sorrow for [her] enslaved sisters."[83] Angelina Grimké identified female slaves as "our countrywomen—*they are our sisters.*" Women had to speak up, Angelina insisted: "The denial of our duty to act in this case is a denial of our right to act; and if we have no right to act, then may *we* well be termed 'the white slaves of the North,' for like our brethren in bonds, we must seal our lips in silence and despair."[84] Yet not all white women abolitionists were prepared to act on this sense of sisterhood to the extent of working and socializing with blacks. Women in the bi-racial Philadelphia Female Anti-Slavery Society, such as Lucretia Mott, Charlotte Forten, and Grace and Sarah Douglass, took a firm stand against racism, but women in antislavery groups in New York refused to work with African Americans. They ignored the pledge suggested by Angelina Grimké at the 1837 women's national antislavery convention that every woman deem it her duty "to be delivered from such an unholy feeling [as racial prejudice]."[85] Even when black women were allowed to join white women's antislavery organizations they frequently experienced discrimination, and black men were more often welcomed than black women.

Women's Rights in the United States

One impetus for a self-conscious feminism in the United States thus came from within the abolition movement, as women like the Grimkés were drawn to defend women's rights in the course of defending their own right to speak in public. For them, abolition was what later feminists would call a consciousness-raising experience. Abby Kelley observed that "in striving to strike [the male slave's] irons off, we found most surely that *we* were manacled *ourselves.*"[86]

In 1838, in her published Letters to Catherine Beecher: In Reply to an Essay on Slavery and Abolitionism, Addressed to A.E. Grimké, Revised by the Author, *Angelina Grimké defended her understanding of woman's mission against Beecher's insistence that it be constrained to the private sphere.*

The investigation of the rights of the slave has led me to a better understanding of my own. I have found the Anti-Slavery cause to be the high school of morals in our land—the school in which *human rights* are more fully investigated, and better understood and taught, than in any other. Here a great fundamental principle is uplifted and illuminated, and from this central light, rays innumerable stream all around. Human beings have *rights,* because they are *moral* beings: the rights of *all* men grow out of their moral nature; and as all men have the same moral nature, they have essentially the same rights. These rights may be wrested from the slave, but they cannot be alienated: his title to himself is as perfect *now,* as is that of Lyman Beecher: it is stamped on his moral being, and is, like it, imperishable. Now if rights are founded in the nature of our moral being, then the *mere circumstance of sex* does not give to man higher rights and responsibilities, than to woman. To suppose that it does, would be to deny the self-evident truth, that the "physical constitution is the mere instrument of the moral nature." To suppose that it does, would be to break up utterly the relations, of the two natures, and to reverse their functions, exalting the animal nature into a monarch, and humbling the moral into a slave; making the former a proprietor, and the latter its property. When human beings are regarded as *moral beings, sex,* instead of being enthroned upon the summit, administering upon rights and responsibilities, sinks into insignificance and nothingness. . . .

. . . Now, I believe it is woman's right to have a voice in all the laws and regulations by which she is to be *governed,* whether in Church or State; and that the present arrangements of society, on these points, are *a violation of human rights, a rank usurpation of power,* a violent seizure and confiscation of what is sacredly and inalienably hers—thus inflicting upon woman outrageous wrongs, working mischief incalculable in the social circle, and in its influence on the world producing only evil, and that continually. *If* Ecclesiastical and Civil governments are ordained of God, *then* I contend that woman has just as much right to sit in solemn counsel in Conventions, Conferences, Associations and General Assemblies, as man—just as much right to sit upon the throne of England, or in the Presidential chair of the United States.

It is interesting to note that although British women also played a key role in writing petitions and raising funds for their antislavery cause, they did not make the same transition to feminism as did American abolitionists. Perhaps this was because slavery was outlawed earlier in the British empire, or perhaps because slavery was so much a part of American society. The women who were determined to speak out had their commitment tested by clerical opposition and mob violence. In 1972, Kate Millett, a feminist of the "second wave," wrote, "Slavery was probably the only circumstance in American life sufficiently glaring in its injustice and monumental evil to impel women to break that taboo of decorum which stifled and controlled them more efficiently than the coil of their legal, educational, and financial difficulties."[87] Even then, not all feminists were drawn to the campaign, nor did all women abolitionists become feminists. Women and men alike were split over the role of women in the antislavery movement.

Opponents accused feminists of diverting attention away from slavery by embarking on "a selfish crusade against some paltry grievance of [their] own." When so rebuked, Lucy Stone responded, "I was a woman before I was an abolitionist. I must speak for the women."[88] Whereas the Grimkés in the late 1830s fought for women's right to speak as abolitionists, Lucy Stone (1818–93) in the late 1840s was an abolitionist speaking for women's rights. In background and temperament, she was similar to many others in reform movements: New England born, from an old, respectable, financially secure family, she was conscious of her heritage, idealistic, self-righteous, and terribly earnest. Like Sarah Grimké, she watched her brothers get the education she yearned for. Unlike Grimké, she was able to work and save for nine years in order to enter Oberlin College, the first college in the United States to admit blacks and women. But female students were not admitted under equal conditions: Stone fretted at having to take a shorter and easier program of studies, at being denied participation in the debating program, and at having to do the weekly laundry, along with the other women, for the whole school. When she became a teacher, she found herself earning $14 per month while her brother had earned $30 in the same post. Her earliest experiences, she said, made her "a disappointed woman." From this came her commitment to feminism: "In education, in marriage, in religion, in everything, disappointment is the lot of woman. It shall be the business of my life to deepen this disappointment in every woman's heart until she bows down to it no longer."[89]

When at the age of nineteen Stone listened to her clergyman read aloud a minister's letter attacking the Grimkés for public speaking, she claimed that it "broke my bonds." She joined the antislavery campaign but could not resist speaking on women's issues. She finally worked out a compromise with the Anti-Slavery Society that allowed her to lecture on abolition on the weekends, when large crowds attended, and on women's rights on her own time, during the week. Her primness and childlike demeanour masked her determination: "I expect to plead not for the slave only, but for suffering humanity everywhere. ESPECIALLY DO I MEAN TO LABOR FOR THE ELEVATION OF MY SEX."[90]

In her private life as well, Stone was representative of American feminists. Unlike many European feminists, the Americans tended to marry late and to enjoy supportive, near-egalitarian relationships with husbands sympathetic to and often active in women's causes. Wary of losing her independence, Lucy Stone was finally won over by Henry Blackwell, an antislavery reformer and advocate of women's equality. At their wedding in 1855 they read a protest against the laws that oppressed women in marriage. Stone insisted on keeping her own name, even later refusing the opportunity of voting for school elections in Massachusetts rather than registering under her married name as the law required.

Lucy Stone and Henry Blackwell seem to have enjoyed a happy, companionate marriage, editing together the *Woman's Journal.* Nonetheless, Stone, like Angelina Grimké before her and so many after her, felt bound to prove that feminism was not incompatible with homemaking. She prided herself on making her own bread, soap, and preserves. When her daughter was born, she gave up lecturing temporarily rather than leave her with a nursemaid. On one night out she went to hear a lecture on Joan of Arc, which left her feeling "as though all things were possible to me." But when she came home and looked at her sleeping child, so vulnerable, "I shrank like a snail into its shell and saw that for these years I can be only a mother."[91] All feminists struggled to balance their private and public duties. Most, like Stone, were prepared to step aside from reform work until their childrearing duties were over.

The rights of women to participate freely in the abolition struggle and to speak out in public were not the only items on the white feminist agenda. In the 1840s, women's health became an issue, widely discussed in female physiological societies. Reform also came from a different direction, in the form of a protest against the lack of married women's property rights. Among the campaigners in New York State were Ernestine Potowski Rose, Paulina Wright Davis, and Elizabeth Cady Stanton, all to be influential in the subsequent women's rights movement. Women's advocates also registered their dislike of sexist language: Antoinette Brown spoke of "our sisternity," and Maria Weston Chapman wrote in 1839, "Let us strike manful and womanful for justice and freedom."[92]

Yet white Americans were not as attentive to working women's needs as were the French feminists. Their rural and small town New England or New York background isolated them from urban and industrial problems and made it easier to focus on moral reforms than on material ones. Although class and sectarian differences were to be found among white reformers, their common ethnicity and Protestantism limited their tolerance for Catholics, Natives, Irish, and the "inferior classes" as well as for blacks. Angelina Grimké, who criticized viewing the poor as "unfortunate *in*feriors, not as our *suffering equals*"[93] was in this regard unique.

The first wave of feminism, that is, the organized women's movements and in particular the suffrage campaign, has usually dominated accounts of nineteenth-century feminism. But feminism was well represented earlier in the century by courageous and imaginative pathbreakers, who were among the first to act on their conviction that women suffered under male dominance.

Four aspects of this phase of feminism are noteworthy. First, it was tied to other movements, both radical and reformist. Feminists could and did exist in isolation. One hears, for example, of the North American bride in the early nineteenth century "who simply walked out of the church when she discovered that the wedding ceremony required that she promise to obey."[94] But only when feminists became part of a context that legitimized demands for change did they find the inspiration and support they needed to begin working together actively together on behalf of women.

Second, participants in early nineteenth-century feminism came from varied backgrounds. Whereas white American feminists tended to come from rural or small town backgrounds, sharing a common culture and heritage as well as economic security, the background of black Americans was more varied. Europeans were frequently lower middle or upper working class, often crossing class lines in their quest for economic independence. Whether American or European, feminists saw themselves as spokespeople for all women, a position that would become more difficult as class and racial tensions increased in the second part of the century.

Third, and following from both the preceding points, feminists embraced a wide range of concerns. The vision of feminists mirrored the hopes of their radical and reformist associates; it was an optimism born of the first flush of political and economic change, which seemed amenable to direction by dedicated people, working together. Experience modified this vision: the sexual freedom advocated by Fourier and the early Saint-Simonians gave way to concerns for economic independence or for an idealized family. By the late 1840s, feminists were more concerned to elevate their role within the family than to challenge the importance of family as an institution.

Perhaps this evolution helps us to understand those aspects of nineteenth-century feminism that seem conservative to us today. In the context of lack of women's rights in marriage, increased desertions, decreased opportunities, and continuing evidence of traditional misogyny, talk about an idealized family had revolutionary overtones. Nineteenth-century women saw their emancipation in society's recognition of their special contribution and the elimination of any barriers to it. Control over family life was a feminist goal. Modern feminists have been disappointed and frustrated by earlier feminists' reluctance to challenge traditional gender roles, but the political significance of such reluctance must be weighed in their context, not our own. While celebrating gender differences, these advocates never backed away from insisting on identical moral responsibilities. This had been Mary Wollstonecraft's argument fifty years earlier; now feminists had begun to put it into practice.

Fourth, we must keep in mind that the feminists we have been describing formed a relatively small minority, as was true of the members of the reform movements in general. In each country there were no more than a few hundred women at the most who discussed and popularized feminist ideas. The unsettled political and economic conditions that inspired radicals and reformers encouraged most of their contemporaries to dedicate their lives to finding security rather than jeopardizing it. For most North Americans the early nineteenth century meant an opportunity for material as well as moral improvement. For many Europeans the beginnings of the transition to an urban, industrial society left little energy or time for radical politics. The great bulk of the population on both sides of the Atlantic still lived in rural areas, well isolated from new ideas or aspirations. In such a context, what is remarkable is the existence of feminism rather than its lack of widespread support.

NOTES

1 Barbara Taylor, *Eve and the New Jerusalem: Socialism and Feminism in the Nineteenth Century* (London: Virago Press, 1991), 153.

2 "Louise Otto (1849)," in *Women, the Family, and Freedom: The Debate in Documents*, ed. Susan Groag Bell and Karen M. Offen, vol. 1, *1750–1880* (Stanford: Stanford University Press, 1983), 263.

3 Kathryn Kish Sklar, *Catharine Beecher: A Study in American Domesticity* (New York: W.W. Norton, 1973), 83.

4 Quoted in Ellen Carol DuBois, ed., *Elizabeth Cady Stanton, Susan B. Anthony: Correspondence, Writings, Speeches* (New York: Schocken, 1981), 8.

5 Quoted in Sklar, *Catharine Beecher*, 135.

6 Quoted in Jane Rendall, *The Origins of Modern Feminism: Women in Britain, France, and the United States 1780–1860* (Basingstoke: Macmillan, 1985), 120.

7 Taylor, *Eve and the New Jerusalem*, 123–24.

8 Ibid., 165.

9 Quoted in Elaine Showalter, "Florence Nightingale's Feminist Complaint: Women, Religion, and *Suggestions for Thought*," *Signs: Journal of Women in Culture and Society* 6, 3 (1981): 405.

10 Nancy F. Cott, *The Bonds of Womanhood: "Woman's Sphere" in New England, 1780–1835* (New Haven, CT: Yale University Press, 1977), 194.

11 Taylor, *Eve and the New Jerusalem*, 72.

12 Quoted in ibid., 20.

13 Quoted in Jonathan Beecher, *Charles Fourier: The Visionary and His World* (Berkeley: University of California Press, 1986), 206.

14 "Charles Fourier (1808)," in *Women, the Family, and Freedom,* ed. Bell and Offen, 41. Fourier has long been unjustifiably credited with coining the word "feminism."

15 Richard Pankhurst, "Introduction," in William Thompson, *Appeal of One Half the Human Race, Women, Against the Pretensions of the Other Half, Men, to Retain Them in Political, and thence in Civil and Domestic Slavery* (London: Virago, 1983), i.

16 Thompson, *Appeal*, xxi, xxiii, xxx, 63.

17 Taylor, *Eve and the New Jerusalem*, 63.

18 Thompson, *Appeal*, 73.

19 Harriet Jacobs, *Incidents in the Life of a Slave Girl: Written by Herself* (1861; reprint, Cambridge, MA: Harvard University Press, 1987), 77.

20 Thompson, *Appeal*, xxiii.

21 Quoted in Taylor, *Eve and the New Jerusalem*, 218.

22 Quoted in ibid., 153.

23 Ibid., 133.

24 "Charles Fourier (1832)," in *Women, the Family, and Freedom,* ed. Bell and Offen, 145.

25 Quoted in Taylor, *Eve and the New Jerusalem,* 214.

26 Carl Guarneri, *The Utopian Alternative: Fourierism in Nineteenth-Century America* (Ithaca, NY: Cornell University Press, 1991), 200. In the United States alone there were about fifteen Owenite communities set up in the 1820s and about thirty Fourierist communities in the 1840s.

27 Carol A. Kolmerten, *Women in Utopia: The Ideology of Gender in the American Owenite Communities* (Bloomington: Indiana University Press, 1990), 79, 171.

28 Quoted in Guarneri, *The Utopian Alternative,* 209.

29 Quoted in Kolmerten, *Women in Utopia,* 53.

30 Quoted in Guarneri, *The Utopian Alternative,* 209–10.

31 Quoted in Malcolm L. Thomis and Jennifer Grimmett, *Women in Protest 1800–1850* (London: Croom Helm, 1982), 92.

32 Quoted in ibid., 134, 107.

33 Quoted in Taylor, *Eve and the New Jerusalem,* 96.

34 Quoted in Thomis and Grimmett, *Women in Protest,* 86.

35 Quoted in Taylor, *Eve and the New Jerusalem,* 99, 109.

36 Ibid., 73, 74.

37 Quoted in Thomas Dublin, *Women at Work: The Transformation of Work and Community in Lowell, Massachusetts, 1826–1860* (New York: Columbia University Press, 1979), 91.

38 Claire Goldberg Moses, *French Feminism in the Nineteenth Century* (Albany: State University of New York Press, 1984), 47, 50.

39 Suzanne [Voilquin] in *Tribune des femmes,* in *Feminism, Socialism, and French Romanticism,* ed. Claire Goldberg Moses and Leslie Wahl Rabine (Bloomington: Indiana University Press, 1993), 303.

40 Quoted in Moses, *French Feminism,* 70.

41 Moses and Rabine, eds., *Feminism, Socialism, and French Romanticism,* 7 and Joséphine-Félicité [Milizet] in *Tribune des femmes,* in ibid., 291.

42 Marie-Reine [Reine Guindorf] in *Tribune des femmes,* 287 and Suzanne [Voilquin] in *Tribune des femmes,* 294, both in *Feminism, Socialism, and French Romanticism,* ed. Moses and Rabine.

43 Jeanne-Désirée [Veret] in *Tribune des femmes,* in ibid., 296.

44 Suzanne [Voilquin] in *Tribune des femmes,* in ibid., 306.

45 Claire Goldberg Moses, "'Difference' in Historical Perspective: Saint-Simonian Feminism," in ibid., 43. Claire Démar was an exception. She proposed to Enfantin that "women should head families and men raise children" (p. 59).

46 Quoted in Moses, *French Feminism,* 148.

47 Marie-Reine [Reine Guinsdorf], "To Women," in *Feminism, Socialism, and French Romanticism,* ed. Moses and Rabine, 315.

48 Quoted in Maïté Albistur and Daniel Armogathe, *Histoire du féminisme français du moyen âge à nos jours* (Paris: des femmes, 1977), 285 (my translation).

49 Flora Tristan, *Women Travelers* (1835), 2 and *Méphis* (1838), 46, in *Flora Tristan, Utopian Feminist: Her Travel Diaries and Personal Crusade,* ed. and trans. Doris and Paul Beik (Bloomington and Indianapolis: Indiana University Press, 1993).

50 Flora Tristan, *Workers' Union* (1843), in ibid., 121, 106.

51 Quoted in S. Joan Moon, "Feminism and Socialism: The Utopian Synthesis of Flora Tristan," in *Socialist Women: European Socialist Feminism in the Nineteenth and Early Twentieth Centuries,* ed. Marilyn Boxer and Jean H. Quataert (New York: Elsevier, 1978), 24–25.

52 Quoted in Máire Cross and Tim Gray, *The Feminism of Flora Tristan* (Oxford: Berg, 1992), 105.

53 Quoted in Moses, *French Feminism,* 128.

54 Quoted in ibid., 130

55 "Jeanne Deroin (1849)" in *Women, the Family, and Freedom,* ed. Bell and Offen, 263.

56 Quoted in Rendall, *Origins of Modern Feminism,* 294.

57 David A. Powell, *George Sand* (Boston: Twayne Publishers, 1990), 29.

58 Quoted in Albistur and Armogathe, *Histoire du féminisme français,* 302 (my translation).

59 "Louise Otto (1851)," in *Women, the Family, and Freedom,* ed. Bell and Offen, 297, 298, 297.

60 Moses, *French Feminism,* 147, 149.

61 "Jeanne Deroin and Pauline Roland (1851)," in *Women, the Family, and Freedom,* ed. Bell and Offen, 289.

62 Quoted in Celia Morris Eckhardt, *Fanny Wright: Rebel in America* (Cambridge, MA: Harvard University Press, 1984), 148, 11, 166.

63 Quoted in Kolmerten, *Women in Utopia,* 119.

64 Quoted in Eckhardt, *Fanny Wright,* 156, 172.

65 Frances Wright, "Of Free Enquiry," (1829) in *The Feminist Papers: From Adams to de Beauvoir,* ed. Alice S. Rossi (New York: Columbia University Press, 1973), 109.

66 Quoted in Eckhardt, *Fanny Wright,* 3, 265, 250, 290.

67 Quoted in Blanche Hersh, *The Slavery of Sex, Feminist-Abolitionists in America* (Urbana: University of Illinois Press, 1978), 206.

68 Quoted in Barbara J. Berg, *The Remembered Gate: Origins of American Feminism: The Woman and the City 1800–1860* (New York: Oxford University Press, 1978), 181, 185.

69 Quoted in ibid., 204, 206, 255.

70 Quoted in ibid., 257, 258, 231.

71 Maria W. Miller Stewart, "Lecture Delivered at the Franklin Hall" (1832), in *Man Cannot Speak for Her,* ed. Karlyn Kohrs Campbell, vol. 2, *Key Texts of the Early Feminists* (New York: Greenwood Press, 1989), 3.

72 Ibid., 5, 7, 4.

73 Maria W. Stewart, "Religion and the Pure Principles of Morality" (1831), in *Black Women in Nineteenth-Century American Life: Their Words, Their Thoughts, Their Feelings,* ed. Bert James Loewenberg and Ruth Bogin (University Park: Pennsylvania State University Press, 1976), 189.

74 Hersh, *Slavery of Sex,* 4.

75 Quoted in Catherine M. Prelinger, *Charity, Challenge and Change: Religious Dimensions of the Mid-Nineteenth-Century Women's Movement in Germany* (New York: Greenwood Press, 1987), 38.

76 Quoted in ibid., 80.

77 Quoted in ibid., 135.

78 Quoted in Gerda Lerner, *The Grimké Sisters from South Carolina: Pioneers for Woman's Rights and Abolition* (New York: Schocken Books, 1967), 153.

79 Quoted in Hersh, *Slavery of Sex,* 43, 42.

80 Quoted in Lerner, *The Grimké Sisters,* 191–92.

81 Quoted in Shirley J. Yee, *Black Women Abolitionists: A Study in Activism, 1828–1860* (Knoxville: University of Tennessee Press, 1992), 144.

82 Ibid., 137.

83 Quoted in Julie Winch, "'You Have Talents—Only Cultivate Them': Philadelphia's Black Female Literary Societies and the Abolitionist Crusade," in *The Abolitionist Sisterhood: Women's Political Culture in Antebellum America,* ed. Jean Fagan Yellin and John C. Van Horne (Ithaca, NY, and London: Cornell University Press, 1994), 114.

84 Quoted in Lerner, *The Grimké Sisters,* 161, 162.

85 Quoted in Carolyn Williams, "The Female Antislavery Movement: Fighting against Racial Prejudice and Promoting Women's Rights in Antebellum America," in *The Abolitionist Sisterhood,* ed. Yellin and Van Horne, 169.

86 Quoted in Hersh, *Slavery of Sex,* 34.

87 Kate Millett, *Sexual Politics* (New York: Avon Books, 1969, 1970), 80.

88 Quoted in Hersh, *Slavery of Sex,* 22, 40.

89 "Lucy Stone, Speech (1855)," in *Up from the Pedestal: Selected Writings in the History of American Feminism,* ed. Aileen S. Kraditor (Chicago: Quadrangle Books, 1968), 71.

90 Quoted in Hersh, *Slavery of Sex,* 23, 86.

91 Quoted in Ellen Carol Dubois, *Feminism and Suffrage: The Emergence of an Independent Women's Movement in America 1848–1869* (Ithaca, NY: Cornell University Press, 1978), 27.

92 Quoted in Hersh, *Slavery of Sex,* 200.

93 Quoted in ibid., 127.

94 Alison Prentice, Paula Bourne, Gail Cuthbert Brandt, Beth Light, Wendy Mitchinson, and Naomi Black, *Canadian Women: A History* (Toronto: Harcourt Brace Jovanovich, 1988), 90.

7

The Beginnings of
Organized Feminism

Are we here only for the sake of men?

AMALIE HOLST, 1802

*It is not for men, but for woman alone, to determine what
[her] sphere is, or is not.*

SUSAN B. ANTHONY, 1875

*[Feminism] is about having the opportunity to make your own decisions
and living your life as you want to live it, not in a way that society (men in
particular) wants you to live.*

LETTER TO THE *VANCOUVER SUN*, 1995

Whereas earlier activists appear for the most part isolated or eccentric, by
the 1850s and 1860s reformers in Europe and North America were organizing groups to campaign specifically on issues identified with women. This
development marks the beginning of what historians have called the first
women's movement, or first-wave feminism. Spanning three generations and
culminating in the vote for women during or just after World War I, this
movement was in fact many movements that seem surprisingly broad-
ranging. Participants attacked the male monopoly of education, professional
careers, and culture; married women's economic and legal dependence; sexual and moral double standards; women's lack of control over their bodies;
the drudgery of housework; low wages; and, not least, women's exclusion
from politics. Unifying all these campaigns was the determination that
women be allowed to define their own capabilities and goals.

By contrast, however, most reformers were content to accept the
restraints of race and class as natural and inevitable. In comparison to the

1854–56	Crimean War
1859	Charles Darwin writes *Origin of Species*
1859–70	Unification of Italy
1861	Emancipation of Russian serfs
1861–65	United States Civil War
1865	General German Women's Association founded
1867	Canadian Confederation
	First debate on women's suffrage in British parliament
1869	John Stuart Mill writes *The Subjection of Women*
	Josephine Butler launches Repeal Campaign in England
	National Woman Suffrage Association formed in United States
1871	French Third Republic founded
	Unification of Germany
1873	Woman's Christian Temperance Union founded in United States
1874	Girton College, Cambridge, founded in England
1875	Alexander Graham Bell invents the telephone
1879	August Bebel writes *Woman and Socialism*

association of feminism earlier in the century with movements for freedom from racial or economic oppression, such as antislavery or communitarian socialism, the women's movements of the mid- to late nineteenth century exhibit a narrower focus, what one might call a "status-oriented" feminism.[1] Since the participants were largely white and middle class, their goals reflected their desire for self-fulfilment and for greater influence in both family and public life. This chapter discusses, first, the background of these movements, second, the varied issues around which reformers organized, and, third, the extent to which they did or did not accomplish their goals.

THE CONTEXT OF WOMEN'S MOVEMENTS

By the 1850s industrialization was beginning to pay off in the form of increased wealth for many groups in society. The collapse of the early radical movements in Europe and the determination of governments and business to consolidate the gains of industrialization left the field open to liberal reformers. Advances in science and technology reinforced the conviction of the middle classes that this was an age of progress, as did reforms such as the abolition of slavery in the United States and of serfdom in Russia, nationalist movements in Germany, Italy, and Scandinavia, and the gradual extension of voting rights to adult white men.

Many observers, like John Stuart Mill in England, saw women's emancipation as an essential stage in the progressive liberalization of society. Similarly, the American feminist Elizabeth Cady Stanton reasoned, "This same law of equality that has revolutionized the state and the church is now knocking at the door of our homes and sooner or later there too it must do its work." The expansion of government and industry opened up possibilities to upwardly mobile men whose wives and daughters chafed at the gender restrictions that kept them from the same opportunities. Stanton raged at seeing women who "ignorantly made ladders of themselves by which fathers, husbands, brothers, and sons reached their highest ambitions."[2] Women like Stanton may very well have experienced a sense of decreased opportunity in comparison to their male counterparts, but perhaps more important was the optimistic climate. It created expectations of change that, when stymied by parental restrictions or professional barriers, sent conflicting messages to privileged women.

Most women activists were raised in some degree of material comfort; their fathers were usually business or professional men. Yet the term *middle class* can be misleading when applied to women who had few financial resources of their own or means of gaining them. Those born into economic security did not necessarily continue to live in it. Some, like Barbara Smith Bodichon in England or Maria Deraismes in France, inherited money and could live independently. Frances Power Cobbe, although from the English gentry, received only a modest allowance. Hubertine Auclert in France inherited an income that would have allowed her to live comfortably, but she preferred a self-imposed austerity, lecturing by candlelight and spending precious time searching out street people to sell her newspaper, few of whom returned with the proceeds. The American Susan B. Anthony also struggled to make ends meet although, unlike Auclert, she had no assets until near the end of her long life. Still, women who had worked as factory hands, domestic servants, or as farmers were conspicuously absent from feminist organizations.

Progress brought with it poverty, class, and racial tensions as the social consequences of industrialization, urbanization, and migration. The optimism and increased expectations that the middle classes enjoyed were rarely experienced by the working classes, whose members expended their energies in efforts to feed and clothe their families. Skilled workers aspired to join the ranks of the middle class, whose status was confirmed by homes in neighbourhoods far from city centres, at least one servant, smaller family size, elevated patterns of consumption, and, not least, by a wife and mother who did not work outside the home. While social inequality remained very much what it had been before the Industrial Revolution, society became more diverse, with a wide range of subgroups between the rich and the very poor.

Liberal reformers responded to these conditions with an alternative rationale for women's emancipation, seeing it not as the consequence of progress but rather as the guarantee for its continuation. The same process of modernization that produced factories and slums also created the possibility of women organizing for social reform and thereby another route to feminism. Those who were convinced of irreconcilable class tensions and the impossibility of reforming society were attracted instead to socialist movements that forecast revolution; they generally kept their distance from organized feminism. African-American women, dismayed by the indifference of most white women to racial issues, formed their own groups to deal with the effects of poverty and racism on black communities. As Frances Ellen Watkins Harper observed, "The white women go all for sex, letting race occupy a minor position."[3]

The immediate context for women's movements, the political environment, differed dramatically in different countries. The defeat of liberalism in Germany in 1848 and the country's unification under Bismarck by 1871 forced reformers to cope with a militaristic and authoritarian climate. In most parts of the country women were not permitted to join political parties or even to attend public meetings where politics were discussed. In France also, women were forbidden to participate in political clubs, and newspapers were subject to government censorship during the 1850s and 1860s. During the workers' uprising in Paris in 1871 many feminists were arrested and subsequently exiled. The first priority for French liberals in the 1870s and 1880s was safeguarding the fragile Third Republic, a task sometimes seen as at odds with women's rights because women were identified as sympathetic to the Catholic clergy, considered enemies of the Republic. The United States and Britain, in contrast, had long-standing liberal, representative governments, fortified by economic growth. The extension of male suffrage in the 1860s in both countries gave educated women with powerful connections the possibility of influencing constitutional change by appealing both to sympathetic politicians and to public opinion. The Civil War in the United States in 1861–65 had given a great boost to women's activism by encouraging the formation of thousands of aid societies, a massive petition drive to abolish slavery, and postwar reconstruction work in teaching and community welfare. Women's groups flourished after the war and by 1887 Susan B. Anthony began organizing the International Council of Women, an international federation that inspired and supported feminists elsewhere. Organization was dependent on urbanization and communications, however, and for that reason, feminist movements did not develop until the end of the century or later in rural areas such as southern Europe or the Canadian prairies.

GOALS AND CAMPAIGNS

Movements that spanned three generations, from the 1850s to the 1910s, necessarily varied their aims and direction. Nonetheless, one fundamental purpose united these activists: women must be allowed to set their goals and control their lives. The words used in a resolution written by the participants at an 1851 woman's rights convention in the United States echoed throughout this period and are worth quoting in full:

Resolved, that we deny the right of any portion of the species to decide for another portion, or of any individual to decide for another individual, what is and what is not their "proper sphere"; that the proper sphere for all human beings is the largest and highest to which they are able to attain; what this is, can not be ascertained without complete liberty of choice; woman, therefore, ought to choose for herself what sphere she will fill, what education she will seek, and what employment she will follow, and not be held bound to accept, in submission, the rights, the education, and the sphere which man thinks proper to allow her.[4]

Bold as this statement was, we should consider that it came from a political culture that still legitimized slavery and in which one could read chilling accounts by ex-slaves such as Sojourner Truth and Harriet Jacobs of what lack of "liberty of choice" could mean.

This attempt by upper- and middle-class women to define woman's sphere was a challenge to the separate spheres ideology that made politics and business the proper activities of men but which confined women to the home, to a life perceived as boring and useless. A year after the above resolution, Florence Nightingale in England made her own poignant appeal: "Why have women passion, intellect, moral activity—these three—and a place in society where no one of the three can be exercised?"[5] Thirty-six years later a young German, Lily von Kretschmann (Braun), under pressure from her parents to marry, echoed Nightingale's anguish: "I am twenty-three years old, healthy in mind and body, perhaps more able to achieve than many others and not only do I not work, I don't even live, rather my life is being arranged."[6] The American reformer Rheta Childe Dorr, subsequently a labour organizer, similarly described herself and her acquaintances: "We all lived in dolls' houses and I for one wanted to get out into the world of real things."[7]

Biological inferences from separate spheres ideology threatened to limit the options of women who were otherwise privileged. The Englishman George Hastings, in other respects sympathetic to feminism, saw woman's "destiny in life" as "dissimilar [to man's]. Man . . . is eminently a working animal, one intended to earn wages to maintain himself and those dependent upon him; whereas a married woman is eminently, essentially, and primarily a child-bearing animal."[8] Feminists found this distinction arbitrary and unjust. John Stuart Mill protested that "we ought . . . not to ordain that to be born a girl instead of a boy, any more than to be born black instead of white, or a commoner instead of a nobleman, shall decide the person's position through all life."[9] Mill's essay, *The Subjection of Women* (1869), was widely translated when it appeared and was instrumental in bringing many women and men to feminism.

The issues generally associated with first-wave feminism reflect the importance of property and status rather than racial struggle or economic survival. Feminists identified laws that gave husbands control over their wives' property, denied women access to education and jobs, and made men their legal guardians and political representatives as the immediate hindrances to women's self-determination. The result was a series of campaigns that targeted those inequities. The drive for personal autonomy further entailed an analysis of the extent to which institutions and social values were male dominated. "Woman is showing her innate wisdom," wrote American reformer Matilda Joslyn Gage, "in daring to question the infallibility of man, his laws, and his interpretation of her place in creation."[10] The attempt by these women to control their lives was simultaneously a rejection of the arbitrary boundary between public and private. Feminist reformers were united by a commitment to take control of their lives, influence society, and thereby break the hold of patriarchy as they experienced it. Let us turn from these common goals to look at the specific campaigns.

Education and the Professions

The twin goals of nineteenth-century women's movements were to improve the legal position of married women and to create the possibility of economic independence for single women. From the 1840s through to the end of the 1860s, reformers launched campaigns for married women's property rights and improved educational and employment opportunities. In 1848, American activists initiated a series of local and national equal rights conventions or open meetings to address a variety of issues. In the 1850s, women in Canada West (Ontario) lobbied for a married women's property act. In England, the 1856 petition drive of Barbara Smith Bodichon (1827–91) and Bessie Raynor Parkes (1829–1925) for married women's property reform was followed by the founding of the *English Woman's Journal* in 1858—with Bodichon as patron and Parkes as editor—and of the Society for Promoting the Employment of Women in the following year. Their partnership attracted other women from the same social and reformist background, who collectively became known as the Langham Place circle after the location of Bodichon's house.

In 1865, German feminists regrouped from the political repression following the failed revolution of 1848 to form the General German Women's Association and to renew their lobbying for educational and employment opportunities as a first step to securing other rights. Austrian feminists, worried about the plight of middle-class women following the economic ruin of many families after the military victory of Prussia in 1866, called for girls' education and the opening of civil service jobs to women. In France, the Society for the Amelioration of Woman's Condition, founded by Léon Richer and Maria Deraismes in 1870, lobbied for better education, the re-establishment of the right to divorce, and property rights for married women. Danish feminists founded the Danish Women's Union in 1871, and in Sweden feminists launched a Society for Married Women's Property Rights in 1873. In Russia as well, the 1860s and 1870s saw successful agitation for university education for women and attempts to solve the problem of female unemployment, an indirect consequence of the emancipation of the serfs. Even in such an isolated place as the Mexican Yucatán, feminists formed a society in 1870 and sponsored a secondary school for girls and a newspaper that was completely owned and operated by women.

Better education promised a beginning. Emily Davies, whose efforts in Britain culminated in the founding of Girton College for women at Cambridge in 1874, pointed out that it was not surprising that women who had no learning could find nothing to do. As had been the case for centuries, the "daughters of educated men," as the twentieth-century novelist Virginia Woolf would call them, hungered for the education reserved for their brothers and managed to secure it in informal ways, thanks to their high motivation and the co-operation of family members, usually fathers. Now more formal channels were in place. In 1865 the University of Zurich in Switzerland became the first European university to admit women. By the 1880s, the American women's colleges of Vassar, Smith, and Wellesley were offering women as tough an academic education as their male counterparts could get elsewhere; and Girton College provided the same kind of academic challenge to English women. Although secondary school education was available to French girls after 1880, it did not prepare them for university entrance. The few women who graduated from French universities had to study privately for the qualifying degree. Admission to German and Austrian universities did not come until the turn of the century.

The case for women's education was not self-evident to most educators. Stark financial considerations helped them to make up their minds. In most countries the expansion of ,public schooling created a demand for women teachers who would replace men at lower wages. Financial pressures led universities in the American Mid-west to admit women. European reformers dramatized the plight of "surplus" women, those unable to find suitable marriage partners as eligible men either delayed marriage or emigrated to colonies or the American West. These women needed new job opportunities and adequate training if they were to earn their own livelihoods, feminists pointed out. They envisioned preparation for professional careers, which would necessitate entry to academically oriented secondary schools, universities, and professional programs.

Arguments from utility rather than from justice tended also to shape demands for entry into the professions. In Germany, where men continued to monopolize public teaching, feminists argued that women were especially suited for educating girls. They rejected co-education since it would mean integrating girls into boys' schools taught by men. In all countries, reformers touted medicine as particularly appropriate for women, not only because of women's traditional association with nurturing and healing but also because Victorian modesty posed practical barriers between male doctors and female patients. Feminists stressed the benefit of having doctors who understood women's problems and could teach them about their bodies. In England, Josephine Butler greeted the medical practice of Elizabeth Garrett Anderson with great relief: "I gained more from her than from any other doctor . . . *because* I was able to *tell* her so much more than I ever could or would tell to any *man*."[11]

The women's movement offered crucial material and emotional support for the few women who were medical pioneers. One success story, a so-called feminist showplace, was the New England Hospital for Women and Children in Boston, established in 1862. Within ten years it had become one of the largest hospitals in Boston, and by 1887 it was completely run by women, "an island of feminist strength and sisterhood."[12] It offered unique benefits to both patients and physicians, dramatically reducing the incidence of puerperal disease in maternity patients by taking sanitary precautions and giving women doctors an opportunity for practical study that they could not get elsewhere. Sadly, the hospital's support for women doctors was limited by racism: when Dr. Caroline V. Still Anderson applied for a position, she was initially refused admission because she was black.

At a time when the medical profession was trying to establish its claim to scientific legitimacy and the exclusive right to make definitive pronouncements about women's sexuality, women doctors symbolized a challenge to male expertise. Josephine Butler challenged the attempt of doctors to extend their influence into local government through medical councils attached to government boards. "It is coming to be more & more a deadly fight for *our bodies*," she wrote.[13] Butler also led the drive, discussed below, to repeal the laws regulating prostitution in Britain. These laws authorized arbitrary detention of prostitutes but not their clients and compelled women to submit to medical examinations.

Successful professional women were under enormous pressure to defend their respectability. Martha Hamm Lewis, in the 1850s the only woman to attend a training school for teachers in New Brunswick, Canada, had to comply with requirements that she arrive ten minutes before the other students, sit alone at the back, wear a veil, and leave five minutes before the end of the lecture. The importance of ladylike decorum was stressed by all educators in an effort to tone down the dangers of any departure from tradition. In the late 1880s, student Janet Courtner agonized over whether to enter an Oxford University lecture hall alone when her chaperon failed to appear. (Courtner did.) Female students at Oberlin College in the United States were not allowed to appear before mixed audiences nor to read their own essays aloud in class until 1859. When Oberlin students elected Lucy Stone to give a graduation address in 1847, Stone refused to write one rather than have a man deliver it for her. The British educational pioneer Emily Davies avoided associating with "'masculine looking' women as a liability to the cause." Nor did successful completion of studies encourage behavioural non-conformity. Mary Putnam Jacobi, an American who was the first woman to attend the École de Medicine in Paris, was advised by her normally supportive father, "Be a *lady* from the dotting of your i's to the color of your ribbons—and if you must be a doctor, be an attractive and agreeable one."[14]

Fitness and Fashion

Critics found higher education not only unladylike but unhealthy for women. To the objection that women's fragile constitution was not suitable for such mental exertions, defenders of women's education insisted that nervous and physical breakdowns resulted from the lack of mental stimulation. British and American educators introduced physical fitness, usually in the form of gymnastics, into the curriculum in order to ensure the physical health of their female students. The American movement for women's health and fitness inspired Charlotte Perkins Gilman to keep as her "bedside Bible" William Blaikie's *How to Get Strong and How to Stay So* (1879). As a young woman, Gilman was exhilarated by long hikes, weightlifting, and running a seven-minute mile; at age eighteen she described herself in her diary as "Health, Perfect. Strength amazing."[15] Englishwoman Winifred Peck remembered sports as the high point of her school days: "But what freedom, what glory, to scamper about after one ball or another in sun or rain or wind as one of a team, as part of the school, on an equality, I felt, with my brothers at last."[16]

Health and practical considerations encouraged feminists to agitate for dress reform at a time when fashion dictated tightly laced corsets, heavy petticoats and crinolines or hoops, long trailing skirts, and dropped shoulders that restricted arm motion. Yet most would-be dress reformers found social pressures too formidable. According to the report of the Woman's Rights Convention held in Syracuse, New York, in 1852, "In no one respect were the participants in these early Conventions more unsparingly ridiculed, and more maliciously falsified, than in their personal appearance." The reporter hastened to reassure that the participants were in fact "superior" in their dress "to the mass of women."[17] Similarly defensive, Elizabeth Garrett Anderson, in her efforts to enter the medical profession, said of her detractors, "I am glad they cannot say I am masculine. . . . I am very careful to dress well habitually, rather more richly in fact than I should care to do if I were not in some sort defending the cause by doing so."[18]

In the United States, a few women, including Elizabeth Cady Stanton and Amelia Bloomer, bravely adopted the outfit of tunic and short skirt over long loose trousers named after Bloomer but designed by Elizabeth Smith Miller in 1850. Stanton enjoyed two years of what she called "incredible freedom" before succumbing to "the persistent persecution and petty annoyances suffered at every turn."[19] Nor was the Rational Dress Society in England any more successful in promoting its combination of skirt and knee-length trousers. By the end of the century, the bicycle succeeded where decades of discussion failed; it, more than anything else, promoted dress reform and prompted the ever-hopeful Stanton to remark, "Many a woman is riding to the suffrage on a bicycle."[20]

Culture and Careers

Other women challenged the male monopoly on literature and ideas by founding literary clubs and pursuing careers as authors. As early as 1836, the city of Philadelphia boasted three African-American women's literary societies. A New York club, Sorosis, begun in 1868 by Jane Cunningham Croly, provided professional contacts and support for women journalists. A study of 194 British feminists found that the largest occupational group of women after teachers comprised poets, novelists, writers, editors, and translators. Careers in education and writing, which did not necessarily involve a life-long commitment, facilitated the work pattern of middle-class women with intermittent family responsibilities.

The growing acceptance of the connection between women and literature by the 1870s helped alleviate women's "anxiety of authorship," discussed
in Chapter 3. For many women the novel became a vehicle of protest, however indirect, against male privilege. The domestic novel, which appeared in
the United States between the 1820s and the 1870s, dramatized the lives of
ordinary women and depicted strong female communities. Louisa May
Alcott's *Little Women* (1868) is an enduring example. American suffragist
Susan B. Anthony read and re-read the novels of British writer Charlotte
Brontë and poet Elizabeth Barrett Browning, inspired by their portrayal of
"strong-minded women." Fredrika Bremer in Sweden used her novel *Hertha*
(1856) to describe "the patriarchal bonds which keep back the growth of
woman's mind and social life in Sweden, and which sometimes amounts [*sic*]
to the most crushing tyranny."[21] Olive Schreiner's novel *The Story of an
African Farm* (1883) featured a young women often described as the first real
feminist heroine, who refused to give up her independence to marry, even
when she became pregnant.

Journalism also attracted women. African-Canadian Mary Ann Shadd
Cary, the first woman to establish and produce a newspaper in Canada,
began editing the *Provincial Freeman* in 1853; it dealt with antislavery, temperance, and women's rights. Swedish feminists began publishing the *Home
Journal* in the 1860s. In 1867 Angela Grassi began directing the Spanish journal *El Correo de la Moda*. From 1868 the fortnightly *La Donna,* founded by
eighteen-year-old Alaide Gaulberta Beccari, gave readers news of feminist
activity throughout Italy. Betsy Perk of the Netherlands published women's
news magazines in the 1870s. Near the end of the century, Pauline Elizabeth
Hopkins helped found the *Colored American Magazine*. The articles she
wrote for the journal included a biographical series titled "Famous Women
of the Negro Race" and her reflections on "Heroes and Heroines in Black."
British journalists published over one hundred weekly and monthly feminist
periodicals between 1850 and 1930, and in France journalists put out approx-
imately fifty feminist periodicals between 1868 and 1914. The most famous
was *La Fronde,* founded in the 1890s. Its name referred to the seventeenth-
century war against the French monarchy, and it was the first daily newspaper to be directed, edited, written, and printed entirely by women. The
quality of its literary reviews, informational articles, news, features on sports,
health, and spiritualism gained it an international reputation. As a model of
non-sectarianism, the paper each day printed the date according to the
Gregorian, republican, orthodox, and Jewish calenders.

Marriage Reform

The fight for equal education and career opportunities was designed to benefit single rather than married women, but the ideal of self-determination
applied to both groups and its implications for married women threatened to
radicalize relations between the sexes. American feminists held marriage
reform to be of paramount importance in comparison to other issues. Laura
Bullard, in a newspaper run by Elizabeth Cady Stanton and Susan B.
Anthony and appropriately titled *The Revolution,* wrote in 1870,

Olive Schreiner's Story of an African Farm *(1883) shocked its readers with a heroine who became a mother but refused to marry. Here Lyndall tries to describe to her childhood friend what it means to be a woman.*

"Look at this little chin of mine, Waldo, with the dimple in it. It is but a small part of my person; but though I had a knowledge of all things under the sun, and the wisdom to use it, and the deep loving heart of an angel, it would not stead me through life like this little chin. I can win money with it, I can win love; I can win power with it, I can win fame. What would knowledge help me? The less a woman has in her head the lighter she is for climbing. I once heard an old man say, that he never saw intellect help a woman so much as a pretty ankle; and it was the truth. They begin to shape us to our cursed end," she said, with her lips drawn in to look as though they smiled, "when we are tiny things in shoes and socks. We sit with our little feet drawn up under us in the window, and look out at the boys in their happy play. We want to go. Then a loving hand is laid on us: 'Little one, you cannot go,' they say; 'your little face will burn, and your nice white dress be spoiled.' We feel it must be for our good, it is so lovingly said; but we cannot understand; and we kneel still with one little cheek wistfully pressed against the pane. Afterwards we go and thread blue beads, and make a string for our neck; and we go and stand before the glass. We see the complexion we were not to spoil, and the white frock, and we look into our own great eyes. Then the curse begins to act on us. It finishes its work when we are grown women, who no more look out wistfully at a more healthy life; we are contented. We fit our sphere as a Chinese woman's foot fits her shoe, exactly, as though God had made both—and yet he knows nothing of either. In some of us the shaping to our end has been quite completed. The parts we are not to use have been quite atrophied, and have even dropped off; but in others, and we are not less to be pitied, they have been wakened and left. We wear the bandages, but our limbs have not grown to them; we know that we are compressed, and chafe against them."

The ballot is not even half the loaf; it is only a crust—a crumb. The ballot touches only those interests, either of women or men, which take their root in political questions. But woman's chief discontent is not with her political, but with her social, and particularly her marital bondage. The solemn and profound question of marriage . . . is of more vital consequence . . . than any such superficial and fragmentary question as woman's suffrage.[22]

The preoccupation with marriage reform is a good example of the racial and class bias of feminism at this time because for African-American, African-Canadian, and working-class women the family could be a source of strength. Emancipation brought ex-slaves their first opportunity to create legal and stable families; they luxuriated in the novelty of freely entering into marriage and establishing two-parent households. Women who had been valued principally as workers took pride in their roles as wives and mothers and in their husbands' ability to provide for them. Their obligations to family and kin took priority over individualist claims for self-fulfilment. Linda Brent, the protagonist of an autobiographical narrative written by ex-slave Harriet Jacobs in 1861, recounts her ordeal in escaping from slavery in the American South but at the book's end yearns to cap her freedom with "a hearthstone of my own, however humble."[23] For all working-class women, attention to domestic duties could be a form of resistance against economic compulsion and the stereotypes that defined them primarily in terms of their work outside the home, at least outside their own homes. Because most of them continued to work outside the home they were probably not as dependent on their husbands as white, middle-class women.

In Britain, the United States, and English Canada, the subjection of free women in marriage according to common law had been summarized in the eighteenth century by the English jurist William Blackstone, who had described the wife's legal existence as incorporated into that of her husband. Frances Power Cobbe, an English feminist, used an unforgettable analogy, comparing marriage to the enclosure of two tarantulas in a bell jar: "When one of these delightful creatures is placed under a glass with a companion of his own species, a little smaller than himself, he forthwith gobbles him up."[24] Feminists were determined to transform this hierarchical relationship, so at odds with the principles of liberalism, into one of equality.

An attack on inequality in marriage was an attack on both the patriarchal family and the notion that women's domestic powers were a compensation for their legal disabilities. Securing married women's right to own property was thus a priority. In the United States it may have been more important than the antislavery campaign in precipitating the 1848 meeting in Seneca Falls, New York, which initiated women's rights conventions. Reformers such as Ernestine Potowski Rose, a Polish newcomer to America, had campaigned hard for property rights in New York State, and a Married Women's Property Law was adopted just a few months before the historic women's rights meeting. In Britain married women's property reform was initially the first priority, but feminists fell back on education and employment issues in the 1860s, perhaps because their attack on marriage proved too threatening, just as the Americans would retreat from a radical position on divorce reform. Elizabeth Cady Stanton, who championed a more radical approach to marriage, found it "galling" for a "proud woman" to be "dependent upon a husband's bounty."[25] The matter was even more vital to married wage earners, who had no control over their earnings, and the campaign in England highlighted the plight of working women.

Property law reform also raised the issue of suffrage, as the right to vote was closely linked to ownership of property. Acknowledgment of married women's economic rights could serve as a basis for arguing for their political rights. Other related issues were child custody, guardianship rights for mothers, and equality in divorce, although feminists were divided over the last of these issues, being aware of the adverse economic effects women often suffered from divorce.

Feminists were concerned not only to improve women's status once they married but also to give middle-class women a realistic choice, supported by the possibility of economic independence, of whether to marry or not. "Marriage, to women as to men," asserted Susan B. Anthony, "must be a luxury, not a necessity; an incident of life, not all of it."[26] Anthony, who concluded that "the women who *will not be ruled* must live without marriage,"[27] was one of the few American feminists of her generation to remain single. Married women were prominent, usually a majority, in feminist movements at this time in all countries, but those who married often did so late and after much deliberation. Olive Schreiner, for example, did not marry until she was nearly forty, and even then she insisted on being financially independent and keeping her own name. Hannah Mitchell, a working-class English woman who married in 1895, reflected, "Perhaps if I had really understood my own nature, as I came to do later, I should not have married, for I soon realized that married life, as men understand it, calls for a degree of self-abnegation which was impossible for me. I needed solitude, time for study, and the opportunity for a wider life."[28]

Most feminists were more hopeful about their ability to marry without compromising their ideals. Some couples followed the precedent established by Robert Dale Owen and Mary Jane Robinson in 1832 in writing a marriage contract. Prior to marrying Harriet Taylor in 1851, John Stuart Mill put in writing his protest against "the odious powers" that the law conferred upon him as a married man and promised "never in any case or under any circumstances to use them."[29] In France, Hubertine Auclert interrupted civil marriage ceremonies to denounce marriage as women's subservience until the courts prohibited her demonstrations. Auclert later enjoyed a happy and affectionate marriage, cut short by her husband's death.

Women like Schreiner were following an earlier precedent in refusing to adopt their husbands' names. One hapless man who nominated Mrs Stephen Smith to a committee at an American Woman's Rights Convention in 1852 was sternly reminded by the president that "Woman's Rights' women do not like to be called by their husbands' names, but by their own."[30] Hubertine Auclert compared the custom of wives changing their names to that of Roman slaves taking the names of their masters. She proposed instead that all adult French women be called madame, regardless of marital status. Participants at international women's congresses held at Paris between 1878 and 1913 agreed that married women should be able to keep their maiden names. British and German feminists often added their husbands' names to their own, and some men added their wives' names to their own, as did Olive Schreiner's husband, Samuel Cronwright Schreiner.

Work and Home-Work

Although their attack on traditional marriage makes clear that nineteenth-century feminists did not simply confine themselves to improving women's position in public life, as historians have sometimes argued, it is true that they generally failed to recognize the extent to which male privilege rested on men's exemption from parenting and household duties. With some exceptions, such as the American Anna Denton Cridge's utopian novel, *Men's Rights; or, How Would You Like It?* (1870), the attack on separate spheres ideology usually stopped short of questioning the division of labour in the home. For this reason, while feminists spoke of women's sphere as unlimited, in practice it could come uncomfortably close to how society conventionally defined it. French feminist Léon Richer explained, "The family is [woman's] primary home for action, her preferred environment, her natural atmosphere; yes, this is primarily where her influence must be felt." He added, "By liberating woman . . . nobody intended by that to give her the absurd advice to abandon her sex. Nobody said that she should stop caring for her children or having her husband support them. . . . No, woman must remain woman; she can do nothing better."[31]

Although the more conservative political and social environment in Europe made it difficult for feminists to criticize the family, its reform nonetheless became their goal. Under the twin influences of Saint-Simonian idealism and the pedagogy of Friedrich Froebel, German reformers attempted to counter the militaristic ethos prevailing in society with a vision of "spiritual motherhood." Froebel, an innovator in early childhood education, stressed the importance of the mother–child bond. Maternal love would encourage the independence and self-reliance of the child while harmonizing the relations between the individual and the community. The goal of reformers was a woman-centred family, which would act as an agent of social harmony and progressive influence, similar to the republican motherhood ideas promulgated earlier in the United States and France. Female values would offset the masculine emphasis on warfare and politics, and women's social service would rank as the equivalent of men's military service. Some historians see this as a retreat from an earlier equal rights position, citing as an example the modest goal of Auguste Schmidt, co-founder of the General German Women's Association: "And surely as the only true family is one in which the woman takes on the respected role of a helper, so our associations will achieve their full effect only when women become helpers for the social tasks of the time."[32]

Yet even this position appeared radical to conservatives. The organization's petition in 1876 pressing for mothers' custodial rights was unsuccessful. A later petition asking the Prussian minister of education in 1886 to allow girls' education under women's control in order to encourage girls to develop their potential, encountered the response that "women should be educated only for the role of wifely 'helpmate.'"[33]

Defence of the traditional family also came from socialists in the 1860s and 1870s. Dismayed at the changes they attributed to capitalism, they substituted a sentimentalized version of family life for the feminist critique of the earlier utopian socialists. Pierre Joseph Proudhon, who had argued that women had one-third the physical, moral, and intellectual capacity of men, so influenced the French section of the International Workingman's Association that in 1866, one year after his death, it honoured his memory by resolving that women be barred from work outside the home. Influenced by Ferdinand Lasalle, German socialists who emigrated to the United States regarded "the restoration of family unity" as "one of the most beautiful aims"[34] of socialism and in 1875 called for statutory restriction of women's work. The divisive nature of the issue was apparent at the founding congress of the Social Democratic Party in Germany in 1869 when dual motions were presented, one supporting equal wages for women, the other proposing the abolition of female labour in the workforce.

By the 1880s, due to the growing influence of Marxism, Lasalle's and Proudhon's views had become less popular. Karl Marx described women's entry into the labour force as part of the relentless development of capitalism, which would prepare the way for the inevitable victory of the proletariat. Although Friedrich Engels in particular was sympathetic to women's oppression and analyzed its historical origins in *The Origins of the Family, Private Property, and the State* (1884), he tied women's emancipation to that of all workers and subordinated it to the class struggle. Demands for equal rights for women were regarded as bourgeois distractions, irrelevant to the larger issue. The famous German revolutionary, Rosa Luxembourg, dismissed female emancipation as "old ladies' nonsense."[35] The German socialist August Bebel took a more positive position. His *Woman and Socialism* (1879) proved enormously popular, inspiring many women to join the socialist movement and influencing the socialist groups in the Second International of socialist workers (1889–1914) to support equal pay for women, protective legislation, and equal rights. Although he advocated the complete equality of women in the public sphere, Bebel nonetheless foresaw a clear division of labour in the future: men "would shoulder responsibility for the 'defence of the realm' and women the 'care of hearth and home.'"[36]

Not only did most feminists accept their responsibility for the home, but at this time they also generally saw marriage and especially motherhood as incompatible with a full-time career outside the home. New ideas about childhood stressed the importance of the early years and the special role of mothers, who alone could respond to the child's psychological needs and develop its social and creative potential.

Of course, not all married women were mothers, and not all mothers were content at home. As early as 1857 Barbara Smith Bodichon had suggested that married women could make important contributions to society, and she also valued women's domestic work. "Women who act as house keepers, nurses, and instructors of their children," she wrote, "often do as much for the support of the household as their husbands; and it is very unfair for men to speak of supporting a wife and children when such is the case."[37] Always unconventional, Bodichon wrote home from her New Orleans honeymoon that her husband was doing the housekeeping, marketing, and cooking. To her regret she never had children.

In the 1880s the views of another English woman, Mona Caird, on the importance of economic independence for all women anticipated the ideas of Charlotte Perkins Gilman and Olive Schreiner some years later. Caird insisted that a free marriage had to be founded on women's economic independence and that women should not be tempted to marry or stay married "For the sake of bread and butter."[38] Similarly Dr. Elizabeth Garrett Anderson boldly concluded that "the woman question will never be solved in any complete way so long as marriage is thought to be incompatible with freedom and with an independent career."[39] She defied the dire predictions of her contemporaries by continuing her career while married and raising three children, albeit with the help of a wet nurse, nanny, and other servants. In the 1890s, the African-American crusader Ida B. Wells-Barnett brought her infant son along on a speaking tour. In her autobiography she wrote, "I honestly believe that I am the only woman in the United States who ever travelled with a nursing baby to make political speeches."[40] Nonetheless, when her second child was born, Wells-Barnett decided to remain at home.

While no one at this time suggested abolishing the division of labour in the home, many complained about the enervating effects of housework. Innovations such as piped water, gas stoves and lighting, and manufactured goods, as well as an increase in female servants and a decline in the birth rate, eased many traditional household tasks for urban middle-class women, but higher standards of housekeeping, child rearing, and consumerism left many with little time or energy for other work. Charlotte Perkins Gilman, who found housework particularly debilitating, observed, "If each man did for himself the work he expects of his woman, there would be no wealth in the world; only millions and millions of poor tired men, sweeping, dusting, scrubbing, cleaning, serving, mending, cooking, washing, ironing."[41] The relatively well-off Elizabeth Cady Stanton wrote, "How much I do long to be free from housekeeping and children, so as to have some time to read, and think, and write." Overwhelmed with the burden of caring for seven children, she deferred full-time work in the movement until her children were older. "I pace up and down these two chambers of mine like a caged lioness," she admitted, "longing to bring to a close nursing and housekeeping cares."[42] She received help from her co-worker, Susan B. Anthony, but not from her husband, who was away from home up to ten months of the year on business or politics.

In 1868 the American Melusina Fay Peirce had suggested wages for housewives as a solution. She declared it "just as necessary and just as honorable for a wife to earn money as it is for her husband." Peirce attempted to translate her idea into reality by organizing the Cambridge Cooperative Housekeeping Society. The members would do their domestic work cooperatively and charge their husbands for their services. The scheme was sabotaged by the husbands in a show of what Peirce disgustedly called "HUSBAND-POWER."[43] In Britain in the 1880s, Jane Hume Clapperton, inspired by earlier utopian socialist communities, advocated co-operative family living arrangements with communal kitchens and laundries. In subsequent decades others would pick up on Peirce's and Clapperton's suggestions, but at this time most married feminists made the care of their households their first priority.

Sexual Standards and Social Purity

If feminists did not dispute the desirability of motherhood, they did affirm the right of most women to decide if and when to bear children, what they called "voluntary motherhood." Victorian ideology associated sexual initiative and pleasure with men, sexual reserve and reproductive duties with women. Defying medical authorities who insisted that the male sexual drive was natural and therefore unalterable, feminists recognized the political context of heterosexual relations as an issue of male power.

The sexual vulnerability of slave women to their owners was a glaring example of male abuse, even though the idea of female passionlessness did not usually extend to black women, whether slave or free. *Incidents in the Life of a Slave Girl* (1861), by Harriet Jacobs, documents the author's stubborn resistance to the attempts of her owner's father to make her submit sexually. When he struck her, she retorted, "How I despise you" and met his threats to kill her with the rejoinder, "You have no right to do as you like with me." Jacobs was bold for her times in openly discussing the sexual aspects of slavery in her writing. Although Linda Brent, Jacobs' pseudonymous heroine, successfully staved off her master, she violated Victorian norms in the process. She had an illicit love affair as a deliberate strategy, correctly believing that her master would leave her alone if he knew that she had given herself to another. It seemed "less degrading," she explained, "to give one's self, than to submit to compulsion."[44] Jacobs' account notwithstanding, assumptions of black women's immorality would continue well into the twentieth century. Its persistence meant that free black women continued to contend with the probability of sexual abuse by white men.

Within the context of white feminism, voluntary motherhood became an issue early on. It was openly discussed in the 1860s in the United States in the religious movement known as Spiritualism. Spiritualists were strong individualists and thus attracted to ideas of radical reform. In the following decade Elizabeth Cady Stanton broached the subject of "self-sovereignty" in small afternoon meetings open only to women. Women did more than discuss the possibility, according to historian Daniel Scott Smith. He cites the radical fall of the marital fertility rate throughout the century as proof that women had appropriated power within their families, a move he calls "domestic feminism."[45] The decision to restrict family size was not necessarily made by women, however, nor with their interests in mind. Birth control practices had first appeared in Europe in the late seventeenth and eighteenth centuries among propertied and upwardly mobile groups and had most likely resulted from considerations of the family's resources and ambitions.

For feminists, control of maternity meant control over sexual intercourse. Their demand that women be allowed to set the standards for sexual

> *In describing her girlhood in* Incidents in the Life of a Slave Girl, Written by Herself *(1861), Harriet Jacobs raised the issue of sexual abuse, which few women dared to address in public at this time.*
>
> Every where the years bring to all enough of sin and sorrow; but in slavery the very dawn of life is darkened by these shadows. Even the little child, who is accustomed to wait on her mistress and her children, will learn, before she is twelve years old, why it is that her mistress hates such and such a one among the slaves. Perhaps the child's own mother is among those hated ones. She listens to violent outbreaks of jealous passion, and cannot help understanding what is the cause. She will become prematurely knowing in evil things. Soon she will learn to tremble when she hears her master's footfall. She will be compelled to realize that she is no longer a child. If God has bestowed beauty upon her, it will prove her greatest curse. That which commands admiration in the white woman only hastens the degradation of the female slave. I know that some are too much brutalized by slavery to feel the humiliation of their position; but many slaves feel it most acutely, and shrink from the memory of it. I cannot tell how much I suffered in the presence of these wrongs, nor how I am still pained by the retrospect. My master met me at every turn, reminding me that I belonged to him, and swearing by heaven and earth that he would compel me to submit to him. If I went out for a breath of fresh air, after a day of unwearied toil, his foot-steps dogged me. If I knelt by my mother's grave, his dark shadow fell on me even there. The light heart which nature had given me became heavy with sad forebodings. The other slaves in my master's house noticed the change. Many of them pitied me; but none dared to ask the cause. They had no need to inquire. They knew too well the guilty practices under that roof; and they were aware that to speak of them was an offence that never went unpunished.

relationships helps to explain the repugnance most feminists felt for artificial methods of contraception. Such methods, they feared, would mean sex on men's terms, further reducing women's control over their bodies. Those who proposed free love defined it as freedom from the obligations imposed by legal marriage, what Paulina Wright Davis in 1871 called "the rendering of marital rights and compulsory maternity."[46] Although they saw free-love relationships as an alternative to marriage, they understood them as heterosexual, monogamous, and disciplined in restricting sexual intercourse to procreation. This was in marked contrast to some individuals, such as the American Victoria Woodhull, and to various radical reform groups that believed free love encompassed unrestricted heterosexual relationships.

Problematically, marriage was often women's only source of economic security and the only guarantee of support for their children. Given women's lack of options, voluntary motherhood in conventional marriage was probably a more realistic alternative than free love, but both were attempts to strengthen women's position by controlling sexual access rather than by expanding it. For this reason, most feminists opposed the ideas of sexual radicals such as Woodhull, who achieved notoriety in the United States in the 1870s by vigorously championing women's sexual freedom. Annie Besant, who publicly advocated birth control in England, did so largely in isolation from other feminists. Many women, of course, continued to find an alternative to heterosexual marriage in stable and intimate relationships with other women.

At stake was women's protest against the centuries-old definition of woman as a sexual animal, or more simply, "the sex." Much of the feminist drive for self-determination can be understood as a protest against women's reduction to sexual objects. "Man has inflicted an unspeakable injury upon woman," Sarah Grimké had insisted, "by holding up to her view her animal nature, and placing in the back ground her moral and intellectual being."[47] More than seventy years later, in 1911, the British feminist Ethel Snowdon made the same appeal: "For the woman as a human being, and not as an animal, the feminist demands opportunity and freedom."[48]

As part of the attempt to give women control of their bodies, feminists tackled the problem of family violence. In England, John Stuart and Harriet Taylor Mill protested wife beating, an objection repeated in 1878 by Frances Power Cobbe in her article, "Wife-torture in England." Americans Elizabeth Cady Stanton and Susan B. Anthony publicized and condemned domestic violence and demanded the death penalty for rape. Lucy Stone in the United States and Lydia Becker in England both reported "crimes against women" such as wife beating and incest in their respective women's journals. Stone sought legal protection for battered wives; others lobbied for more liberal divorce laws or set up shelters for abused women. The Protective Agency for Women and Children, founded in Chicago in 1885, established a legal aid office for battered women and provided assistance for rape victims in the form of emotional support, legal help, and court appearances on the victims' behalf. Aside from these examples, most feminists dealt with family abuse only indirectly, in temperance or social purity campaigns that attempted to reform the morals of society.

The most important social purity campaign in Britain was the effort to repeal the Contagious Diseases Acts, which permitted the detention and compulsory medical examination of prostitutes. Excluded from the national repeal association, much as American women had been earlier excluded from temperance and antislavery societies, British women formed their own repeal organization in 1869. Repealers had a wide variety of motives. Some worried that the acts condoned prostitution by regulating it; others believed that the legislation was simply ineffective. Feminist repealers in particular saw prostitution as the paradigm for the female condition; they attacked the double standard by pointing out how the laws unjustly punished the victims instead of the perpetrators. Unlike those who condemned prostitutes as morally flawed, feminist repealers regarded them as victims of male oppression. A spokeswoman for the organization viewed the laws as "an insult to the whole womanhood of England" in their "ruthless sacrifice of female liberties to the supposed interest of profligate men."[49]

Were the middle-class managers of the repeal campaign unable to imagine women who did not conform to conventional moral standards except as victims of male immorality? Maybe, but it is also true that Josephine Butler (1828–1906), the charismatic leader of the women's repeal organization, thought of prostitutes as sisters, in much the same way that some American abolitionists had thought of female slaves. To her the acts evoked "a deeply awakened common womanhood. Distinctions are levelled," she declared. "We no more covet the name of ladies; we are all *women*."[50] Middle-class reformers made many pronouncements about sisterhood across class lines; the British repeal campaign was one area where they acted on it.

Repealers also criticized the arbitrary authority that the laws gave to police and doctors. They condemned the requirement of examinations for prostitutes but not for their soldier or sailor clients and denounced the exams themselves as degrading, a form of "instrumental rape" with the speculum used as a "steel penis."[51] This indelicate language and their insistence on the right to address mixed audiences on such issues subjected the advocates to recriminations, even violence. In one confrontation a mob covered Josephine Butler "with flour and excrement, her clothes had been torn off her body, her face was discoloured and stiff with dried blood and she was so bruised that she could hardly move."[52] Her persistence and courage was an inspiring example of feminist activism and stimulated the founding of similar organizations in other European countries.

The social purity campaign in Britain did not end with the repeal of the acts in 1886. Rather it broadened to include protests against marital rape and the sexual abuse of children. Reformers attempted to secure legislation to raise the age of consent and to make incest a crime under English law. At this time, father–daughter incest was often punished less severely than the theft of a loaf of bread. Ellice Hopkins publicized horrendous examples of the failure of police to take reports of sexual abuse seriously and of the tendency of judges to punish the abusers of boys more heavily than those of girls. Few reformers spoke as frankly about the double standard, however, as the African-American Ida B. Wells-Barnett was to do in the 1890s, as we will see in Chapter 8.

Social Reform

The social purity movement was part of a general broadening of reform activities in the 1870s and 1880s, notably in Britain, the United States, and English Canada. Reformers saw contemporary social problems as largely caused by the "selfish individualism" that accompanied industrialization. They were inspired in part by Auguste Comte, a French philosopher who had been convinced that scientific laws were at work in society. Comte, who called his philosophy positivism, believed that social scientists, or experts, could identify the laws of human relations and use them to discipline individuals and achieve social harmony. Paradoxically, there was a heady dose of romanticism in Comte's social science, a holdover from the views of earlier utopian socialists who had designated woman as "Priestess of Humanity." Science and rationalism thus seemed to lend support to reformers' hopes of organizing society to achieve a social balance between masculine and feminine values.

By the 1880s in the United States, these ideas had blossomed into a wide-ranging reform program, what one historian calls an "holistic program of woman's reform—a consciousness in the broadest sense of woman's role in civilization."[53] At its centre was the temperance movement. Though present in most Western countries, temperance was most closely allied with feminism in North America. In the United States, it was known "as the woman's revolution." Led by the Woman's Christian Temperance Union (WCTU), the movement targeted alcohol as the major cause of poverty and family abuse. The WCTU perceived men as the perpetrators and women and children as the victims. The temperance movement built on and exploited the Victorian cult of domesticity, associating women with domestic life and in the process attributing to them a moral purity appropriate to the home, in contrast to the dirty world of politics and business. One obvious conclusion was that women would lose their moral purity if they came into contact with the outside world. Another, however, was that women had a duty to extend their moral influence to clean up the mess made by men. This inference was preferred by feminists. Confident that "women are fortunate in belonging to the less tainted half of the race," the American leader Frances Willard described "the mission of the ideal woman" as "TO MAKE THE WHOLE WORLD HOMELIKE."[54] In the same vein, Mary Livermore, also an American temperance leader, called on reformers to create "a republic of women" whose purpose would be to "train women for the next great step in the evolution of humanity, when women shall sit side by side in government, and the nations shall learn war no more."[55]

Temperance offered a deceptively easy solution to problems posed by urban poverty and immigration, but it may also have held special appeal for women as a way to attack male dominance indirectly. In the "women's crusade" of 1873–75, American women demonstrated against saloons as examples of male culture, organizing what may have been the first sit-ins in history. Their criticism of alcohol abuse thinly veiled their resentment of women's vulnerable position within the family. The campaign served to bring many women into public life who may have been hesitant to endorse more radical causes, including women from rural and small town backgrounds throughout North America. Undoubtedly many were thereby politicized. "The seal of silence is removed from Woman's lips by this crusade, and can never be replaced," a WCTU member declared in 1874.[56]

As governments failed to legislate the desired prohibition, supporters came to promote women's suffrage as the answer. A temperance organizer proudly concluded that she and her co-workers were "doing more for Woman

Suffrage than any of you [suffragists] dream."[57] The call that Susan B. Anthony sent out in the 1880s to women's groups to organize an international council of women reflected her hope that the recognition of women's moral contributions would result in their political equality. Under the feminist leadership of Frances Willard, the national American WCTU formally endorsed suffrage in 1881; the Canadian WCTU followed suit ten years later.

The reverse also happened. Temperance not only brought participants to suffrage but also appealed to those who found the suffrage movement too narrow and frustrating and turned to social reform instead. Inasmuch as social reform revealed the class bias of middle-class reformers and their desire to extend the values of sobriety and industry to the working classes, it represented a conservative aspect of the women's movement. By building on contemporary assumptions of gender difference, it also strengthened the association of women with selflessness: "Forever be silenced the self assertion, 'all the rights I want,'" declared the president of the Illinois Woman's Suffrage Association in 1883. "The time has come when the patriot men of America must call in the reserves and summon women to the glorious service of aiding to save our country from the combination of vice and selfishness. . . . Our hour for self-sacrificing service is here."[58] Evident already in the American Mid-west in the 1870s, this conservative drift characterized the national women's movement by the 1890s. The Canadian and French women's movements would be similarly affected by or after the turn of the century.

Sisterhood in Action

The social reform movement brought reformers face to face with problems encountered by the working classes. The Victorian belief in gender difference and the close sustaining friendships and family ties that women enjoyed reinforced the idea that gender could unite women of different backgrounds. In 1888, representatives of fifty-three women's organizations met in Washington, DC, to form the International Council of Women. They declared, "Much is said of a universal brotherhood, but, for weal or for woe, more subtle and more binding is universal sisterhood."[59] Middle-class reformers established cross-class alliances in the form of services aimed at working women, such as the lunchrooms, legal services, employment bureau, health clinic, co-operative exchanges, and courses in dressmaking, sales work, and housekeeping provided by the Women's Educational and Industrial Union, founded in Boston in 1877. In Germany, the Union of German Women similarly organized classes, clubs, day care, and cultural activities for working women.

To historians the dual purpose of these endeavours is evident. They earned praise and respect for middle-class reformers while benefiting the women they assisted. German women hoped that their record of community service would silence those who believed that voting rights should be based only on military service. Less consciously, reformers in general hoped to give working-class and poor women "good" role models and to inculcate middle-class values. The result was often a one-way process, reformers benefiting more from their own influence in the community than did those they were supposed to be assisting.

Like Josephine Butler, some feminists were capable of appealing to universal sisterhood without hypocrisy. Many "hoped to leap social barriers and welcome working-class women on their own terms," in marked contrast to earlier, patronizing philanthropists. Nevertheless, historian Mari Jo Buhle judges that class distinctions were often insurmountable. This was true even in the United States, where class divisions were less pronounced than in Europe, as was evident in the attempt of Elizabeth Cady Stanton and Susan B. Anthony to form a political alliance with working women in 1868. Even the distinctively skilled workers they approached placed economic issues such as wage parity with men and admittance into apprenticeship programs above political rights such as the vote. Class tensions within the group quickly became obvious, and within a year the working-class women dropped out, enabling the others to concentrate on literary and political matters and benevolent activities.

More successful were African-American and African-Canadian women, who built on a long tradition of community service to supply social welfare programs for women and families who lacked government assistance. Often barred from professional teaching programs because of racism, black women teachers directed their efforts into neighbourhood schools, which did not require certification. But even middle-class black women could not always avoid sounding patronizing. Mary Church Terrell, who was to be first president of the National Association of Colored Women (NACW) in 1896, declared, "Self-preservation demands that [black women] go among the lowly, illiterate and even the vicious, to whom they are bound by ties of race and sex . . . to reclaim them."[60] Language aside, the NACW would have an impressive record of reaching out to the black community in an attempt to bridge class divisions.

Some groups managed to avoid condescension and to understand and promote the concerns of working women successfully. The Illinois Woman's Alliance of 1888, composed of middle-class club women and socialist-inclined working women, succeeded in persuading the state legislature to limit the sweatshop system. In Britain, women appointed as factory inspectors effected small improvements in women's working conditions. Although there was no consistent split along class lines on the question of protective legislation for women workers, the issue divided feminists in the 1880s. Reformers with close ties to working women tended to support laws that would improve their working conditions; other feminists deplored any attempt to legislate on the basis of gender difference.

Middle-class feminists also assisted women to unionize. There are many examples of demonstrations by working women in these years: black women launderers struck to establish a price code for their services in Jackson, Mississippi, in 1866; eight thousand French silk winders walked out in Lyon in the late 1860s; seven hundred match girls successfully demanded higher wages and their own union in London in 1888. But most unions formed by working women tended to be small and short-lived, and not just because they lacked resources. Impediments to organization included the usually fragmented and temporary nature of women's paid work, their lack of public space equivalent to the pubs and saloons where men could meet, longer working hours, a double burden of domestic chores, inability to afford union dues, and vulnerability to intimidation from male bosses. Not least important was the reluctance of working-class men to accept women in the workforce, a reluctance that convinced middle-class women to take up the slack to promote unionism. Male workers continued to fear women as cheap competition and to idealize a family headed by a male breadwinner supporting his dependants.

A notable exception was the Knights of Labor, a workers' association that spread rapidly in Canada and the United States in the 1880s. The Knights recruited all workers, women and men, skilled and unskilled, whites and blacks. They supported women's suffrage and equal pay for equal work and regarded housework as productive labour, although their progressive ideas existed in uneasy tension with the ideal of domesticity. In Britain, two successful feminist-initiated unions, the Women's Protective and Provident League and the National Union of Women Workers, were founded in 1874. Similar organizations in Germany dated from the 1880s. In spite of these efforts, the percentage of women workers who were unionized remained very small.

The Suffrage Issue

When it was first considered by feminists, women's suffrage had been rejected by most as too radical. This was true even in the United States, where suffrage was first endorsed by an organized movement. When Elizabeth Cady Stanton, Lucretia Mott, and some three hundred other women and men met in 1848 at Seneca Falls, suffrage was the only resolution not adopted unanimously. The participants feared that the "demand for the right to vote would defeat others they deemed more rational, and make the whole movement ridiculous." It was included only through the persistence of Stanton and Frederick Douglass, who insisted "that the power to choose rulers and make laws, was the right by which all others could be secured."[61]

Elsewhere as well, reformers shied away from the suffrage issue. In England, meeting a decade after Seneca Falls, the Langham Place group initially refused to discuss suffrage because it was too radical. Barbara Smith Bodichon, desiring to form a Women's Suffrage Committee in 1865, was at first dissuaded by her colleague, Emily Davies, who feared that the suffrage issue would adversely affect educational reform—in this case, the founding of Girton College—and gave up her own suffrage work accordingly. Two years later in Germany, Friedrich von Holtzendorff, leader of an organization that promoted employment opportunities for women, reported, "In

Germany woman's suffrage does not even have a place among the subjects for political discussion."[62] In Canada, a small group of professional women who came together in 1876 chose to mask their political purpose by calling themselves the Toronto Women's Literary Club. Not until 1883 did they dare to organize openly as the Toronto Women's Suffrage Association. At the same time, almost no one in France supported the idea of women's suffrage. The mere mention of it could provoke laughter in the national assembly. In 1878 and again in 1889, at two international women's rights congresses held in Paris, the organizers refused to allow suffrage, "this dangerous question,"[63] to be discussed. In Europe feminists who concentrated on economic, educational, and legal rights were labelled moderate; those who demanded the vote were called radical.

Why was the demand for the vote perceived to be so extreme? Historian Ellen DuBois has pointed out that by circumventing women's position in the family, political rights—and suffrage as a symbol of them—threatened the basis of women's subordination in society. The right of suffrage would establish a direct relationship between women as citizens, or individuals, and the state. "By demanding a permanent, public role for all women," explains DuBois, "suffragists began to demolish the absolute, sexually defined barrier marking the public world of men off from the private world of women."[64] A committee report at the 1867 Constitutional Convention in New York State, attended by members of the judiciary committee and the legislature, announced that "public sentiment does not demand and would not sustain . . . an innovation so revolutionary and sweeping [as suffrage], so openly at war with a distribution of duties and functions between the sexes as venerable and pervading as government itself, and involving transformations so radical in social and domestic life."[65]

The prospect that terrified the committee members would probably have impressed suffragists as simply too optimistic. The idea seemed even more radical in Canada and Europe, where property qualifications for male voters were maintained until the late nineteenth or early twentieth century. France was an anomaly because even though all men received the vote in 1848, women had to wait almost another hundred years. French feminists faced unusual circumstances, but developments everywhere belied John Stuart Mill's optimistic prediction that suffrage would be easily won.

In the United States and Britain, the issue acquired significance in the context of laws that extended the male franchise. In the United States, the word "male" was introduced for the first time into the federal constitution in 1868 by supporters of the enfranchisement of black men. Reformers who had fought both for the abolition of slavery and for women's rights saw the decision of their abolitionist allies to promote the rights of black men over those of women as a bitter betrayal. Some, like Lucy Stone, agreed to postpone women's suffrage, but others, including Elizabeth Cady Stanton, Susan B. Anthony, and Sojourner Truth, refused to separate the issues. Stanton ominously predicted that "if that word 'male' be inserted, it will take us a century at least to get it out."[66] Determined to carry on the fight, Stanton and

Anthony broke with their former allies. Their decision to accept funding from a politician who was also a racist resulted in the verdict of both their contemporaries and historians that Anthony and Stanton were opportunists and racists at heart. A recently discovered letter from Henry Blackwell admitting that their association with the politician was his idea supports an alternative interpretation, however, that Anthony and Stanton fell victim to the manipulation of Blackwell and other male politicians who sought to discredit their leadership.

These same men failed to respond to Anthony's appeal "to broaden our Woman's Rights platform, and make it in—*name* what it ever has been in *spirit*—a Human Rights platform" and forced the separation of race and gender issues. But it is also true that Stanton revealed her willingness to resort to any argument, even a racist one, if it would advance women's rights. "What kind of a government, think you, American statesmen, you can build, with the mothers of the race crouching at your feet," she asked rhetorically, "while iron-heeled peasants, serfs, and slaves, exalted by your hands, tread our inalienable rights into the dust?" She added bitterly, "It is an open, deliberate insult to American womanhood to be cast down under the iron-heeled peasantry of the Old World and the slaves of the New."[67] Although that language temporarily subsided, Ellen DuBois concedes that "the more subtle habit of seeing women's grievances from the viewpoint of white women had been firmly established within the suffrage movement."[68] Once slavery was abolished, race was not a major issue for white feminists, and middle-class African Americans found it more empowering to form their own equal rights organizations, such as the Colored Women's Progressive Association, established in 1880.

That suffrage had a wide appeal for American women is obvious from the letters Susan B. Anthony (1820–1906) received in support of her 1888 campaign for a constitutional amendment to extend the franchise. The campaign was just one of Anthony's many strategies during her lifelong mission as a women's rights activist. In 1872 Anthony had voted in a presidential election and was subsequently tried in court for this illegal act. Although she refused to pay the resulting fine, the judge decided that it was not in the court's interest to pursue the case. The National Woman Suffrage Association devised another strategy, and in 1878 Anthony drafted a proposed constitutional amendment; it was introduced in the American congress regularly and unsuccessfully through the 1880s. Among the women who responded to her 1888 campaign were those who described themselves as "the mother of 9 children and still struggling for my freedom," "your Sister though Colored," and "only a working woman."[69]

The extension of male suffrage in Britain in the late 1860s and again in the 1880s raised the issue of female suffrage there. In 1866, Barbara Smith Bodichon and associates from Langham Place launched their fifty-two-year campaign by drafting a petition that the recently elected John Stuart Mill presented to parliament. Mill's unsuccessful attempt to amend the 1867 Reform Bill by replacing "men" with "persons" was followed by another attempt to include women's suffrage in the Reform Bill of 1884. The suffrage societies that had formed in the interim brought considerable pressure to bear on the government. Even though a majority of liberal MPs favoured women's suffrage, the prime minister was fearful of jeopardizing the bill's chances for success and the proposal was dropped. At the same time, newly legislated limits on electoral funding forced political parties to turn to unpaid volunteers. As a result, many women opted to work in women's auxiliaries to the major parties, and the organized suffrage movement lost ground.

Unlike the Americans, British suffragists had to deal with the existence of a property qualification for male voters. They therefore concentrated on breaking the "sex barrier" by extending the franchise to women on the same terms as applied to men. While more realistic than a demand for full adult suffrage, this policy weakened their support among leftist politicians, who feared a "class vote" of propertied women. It also meant the exclusion from the franchise of married women, who were still prohibited from owning property in their own names. By 1882, married women's property acts had changed the situation, but suffragists remained divided over the issue and most still feared that married women's enfranchisement was unrealistic.

French feminists faced greater political obstacles. While the United States and Britain had stable, essentially liberal governments, France between 1790 and 1870 experienced two constitutional monarchies, two republics, and two imperial regimes. Rather than ushering in the reign of republicanism, the French Revolution had divided the nation into two camps, one endorsing equality of rights and opportunity, the other glorifying the monarchy, church, and army. The Third Republic was born of national defeat in the Franco-Prussian war of 1870–71 and was immediately tested by a bloody workers' uprising in Paris. The violence and failure of the revolt were captured in the symbol of *la Pétroleuse,* a raging woman setting homes ablaze, a woman out of male control, a feminist. Not surprisingly, feminists were not allowed unrestricted freedom of assembly and freedom of the press for two decades; until then they needed government permission to meet, hold public lectures, or publish a political newspaper.

Wary of the chaos that they attributed to broad male suffrage, conservatives were fearful of extending the factionalism of French politics into the family. One commentator recoiled in horror from a vision of each household as "a little constitutional state where the dinner menu will be decided by majority vote."[70] In this climate even the name of the Association for Women's Rights, founded by Maria Deraismes and Léon Richer in 1870, was too threatening; officials approved only when it was changed to the Association for the Future of Women.

Opposition did not come only from the right. Léon Richer (1824–1912) endorsed educational and civil reforms but vehemently opposed female suffrage. Like other republicans, he feared, probably correctly, that women were supporters of the church and would use their vote to strengthen clerical influence. "It is enough for us to have to struggle against reactionaries of the masculine sex," warned Richer, "without giving to these partisans of defeated regimes the support of millions of female ballots subject to the occult domination of the priest, the confessor." Assuming that women took their orders from the confessional, he predicted that "if they voted today, the Republic would not last six months."[71]

The torch of suffragism was carried by the indefatigable activist Hubertine Auclert (1848–1914), France's counterpart to Elizabeth Cady Stanton. As dedicated to the republic as Richer and Deraismes but convinced that a true republic would not exist until the "aristocracy of sex" was abolished, she resolved to go to Paris "to fight for the liberty of my sex." She became impatient with the willingness of Richer and Deraismes to postpone the demand for the vote until women were better educated. While Deraismes declared that suffrage "will be the business of our nieces,"[72] Auclert protested, "It is not education that makes the voter; it is pants."[73] In 1876, she founded the Women's Rights Society, which in 1883 became the Women's Suffrage Society.

Auclert's efforts were tireless, leading her biographer to call her the most militant and certainly most energetic feminist in late-nineteenth-century France. In addition to writing and lecturing, she edited a suffragist newspaper, pressured socialists for their support, led a campaign to register female voters, organized a shadow slate of fifteen women candidates, engineered a tax strike and a census boycott, fought two court cases, conducted six petition campaigns, and issued suffrage stamps and postcards. She urged replacing the French national holiday of 14 July, which she called the "Day of Dupes," with May 30, the anniversary of the death of Joan of Arc. The first activist to adopt the label *feminist,* she believed what she wrote: "One must act as if one can do everything."[74] According to the files they kept on all feminists, the police regarded Auclert "as afflicted with madness or hysteria; an illness which makes her look on men as her equals."[75]

Auclert's radicalism was too extreme for most other feminists, her followers numbering barely one hundred. Even in the United States, the suffragists were too radical to establish a mass movement. Ellen DuBois describes them as "a guerilla force" in contrast to the Woman's Christian Temperance Union, which "commanded an army."[76] Female suffrage, like other women's rights issues, was a minority cause.

EVALUATING FEMINISM

How successful were these feminist campaigns? By the end of the 1880s many women were benefiting from improved access to higher education, married women's property laws, more equal divorce laws, entry into professions, and in some areas the right to vote in local elections. Nevertheless, most of these changes can be described neither as unequivocal gains nor as the result of feminist agitation. In some countries, such as Sweden, reforms predated the emergence of organized feminism.

Married women's property reform can serve as an example. Studies of American and British legislation have consistently shown the importance of non-feminist motives in initiating change. Paramount in Britain was the desire to systematize a complex and archaic network of laws. When the favourable climate for legal reform waned, the chances for a property bill decreased dramatically. Even with a favourable climate, it still took twenty-seven years of agitation to get an effective act. Before then it simply was not a high priority for government leaders. When reform was finally carried out, it was piecemeal and insubstantial. "Women had gained little [in Britain] by the start of the 1890s in terms of destroying the legal essentials of male superiority," concludes one historian. "Despite the claims that the nineteenth century had been the 'woman's century' . . . the legal inferiority of married women remained largely intact."[77]

Important in the United States, in addition to the motive of legal codification, was the perceived need to protect the family from the fluctuations of an increasingly commercial economy. When the husband's property could be seized for debt, it seemed desirable to find a way to protect family assets. Protection of married women's property could thus mean protection from the husband's creditors rather than from the husband. Reformers could even argue from the antifeminist viewpoint that property law reform would safeguard the family and thereby alleviate the need for married women to enter the labour force. In fact, feminist agitation could impede reform because it raised the possibility of revolutionizing gender relationships, a possibility that most people found threatening.

Worry over family stability also generated support from conservatives for other apparently feminist demands such as equal wages. Moralists feared that low wages would encourage women to resort to prostitution for supplementary income. Higher wages might even put women back in the home if employers had no incentive to hire them in preference to men. In complete indifference to women's rights, others argued that less reliance on cheap labour would force businesses to modernize.

Other issues were also argued from non- or antifeminist motives. The drive to extend higher education to women, for example, was part of a more general middle-class reform program that had nothing to do with feminism. Economic motives often dictated women's admission to universities, as we have seen. Some American medical schools were persuaded to open their doors to women only when wealthy women offered endowments with conditions attached. Important gains for women usually came because of advantages to the male establishment, such as countering a decline in male enrolment. When conditions changed, the doors swung shut. Nor did women's new access to education necessarily promote feminism. Private secondary schools and colleges were dependent on the support of patrons and parents; educators could not afford to rock the boat with innovative curricula or goals. Although education could prove an emancipating experience for young women, promoters cautiously observed only that an educated woman would be a better wife and mother. As for changes in health and dress, these were often promoted as enabling healthier mothers to bear and raise healthier children. Similarly, feminist pressure was not responsible for the decisions of the first American territories to give women the vote. In Utah, for example, the legislature voted for women's suffrage in 1870 in the belief that

Mormon women would support polygamy, which was under attack by the American congress.

Feminist action was not unimportant. It put the issues on the agenda, but it could not force decision makers to act on them. As an historian reminds us, "Reforms, after all, are not carried through by debates but by the machinery controlled by political parties and their leaders."[78] As is true of any disenfranchised group, women could only hope to persuade influential male sympathizers. Given the persistence of patriarchy, it was rarely in the interests of men to change the system from which they so obviously bene-fited. Although there was some perceived need to modernize the family to enable it to cope with economic change, there was no desire to subvert it.

The important gain for feminists could not be measured by an external victory. Thirty years earlier American women's rights campaigners had started out timidly and with trepidation, but by the 1880s they were able to form complex organizations under experienced and confident leadership. At the Seneca Falls convention in 1848, Elizabeth Cady Stanton noted that the par-ticipants, faced with the task of writing a declaration, were "as helpless and hopeless as if they had been suddenly asked to construct a steam engine." The women "shrank" from organizing the meeting or leading the discussions and arranged for a male chair. Frances Gage, recruited to chair a convention in Akron, Ohio, in 1851, later recalled having to face a hostile and jeering audi-ence. According to Gage, the women were rescued from humiliation only through the timely intervention of the ex-slave and abolitionist Sojourner Truth, who "with the air of a queen"[79] walked up to the front and delivered her famous speech, "Ar'n't I a Woman?" Yet none of twenty-seven contem-porary descriptions of the convention nor an earlier account from Gage her-self confirms either the exact words that she later attributed to Truth or the hostile atmosphere from which the participants needed to be rescued. Gage's trepidation in mounting a public platform doubtless accounts for her later embellishment of the occasion.

A significant if unusual contribution to easing American women's entry into public speaking was their participation as mediums or trance speakers in the religious movement known as Spiritualism, which began in 1848. Audiences that jeered at women reform lecturers listened raptly to women speaking as conduits of divine truth. By the end of the 1850s women trance speakers outnumbered women reform lecturers. Many Spiritualists went on to become suffragists, their stint under divine guidance having given them the necessary confidence to speak in their own voices.

Building on experiences like these, by the mid-1850s reformers were conducting a sophisticated campaign in New York State for women's suffrage and property rights, holding local meetings, organizing systematic petition drives, speaking before the legislature, lobbying politicians, keeping meticu-lous records, raising funds, and awakening significant support. Although no women's rights meetings were held during the Civil War from 1861 to 1865, the Women's National Loyal League was formed and became, under Elizabeth Cady Stanton's leadership, a national feminist network that laid much of the groundwork for postwar organizing.

As a result of disagreement over the issue of black men's suffrage in the late 1860s, American suffragists formed two national organizations, the National Woman Suffrage Association (NWSA) and the American Woman Suffrage Association (AWSA). The former concentrated on attempting to secure a federal constitutional amendment, the latter worked mainly on local campaigns. More important, the NWSA was founded as an autonomous organization, relying for support on women rather than on any association with other reform movements. Whereas the AWSA sought male allies and alternated its presidency between a man and a woman, the NWSA rejected the idea of male leadership. Its policy, according to Ellen DuBois, significantly advanced the cause of women's autonomy by allowing feminists to find their true constituency, namely, white middle-class women who had not previously been associated with reform but who were receptive to winning political rights. One such woman, Sarah Williams, described the suffragists' impact: "A large circle of intelligent and earnest women were longing and waiting to do something to spread the movement for woman suffrage, when the coming of these pioneers of reform roused them to action. It was like the match to the fire all ready for kindling." The resulting movement was a "powerful political force" that sustained itself for more than half a century.[80]

The NWSA's exclusion of men from leadership positions was in sharp contrast to the usual pattern in feminist groups; men not only usually participated as members but were often chosen as speakers and leaders. The fact that wives would have found it difficult to participate without their husbands' support explains the frequent presence of married couples, but women's rights was not considered of interest only to women. "This is no woman's movement," declared an American man in 1854, "It is a reformation intended to advance and improve the happiness of *men* and *women* equally."[81]

Women found men's support helpful but sometimes only up to a point. In the Men and Women's Club, organized by British intellectuals in the late 1880s to facilitate discussion between the sexes on social and moral issues, the women felt intimidated in spite of the group's commitment to equality. Although within two years of the 1857 founding of the National Association for the Promotion of Social Science in Great Britain, women had begun to read their own papers at meetings, many still found it necessary to state reassuringly that "there is no fear of English women flinging themselves recklessly into the arena of public speaking."[82] At least one woman in the association continued to rely on men to deliver the thirty-two papers she wrote over twenty years. In the context of the Canadian suffrage movement, Emily Stowe reported her experience: "We admitted the opposite sex as members and the effect was demoralizing. The old idea of female dependence crept in and the ladies began to rely on the gentlemen rather than upon their own efforts."[83] Stowe also found the presence of male speakers at temperance meetings daunting.

In European organizations, women and men worked closely together. Sometimes the men were dominant. In the German Lette Federation, which sought to expand women's employment, men held all the offices. Feminist politics in Sweden before 1890 have been described as "a man's affair," the work of male liberal politicians.[84] Men outnumbered women in the French contingent at the Congress for Women's Rights held in 1878 and formed the majority of members of Léon Richer's French League for Women's Rights in 1882, at that time the largest feminist organization in France. This strategy was deliberate, part of Richer's tactic of seeking the support of politicians and other influential people as a realistic way to gain gradual reforms. It also reflected his own disappointment in French women, whom he believed generally indifferent to politics.

The General German Woman's Association, in contrast, constituted itself as a women-led organization, much to the distress of contemporaries who were not used to seeing women conducting meetings and speaking in public. The group took as "the first demand, that if women want to reach the goals of progress and independence that are appropriate to their sex, they must show that they will and can help themselves."[85] Men were permitted to become honorary members with an advisory status, however, and the founder, Louise Otto-Peters, hastened to state that the exclusion of men as full members was adopted not out of hatred but with the approval, even encouragement, of the men themselves.

British feminists were helped by their strong ties and community of interests. As sisters or cousins or intimate friends, often sharing family backgrounds of participation in earlier reform movements such as antislavery, they gave to this phase of activity a "strong sense of mutuality."[86] They created an alternative social milieu to the home in all-women clubs and reading rooms. Female culture constituted a counterpoint both to the idea of competitive individualism that prevailed in Victorian society and to the organizational model of powerful groups with strong leaders. Feminist disdain for the latter explains the absence of a centralized organization, an official ideology, and an acknowledged leader within the movement. As the ideological differences of established political parties became more pronounced in the second half of the century, so did feminist pragmatism and cynicism about male party politics.

Religious differences among British feminists were blunted, freethinkers and believers working hand in hand. This was the case in Germany as well but was not true everywhere. For example, the religious scepticism of Emily Stowe, the founder of the Toronto Women's Literary Club, may have deterred the growth of the suffrage movement in English-speaking Canada. In Quebec, lay women exploited the idea of an innate womanly disposition to charitable work in order to penetrate the network of social activities previously monopolized by nuns and to work closely with them, but French feminists, who were predominantly Protestant, Jewish, or anticlerical, were unable to make common cause with devout Catholic women. Religious differences became even more pronounced as the feminist movement broadened to include more conservative women in the decades leading up to World War I.

How could women's groups be both autonomous and effective? Even though Elizabeth Cady Stanton and Susan B. Anthony worked hard to build their own constituency of white middle-class women, the suffrage movement remained small, as we have seen. Thus, by the 1880s American suffragists were seeking allies among social reformers, usually more conservative women, and couching their appeal in language acceptable to a broader group. Feminists in other countries faced the same problem. Like Stanton, Hubertine Auclert in France was prepared to court unorthodox allies, but there was no comparable social reform movement in France at that time. Auclert's goal of immediate suffrage was too radical for most feminists, so she approached the socialists, shouting out at one socialist meeting, "Enough centuries of submission! We must revolt, we must cease to obey!"[87] Auclert was successful in persuading the French Workingman's Party to pass a motion supporting women's suffrage; it was the only party in France to do so. She realized the tokenism of the gesture, however, when in the ensuing internecine conflict her feminism was rejected as bourgeois reformism. Auclert refused to compromise by subordinating her feminism to the goal of the workers' revolution. To her the means were as important as the ends. As historian Olive Banks has observed, "Perhaps the most striking thing about feminism is the extent to which it has been a movement *of* women and not just *for* women."[88]

From the 1850s, middle class women in North America and Europe began to organize in an attempt to achieve personal autonomy and exert influence on public life. Their campaigns embraced educational and employment opportunities, dress reform, married women's property laws, co-operative housekeeping, the right to set sexual standards and control their bodies, and the right to civic equality through exercise of the vote. These issues largely reflected their interests as privileged women. The idea of women's self-determination that united these activities was for the benefit of those not encumbered by racial oppression or by the daily struggle to survive. Although women's success in achieving specific goals is arguable, the most important gains were their ability to organize and their newly found self-confidence and expertise. By the end of the 1880s, feminists had mounted an impressive attack on patriarchal oppression as they experienced it.

NOTES

[1] Susan M. Hartmann uses this term in a different context, contrasting it to "survival-oriented" feminism, in *American Women in the 1940s: The Home Front and Beyond* (Boston: Twayne Publishers, 1982), 315.

[2] Elizabeth Cady Stanton, "Home Life" (ca. 1875), 133 and "Address of Welcome to the International Council of Women" (1888), 209, in *Elizabeth Cady Stanton, Susan B. Anthony: Correspondence, Writings, Speeches,* ed. Ellen Carol DuBois (New York: Schocken, 1981).

[3] Quoted in Hazel V. Carby, *Reconstructing Womanhood: The Emergence of the Afro-American Woman Novelist* (New York and Oxford: Oxford University Press, 1987), 68.

4   "Second National Convention, Worcester, Massachusetts, October 15–16, 1851. Resolutions," in *The Concise History of Woman Suffrage: Selections from the Classic Work of Stanton, Anthony, Gage, and Harper,* ed. Mari Jo Buhle and Paul Buhle (Urbana: University of Illinois Press, 1978), 113.

5   Florence Nightingale, "Cassandra," in Ray Strachey, *"The Cause": A Short History of the Women's Movement in Great Britain* (1928; reprint, Port Washington, NY: Kennikat Press, 1969), 396.

6   Quoted in Jean H. Quataert, *Reluctant Feminists in German Social Democracy, 1885–1917* (Princeton, NJ: Princeton University Press, 1979), 89.

7   Quoted in Nancy Schrom Dye, *As Equals and As Sisters: Feminism, the Labor Movement, and the Women's Trade Union League of New York* (Columbia: University of Missouri Press, 1980), 9.

8   Quoted in Mary Lyndon Shanley, *Feminism, Marriage, and the Law in Victorian England, 1850–1895* (Princeton, NJ: Princeton University Press, 1989), 101.

9   John Stuart Mill, *The Subjection of Women,* in *Essays on Sex Equality: John Stuart Mill and Harriet Taylor Mill,* ed. Alice Rossi (Chicago: University of Chicago Press, 1970), 145.

10 Quoted in Lynne Spender, "Matilda Joslyn Gage: Active Intellectual (1826–1898)," in *Feminist Theorists: Three Centuries of Key Women Thinkers,* ed. Dale Spender (New York: Pantheon Books, 1983), 139.

11 Josephine Butler, "On Dr. Elizabeth Garrett Anderson" (1868), in *Strong-Minded Women and Other Lost Voices from Nineteenth-Century England,* ed. Janet Horowitz Murray (New York: Pantheon Books, 1982), 317.

12 Mary Roth Walsh, *"Doctors Wanted: No Women Need Apply": Sexual Barriers in the Medical Profession, 1835–1975* (New Haven and London: Yale University Press, 1977), 76, 103.

13 Quoted in Susan Kingsley Kent, *Sex and Suffrage in Britain, 1860–1914* (Princeton, NJ: Princeton University Press, 1987), 120.

14 Quoted in Christine Bolt, *The Women's Movements in the United States and Britain from the 1790s to the 1920s* (Amherst: University of Massachusetts Press, 1993), 118, 160. A Miss M. Colborne, a medical pioneer, described her experiences in Britain in 1865 in trying to attend a lecture on physiology, in a letter to Emily Davies: "As the lecturer was explaining something when I entered, he did not discover me until the looks and coughs of the students had attracted his attention to my corner—he broke off in his lecture, and said he should like to decide whether the lecture should be continued or not, there was a show of hands against the continuance, the lecturer then bowed, pronounced the lecture discontinued, and the students left the room. I intend to try the Chemistry lecture tomorrow morning" (quoted in Philippa Levine, *Victorian Feminism 1850–1900* [London: Hutchinson, 1987], 49).

15 Quoted in Mary A. Hill, *Charlotte Perkins Gilman: The Making of a Radical Feminist, 1860–1896* (Philadelphia: Temple University Press, 1980), 50.

16 Quoted in Paul Atkinson, "Fitness, Feminism and Schooling," in *The Nineteenth-Century Woman: Her Cultural and Physical World,* ed. Sara Delamont and Lorna Duffin (London: Croom Helm, 1978), 118.

17 "Syracuse National Convention, September 8, 9, and 10, 1852," in *History of Woman Suffrage,* vol. 1, *1848–1861,* ed. Elizabeth Cady Stanton, Susan B. Anthony,

and Matilda Joslyn Gage (1881; reprint, New York: Arno and New York Times, 1969), 517.

18 Quoted in Philippa Levine, *Feminist Lives in Victorian England: Private Roles and Public Commitment* (Oxford: Basil Blackwell, 1990), 141.

19 Elizabeth Cady Stanton, *Eighty Years and More: Reminiscences 1815–1897* (New York: Schocken Books, 1971), 201, 202.

20 Quoted in Atkinson, "Fitness, Feminism and Schooling," 121.

21 Quoted in Donald Meyer, *Sex and Power: The Rise of Women in America, Russia, Sweden, and Italy* (Middletown, CT: Wesleyan University Press, 1987), 165.

22 Quoted in William L. O'Neill, *Feminism in America: A History,* 2nd ed. (New Brunswick and Oxford: Transaction Publishers, 1989), 19–20.

23 Harriet Jacobs, *Incidents in the Life of a Slave Girl: Written by Herself,* ed. Jean Fagan Yellin (Cambridge, MA: Harvard University Press, 1987), 201.

24 Frances Power Cobbe, "Criminals, Idiots, Women and Minors. Is the Classification Sound?" (1868), in *Barbara Leigh Smith Bodichon and the Langham Place Group,* ed. Candida Ann Lacey (New York: Routledge and Kegan Paul, 1987), 394.

25 Quoted in Norma Basch, *In the Eyes of the Law: Women, Marriage and Property in Nineteenth-Century New York* (Ithaca and London: Cornell University Press, 1982), 178–79.

26 Quoted in Bolt, *Women's Movements,* 133.

27 Susan B. Anthony, "Homes of Single Women" (1877), in *Elizabeth Cady Stanton,* ed. DuBois, 148.

28 Hannah Mitchell, *The Hard Way Up: The Autobiography of Hannah Mitchell, Suffragette and Rebel,* ed. Geoffrey Mitchell (London: Faber and Faber, 1968), 88.

29 Quoted in Alice S. Rossi, "Sentiment and Intellect: The Story of John Stuart Mill and Harriet Taylor Mill," in *Essays on Sex Equality,* ed. Rossi, 45.

30 "Syracuse National Convention," in *History of Woman Suffrage,* ed. Stanton, Anthony, and Gage, 1:528.

31 Quoted in Claire Goldberg Moses, *French Feminism in the Nineteenth Century* (Albany: State University of New York Press, 1984), 202.

32 Quoted in Herrad-Ulrike Bussemer, *Frauenemanzipation und Bildungsbürgertum: Sozialgeschichte der Frauenbewegung in der Reichgründungszeit* (Weinheim und Basel: Beitz Verlag, 1985), 188 (my translation).

33 Quoted in Ann Taylor Allen, *Feminism and Motherhood in Germany, 1800–1914* (New Brunswick, NJ: Rutgers University Press, 1991), 124.

34 Quoted in Mari Jo Buhle, *Women and American Socialism, 1870–1920* (Urbana: University of Illinois Press, 1981), 9.

35 Quoted in Richard J. Evans, *The Feminists: Women's Emancipation Movements in Europe, American and Australia 1840–1920* (New York: Barnes and Noble, 1977), 161.

36 Ute Frevert, *Women in German History, from Bourgeois Emancipation to Sexual Liberation,* trans. Stuart McKinnon-Evans (Oxford: Berg, 1988), 141.

37 Quoted in Sheila R. Herstein, *A Mid-Victorian Feminist: Barbara Leigh Smith Bodichon* (New Haven and London: Yale University Press, 1986), 128.

38 Quoted in David Rubinstein, *Before the Suffragettes: Women's Emancipation in the 1890s* (Brighton: The Harvester Press, 1986), 38.

39 Quoted in Jo Manton, *Elizabeth Garrett Anderson* (London: Methuen, 1965), 213. When she became engaged, the *British Medical Journal* commented ominously, "The problem of the compatibility of marriage with female medical practice . . . will thus be partly tested" (p. 214).

40 Quoted in Joanne M. Braxton, *Black Women Writing Autobiography: A Tradition Within a Tradition* (Philadelphia: Temple University Press, 1989), 132.

41 Quoted in Hill, *Charlotte Perkins Gilman,* 251.

42 Elizabeth Cady Stanton, "Letter" (1852), and "Letter" (1856), in *Elizabeth Cady Stanton,* ed. DuBois, 55, 63. Married only to the women's movement herself and frustrated at Stanton's inability to get away from home, Anthony at one time wrote to her, "I shall make a contract with the Father of my children to watch & care for them one half the time" (quoted in Kathleen Barry, *Susan B. Anthony: A Biography of a Singular Feminist* [New York: New York University Press, 1988], 157).

43 Dolores Hayden, *The Grand Domestic Revolution: A History of Feminist Designs for American Homes, Neighborhoods, and Cities* (Cambridge, MA: MIT Press, 1981), 17, 82.

44 Jacobs, *Incidents in the Life of a Slave Girl,* 39, 55.

45 Daniel Scott Smith, "Family Limitation, Sexual Control, and Domestic Feminism in Victorian America," in *Clio's Consciousness Raised: New Perspectives on the History of Women,* ed. Mary Hartman and Lois W. Banner (New York: Harper and Row, 1974), 132.

46 Quoted in Linda Gordon, *Woman's Body, Woman's Right: Birth Control in America,* rev. ed. (New York: Penguin Books, 1990), 101.

47 Sarah Grimké, "Letter IV," in *Letters on the Equality of the Sexes and Other Essays,* ed. Elizabeth Ann Bartlett (New Haven: Yale University Press, 1988), 42.

48 Quoted in Kent, *Sex and Suffrage in Britain,* 13.

49 Quoted in Judith R. Walkowitz, *Prostitution and Victorian Society: Women, Class, and the State* (Cambridge: Cambridge University Press, 1980), 170.

50 Quoted in Kent, *Sex and Suffrage in Britain,* 75.

51 Walkowitz, *Prostitution and Victorian Society,* 114, 146.

52 Quoted in Kent, *Sex and Suffrage in Britain,* 72.

53 Buhle, *Women and American Socialism,* 65.

54 Frances E. Willard, *How to Win: A Book for Girls* (1888), in *Up from the Pedestal: Selected Writings in the History of American Feminism,* ed. Aileen S. Kraditor (Chicago: Quadrangle Books, 1968), 318.

55 Quoted in Buhle, *Women and American Socialism,* 68–69.

56 Quoted in ibid., 61.

57 Quoted in ibid.

58 Quoted in Steven N. Buechler, *The Transformation of the Woman Suffrage Movement: The Case of Illinois, 1850–1920* (New Brunswick, NJ: Rutgers University Press, 1986), 116.

59 "The International Council of Women (1887)," in *Women, the Family, and Freedom: The Debate in Documents,* ed. Susan Groag Bell and Karen M. Offen, vol. 2, *1880–1950* (Stanford: Stanford University Press, 1983), 99.

60 Quoted in Paula Giddings, *When and Where I Enter: The Impact of Black Women on Race and Sex in America* (Toronto: Bantam Books, 1984), 97.

61 "Seneca Falls Convention, Seneca Falls, New York, July 19, 20, 1848, including the Declaration of Sentiments and Resolutions," in *Concise History of Woman Suffrage,* ed. Buhle and Buhle, 97.

62 Quoted in Bärbel Clemens, *"Menschenrechte haben kein Geschlecht!" Zum Politikverständnis der bürgerlichen Frauenbewegung* (Pfaffenweiler: Centaurus-Verlagsgesellschaft, 1988), 26 (my translation)

63 Quoted in Steven C. Hause, *Hubertine Auclert: The French Suffragette* (New Haven: Yale University Press, 1987), 44.

64 Ellen DuBois, "The Radicalism of the Woman Suffrage Movement: Notes Toward the Reconstruction of Nineteenth-Century Feminism," *Feminist Studies* 3 (Fall 1975): 65.

65 "New York Constitutional Convention," in *History of Woman Suffrage,* vol. 2, *1861-1876,* ed. Elizabeth Cady Stanton, Susan B. Anthony, and Matilda Joslyn Gage (1882; reprint, New York: Arno and New York Times, 1969), 285.

66 Quoted in Ellen DuBois, *Feminism and Suffrage: The Emergence of an Independent Women's Movement in America 1848–1869* (Ithaca, NY: Cornell University Press, 1978), 61. In Britain voters were first defined as "male persons" in the 1832 Reform Bill.

67 "National Conventions in 1866–67," 2:172 and "National Convention—1869," 2:351, in *History of Woman Suffrage,* ed. Stanton, Anthony, and Gage.

68 DuBois, "Radicalism," 92.

69 "Letters to Anthony in Support of Woman Suffrage, 1880," in *Elizabeth Cady Stanton,* ed. DuBois, 202, 205, 206.

70 Quoted in Pierre Rosanvallon, *Le sacre du citoyen: Histoire du suffrage universel en France* ([Paris]: Gallimard, 1992), 396–97 (my translation).

71 Quoted in Patrick Kay Bidelman, *Pariahs Stand Up! The Founding of the Liberal Feminist Movement in France, 1858–1889* (Westport, CT: Greenwood Press, 1982), 92, 155.

72 Hause, *Hubertine Auclert,* 29, 19, 24.

73 Quoted in Steven C. Hause with Anne R. Kenney, *Women's Suffrage and Social Politics in the French Third Republic* (Princeton, NJ: Princeton University Press, 1984), 18.

74 Hause, *Hubertine Auclert,* 79.

75 Quoted in Felicia Gordon, *The Integral Feminist: Madeleine Pelletier, 1874–1939: Feminism, Socialism and Medicine* (Minneapolis: University of Minnesota Press, 1990), 85.

76 DuBois, "Radicalism," 69.

77 Rubinstein, *Before the Suffragettes,* 52.

78 Lee Holcombe, *Wives and Property: Reform of the Married Women's Property Law in Nineteenth-Century England* (Toronto: University of Toronto Press, 1983), 215.

79 "Seneca Falls Convention," 1:68–69 and "Rochester Convention, 2 August 1848," 1:76 in *History of Woman Suffrage*, ed. Stanton, Anthony, and Gage. At a convention in 1852 Susan B. Anthony introduced a motion requiring soft-spoken women to let others read their speeches. But the motion was voted down. Paulina Wright Davis opposed it because "ladies did not come there to screech; they came to behave like ladies and to speak like ladies" (quoted in Ann Braude, *Radical Spirits: Spiritualism and Women's Rights in Nineteenth-Century America* [Boston: Beacon Press, 1989], 97).

80 DuBois, *Feminism and Suffrage*, 182, 18.

81 Quoted in William Leach, *True Love and Perfect Union: The Feminist Reform of Sex and Society* (New York: Basic Books, 1980), 301. In Britain an article in the *Englishwoman's Review* reassured readers that suffrage was not about "Women's Rights—an unlucky phrase fostering bitterness. It is a question of men's and women's rights" (quoted in Bolt, *Women's Movements*, 142).

82 Quoted in Kathleen E. McCrone, "The National Association for the Promotion of Social Science and the Advancement of Victorian Women," *Atlantis* 8, 1 (1982): 47.

83 Quoted in Alison Prentice, Paula Bourne, Gail Cuthbert Brandt, Beth Light, Wendy Mitchinson, and Naomi Black, *Canadian Women: A History* (Toronto: Harcourt Brace Jovanovich Canada, 1988), 178.

84 Meyer, *Sex and Power*, 195.

85 Quoted in Bussemer, *Frauenemanzipation und Bildungsbürgertum*, 123 (my translation). A member of the Leipzig Association for Women's Education, which also excluded men, complained of the difficulties women faced: "If any other group has a budget deficit, it's no big deal—it's just a deficit like any other—however, for us, because we have undertaken to lead a group without male members, it would be a deficit of women's ability, a bankruptcy of the whole women's movement" (p. 125, my translation).

86 Quoted in Levine, *Feminist Lives*, 41.

87 Quoted in Hause, *Hubertine Auclert*, 55.

88 Olive Banks, *Becoming a Feminist: The Social Origins of "First Wave" Feminism* (Brighton: Wheatsheaf Books, 1986), 106. Not all women were "woman-centred." Emily Davies, for example, valued her close work with men: "The new and difficult thing," she felt, "is for men and women to work together on equal terms" (quoted in Barbara Caine, *Victorian Feminists* [Oxford: Oxford University Press, 1992], 96).

8

Issues in First-Wave Feminism

In many of the campaigns first-wave feminists launched—for employment opportunities, legal rights, better education, and reform of family life and sexual standards—they confronted issues that are still relevant to modern feminists. That so many of these issues were still on the agendas of second-wave feminists led historians of the late 1960s and early 1970s to criticize first-wave feminists for not having achieved more than they did. Their "mistakes" were, first, letting themselves become sidetracked by the suffrage campaign, second, perpetuating a conservative view of the family and women's role that substantiated rather than subverted separate spheres ideology, and third, failing to overcome a white, middle-class orientation. Over the last twenty years historians have debated these issues, attempting to understand feminist goals and strategies within their historical context but also to assess their impact. This chapter investigates each issue in turn, beginning with the importance of the suffrage issue after 1890.

THE IMPORTANCE OF SUFFRAGE

Kate Millett, whose book *Sexual Politics* (1969) was one of the key writings of second-wave feminism, judged the suffrage campaign in the United States to be

> the red herring of the revolution—a wasteful drain on the energy of seventy years. Because the opposition was so monolithic and unrelenting, the struggle so long and bitter, the vote took on a disproportionate importance. And when

1880–1914	Height of imperialism
1889	Second Socialist International founded
1889–1914	German naval race with England
1892	Ida B. Wells launches anti-lynching campaign
1895	Elizabeth Cady Stanton writes *The Woman's Bible*
1903	First airplane flight
	Women's Social and Political Union (WSPU) forms in Britain
1906	Finland passes women's suffrage
1911	First celebration of International Proletarian Women's Day in Europe
	Olive Schreiner writes *Woman and Labour*
1912–13	Balkan Wars
1914	World War I begins

the ballot was won, the feminist movement collapsed in what can only be described as exhaustion. The suffrage campaign reminds one of nothing so much as a flat tire encountered early on a long journey—a flat which takes so much time, labor, and expense to repair that the journey is dejectedly abandoned.[1]

The struggle was certainly long and bitter. It took American women seventy-two years from the time they first claimed the franchise in 1848 until the federal government granted it in 1920. During that time, according to suffrage leader Carrie Chapman Catt, they waged 56 state referendum campaigns, 480 campaigns directed at state legislatures, 277 campaigns directed at state party conventions, 19 congressional campaigns, and 41 state amendment campaigns. In Britain suffragists were better able to concentrate their energies, but even there fifty-three years lapsed between the first campaign in 1865 and the grant of a limited franchise in 1918; full suffrage followed in 1928. The time lag was greatest in France, where the first appeal for women's suffrage was made in 1787, before the French Revolution. Feminists mounted sporadic campaigns throughout the nineteenth century, but although the first suffrage bill was introduced in the legislature in 1901, women's suffrage was not granted until 1944. In Switzerland, the Federation for Women's Suffrage dated from 1909, but Swiss women received the vote only in 1971.

Women's suffrage was granted in most Western countries in the context of World War I and its aftermath and will be discussed, accordingly, in the following chapter. Here, it is important to note the prewar growth of suffrage movements. In the United States suffrage became a mass movement. Ray Strachey reported that in Britain there were more than fifteen different suffrage societies, including a Men's League for Women's Suffrage, an Actresses' Franchise League, a Catholic Women's Suffrage Society, "and so on, until there was no group of people left in the country for whom an appropriate suffrage society could not be found."[2] Even in France, where women's suffrage was still considered very radical, at least 15,000 suffragists were active by 1914 and votes for women had become a public issue, discussed in the press and supported by women's groups ranging from Catholic to socialist. In a write-in poll conducted by the newspaper *Le Journal* over the question of whether women wanted suffrage, 505,912 voted in favour, 114 against.

International encouragement came from the American-initiated International Woman Suffrage Alliance, which held its first meeting in Berlin in 1904, and also from the decision of the international socialist movement in 1907 to support women's suffrage. Especially heartening was the granting of the vote to women in Finland in 1906 and in Norway in 1907. Although organized feminist movements in both countries began relatively late, they were closely associated with the struggle for national liberation against Russian and Swedish rule respectively. In Finland leading political parties united to demand a constitution from the czar, which, when granted, extended suffrage to all women and men. In Norway the nationalist movement stimulated hundreds of thousands of women to demonstrate their political acumen by unofficially voting in a plebiscite on the future of the monarchy. The government responded by giving propertied women the vote in 1907 and extended it to all women in 1913.

Why Suffrage?

Why was the vote so important to so many women? Kate Millett, in the above quotation, described the focus on the vote as a response to the strength of the opposition. It is certainly true that frustration bred militancy. Hubertine Auclert, who at the age of sixty smashed a voting urn at a polling station during the Parisian municipal elections of 1908, described herself as "driven to desperation by seeing my legal efforts lead to nothing."[3]

The most dramatic actions were those adopted by the Women's Social and Political Union (WSPU) in Britain from 1905. The suffragettes, so labelled by a journalist to distinguish them from the moderate suffragists, resorted to spectacular and violent means to pressure the government, beginning with heckling politicians and escalating to attacks on property: breaking windows, burning mail boxes, destroying paintings, cutting phone wires, and even planting bombs. The WSPU also pioneered non-violent tactics, utilizing banners, postcards, even military regalia such as uniforms—white dresses with sashes in the suffragette colours of green and purple—and a fife-and-drum band. At one meeting it marshalled 150 brass bands and twenty speakers' platforms. On another occasion a member flew across London in a balloon, releasing thousands of leaflets. At times confrontations turned ugly. In 1910, British police brutally clashed with suffragettes in a six-hour battle, beating the women and grabbing their breasts, on what became known as

Black Friday. Most other times the police stood back as hecklers and rowdies drowned out suffragette speakers with jeers and obscenities, threw rotten eggs or manure, or grappled with them, tearing clothes and even breaking ribs.

Eventually the government began arresting the demonstrators, a move that suffragettes welcomed for the added publicity. When arrests became too frequent to make headlines, WSPU prisoners resorted to hunger strikes. Prison authorities countered with forced feeding, several wardens holding a prisoner down in order to insert a twenty-inch tube down her nostril or throat. Trying to keep one step ahead, the government passed legislation allowing hunger strikers to be freed only until they were well enough to be rearrested. The WSPU, undaunted, commemorated the occasion by marketing a card game, called "Suffragettes in and out of Prison." As a result of these efforts, the women's suffrage campaign achieved high public visibility and challenged contemporary notions of female passivity and fragility. It "broke down hitherto infrangible tabus," English feminist Winifred Holtby recalled in 1935. "An emotional earthquake had shattered the intangible yet suffocating prison of decorum."[4] To heighten the effect, the suffragettes, most of whom were upper- or middle-class ladies, dressed for the occasion with long, fitted, lace-trimmed dresses, ribboned hats, and upswept hairdos.

In the United States suffragists like Harriot Blatch, daughter of Elizabeth Cady Stanton, began introducing attention-getting tactics in 1907. The American suffragists became skilled at adapting their tactics to each situation. In Washington State in 1910, for example, strategists avoided large demonstrations in order to avoid antagonizing or alarming the opposition, although a banner inscribed "Votes for Women" did grace the summit of Mount Rainier. In the Illinois campaign of 1913, in contrast, organizers arranged for thousands of letters and telegrams to be sent to legislators, a telephone brigade to call the speaker of the legislature every fifteen minutes, and guards at the entrance to the legislature to keep supporters from leaving and unfriendly lobbyists from entering. The New York State campaign of 1915 featured open air meetings, torchlight rallies, street dances, ethnic block parties, and outdoor concerts. In Canada, suffragists organized mock parliament skits, in which sex roles were reversed and women politicians debated the wisdom of granting men the vote. All of these activities were daring and empowering for women not accustomed to promoting their self-interest, let alone doing so in public.

Women elsewhere were more cautious. Anita Augspurg, visiting England from Germany, wrote home, "What is known here as moderate would still be the summit of outrageousness in Germany."[5] When the French feminist Madeleine Pelletier urged her colleagues to adopt militant tactics, one suggested that throwing potatoes would be safer. Pelletier retorted, "Potatoes! People would think we want to *feed* the voters."[6] Nonetheless, German suffragists held their first procession in 1912, and in France in 1914 more than five thousand marched to pay homage to the eighteenth-century advocate of women's suffrage, the Marquis de Condorcet, in a "feminist day" celebration.

A second reason for emphasizing suffrage—in addition to growing frustration over the difficulty of obtaining the franchise—was the limited success of other campaigns. While some feminist reforms had been won by the 1890s, such as laws allowing married women control over their property, they neither went far enough to suit their proponents nor necessarily recognized the validity of feminist arguments. Activists therefore stiffened their determination to obtain the vote as the route to more substantial gains, ranging from full civil rights to measures promoting maternal or child welfare or prohibiting alcohol. "If we dropped every other Department in our organization, and worked for woman's enfranchisement," the president of the Ontario Woman's Christian Temperance Union (WCTU) announced in 1904, "we should be farther ahead in ten years than we will be in fifty years without it."[7] In the United States and Britain many working women became convinced that suffrage was the means to ameliorate poor working conditions and low salaries. African-American and African-Canadian women looked to suffrage not only as a symbol of equal rights but also to meet their specific needs, such as access to education or fighting sexual exploitation. By the early 1900s African-American women had formed suffrage groups in major cities as well as at least seven state suffrage societies.

The third reason for focusing on the vote was its tremendous symbolic importance. It signified the citizen's relation to the state. For women, this was public confirmation of their identities other than as members of families. Writing in 1914 the British feminist Beatrice Hale described the vote as "a fragment of sovereignty."[8] Antisuffragists also understood its symbolic importance; for them women's suffrage threatened to dissolve the distinction between the public and private spheres and to subvert the family as a hierarchical unit under the husband's authority. The state would come between the husband and wife, they feared, and suffrage would provide the occasion for family friction. For both sides fundamental issues of gender roles and relationships, the family, and authority were at stake. It is not surprising, then, that the struggle was so long; it was not unusual for comparable social movements, such as Chartism in nineteenth-century England, to take three-quarters of a century to achieve their goals.

As national movements became more diverse, it became harder to accommodate the divergent interests that supporters represented. From the 1890s younger women and women from widely different social backgrounds came on board. Feminists, labour organizers, and social reformers all had their different reasons for supporting women's suffrage. The diversity was, to a certain extent, welcome proof of feminist claims that all women had interests in common. The gradual implementation of adult male suffrage and the heated political debates it occasioned throughout the century heightened the discrepancy of women's exclusion. So did the visibility of women in public life as they swelled the labour force as wage workers. An American observer took heart that "women who on every other possible opinion were as far apart as the two poles, worked together . . . . It was as though, among an archipelago of differing intellectual interests and social convictions, [suffragists] had found one little island on which they could stand in an absolute unanimity."[9] That this "absolute unanimity" was sometimes wishful thinking was apparent to one veteran American suffragist, the Reverend Olympia Brown, who complained bitterly of the "shallow false talk of love excellence harmony &c" which was "so false that it makes me vomit."[10] In particular, it veiled the extent to which suffragism might diverge from feminism.

Suffrage Without Feminism?

The example of the Canadian suffrage movement has been used to argue that suffragists were not necessarily feminists. Historian Carol Bacchi has analyzed the movement's "capture" in the early twentieth century by white middle-class social reformers, notably temperance workers. Their aim was the restoration, not the reformation, of the traditional family, which they saw as a bulwark against social change. Reformers hoped to recreate an earlier community, rooted in a nostalgic image of the patriarchal family as a means of social control. The enfranchisement of women, they hoped, would double the family vote. Other results were undesirable or irrelevant; when asked if the Toronto Local Council of Women supported suffrage, its president Mrs. A.H. Huestis replied, "Yes, but that is the last plank on our platform. We put the reforms first."[11] She was referring to such issues as improved child labour laws and better housing for immigrants.

While association with temperance made suffrage respectable, it simultaneously tamed it. Temperance advocate and suffragist Nellie McClung offered the reassurance that women voters would not "mix their tricks and lose interest in husband, home, and child."[12] Any critique of male oppression remained latent, never impeding the agreement of women and men reformers on identical goals; the real division in the suffrage movement was one of class, not gender. By succumbing to the rhetoric of social reform, feminists lost sight of the real issue, women's deprivation and oppression in a patriarchal society. Bacchi's analysis also explains why white North American feminists failed to respond to the heightened racist climate that confronted ethnic minorities in the late nineteenth and early twentieth centuries, but it underestimates both the extent to which temperance workers and suffragists had common feminist goals and the need of the latter to tone down an implicitly radical message.

A tendency towards reformism also predominated in the American suffrage movement as second-generation feminists succeeded to its leadership. The movement broadened in attracting women from outside the middle class and became more narrowly focused on winning the vote, growing more conservative in the process. In Illinois, for example, upper-class women, motivated to "fine-tune" the social order, lent their influential support. American suffrage leaders after 1895 were more likely to be socially prominent. Such support may have been decisive in the eventual winning of the vote, but it is questionable whether these new members contributed any insights about male dominance.

If not all suffragists were feminists, not all feminists agreed with the emphasis on the vote. Some, such as Teresa Billington-Grieg, who helped found the WSPU but left in 1910, criticized the narrowness of the suffragettes: "The suffragette who is content with the home as it is, built on the subjection of the woman," she believed, "is not a true rebel . . . . Any woman who is really a rebel longs to destroy the conventions which bind her in the home as much as those that bind her in the State." She further complained that many "fail to see that large areas in which emancipation is needed lie entirely outside the scope of the vote."[13] Billington-Grieg was one of a small number of feminists who interjected a more radical stance into feminism after 1910, analyzing women's economic oppression and questioning the sexual division of labour. Most feminists, in contrast, would have responded positively to the warning of long-standing British suffrage leader Millicent Garrett Fawcett, not to "give up one jot or tittle of your womanliness, your love of children, your care for the sick, your gentleness, your self-control, your obedience to conscience and duty, for all these things are terribly wanted in politics."[14] In 1891 Fawcett reiterated that women should be represented in government precisely because they were different from men rather than because they were not. Did Fawcett's outlook represent a conservative current at odds with the real interests of feminists?

A CONSERVATIVE IDEOLOGY?

First-wave feminism had a long intellectual tradition but no official ideology. Feminist analysis was not created full blown by any one founder but emerged out of different situations and contexts. Leading theorists such as John Stuart Mill, August Bebel, Charlotte Perkins Gilman, Olive Schreiner, or Clara Zetkin were also activists; they gave speeches, presented petitions, raised money, or edited newspapers. The context was strategic, not academic. Two of the most systematic and thorough works, Mill's *The Subjection of Women* and Bebel's *Woman and Socialism,* were remembered for their effect in securing support and popularizing the cause. An historian's characterization of early American feminists applies to others: "They disagreed with each other, were agitators before they were theorists, and produced no single spokeswoman or unifying text."[15] Given the traditional exclusion of women and women's issues from academia it is not surprising that the production of systematic theory was not a high priority.

Nonetheless, historians have persistently identified two major strands in the movement, generally described as maternal or social feminism and liberal or equal rights feminism. Maternal feminists argued that women, because of their maternal instincts or experiences, had a unique and vital contribution to make to society. They argued from the differences rather than the similarity between the sexes and urged that the values of female culture be used to counter the competitive, destructive aspects of a male-dominated industrial order. Liberal feminists, on the other hand, remained inspired by the liberal ideology of equal rights, based on the assumption of the essential similarity of all human beings. As the German writer Hedwig Dohm put it, "Human rights have no gender."[16]

The American Elizabeth Cady Stanton (1815–1902) is usually included in the camp of the liberal feminists. Stanton fumed against those who "can not take in the idea that men and women are alike."[17] A daughter from an old and wealthy New York family, she was very conscious of the republican tradition enshrined in the Declaration of Independence and had paraphrased it in the Declaration of Sentiments produced by the Seneca Falls Convention in 1848. In a speech delivered in 1892 when she was seventy-six, Stanton described the essential aloneness of each individual and the necessity to develop one's personal resources. Woman's family relationships, she declared, were no more than "the incidental relations of life."[18]

Maternal feminists, on the other hand, believed strongly in gender differences rooted in women's family situation. They were convinced of the existence of a uniquely female moral sensitivity and spirit of selflessness, what one historian has called "the power of love, rather than a love of power."[19] The more reformers became aware of the problems caused by industrialism, urbanization, and large-scale migration, the more they saw women's intervention as the answer. The American reformer Mary E. Lease spoke what many thought: "Thank God we women are blameless for this political muddle you men have dragged us into."[20] Across the Atlantic the French feminist Maria Deraismes added her indictment of male-dominated politics: "What! Women in politics would spoil everything? Alas! It seems to me that in this regard things have already progressed quite far!"[21] Women could not continue to sit on the sidelines and watch civilization disintegrate. While liberal feminists wanted to extend liberal ideas to the family, maternal feminists wanted to extend the virtues of the family to society. They recognized a moral obligation conferred by women's nature and experience. As the African-American poet and lecturer Frances Ellen Watkins Harper eloquently put it, "Through weary, wasting years men have destroyed, dashed in pieces, and overthrown, but to-day we stand on the threshold of woman's era, and woman's work is grandly constructive. In her hand are possibilities whose use or abuse must tell upon the political life of the nation, and send their influence for good or evil across the track of unborn ages."[22]

Although Stanton and Harper seem to represent polar extremes, we know now that the distinction between these two kinds of feminism has been overdrawn. There is no simple contrast between Americans and Europeans or between maternalist reformers and individualist radicals within any national movement. Throughout the second half of the nineteenth century feminists typically referred to the natures of women and men as both equal and complementary. Even Elizabeth Cady Stanton rhapsodized about "the feminine element"[23] and the changes that would occur under its influence. The following poem, written in 1885 to commemorate women workers on strike in Philadelphia, exemplifies how easily one could appeal to both equality and difference:

> We ask not your pity, we charity scorn,
> We ask but the rights to which we were born.
> For the flag of freedom has waved o'er our land,
> We justice and equality claim and demand.
> Then strive for your rights, O, sisters dear,
> And ever remember in your own sphere,
> You may aid the cause of all mankind,
> And be the true women that God designed.[24]

> *Charismatic, energetic, and witty, the Canadian suffragist Nellie McClung (1873–1951) is a good example of a maternal feminist who felt that women could and should clean up the mess men had made.*

If politics are too corrupt for women, they are too corrupt for men; for men and women are one—indissolubly joined together for good or ill. Many men have tried to put all their religion and virtue in their wife's name, but it does not work very well. When social conditions are corrupt women cannot escape by shutting their eyes, and taking no interest. It would be far better to give them a chance to clean them up.

What would you think of a man who would say to his wife: "This house to which I am bringing you to live is very dirty and unsanitary, but I will not allow you—the dear wife whom I have sworn to protect—to touch it. It is too dirty for your precious little white hands! You must stay upstairs, dear. Of course the odor from below may come up to you, but use your smelling salts and think no evil. I do not hope to ever be able to clean it up, but certainly you must never think of trying."

Do you think any woman would stand for that? She would say: "John, you are all right in your way, but there are some places where your brain skids. Perhaps you had better stay downtown today for lunch. But on your way down please call at the grocer's, and send me a scrubbing brush and a package of Dutch Cleanser, and some chloride of lime, and now hurry." Women have cleaned up things since time began; and if women ever get into politics there will be a cleaning-out of pigeon-holes and forgotten corners, on which the dust of years has fallen, and the sound of the political carpet-beater will be heard in the land.

Source: Nellie L. McClung, *In Times Like These*, intro. Veronica Strong-Boag (Toronto: University of Toronto Press, 1972). Reprinted with the permission of the publisher.

As a result of this flexibility, the women's movement has been charged with lacking ideological clarity. Various historians have remarked on the confusion, contradiction, or ambivalence of arguments based on both gender difference and equality. In the view of one critic, the predominance of maternal feminist rhetoric from the 1890s proves that feminists "were insufficiently alert to the danger presented by even a partial accommodation to the maternal mystique."[25] They succumbed to the dominant values of their culture, failing to understand that their true interests lay in criticizing the division of labour in the family rather than perpetuating it. The second wave therefore inherited the unfinished agenda of the first wave of feminism. More recently but in the same vein, historian Nancy Cott has suggested that maternal feminism was not really feminism and is more accurately described by the terms *municipal housekeeping* or *civic maternalism*. Feminism should be reserved for "something more specific than women's entrance into public life or efforts at social reform," she maintains, namely an expressed "intention to alter gender hierarchy."[26] Why, after all, should temperance workers be called feminists? One might add that while maternal feminism had the laudable goal of separate but equal, can separate ever be equal, given the context of a male-dominated society? Does not any stance that accepts given sex roles contribute to perpetuating them?

In Defence of Maternal Feminism

Historians who defend maternal feminism argue that it was a necessarily and skilfully adaptive ideology and that it posed a radical alternative to male-defined values. They insist that it is important to understand the context of the movement, a context not only of male politics and intellectual traditions but also of women's lives and experiences. Although women had to depend on men for any change in their situation, they could and did resist becoming like men in order to bargain for their rights. Some maternal feminists explicitly dismissed the ideology of liberalism as androcentric. They saw equal rights theory, which posits an abstract individual free of gendered characteristics, as a male-centred ideology, running counter to women's social experiences as mothers, daughters, wives, and sisters. As the German feminist Helene Stöcker put it, "No, no, not to be a man or to want to be a man, or to be mistaken for a man: how should that help us!"[27] Those who spoke in favour of equal rights and opportunities were simply integrating women into a male ideology, whereas those who argued from difference were attempting to create an alternative ideology based on female experience and values. The latter project was inherently radical, argues scholar Naomi Black. By re-evaluating male categories rather than simply broadening them to include women, maternal feminists in her judgment were "committed, whether they [knew] it or not, to a basic transformation of patriarchal structures and values."[28]

How did this work in practice? In Britain and North America maternal feminism came from and nourished a distinct female political culture. What critics would label inconsistency, historian Philippa Levine describes as a collectivist and pragmatic alternative to male politics, both to the ideology of individualism and to the deepening doctrinal differences between established political parties. Feminists wanted nothing less than to redefine politics by "feminizing political values, as opposed to masculinizing women to fit them for public office."[29] The rejection of male categories was an attempt to define and celebrate what was uniquely female. Levine is referring to the British context, but American scholars have also described how women working through voluntary associations created an alternative political culture to the exclusively male realm of electoral politics. Paradoxically, in the four decades before American women got the vote they had enormous political influence.

The components of this culture—the women's clubs that proliferated throughout the second half of the nineteenth century and the national network they forged—ranged from missionary societies to cultural or social action groups. Unique to North America, these institutions lent the New World a sense of national mission and community identity lacking in an immigrant society. Clubs that started out as literary or cultural organizations turned to social problems and from there to feminism. In 1904, the president of the American umbrella organization of white women's clubs exhorted, "Ladies, you have chosen me your leader. Well, I have an important piece of news to give you. Dante is dead. He has been dead for several centuries, and I think it is time that we dropped the study of his Inferno and turned our attention to our own."[30]

Club feminism was characteristically maternalist; these grass-roots organizations extended the moral concern implied in the concept of motherhood into the public realm. For African-American women this meant addressing problems specific to southern black communities, such as high infant mortality rates. Maternalist language could simultaneously enhance black women's commitment to their race and their sense of self in a culture still cognizant of the reproductive coercion of mothers under slavery. Mary Church Terrell, first president of the National Association of Colored Women (NACW), explained the race-specific aspects of motherhood to a predominantly white audience in 1899: where a white mother will experience "feelings of hope and joy," a black mother sees "the thorny path of prejudice and proscription," leading her to tremble "with apprehension and despair."[31] The NACW understood the needs of mothers in paid labour and gave priority to mothers' clubs and day nurseries, orphanages, old-age homes, and other essentials for communities that rarely received government assistance.

White middle-class women focused on problems in industrial, urban communities and were able to secure the co-operation of local governments in subsidizing and eventually taking over their programs. As a result, amenities such as clean water and pasteurized milk, parks and kindergartens, and libraries and hospitals enhanced urban life for tens of thousands of Americans. Under their pressure, governments addressed the needs of mothers and children as legitimate objects of public policy. The concept of government attentive to the welfare of its citizens emerged as a result. This concept, along with the incorporation of these services into state bureaucracies, laid the basis for the modern welfare state.

The pre-eminent example of a female professional culture was the group associated with Jane Addams and Hull House, a settlement house, or centre offering community services. Hull House was established in a Chicago working-class neighbourhood in 1889. Rather than compete with male professionals, the women reformers and researchers from Hull House lobbied for their own area of expertise within the federal government and won it with the establishment of the Children's Bureau in 1912. Staffed and administered by women, the Children's Bureau gained a reputation for its unique ability to communicate with women throughout the country and to champion their interests. Hull House also represents the success of maternal feminism in justifying a separatist culture, which gave women the support system they needed to remain single and devote their time and energy to reform causes or professional careers rather than to families. This might seem ironic given the emphasis on motherhood, but motherhood was never understood by feminists as limited to or even exemplified by *biological* maternity; they understood it as spiritual or social motherhood.

Nineteenth-century Britain and North America had relatively weak central governments that, correspondingly, allowed space for women to initiate and run their own programs. The situation in continental Europe was different. In Germany, for example, the state pioneered the introduction of social welfare policies; women could have little access to or impact on the male bureaucracy. In France, upper- and middle-class women had a long tradition as philanthropists, but their charity work was usually directed by the state or the church. In these contexts, maternal feminism appeared as a radical demand for women's input into public policies and for state intervention on behalf of mothers and children instead of fathers, who were still legally the head of the household. In fact, Americans critical of the feminist emphasis on suffrage in their own country considered Europeans more radical in tackling issues that went to the heart of family relations.

The way feminists in France, Italy, and Germany used maternalist rhetoric from the 1890s illustrates the type of action that Americans admired. In these countries, as elsewhere, the declining birth rate seemed to reach alarming proportions. When blamed for the decline, French feminists turned the argument around, insisting that the best way to encourage population growth was to support mothers. They agitated successfully, as did Italian feminists, for compulsory maternity leave, introduced in some measure in both countries by the early 1910s. Other European countries—the Netherlands, Denmark, and Norway—also provided some form of maternity benefits before or during World War I, although it is difficult to assess to what extent feminism contributed to the result. In Germany at the turn of the century feminists used motherhood to claim a voice for women in public debates about venereal disease, prostitution, and abortion. The discussions were dominated by male experts, who spoke as politicians, doctors, lawyers, inspectors, or ministers. They did not, however, speak as fathers. Women, lacking professional expertise—they could not be certified as doctors until 1899 in Germany—professionalized motherhood in an attempt to overcome their exclusion from the discussion.

Maternal feminists were not in full agreement about their goals, although most welcomed paid maternity leave as well as services such as free milk and health clinics. The most radical argued that state recognition should extend to all mothers regardless of marital status and that women should control all aspects of maternity, including access to birth control and abortion. As expressed in the philosophy of the Norwegian feminist Kati Anker Møller: "We love motherhood, we want to promote motherhood, but it should be voluntary and the responsibility should all be ours."[32] Though they might differ among themselves about the meaning and importance of motherhood, women were united in using it to represent women's interests, to demand input into the decisions that affected them. Their overall aims were to gain public acknowledgment of the issues central to most women's lives and to channel that acknowledgment into material improvements, whether in the name of feminism or of pronatalism, that is, of arguments concerned solely with increasing the birth rate.

The Swedish writer Ellen Key (1849–1926) made one of the strongest arguments for a feminist evaluation of motherhood. Key has presented a dilemma for modern feminists because of the centrality of motherhood in her thought. She regarded it as women's "highest cultural task" and rejected the idea of mothers working outside the home. Yet she was by her own claim the first Swedish feminist to speak in public for female suffrage, and she advocated "complete freedom for every woman to follow her individuality." Unifying Ellen Key's views was a commitment to a new social order that placed the mother–child relationship at its centre. It was society's responsibility to support mothers economically and psychologically. Women's rights meant women's right to full-time motherhood. "It was thus not motherhood itself that was debilitating to women as social beings," observes one critic, "but the patriarchal structure in which it was contained."[33] This is a surprising anticipation of second-wave ideas on motherhood. In her own context, Key was controversial, even notorious, because of her elevation of motherhood over marriage. Radical American feminists of the 1910s greeted Key as a sister radical who promoted women's sexual liberation. One might argue that any demand, even from less controversial figures, that public life accommodate motherhood implicitly challenged the ideology of separate spheres.

The above discussion presents maternal feminism as a conscious alternative to liberal feminism, but many, perhaps most, first-wave feminists refused to accept that liberal and maternal feminism were mutually exclusive. The liberal goal of self-realization was never an abstraction. Women claimed equality as part of the larger freedom to develop themselves, although not necessarily along the same lines as men. Feminists generally viewed equal rights, including the right to vote, as a means for self-fulfilment and social reforms rather than as an end in itself. Women increasingly came to define fulfilment in terms of service to their community. For them equal rights and service were complementary rather than contradictory.

The arguments of difference and equality are interwoven in a book by the South African writer Olive Schreiner, *Woman and Labor* (1911), which became a bible for many in the women's movement. Schreiner (1855–1920) passionately denounced any division of labour on the basis of gender difference. "Any attempt to divide the occupations in which male and female intellects and wills should be employed," she objected, "must be to attempt a purely artificial and arbitrary division." She demanded that all work be open to women: "From the judge's seat to the legislator's chair; from the statesman's closet to the merchant's office; from the chemist's laboratory to the astronomer's tower, there is no post or form of toil for which it is not our intention to attempt to fit ourselves; and there is no closed door we do not intend to force open." At the same time Schreiner claimed for women "a distinct physic attitude" based on the division of labour in reproduction: "No step in the reproductive journey, or in their relation to their offspring, has been quite identical for the man and the woman." Acknowledging areas "in which sex does play its part," Schreiner determined that "woman, the bearer of the race, must stand side by side with man, the begetter."[34] Neither can act for the other.

Uniting these different strands in Schreiner's work was her assertion that child bearing should enhance but not limit women's role, rather a matter of women having their cake and eating it too. While describing motherhood as the "crowning beatitude of the woman's existence," Schreiner happily put it into perspective. Nowadays, she wrote, the experience of motherhood in child bearing and rearing, "instead of filling the entire circle of female life from the first appearance of puberty to the end of middle age, becomes an episodal occupation, employing from three or four to ten or twenty of the threescore-and-ten-years which are allotted to human life."[35] Valuing the experience was essential; allowing it to determine all of women's existence was foolish and wrong.

Maternal Feminism as Strategy

Utilitarian motives also played a part in the employment of maternalist rhetoric. No matter how daring feminists' ideals might be, they had to make their ideas acceptable to men if they wanted to have any impact. American author Sara Willis Parton, who wrote under the pen name Fanny Fern, defended pragmatic tactics: "Better policy to play possum, and wear the mask of submission. No use in rousing any unnecessary antagonism. . . . I shall reach the goal just as quick in my velvet shoes, as if I tramped on rough-shod as they [suffragists] do with their Woman's Rights Convention brogans."[36] Similarly, the Canadian temperance leader Letitia Youmans recognized "the necessity of being as wise as a serpent and as harmless as a dove."[37] While not all feminists were so frank, all had to consider the public impact of their ideas.

Reference to women's maternal and moral virtues could be especially helpful in specific contexts. In France, it helped defuse the tenacious view of woman as politically disruptive, a view strengthened by the workers' uprising in Paris in 1871, when women such as Louise Michel and Paule Mink fought on the barricades alongside men. Two decades later, in the nearly hysterical climate of concern over the declining birth rate, maternalist rhetoric was a necessity. A recent study judges that feminist use of it was "politically astute," "realistic, even astute," "appropriate," "logical and necessary."[38] In Germany as well, feminists were aware of the need to tread carefully. The Federation of German Women's Associations wrote to the Founding Congress of the International Council of Women in 1888 explaining how life under a monarchy necessitated tact and caution. Across the Atlantic, the conservative social atmosphere of the Maritime provinces in Canada persuaded Edith Archibald of Halifax to suggest that she and her colleagues speak of children's rights rather than women's rights. Like so many other women, Archibald discovered that men who would rally on behalf of children would raise their hackles at any attempt by women to promote their own interests. African-Canadian and African-American women found the idea of inherent female virtue a useful weapon to counter white accusations of sexual immorality. All women could find a sense of righteousness comforting when faced with the hostility and ridicule of their opponents.

Feminists could also utilize maternal feminism to reach more conservative women. In Germany, Henriette Goldschmidt recognized its practical importance: "To reach our aim of a large women community [*sic*] our programme has to be moderate and not rash; we especially should not touch the woman's role as wife and mother but always have to stress its value and importance."[39] Another German leader, Gertrud Bäumer, also understood that for most women fulfilment meant motherhood and concluded, "Room has to be made for it."[40] As a result, motherhood played the same role in uniting German women of different political persuasions that suffrage played in North America and Britain.

The attempt to unite women with different agendas under maternal feminism could, however, result in strange bedfellows. German radicals were encouraged by the freer political atmosphere of the 1890s and contacts with the international women's movement. Although they managed briefly to capture the leadership of the Bund Deutscher Frauenvereine, or BDF (Federation of German Women's Associations), moderates rallied to oust them and secure the group's direction under the presidency of Gertrud Bäumer. The struggle reveals dissension in the movement at the same time that the spectacular growth of the German socialist party provoked a conservative reaction in the nation. The BDF grew in numbers, but its member groups included a colonial society that urged the emigration of white women in order to keep German colonies racially pure, a temperance society whose membership was mostly male, and a group of Prussian rural housewives who described their motives in appropriate preindustrial imagery as "taking up [the movement's] reins in order to drive it themselves."[41]

In France the ideology of maternal feminism opened up the possibility of alliance with Catholic women, whose support was vital if feminists hoped to create a mass movement. (Most French feminists were anticlerical, Protestant, or Jewish.) Although Marie Maugeret, a self-styled Christian feminist, resolutely rejected "free thinker feminism" and called on women to help re-Christianize the country, she supported women's right to work, equal pay, married women's property rights, reform of the civil code, and the right to vote. Taking the Bible as her inspiration, she understood feminism, as did most other French feminists, in terms of duties rather than rights. The battle lines between Catholics and anticlerical republicans throughout the nation remained strong, however, and even increased at the end of the century. Collaboration was impossible, and Maugeret remained as atypical among feminists as among Catholics. In Quebec, maternal feminists were much more successful in forging bonds with Catholic women, albeit nuns whose tradition of activism within the community served as an inspiration and model for secular feminists.

Although the argument of gender difference proved useful, it would be a mistake to assume that feminists adopted it for wholly utilitarian reasons. They, along with their opponents, shared the social and intellectual milieu of the late nineteenth and early twentieth centuries, in which the conviction of sexual differences was deeply rooted. Science appeared to lend authority to the notion of inherent gender distinction. Partly as a result of Charles Darwin's theory of evolution, which incorporated the idea that sexual characteristics grow more pronounced over time, the ideology of separate spheres became stronger rather than weaker in the late nineteenth century. Medical "experts" added their view that difference meant deficiency, labelling menstruation and child bearing as debilitating weaknesses. As medicine and science strengthened or even replaced religious authority, the law of nature appeared just as unalterable as any law of God. The English doctor Elizabeth Sloan Chesser pronounced in 1913, "The longing of every normal woman to find happiness in sex union and to exercise her functions physically and psychically in marriage and motherhood is an ineradicable instinct which cannot be altered by any external circumstances of education or environment whatsoever."[42] Or, as Nellie McClung more crisply put it, "Every normal woman wants to have children."[43]

By the turn of the century social Darwinism, the idea that nations or races were engaged in a struggle for survival, was pervasive in Western countries. Lord Cromer, the British minister of war and an antisuffragist, warned in 1910, "Can we hope to compete with such a nation as this [Germany], if we war against nature, and endeavour to invert the natural roles of the sexes? We cannot do so."[44] Abetting this nationalist-imperialist mood, statistics revealing a declining birth rate among the upper and middle classes spurred fears of "race suicide" throughout North America and Western Europe.

As well, the turn of the century brought an antifeminist backlash, in part caused by what successes the movement had. Hostility to those who seemed to threaten marriage and motherhood was provoked in several ways: "New Woman" novels appeared in the 1890s, celebrating an independent, cycling, and smoking heroine who would marry only after due consideration or perhaps not at all; increasing numbers of women entered the workforce; reports of university-educated women shunning marriage circulated—a stunning 75 percent of women who graduated from American colleges before 1900 remained single—and the numbers of female students and even of female faculty rose; divorce rates went up; and the medical community condemned homosexuality as abnormal, associating lesbianism with feminism. In this context one can appreciate the 1915 American suffrage banner that promised,

> For the safety of the nation to
> Women give the vote
> For the hand that rocks the cradle
> Will never rock the boat.[45]

Rather than reject outright "scientifically" supported notions of sexual difference, reformers tried to turn them to their advantage. The theory of evolution could justify keeping women in the home by reinforcing separate spheres, but it also could be turned around to justify women's entry into the public sphere. If women's qualities were innate rather than the result of social conditioning, there was no rationale for excluding women from the public sphere in order to keep them womanly. This was an attractive argument to defuse the opposition; but, we have to ask, was this always the intent? Were maternal feminists hostage to the ideology they thought they were challenging? Maternalist language may have seemed to Gertrud Bäumer the way to broaden the German women's movement, but was it strategy or conviction that led her to add, "Good for a woman who restricts herself to home and family! In many ways she acts more in the spirit of the women's movement than if she took up some male career"?[46]

From our distance it is difficult to judge the sincerity of motives or strategies, although we can assess their impact. Maternal feminists may have hoped to subvert patriarchal values, but maternalism could be and was adapted to serve those values. Feminists argued that attention to the interests and needs of mothers and children would reorient society, but male politicians and governments were able to separate the needs of children from those of mothers and to foster them in the interest of producing future workers and soldiers. Although the German women's movement championed the idea that women's emancipation was bound up with the promotion of social reform, female social work was co-opted by the state under the impact of World War I and redirected to support the war effort, the ultimate expression of male culture. Even in the United States, the Children's Bureau maintained its monopoly only until the 1930s. When its concerns became more central to the government, it fell under the control of male bureaucrats. Women had the most influence in policy decisions when they worked from parallel structures, which in the long run marginalized them; nowhere were women able to penetrate the male bastions of politics. Nor did they necessarily want to. Some shunned the dirty world of men's politics, convinced of their own moral superiority even when they had an opportunity to exert influence. As well, although advocates could not have foreseen it, inviting state intervention into matters of family welfare could bring an unwelcome intrusion of (male) experts.

Promoting maternalism could backfire in other ways. Some legislators may have been reassured by maternalist arguments with respect to how women would use the vote; others opposed women's suffrage precisely because they objected to the imposition of "feminine" values such as temperance. And while insistence on woman's special attributes was used to open up occupations from medicine to factory inspection, it could also act as a barrier. Women doctors, for example, were ultimately isolated in their profession and hindered from entering medical specialties other than those dealing with women and children. The same pattern occurred in other professions. British women journalists were poorly paid and limited to writing about women's topics. In Canada, female educators, nurses, journalists, and social workers were "systematically shunted into specialized job ghettos which reaffirmed their subordination rather than autonomy." These pioneering women became hostages to the ideology that helped them enter and survive in a hostile environment. In 1884, a Canadian male author spoke with regrettable foresight: "Busy people are the happiest. Give occupation to the woman with no duties, and we shall have fewer busy-bodies and happier women. Never fear that throwing open the gates of learning will deluge the world with advocates of 'female rights.'"[47]

By using maternalist rhetoric, therefore, feminists may have allowed themselves to be co-opted or marginalized. Yet it is difficult to see what else they could have done. At the time, it seemed to work. By the early twentieth century, depending on the context, women had introduced measures that improved life in countless ways for needy people; they had contributed a woman's voice to public debates, even if they were ultimately overridden; and they had made suffrage a more respectable cause, perhaps even making its ultimate victory possible. As the authors of a recent study judge, the fact that women "ultimately lacked the political power to refashion the state according to their own visions does not diminish the importance of those visions, their accomplishments, or their legacy."[48] As to whether maternal feminism was indeed feminist, that judgment can be made only by considering what it meant in each political context.

CONTINUED CHALLENGES

The debate over maternal feminism should not obscure the other ways in which feminists continued to challenge contemporary values. Many younger, college-educated, and economically independent women who joined the movement after 1890 were ready to experiment with new ideas and practices and to contribute to the rebellion against Victorian mores that marked fin-de-siècle culture. The group of twenty-five self-styled feminists who were members of the Heterodoxy club in Greenwich Village, New York, in 1912, described themselves as "the most unruly and individualistic females you ever fell among."[49] In Britain, feminist journals such as *Shafts* or *The Freewoman* held lively discussions on unorthodox views. In France, Madeleine Pelletier defied her mother and society by cutting her hair and wearing a man's jacket with a straight skirt. The ideas of the more radical first-wave feminists on marriage, work outside of and inside the home, sexuality, religion, and sex role theory are of interest here and merit attention.

The "new woman" literature of the 1890s fuelled an intense discussion of heterosexual relationships, even if the new woman herself was more a literary caricature than a reality. Shocked theatre audiences debated the ethics of Nora's move in leaving her family in Henrik Ibsen's play *A Doll's House* (1879), and sympathetic women formed "Nora's groups." Although it is true that first-wave feminists did not make the personal political in the same way as second-wave feminists were to do, they did understand the idea of oppression within the family. Elizabeth Wolstenholme, for example, who established the Women's Emancipation Union in England in 1891, found "injustice within the family" to be "the perennial source of all other injustice."[50] She had been prepared to bear a child in a common-law relationship until her colleagues urged her to marry so as to not tarnish the image of the suffragists. (She did marry, and she and her husband took the name Wolstenholme Elmy.) Many younger feminists in Britain seemed altogether hostile to the idea of marriage, and indeed the number of married women in the movement declined. In 1913 single women formed 63 percent of the WSPU. Teresa Billington-Grieg and Cicely Hamilton believed that only women free from marriage could adequately carry on the fight for emancipation. To them the deliberate choice of singlehood was the only way to personal independence and fulfilment. Others referred to the refusal of women to marry as a "silent strike" against male power in the family and sexual relations. In the United States within the same generation, a higher number of women than usual remained single, devoted to reform causes and careers.

To allow married women to take advantage of new professional employment opportunities, the home environment had to be altered. The solution, as earlier, seemed to lie in changing the way domestic work was valued, or at least performed. In Germany, Käthe Schirmacher proposed wages for housework and insisted on its social value: "Without the patient work of millions of women, who are never named in song or heroic legends, an intellectual culture, a development of the arts and sciences would be unimaginable." "Where is the recognition for all our work in this area?" she asked rhetorically. "Nowhere! . . . Our work gains us nothing, for here suddenly the principle ceases to apply: equal work, equal rights, more work, more rights: instead it's more work, fewer rights."[51]

Many were inspired by the suggestions made by Charlotte Perkins Gilman in the United States for professionalizing housework or by Lily Braun in Germany for collectivizing it. These ideas were popularized in England and taken up by the Fabian Society Women's Group, which researched the issue. The result was an impressive series of publications that included the classic monographs of Olive Schreiner and Alice Clark on women and work. Members of the more mainstream National Union of Women's Suffrage Societies discussed Lady McLaren's *Women's Charter of Rights and Liberties* of 1910, which proposed wages for housework and state-run child care. Although the Union did not adopt the proposals, the exchange in its journal, *Common Cause,* was lively.

Others preferred a more hands-on approach. In the fifty years before 1917, some five thousand people participated in feminist schemes for collectivizing domestic work. One plan was the Feminist Apartment Hotel proposed by Henrietta Rodman, a disciple of Charlotte Perkins Gilman. The design for the twelve-storey building with kitchenless apartments and a nursery school featured details such as fold-up beds and built-in bathtubs to minimize housekeeping. Alice Constance Austin more ambitiously planned a feminist city in California of ten thousand people with an underground delivery system to provide hot food and clean laundry. Although these more ambitious projects were never built, there were at least thirty-three experiments in the United States with community dining clubs and cooked food delivery services.

Schemes such as these had in common the assumption that women would continue to bear the responsibility for domesticity; women would supervise trained, paid female workers. Community kitchens, cooked food delivery services, and domestic science courses were meant to free white middle-class women from domestic cares by passing them on to other women. There was no attack on the gendered division of labour, just a desire to make it more efficient. Alice Austin, for example, expected that married women in her feminist city would put their time into raising children rather than into careers. A few, like the German socialist Clara Zetkin, did call on men to share housework and parenting. Some of the most radical discussions took place in British feminist circles. One contributor to *The Freewoman,* a weekly feminist review published in 1911–12, proposed state-run nurseries for infants of two weeks or more. Another asked, "Might not the advice to go home and mind the baby sometimes be applied to the fathers?"[52] For most feminists, however, the assumption of a continued reliance on servants prevented a more thorough analysis; even a working-class woman like Hannah Mitchell, who hated housework, assumed that she was an exception and resigned herself accordingly.

British feminists protested the physical as well as the economic consequences of marriage. In feminist and non-feminist circles the extent of venereal disease was greatly, if exaggeratedly, publicized in the early twentieth century. The WSPU increasingly targeted heterosexual relations as physically destructive for women and linked the issue of sex and suffrage in Christabel Pankhurst's slogan, "Votes for women, chastity for men." As in North America, social purity and suffrage were joined. From the 1880s, a large majority of old campaigners in the women's movement supported the National Vigilance Association for the Repression of Criminal Vice and Immorality, the goals of which were as ominous as its name indicates, including, for example, censorship and opposition to birth control. These reformers also turned to suffrage as the answer. By 1914, suffrage organizations commonly addressed heterosexual issues in their propaganda. At times the resulting condemnation of male sexual morality amounted to what contemporaries saw as an explicit "sex war."[53]

Although family violence and marital rape found some discussion with veiled references to husbands' rights, few dared to raise the issue of rape per se. In the African-American community, however, journalist Ida B. Wells-Barnett (1862–1931) exposed the political and racial context of rape. Wells-Barnett, born a slave, in the 1890s published her meticulously researched findings on the connection between rape accusations and lynchings of black men in the American South. Her antilynching campaign, she later claimed, was the beginning of black women's organization, and it is true that in some cities her speeches inspired women to form clubs. Wells-Barnett saw allegations, usually made by white men, of black men raping white women as a way for white men to re-establish their control over blacks. As she and others pointed out, in the reverse situation, black women were not in a position to protect themselves from white men by threatening to expose rape. Fannie Barrier Williams observed meaningfully, "We have never been taught to understand why the unwritten law of chivalry, protection, and fair play that are everywhere the conservators of women's welfare must exclude every woman of a dark complexion."[54] Wells-Barnett went further, "exposing the rawest nerve in the South's patriarchal bosom"[55] by suggesting that many interracial liaisons were actually conducted at the initiative of white women.

Most feminists continued to assume female virtue and male vice. As earlier, they associated male sexuality with artificial methods of birth control, fearing that these would make women more vulnerable to male demands. Writing at a time when many women were rejecting Victorian sexual standards, the Canadian feminist Alice Chown, a rebel in other ways, wrote, "So long as woman accepts indiscriminate sex relations, so long as her physical relation to man is stronger than her intellectual or spiritual, so long will she be subject to him."[56] Most women preferred to regulate intercourse by methods that they controlled, such as douches or reliance on "safe" periods. Whatever the method, feminists were adamant that motherhood should be voluntary. Ethel Snowden described "a woman's absolute right over herself after marriage" as the "last and greatest" demand of the women's movement. Stella Browne and Cicely Hamilton both condemned the idea of women as breeding machines. "Motherhood," Hamilton declared, "can be sacred only when it is voluntary, when a child is desired by a woman who feels herself fit to bear and rear it."[57]

Implicit in Hamilton's statement are the eugenic arguments about improving race through the science of heredity that were common in all Western countries in the early twentieth century. Eugenicists worried about the declining birth rate of their own ethnic population and blamed it on women's emancipation. The English author S.H. Halford declared women's "sexlessness" a wrong committed against both society and men, whose "inevitable need calls for preferential consideration over the sentimental grievances of women."[58] In a manner similar to their radicalization of separate spheres ideology, feminists appropriated eugenics to claim that the race benefited most from quality, not quantity. Large unhealthy families were a detriment to the race, and mothers knew best how to produce superior children. Such reasoning could reinforce a racist outlook but it could also stress the cultural and social rather than the biological. It gave women the grounds to argue the interests of unborn children against husbands who might carry venereal disease. Some even linked motherhood to heterosexual radicalism, defending the right of women to have children outside of marriage by underlining the importance of child bearing to the state, or by justifying birth control in the interest of the higher development of the race.

Women such as Madeleine Pelletier and Nelly Roussel in France, Stella Browne and Marie Stopes in England, Aletta Jacobs and Marie Rutgers-Hoitsema in the Netherlands, Marie Stritt and Helene Stöcker in Germany, and Emma Goldman in the United States took a public position in favour of birth control and even abortion. France, where both topics were openly discussed by feminists, had long had the lowest birth rate in the Western world. In Germany in 1908, the Federation of German Women's Associations debated the proposed decriminalization of abortion. Gertrud Bäumer denounced decriminalization as a betrayal of the essential principles of the women's movement, but Camilla Jellinek and Käthe Schirmacher claimed that the movement could be true to itself only by defending women's right to abortion as part of their right to self-determination. The radicals lost the vote, but only because the Federation manoeuvred the last-minute membership of a conservative religious women's group, which voted against it.

Encouraged by the writings of sex reformers such as Havelock Ellis and Richard von Krafft-Ebing in the 1880s and 1890s, some feminists publicly acknowledged women's right to express heterosexuality just as men did. In Germany, the League for the Protection of Motherhood and Sexual Reform, under the direction of Helene Stöcker, advocated sex education and contraception, legalized abortion, and the recognition of heterosexual activity as a "natural and self-evident right."[59] Antifeminists could also promote female heterosexuality, however. In Britain, Walter Gallichan, author of *Modern Woman and How to Manage Her* (1909), stereotyped all women who fought for women's rights as frigid and man hating: "the cold woman frequently becomes a militant man-hater," he reasoned, "and especially so when she is beautiful."[60] Not surprisingly, most feminists continued to assume that the promotion of female heterosexuality, as Anna Papritz in Germany suggested, represented "a man's point of view."[61]

The discussion of sexuality had both negative and positive implications for lesbians. Throughout most of the nineteenth century, women had continued to enjoy intense romantic friendships with other women. The feminist movement indirectly encouraged such relationships through its critical analysis of heterosexual relations. By the late nineteenth century, however, both medical researchers and artists had begun to characterize homosocial relations as explicitly sexual and biologically abnormal. Whereas many homosocial women were undoubtedly dismayed by such criticism, others found solace in the idea that their sexual preference was due to nature rather than to a moral failing. At the same time, their conviction of belonging to a "third sex" weakened their sense of solidarity with other women. An exception was Anna Rueling in Berlin, who in 1904 identified common interests of lesbians and feminists and called on the women's movement to support the rights of homosexuals.

Scarcely less controversial than sexuality was the issue of religion. Most feminists disavowed religious radicalism not only because they wished to appear respectable but also because many continued to find inspiration in their faith. All the more noteworthy, then, was Elizabeth Cady Stanton's critique of organized religion, which she believed was the root of woman's oppression. In 1895 and 1898, when she was over eighty years old, Stanton published *The Woman's Bible*, a collection of international feminist commentaries. She and the other authors gave a very unflattering account of the Old Testament as "emanating from the most obscene minds of a barbarous age" and labelled passages in St Paul on women's subordination "bare-faced forgeries, interpolated by unscrupulous bishops." While drawing attention to the importance of women in early Christianity, the commentators criticized the omission of women's names in the Old Testament ("Then as now names for women and slaves are of no importance. . . . To-day the woman is Mrs. Richard Roe, to-morrow Mrs. John Doe."), and included a sampling of women's responses to the question, "Have the teachings of the Bible advanced or retarded the emancipation of women?"[62] Other feminists spoke out against organized religion—among them Frances Power Cobbe in England, Hubertine Auclert in France, Flora MacDonald Denison in Canada, and Auguste Fickert in Austria—but few were as bold as Stanton in an age that was still fundamentally religious. In 1896, the National

American Woman Suffrage Association, which had earlier elected Stanton president, voted after an acrimonious debate to disavow any association with *The Woman's Bible.*

One of the most interesting challenges to social attitudes, and thereby to assumptions of first-wave feminists, was posed by academic women in the United States whose research in psychology and anthropology helped refute the notion of inherent sex differences. They faced financial and other obstacles in pursuing their studies, but the work of researchers such as Helen Bradford Thompson and Elsie Chews Parsons helped to replace Victorian orthodoxy about separate spheres with widespread scepticism by 1914. It also had an unforeseen consequence: their challenge to gender roles undermined the sense of sisterhood and homosocial support networks that had fed the women's movement. This implication would be more fully developed after World War I.

In spite of its increasing concentration on suffrage, then, feminism after 1890 seems as multifaceted as before. Having won some capitulation to their demands for property laws, educational access, and employment opportunities, activists felt both more confident and more impatient. Conservatives and radicals, older women and younger, agreed on the need to improve women's situation, even if they disagreed on immediate targets and tactics. The diversity of a movement that by now had spanned three generations remains impressive. These were the years in which the term *feminist* appeared, first in France and England in the 1890s and by the 1910s in North America, although only a small minority so identified themselves. Whether the reference to feminism marks a new phase or a change of direction within the movement, the vitality and diversity of women who were organizing to change women's position belie any simple indictment of first-wave feminism as conservative.

BARRIERS AND BRIDGES

Is it true that first-wave feminism was an elitist movement, unable to transcend class or racial barriers? The political climate in Western countries at the turn of the century was certainly not conducive to the promotion of sisterhood across class and race lines. Feminist responses to this climate reflected the divisions within women's movements. On the one hand, most suffragists mirrored the prejudices of the age as they pursued their adaptive strategy. On the other, women who tended to be socially radical also tended to be politically radical. Many turned to socialism and a significant number devoted their efforts to bridging the gap between working and middle classes. Others were caught somewhere between these two poles, continuing their efforts to assist the less privileged but with mixed motives and mixed results. Let us look at four examples of how feminism combined with racial or class struggles: race and suffrage in North America; class and suffrage in Britain; the cross-class efforts of social reformers; and attempts in Germany and France to connect socialism with feminism.

Suffrage and Sisterhood in North America

Whereas European suffragists could pander to contemporary imperialist sentiments with the vague claim that women's suffrage would improve the race, white North American suffragists worried specifically about large-scale immigration from Central and Southern Europe, which began in the United States in the mid-1800s and a decade later in Canada. Most easily adopted or shared the racist views of their contemporaries. They used statistics to prove the numerical superiority of native-born Anglo-European women in the population, contending that the enfranchisement of all women would offset the "foreign vote." Margaret McAlpine of the Canadian Suffrage Association advised the prime minister in 1911 that "Canadian women have the well-being of the country more at heart than the average foreign immigrant."[63] One reason why provinces in the Canadian West were the first to legislate women's suffrage may have been because those areas had the heaviest immigration.

In case the quantitative argument was not persuasive, some white middle-class suffragists suggested using literacy or education as measures to determine qualified voters. The advantages for southern whites was made clear by a resolution of the National American Woman Suffrage Association in 1893 calling attention to the fact

> that in every State there are more women who can read and write than the whole number of illiterate male voters; more white women who can read and write than all negro voters; more American women who can read and write than all foreign voters; so that the enfranchisement of such women would settle the vexed question of rule by illiteracy, whether of home-grown or foreign-born production.[64]

One southern white suffragist wrote even more plainly that the vote of white women would guarantee the racial supremacy of whites over blacks and foreigners. In vain did Fannie Barrier Williams counter, "We believe that the world always needs the influence of every good and capable woman, and this rule recognizes no exceptions based on complexion."[65]

Even Susan B. Anthony, who was otherwise sympathetic to African Americans, found southern whites a more important constituency. When suffragists were asked to take a stand against segregation on trains, a practice that forced black women to ride in smoking cars where they were vulnerable to sexual harassment, Anthony attempted to avoid a split, declaring, "Our hands are tied."[66] A few years earlier, in 1894, she had deferred to southern whites by asking the veteran suffragist and black leader Frederick Douglass not to attend a suffrage convention held in a southern city. The same principle of expediency surfaced again in 1913 when organizers of a suffrage parade in front of the White House asked Ida B. Wells-Barnett, famous for her anti-lynching campaign and now representing a black women's suffrage club, not to march with the mostly white delegation from her city. To Wells-Barnett's credit, when the march began, she took her place in line exactly as she had planned.

Although many white suffragists never openly welcomed black women in the movement, they did become more conciliatory to immigrants and workers after the turn of the century. The support of recent immigrants such as Jews and Italians was essential in areas like New York City and was to prove decisive in the state vote for women's suffrage. The suffrage movement was also broadened by the new participation of activists with experience organizing women workers or those familiar with the British experience, such as Harriot Stanton Blatch. By the late 1890s, even American farm women were rallying for suffrage, buoyed by their participation in farmers' movements to extend their political influence. Although, as we have seen, American women's suffrage had become a mass movement by 1910, accommodating many different groups, each had its own reasons for joining and the unity was never more than superficial.

Class and Suffrage in Britain

The comparable divisions in European society were based on social class. Suffragists in Britain were uniquely successful at incorporating women workers into the movement from the 1890s. Much of the initiative came from Esther Roper and Eva Gore-Booth, both from privileged backgrounds, who targeted mill workers in the textile towns of Lancashire. They went to workers' homes, factory gates, and unions in a radical break with previous "parlour room" strategy. Among their recruits was Selina Cooper, a mill worker since the age of ten, a strong and courageous woman who was the only one with "the confidence to stand up at Labour [Party] conferences and try to push through motions on women's suffrage." Cooper and a few other women who had been trade union organizers were convinced that the vote would be more effective than their union in securing higher wages and improved working conditions. As Cooper announced at an open-air meeting, "[Women] do not want their political power to enable them to boast that they are on equal terms with the men. They want to use it for the same purpose as men—to get better conditions. . . . We do not want [the vote] as a mere plaything!"[67]

As a result partly of this development and partly of frustration with the continued intransigence of parliament, the British suffrage movement moved to the left in the early twentieth century, unlike the ones in North America. The move was easier in Britain because it had a Labour Party growing in strength and more receptive to women's suffrage than either the Liberal or the Conservative Party. The Fabian socialist Beatrice Webb observed in 1914 that "the whole of the women's movement finds itself side-slipping, almost unintentionally, into Labour and Socialist politics."[68]

The exception was the militant Women's Social and Political Union (WSPU), whose co-founder, Emmeline Pankhurst (1858–1928) ironically, had begun as a socialist activist. Initially drawing support from the working class, the Pankhursts soon found that arrests of middle-class women made more headlines. Women without domestic servants generally had neither the time nor the taste for such antics, which seemed the self-indulgent behaviour of a few women with time and money. Working-class women, whether employed outside the home or not, had to juggle housekeeping and politicking. Hannah Mitchell reported facing "arrears of work, including the weekly wash," on her return from campaigning. Many women, she admitted, "faced with this accumulation of tasks, often resolve never to leave home again."[69] Another activist who knew she was going to prison baked enough bread ahead of time to meet her family's needs for two weeks. To her dismay, she was sentenced to six weeks; her agitation was so great that she had to be bailed out so that she could return to light her oven. Not surprisingly, then, the WSPU London office was usually "full of fashionable ladies in silks and satins. Tea and cakes were handed round."[70]

The enthusiasm of the Lancashire textile workers for suffrage did not mask the deep divisions in the British suffrage movement, as in North America. Similar to other European countries where full adult male suffrage had not yet been granted, the question was who should get the vote when. Many suffragists feared that the goal of full adult suffrage was unrealistic. Reasoning that "half a loaf was better than none," they wanted women to vote under the same qualifications as men. They also worried that any grant of adult male suffrage would settle the question of general suffrage reform, thereby retarding the special cause of women's suffrage, as had happened in France. For its part, the working class expected that propertied women voters would no longer push to extend the franchise. Had not the women's rights' advocate Frances Power Cobbe feared enfranchising "a rabble of illiterates"?[71] A suffragist who was sympathetic to workers, agreeing that it might be "easier and quicker to get a half-loaf than a whole one," asked pointedly, "why choose the top half?"[72] These class-related issues were not resolved before the war and re-emerged more strongly after it, no longer camouflaged by the drama of the suffrage campaign.

Motherhood and Sisterhood

The ideology of maternal feminism, which assumed an identity of interests of all women, inspired hundreds of thousands of upper- and middle-class women to promote changes in the living and working conditions of those who were less privileged. Women supposedly best understood the sufferings of other disadvantaged members of society, in particular, other women and children. They worked through service clubs, settlement houses, elected offices in local government, or trade unions. The extent to which these efforts represented successful cross-class co-operation depended on the degree to which privileged women could identify and work with those they wanted to help.

The pitfalls were many. Charles Sowerwine, in his history of women and socialism in France, identifies three reasons for the failure of such cross-class enterprises. The first was the desire of the organizers to remain in control, the second was their inability to understand working women's experiences, and the third was their reformist perspective. As for the first, many organizers were frankly elitist. Elizabeth Cady Stanton, for example, admitted that she saw "no hope of any general self-assertion among the masses. The first steps for their improvement must be taken by those who have tasted the blessings of liberty and education."[73] Her views were echoed in France by Marguerite Durand, whose newspaper La Fronde gave material and emotional support to striking seamstresses and tailors. While praising working women as "the only ones yet to have shown bravery . . . who will make the revolution for their bourgeois sisters," she added, "but what good are arms which flail about when there are no brains to guide them?"[74]

Speaking in 1906, the American Gertrude Barum, secretary of the Women's Trade Union League (WTUL), chided her audience of privileged women for not inviting wage-earning women to speak at the convention: "We have been preaching to them, teaching them, 'rescuing' them, doing almost everything for them except knowing them and working with them. . . . They will speak much better for themselves than you can get any one to speak for them."[75] The league Barum represented was a typical coalition between workers and middle-class reformers, but its constitution was unusual in requiring a majority of executive board members to be trade unionists rather than their middle-class "allies." It was many years, however, before parity was achieved on the board. President Margaret Dreier Robins, who although from a well-to-do background chose to live in a cold-water tenement, illustrated the commitment of the reformers. Even so, the obvious affluence of most allies, or as some workers called them, "the mink brigade,"[76] as well as their ability to be articulate and innovative, intimidated their colleagues and contributed to divisions within the group over strategy and objectives.

In contrast to the WTUL, most reform organizations were consciously designed by middle-class women for working-class women rather than with them. In Britain and Germany, for example, most women's unions were established on the initiative of bourgeois women, who could supply vital financial resources. On their own, working women had enormous difficulties attempting to organize, which did not abate in spite of the surge of labour activity in the 1880s and around 1910. Nonetheless, there were some dramatic successes. In the United States, women workers, including cigar makers, laundry workers, and corset makers, staged eighty-three strikes from 1895 to 1905. The most successful group was garment workers; hundreds of thousands of women walked out on strike between 1905 and 1915, challenging middle-class women to "Make Sisterhood a Fact!"[77] by supporting them.

The success of women garment workers was exceptional. Most male workers continued to be unhelpful at best over the integration of women into the labour movement and often actively hostile to the prospect. Their opposition spurred middle-class women to step in to help working women organize. The goal remained integration into the labour movement, but women organizers who worked in mixed unions usually found themselves isolated and exploited. Partly because of these experiences and also because of the formidable ethnic and language barriers among New York workers, the WTUL by 1914 turned to the suffrage campaign as an alternative to union organizing. As Mary Dreier wrote in a letter, "The attitude of the labor men to the working women has changed me from being an ardent supporter of labor to a somewhat rabid supporter of women and to feel that the enfranchisement of women and especially my working-class sisters is the supreme issue."[78] Then, too, middle-class reformers were more comfortable with the prospect of change through legislation than change through labour organizing.

A very different, and successful, cross-class enterprise was Hull House, the settlement house founded by Jane Addams and Ellen Starr in Chicago. It provided child care, a cooked food service for working women, self-improvement classes, cultural activities, and union and strike assistance. Called "one of the most politically effective groups of women reformers in U.S. history,"[79] the women associated with Hull House spearheaded a successful drive to abolish the worst conditions of sweated labour and establish the eight-hour day for female workers in Illinois. Hull House served as a "halfway house between domestic tradition and the political world"[80] for its middle-class founders and its staff. Jane Addams was able to enter into unique sympathy with the people she served, and Hull House backed all prudent efforts that workers made to improve their position. As a sign of her fame and respect, readers of *Independent Magazine* in 1913 voted Addams "the second most useful American, after Thomas Edison."[81]

Like white North Americans, African-American and African-Canadian middle-class women served their communities, necessarily sensitive to the problems of racism, sexual violence, harassment, and poverty that working-class black women experienced. Both the tradition of interdependence within black communities and pride in individual achievements motivated middle-class black women to social activism. They could point to successes like the Neighborhood Union in Atlanta, Georgia, which sponsored a wide variety of projects, or fundraising for the antilynching crusade. Such experience must have made the discrimination they experienced from white reformers particularly wounding. The National League on Urban Conditions, for example, reserved leadership posts for black men and white women. Similarly, the General Federation of Women's Clubs barred blacks from membership in an attempt to placate southern whites. The noted African-American educator Anna Julia Cooper, hearing of discrimination practised by a southern club named Wimodaughsis—for wives, mothers, daughters, sisters—suggested that it should really be named Whimodaughsis, for *white* wives, mothers, daughters, and sisters.

In Britain, women won election to school boards, poor law boards, and local councils. With courage they faced the ridicule of the public, the hostility of male colleagues, and the indifference of their constituencies. The extent to which they understood and championed the needs of those they served is remarkable. In small but vital ways they helped to make life better for those who lived on the margins of society. They organized summer playgrounds and school lunches, provided special care for disabled students, promoted girls' education or equal wages for female teachers and staff, and furnished workhouse inmates with better clothing, food, and medical care. According to one study, their "feminist perspective" was used explicitly on behalf of women and children, the sick, elderly, or disabled. Most important for our discussion, they were less judgmental of and more respectful and supportive towards the poor than were their male colleagues. The Countess of Carlisle was typical in her rejection of a patronizing attitude: "We want no Lady Bountifuls in this last end of our nineteenth century; we want Radical women in whatever class they may chance to live giving to the people their legitimate rights."[82]

The women at Hull House and in British local government successfully avoided the second common shortcoming mentioned above: the failure to understand working women's experiences, which at times clashed with more general feminist goals. For example, a feminist priority was to expand employment opportunities for women, but working-class women often understood economic improvement as freedom *not* to work. Few would have appreciated the praise of the American feminist Henrietta Rodman: "Our sisters of the poor class have the most fundamental right for which we are struggling—the right for economic independence, the right to continue their chosen work after marriage."[83] In contrast, socialist working women in Hamburg, Germany, in 1887 looked forward to a time "when our men will earn more, so that we don't need to work any more and can devote ourselves more to bringing up our children."[84] Black clubwomen were more sympathetic than whites to the problems of women who had to earn money at home; white middle-class women usually did not think of organizing either those women or domestic servants.

The issue of protective legislation to limit the hours and conditions of women's work caused great division, but it was not simple class division. Many workers welcomed any legislated improvement; others feared the loss of income that might ensue if they were prohibited from taking night work, for example. Many liberal feminists adamantly opposed gender-specific legislation, preferring, as the Langham Place women in Britain had described, "a fair field and no favour." Socialist-leaning women such as Beatrice Webb, on the other hand, agreed with the labour movement's support of such laws. Webb denounced her opponents as "capitalist's [*sic*] wives and daughters."[85] The whole issue was further complicated because both feminists and antifeminists could advocate protective laws to safeguard the health of mothers and children, antifeminists justifying them for the good of the race.

The third shortcoming of reformers seems more clear cut: middle-class women tended to adopt a "reformist perspective" that contrasted with the sense of class conflict understood by workers. Reformers often had a romanticized notion of themselves as the agents of class reconciliation. The French feminist Eugénie Poutonié-Pierre, co-founder of the Women's League in 1889, proposed to unite women and workers in "one single cause, the humanitarian cause" in order to ensure that "social evolution may proceed peacefully."[86] Similarly, members of the National Council of Women of Canada saw their mission as "to further the application of the Golden Rule to society, custom and law."[87] Their idealism reflected the value that women's culture gave to selflessness and service but also revealed the stake that university-educated and professionally trained women had in perpetuating the status quo. The lack of inclination to challenge the system was embarrassingly evident at an international congress held in Paris in 1900, when middle-class delegates refused to back a proposal to give their maids one day off each week. Perhaps also, elite women could talk of harmony because they expected deference from working-class women.

Reformism seemed particularly promising in Germany, where middle-class women hoped to heal the social strains resulting from recent unification and rapid industrialization. As indicated by Henriette Schmidt, one of the leaders of the German women's movement, they intended "to smooth over social contradictions and thus to stabilize the inner unity of the new Germany."[88] Through welfare work and reform activities they would turn the masses into a people. Although the German women's movement had originally recognized the links between women and workers, both lacking full rights and social status, it increasingly emphasized not misery and poverty but their political consequences. One critic's cynical observation that this kind of feminism was nothing more than "a movement destined to help capitalist society survive by suppressing the most glaring inequalities and by combatting misery with charity"[89] seems not far off the mark in this case.

Feminists and Socialists

What about those who took the class struggle more seriously? Many of the younger, educated women who joined the feminist movement around the turn of the century were sympathetic to socialism. Some, such as Sylvia Pankhurst in England, Lily Braun in Germany, and Madeleine Pelletier in France, founded or joined socialist parties. For feminists interested in pursuing their cause politically, socialists seemed natural allies, dedicated as they were, at least in theory, to the equality of women. These alliances were rarely successful. Historian Richard Evans titled his chapter on the relationship between feminists and socialists "The Impossible Alliance." Other historians have agreed that the gulf was "unbridgeable."[90]

Why was this the case? Since August Bebel's study of the woman question (see Chapter 7), European socialist parties had endorsed full economic and political equality for women, and were usually the only parties to do so. Many socialists, however, persisted in viewing feminist demands as bourgeois and diversionary. Middle-class feminists wanted to integrate women as full citizens into a reformed capitalist state, whereas socialists aimed for a revolutionary transformation of society and the liberation of all oppressed groups, men and women. A French socialist colleague explained to Madeleine Pelletier, "Socialism would free women, but before [the revolution] one must not instigate a battle of the sexes—this would be deviationism."[91] Then, too, the ideology of the patriarchal family was still very much a part of working-class culture, as suffragette Hannah Mitchell discovered when she married: "Even my Sunday leisure was gone for I soon found that a lot of the Socialist talk about freedom was only talk and these Socialist young men expected Sunday dinners and huge teas with home-made cakes, potted meat and pies, exactly like their reactionary fellows."[92] The story in France, Germany, Russia, and Italy was the same; in this context, it is not surprising that socialist politicians were as ready as others to sacrifice women's issues to more pressing concerns, especially as their stake in parliamentary politics grew. The response of Russian Bolsheviks to Alexandra Kollontai's idea of organizing a club for women following the 1905 revolution symbolizes socialist attitudes in general; although she secured the reluctant agreement of the St Petersburg committee for the meeting, Kollontai arrived to find the room locked and a notice reading, "Meeting for Women only—Cancelled / Tomorrow, Meeting for Men Only."[93]

Women socialists were as responsible as their male colleagues for the unbridgeable gulf. To be a socialist meant to dedicate oneself first and foremost to the cause of the working class. In Russia, for example, Marxist women attended women's congresses with the specific intent of disrupting them in order to prove that cross-class collaboration was impossible. They convinced one of the organizers of the 1908 All-Russian Congress of Women of their point, and she then agreed, "As for unity . . . I regard it as impossible in a class society. I regard the constant appeals of [the Marxists] for disunity as useful, in forcing us to renounce a vain hope."[94] Socialists could become enthusiastic about recruiting women in order to hasten the revolution but not to detract from it. Socialist feminism in practice meant giving priority to socialism.

Clara Zetkin in Germany and Louise Saumoneau in France illustrate the predicament of women caught between the ties of class and gender. Zetkin (1857–1933) was the leader of the women's section of the Second International and an impressively large German socialist women's movement. She insisted on the autonomy of that movement from the party. It must "possess a certain measure of independence and freedom of movement," she warned, and "if the male comrades are not judicious enough to provide this vital necessity, it must be fought for."[95] Apparently inspired by an American precedent in 1908 or 1909, Zetkin introduced International Proletarian Women's Day as an expression of the solidarity of all socialist women. Held in German cities on 19 March 1911 in spite of police obstruction, the successful demonstrations inspired celebrations in following years in Sweden, France, and Russia.

Clara Zetkin nonetheless remained a self-styled "inveterate Marxist." Her success was to convince her male colleagues that rather than being a diversion, socialist efforts on behalf of women ensured that feminism would not lure them away. Those who endangered the unity of party policy on the family—like Lily Braun, who came to socialism from feminism and pioneered ideas of collective child care—were unceremoniously "hounded" from the party by Zetkin. Ideas such as collective housekeeping or birth control might serve to reconcile the individual to the status quo, feared Zetkin. While liberating for individuals, such reforms could inhibit the collective goals of the movement, always the first consideration. Clara Zetkin's outlook was shared by trade union leader Gertrud Hanna, who described herself and her associates as "in the first place Party members, secondly unionists, and finally, if at all, feminists."[96]

Few German socialists were willing to take a stand for feminism. Large as the socialist women's movement was—over 16 percent of the membership of the party in 1914, in contrast to less than 3 percent in France—the majority of members were housewives married to party men. If the men encouraged their participation, it was with a view to strengthening family solidarity; the enemy was capitalism, not, as bourgeois feminists would have it, men. Socialist women were therefore understandably reluctant to challenge party policy or priorities. They remained content to deal with women's issues such as protective legislation and health matters rather than with issues of general party policy.

The unwillingness of German socialists to forward feminist aims was matched by an unwillingness to co-operate on the part of middle-class feminist organizations. The Federation of German Women's Associations, in a high-minded rejection of partisan politics, refused to admit socialist member groups. Socialist women, for their part, refused to participate in middle-class international congresses. After 1894, there were no further attempts at co-operation between the two wings of the women's movement. Historians have agreed that the result decisively weakened the German women's movement.

▶ *Clara Zetkin, the German socialist, addressing the International Workers' Congress in 1889, defended the importance of women's paid work outside the home.*

Women's emancipation is basically a question of women's work. . . . Socialists must know that women's work is a necessity for present-day economic development; they must know that women's work will result in shortening the working hours dedicated to society by individuals and will increase that society's wealth; they must know that it is not the competition of women's work per se, but rather capitalistic exploitation of women's labor that depresses the wages of men. Socialists must know, above all, that slavery or freedom depend upon economic dependence or independence.

Those who have inscribed the liberation of mankind upon their banners must not condemn half of humanity to political and social slavery through economic dependence. As the worker is subjected to the capitalist, so is woman subjected to man; and she will remain subjected as long as she is economically dependent. Work is the essential condition upon which this economic independence of woman is based. If we wish women to be free human beings, to have the same rights as men in our society, women's work must be neither abolished nor limited except in certain quite isolated cases.

Women workers who aspire to social equality do not expect emancipation through the bourgeois women's movement, which claims to be fighting for women's rights. This structure is built upon sand and has no basis in reality. Working women are absolutely convinced that the question of women's emancipation cannot be isolated and exist in a vacuum, but that it must be seen as part of the great social question. They understand clearly that this question will never be resolved in our society as presently constituted, but only following a complete overthrow of this society. . . .

While women go forward hand in hand with the Socialist Workers' Party, they are prepared to take part in the struggle and sacrifices of the battle. They are, however, also firmly determined to demand all their rights once victory is achieved. Regarding sacrifices and duties as well as rights, they want to be no more and no less than comrades in arms who have been accepted under equal conditions into the ranks of the combatants.

Source: Clara Zetkin, "Für die Befreiung der Frau! Rede auf dem Internationalen Arbeiterkongress zu Paris, 19 Juli 1889," *Protokoll des Internationalen Arbeiter-Congresses zu Paris, 14–20 Juli 1889* (Nürnberg, 1890), 80–85, trans. SGB in *Women, the Family, and Freedom: The Debate in Documents,* ed. Susan Groag Bell and Karen M. Offen, vol. 2, *1880–1950* (Stanford, CA: Stanford University Press, 1983). Reprinted with the permission of the publisher.

The same division plagued the Austrian women's movement. Auguste Fickert, a leading figure of the General Austrian Women's Association, defined women's rights as narrowly bourgeois and supported socialist candidates and goals. "We do not want to imitate men who in the course of history have generally used their attained rights only to oppress those weaker than themselves,"[97] she explained. She believed that women could maintain their political independence by refusing to affiliate with a party though they might support its policies. In 1892, believing class co-operation to be crucial, she attempted to organize an Austrian Women's Day that would address issues of both working- and middle-class women, but the idea of appearing on the same platform as socialist speakers proved too radical for the middle-class women, and the plan fell through. Socialists for their part generally refused to co-operate with reformist groups and in 1907 were forbidden by the Second International to do so. In areas with a long-standing tradition of leftist co-operation, however, such as parts of Switzerland, socialists and bourgeois feminists continued to work together on women's suffrage.

As in Germany, French socialists became a major political force. They were much less successful at recruiting women, however, partly because there was at first no separate section for them as there was in Germany. The few women who rose through the ranks were not disposed to stress sisterhood on behalf of their more timid sisters. Charles Sowerwine asks us to imagine how intimidating "the tobacco-filled air, the male complicity troubled by the presence of a woman, in short, the male club atmosphere of the socialist sections"[98] could be. French male socialists were no more inclined than their German comrades to push women's interests; they "kept a good record of verbal support for women's suffrage, a poor record of actual work for the vote, and a hidden record of opposition to the reform."[99]

The French counterpart to Clara Zetkin was Louise Saumoneau (1875–1950), who in 1899 co-founded a socialist women's group. Like Zetkin, Saumoneau distrusted feminists. As a poor seamstress, she had taken a precious half day off work to attend a feminist meeting where the burning issue was whether dowries were moral. In disgust, she decided to form her own group as an alternative to "feminist confusionism." Although Saumoneau recognized the double oppression of working women, the masthead of the group's newspaper reassured male socialists that "there need be no antagonism between men and women of the proletarian class."[100] Her purpose, in fact, was to recruit women to socialism. "The women of the people," she warned, "must not abandon the terrain of class struggle . . . to run after a chimerical . . . emancipation on the bourgeois terrain." Even less charitably, she referred to feminists as "intriguing, naïve, deranged, and hysterical women"[101] who were only interested in perpetuating their economic interests and class privilege. They, rather than men, were the enemy.

Louise Saumoneau's effort did fulfil one criterion for a successful socialist-feminist women's movement: it was based on women's practical experience, which was closer to that of their fathers, brothers, and husbands than to that of their female employers. Her approach in effect necessitated a class analysis, which reformist feminists were unwilling to endorse. An organization would have to be closely enough linked to mainstream socialism to have an impact but independent enough to provide an alternative to the all-male atmosphere of the party. How could a women's group be both autonomous and influential? In the end, Saumoneau's group was neither, becoming simply a women's auxiliary.

Madeleine Pelletier (1874–1939) has been called the most radical feminist of her generation. Perhaps her squalid working-class home or her mother's religious zeal spurred her to rebel. In any case, from the age of thirteen she frequented radical political and intellectual circles. Later she would declare, "I can say that I have always been a feminist, at least since I was old enough to understand." Self-taught, she became a doctor and was the first woman employed by the state psychiatric service in France. She went on to become one of the few women to reach an executive post within the Socialist Party. She found that her socialist colleagues were no more receptive than the medical establishment to her cropped hair, semi-masculine dress, and uncompromising feminist views. Although she did succeed in having a resolution supporting women's suffrage passed by her party, she was told by a delegate, "I hope you realize that we vote in favour of your motion because votes for women has no chance whatever of succeeding. If it had, you would see some real opposition."[102] Like Auguste Fickert in Austria, Pelletier believed that cross-class co-operation was essential. Also like Fickert but unlike Clara Zetkin and Louise Saumoneau, she held feminism dearer than socialism. "A woman, like any other individual," she declared, "can be a socialist, a republican or a monarchist according to her convictions; but above all she should be a feminist."[103] Disenchanted with socialism, Pelletier turned to anarchism. "The working class," she believed, "will be the last to accept feminism."[104]

In the end, feminists refused to give up their feminism and socialists refused to give up their socialism. Only in times of crisis or where a clear victory was at hand, as in Sweden in 1909–12 or in Germany and Russia during World War I, did the two groups co-operate. In Britain, where party lines were more fluid, the women's movement made a general shift towards socialism and towards issues important to working women, such as protective legislation, trade unions, and family welfare. Although the British context was very different from that on the continent, historian Olive Banks comes to the provocative conclusion that the result for feminism was much the same: the concentration on class rather than on gender issues was disastrous. Preoccupation with economic exploitation sidestepped the importance of sexual oppression. Class seemed to matter more than gender both for women who were able to bridge class divisions and for those who were not.

In summary, although first-wave feminists were not very successful in overcoming the racial and class divisions among women, it is important to understand that their failure was grounded in the realities of their society rather than in their motives and ideals. The feminists who did challenge those realities put the lie to Alexandra Kollontai's assumption that "between the emancipated woman of the intelligentsia and the toiling woman with calloused hands, there was such an unbridgeable gulf that there could be no question of any sort of point of agreement between them."[105]

❖

The feminist movement stands condemned for being too centred on suffrage, too timid about gender roles, and too accepting of class and race divisions. It was, however, a very complex movement, or coalition of movements. Clubwomen, reformers, farm women, trade unionists, socialists, and equal rights activists all endorsed women's suffrage as the means to an end; and while the suffrage campaign was colourful and newsworthy, the divisions within it were never far from the surface. The same tactical considerations that led reformers to suffrage encouraged them to describe their aims in terms understandable to their contemporaries and reflective of the scientific, imperialist, and racist values of the period. The concepts of motherhood, community, and social harmony made feminist demands respectable and, by definition, less revolutionary. To indict feminism for failing to create a more radical movement is to underestimate seriously the depth of resistance to the restructuring of fundamental values that it represented. Although a radical like Madeleine Pelletier could say of herself, "I decidedly was born several centuries too early,"[106] most feminists were of their age as well as ahead of it.

NOTES

1   Kate Millett, *Sexual Politics* (New York: Avon Books, 1969, 1970), 83–84.

2   Ray Strachey, *"The Cause": A Short History of the Women's Movement in Great Britain* (1928; reprint, Port Washington, NY: Kennikat Press, 1969), 320.

3   Quoted in Steven C. Hause, *Hubertine Auclert: The French Suffragette* (New Haven: Yale University Press, 1987), 199.

4   Winifred Holtby, *Women and a Changing Civilization* (1935; reprint, Chicago: Academy Press, 1978), 52, 53.

5   Steven C. Hause with Anne R. Kenney, *Women's Suffrage and Social Politics in the French Third Republic* (Princeton, NJ: Princeton University Press, 1984), 109.

6   Quoted in Felicia Gordon, *The Integral Feminist: Madeleine Pelletier, 1874–1939: Feminism, Socialism and Medicine* (Cambridge: Polity Press, 1990), 101. Some of the British suffragettes, fearful of hurting people, had at first tied strings to the rocks they threw at windows in order to have more control over the missiles.

7   S. McKee, quoted in Catherine L. Cleverdon, *The Woman Suffrage Movement in Canada,* 2nd ed. (Toronto: University of Toronto Press, 1974), 27.

8   Quoted in Susan Kingsley Kent, *Sex and Suffrage in Britain, 1860–1914* (Princeton, NJ: Princeton University Press, 1987), 211.

9   Inez Irwin, quoted in Dorothy Schneider and Carl J. Schneider, *American Women in the Progressive Era, 1900–1920* (New York: Facts On File, 1993), 171. Irwin was speaking of one group but her words are generally applicable.

10   Quoted in Nancy F. Cott, *The Grounding of Modern Feminism* (New Haven and London: Yale University Press, 1987), 28–29.

11   Quoted in Carol Lee Bacchi, *Liberation Deferred? The Ideas of the English-Canadian Suffragists 1877–1918* (Toronto: University of Toronto Press, 1983), 32.

12   Quoted in ibid., 81.

13   Teresa Billington-Grieg, *The Militant Suffragette Movement: Emancipation in a Hurry* (London: Frank Palmer, n.d.), 159–60, 173.

14   Quoted in Sandra Holton, *Feminism and Democracy: Women's Suffrage and Reform Politics in Britain 1900–1918* (Cambridge: Cambridge University Press, 1986), 15. This quotation should not mislead us; Fawcett was actually a liberal rather than a maternal feminist.

15   Christine Bolt, *The Women's Movements in the United States and Britain from the 1790s to the 1920s* (Amherst: University of Massachusetts Press, 1993), 91.

16   Quoted in Bärbel Clemens, *"Menschenrechte haben kein Geschlecht!" Zum Politikverständnis der bürgerlichen Frauenbewegung* (Pfaffenweiler: Centaurus-Verlagsgesellschaft, 1988), 39 (my translation).

17   Elizabeth Cady Stanton, "Address to the Legislature of New York on Women's Rights" (1854), in *Elizabeth Cady Stanton, Susan B. Anthony: Correspondence, Writings, Speeches,* ed. Ellen Carol DuBois (New York: Schocken, 1981), 50.

18   "National-American Convention and Hearings of 1892," in *History of Woman Suffrage,* vol. 4, *1883–1900,* ed. Susan B. Anthony and Ida Husted Harper (1902; reprint, New York: Arno & The New York Times, 1969), 190.

19 Carolyn Johnston, *Sexual Power: Feminism and the Family in America* (Tuscaloosa: University of Alabama Press, 1992), ix.

20 Quoted in Mari Jo Buhle, *Women and American Socialism, 1870–1920* (Urbana: University of Illinois Press, 1981), 89.

21 Quoted in Claire Goldberg Moses, *French Feminism in the Nineteenth Century* (Albany: State University of New York Press, 1984), 220.

22 Frances Ellen Watkins Harper, "Woman's Political Future" (1893), in *Black Women in Nineteenth-Century American Life: Their Words, Their Thoughts, Their Feelings,* ed. Bert James Loewenberg and Ruth Bogin (University Park: Pennsylvania State University Press, 1976), 245.

23 "National Conventions—1869," *History of Woman Suffrage,* vol. 2, *1861–1876,* ed. Elizabeth Cady Stanton, Susan B. Anthony, and Matilda Joslyn Gage (1882; reprint, New York: Arno & The New York Times, 1969), 351.

24 Quoted in Susan Levine, "Labor's True Woman: Domesticity and Equal Rights in the Knights of Labor," *Journal of American History* 70, 3 (1983): 330.

25 William O'Neill, "Feminism as a Radical Ideology," in *Dissent: Explorations in the History of American Radicalism,* ed. Alfred F. Young (DeKalb: Northern Illinois University Press, 1968), 285.

26 Nancy F. Cott, "What's in a Name? The Limits of 'Social Feminism': or, Expanding the Vocabulary of Women's History," *Journal of American History* 76 (1988): 820–21, 826.

27 Quoted in Theresa Wobbe, *Gleichheit und Differenz. Politische Strategien von Frauenrechtlerinnen um die Jahrhundertwende* (Frankfurt: Campus Verlag, 1989), 127 (my translation).

28 Naomi Black, *Social Feminism* (Ithaca: Cornell University Press, 1989), 53.

29 Philippa Levine, *Feminist Lives in Victorian England: Private Roles and Public Commitment* (Oxford: Basil Blackwell, 1990), 106.

30 Sarah Platt Decker, quoted in Barbara Kuhn Campbell, *The "Liberated" Woman of 1914: Prominent Women of the Progressive Era* (n.p.: Umi Research Press, 1979, 1976), 152–53.

31 Quoted in Eileen Boris, "The Power of Motherhood: Black and White Activist Women Redefine the 'Political,'" in *Mothers of a New World: Maternalist Politics and the Origins of Welfare States,* ed. Seth Koven and Sonya Michel (New York: Routledge, 1993), 223.

32 Quoted in Ida Blom, "Voluntary Motherhood 1900–1930: Theories and Politics of a Norwegian Feminist in an International Perspective," in *Maternity and Gender Policies: Women and the Rise of the European Welfare States, 1880s–1950s,* ed. Gisela Bock and Pat Thane (London: Routledge, 1991), 23.

33 Cheri Register, "Motherhood at Center: Ellen Key's Social Vision," *Women's Studies International Forum* (Special issue, "Reassessments of 'First-Wave' Feminism," ed. Elizabeth Sarah) 5, 6 (1982): 601, 606.

34 Olive Schreiner, *Woman and Labor* (New York: Frederick A. Stokes Company, 1911), 164, 172, 197, 198, 203.

35 Ibid., 128, 62.

36   Quoted in Karen J. Blair, *The Clubwoman as Feminist: True Womanhood Redefined, 1868–1914* (New York: Holmes and Meier, 1980), 11.

37   Letitia Youmans, "Campaign Echoes" (1893), in *Canadian Women on the Move 1867–1920,* ed. Beth Light and Joy Parr (Toronto: New Hogtown Press and Ontario Institute for Studies in Education, 1983), 219.

38   Karen Offen, "Depopulation, Nationalism, and Feminism in Fin-de-Siècle France," *American Historical Review* 89, 3 (1984): 674–75.

39   Quoted in Ute Gerhard, "A Hidden and Complex Heritage: Reflections on the History of Germany's Women's Movements," *Women's Studies International Forum* 5, 6 (1982): 563.

40   Quoted in Wobbe, *Gleichheit und Differenz,* 116 (my translation).

41   Elisabeth Boehm, quoted in Barbara Greven-Aschoff, *Die bürgerliche Frauenbewegung in Deutschland 1894–1933* (Göttingen: Vandenhoeck & Ruprecht, 1981), 113 (my translation).

42   Quoted in Lorna Duffin, "Prisoners of Progress: Women and Evolution," in *The Nineteenth-Century Woman: Her Cultural and Physical World,* ed. Sara Delamont and Lorna Duffin (London: Croom Helm, 1978), 79. Patrick Geddes and J. Arthur Thomson, two biologists, wrote in *The Evolution of Sex,* rev. ed. (London: Walter Scott Publishing, 1914), 31, "What was decided among the prehistoric Protozoa cannot be annulled by Act of Parliament."

43   Nellie McClung, *In Times Like These* (Toronto: University of Toronto Press, 1972), 22.

44   Quoted in Les Garner, *Stepping Stones to Women's Liberty: Feminist Ideas in the Women's Suffrage Movement 1900–1918* (London: Heinemann, 1984), 9.

45   Quoted in Gerda Lerner, *The Majority Finds Its Past: Placing Women in History* (New York: Oxford University Press, 1979), 34.

46   Quoted in Wobbe, *Gleichheit und Differenz,* 117 (my translation).

47   Wayne Roberts, "'Rocking the Cradle for the World': The New Woman and Maternal Feminism, Toronto 1877–1914," in *A Not Unreasonable Claim: Women and Reform in Canada, 1880s–1920s,* ed. Linda Kealey (Toronto: Women's Educational Press, 1979), 31, 30.

48   Seth Koven and Sonya Michel, "Womanly Duties: Maternalist Politics and the Origins of Welfare States in France, Germany, Great Britain, and the United States, 1880–1920," *American Historical Review* 95 (1990): 1078.

49   Quoted in Judith Schwarz, *Radical Feminists of Heterodoxy: Greenwich Village 1912–1940,* 2nd ed. (Norwich, VT: New Victoria Publishers, 1986), 103.

50   Quoted in Sheila Jeffreys, *The Spinster and Her Enemies: Feminism and Sexuality 1880–1930* (London: Pandora, 1985), 28.

51   Quoted in Wobbe, *Gleichheit und Differenz,* 135, 130 (my translation).

52   Fanny Johnson, quoted in Garner, *Stepping Stones to Women's Liberty,* 71.

53   Kent, *Sex and Suffrage,* 159.

54   Frances Barrier Williams, "The Intellectual Progress of the Colored Women of the United States since the Emancipation Proclamation" (1893), in *Black Women in Nineteenth-Century American Life,* ed. Loewenberg and Bogin, 276.

55 Paula Giddings, *When and Where I Enter: The Impact of Black Women on Race and Sex in America* (Toronto: Bantam Books, 1984), 28.

56 Alice A. Chown, *The Stairway* (Toronto: University of Toronto Press, 1988), 89. Although Chown dated this journal entry 1910, it most likely was written shortly before the book's publication in 1921.

57 Quoted in Angus McLaren, *Birth Control in Nineteenth-Century England* (London: Croom Helm, 1978), 205.

58 Quoted in ibid., 207.

59 Quoted in Richard J. Evans, *The Feminist Movement in Germany 1894–1933* (London: Sage Publications, 1976), 125.

60 Quoted in Jeffreys, *The Spinster and Her Enemies,* 145. Gallichan was actually married to a feminist.

61 Quoted in Evans, *Feminist Movement in Germany,* 119.

62 Elizabeth Cady Stanton and the Revising Committee, *The Woman's Bible,* Part 1, *The Pentateuch;* Part 2, *Judges, Kings, Prophets and Apostles* (1895, 1898; reprint, Seattle: Coalition Task Force on Women and Religion, 1974), 1:126; 2:150; 1:73; 2: "Appendix," 185–214.

63 Quoted in Bacchi, *Liberation Deferred?* 54.

64 "The National-American Convention of 1893," in *History of Woman Suffrage,* ed. Anthony and Harper, 4:216n.

65 Williams, "The Intellectual Progress of the Colored Women of the United States," 276.

66 Quoted in Nancie Caraway, *Segregated Sisterhood: Racism and the Politics of American Feminism* (Knoxville: University of Tennessee Press, 1991), 150.

67 Quoted in Jill Liddington and Jill Norris, *One Hand Tied Behind Us: The Rise of the Women's Suffrage Movement* (London: Virago, 1978), 21, 29.

68 Quoted in Garner, *Stepping Stones to Women's Liberty,* 42.

69 Hannah Mitchell, *The Hard Way Up: The Autobiography of Hannah Mitchell, Suffragette and Rebel,* ed. Geoffrey Mitchell (London: Faber and Faber, 1968), 162.

70 Liddington and Norris, *One Hand Tied Behind Us,* 206.

71 Quoted in Philippa Levine, *Victorian Feminism 1850–1900* (London: Hutchinson, 1987), 61.

72 Julia Dawson, quoted in Liddington and Norris, *One Hand Tied Behind Us,* 181.

73 Quoted in Ellen Carol DuBois, *Feminism and Suffrage: The Emergence of an Independent Women's Movement in America 1848–1869* (Ithaca: Cornell University Press, 1978), 119.

74 Quoted in Charles Sowerwine, *Sisters or Citizens? Women and Socialism in France Since 1876* (Cambridge: Cambridge University Press, 1982), 75.

75 "National American Convention of 1906," in *History of Woman Suffrage,* vol. 5, *1900–1920,* ed. Ida Husted Harper (1922; reprint, New York: Arno & The New York Times, 1969), 165–66.

76 Quoted in Schneider and Schneider, *American Women in the Progressive Era,* 62.

77 Quoted in Cott, *Grounding of Modern Feminism,* 23.

78 Quoted in Nancy Schrom Dye, *As Equals and As Sisters: Feminism, the Labour Movement, and the Women's Trade Union League of New York* (Columbia: University of Missouri Press, 1980), 122.

79 Kathryn Kish Sklar, "Hull House in the 1890s: A Community of Women Reformers," *Signs: Journal of Women in Culture and Society* 10, 4 (1985): 658.

80 Rosalind Rosenberg, *Beyond Separate Spheres: Intellectual Roots of Modern Feminism* (New Haven: Yale University Press, 1982), 33.

81 Bolt, *Women's Movements,* 218–19.

82 Patricia Hollis, *Ladies Elect: Women in English Local Government, 1865–1914* (Oxford: Clarendon Press, 1987), 10, 28.

83 Quoted in Dye, *As Equals and As Sisters,* 9.

84 Quoted in Richard J. Evans, *Comrades and Sisters: Feminism, Socialism and Pacifism in Europe, 1870–1945* (Sussex: Wheatsheaf Books, 1987), 25–26.

85 Quoted in Carol Dyhouse, *Feminism and the Family in England, 1880–1939* (Oxford: Basil Blackwell, 1989), 82.

86 Quoted in Sowerwine, *Sisters or Citizens?* 69.

87 Quoted in Veronica Strong-Boag, "'Setting the Stage': National Organization and the Women's Movement in the Late 19th Century," in *The Neglected Majority: Essays in Canadian Women's History,* ed. Susan Mann Trofimenkoff and Alison Prentice (Toronto: McClelland and Stewart, 1977), 101.

88 Paraphrased by Herrad-Ulrike Bussemer, *Frauenemanzipation und Bildungsbürgertum. Sozialgeschichte der Frauenbewegung in der Reichgründungszeit* (Weinheim und Basel: Beitz Verlag, 1985), 171 (my translation).

89 Marie Hélène Zylberberg-Hocquart, quoted in Maïté Albistur and Daniel Armogathe, *Histoire du féminisme français du moyen âge à nos jours* (Paris: Des femmes, 1977), 357 (my translation).

90 Evans, *Comrades and Sisters,* ch. 2; Jean H. Quataert, *Reluctant Feminists in German Social Democracy, 1885–1917* (Princeton, NJ: Princeton University Press, 1979), 108.

91 Quoted in Gordon, *The Integral Feminist,* 108.

92 Mitchell, *The Hard Way Up,* 96.

93 Quoted in Evans, *Comrades and Sisters,* 110.

94 Olga Shapir, quoted in Linda Harriet Edmondson, *Feminism in Russia, 1900–1917* (Stanford, CA: Stanford University Press, 1984), 100.

95 Quoted in Sowerwine, *Sisters or Citizens?* 19.

96 Quoted in Quataert, *Reluctant Feminists,* 65, 11.

97 Quoted in Harriet Anderson, *Utopian Feminism: Women's Movements in Fin-de-siècle Vienna* (New Haven, CT: Yale University Press, 1992), 10.

98 Sowerwine, *Sisters or Citizens?* 105.

99 Steven C. Hause and Anne R. Kenney, "The Limits of Suffragist Behaviour: Legalism and Militancy in France, 1876–1922," *American Historical Review* 86, 4 (1981): 792.

100 Marilyn Boxer, "Socialism Faces Feminism: The Failure of Synthesis in France, 1879–1914," in *Socialist Women: European Socialist Feminism in the Nineteenth and Early Twentieth Centuries,* ed. Marilyn J. Boxer and Jean H. Quataert (New York: Elsevier, 1978), 92, 94.

101 Quoted in Hause and Kenney, "Suffragist Behaviour," 793.

102 Gordon, *The Integral Feminist,* 7, 111.

103 Quoted in ibid., 113.

104 Quoted in Boxer, "Socialism Faces Feminism," 103.

105 Quoted in Evans, *Comrades and Sisters,* 58.

106 Quoted in Gordon, *The Integral Feminist,* 140.

9

Wartime
and
Interwar Feminism

There were plenty of feminists and you knew who they were and they wrote individually, or spoke individually, but there was no organized movement outside of birth control. There was nothing for them, they had no organ, no avenue, to speak through. All they could do would be on their own and it was only writers you'd know about, because they could write. . . . I didn't change any of my own feelings but there wasn't anything, no movement, nothing to join.

Miriam Allen deFord, 1973

The absence of highly visible, organized feminist movements in the interwar years has been confirmed by most historical accounts. American feminism is the prime example: after reaching its high-water mark with women's entry into non-traditional jobs during World War I and the suffrage victory in 1920, feminism ebbed until the second wave began in the 1960s. Flavoured with such words as "faltering," "marginal," "disorganized and fragmented," "disarray," and "doldrums," historical accounts give an emphatic and unflattering picture. Even the term *feminism* practically disappeared except for pejorative associations. A history of the American movement published in 1968 bore the subtitle, *The Rise and Fall of Feminism in America.*

Historians are now revising this account. Although no country had a single, unified national feminist movement, feminists continued to articulate their concerns and press their campaigns from 1914 to 1940. For two reasons, however, they appeared to be, and were, less successful. First, the aftermath of the war saw not only political and economic instability but also a conservative backlash. As the English feminist Winifred Holtby described in

1914–18	World War I
1915	Women's Peace Conference at The Hague
1915–20	Women's suffrage granted in most western countries
1917	Bolshevik Revolution in Russia
1919	Treaty of Versailles ends World War I
	Sex Disqualification Act in Great Britain
1919–33	Weimar Republic in Germany
1922	Benito Mussolini comes to power in Italy
1923	First submission of Equal Rights Amendment to United States Congress
1928	Persons Case in Canada
1929	Beginning of the Great Depression
1933	Adolf Hitler becomes German chancellor
	Franklin D. Roosevelt becomes United States president, introduces New Deal
1936–39	Spanish Civil War
1938	Germany annexes Austria
1939	World War II begins

1934, she and her contemporaries were witnessing a reaction "not only against feminism, but against democracy, liberty, and reason, against international co-operation and political tolerance."[1] Measured against the crises of the 1920s and 1930s, women's rights seemed a parochial cause. Second, the postwar disarray within feminist ranks contrasts unfavourably with the well-organized prewar suffrage campaigns in countries such as the United States, Canada, and Great Britain. As we have seen, however, suffrage movements were unstable alliances of very different groups. In countries where their mission was successful, social reformers and more radical feminists subsequently went their separate ways.

The traditional interpretation of feminism's "ebb" must also be modified by taking into account the variety of ways in which feminism can flourish, whether the pragmatic feminism of women fighting for survival during the depression years or the working-class feminism of women determined to ameliorate their situation in the labour force. From this perspective the 1930s and 1940s brought a renewal, or a continuation, of women's activism, throwing into question the notion of sequential "waves."

This chapter will examine the impact of World War I (1914–18) on feminists and feminist movements and then consider the issues of the interwar years. Political participation of women both as voters and as politicians was an absorbing issue of the 1920s, as were divisions within feminism, primarily of ideology and age. In the 1930s external events took their toll, namely the Great Depression and the rise of fascism, both of which eventually culminated in World War II.

THE WAR AND ITS IMPACT

The hostilities that signalled the beginning of World War I in August 1914 brought consternation and hard decisions to feminists and suffragists in the belligerent countries. Most suffrage organizations changed gears immediately, redirecting their energies into war-related work. Millicent Garrett Fawcett, leader of British suffragism, without hesitation resolved to put her large organization into the service of her country, to help ease the strains of war. The Women's Social and Political Union (WSPU) transferred its militant suffragism into militant patriotism, changing the name of its newspaper from *The Suffragette* to *Britannia* and declaring itself "Second to none in Patriotism."[2] French feminists spoke of duty rather than rights. The Federation of German Women's Associations (BDF), like women's groups elsewhere, intended to take advantage of the opportunity the war presented: women who still lacked full civic rights could now prove themselves to be responsible citizens. Members of the BDF sprang into action, taking over a wide range of charitable activities; this "home service" was defined by BDF leader Gertrud Bäumer as "the wartime equivalent of 'women's movement.'"[3]

The Pursuit of Pacifism

Not all feminists equated citizenship with patriotism. In both warring and neutral countries, a small number of radicals broke ranks to support the cause of peace. The notion that women were more inclined to pacifism than were men was common throughout the late nineteenth and early twentieth centuries, a corollary of the emphasis on gender difference at the root of maternal feminist ideology. In 1915 Canadian feminist and doctor Augusta Stowe claimed grandly that "when women have a voice in national and international affairs, war will cease forever."[4] Although such views had been a staple of prewar feminist ideology, only the most radical activists were prepared to act on them to promote pacifism in wartime. Many were already socialists or were radicalized by the war and the antidemocratic measures taken by nervous governments. Gertrude Richardson in Canada, for example, combined maternal feminism with Marxist ideology, calling on the "Women of Canada" to "arise and save our men" while condemning the war as arranged by "the blood-stained Capitalists of the world."[5]

Antifeminists were quick to note and denounce the convergence of radical causes. In the United States, the National Association Opposed to

Woman Suffrage pointed out the connection: "Pacifist, socialist, feminist, suffragist are all parts of the same movement—a movement which weakens government, corrupts society and threatens the very existence of our great experiment in democracy."[6] In Germany the Bavarian War Ministry saw the female suffrage movement as closely connected with the pacifist movement and forbade feminist activity in the interests of public security. By 1916 the Munich branch of the Women's Suffrage League was not permitted to hold any meetings, either public or private, and its leaders were forced underground with their activities. Police spies infiltrated meetings of the New York feminist group Heterodoxy although its members were in fact split over the issue of pacifism. In Toronto a letter that Alice Chown wrote to local newspapers revealing her feminist pacifism provoked suggestions by angry respondents that she be jailed or interned in an asylum.

Although European socialist parties fell in behind their governments, Clara Zetkin, head of the international socialist women's organization, summoned women to meet on neutral territory in March 1915. Some seventy women managed to come to Berne, Switzerland, a remarkable achievement in the midst of war. (Not until six months later did socialist men undertake a similar initiative.) In an uncharacteristic move Zetkin called on bourgeois women to join ranks with German socialists to work for peace. But the patriotic sentiments of the majority of feminists precluded any nation-wide anti-war movement in Germany, as in other countries. In fact, the BDF expelled its pacifist members. In England Ray Strachey, Millicent Garrett Fawcett's colleague and friend, denounced her pacifist opponents as "the lunatic section."[7]

Those mainstream feminists who were pacifists utilized their international contacts, long established in such groups as the International Woman Suffrage Alliance. Dr. Aletta Jacobs of the Netherlands spearheaded the call for a women's peace conference, which was held at The Hague in April 1915. Not all countries or major women's groups were represented. The National Council of French Women declared attendance impossible, and the German BDF similarly rejected the idea as "irreconcilable with patriotic sentiment and national duty of the German woman's movement."[8] Some women were prevented by their governments from attending; others, as in the case of Canada, were unofficial delegates. Even so, some nine hundred women participated from twelve countries, including Germany, Austria-Hungary, and Belgium. The delegates not only passed resolutions calling for an international peacekeeping body and the peaceful adjudication of international conflicts but also boldly travelled to fourteen capitals to present their plans for a negotiated peace to twenty-one ministers, two presidents, one king, and the pope. Amazingly, women who could not even vote on national affairs were received as international envoys. The advisers of the Canadian prime minister dismissed their suggestions as impractical, but the Austrian prime minister declared them the first sensible words that he had heard in months. Although the ideas presented by the women were familiar in pacifist circles, Jane Addams emphasized them in a conversation she had with the American president, Woodrow Wilson, who found her formulation the best anyone had yet put out. Wilson would be the chief promoter of a League of Nations at the Versailles peace talks which ended the war.

Following the Hague Congress, Jane Addams formed the Women's International League for Peace and Freedom (WILPF), still in existence today. The daughters and granddaughters of the League's first members continued its tradition of peace activism in the 1970s and 1980s. National and local organizations undertook a wide range of peace education in the interwar years, and branches in Canada, Britain, and Germany became associated with broader movements for social reform and racial justice. For her efforts Jane Addams won the Nobel Peace Prize in 1931; she wished to be remembered by the words engraved on her tombstone, "Jane Addams of Hull-House and the Women's International League for Peace and Freedom."[9]

The War and Women's Suffrage

The majority of feminists in all countries placed war activities before suffrage work. Yet it was precisely during or just after the war that most Western governments extended suffrage to women: Iceland (partial) and Denmark in 1915; the new Soviet Union in 1917; Canada in 1918, although not to Asian and First Nations women; Germany and Austria also in 1918 and Great Britain (partial) in the same year; the Netherlands and Sweden in 1919; the United States and Belgium (partial) in 1920.[10] Was this, as many have suggested, a reward for women's war effort? This question raises the larger issue of who gets credit for the result. Were women *given* the vote or is it more accurate to say that women were successful in *getting* the vote?

At first glance it seems difficult to generalize for all cases. In Germany, the Netherlands, and Sweden, for example, women's suffrage seems to have been an attempt to ward off more radical changes. In Germany it was a last-minute decision made by the Joint Parliamentary Committee. Historian Richard Evans categorically rejects the idea that the war improved women's political position.[11] Although the Federation of German Women's Associations had renewed its demand for suffrage when discussion of political reform began in 1917, it was the revolutionary events of 1918 ending imperial rule and establishing a new government that made female suffrage seem advisable. Evans thus claims that female suffrage in Germany was merely the product of men's political instrumentality. In Canada as well, the federal government used female suffrage as a political tool, enfranchising army nurses and female relatives of soldiers serving overseas in order to secure an election victory. Once the gender bar had been broached, enfranchisement for most other Canadian women was a matter of course, though status Indians and Asian Canadians did not gain the vote until after World War II.

It is fruitful in this context to look at the situation in Mexico, although we have to jump ahead to the 1930s to do so. The Mexican Revolution of 1910 had ushered in a decade of political upheaval. Although feminists had been active from the 1870s, they had to contend with an overwhelmingly illiterate and impoverished rural population and a strong Catholic Church. Progressive or socialist government leaders had fostered feminism in an attempt to recruit allies for their anticlerical reform programs. In that tradition General Lázaro Cárdenas, who became president in 1934, drafted a bill to implement female suffrage. The bill was passed by both the Senate and Chamber of Deputies and by 1939 it had been ratified by the states, awaiting only formal declaration to be made into law. That declaration never came. Instead, the matter was dropped, and Mexican women did not receive the federal vote until 1958. What happened? A last-minute threat from a right-wing presidential candidate supported by the Feminine Idealist Party apparently unnerved Cárdenas, who feared a clerical vote by newly enfranchised women voters. Feminist agitation in the form of street demonstrations, picketing, marches, and threatened hunger strikes was not enough to compel the government to act. Here, as in Germany, Richard Evans's verdict on the political instrumentality of female suffrage holds good.

In Germany, Canada, and Mexico, suffrage was not a mass movement. What about those countries where it was? In Britain, the prewar suffrage movement made the issue unavoidable. The war provided an opportunity for the government to act on it without seeming to capitulate to the violent tactics of the WSPU. Winston Churchill may have been right when he declared that women's war work had been essential to victory, but the notion of a reward seems hollow when one considers that the bill excluded most of the women who worked in war-related industry. Until 1928 suffrage was restricted to most women over thirty. The refusal to enfranchise almost half of all adult women while enfranchising younger soldiers was designed to offset the fact that women outnumbered men in the adult population. Here, as in Mexico, the government was leery about the impact of female voters.

Immediate action on suffrage in Britain was necessary because the war made it impossible for soldiers to fulfil the one-year continuous residency rule. That political reform included female suffrage was the result of the long-standing campaign mounted by moderate suffragists along with the incendiary tactics of the WSPU, which if nothing else made the moderates look respectable. As Claire Duchen, an historian of the French women's movement, has remarked, "Legislation improving women's status does not happen by itself or through the good nature of lawmakers: women have had to fight for change every inch of the way."[12] We might add that it also does not happen *without* the good nature of lawmakers. Perhaps in the backs of their minds, British politicians feared a renewal of militancy. Like German politicians, they may have acted to forestall more radical change. Nineteenth-century conservative governments in Britain, Germany, and France had paved the way in initiating reforms in order to increase citizens' loyalty to traditional institutions, by, for example, extending male suffrage.

Like Winston Churchill, President Woodrow Wilson in the United States viewed women's work as vital to winning the war. That admission plus the apparent hypocrisy of a nation fighting for democracy abroad while restricting it at home fuelled the pickets that the small and militant Woman's Party had posted at the White House. A Colorado woman wrote, "I have no son to give my country to fight for democracy abroad, and so I send my daughter to Washington to fight for democracy at home." The combination of militancy and organized lobbying came to characterize the American scene as it did the British. Under the effective leadership of Carrie Chapman Catt, American suffragists regrouped from a series of failures at the turn of the century and mounted a successful campaign that, as in Britain, put suffrage on the national agenda. Harriot Stanton Blatch crowed, "All honor to women, the first disfranchised class in history who unaided by any political party won enfranchisement by its own effort alone."[13]

As in Britain, therefore, American women's suffrage was the culmination of decades of effort along with the opportunity provided by war. But American historians have raised provocative questions about the long-range causes of the suffrage grant. Compare President Wilson's wartime receptivity to suffrage to the ridicule experienced by the writers of the Seneca Falls Declaration some seventy years earlier. Since then, the suffrage movement had become respectable, accepted as part of a broad social reform movement. Two circumstances prompted the transformation. First, maternalist rhetoric, discussed in the previous chapter, stressed the continuity between woman's domestic responsibilities and the need for reform in public areas of social welfare. Second, earlier grants of female suffrage at the state level reassured lawmakers that no major changes were in store. That these two arguments contradicted each other was apparently not widely noticed.

Even more decisive was the transformation of American electoral politics at the beginning of the twentieth century. Throughout the nineteenth century two political subcultures had existed, separated by gender. Whereas women worked through reform organizations and lobbying campaigns, men monopolized electoral politics, dominated by parties and based on partisanship and patronage. By the twentieth century, local issues and loyalties had faded under the impact of urbanization and industrialization, and governments had become insulated from voters. As well, more abstract issues resolvable only by national resources lessened the attraction of party politics for voters. Disillusion with the ballot resulted, measured by a downturn in voting participation. Not coincidentally, this was precisely when the vote was extended to women. In 1926 feminist Suzanne LaFollette acknowledged that the woman's movement had "succeeded in securing political rights for women at the very period when political rights . . . [were] worth less than they . . . [had] been at any time since the eighteenth century."[14] Only in areas where voter turnout was still high, such as the South, did women's suffrage meet with resistance.

Does this change in electoral politics apply to Britain? Politicians may have feared the female vote in 1918, but ten years of partial enfranchisement calmed their fears just as the grants of state suffrage had reassured American politicians. When suffrage was enacted for all adult women in 1928, feminist Vera Brittain wondered, "Does [this final triumph] signify the final triumph of the feminist idea . . . or . . . is the acquiescence in equal franchise due more to a growing scepticism as to the importance of votes than to a growing conviction as to the justice of women's rights?"[15]

The example of France should put the axe once and for all to the notion of suffrage as a reward for women's war work. Although a suffrage bill passed overwhelmingly in the Chamber of Deputies in 1919, it was defeated by the Senate three years later by a narrow margin of twenty-two votes. A similar scenario was to occur three more times before 1936. In 1931 the margin of support in the Chamber was 319 to one. It may be that the deputies supported those bills because they knew full well that they would never pass the Senate. Indeed the arguments from both conservatives and republicans were little different from those that had been uttered over a century earlier, during the French Revolution. The specific situations that elsewhere motivated lawmakers—revolution in Germany, general suffrage reform in Britain, a federal election in Canada—were lacking. Senators thus saw no political advantage to be gained from a still-controversial innovation and were disinclined to act out of gratitude or generosity.

Accounting for female suffrage involves much more, therefore, than evaluating the suffrage movements themselves. French feminists may have been badly divided and relatively lacking in financial resources, but the suffrage movement in prewar France was nonetheless large, organized, and active. French suffragists, like others, deserve credit, but not as much as Harriot Stanton Blatch would give them. Simone de Beauvoir, a twentieth-century French feminist who generally downplayed women's agency, was perhaps not unduly cynical when she concluded, "Neither the Roman matrons uniting against the Oppian law nor the Anglo-Saxon suffragettes could have succeeded with their pressure unless the men had been quite disposed to submit to it."[16]

Backlash

From the foregoing, it might seem that the effect of World War I on feminism was somewhat minor. In fact, it had a profound impact by creating an antifeminist reaction that, along with the backlash generated by World War II, crippled the appeal and effect of feminism for almost half a century. Sandra Gilbert, a literary historian, has described how different the war experience could be for women and men. For everyone of that generation it represented a turning point, the shattering of the easy optimism and complacency they had known before the world "crashed into chaos."[17] But the death and destruction associated with the war were tempered for many women by a sense of freedom and new responsibilities. Whereas warfare brought home to the soldiers their vulnerability and powerlessness, some women experienced an exhilarating empowerment. A young British woman said it was "like being let out of a cage."[18] Paola Baronchelli Grosson in Italy believed that middle-class women "had obtained more from three years of war than from several decades of feminism."[19] From France Madeleine Pelletier reported that the war was a "paradise for working-class women. Never have they been as happy. . . . Never have they earned so much money."[20]

We know now that the extent of women's wartime employment has been vastly overrated. The percentage of women entering the paid labour force for the first time during the war was small in comparison to women who transferred from other sectors into war industries. Most women worked not because of new opportunities but because a centuries-old pattern of need drove them to contribute to their family's income. Whatever their motives, women throughout the war still earned less than men and worked largely in sex-segregated fields. And both women and men assumed that when the war ended, demobilized men would have priority for jobs.

For all that, many experienced their situation as an improvement. "During the wartime period," Lorine Pruette recalled in 1931, "the women of [the United States] were happier, probably, than at any other time in this twentieth century."[21] A transformation in fashion that replaced corsets, long skirts, and elaborate hairstyles with short skirts and bobbed hair was one positive change for women. Another was greater access to public space. It was no longer practical to insist that young, respectable women be constantly chaperoned. Women rejoiced in this freedom and, once the war was over, determined to keep it and use it to enjoy life.

Although most young women did marry, contemporaries worried whether the "flappers" would settle down to domestic responsibilities, or in other words, motherhood. In the European countries touched by the war the death toll intensified long-standing concern over declining birth rates and contributed to a backlash against single and working women even before the war ended. The war worked also in more subtle ways to drive a wedge between women and men. Many soldiers resented the prowar sentiments of those at home, particularly women who pinned the white feather of cowardice on "slackers." Others felt irrevocably alienated from those who could never understand what combat was like, an alienation that could take the form of repressed anger and a renewed misogyny. The war put "a barrier of indescribable experience," testified Vera Brittain, "between men and the women whom they loved."[22] Some women, for their part, blamed men for the war: Christabel Pankhurst, WSPU leader, saw it as "God's vengeance upon the people who held women in subjection."[23] Others, more sensitive, felt shame and guilt for having experienced the war as something positive, or even for having survived it. In Germany dismay over the provisions of the Treaty of Versailles nourished a "stab in the back" theory, which attributed the country's defeat not to the military but to betrayal on the home front, including women along with self-serving politicians. Many women wondered if in fact they were somehow to blame.

Whatever their experiences, both sexes felt a profound desire for a return to normality at war's end, normality meaning traditional gender roles and the security of a familiar domesticity. Such a climate made it difficult for feminists to take up the "sex antagonism," to use Rebecca West's phrase, of the prewar years. It was more comfortable to talk of the complementarity of the sexes, but this reinforced the notion of restricted separate spheres that feminism had set out to undermine. The 1920s and 1930s saw a full flowering of the ideology of domesticity, which was to recur in the late 1940s and 1950s following in the aftermath of World War II and which Betty Friedan later dubbed "the feminine mystique." "The peace in our time, for which we all crave," the English feminist Cicely Hamilton soberly predicted, "will mean a reaction, more or less strong, against the independence of women."[24]

British novelist and journalist Rebecca West (1892–1983) disagreed with the tendency of interwar feminists to mute what she called "sex-antagonism," as she wrote in "On a Form of Nagging," an article appearing in the 31 October 1924 issue of the feminist journal Time and Tide.

I am an old-fashioned feminist. I believe in the sex-war. I am, to use an expression that for some reason that I never can understand is used as a reproach, anti-man. When those of our army whose voices are inclined to coo tell us that the day of sex-antagonism is over and that henceforth we have only to advance hand in hand with the male I do not believe it. . . . When such a one says in a speech . . . that "women must learn to work with men," I disagree. I believe that women know how to work with men. But I believe that it is the rarest thing in the world for a man to know how to work with women without giving way to an inclination to savage his fellow-workers of the protected sex. This springs I admit, from a perfectly understandable and human cause. Man, baffled and fatigued by his struggle to establish and perpetuate human life in the universe, becomes afraid of judging his progress by the standard of approach to the absolute good. He prefers a relative standard. He wants to feel that however badly he is doing someone else is doing worse. As the only person with whom man can compare himself is woman, it is desirable that she should do worse. In fact, by the Lord Harry, she *shall* do worse. Therefore he harries and frustrates every sign of power that makes its appearance in women and deprives it of any opportunity to justify itself in contributions to the development of humanity. There are, of course, innumerable men of whom this is not true. The man who is really virile, who is a person of power, never fears any accession to power on the part of women. But all those who are not, indulge in anti-feminism. The woman who forgets this, who does not realise that by reason of her sex she lives in a beleaguered city, is a fool who deserves to lose (as she certainly will) all the privileges that have been won for her by her more robustly-minded sister. This is not to say that feminism need be shrill or hysterical. One can be as serene in a beleaguered city as anywhere else; but one must be vigilant.

ISSUES OF THE 1920S AND 1930S

The postwar political climate was not auspicious for feminist politics. Critics of the new German government lamented a topsy-turvy world, where groups previously excluded from influence—socialists, women, and Jews—now held sway. The Nazis and other right wingers branded feminism part of a worldwide Jewish conspiracy. Even non-Nazis saw the "new woman" as the symbol of a supposedly immoral and degenerate modern culture that flourished in the newly established Weimar Republic. Many moderate feminists for their part held back from participating in a government forged in defeat. Gertrud Bäumer, although she was later to hold a ministerial position, found it impossible at first to rejoice over the concession of women's suffrage: "We feel ourselves too much a part of our people to consider at this time only the progress that we have made for our own goals."[25] Although women's religious organizations were encouraged to rally to defeat the forces of socialism and atheism, many women fell back on the old concept of women as culture bearers, able to restore social harmony to a divided nation only by remaining above politics.

In the victorious nations practical issues of postwar reconstruction, national security, and depopulation had priority over women's rights. Economic chaos decimated feminist finances, reducing individuals to penury and leaving organizations and periodicals underfunded. While the European countries struggled to rebuild, labour unrest and racial tensions in North America coincided with a red scare triggered by the Russian Revolution and the fear of an international Bolshevik conspiracy. Most Canadian women became full citizens at a time when the country was more divided by class, language, and region than it had ever been. In the United States, the popularity of pacifism after the war provoked a counterattack by the military, determined to maintain the scale of wartime appropriations.

The worst of this smear campaign was the notorious Spider-Web Chart, compiled in 1923 reputedly by the librarian of the Chemical Warfare Service, Lucia Maxwell. Under the heading, "The Socialist-Pacifist Movement in America Is an Absolutely Fundamental and Integral Part of International Socialism," the chart listed and described fifteen women's organizations and twenty-nine leaders, drawing a web of lines to show how they were linked to one another and to two umbrella organizations. Among the groups were the National League of Women Voters, the YWCA, the WCTU, the American Association of University Women, and even, initially, the Daughters of the American Revolution. At the bottom of the chart Maxwell appended her poem:

> Miss Bolsheviki has come to town,
> With a Russian cap and a German Gown,
> In *women's clubs* she's sure to be found,
> For she's come to *disarm* AMERICA.[26]

Although this particular chart was withdrawn after it had circulated among government agencies and journalists, right-wing pressure groups, including women's patriotic societies, continued to attack feminism and pacifism throughout the decade, taking a high toll on individuals and organizations. Crystal Eastman, a pacifist as well as a lawyer and journalist, was included on a list of "dangerous Reds"[27] along with Jane Addams and found herself unable to get enough work in the United States; she ended up dividing her time between New York and England. Feminist organizations had to expend endless energy in defending themselves and, intimidated, they moderated their goals.

Women and Politics

Considering the antifeminist climate, the grant of suffrage to women in most Western countries seems less momentous to us than it did to contemporaries. The rhetoric of the suffrage campaign had promised that women would make a difference when admitted to full citizenship. Both women and politicians had high expectations as a result. Did women voters live up to their potential? We know that suffrage did not become a stepping stone to full equality for women. Although the British parliament passed twenty-one pieces of legislation for women between 1918 and 1929, including equal divorce and guardianship laws, no feminist today would agree with Ray Strachey, who wrote in her 1928 history of the British suffrage movement that "the main fight is over, and the main victory is won."[28] Across the Atlantic, the Royal Commission on the Status of Women in Canada would report in 1970 that in the fifty years since women's suffrage there had been no major changes in women's political activities other than their exercising the right to vote. But to optimistic feminists at the time, it seemed, as Vera Brittain observed in England, that there were no antifeminists left of any importance.

Even where gender equality was legislated, it did little to vanquish the persistence of patriarchy. In Germany, for example, the Weimar Constitution declared that "men and women have basically the same rights and duties," but specific legislation enacting that article into law was not forthcoming. The 1896 law code, which had confirmed married women's dependency, continued unchanged. Organized political life remained essentially what it had been before the war. None of the fundamental institutions, such as the state bureaucracy or the judiciary, was altered. As in many other countries women were kept from serving on juries on the grounds that they were too emotional, and married women could be and were dismissed from teaching and civil service positions. The word *basically* in article 109 was in fact an equivocation; it meant "not really."

In Austria, where the equality clause in the constitution was not qualified, the judiciary refused to enforce it. In Britain, the Sex Disqualification (Removal) Act of 1919 prohibited sex discrimination in public or civil positions. Nonetheless, as in Germany and Austria, the marriage bar remained in effect for civil service employees and professionals such as teachers and nurses. Because the act did not explicitly prohibit the dismissal of employed married women it was in effect a dead letter. Viscountess Rhondda used the

Sex Disqualification Act to sue the House of Lords for not allowing her to take her seat as a peeress, but her opponents successfully claimed that the act did not compel compliance given the absence of specific language to that purpose.

British lords were more generous in their response to an appeal by Canadian feminists, who in 1928 asked the Judicial Committee of the British Privy Council for a legal interpretation of the British North America Act. The act, which had established the Dominion of Canada in 1867, specified that only "persons" could be appointed to the Canadian Senate. After lobbying in vain for a female appointment, Emily Murphy, Nellie McClung, and three other women petitioned the Canadian Supreme Court asking for an interpretation of the BNA Act. The Court found that women were not "qualified persons." Evidently the judges were convinced by the suggestion of the solicitor general that otherwise the act would have referred to senators and *senatresses*. The petitioners then successfully appealed to England, although the Judicial Committee felt it necessary to warn that it was not endorsing women's rights. When the Canadian prime minister finally did appoint a woman senator in 1930, he did not choose the feminist Emily Murphy, to many the obvious candidate, but instead Cairine Wilson, a woman whom journalists described approvingly as a "lady of retiring disposition,"[29] and "first, last, and always a woman—a wife and mother of eight children."[30]

Although female voters brought about neither world peace nor full equality for women, there is evidence to suggest that they were decisive in the adoption of important welfare reforms in the 1920s. One example is the Sheppard–Towner bill in the United States. Passed in 1921 the bill set up mother and child health clinics, the first American instance of federally supported welfare. Its passage led the American Medical Association, which opposed it, to fret that women had created one of the strongest lobbies it had ever seen. Even before the grant of federal suffrage, American women had used their state and municipal votes, as well as the techniques of public education and lobbying perfected through their network of voluntary associations, to enact mothers' pensions and protective laws for working women. Canadian women also successfully lobbied for provincial legislation such as mothers' allowances, factory acts, infant protection, minimum wage laws for women, and better public health and educational facilities.

It is difficult, however, to gauge the long-range impact of women's groups. In the United States, it had become obvious by mid-decade that the anticipated female voting bloc would not materialize. In 1924 an American reporter shared his perception that nothing had changed: "not a boss has been unseated, not a reactionary committee wrested from old-time control."[31] The Sheppard–Towner Act, passed by a huge margin in 1921, failed to get enough support in 1929 to secure its renewal. In Britain the story was much the same; the only concrete welfare benefit that women gained in the 1920s was a Widows' Pensions Act. In contrast to endowments for mothers, which would help make them financially independent, the Pensions Act confirmed the norm of a family headed by a male breadwinner by supplying aid only for those women who had lost their providers through death. Any more radical reform was not forthcoming. A feminist-sponsored bill to exempt public employees from the marriage bar was handily defeated in 1927. Even though the Labour Party women's conference voted three times for legalizing birth control, the party refused to take it up until city councils joined the campaign. In short, while admitting the possibility of a female voting bloc, politicians were willing to make only those concessions consistent with the postwar reactionary climate.

Women in Politics

Why did the expected women's bloc fail to materialize? If women could unite in a mass movement to put suffrage on national political agendas, why could they not do the same with other feminist demands? Putting the question that way ignores the divisions within the suffrage movement, mainly the one between what Crystal Eastman called the "humanitarian" (maternal feminist) and the "pure feminist" (equal rights feminist). In the postsuffrage period, each "reverted to type." As Eastman put it,

> The humanitarian type said to itself, "Thank God, that's over. Now we can stop demanding our rights . . . and turn once more to the various reforms which we believe will benefit the human race.". . . The "pure feminist" type said, "Thank God, that's over. Now we can go on with the programme of feminism. We can begin to attack the subjection of women in its other forms, many of them as deep-rooted and menacing to freedom as was our disfranchisement."[32]

Eastman was writing after the divisions among American feminists had hardened into enmity, but even earlier some had perceived that there would be difficulty organizing for postsuffrage goals. British suffrage leader Millicent Garrett Fawcett had foretold in 1917 how from her retirement she would watch the movement floundering. The issue of suffrage had created a common ground among women, disenfranchised on the basis of gender. Once that reform was achieved, no obvious issue would have the same function. A veteran of the American suffrage campaign, Anna Howard Shaw, told a colleague, "I am sorry for you young women who have to carry on the work in the next ten years, for suffrage was a symbol, and now you have lost your symbol. There is nothing for the women to rally round."[33] The issue of peace was, as we have seen, divisive. So, for reasons explored below, were birth control and protective laws for working women.

Still, women could unite around the concept that they had a particular contribution to make to politics. Consistent with presuffrage ideology, many distrusted party politics as corrupting and divisive. Did women have the potential to transform politics? Could they not do better than men, rising above party factionalism in order to work for the common good? The specific question for politically minded women was whether they should work from within the traditional parties or form an independent bloc. In retrospect we can say it was very much a choice between a rock and a hard place. Neither option proved to be effective for promoting feminist goals.

Both in Canada and in the United States attempts were made to organize an independent bloc. In Ontario the Woman's Party formed in 1918 but was not able to withstand opposition from women in Western Canada. The National Woman's Party in the United States, formed originally in 1913 as the Congressional Union to introduce militant tactics into the suffrage campaign, continued after the war with a feminist agenda. A narrow focus on equal rights determined its fate as a minority party, uncongenial to women who had broader interests in, for example, birth control, pacifism, or the working conditions of women wage earners.

More representative was the National League of Women Voters, successor to the main American suffrage organization, which wanted to educate women so that they could work within conventional channels. "The only way to get things done is to get them done on the inside of the political party," Carrie Chapman Catt told the members bluntly.[34] Anne Martin, who had worked for the Woman's Party, vehemently disagreed: "There is no doubt that Mrs. Carrie Chapman Catt sounded the doom of feminism for many years to come when she urged the newly enfranchised American women . . . 'to work with the party of your choice,'—exactly where men political leaders wanted them, bound, gagged, divided, and delivered to the Republican and Democratic parties."[35] She urged instead that women organize as a separate political force. But the problems seemed insurmountable. How could women overcome the divisions within their ranks? How could they command resources or reliable allies? How could they gain access to the levers of power?

Those women who chose to work from within did not find the obstacles any less formidable. Although British political parties obligingly ran women candidates, more than 80 percent of them were placed in ridings where their party had no chance of winning. An outspoken feminist would have had difficulty even securing a nomination. The first English woman to be elected to the House of Commons, Nancy Astor, announced reassuringly, "I am not in public life for a career. I have six children and many interests."[36] One has great difficulty imagining a male MP making that remark.

In the course of her political career, Nancy Astor actually became somewhat feminist, undoubtedly as a result of her exposure to the chauvinism of her colleagues and the press, which commented relentlessly on her wardrobe. The same happened to the first woman to hold a seat in the Canadian parliament, Agnes Macphail (1890–1952). For fourteen years Macphail served as the sole female member, first in the House of Commons and later in the Ontario legislature. Looking back on her experience Macphail observed, "I couldn't open my mouth to say the simplest thing without it appearing in the papers. I was a curiosity, a freak. And you know the way the world treats freaks."[37] At times lonely, Macphail was always feisty. When heckled by a man in the audience who taunted, "Don't you wish you were a man?" she fired back, "Yes, don't you?" Although Macphail considered herself a representative of her farm and labour constituency rather than of women, by 1927 she declared, "I am a feminist and I want for women the thing men are not willing to give them—absolute equality."[38]

Agnes Macphail's political independence marginalized her. There was the opposite danger also, that women would try to fit in, to become accepted as "one of the boys." The American editor Henry Lewis Mencken, expressing a widespread disillusionment with party politics, warned in 1922, "A woman who joins one of these [political] parties simply becomes an imitation man, which is to say, a donkey. Thereafter she is nothing but an obscure cog in an ancient and creaking machine, the sole intelligible purpose of which is to maintain a horde of scoundrels in public office."[39] In describing the tensions women faced, historian Olive Banks suggests that it is "only those women who are prepared to compromise their feminism or, possibly, who were never feminist in the first place, who are able to command sufficient confidence from the men that surround them to rise to power at all."[40]

Contributing to Agnes Macphail's isolation was the fact that before 1950 only five women were elected to the Canadian parliament, two of whom stood in for their husbands. In Germany the situation was very different; forty-one women took seats in the national assembly in 1919, almost 10 percent of the total. It appears that German politicians, like their American counterparts, acted prudently at first, placing women high on the electoral lists. Thereafter, women had great difficulty securing places as priority candidates, nor were they able to gain direct support in electoral districts. In fact, the high number of women deputies in 1919 was not duplicated again until 1983.

Once in the German parliament, women were able to act as a group on occasion. Liberals and socialists joined in unsuccessful attempts to strike the word *basically* from Article 109 and to eliminate the marriage bar. They also united in support of state maternity benefits and money for nursing mothers. On more contentious issues, predictably, such as reform of the abortion law, there was no united bloc even when the parties allowed an open vote. The Federation of German Women's Associations (BDF), like the American League of Women Voters, thought of itself as educational and nonpartisan. It was committed to getting more women into politics but was unable to marshall the necessary clout. The heterogeneity of its member organizations, which ranged from housewives to civil servants, kept it from acting as a coherent interest group or from tackling hard issues that would have divided the membership. Although the BDF considered forming a women's party it never did. Perhaps its leaders realized that it lacked the resources or coercive sanctions to make such a strategy effective.

In short, political women were either isolated if they were feminists or invisible if they toed the party line. Participating in electoral politics was only one way to exercise political influence, however. The alternative was to work as a lobby or interest group. This was the mode of choice for most North American activists. Specialized groups, such as parent–teacher associations, the YWCA, professional and business organizations, city clubs, and the like, replaced the large suffrage coalitions. Rather than retreating from politics once they had won the vote, women continued to organize as they had for decades, perfecting the method of pressure-group politics. In fact, given their greater access to education and the fall in the birth rate, American women in this period may have participated more in associational activities than at any other time.

For all that, few of these groups, if any, thought of themselves as feminist, and if there was agreement on methods, there was little consensus on goals. As a result, historians concur, interwar feminism lacked coherence and direction, degenerating into multiple, fragmented organizations. Let us now look at the divisions that splintered and weakened the movement.

Equal or Different?

The most divisive issue for feminists in the United States and Great Britain spilled over to bedevil international feminist politics as well and had long been latent in organized feminism: Should women emphasize difference or equality? Before the 1920s, the issue had tended to characterize feminism rather than feminists, activists employing one or the other argument as the occasion demanded. In the 1920s, however, differences of personality combined with questions of ideology and tactics to thrust the question to the front and render the responses irreconcilable.

The opening skirmish in the United States came when Alice Paul of the National Woman's Party (NWP) drafted an equal rights statement, which was submitted to congress in 1923 as a proposed constitutional amendment. The Equal Rights Amendment (ERA) read: "Men and women shall have equal rights throughout the United States and every place subject to its jurisdiction." Fearful that the principle of equal rights had the potential to nullify reforms that maternal feminists had worked for over decades, seven national women's organizations protested against it almost immediately. Because legislation such as minimum wage laws or restrictions on night work was sex-based, reformers were apprehensive that an equal rights standard would abrogate their work. That was not Alice Paul's intention; in fact, she at first expressed a willingness to exclude laws that benefited women. But smouldering resentment among former suffragists of the NWP's militancy and continued suspicion of its goals, along with Paul's lack of tact, jeopardized any possibility of co-operation between the NWP and other groups.

It was not just a matter of personalities, for the same split occurred in Great Britain between equal rights feminists and "new" feminists, as they dubbed themselves. The former group gathered around Viscountess Rhondda, who founded the distinguished feminist weekly *Time and Tide* and organized the Six Point Group, a nonpartisan pressure group, to push for such reforms as equal pay. Although twenty-four major women's organizations subscribed to the Six Point Group's goals, by 1927 the split among British feminists resembled the one among the Americans. The "new," or maternal, feminists were led by Eleanor Rathbone (1872–1946). Rathbone campaigned for family allowances to be paid to mothers as a way to give them economic independence and social recognition. She also supported labour legislation protecting women workers. When the International Labour Bureau of the League of Nations promoted protective laws, Rhondda founded yet another group, the Open Door Council, to oppose them. The increasingly acrimonious dispute also split the International Alliance of Women for Suffrage and Equal Citizenship.

A good case could be made for protective legislation. Crystal Eastman, an equal rights feminist, admitted, "A great deal can be said for minimum wage laws and laws limiting the hours of labor for women on the ground that woman's labor is the least adapted to organization and therefore the most easily exploited and most in need of legislative protection."[41] Although equal rights feminist—or, as the "new" feminists dubbed them, the "Me Too feminists,"[42]—envisioned a perfect world in which gender did not matter, in reality women workers faced appalling conditions without the means to compel the attention of male-dominated unions. Protective legislation can be seen as a 1920s version of affirmative action, the state doing what male-dominated unions were unwilling to do. While professional and business women had the most at stake in equal rights legislation, the majority of women were either wage earners or housewives, frequently both. To them equal rights legislation was abstract, naïve, and irrelevant; minimum wage laws and shorter working hours would have a positive and dramatic effect on their lives. So would family allowances, by reducing wives' economic dependency, easing their double burden, and raising their self-image. "At last we have done with the boring business," reported Eleanor Rathbone in 1925,

> of measuring everything that women want, or that is offered them by men's standards, to see if it is exactly up to sample. At last we can stop looking at all our problems through men's eyes and discussing them in men's phraseology. We can demand what we want for women, not because it is what men have got but because it is what women need to fulfil the potentialities of their own natures and to adjust themselves to the circumstances of their own lives.[43]

Such an approach had the potential to reach ordinary women in a way that liberal feminism could not; by its focus on family life and refusal to define equality in men's terms, perhaps its potential was more radical as well. Women's economic dependency in marriage, believed Rathbone, was the last stronghold of male dominance.

For their part, equal rights feminists argued that family allowances would discourage women from working outside the home and encourage employers to eliminate wage increases for men. Many working women stood to lose by minimum wage laws and restricted hours that would make them less competitive than men. Further, reforms should benefit all workers by being job rather than gender specific. "You can't protect women without handicapping them in competition with men," reasoned a labour leader interviewed by Crystal Eastman. "If you demand equality you must accept equality. Women can't have it both ways."[44] Why treat all women as if they were permanently pregnant, wondered Cicely Hamilton. Elizabeth Abbott put it more bluntly, declaring, "The issue is not between 'old' and 'new' feminism. (There is no such thing as 'new' feminism, just as there is no such thing as 'new' freedom. There is freedom; and there is tyranny.) The issue is between feminism—equalitarianism—and that which is *not* feminism."[45]

Although middle-class women tended to support equal rights legislation and working women to oppose it, the lines were not drawn hard and fast. The major black women's groups in the United States lined up on either side, with the National Association of Colored Women supporting the ERA and the National Council of Negro Women opposing it. For many individuals it was more a matter of priorities than principles. The narrow focus of the NWP precluded other issues important to women, such as pacifism, birth control, and race relations. Just as socialist parties argued that feminism was diversionary, so to Alice Paul was anything other than the ERA. This restricted focus and Paul's claim that her position alone was "feminist" ensured that most American reformers would shun the term for themselves.

Mary Beard (1876–1958), an American historian, refused to endorse either approach but instead recognized their defects. Protective legislation would clearly be used to discriminate against women, but equal rights written into law at a time when conditions were manifestly unequal "would be equality in disaster rather than in realistic privilege." Few understood her preference for humanism instead of "feminism as the companion-piece of manism,"[46] however, and Beard was isolated in her attempt to steer a middle path.

Was the "new" feminism a shrewd move to exploit contemporary social currents, in particular the emphasis on domesticity? Or was it a capitulation to conservatism? Late nineteenth-century maternal feminism, represented by Frances Willard's campaign against alcoholism in the United States and by Josephine Butler's crusade against state regulation of prostitution in Britain, had sought to extend women's familial role to the public arena. The goal was to curb masculine practices and replace them with a single moral standard supplied by women. Regardless of whether gender-based values were seen as primarily biological or cultural in origin, maternal feminists had assumed that men could change and that it was women's duty to prod them. The goals of the "new" feminism, in contrast, seem much more modest. There was no attempt to challenge the idea of woman in the home or to encourage women's entry into the public sphere. On the contrary, the point was to elevate women's role within the home and to protect them when necessity demanded that they work outside it.

Did interwar feminism, then, trap women in the cult of domesticity from which earlier feminists had tried to free them? To assess this development, we have to examine another difference between feminists: age, or the generation gap.

The Generation Gap and the New Morality

In the interwar years, feminism appeared to be the obsession of a minority of aging women. What had once been associated with adventure and rebellion now seemed dull and old-fashioned. Vera Brittain described the unflattering public perception of feminists as "spectacled, embittered women, disappointed, childless, dowdy, and generally unloved."[47] In Italy they were called "old carcasses."[48] In all countries, feminist organizations failed to attract the younger generation, which in Germany drifted towards the Nazis. This failure has been described as the main problem of interwar feminism.

Did the generation gap result from a perception that there was nothing left to be done once the vote had been won? Suffrage reform eliminated the blatant and harsh inequality that earlier women had known. In trying to account for young women's "strong hostility to the word 'feminism' and all which they imagine it to connote," Ray Strachey agreed that it was due to their ignorance of "what life was like before the war."[49] Alternatively, the generation gap, suggests historian Alice Rossi, may be part of a pendulum swing or generational dialectic between mothers and daughters. Feminism was still present in the daughters but in a different form. Although it lost its public visibility, the younger generation was busy consolidating it into the fabric of their inner lives. American professional women, for example, rejected the public face of feminism but never wavered in their desire for independence and fulfilment.

It certainly is true that young women were more interested in personal fulfilment than in public crusades. Vera Brittain (1893–1970), part of that generation but somewhat removed because of her wartime service, explained that older people failed to understand "that reckless sense of combined release and anti-climax which set my contemporaries, who had lived a lifetime of love and toil and suffering and yet were only in their early twenties, dancing in the vain hope of recapturing the lost youth that the War had stolen."[50] Even in countries less traumatized by war, the flapper came to signify a carefree, pleasure-seeking, uninhibited young woman who baffled veteran feminists. The puzzlement was mutual. "The attitude of the nineteenth- and pre-war–twentieth-century 'feminist' seemed incomprehensible to [young women]" explained Winifred Holtby in 1934, "something unnecessary, exaggerated and more than a little ugly."[51]

To contemporary observers the younger generation seemed to reduce personal fulfilment exclusively to sexual freedom. Although new patterns of premarital and extramarital sexuality had been present before the war, they were mainly limited to university or bohemian circles. After the war what had previously been radical became mainstream. In the United States, for example, women born after 1900 were twice as likely to have had premarital sex as those born before 1900. British women born after 1904 also admitted to increased heterosexual activity. Sexual experimentation in sophisticated neighbourhoods like Harlem and Greenwich Village in New York included homosexuality although even there bisexuality was more acceptable for women than lesbianism.

Doubtless many wanted to extend women's demands for equal rights to include sexual equality. Older feminists, however, were not amused. Jane Addams objected to the "astounding emphasis upon sex." Charlotte Perkins Gilman condemned it as "selfish and fruitless indulgence," "sickening," and "as a mere imitation of masculine weakness and vice."[52] Ray Strachey was dismayed to see young women putting make-up on in public and in other ways showing their eagerness to please men. (Strachey, it must be noted, was not particularly concerned with her appearance, having once worn a dress to dinner without noticing that it was inside out.) The key to older feminists' rejection of the new morality lies in Strachey's observation that sexual freedom was more about pleasing men than about giving women equal rights. She and the others of her generation were not convinced that the new heterosexual freedom stood to benefit women. Although sex reformers such as Havelock Ellis acknowledged women's sexuality, they saw it exclusively in terms of heterosexual intercourse. One historian terms sex reform a kind of "sexual first aid" which "did not challenge the sexual status quo, in which women were expected to be dependent on men and to do sexual intercourse whether they liked it or not."[53] This criticism is not quite accurate since the emphasis in new marriage manuals was to get women to like it. Authors wrote for husbands, who were to instruct child-like wives; one author, addressing women directly, told them, "you *must* be willing to be awakened."[54]

Before sex reform and before Freud women had enjoyed intense, intimate relationships with other women. Now most experts considered such an orientation pathological and associated lesbianism with feminism. Sigmund Freud, for example, in 1920 described a young woman who exhibited what he termed "lesbian masculinity." Freud based his diagnosis not on any experience she had or preference she showed for sex with other women but rather on her "masculine" intellectual attributes such as "her acuteness of comprehension and her lucid objectivity." Freud called her "a spirited girl, always ready for romping and fighting," and unwilling to take second place to her brother. "She was in fact a feminist," Freud pronounced, "She felt it to be unjust that girls should not enjoy the same freedom as boys and rebelled against the lot of women in general."[55]

Both sexologists and novelists made the link between abnormality, lesbianism, and feminism, on the one hand, and health, heterosexuality, and female submissiveness, on the other. In the second volume to his best seller *Ideal Marriage* (1928), titled *Sex Hostility in Marriage* (1931), Theodore Van de Velde wrote approvingly, "The sexual impulse is associated in the woman with a tendency to submit herself."[56] It may not be accidental that sex reform coincided with the peak of the suffrage movement, a rise in the number of single women, and World War I, which as we saw was a liberating experience for many women. The acceptance of female sexual pleasure was a way to reconcile the "new woman" to marriage and motherhood. Marital harmony, not self-indulgence, was the goal. Dora Russell, active in the British birth control movement, wrote reassuringly that an understanding of the dignity and beauty of sex "is the bridge that will span the breach" between the sexes.[57]

What effect did these ideas have on the woman-centred institutions and relationships that were so important to first-wave feminism? Female students no longer looked to their unmarried women professors as role models. The fear of English birth controller Marie Stopes that sex-starved spinster teachers would corrupt girls became the theme of antilesbian novels. Some lesbian writers, such as British novelist Radclyffe Hall, internalized these negative values. Stephen, the lesbian heroine of Hall's *The Well of Loneliness* (1928), exemplifies the self-loathing and masculinity that were to become stereotypical attributes. One reader described the book's impact: "I had found a copy of [it] in the library, and for the first time in my life, I felt a certain shame about my feelings towards women."[58] Nonetheless, lesbian culture flourished in the cosmopolitan centres of Paris, Berlin, Vienna, London, and New York. Natalie Barney's Paris salon provided well-off and talented lesbians with a supportive network.

Women still treasured their female friendships, but they became more cautious about the implications. Vera Brittain wrote disarmingly of her close friendship with Winifred Holtby, with whom she lived for many years,

> From the days of Homer the friendships of men have enjoyed glory and acclamation, but the friendships of women . . . have usually been not merely unsung, but mocked, belittled and falsely interpreted. I hope that Winifred's story may do something to destroy these tarnished interpretations, and show its reader that loyalty and affection between women is a noble relationship.

She went on, however, to express her hope that her book would show that such a relationship, "far from impoverishing, actually enhances the love of a girl for her lover, of a wife for her husband, of a mother for her children." As well, Brittain stressed Holtby's relationship with "Bill" in order to put to rest "the scandalmongers"[59] who imagined a homosexual relationship between Holtby and her or between Holtby and Viscountess Rhondda. When Rhondda herself began a living arrangement with Theodora Bosanquet in 1933, which was to last twenty-five years, she took pains to deflect gossip by describing it as a housekeeping arrangement. In New York, the freewheeling discussions of the feminist club Heterodoxy in the 1910s became in the 1920s more narrowly restricted to the themes of marriage and motherhood. Although lesbians participated in the group, they no longer felt as comfortable.

While individual friendships could and did flourish, the new climate weakened women's gender consciousness. One historian has even suggested that the erosion of separatist ideology and institutions was responsible for the decline of postsuffrage feminism. One must balance this assessment against the evidence of women's ongoing activity in voluntarist associations, which continued to nourish a female culture.

From the above we can understand why feminists regarded the new sexual freedom with ambivalence or even distaste. When we look at another prop of the new morality, birth control, we find that it too had ambiguous and sometimes negative implications for feminism. This conclusion seems curious given the obvious benefits for women anxious to control reproduction. Some feminist groups, such as branches of the Women's International League for Peace and Freedom in Germany and Canada, vigorously championed birth control, but most feminist organizations kept their distance. Why was this so?

For one, the postwar climate was hardly conducive to discussions of women's reproductive freedom. Quite the opposite was true, in view of the toll that war had taken on the male population and of the already declining birth rate. The concern was apparent even in England, where the male population actually rose in spite of war deaths because of a drop in male emigration. In France pronatalist fervour helped defeat women's suffrage. Feminists themselves appeared more concerned with discussing how to raise the birth rate than with gaining the vote. Severe laws in 1920 and 1923 stiffened the penalties for doctors performing abortions and dispensing contraceptive information. One victim was the militant feminist Madeleine Pelletier, who had courageously written that abortion "is the woman's right. She is free to control her body and if the born child is sacred, the foetus in her belly belongs to her. She ought to be able, at will, to keep it or reject it."[60] A doctor and presumed abortionist, Pelletier saw her clinic raided in 1939 although she had been partially paralyzed from a stroke for two years. Six weeks later she was committed to an insane asylum where she died, alone and penniless after the government confiscated her assets. Most certainly, her confinement was the government's way to avoid the publicity of a formal arrest.

Weimar Germany seems to have been unique in witnessing a spontaneous, grass-roots protest on the part of working women against the law that forbade abortions and imposed penal servitude on convicted women and their accomplices. Women doctors joined the protest, speaking both as professionals and as women. The socialist and communist parties, prodded by their female members, responded by making abortion reform a priority and keeping the issue in the public eye. Although the socialists pressed for abortion on demand, they could only effect a compromise that substituted jail sentences for penal servitude. This change, however, gave Germany the most lenient abortion law in Western Europe.

Birth control was not necessarily feminist. The two best-known proponents of birth control in English-speaking countries were Margaret Sanger in the United States and Marie Stopes in England. Sanger (1883–1966), who coined the phrase *birth control*, had started out as a radical socialist and a feminist. "No woman can call herself free," she wrote in 1920, "who does not own and control her body."[61] At one point interested in radical labour organizing, she then adopted birth control as her *cause célèbre* and sought to make it respectable by cultivating the support of physicians. Although there was no inherent reason why birth control clinics needed medical supervision, Sanger's direction ensured that white women would now appeal to professional men for advice rather than to female relatives, friends, or neighbours. In place of traditional methods such as douches and withdrawal, both Sanger and Stopes promoted diaphragms or cervical caps, which needed to be fitted by doctors. In African-American communities, in contrast, physicians were more sensitive to the involvement of midwives and women volunteers, and women continued to rely on douching as the preferred method of contraception.

As with sex reform, birth control was intended to promote heterosexuality. Armed with the new manuals and the proper protection, a woman now had no excuse not to enjoy intercourse, unless of course she was lesbian, frigid, or a man-hating feminist, most likely all three in one. Birth control was not meant to free her from her traditional responsibilities but to enable her to fulfil them better. For both Stopes and Sanger birth control meant better sex in better marriages, which in turn meant happier wives and mothers and, not incidentally, happier children. Neither one disdained using eugenic arguments to support their cause, pointing out that birth control could improve the race by reducing the number of the "unfit." Both opposed abortion even though women continued to choose it as back-up birth control when other methods failed.

Compared to the first-wave campaign to curb male sexuality, the new morality accepted the male sex drive as given and encouraged women to adapt to it. Hence the disdain of older feminists for sex reform. The Federation of German Women's Associations (BDF), motivated by what it considered the moral laxity of the Weimar Republic, continued its opposition to state-regulated prostitution, contraception, abortion, and sexual permissiveness. Understandably, this campaign attracted few young women and confirmed the impression of a generation gap. Ironically, the Nazis did better by promising to equalize the status of unmarried and married mothers, a reform opposed by the BDF. In Mexico attempts after 1922 by the socialist governor of the Yucatán to promote free love, easy divorce, and birth control foundered on the resistance of Mexican feminists. Although the governor was keen to set up birth control clinics, feminists voted instead for prenatal and postnatal clinics to reduce infant mortality and maintained their insistence that men be raised to women's moral standards.

One last example of older social purity ideas comes from the American south and the antilynching campaign that Jessie Daniel Ames organized among white women in the 1930s. The campaign was a deliberate attempt to explode the myth of white women as helpless victims of black rapists, a myth that racists used to justify the lynching of black men. To do so Ames exploited another cultural symbol, that of the southern lady's moral superiority. The campaign was inspired both by Ames's own feminist antipathy to the white man's assumption that women, white and black, were his property and by the antilynching struggle waged for years by the black community. White women were finally taking up the challenge issued by black women to "control your men"[62] and stop them from lynching blacks. Ames's campaign is reminiscent of nineteenth-century social purity movements, which also sought to curb male sexuality and violence by imposing women's higher moral standards.

One bridge across the generation gap was the popularity of women film stars and sports figures. Both older and younger women thrilled to the accomplishments of figures such as actor Katharine Hepburn or aviator Amelia Earhart. Such individuals helped popularize the idea that any woman could be successful if she tried hard enough now that women had achieved equality through the vote. Indifferent to structural and social barriers to equality, this emphasis on individual achievement both revealed and contributed to the weakness of feminism as a collective movement during the period. The emphasis on individualism and personal solutions characterizes the interwar feminist approach to marriage as well.

Marriage, New Style

Infused with the relaxed sexual intimacy promised by sex reformers and birth controllers, marriage appeared more enticing than ever. Not that young women needed to be enticed. Education or working experience notwith-standing, most looked forward to marriage as the most important step in their lives. Understandable for working-class women, who continued to experience the disadvantages of low pay, long hours, and little job security, this expectation also characterized their college-educated and professional sisters. In previous decades a high percentage, from one-half to two-thirds at some colleges, of American graduates had not married. In the early 1920s, two of those colleges saw 80 to 90 percent of their graduates marrying. A survey of American teenagers taken during this period found that more than one-third of female respondents wanted a career, but by end of the decade few were willing to renounce marriage for it.

Throughout the interwar period popular magazines did their share to promote marriage and domesticity. British publications such as *Good Housekeeping, My Home,* and *Woman's Own* enjoyed an enormous readership, which reached into the millions by the mid-1930s. The message was clear and insistent: as *Woman's Own* put it, "Any girl worth her salt wants to be the best housewife ever—and then some!" or, "A bad husband is better than no husband at all." As for women's financial independence, "a marriage in which the wife is also a breadwinner isn't a true marriage at all."[63] Readers were bombarded by advertisements and articles targeting "Mrs Consumer." The result, reinforced by "science," was higher standards for housekeeping and mothering that offset any reduction in workload promised by the introduction of prepared foods, electric appliances, and such cleaning innovations as vacuum cleaners and washing machines. Housewives were urged, for example, to move to the front lines in the war against germs, believed to thrive in dust; an advertisement for Lysol cleaner warned, "Germs live on every door knob." And even though family size continued to shrink throughout this period, experts berated women inclined to take a casual or traditional approach to child rearing. While women were assured that motherhood was "the highest of all professions," they were also cautioned that "if your child is a problem child, probably you are a problem mother."[64] The media blitz and the intrusion of experts made it impossible to maintain the older image of women as arbiters of private life.

Is it too cynical to see this as a campaign to keep women out of the labour market in light of the high unemployment of the postwar years? Home, family, and marital sex—these private satisfactions would reconcile social tensions in a manner reminiscent of Catharine Beecher's approach in the nineteenth century (see Chapter 6). One should beware of imagining women as passive victims, however. Many could for the first time look forward to improving their standard of living, to have the clean and attractive homes their mothers had lacked. Their desire to make life better for themselves and their families can be viewed in the same way as their determination to control family size, which they did in the face of insistent pronatalist sentiment.

Independent-minded women were determined not to submerge themselves in marriage. Comparing themselves to first-wave feminists, who were commonly thought to be dedicated spinsters, interwar feminists were intent on having *both* marriage and careers. Their perception of the past was in fact false. The majority of women in feminist movements in all countries had been married, and the debate on how to reconcile marriage and career was an old one. Nonetheless, many women of the 1920s and 1930s had new expectations for emotional and sexual satisfaction in marriage. The radical couples of Greenwich Village, New York, for example, wanted relationships that were emotionally, intellectually, and sexually satisfying. Yet even here the ambivalence of the men towards their wives' independence meant that these marriages ultimately resembled more traditional ones.

When Amelia Earhart made her future husband promise to release her after a year if she found their relationship unsatisfactory, her fears about losing her independence were no different from those of feminists fifty years earlier. Nor was her resolve to keep her birth name new. The American Ruth Hale appealed to historical precedent when she formed the Lucy Stone League, which had as its motto, "My name is the symbol of my identity and must not be lost."[65] No feminist or feminist organization at this time went beyond any earlier feminist critique of marriage; they developed no ideology that called for its radical reformation or abolition. Vera Brittain, as ambivalent about marriage as Amelia Earhart was, nonetheless affirmed that "one happily married wife and mother is worth more to feminism . . . than a dozen gifted and eloquent spinsters."[66]

The real test came not with marriage but with motherhood; or, as the American Henrietta Rodman wrote in 1915, "At the present time the care of the baby is the weak point in feminism."[67] A disciple of Charlotte Perkins Gilman, Rodman advocated a social solution, co-operative housing. Nonetheless, most women believed that it was up to them to find the answer. Vera Brittain told her fiancé, "I want to solve the problem of how a married woman, without being inordinately rich, can have children and yet maintain her intellectual and spiritual independence as well as having . . . time for the pursuit of her own career."[68] Revealingly, Brittain did not regard the problem as one that both parents had to face. Although her own marriage was, to use her phrase, "semi-detached," she assisted by her domestic staff she took responsibility for the house and children even when she and her husband were living together.

Crystal Eastman (1881–1928) grappled with the same dilemma. As a child she persuaded her parents that she and her brothers should share the household chores. "Men will not give up their privilege of helplessness without a struggle," she recognized and called on women to "bring up feminist sons." Like Vera Brittain, she and her husband practised what Eastman called "Marriage under Two Roofs,"[69] but while she allowed the father to retreat to his own flat, the children stayed with their mother.

At times Eastman did consider the problem in social terms, advocating that both boys and girls be taught domestic science, for example. More usually she, like Brittain, looked for a personal solution. So did the seventeen women who were invited by an American magazine, *The Nation,* in 1926–27 to share their thoughts on why and how they became feminists. The theme that emerges from their essays is their awareness of their failure to solve the problem of women's dual burden. Cognizant of men's privilege, they were pessimistic about changing it. After marriage "men appear to lose a large part of their capacity as adults," Lorine Pruette remarked drily, "they can no longer feed themselves, house themselves, look after their health, or attend to their social responsibilities (most of them upon marriage lose the capacity even of writing to their own mother)."[70] As Crystal Eastman had earlier put it, women "must make up their minds to be a sort of supermen [*sic*], I think."[71] Not surprisingly, fully twelve of the seventeen writers were childless. Over half lived by writing, because of its flexibility one of the best careers to combine with homemaking and motherhood.

That these women saw their failure as a personal one reveals the weakness of interwar feminism. The few radicals who experimented with lifestyles lacked the support of a movement concerned with politicizing the personal. "What was missing," summarizes Elaine Showalter in her study of the *Nation* series, "was a sufficiently sizable base of employed married women, experiencing firsthand the role conflict which the *Nation* women understood; and a feminist analysis which could interpret the role conflict and the discrimination as a collective political phenomenon rather than as a personal problem."[72] As a result feminists were disillusioned and perhaps more inclined to support Eleanor Rathbone's version of feminism, based as it was upon the hard reality of women's double burden.

There were a few experiments with an institutional solution to the problem of how to reconcile marriage and careers. Vassar College in the United States introduced an imaginative program in euthenics designed to raise the status of homemaking and child care through the practical application of science. A dramatic departure from the college's commitment to give its students an education identical to that of men's colleges, the 1924 program raised the ire of faculty members, one of whom protested, "You are driving women back into the home, from the slavery of which education has helped us to escape."[73] Ethel Puffer Howes encountered the same opposition with her short-lived Institute for the Coordination of Women's Interests, established at Smith College in 1925. Convinced that women should not be asked to sacrifice either professional or domestic interests, Howes attempted to create an alternative to the male-defined career model. Her institute promoted co-operative approaches to housework and child care and part-time or freelance work for mothers. As at Vassar, faculty resisted what they saw as an adulteration of standards, and Howes' Institute was disbanded in 1931.

Feminism and Work

The self-conscious efforts of a few literary and professional women to combine home and work did not exhaust the attempts of women to fight the injustice of their double burden. Canadian prairie women in the 1920s and

1930s, for example, developed a feminism of private life, not as organized or as visible as the suffrage movement but nonetheless based on a sense of gender oppression and a determination to change it. Although these women rarely transformed their anger at male privilege into political action in the traditional sense, they wrote letters to local newspapers asking about their rights or seeking mutual encouragement. They formed co-operatives, demanded higher status for homemaking, insisted that family members share chores, campaigned for improved property rights, and argued for birth control clinics. They recognized, as did self-declared feminists, that the key issues for women now that they had the vote centred around their work.

Married women's paid work was the most hotly debated issue of the 1920s and 1930s. Hostility towards married women in the workplace was an understandable if lamentable response to the massive unemployment of the Great Depression, which began in 1929. High unemployment had been characteristic as well of the 1920s in most Western countries, and married women even then faced the charge that they were taking jobs away from men who had families to support. With the depression, marriage bars became even more widespread. As did many other countries, the United States passed legislation in 1932 excluding married employees' "spouses" from civil service jobs. Sex-neutral language veiled what was openly understood as discrimination against married women. A Gallup poll taken in 1936 revealed that more than 80 percent of the respondents opposed wives working if their husbands had jobs. George Gallup himself remarked that he had never seen respondents "so solidly united in opposition [to employment of married women] as on any subject imaginable including sin and hay fever."[74] In Quebec, a measure was introduced into the legislature denying women the right to work except on farms, in forests, or in homes. It was defeated, but sixteen out of forty-seven delegates voted for it. The premier took the position not that the bill was undesirable but that it was simply impractical.

Postwar economic dislocations had severely affected European countries, none more so than Germany, which had to pay heavy reparations to Britain and France. Runaway inflation in the early 1920s resulted in a law, in violation of the German constitution, permitting the dismissal of married women government employees with some other means of support, presumably their husbands. Whereas men were temporarily laid off rather than fired, women were dismissed with a small compensation in lieu of pension rights. Even after the emergency the law was extended and then reinstated in 1932 to deal with the depression. The effect of such a measure was dubious, given that women civil servants numbered less than one thousand compared to the 6.5 million unemployed, but it did score points for politicians. Not one political party, not even the socialists, opposed it. Gertrud Bäumer, then a deputy in the assembly but still associated with the BDF, abstained rather than vote against it. The BDF had earlier warned against women competing with men and backed an "appropriate" gendered division of labour. Sex segregation was in fact a workplace reality of long standing and contradicted the illusion that women were taking jobs away from men.

Not all women gave up easily. A national advice columnist in the United States reported that her most frequently asked question was, "Should a woman work outside of the home after marriage?"[75] Three-quarters of participants in a British essay competition on the question, "Should Married Women Work?" said yes, and that in 1934. In the face of severe economic hardship, however, few voices were heard asserting women's *right* to paid employment. Defenders of working women usually argued from expediency, maintaining that women worked out of need. An American journalist who defended wives' employment did so with the conviction that "90 percent of these women would rather be at home sewing on buttons, arranging flowers, and baking beans for their families."[76] While largely true, this line of defence was dangerous for feminism, and its effects outlasted the depression itself. Although massive unemployment ended with World War II, a feminist rhetoric supporting women's occupational equality failed to survive the economic pressures of these years.

Women facing tough economic times could choose from a variety of strategies, depending on their situation. They could continue a pragmatic feminism, like the Canadian prairie women mentioned above. If they were in paid employment they could organize within the workplace. Alternatively, they could affiliate themselves with political parties that addressed their needs. What were the consequences of each kind of action and what did they mean for feminism? Let us look at each in turn.

Exercising the first option, women responded to the Great Depression with the same determination and inventiveness that people have always summoned in hard times. They faced down relief workers, boycotted businesses, or found ingenious ways "to make do." Since women were paid less than men and thus preferred by some employers, many became the breadwinners for their families. Gender stereotypes were thus frequently challenged. A Canadian farm woman reported matter-of-factly, "I've helped outside with anything I lay hands on, and have milked up to six cows myself when the good man was away or busy. I get help with washing and other housework when he is not busy. And I can leave him to do a baking of bread and take care of six children when I go anywhere."[77] An American southern woman said it for many: "When you see your child not having enough to eat, it is enough to put a fight in anybody."[78]

If this was feminism, it remained on the level of the individual and lacked reference to women as an oppressed social *group*. Useful here is the distinction between liberal and individualist feminism. The former describes a woman who sees her self-advancement as beneficial to all women; the latter, a woman who is simply looking out for herself. While they could certainly help change women's consciousness of themselves, pragmatic strategies pursued by women as individuals without an ideological framework did not, I believe, constitute feminism. A study of the impact of the depression on women in San Antonio, Texas, concludes, "Rather than undermining their roles, the Depression challenged housewives to do their very best. While the Depression jeopardized men's positions as primary breadwinners, it reinforced women's importance as home managers even if they were also paid workers."[79]

Collective actions, the second option mentioned above, were not necessarily feminist either. In recent years North American scholars have documented the interwar activism of women from a wide range of ethnic and cultural backgrounds: Jewish housewives in Toronto; Mexican-American industrial workers in San Antonio; Finnish-Canadian women; Appalachian women; cannery workers in California, African-American domestic workers in Washington, DC; tobacco factory workers in Richmond, Virginia. These actions were usually centred around the community or the workplace and put class or race issues above those of gender. Mexican-American cannery workers in California, for example, were assisted by Communist Party organizers; as usual, the workers' struggle came first. African Americans disillusioned with voting literacy requirements and poll taxes, which made a mockery of voting rights, and with the general indifference of white feminists to race issues, preferred to put their energies into mixed groups to fight racism. Such was the case with Mary McLeod Bethune, who founded the National Council of Negro Women in 1935, the largest black women's organization in the United States. Other groups, such as housewives' organizations that protested high prices during the depression, remind one of the association in preindustrial Europe of working-class women with food rebellions. Collective protest was not novel in itself, but its geographic range and ethnic diversity in the United States of the 1930s were.

The fifty-year history of unionized waitresses in the United States provides a contrast to the usual experience of women in unions. Dating back in some cases to the 1880s, waitresses formed all-female unions as well as ones including men. Often widowed, divorced, or separated, waitresses were as concerned with economic independence as were middle-class women who fought for entry into universities and professions. The union was their equivalent to a reform society or women's club and, in the early years, as concerned with morals and social activities as with employment rights. Necessarily assertive in interactions with male clientele and co-workers and having fought their way to a respectable status, waitresses took pride in their occupation and in their unions. A slogan printed by a Los Angeles local in 1940 proudly stated, "Who Says 'Women are the Weaker Sex?' We are the largest culinary craft union in the World." The key to their success was their sense of gender solidarity and confidence, which enabled them to assume leadership in the international union with which they were affiliated even though they composed only a small minority of its members. Their woman-centred separatist strategy made their union a vehicle for a "working-class feminism."[80]

A similar example of "job-oriented" or working-class feminism was the United Cannery, Agricultural, Packing, and Allied Workers of America. During its heyday in the 1930s and 1940s it united women from a variety of ethnic backgrounds, including Mexicans, Asians, and blacks. The union grew out of a women's, or "cannery" culture, somewhat similar to the female work culture created by Lowell textile workers in the 1840s, discussed in Chapter 6, although the latter had the advantages of common ethnic background and living quarters. To deal with their diversity, the cannery workers pledged themselves never to discriminate against a fellow worker. Encouraged by women organizers, the members won such benefits as paid vacations, maternity leaves, and company-provided day care. Locals were democratic and autonomous, and women held leadership positions at every level. For some this sense of empowerment was just the beginning; as one Mexican-American woman reported with pride, "I felt like I could do more things. I learned how to fight."[81]

Women also joined union auxiliaries but with dramatically different consequences. Usually the wives of union men, auxiliary members could develop a sense of solidarity and leadership skills, but the auxiliaries were formed to provide supportive roles for the main actors, the men. These roles were not always the stereotypically female ones of providing food or services for strikers; sometimes the women went out to canvass or even to defy police on the picket lines. Yet the organizations were not usually permanent, nor, oriented as they were around women's roles within the traditional family, did they pose any challenge to gender hierarchy.

Teamsters' strikes in Minneapolis in 1934 illustrate the failure of auxiliaries to develop feminist consciousness. Although a Ladies' Auxiliary was organized to provide cooking, medical care, and fundraising, its underlying purpose was to enlist the support of wives and thus eliminate the "nagging wife syndrome," which could sap the strikers' morale. The women assumed authority during crises and suffered police beatings and arrests, but these experiences had no long-term consequences. When the crisis was over, the women slipped back into traditional ways, comforted perhaps by the memory of their former militancy. Auxiliaries may have nourished a female culture, but they did not lead to feminism.

Depression Politics

What about the third option for women, of affiliating with a political party? Once the initial novelty of women voters wore off, mainstream political parties were not particularly sensitive to women's issues, as has been noted. The response of socialist and communist parties was more complex, guided as it was by a mix of traditional attitudes, socialist theory, and political expediency. Tradition and socialist theory were not especially friendly to feminism, reinforcing as they did the conventional family and the primacy of the class struggle respectively. Inspired by political expediency, however, leftist parties made specific efforts to recruit women and to raise their consciousness. Even then, sexual stereotypes and gender hierarchy were reinforced.

The Communist Party of Canada, for example, set up a women's department in 1922 and organized women's labour leagues for working-class women, mostly housewives who came from Finnish, Ukrainian, Jewish, and English backgrounds. In these groups women were encouraged to read and discuss socialist issues and to organize events such as International Women's Day, which was celebrated in small towns all across Canada. As with union auxiliaries, all-women political groups gave their members confidence. "To be in the same organization as men," explained a Ukrainian member, "would be again to subordinate our thoughts and wishes to men."[82] Although theoretically controlled by the party, local groups were able to set their own agendas. In 1933, for example, Jewish women in Toronto organized a boycott of kosher butchers who had raised their prices. It was quite a novelty for these women to go on picket lines, defy their butchers, and go to court. Vancouver housewives took the same action against meat retailers later in the decade.

Although the Communist Party throughout North America led thousands of women workers in strikes, it encouraged a class rather than a feminist consciousness. Remember that according to socialist theory feminism was a bourgeois diversion. Ideology aside, however, women's experience in the party and in the labour leagues did not lead to feminist consciousness. Men dominated leadership positions, women were isolated and marginalized in their separate groups, and the party appealed to women on the basis of where it thought women's interests lay, in the household and family. The party thus reinforced women's domestic role, offering household hints and consumer information in the women's column of its newspaper, for example. Occasionally one hears a grumble of protest, as from one reader who angrily called for a "little Communism in action," meaning that men should do the dishes. But most women members, as housewives, were conscious of economic hardship primarily as it affected their families. As one recalled, "The question of women just never came up. Economics and war overshadowed everything else. I never thought about the woman question . . . except for resenting always being the stenographer of the group."[83]

In Europe as in North America the most radical women were drawn to the class struggle and put class before gender. Socialists Margarita Nelken in Spain and Angelica Balabanoff in Italy were sympathetic to feminism but ultimately loyal to their parties—considering the political crises in both countries, understandably so. Their politics, like that of their male colleagues, was driven by expediency.

A unique example of radical women organizing against gender and other forms of oppression comes from Spain in the 1930s. Spain had the largest anarchist movement in Europe, dedicated to the struggle against all forms of hierarchy and domination. Anarchists believed that oppression was multidimensional, not solely economic, as socialists would have it. Such an ideology would seem ideally suited to women, but like other groups whose practice contradicted theory, anarchist leaders primarily recruited men organized in unions. In their family life, these men were no different from their counterparts elsewhere, dropping their pose as supporters of female liberation at the threshold of their homes and, the women complained, behaving like masters inside. Anarchist women therefore began meeting in small groups throughout the country in the late 1920s and early 1930s; in 1933 three women formed Mujeres Libres (Free Women), consciously or not taking the same name as the first French feminists to organize autonomously a century earlier. Completely dedicated to the struggle for a social revolution, they believed nonetheless that women had to organize on their own. The group had two goals: to enlist women in a common cause and to awaken their consciousness of gender oppression. The latter purpose distinguished Mujeres Libres from other leftist groups formed during the Spanish Civil War to recruit women for the war effort.

Mujeres Libres did not call themselves feminists. Indeed, most had never heard of feminism. Moreover, they declared themselves hostile to the goals of feminism, uninterested in seeking "equality for women within an existing system of privileges." As Suceso Portales insisted in a 1979 interview, "We are not—and we were not then—feminists. We were not fighting against men. We did not want to substitute a feminist hierarchy for a masculine one. It's necessary to work, to struggle, *together* because if we don't we'll never have a social revolution. But we needed our own organization to struggle for ourselves." They preferred to think of their goal as an "integral humanism,"[84] which would unite masculine and feminine elements without specifying what these were.

Believing in raising consciousness through action, the group organized an impressive variety of projects, including maternity clinics, mutual support groups for women workers, child care so that they could attend union meetings, a magazine produced exclusively by women, a crusade against illiteracy, and technical training in such areas as mechanics, nursing, and agriculture. While Mujeres Libres reached out to all kinds of women and remained respectful of those with household duties, the organization considered it essential to bring women into the labour force in order to create a sense of self outside the home and a start towards economic independence. The response was enthusiastic and energizing; on propaganda tours Mujeres Libres speakers found women who proudly told them that they could now articulate what they had always felt.

Mujeres Libres enjoyed more success than the socialist women's groups discussed in Chapter 8. It spoke to women on the basis of their practical experience, through a class analysis, and it insisted on autonomy. Yet it was unable to get the financial and organizational support it needed from male colleagues. Supportive up to a point, anarchist men simply could not understand the need for women to organize separately and felt threatened, accusing the women of feminism and on occasion resorting to sexual slurs. In any event, the political defeat of the anarchists by the communists and then by General Franco in 1939 ended the experiment.

A very different experiment was under way in the United States during the mid-1930s with the New Deal of President Franklin D. Roosevelt. These years saw the peak of women's input into state welfare policies. Women who had campaigned for suffrage and had kept their network alive through the 1920s now had access to the government via First Lady Eleanor Roosevelt. Eleanor Roosevelt was the quintessential maternal feminist: "When all is said and done," she believed, "women *are* different from men. They are equals in many ways, but they cannot refuse to acknowledge the differences." Identified with humanitarian reforms, women like her were able to take advantage of a favourable political climate in the 1930s to

> Mujeres Libres, *the Spanish anarchist women's group, recognized that a woman had to fight two battles, one along with men for "freedom, equality, and social justice" in the world and one by herself for her own interior freedom. Here, "Ilse" describes women's struggle against parents and husbands.*

It is not easy to let go of the strong cords which, by education and tradition, exist between the woman and the family. It is hard to make one's dear parents suffer when they are not able to agree with the desire for freedom of their daughter, when they do not want to aid in the fight, when they deny the adolescent girl enlightenment on sexual matters, and want to induce a passive and virginal state so that a man will offer her marriage and ensure that the woman, filled with ignorance and prejudice, encounters not happiness, but a desolate and sad life. Such marriages make a mockery of the model marriage, and encourage insincerity and cowardly deceit. . . .

In the subconscious of the woman all these loved ones—parents, husband, children—exist as enemies of her freedom. And the woman has to fight these enemies, modifying her attitude in front of them, struggle against prejudice and tradition and, now internally free and in a unique condition, really join with her companions of the other sex to fight together against the exterior enemy, against servitude and oppression. . . .

With such obstacles, it is understandable that there is a tendency to abandon the fight. But remain strong and do not give in, women of the Revolution. When we have overcome, we will belong to ourselves; when our everyday decisions come from our own convictions and not from old-fashioned customs; when our emotional life is free of sentimental and traditional considerations; when we are able to offer our love freely, our friendship or sympathy as genuine expressions of ourselves, then it will be easy to overcome the external obstacles. Automatically we will become people of free will and equal social rights, free women in a free society able to work together with men as true companions.

The Revolution has to begin at the bottom. And within. Open to the air the old and painful family life. Educate the children in freedom and happiness. Life will be a thousand times more beautiful when the woman is really a free woman.

Source: "Mujeres Libres": España 1936–1939, selección y prólogo de Mary Nash (Barcelona: Tusquets Editor, 1975). Excerpt translated by Sandra Moe. Reprinted with permission.

institutionalize the social reforms that they had been working for since before the First World War. They thereby acquired a public visibility that was not to be equalled until the 1960s. Molly Dewson, one of the key figures in the network, described as "unbelievable" the growth in public recognition of women.[85] Both she and Eleanor Roosevelt lobbied for women's appointments, with the result that women were appointed to high-level government positions, including one in the cabinet. Roosevelt drew attention to the impact of the depression on women, organizing the White House Conference on the Emergency Needs of Women in 1933 as well as holding news briefings for women journalists as a form of 1930s affirmative action. She was an inspirational role model for all women interested in public life. A journalist once said of her that "she talks like a social worker and acts like a Feminist."[86]

Unfortunately, not all members of Franklin Roosevelt's administration shared the president's interest in working with women. Most women were appointed to new programs rather than to the older departments, and they never became a part of the inner political circle. In 1935 the New Deal began to wind down, and with it, women's influence. Cutbacks affected the new agencies and the programs created by them. As well, North America was not immune to the antifeminism generated in fascist Europe. Although Eleanor Roosevelt became preoccupied with European developments later in the decade, her service as chair of John Kennedy's Presidential Commission on the Status of Women in 1961 would provide a link between first-wave feminists and their granddaughters of the second wave.

Many European countries also adopted or improved welfare measures during the 1930s. How much this was due to feminist agitation is difficult to say because of the influence of other motives. In Sweden, for example, Social Democratic women's groups had been advocating maternity benefits for several decades, but when the government introduced family welfare measures in the 1930s it was responding not to feminist but to pronatalist demands. In France as well, help to families with children was a response to pronatalist, Catholic, and patriotic pressure. French feminists were so marginal to the debate that policy makers did not even see the issue in terms of gender, even though feminists had framed their ideology in the most acceptable maternalist terms. It was strictly a family issue.

The opposite was the case in Britain. There, feminists and socialists so alarmed policy makers that their initiatives were doomed to failure: "If feminist campaigns succeeded in identifying family policy with women's emancipation," judges historian Susan Pedersen, "they did so at the cost of reminding politicians, civil servants, trade unionists, and social scientists of exactly why they found such policies objectionable and of deepening these groups' attachment to the defense of men's breadwinner status."[87] The reforms that were enacted classified housewives as "non-working" and awarded fewer benefits to single working women than to working men.

It seems, then, that maternal feminism was successful in the United States, a failure in Britain, and largely irrelevant in France and Sweden. What about in fascist countries, where maternalist rhetoric was co-opted by antifeminist governments? The language of self-sacrifice helped Italian feminists reconcile themselves to fascism. Was the failure of German women to recognize the threat of Nazism the consequence of failing to develop a feminist ideology that went beyond separate spheres?

Feminism and Fascism

The debate among historians over the relation between the German women's movement and the rise of fascism centres on the ideology of the Federation of German Women's Associations (BDF), a conservative set of principles that one historian has even labelled protofascist. Comparable to the National Councils of Women in other countries, the BDF was an umbrella organization, which included conservative women's groups in an effort to get mass support. The most conservative were by no means feminist. One of them, a Protestant women's group, quit the BDF when the latter renewed its campaign for female suffrage in 1918. In its place came professional associations and occupational unions, representing their own economic interests. These groups, allied with right-wing political parties, pulled the BDF to the right during the 1920s and early 1930s.

More decisive than the events of the interwar years in Germany, according to historian Richard Evans, was the failure of the BDF to develop a thoroughgoing feminist ideology either before or after World War I. A testimony to maternal feminism, its program read, "The special civil tasks of women lie . . . in the maintenance of German unity, in the promotion of internal peace, and in the conquest of social, confessional and political antagonisms through a spirit of self-sacrifice." Whereas in North America maternal feminism led to women's involvement with politics, German maternal feminists disdained party politics as divisive and remained detached from or even hostile to the Weimar Republic. In large measure this disdain carried over from the origins of the BDF in the nineteenth century, when women were forbidden to participate in politics. Political impotence thus shaped the ideology of the BDF and left it unable to adapt to a different situation later on. "When Adolf Hitler declared that 'equal rights for women means that they experience the esteem that they deserve in the areas for which nature has intended them,' he could only be applauded by the women's movement. It had after all been saying the same thing for years."[88] The BDF decision to dissolve itself when ordered to submit to Nazi rule in 1933 thus cannot be seen as an act of defiance, Evans believes, since it had already expressed basic agreement with Nazi policies. In 1933, after the Nazis had come to power, Gertrud Bäumer (1873–1954), leader of the BDF throughout much of its history, affirmed, "We are ultimately completely indifferent to the posed question of what form the state takes . . . whether it's a parliamentary, a democratic or a fascist state. For each one the basic requirement is the same . . . how to bring the cultural influence of woman to its full inner development and free social effectiveness."[89] All too similarly, a Nazi women's organization in 1935 declared that its task was to direct women away from the confusion of party politics to the social sphere.

Yet the BDF has its defenders. One interprets its touted indifference to party politics as a genuinely feminist resistance to a masculine state. Women attempted to create an alternative politics, in vain. That they failed was due to the harsh realities of the economic and political situation rather than to any inherent weakness of the belief in woman's ability to create a gender-based alternative. The problem of women's political helplessness was "*not* ultimately a problem of the relations between women."[90]

I doubt that German Jewish women would have agreed. They were represented in the BDF through the Jüdischer Frauenbund, or JFB (League of Jewish Women). Its founder, Bertha Pappenheim, wrote in 1925, "To know of wrong and to remain silent makes one an accomplice."[91] The JFB was the most feminist Jewish women's group in Western Europe and the only religious group in Germany to identify with feminism, although its members felt that their Jewishness was uncomfortable for other BDF women. Alice Salomon, on the BDF executive, was refused the presidency because of her Jewish name. When under Nazi pressure the BDF suggested that the JFB leave the group, the latter agreed that co-operation was no longer possible but averred their continuing commitment to the women's movement.

Other defenders of the BDF challenge the thesis that it was indifferent to fascism. According to this view, the BDF did not speak with one voice; if it had been protofascist, divisiveness within its ranks over such issues as international co-operation, pacifism, and disarmament would not have arisen. Nor was it politically detached. The stand of political neutrality was an attempt to unite groups with different political and religious outlooks. In fact, Gertrud Bäumer was deeply involved in Weimar politics. The BDF urged members to vote, educated them on women's issues, and exhorted them to defend democracy against dictatorship and to keep faith in the Weimar Republic. For most German feminists maternalism was an assertion of women's civic responsibility and compassion for the weak. In retrospect, it was a mistake to enrol groups with an explicitly conservative agenda, but Gertrud Bäumer and other leaders believed strongly that the women's movement should include those who were primarily housewives and mothers. "The idea of the women's movement," Bäumer wrote, "can have value only in a federation which includes women working outside the home and women whose world consists of home and family. If one of these two large groups of women relinquishes its inner communality with the other, it loses the consciousness of a decisive solidarity in the face of differences of lifestyles and cultural tasks."[92] Neutrality did not mean indifference, and even the posture of neutrality was abandoned as the Nazi threat advanced. Further, to argue that maternal feminists and Nazis shared the same ideology is to ignore the racism of Hitler's population policies, which were profoundly antinatalist. Under them, some 200,000 women were forced to undergo compulsory sterilization. In apparent agreement with the maternal feminist claim that women were more compassionate than men, the Nazis specified that female doctors should be the ones to break the news to women who were selected for sterilization and that fathers, not mothers, should make decisions about the sterilization of children.

The debate over the BDF and German feminism will doubtless continue, but it has brought to light a curious by-product of the Nazi years: a group of fascist women who, unlike the BDF, rejected separate spheres ideology and even patriarchy. These women viewed patriarchy as the cause of Germanic decline; they saw so-called Jewish hegemony and socialism as the consequences of male domination. Mythologizing ancient Germanic society as matriarchal, they insisted that women should be free and equal to men and equally represented in all areas of public life, including the military. They dismissed antifeminism as Jewish or "oriental," in other words, as un-German, and called for co-education and domestic training for boys and girls. They combined their "feminism" with fervent nationalism, following the lead of the once radical feminist Käthe Schirmacher (see Chapter 8), who wrote after World War I, "Until the war I fought for the freedom of women, since the war for the freedom of Germany: both are one."[93] Not surprisingly, they were also elitist, referring only to those women who along with their men constituted a "natural aristocracy." Also not surprisingly, the Nazis remained unimpressed, and we hear no more of this group after 1937.

A very different version of feminism was urged by Virginia Woolf (1882–1941) in her brilliant 1938 essay *Three Guineas.* Aware of the overlap between patriarchy and fascism, Woolf suggested a separatist feminist politics that would allow women to assert their pacifist values without compromise. When she called on women "to maintain an attitude of complete indifference" to men's conflicts, she carefully qualified it as based not "upon instinct, but upon reason." Whose reason? The reason of women aware of their outsider status, women so far excluded from the social and economic benefits of traditional culture that war fought for "their country" is irrelevant to their (non)possession of land, wealth, and property. "As a woman my country is the whole world,"[94] Woolf's outsider concluded. Woolf's feminism more accurately gauged the oppressive effects of male dominance than did the maternal feminism of the German women's movement, but then she was writing in 1938 and from outside Germany.

Maternalist rhetoric could either challenge or reinforce the status quo, depending on the context. It is unfair to blame the ideology itself rather than the circumstances of political life that conditioned how it might be used. Still, historian Christine Wittrock makes a telling point when she reflects, "Any thought of polarity, any emphasis of 'difference'—even if to the advantage of the oppressed—is the first step in the direction of an antihumanist, biologistic image of humanity, thus the first step in the direction of legitimizing an ultimately racist or sexist approach to inequality."[95] Tragically, Jewish women in Germany shared both the maternal feminism and the helplessness of the BDF. In 1934 the last leader of the JFB wrote pathetically, "The united will of mothers is a force which . . . is capable of changing the ideas of the world."[96] Even outside Germany the ideology of difference had its limits. As we have seen, the influence of women in America's New Deal lapsed after a few years. A British historian's evaluation of interwar feminism is remarkably similar to earlier historians' indictment of first-wave feminism: "Success had been won without a *fundamental* reassessment of attitudes on the part of either sex. . . . Women had capitalised effectively on the differences rather than the similarities between the sexes. Domesticity had been used as a Trojan Horse; but once inside the citadel it proved difficult to escape from the successful stratagem."[97] Not surprisingly, then, second-wave feminism began with a forceful rejection of the ideology of difference.

The years from the beginning of World War I to the beginning of World War II were difficult for feminists, indeed for reformers or radicals of any kind. Postwar political tensions, economic downturn, and the rise of fascism all made it seem reasonable to cling to what one had rather than to try for more. Young women and men valued pleasure; older ones valued families. In this milieu women's wartime work and the voting rights granted to them during or after the war did not seem to have much impact in changing their lives or in creating a more caring society.

Nonetheless, in small and countless ways, and in spite of feeling the divisions of age, class, race, sexual preference, politics, and ideology, women continued to press for change. They tried to improve their lives and the lives of others around them through many channels: pacifism, antiracism, unions; leftist or mainstream political parties; business and professional organizations; birth control leagues, housewives' auxiliaries, and co-operatives; and equal rights groups. This level of activity would continue in the years following World War II, but women's lives would never be the same.

NOTES

[1] Winifred Holtby, *Women and a Changing Civilization* (1935; reprint, Chicago: Academy Press, 1978), 151.

[2] Quoted in Les Garner, *Stepping Stones to Women's Liberty: Feminist Ideas in the Women's Suffrage Movement 1900–1918* (London: Heinemann, 1984), 55.

[3] Quoted in Bärbel Clemens, *"Menschenrechte haben kein Geschlecht!" Zum Politikverständnis der bürgerlichen Frauenbewegung* (Pfaffenweiler: Centaurus-Verlagsgesellschaft, 1988), 105 (my translation).

[4] Quoted in Robert Craig Brown and Ramsey Cook, *Canada, 1896–1921: A Nation Transformed* (Toronto: McClelland and Stewart, 1974), 298.

[5] Quoted in Barbara Roberts, *"Why Do Women Do Nothing to End the War?" Canadian Feminist-Pacifists and the Great War* (Ottawa: Canadian Research Institute for the Advancement of Women, 1985), 23.

[6] Quoted in Nancy F. Cott, *The Grounding of Modern Feminism* (New Haven: Yale University Press, 1987), 61.

7   Quoted in Jo Vellacott, "Feminist Consciousness and the First World War," in *Women and Peace: Theoretical, Historical and Practical Perspectives,* ed. Ruth Roach Pierson (London: Croom Helm, 1987), 115.

8   Quoted in Ute Gerhard, *Unerhört: Die Geschichte der deutschen Frauenbewegung* (Reinbeck bei Hamburg: Rowohlt Taschenbuch, 1991), 311 (my translation).

9   Margaret Hope Bacon, *Mothers of Feminism: The Story of Quaker Women in America* (San Francisco: Harper and Row, 1986), 208.

10 The reader may note a discrepancy between these dates and other sources. Sometimes it is difficult to pinpoint a date. In Austria, for example, a law in November 1918 proclaimed that women would gain the right to vote in the next election, which was held in 1919. For an authoritative list see the appendix in Caroline Daley and Melanie Nolan, eds., *Suffrage and Beyond: International Feminist Perspectives* (Washington Square, NY: New York University Press, 1994), 349–52.

11 Richard J. Evans, *The Feminist Movement in Germany 1894–1933* (London: Sage Publications, 1976), 227.

12 Claire Duchen, *Women's Rights and Women's Lives in France 1944–1968* (London and New York: Routledge, 1994), 165.

13 Dorothy Schneider and Carl J. Schneider, *American Women in the Progressive Era, 1900–1920* (New York: Facts On File, 1993), 183, 190.

14 Quoted in Nancy Cott, "Across the Great Divide: Women in Politics Before and After 1920," in *Women, Politics, and Change,* ed. Louise A. Tilly and Patricia Gurin (New York: Russell Sage Foundation, 1990), 160.

15 Quoted in Deborah Gorham, "'Have We Really Rounded Seraglio Point?': Vera Brittain and Inter-War Feminism," in *British Feminism in the Twentieth Century,* ed. Harold L. Smith (Aldershot: Edward Elgar, 1990), 93.

16 Simone de Beauvoir, *The Second Sex,* trans. H.M. Parshley (New York: Random House, 1952), 144.

17 Vera Brittain, *Testament of Youth: An Autobiographical Study of the Years 1900–1925* (New York: Macmillan, 1934), 92.

18 Lilian Miles, quoted in Gail Braybon and Penny Summerfield, *Out of the Cage: Women's Experiences in Two World Wars* (London and New York: Pandora, 1987), 58.

19 Quoted in Victoria De Grazia, *How Fascism Ruled Women: Italy, 1922–1945* (Berkeley: University of California Press, 1992), 26.

20 Quoted in Felicia Gordon, *The Integral Feminist: Madeleine Pelletier, 1874–1939: Feminism, Socialism and Medicine* (Cambridge: Polity Press, 1990), 141.

21 Quoted in J. Stanley Lemons, *The Woman Citizen: Social Feminism in the 1920s* (Urbana: University of Illinois Press, 1973), 15.

22 Brittain, *Testament of Youth,* 143.

23 Quoted in James Longenbach, "The Women and Men of 1914," in *Arms and the Woman: War, Gender, and Literary Representation,* ed. Helen M. Cooper, Adrienne Auslander Munich, and Susan Merrill Squier (Chapel Hill and London: University of North Carolina Press, 1989), 104.

24 Cicely Hamilton, "The Return to Femininity" (1927), in Dale Spender, *Time and Tide Wait for No Man* (London: Pandora Press, 1984), 79.

25 Quoted in Barbara Greven-Aschoff, *Die bürgerliche Frauenbewegung in Deutschland 1894–1933* (Göttingen: Vandenhoeck & Ruprecht, 1981), 156 (my translation).

26 Quoted in Joan M. Jensen, "All Pink Sisters: The War Department and the Feminist Movement in the 1920s," in *Decades of Discontent: The Women's Movement, 1920–1940,* ed. Lois Scharf and Joan M. Jensen (Westport, CT: Greenwood Press, 1983), 212.

27 Blanche Wiesen Cook, "Introduction," in *Crystal Eastman on Women and Revolution,* ed. Blanche Wiesen Cook (New York: Oxford University Press, 1978), 22.

28 Ray Strachey, *"The Cause": A Short History of the Women's Movement in Great Britain* (1928; reprint, Port Washington, NY: Kennikat Press, 1969), 385.

29 Quoted in Mary Hallett and Marilyn Davis, *Firing the Heather: The Life and Times of Nellie McClung* (Saskatoon: Fifth House, 1994), 213.

30 Quoted in Sylvia B. Bashevkin, "Independence versus Partisanship: Dilemmas in the Political History of Women in English Canada," in *Rethinking Canada: The Promise of Women's History,* 2nd ed., ed. Veronica Strong-Boag and Anita Clair Fellman (Toronto: Copp Clark Pitman, 1991), 430.

31 Quoted in William H. Chafe, *The Paradox of Change: American Women in the 20th Century* (New York: Oxford University Press, 1991), 28.

32 Eastman, "Letter to the Editor of *Time and Tide,*" in *Crystal Eastman on Women and Revolution,* ed. Cook, 224.

33 Quoted in William L. O'Neill, *feminism in America: a history,* 2nd ed. (New Brunswick and Oxford: Transaction Publishers, 1989), 268.

34 Quoted in Naomi Black, *Social Feminism* (Ithaca, NY: Cornell University Press, 1989), 251.

35 Quoted in Susan D. Becker, *The Origins of the Equal Rights Amendment: American Feminism Between the Wars* (Westport, CT: Greenwood Press, 1981), 205–6.

36 Quoted in Martin Pugh, *Women and the Women's Movement in Britain, 1914–1959* (London: Macmillan Education, 1992), 171.

37 Quoted in Bashevkin, "Independence versus Partisanship," 417.

38 Quoted in Terry Crowley, *Agnes Macphail and the Politics of Equality* (Toronto: James Lorimer and Company, 1990), 98, 91. Elizabeth Gurley Flynn, an American activist, tells the same story about the suffragist Maude Malone (Elizabeth Gurley Flynn, *The Rebel Girl: An Autobiography, My First Life (1906–1926)* (New York: International Publishers, 1955), 57.

39 Quoted in O'Neill, *feminism in America,* 265.

40 Olive Banks, *Becoming a Feminist: The Social Origins of "First Wave" Feminism* (Brighton: Wheatsheaf Books, 1986), 122.

41 Eastman, "Equality or Protection" in *Crystal Eastman on Women and Revolution,* ed. Cook, 157.

42 Eleanor Rathbone wrote, "Are women, we ask, to behave for ever like a little girl running behind her big brother and calling out, 'Me, too'?" (quoted in Susan Ware, *Still Missing: Amelia Earhart and the Search for Modern Feminism* [New York: W.W. Norton and Company, 1993], 57).

43 Quoted in Martha Vicinus, *Independent Women: Work and Community for Single Women, 1850–1920* (Chicago: University of Chicago Press, 1986), 283.

44 Eastman, "Protective Legislation in England," in *Crystal Eastman on Women and Revolution,* ed. Cook, 171–72.

45 Quoted in Sheila Jeffreys, *The Spinster and Her Enemies: Feminism and Sexuality 1880–1930* (London: Pandora, 1985), 154.

46 Quoted in Joan Hoff, *Law, Gender and Injustice: A Legal History of U.S. Women* (New York and London: New York University Press, 1991), 217.

47 Quoted in Harold L. Smith, "British Feminism in the 1920s," in *British Feminism,* ed. Smith, 62.

48 Quoted in de Grazia, *How Fascism Ruled Women,* 241.

49 Quoted in Susan Kingsley Kent, "The Politics of Sexual Difference: World War I and the Demise of British Feminism," *Journal of British Studies* 27 (1988): 236.

50 Brittain, *Testament of Youth,* 469; see also ibid., 498.

51 Holtby, *Women and a Changing Civilization,* 5.

52 Quoted in Nancy Woloch, *Women and the American Experience* (New York: Alfred A. Knopf, 1984), 258.

53 Jeffreys, *The Spinster and Her Enemies,* 158–59.

54 Quoted in Margaret Jackson, *The* Real *Facts of Life: Feminism and the Politics of Sexuality c. 1850–1940* (London: Taylor and Francis, 1994), 161.

55 Quoted in Lillian Faderman, *Surpassing the Love of Men: Romantic Friendship and Love Between Women from the Renaissance to the Present* (New York: William Morrow, 1981), 324.

56 Quoted in Jeffreys, *The Spinster and Her Enemies,* 183. This sentence and the rest of the page were printed in capital letters in the original for emphasis.

57 Quoted in Susan Kingsley Kent, "Gender Reconstruction after the First World War," in *British Feminism,* ed. Smith, 75.

58 Quoted in Faderman, *Surpassing the Love of Men,* 323.

59 Vera Brittain, *Testament of Friendship: The Story of Winifred Holtby* (1940; reprint, London: Virago Press, 1970), 2, 328.

60 Quoted in Gordon, *The Integral Feminist,* 174.

61 Margaret Sanger, "Birth Control—A Parents' Problem or Woman's?" in *The Feminist Papers: From Adams to de Beauvoir,* ed. Alice S. Rossi (New York: Columbia University Press, 1973), 533.

62 Jacquelyn Dowd Hall, *Revolt Against Chivalry: Jessie Daniel Ames and the Women's Campaign Against Lynching* (New York: Columbia University Press, 1979), 93.

63 Pugh, *Women and the Women's Movement,* 212, 213–14, 212.

64 Quoted in Veronica Strong-Boag, *The New Day Recalled: Lives of Girls and Women in English Canada, 1919–1939* (Markham, ON: Penguin Books, 1988), 150, 149.

65 Quoted in Becker, *Origins of the Equal Rights Amendment,* 263.

66 Quoted in Gorham, "'Have We Really Rounded Seraglio Point?'" 103, n. 57.

67 Quoted in Elaine Showalter, ed., *These Modern Women: Autobiographical Essays from the Twenties* (New York: Feminist Press, 1978), 18.

68 Brittain, *Testament of Youth*, 653.

69 Eastman, "Now We Can Begin," 54, 56 and "Marriage under Two Roofs," 76, in *Crystal Eastman on Women and Revolution*, ed. Cook.

70 Quoted in Showalter, ed., *These Modern Women*, 19.

71 Eastman, "Birth Control in the Feminist Program," in *Crystal Eastman on Women and Revolution*, ed. Cook, 47.

72 Showalter, ed., *These Modern Women*, 26.

73 Margaret Washburn, quoted in Helen Lefkowitz Horowitz, *Alma Mater: Design and Experience in the Women's Colleges from Their Nineteenth-Century Beginnings to the 1930s* (Boston: Beacon Press, 1984), 297.

74 Quoted in Lois Scharf, *To Work and To Wed: Female Employment, Feminism, and the Great Depression* (Westport, CT: Greenwood Press, 1980), 50.

75 Quoted in ibid., 23.

76 Ibid., 61.

77 Quoted in Strong-Boag, *The New Day Recalled*, 101.

78 Quoted in Jacqueline Jones, "The Political Implications of Black and White Women's Work in the South, 1890–1965," in *Women, Politics, and Change*, ed. Tilly and Gurin, 121.

79 Julia Kirk Blackwelder, *Women of the Depression: Caste and Culture in San Antonio, 1929–1939* (College Station: Texas A & M University Press, 1984), 170.

80 Dorothy Sue Cobble, *Dishing It Out: Waitresses and Their Unions in the Twentieth Century* (Urbana and Chicago: University of Illinois Press, 1991), 180, 10.

81 Maria Rodriguez, quoted in Vicki L. Ruiz, *Cannery Women, Cannery Lives: Mexican Women, Unionization, and the California Food Processing Industry, 1930–1950* (Albuquerque: University of New Mexico, 1987), 121.

82 Quoted in Joan Sangster, *Dreams of Equality: Women on the Canadian Left, 1920–1950* (Toronto: McClelland and Stewart, 1989), 50.

83 Ibid., 128, 121–22.

84 Quoted in Martha A. Ackelsberg, *Free Women of Spain: Anarchism and the Struggle for the Emancipation of Women* (Bloomington: Indiana University Press, 1991), 116, 2, 103.

85 Quoted in Susan Ware, *Beyond Suffrage: Women in the New Deal* (Cambridge, MA: Harvard University Press, 1981), 14, 44.

86 Quoted in Becker, *Origins of the Equal Rights Amendment*, 217.

87 Susan Pedersen, *Family, Dependence, and the Origins of the Welfare State: Britain and France, 1914–1945* (Cambridge: Cambridge University Press, 1993), 422.

88 Evans, *Feminist Movement in Germany*, 235, 239.

89 Quoted in Greven-Aschoff, *Die bürgerliche Frauenbewegung*, 187 (my translation).

90 Irene Stoehr, "Machtergriffen? Deutsche Frauenbewegung 1933," *Courage: Aktuelle Frauenzeitung* 8 (February 1983): 32 (my translation and emphasis).

91 Quoted in Marion A. Kaplan, *The Jewish Feminist Movement in Germany: The Campaigns of the Jüdischer Frauenbund, 1904–1938* (Westport, CT: Greenwood Press, 1979), 35.

92 Quoted in Hiltraud Schmidt-Waldherr, *Emanzipation durch Professionaliserung? Politische Stragegien und Konflikte innherhalb der bürgerlichen Frauenbewegung während der Weimarer Republik und die Reaktion des bürgerlichen Antifeminismus und des Nationalsozialismus* (Frankfurt/Main: Materialis Verlag, 1987), 184 (my translation).

93 Quoted in Christine Wittrock, *Weiblichkeitsmythen: Das Frauenbild im Faschismus und seine Vorläufer in der Frauenbewegung der 20er Jahre* (Frankfurt: Sendler Verlag, 1985), 174 (my translation).

94 Virginia Woolf, *Three Guineas* (San Diego: Harcourt Brace Jovanovich, 1938), 107, 109.

95 Wittrock, *Weiblichkeitsmythen,* 80 (my translation).

96 Quoted in Kaplan, *Jewish Feminist Movement in Germany,* 73.

97 Pugh, *Women and Women's Movements,* 312.

IO

The Origins
of the
Second Wave

*Who among us remembered that there had been feminist movements in the
past and that they had died? Nobody.*

ELISABETH SALVARESI, 1988

*R*oughly one hundred years after women first began organizing for equal
rights, second-wave feminists caught the media's attention with a series of
spectacular actions. The year 1968 marked a coming to feminist consciousness for many women both in Europe and North America. In Atlantic City,
protesters demonstrated against a Miss America pageant, unfolding a banner
announcing "Women's Liberation," and tossing "instruments of torture,"
such as girdles, curlers, false eyelashes, high heeled shoes, *Playboy* magazine,
typing books, and bras into a "freedom" trashcan, thereby inspiring the
media myth of bra-burning. Earlier that year Toronto feminists had protested
against a "winter bikini" contest. May marked a time of violent mass demonstrations of students and workers in France and a turning point for French
feminists. In the same year, German and Italian feminists confronted male
chauvinism in radical student organizations and began forming separate
women's groups.

In most countries this was the first time in two generations that women
unapologetically declared their feminism. These same women were also
largely unaware of the enormous energies their predecessors had put into the
same cause. The bravado that enabled them to challenge the status quo was
for the most part innocent of any sense of a debt owed to the past. Many
young women shared the judgment of Sheila Rowbotham, an English feminist, who recalled, "My recognition of women as a group was as creatures
sunk into the very deadening circumstances from which I was determined to

1939–45	World War II
1941	Japan bombs Pearl Harbor
1944	French women granted suffrage
1945	United States bombs Hiroshima and Nagasaki
	United Nations established
1947	Cold War begins
1949–90	Germany partitioned
1949	North Atlantic Treaty Organization (NATO) created
	Soviet Union develops its atomic bomb
	Simone de Beauvoir writes *The Second Sex*
1950–53	Korean War
1956–62	French–Algerian War
1960s	Civil rights movement in the United States
1961–89	Berlin Wall erected
1961–63	American Presidential Commission on the Status of Women
1962	Cuban Missile Crisis
1963	Betty Friedan writes *The Feminine Mystique*
1964–75	Vietnam War
1966	National Organization for Women (NOW) formed in the United States
1967–70	Canadian Royal Commission on the Status of Women
1968	Second-wave feminists demonstrate in North America
	May uprising occurs in France

escape. Most older women seemed like this to me."[1] French feminists signalled their sense of a new beginning by declaring 1970 "year zero for the liberation of women"[2] just as the French revolutionaries in 1792 had reset the calendar to celebrate year one. In other countries feminists were more cognizant of the continuity of their efforts. In Italy, for example, the second wave was seen to be the culmination of a movement nurtured in more than fifty years of working-class and antifascist struggles.

In fact, of course, nowhere was the second wave unconnected to earlier feminism. The more historians have enquired, the more evidence they have found of feminist activity between World War II and the late 1960s, but rather than challenging the marine analogy of feminist "waves" this evidence supports an account of two crests of actions marked by widespread public acknowledgment. Between the two waves, the movement ebbed rather than disappeared. This chapter will examine, first, the continuing low profile of feminism from World War II (1939–45) through the 1950s and early 1960s and second, the emergence of the second wave in the late 1960s and early 1970s.

THE IMPACT OF WORLD WAR II

World War II was a very different experience from World War I for European women. In the earlier war women at home had found themselves estranged from men at the front. In contrast, World War II did not spare civilians but subjected them to invasion, occupation, and bombing, as well as the economic hardships that any war brings. In France, Italy, the Netherlands, and the Scandinavian countries occupied by the Nazis, women became resistance fighters, undertaking the same dangerous tasks and responsibilities as men; according to one estimate, they formed 40 to 80 percent of the membership of resistance groups. Italian feminists later looked back on women's clandestine activity during the war as "the first feminism."[3] Women were also instrumental in postwar reconstruction. The war's impact lingered in Germany until the end of the 1940s, allowing women a period of individual assertiveness and social influence as they cleared rubble from bomb sites and struggled to provide for their families.

While the differences between men's and women's experiences were not as pronounced in World War II as in World War I, the same tone of sexual hostility predominated in propaganda and wartime literature. Women were both vilified and eroticized in images that ranged from diseased whores to seductive spies or a powerful but sexy Wonder Woman fighting Hitler and his army. In fascist countries a determination to avenge the men whom World War I had supposedly left emasculated and helpless heightened the antifeminism inherent in militarism.

Women, Work, and Family

Women's work experiences in both wars were similar as well. British women in each generation used the same imagery, being let out of a cage, to describe their sense of liberation. But as previously, most women in war-related industries had transferred there from the service sector; they still earned less than men and were expected to relinquish their jobs without protest after the war. In a poll taken in 1942 in the United States, only 13 percent of respondents thought that wives should not work in war industries, in comparison to a poll taken during the depression when 80 percent believed that wives should not work. But would wartime expedients hold good in peacetime? As in 1918, governments worried about making up their population losses. The crucial question was, would women return to marriage and motherhood? In Britain, most unions adopted clauses specifying that women were replacing men for the duration of the war only.

Some American women benefited from a wartime peak in union organizing that had begun with strikes led by the Congress of Industrial Organizations (CIO) in the 1930s. The industries most affected were ones central to the war effort, namely auto and electrical plants. Prewar women workers had exhibited little class consciousness. Isolated in their work, without leaders and without the encouragement of their male colleagues, they were slow to challenge gender inequality. As one worker recalled in reference to women's lower wages, "In those days we didn't think of it."[4] During the war, however, as previously unorganized women replaced men who were drafted, CIO unions scrambled to find ways of educating their new members so as not to lose hard-won benefits. They hired more female staff, encouraged women to fill vacant local leadership posts and to attend national conventions, held women's conferences, published educational materials, and gave special training courses. Women responded enthusiastically. The result was "the emergence of a substantial women's movement within the CIO during the 1940s."[5] Women's activity paid off in the form of maternity leaves, day care, female counsellors in lieu of male shop stewards, and a burgeoning feminist awareness.

A few months after the war ended two hundred women picketed a Ford plant in Detroit with placards reading, "Stop Discrimination Because of Sex."[6] These women were concerned to maintain both their awareness of gender inequity and their sense of empowerment. At least one expressed her determination to use her wartime experience in breaking down job barriers after the war. This wartime development should not be exaggerated, however. Unions continued to be led by men, with few if any women in high offices. Women still encountered hostility from male colleagues on the job. Their lives were unreasonably burdened with domestic responsibilities that had been compounded in wartime and left them little time or energy for other activities. Not surprisingly, the most active union women tended either to be older, with no young children, or to have a previous history of labour activism.

Trade unions still put men's interests first. Although unions were directed by the National War Labor Board not to discriminate by gender, they commonly avoided raising women's wages by such strategies as reclassifying their work as "light" in order to continue paying it less than "heavy" work. The Auto Workers Union maintained separate seniority lists for men and women because, as one union representative worried, "If [women] now become entrenched within our seniority system, how then will we be able to regulate this when this war work is all over?"[7] Women who adopted the union perspective learned to put class before gender. As with socialists, dedicated unionists feared gender consciousness as diversionary. When a delegate at a 1944 United Auto Workers women's conference suggested that "women and Negroes" should have special provisions comparable to those offered to war veterans, her proposal was "rejected overwhelmingly" by the other women as "favoritism."[8]

Women in Britain had similar experiences. Women's trade union membership doubled, and they became shop stewards as they did in the United

States. Yet there were few permanent results. In 1945 women were earning only 52 percent of what men earned. A British economist claimed that unequal pay was necessary to make sure that motherhood would remain a more attractive vocation than professional or industrial work.[9]

Although it would seem that women's wartime work brought few major changes, historians are divided over how to interpret the rise in married women workers that had already begun in the 1930s and that was to continue after the war. Historian William Chafe views World War II as a turning point for white, middle-class American women. Pointing out that almost three-quarters of the new workers in the United States during the war were married, Chafe believes that the war provided the right opportunity for women who were already eager to work outside the home. He considers this part of a long-range trend that would replace the young unmarried woman worker typical of the nineteenth and early twentieth centuries with an older, married woman with children. This shift, by taking more women out of the home, subjecting them to workplace discrimination, and exacerbating the tensions of their lives, would constitute the basis for a renewed women's movement. Polls taken at the end of the war revealing that between 60 and 85 percent of American women in non-traditional jobs did not want to relinquish them at the war's end confirm Chafe's argument.

Black women who had moved into factory work from domestic or agricultural jobs would presumably have found it harder to give up their work than those who had moved into domestic jobs vacated by whites. Black women's organizations fully intended to capitalize on wartime opportunities. The National Council of Negro Women lobbied hard against inequitable federal policies; it also issued a pamphlet that included a pledge for women workers, "I shall never for a moment forget that thirteen million Negroes believe in me and depend on me."[10] Nonetheless, most black women workers had no alternative but to return to service jobs at the war's end.

Polls also provide evidence for those historians who stress the postwar desire for normality, already familiar to us as a reaction after World War I. Seventy-five percent of a group of young American women polled in 1943, for example, indicated that they wanted to be housewives. The baby boom, which began in the United States as early as 1940 independently of pronatalist propaganda, furnishes additional evidence of a desire for domesticity. The logical conclusion is that there were women in both camps; most likely women felt torn between conflicting ideals, enjoying their work yet in the absence of a high-profile feminist movement unable to resist the pressure to return to their homes after the war.

We will come back later to this problem of interpreting women's paid work, but for now it is important to note that for women the war left a legacy of expectation that they would be rewarded for their help. Their experiences gave many a lasting sense of pride in their ability to accomplish something different. The rhetoric of fighting for democracy encouraged members of ethnic groups in North America, such as African Canadians, African Americans, and Natives, to intensify their demands for equal rights. Too often, however, these efforts were met by increased racism and even violence.

If women were ambivalent about issues of family life and work, politicians were not, uniting under a platform of reforms destined to strengthen the traditional family. The Vichy government of occupied France, for example, introduced family allowances for men whose wives stayed at home, as a compensation for lost income. Families with two or more children continued to receive family allowances after the war. The West German government awarded family allowances only to wage earners—assumed to be men—with three or more children, disregarding the fact that most families were small, especially those headed by widowed or divorced women who were the ones most in need of assistance. Thérèse Casgrain in Quebec succeeded in pressuring the federal government to make family allowances payable to mothers rather than fathers (as the heads of families), but only by appealing directly to the prime minister. The British postwar government considered nurseries, co-operative housekeeping services, even contraception and equal wages, in light of their possible impact on family life. The tone was set for the next two decades. As one scholar summarizes, "It is impossible to overemphasize the importance of marriage as a central and organizing idea in both the 1950s and 1960s."[11]

Cold War Fears

A final similarity of the impact of both world wars was a postwar fear of communism. What the Russian Revolution did for the 1920s, Cold War tensions between the West and Eastern bloc European countries, led by the Soviet Union, did for the 1950s. The result was a climate inhospitable to ideas for social change. Daycare centres in Toronto, implemented by the government during the war to provide help for working mothers, were by 1951 seen as subversive rather than patriotic, a plot by the Kremlin to undermine the family. West German politicians visualized a communist front stretching from Asia through Moscow to their East German neighbours, containable only through a vigorous military and familial patriarchy. In the United States, women seemed to lose whatever gains they had made during the war. Who could find courage to call for gender equality in a nation obsessed with national security? At the outbreak of the Korean War in 1950, the president of the National Federation of Business and Professional Women's Clubs echoed the caution of an earlier generation in denouncing the "old, selfish, strident feminism," in favour of a "'new feminism' which emphasized women's responsibilities as citizens rather than women's rights."[12]

Cold War paranoia was particularly hurtful to homosexuals. Ostensibly because of their proclivity to loose morals and susceptibility to blackmail—because of the social stigma attached to homosexuality—gay women and men in North America were dismissed from the military and government jobs, sometimes on the basis of anonymous accusations. A proposal to bar lesbians from entering Canada was eventually dropped from the Immigration Act of 1952, although the act did exclude those "living on the avails of prostitution or homosexualism."[13] This persecution, amounting to a witch hunt, may have also been a response to the gay networks that developed from the social segregation of the sexes during the war. In any event, homosexuality represented a clear threat to the proponents of "normality," for whom communism meant political and moral subversion, atheism, and sexual deviance. In one case at least, stereotypes collided: in Germany lesbians were considered less dangerous than male homosexuals because all women were thought to be less interested in sex and more concerned to maintain privacy and friendship. Thus, male homosexuality carried greater criminal penalties; in fact, the government kept the same draconian measures to punish homosexuals that the Nazis had adopted in 1935.

Women's Rights

For women in France, Italy, and Quebec, the war brought new rights as well as responsibilities, namely the right to vote. Quebec granted provincial female suffrage in 1940, almost one hundred years after women in the province had been explicitly disenfranchised. After an unexpected election win, the Liberal Party found itself barraged by a storm of petitions, letters, and telegrams from suffragists, forcing it to keep its promise to introduce female suffrage. The women who had wrested this concession bequeathed the memory of their struggle to the younger generation who would pick up the torch in the 1960s.

The free French government, meeting in Algiers under General Charles de Gaulle, decreed women's suffrage in 1944, even before the Liberation. The constitution of the Fourth Republic explicitly guaranteed equal rights along with women's right to work, and in 1946 the government established the principle of equal pay for equal work. Rather than signifying any dramatic change in those politicians who had steadfastly rejected the idea of women's equality, the measures reveal the extent of Communist influence in the coalition government. The provisions for equal pay and equal employment in the civil service were enacted under the auspices of Communist cabinet ministers. In fact, women's suffrage passed only because Communists outvoted the other ministers. Even so, the legal emancipation of French women was not complete. Married women remained legal minors until 1965, and the husband was still considered the head of the household until 1975. Nor did women enjoy much political clout. Their influence declined along with that of the Communist Party in the postwar years, and in most parties they remained marginalized in separate women's sections. As elsewhere, parties were reluctant to give women top places on the electoral lists. President de Gaulle reportedly reacted with mock dismay to the suggestion of appointing a woman cabinet minister, "What, appoint an under-secretary of knitting?"[14] The few women who were elected to parliament confined themselves to speaking on what were perceived to be women's issues.

The Communist Party was also influential in Italy in drafting the postwar republican constitution that gave women the vote and equal rights. In part, this was a tribute to women's role in the resistance; it was also testimony to the unusual sympathy such leaders as Antonio Gramsci and Palmiro Togliatti had displayed for women's issues. The mass rallies women organized to pressure the government, utilizing skills they had learned during the war, must have helped as well.

The belated grant of suffrage in Quebec, France, and Italy raises the question of whether Catholicism retarded women's civic rights. If so, it was only indirectly. The pope had declared in favour of women's suffrage in 1919, and women in other Catholic or largely Catholic countries, such as Ireland, Austria, and Denmark, became voters after World War I. When Newfoundland suffragists renewed their campaign in the early 1920s, they were supported by Catholic clergy. A Catholic newspaper editor helpfully argued that newly translated Babylonian tablets proved that Noah, not Adam, ate the apple, thus absolving Eve from responsibility for original sin. Yet leftist politicians in many countries had long feared that women voters would support the church and clergy, a type of thinking that was almost obsessive in France and Italy.

Long-range causes were at work as well. An important factor in women's self-assertion and influence in Protestant countries was their long history of organizing on moral issues, such as temperance or state regulation of prostitution. Catholic women lacked a comparable avenue to political experience. Their activity outside the home was channelled into church work, under clerical control. As well, convents offered single women careers with economic security and social relevance. As a result, middle-class Catholic women were less apt to feel the frustration that brought so many other women to feminism. A final influence may have been the Roman law tradition in Latin countries, which contrasts with the emphasis of English common law on the rights of the individual. In the south of France, for instance, legal tradition and lack of urbanization made for a combination decidedly unfriendly to feminist goals.

It is nonetheless difficult to generalize about the influence of Catholicism in all cases. The women in Quebec whom one would expect to have been the most conservative, rural women, defied bishops' directives in the 1940s to leave their secular organizations, the Cercles des fermières (Farm Women's Societies), and join one under church control. Their study groups have been credited with generating a feminine, if not a feminist, consciousness that played a decisive role in creating modern Quebec. In the end, specific political circumstances in different countries, including the relation of church to state, were more important than any inherent affinity between feminism and Protestantism.

West Germany boasted politicians if anything more hostile to feminism than those in France. Although women were granted unconditional equal rights in the new constitution of 1949, this victory came only as a result of hard lobbying on the part of Elisabeth Selbert, a lawyer and socialist politician, and others who organized a wave of petitions from women's groups. Selbert boldly threatened that women, a decided majority of the population, would reject the constitution if a provision on equal rights were not included. Even so, the clause granting equal rights was balanced by an article protecting the family, assumed to be the "normal" nuclear family under a paternal breadwinner. An attempt to reform the provision in the Civil Code that granted ultimate authority to the husband failed, coming up as it did against the insistence of a Catholic and conservative government majority that human law could not alter the divinely ordained hierarchy of husband over wife. Eventually, in 1957, the German parliament accepted the idea of equality in marriage by a narrow margin of twelve votes but refused to compromise on the principle that the father should rule on matters relating to children. Although the courts overturned that provision two years later, marriage was still considered to be based on a biologically determined division of labour. Until 1977 German women were legally responsible for housework: "The woman shall direct the household on her own responsibility. She is entitled to go to work in so far as this is reconcilable with her duties to her marriage and family." Although this was changed in that year to allow couples to make their own arrangements, the official commentary noted that "as long as there are infants or growing children to be cared for, the legislator nevertheless regards the housewifely marriage as 'appropriate in a special way,' on the basis of the natural difference between the sexes."[15]

Several factors made tradition and conservative Catholicism appealing to postwar West Germans: the sense of social breakdown and rupture with the past occasioned by the war and defeat; the threat of the Communist government of East Germany, which encouraged women to become wage earners and even provided child care; and, not least, the loss of a generation of radicals who had either fled from Hitler or had been killed by him. This discontinuity would hamper the rise and impact of a renewed feminism.

SOMETHING OLD, SOMETHING NEW

In the 1950s and early 1960s the media popularized the ideal family, composed of Father the breadwinner, Mother the homemaker, and two to four children, nestled happily in its single-family suburban home, enjoying the fruits of an expanded consumer economy. It was outwardly a time of material comfort, conservatism, and conformity, but this picture does not do justice to the complexity of a period in which long-established women's groups continued to press for women's rights and new groups coalesced around issues that were to transform the next generation.

Many women continued to be active in organizations that dated from the early twentieth century. One was the National Woman's Party (NWP) in the United States, formed originally as the Congressional Union in 1913. It carried on as a tightly organized coterie of white, middle-class, professional women with strong homosocial ties, dedicated to seeing the Equal Rights Amendment (ERA) adopted by congress. Their age indicated the long-term commitment of the members: by the 1950s most were in their fifties or older. In addition to the ERA, they lobbied for more government appointments of women. One member even protested the practice of giving hurricanes female names. Thanks to the NWP and other women's groups, 236 women's rights bills were introduced in congress during the 1950s.

The NWP exemplified both the persistence and the divisions of American feminism. Like other white professional women's groups, it ignored issues of concern to black and working women, such as the poll taxes required of southern black voters or the need of working parents for child care. Unlike the black film star Lena Horne, who when performing at a military base placed herself in front of the black troops forced to sit behind German prisoners of war, white feminists had failed to condemn racial segregation in the military. The NWP even duplicated the expediency of earlier white feminists when it allied with an antisemitic group that supported the ERA. Its single-minded dedication to the ERA, which most unions opposed as irreconcilable with protective legislation, meant that the NWP missed an opportunity to unite with women workers who had lost their jobs to returning veterans. It thus continued the tradition in American feminism of divorcing gender issues from those of race or class.

Like many other African Americans, Mary Church Terrell, who had helped found the National Association of Colored Women, refused to make those distinctions. She wrote in her autobiography in 1940, "This is the story of a colored woman living in a white world. It cannot possibly be like a story written by a white woman. A white woman has only one handicap to overcome—that of sex. I have two—both sex and race. I belong to the only group in this country which has two such huge obstacles to surmount. Colored men have only one—that of race."[16] Ignored by white feminists, black activists continued to devote themselves to organizing against lynching, segregation, and discrimination. In the United States, then, equal rights feminists, black activists, and union women all struggled in isolation from each other.

In Britain the Six Point Group, dating from the 1920s, continued to represent middle-class, professional women. As in the United States, British feminism smacked of old ladies. Shirley Williams, daughter of feminist and pacifist Vera Brittain, reflected in a 1960 interview: "I'm not a pacifist but I admire my mother's pacifism; I'm not a feminist either, but that's a matter of generations I think, don't you?"[17]

In Germany, few women's groups outlasted the twelve years of Nazi rule, and the priorities of survival disinclined most women from political activity in the first postwar years. An exception was Agnes von Zahn-Harnack, the last president of the Federation of German Women's Associations, who in 1945 organized a new federation in Berlin. During the rest of the decade other groups revived; by 1947 there were already forty-two, not counting professional organizations. In 1959 they came together in an umbrella organization, which cultivated a low profile although dedicated to equal rights. As elsewhere, the younger generation kept its distance, perhaps influenced in this case by its unhappy experience with Nazi-led youth groups.

In France the situation was essentially the same: continuing activity of professional groups, lack of a common agenda or feminist ideology, and a generation gap. The League of Women's Rights, still active since its founding in 1869, was the only French organization to call itself feminist. While groups embraced "women's rights," they hesitated to use the label feminist, fearing its unfeminine connotation. The same was true elsewhere; NWP members, for example, preferred to fight for "Equalism."[18] This has led one historian to describe feminism at this time as leading "an underground or Sleeping Beauty existence in a society that claimed to have wiped out that oppression."[19]

Women and the Peace Movement

In lieu of organizing directly to combat gender oppression, women channelled their activities in other directions. As after World War I, women organized for peace. Some pacifist women's groups with links to communist parties—in Germany and the United States, for example—succumbed to Cold War fears and were declared illegal. Others insisted on non-partisanship. The Westdeutsche Frauenfriedensbewegung (West German Women's Peace Movement), which had formed in 1952 to protest against the rearming of West Germany, went on to protest against nuclear weapons and the Vietnam War. The Golders Green Guildswomen formed in Britain in 1955 in response to the development of the H-bomb. By the end of the decade British peace activism was at its height with the Campaign for Nuclear Disarmament, which laid the groundwork for anti–Vietnam War protests in the 1960s and, indirectly, for the revival of feminism as well.

Fundamental to women's peace organizing was the maternalist ideology that had been such a marked feature of first-wave feminism. When the long-standing but disillusioned Women's International League for Peace and Freedom met after World War II to consider disbanding, the British playwright George Bernard Shaw cabled, "Convinced that the world would never be properly governed until 50 per cent of its rulers were women."[20] When in 1960 Lotta Dempsey, a Canadian newspaper columnist, casually suggested that women at a summit conference would have a better chance than men to establish peace, a group of Toronto women took up the suggestion, founding the Voice of Women. By the following year, the organization had a membership of five thousand as well as international branches. It continued active throughout the 1960s and 1970s, bringing French- and English-speaking Canadians together to oppose the introduction of nuclear weapons into Canada, campaigning against war toys, holding international peace conferences, taking up environmental and human rights issues, and providing continuity between first- and second-wave feminism.

An unabashedly maternalist philosophy also characterized Women Strike for Peace (WSP), an American organization spontaneously founded in 1961 by mothers protesting radioactive fallout from nuclear testing. As did first-wave maternal feminism, WSP encouraged women to leave the home in order to save it. It also gave women a voice in foreign policy, which they had lacked since the interwar period. A high point of the group's history was its appearance before the House Un-American Activities Committee, a congressional committee led by Senator Joe McCarthy, notorious for his red-baiting. In a great show of solidarity, accompanied by babies and flowers, the women sweetly and innocently rebuffed any accusation of communist influence, flustering and embarrassing committee members.

Although many WSP women became radicalized in the mid-1960s through the civil rights movement and Vietnam War protests, some making the transition to second-wave feminism, the group itself, according to participant and later chronicler Amy Swerdlow, was characterized by a female, rather than a feminist, consciousness. WSP women relied on moral rhetoric, disdained traditional politics as corrupt, and deferred to men in the antiwar movement. Its stance reinforced traditional gender roles and perpetrated a voluntarist activism suitable only for those with adequate time and money. It may be that this was the only way women could be effective in a time of political repression and strong attachment to domesticity. As one historian judges, "Self-interested arguments focusing on gender would have been unthinkable"[21] in postwar America and, we may add, in other countries as well.

Women and Labour

Old and new ideas also mixed in the area of women's labour activity. Women were well represented in the National Negro Labor Council, formed in 1951. The Women's Bureau of the United Auto Workers in the United States continued its work in the postwar years, analyzing contracts for sex discrimination, organizing local committees, and encouraging an awareness of gender hierarchy. Although the Bureau recorded few successes in the 1950s and early 1960s, women labour leaders became increasingly sensitive to and critical of gender discrimination. These women were to play a key role in the renewed women's movement.

The Treaty of Rome, which established the European Economic Community in 1957, included a clause on equal wages that put pressure on participating countries to eliminate gender discrimination. It was not, however, designed as a progressive measure in response to feminist demands but as an attempt to prevent countries from undercutting competition by hiring women at lower wages. Actual practice varied widely, as one might expect. Although the Netherlands signed the EEC treaty on equal wages in 1957, for example, they did not ratify it until 1975. In Britain, labour unions mounted an equal wages campaign during the 1950s that paved the way for strike activities in the 1960s. In West Germany, in an environment of economic expansion and political repression, labour militancy was rare. In Austria as late as 1976 husbands could still legally prohibit wives from working outside the home.

An unusual example of women's labour activism in the United States was captured by the 1953 film *Salt of the Earth*. Many members of the film crew had been forced out of Hollywood by red-baiting. In 1952 they learned about a Mexican-American miners' strike in New Mexico. What was unusual about the strike was that the picket line was staffed by the miners' wives. The women had suggested this strategy in order to subvert an injunction issued against the men. By the time the film group learned of the strike, the women had been picketing for five months and had survived threats and harassment, tear gas bombings, attempts to break through the line with cars and trucks, and even a mass arrest in which fifty women and children crowded the local jail. The film, made in co-operation with the community, was a unique example of labour militancy and "outspoken feminism." When the leading character Ramón, played by a miner—most of the parts were played by community members—complains to his wife, "Listen, if you think I'm gonna play nursemaid from now on, you're crazy.... I've had these kids all day!" Esperanza replies simply, "I've had them since the day they were born." Later she warns him that they can never go back to the "old way." He responds fiercely, "What's your 'new way'? What's it mean? Your 'right' to neglect your kids?"[22] In the end Ramón comes to appreciate Esperanza's new dignity and their family grows closer.

The reality was messier. Except for some tokenism, men continued to make the decisions in the union, and women played no role in the negotiations that ended the strike in the miners' favour. In some families husbands became more sensitive to their wives and shared more in domestic work; Mariana Ramírez testified that "ever since in our community there is a certain respect for the ladies." Virginia Chacón was not as optimistic. "The movie was made, fine," she reported. "That's as far as it got. We went back to the old way. And it's still in existence."[23] The film itself was suppressed because it was considered communist propaganda.

Women and Sexuality

Another area of activity, somewhat surprising given the reputation of the 1950s, was birth control. In France, a group of Protestant women called Jeunes femmes (Young Women) encouraged small discussion groups and furnished leaders for the family planning movement. Under their prodding the French began to discuss birth control publicly in the mid-1950s. Another influential lobby addressing controversial issues such as birth control and marriage reform in France was the Mouvement democratique féminin (Democratic Women's Movement), or MDF, founded in 1961 by the non-communist left. The traditionalism of the established political parties was captured in the 1956 warning of the leader of the French Communist Party: "It seems necessary to restate that the path for women's liberation is through social reforms, through social revolution and not through abortion clinics."[24] Ignoring this, the MDF added its voice to growing criticism of the antiquated marriage law, which was finally although only partially revised in 1965. Family planning centres began to open in the early 1960s, although the pill did not become legal until 1967. In Italy, the left-wing Unione Donne Italiane (Italian Women's Union) began discussing abortion openly in 1961.

While most heterosexual women dutifully accepted their destiny of marriage and motherhood, working-class lesbians were creating a culture of resistance in cities throughout North America. Since the 1930s bars had offered the only opportunity for lesbians and gays to socialize outside of their homes; in the 1950s a distinct bar culture emerged, in which lesbians identified themselves either as butches or femmes, appearing to mimic the masculine and feminine stereotypes of the dominant culture. Butches dressed like men, wooed femmes, and characteristically engaged in physical conflict with other butches or straight men, while femmes cultivated a feminine appearance and manner. Yet these women were not so much mirroring as defying cultural norms. By visibly asserting their difference and openly professing love for other women, butches and femmes were creating the basis for gay solidarity and pride, and they were doing so, remarkably, during a time of intense repression. They were pioneers in other ways as well; a study of lesbian bar culture in Buffalo, New York, found that black lesbians began desegregating white bars in the 1950s. Although some middle-class lesbians began to visit the bars as well, they generally kept their distance. In the mid-decade, in San Francisco, middle-class lesbians formed the Daughters of Bilitis, started as a social club but destined to be the first American lesbian political organization.

Women and Racism

African-American women continued to organize to fight segregation and racism. They challenged segregated schools and housing, protested differential pay scales for black teachers, and tackled the problem of illiteracy. Ella Baker, one of the key founders of the Student Nonviolent Coordinating Committee in 1960, had long been active in consumer education, the National Association for the Advancement of Colored People (NAACP), and the Southern Christian Leadership Conference. Rosa Parks, the woman who gained fame in 1955 by refusing to give up her seat on a bus to a white passenger, had a long prior history of civil rights activity in the local NAACP and in voter registration. When accounts of the bus incident described her as having been tired from a long day's work, Parks corrected, "No, the only tired I was, was tired of giving in."[25] Although she had not planned the action, it was exactly the case that the black community in Montgomery, Alabama, had been looking for to test bus segregation in the courts. The catalyst in making Parks's arrest a community issue was Jo Ann Robinson, head of the Women's Political Council, a black women's professional group operating since 1946. For years Robinson had raised protests about the bus company's racism. The Council had long made preparations for a bus boycott; within hours of Parks's arrest, preprinted handbills were updated and distributed throughout the community.

Simone de Beauvoir

There are many other, if less spectacular, examples of women's activism during the 1950s, ranging from organizing farm workers to establishing kindergartens. Ostensibly a period of conformity and conservatism during which few women identified themselves as feminists, the 1950s can also be considered a period of "quiet" feminism. This dualism, or ambivalence, was mirrored in *The Second Sex,* a 1949 work by the French philosopher and writer Simone de Beauvoir (1908–86) that a contemporary called "the single most important event for feminism in the postwar years."[26] De Beauvoir had intended to write her autobiography but had realized that before she could write about herself, she had to find out what it meant to be a woman. This enquiry led her to undertake an analysis of woman's situation, although not from a feminist perspective. "Enough ink," she wrote, "has been spilled in the quarreling over feminism, now practically over, and perhaps we should say no more about it."[27] Not only was de Beauvoir writing in isolation from any feminist movement but she was also isolated from other women intellectuals. As a student she had been encouraged "to cultivate the man"[28] within her.

De Beauvoir applied an analysis of existentialist philosophy, identifying man as the measure of humanity and woman as the Other. Accepting the fact of women's subordination to men, she was primarily concerned to understand it rather than to change it. The book's scope was broad, combining an investigation of three major perspectives on women (the biological, psychoanalytic, and Marxist) with an overview of women's history from prehistoric times to the twentieth century, a discussion of mythology, a literary analysis of five male authors, and a description of contemporary women from childhood to old age. It was "the first radical attack on the oppression of private life—marriage, the family, housework—to be aired in postwar France."[29]

Subsequent feminist critics have pointed out the flaws in de Beauvoir's analysis, how she downplayed woman's agency and how negatively she described the female body, what she called woman's "bondage of reproduction." Nevertheless, as befitted someone who also identified with socialism, de Beauvoir refused to allow "biological considerations" the last word. "They do not condemn [woman] to remain in this subordinate role forever," she insisted. More important than biology was the value that society gives it. Thus, she was able to write, "One is not born, but rather becomes, a woman." De Beauvoir appreciated that woman's "destiny [is] imposed upon her by her teachers and by society."[30]

She was unprepared for the storm of controversy that greeted the book's publication in 1949. Overnight de Beauvoir became notorious, a target of public insults and vilification. At one public appearance, students jeered her, chanting that she should do a striptease. Bookstore owners banned the book as indecent and the Catholic Church placed it on its index of prohibited books. Only slightly more favourable were American reactions to the book's abridged English translation when it appeared in 1952. Perhaps the Cold War context predisposed reviewers to distance themselves from de Beauvoir's socialist–existentialist perspective. Regardless, within two weeks the book became a best-seller.

De Beauvoir was also unprepared for but deeply moved by women's reactions worldwide as the book went through subsequent translations. Readers also responded enthusiastically to the first volume of her autobiography, *Memoirs of a Dutiful Daughter*, when it appeared in 1958. Throughout her extensive travels over the next decade, de Beauvoir was greeted by women who needed to tell her how profoundly her books had affected them; one journalist subsequently described *The Second Sex* as "like a secret code that we emerging women used to send messages to each other."[31] When Jean-Paul Sartre, de Beauvoir's lifetime companion, told her that she had become a feminist in the best way, by writing *The Second Sex,* she corrected him, observing that she

Simone de Beauvoir had wanted to write her autobiography, but she found that she first had to deal with the question of what it meant to be a woman. This is the question she raises in the "Introduction" to The Second Sex *(1952).*

. . . What is a woman?

To state the question is, to me, to suggest, at once, a preliminary answer. The fact that I ask it is in itself significant. A man would never get the notion of writing a book on the peculiar situation of the human male. But if I wish to define myself, I must first of all say: "I am a woman"; on this truth must be based all further discussion. A man never begins by presenting himself as an individual of a certain sex; it goes without saying that he is a man. The terms *masculine* and *feminine* are used symmetrically only as a matter of form, as on legal papers. In actuality the relation of the two sexes is not quite like that of two electrical poles, for man represents both the positive and the neutral, as is indicated by the common use of *man* to designate human beings in general; whereas woman represents only the negative, defined by limiting criteria, without reciprocity. In the midst of an abstract discussion it is vexing to hear a man say: "You think thus and so because you are a woman"; but I know that my only defense is to reply: "I think thus and so because it is true," thereby removing my subjective self from the argument. It would be out of the question to reply: "And you think the contrary because you are a man," for it is understood that the fact of being a man is no peculiarity. A man is in the right in being a man; it is the woman who is in the wrong. It amounts to this: just as for the ancients there was an absolute vertical with reference to which the oblique was defined, so there is an absolute human type, the masculine. Woman has ovaries, a uterus; these peculiarities imprison her in her subjectivity, circumscribe her within the limits of her own nature. It is often said that she thinks with her glands. Man superbly ignores the fact that his anatomy also includes glands, such as the testicles, and that they secrete hormones. He thinks of his body as a direct and normal connection with the world, which he believes he apprehends objectively, whereas he regards the body of woman as a hindrance, a prison, weighed down by everything peculiar to it. . . .

Thus humanity is male and man defines woman not in herself but as relative to him; she is not regarded as an autonomous being.

Source: Simone de Beauvoir, *The Second Sex*, trans. H.M. Parshley (New York: Alfred A. Knopf, 1952), xvii–xviii. Reprinted with the permission of the publisher.

"became a feminist, above all, after the book had existed for other women."[32] It became, subsequently, a key text in the second wave; one biographer views Simone de Beauvoir as largely responsible for second-wave feminism.

We can appreciate de Beauvoir's achievement all the more when we look at an American best-seller published just two years earlier, *Modern Woman: The Lost Sex* (1947), by Ferdinand Lundberg and Marynia Farnham. Characterizing up to one-third of the population of the Western world as "seriously neurotic," the authors focused on the specific case of women, whom technological and economic changes had rendered unhappy and bewildered. Satisfied that women had won equality, the authors warned that feminism was an expression of neurosis, "at its core a deep illness." Its founder, Mary Wollstonecraft, or "Mary," as the authors condescendingly called her, "was an extreme neurotic of a compulsive type . . . . Out of her illness arose the ideology of feminism which was to express the feelings of so many [deeply disturbed] women in years to come."[33]

Ideal and Reality

The dual nature of the postwar period was heightened by a growing contrast between the ideology of domesticity and the reality of most women's lives. At first, the postwar baby boom appeared to harmonize the ideal and the real. Though shorter in Europe the boom lasted in North America from the 1940s to the late 1950s, accompanied, as elsewhere, by earlier marriages and a higher marriage rate. In 1958, more American women married between the ages of fifteen and nineteen than in any other age group. The period 1946–50 saw the highest marriage rate ever recorded in France.

The generation born in the Great Depression understandably feared a postwar slump, but the expected unemployment did not materialize. On the contrary, the number of clerical, sales, and teaching jobs grew, enticing into the workforce white, middle-class married women whose husbands' wages could not keep up with inflation or their families' expectation of a higher standard of living. In Britain, the percentage of working women who were married was the same in 1951 (43 percent) as it had been in 1943, at the height of war production. In the United States, the labour force participation rate for married women almost doubled between 1940 and 1960.

This was ignored by most media, educators, and policy makers, who continued to assume the full-time dedication of married women to their families. As in the 1920s and 1930s, women's magazines lauded domestic fulfilment. A French advice columnist who, like her British predecessor in the 1930s, advised that any husband was better than none, asked rhetorically, "Is it not preferable to an empty life?" A French magazine defined "true feminism" as "the feminism that knows that a woman's being is fulfilled and enriched more by feeding a baby and wiping its bottom than by completing a philosophy thesis or working in a factory."[34] No wonder that a whopping 96 percent of American housewives polled in 1962 described themselves as either extremely or very happy.

Yet these same women were experiencing the tension between reality and ideology. The 1950s, supposedly a time of happy families, were also marked by a high divorce rate and a preoccupation with juvenile delinquency. Revealingly, 90 percent of the housewives in the 1962 sample hoped that their daughters would not lead the same life they did. Similar results were reported from a 1966 poll of French women. The author of a study of white American girls in the 1950s observes that the daughters of these dissatisfied mothers concurred that they did not want to follow in their mothers' footsteps. One young woman feared she would become like her mother, a "Mrs. Him." In words reminiscent of nineteenth-century middle-class women who felt trapped by the ideology of domesticity, one young woman explained, "We were hungry for experience, for some kind of real life, for some way to tap our energy."[35] She and others would defy the sociologist who claimed that girls did not need careers and that their reproductive role was completely self-justifying. These women would come of age in the 1960s and find in second-wave feminism an outlet for their frustrations.

The older generation's resentment of the role expected of them was captured by Betty Friedan (1921–) in her landmark study *The Feminine Mystique* (1963). Through interviews and correspondence with a sample of educated, white, middle-class, suburban housewives and mothers trying vainly to fit themselves into a media image that denied their educational achievements and personal aspirations, Friedan concluded that "the problem that has no name" was shared by thousands. Friedan's own experiences were symptomatic: "I sensed [what was wrong] first as a question mark in my own life, as a wife and mother of three small children, half-guiltily, and therefore half-heartedly, almost in spite of myself, using my abilities and education in work that took me away from home."[36]

Unlike African-American women, 57 percent of whom worked outside the home in 1960, the group represented by Friedan's sample was expected to take the feminine mystique—the postwar version of the cult of domesticity—seriously. In fact, this group was increasing its labour force participation faster than any other group in the 1950s and 1960s. With more education as universities expanded, smaller families as the baby boom tapered off, and growing financial incentives to seek employment, these women increasingly experienced the feminine mystique as a split between ideal and reality. In the absence of a visible feminist movement, they could only interpret their discontent as personal and idiosyncratic rather than rooted in social institutions.

Betty Friedan's tentative solution was to encourage women to seek work, and thus fulfilment, outside the home. For many in the paid labour force, however, the prospect for fulfilment was dim. Even though the numbers of American women working in professions rose in the 1940s and 1950s, their proportion in most fields declined, and they remained segregated in the female ghettos of teaching and nursing. As well, professional women were earning lower wages in 1960 than in 1955 and the wage gap between women and men employed full time was larger in 1966 than it had been in 1956. As did their nineteenth-century foremothers, who formed the first women's movements, these women experienced relative status deprivation when compared to the huge expansion in white-collar jobs for white, middle-class men.

Like *The Second Sex,* the *Feminine Mystique* was an immediate best-seller. Representative was the confession of the book's French translator: "This book was a shock. . . . I recognised [these suffering women]. I saw them every day. They were my neighbours."[37] Recent studies, however, have questioned Friedan's findings. An analysis of almost five hundred magazine articles found that stories celebrating women's public achievements outnumbered those praising domesticity. The dissatisfaction that Friedan identified can be seen as evidence of multiple and conflicting media messages. Another study points to Friedan's tendency to generalize from a very small sample, some two hundred women. "The one-sided picture which Friedan painted of neurotic, unhappy housewives," cautions historian Susan Ware, "does not convey either the complexity of many middle-class women's lives or the contributions such women made to their communities and public life."[38] Ware found that the same kind of women as those in Friedan's sample were leading active and fulfilling lives as volunteers in their communities. Their participation in such organizations as the League of Women Voters was, among other things, a path to involvement in local or state politics. Nonetheless, even those women active in volunteer work regretted not capitalizing professionally on their university educations.

The complexities of the postwar decades can be summarized as follows: unprecedented affluence and consumerism but also a high idealism expressed in civil rights and peace agitation; high marriage rates but an increasing divorce rate; expansion of education but a discrepancy between women's ambitions and opportunities; a feminine mystique but re-entry of white, middle-class women into paid employment; internationally, Cold War conservatism in the West but the rise of anticolonial movements in Africa and Asia. This volatile mix would belie the 1959 prediction of a Canadian news magazine that in the coming decade "conformity will continue to be a cherished goal."[39]

THE RE-EMERGENCE OF FEMINISM

Historians of second-wave feminism in North America commonly identify two main initial currents. The first, liberal or equal rights feminism, was similar to the liberal feminism of the first wave. It assumed the goal of equality between women and men but with an emphasis on combating discrimination and sexist attitudes rather than on gaining political rights. The second current, radical feminism, also had antecedents in the first wave but was essentially new. It identified patriarchy as the root cause of male dominance and focused on the family and personal relationships rather than on the world of politics or paid employment. With some exceptions, such as Italy, where the feminist movement had mass support among working-class women, both currents continued to reflect the perspective of privileged women.

Equal Rights Feminism

The renewed visibility of feminism in the United States has attracted much scholarly interest. Feminist movements in other Western countries reflected their specific contexts, but most found some inspiration in the highly publicized American developments. How can we explain a renewed wave of liberal feminism in the United States? As we have seen, American women's groups such as the National Woman's Party and National Federation of Business and Professional Women's Clubs had continued a low-key but persistent activism since the early twentieth century. With an eye to creating more employment opportunities for their members, these groups had repeatedly urged the creation of a presidential commission on women. Action finally came under President John Kennedy, whose motives ranged from a desire to revitalize the economy by encouraging women's paid employment to a need to forestall criticism of his administration's poor record of appointing women. The Presidential Commission on the Status of Women was formally constituted in December 1961.

The commission was not interested in breaking down gender stereotypes. On the contrary, it firmly endorsed the idea that women's proper role was as housewives and mothers. The subgroup on education blandly reported, "The expectation that a woman will become a wife and mother differentiates the educational requirements of girl and boy from the very beginning." The Committee on Home and Community, another part of the commission, concurred that the responsibility of a mother for children "is not debatable as a philosophy. It is and will remain a fact of life."[40] Nonetheless, the report of the commission detailed the economic and legal discrimination faced by American women. As well, although most of the commissioners were initially opposed to the Equal Rights Amendment, fearing that it would eliminate protective laws for women workers, they came to see such laws as discriminatory. This rapprochement with ERA backers broke the stalemate that had sidetracked American women's groups since the 1920s.

An important result of the 1963 report was the creation of state commissions for the purpose of collecting data to document sex discrimination. The commissions mobilized networks of union women, lawyers, academics, and organization leaders. This was the context that was to breathe life into the inclusion of "sex discrimination" in the Civil Rights Act of 1964. Proposed at the last minute by a southern senator who was a longtime supporter of the ERA, the amendment had the unintended result of uniting ERA backers with opponents of civil rights, who hoped that the sex discrimination clause would discredit the entire piece of legislation. The bill passed nonetheless, perhaps, as some have claimed, because it was regarded as a joke. According to one report, the House of Representatives almost had to be adjourned because of the hysterical laughter that greeted the initial suggestion of including gender rights within civil rights. A commission charged with enforcing the Civil Rights Act was not prepared to take the provision on sex discrimination seriously either, simply failing to compel compliance. A personnel officer for an airline quailed before the possibility of having to hire women: "What are we going to do now," he asked, "when a gal walks into our office, demands a job as an airplane pilot and has the credentials to qualify?"[41] Both the personnel officer and the enforcement commission failed to realize that a women's network was poised to take advantage of any government action, or inaction.

Betty Friedan was among those encouraged by the Presidential Commission on the Status of Women. In *The Feminine Mystique* she wrote that the commission's "very existence . . . creates a climate where it is possible to recognize and do something about discrimination against women."[42] Trying to write a follow-up book that would describe successful patterns for combining careers with marriage and motherhood, she began to come into contact with what she described as an underground network of angry women whose frustration had been growing for the past decade and who were determined not to have their expectations dashed. The inspiration for the next step came from the civil rights movement. At one meeting, Friedan was beseeched by a young woman with tears in her eyes, to "start a national organization to fight for women, like the civil rights movement for the blacks." Friedan agreed: "Watching the blacks refuse to work or ride the bus in less than human dignity, [white women] could finally say, 'Me, too.'"[43]

Thus, in June 1966 Friedan and other women furious with the government's continued trivialization of gender discrimination formed the National Organization for Women (NOW), with Friedan as president. NOW's stated purpose was "to take action to bring women into full participation in the mainstream of American society now, exercising all the privileges and responsibilities thereof in truly equal partnership with men."[44] NOW thus identified itself as an equal rights or liberal feminist organization, since its position assumed both the basic similarity of men and women and the efficacy of working within the system to achieve reform. This was a reasonable stance for the professional women who were its members and who represented the educational elite of their generation. Their personal success was reflected in their commitment to liberal individualism. By December 1967, NOW was picketing government offices to force compliance with the law, the first time in fifty years that an explicitly feminist group had held a public demonstration in the United States.

A similar development occurred in Canada, where thirty-two anglophone women's groups meeting together in 1966 decided to mount a joint campaign with the Fédération des femmes du Québec (Quebec Federation of Women), or FFQ, to pressure the government to appoint a royal commission on women. The FFQ was the result of a two-day conference held in Montreal in 1965 to celebrate the twenty-fifth anniversary of female suffrage in Quebec. Although the Canadian women were inspired by the American precedent as well as by a United Nations declaration on women's rights, they were acting on long-standing grievances of their own. For years Judy LaMarsh, the only woman in the federal cabinet, had lobbied for a commission on women; finally, pressure from the groups meeting in 1966 along with the threat of Laura Sabia, President of the Canadian Federation of University Women, to lead two million women in a march on Ottawa, did the job. The Royal Commission on the Status of Women in Canada reported in 1970, making 167 recommendations. The subsequently formed National Action Committee on the Status of Women (NAC) was determined to see them actualized. Although some critics saw the commission as an attempt to appease and divert feminists, a Toronto journalist called the report a "bomb . . . packed with more explosive potential than any device manufactured by terrorists."[45]

Although the specifics differed from country to country, it is striking to note the extent of government study and public debate on women's issues during the 1960s. Similar enquiries were conducted by Germany from 1962 to 1966, Denmark in 1965, and France, Britain, Finland, the Netherlands, and Austria in 1966. In France, women's work outside the home had become a major public issue that had some effect in securing reform of the marriage law in 1965. Finnish women organized in 1966 to discuss sex roles. In Italy, women and men met jointly in 1966 in the group Demau (demystification of authority) to "demystify" social and sexual relationships as well as to "*search for a new autonomy for women,* through a conscious evaluation of their own essential values and their own historical situation."[46] In Quebec, women were mobilizing to reap their share of the liberal reforms introduced by the Quiet Revolution of the early 1960s. In a 1968 report to the United Nations, the Swedish government suggested that "there are probably few countries in which the roles of men and women in the family and in society have been so thoroughly analysed and discussed as in Sweden during the 1960s."[47]

If the extent of discussion was impressive, it was not clear where it would lead. The article "Dissatisfaction among Women," by Joke Kool-Smit, which appeared in the Netherlands in 1967, has been credited with precipitating second-wave feminism there. Yet Canadian feminist Thérèse Casgrain, attending a 1966 international seminar in Rome on the theme of women's participation in public life, recalled an International Council of Women conference she had attended in Paris some thirty years earlier where exactly the same subjects had been debated.

The discussion was not always encouraging to feminism. The Moynihan Report, which appeared in the United States in 1965, concluded that the pathological state of the black family was due to cowed men and dominant women, a reversal of "normal" family life. Humiliated by racism and discrimination and the resulting high unemployment, black men, Daniel Moynihan concluded, were unable to act as providers for their families. The result was a matriarchal family structure. Why were black women less affected by racism? Moynihan's "scientific" explanation was the inherent need of "the male animal, from the bantam rooster to the four-star general . . . to strut." His solution? To prioritize jobs for black men until "every able-bodied Negro man was working even if this meant that some women's jobs had to be redesigned to enable men to fulfil them."[48] Note that Moynihan specified women's jobs, not white men's jobs. Moynihan's distortion of black family life and his solution spurred black women to embrace feminism.

For white middle-class women in the thirty years since Thérèse Casgrain's Paris conference much had changed. Their expectations had been altered by numerous developments: increased access to education; easier control of reproduction with the advent of the pill in the early 1960s and the concomitant possibility of divorcing sexuality from reproduction; greater stress on personal fulfilment; an increased role for the state in building social programs; and a greater probability that women would return to the labour force either after their children were grown or, as was increasingly the case, with young children in the home. It is tempting to draw an analogy with first-wave feminism, which had developed in response to women's changing role as industrialization took production out of the home while threatening to confine middle-class women to it. One hundred years later women were leaving the home to join or rejoin the paid labour force. In both cases feminist activity had an economic underpinning.

The important difference between the first and second waves in the United States, according to historian William Chafe, is that whereas sex roles had remained stable in the nineteenth century, since the 1940s they had been changing. The impact of this change was muted by the accepted premise that women worked only because they had to. "The expansion of women's economic role," believes Chafe, "depended on circumstances that prevented female employment from being perceived as a feminist threat."[49] The rhetoric thinly masked a change for middle-class white women that was in fact dramatic.

The meaning of married women's re-entry into the paid labour force becomes clouded, however, when we look at European data. One scholar believes there is "ample evidence"[50] that no major changes in women's work patterns have taken place since the war. According to Gisela Kaplan, we should view women's paid work not as gradually expanding but as fluctuating according to the needs of the capitalist economy. What was true during the war years has held true since then, as the family's need to keep up with inflation replaced the nation's need to meet the war emergency. Women have functioned as a reserve army, responding to the need for labour and, above all, for cheap labour. Whether their work pattern will continue as the economy contracts remains to be seen. In any case, Kaplan calls attention to the difficulty of predicating feminism on a situation that most women continue to see as necessary rather than desirable.

Regardless of their motives, women's visibility in the workforce catapulted issues into public debate. Reduced by Ferdinand Lundberg and Marynia Farnham in 1947 to the manifestation of a gender-based neurosis, women's issues were now accepted as valid social concerns. This alone was not sufficient to generate a women's movement, however. All of the above can explain the renewed interest in feminism, but the push for women's "liberation" was to come from a different direction.

Radical Feminism

Like the liberal climate that had accompanied first-wave feminism, the 1960s were marked by the expectation of progressive social change. They were also a decade of violence: the Algerian war of independence; the erection of the Berlin Wall; brutal beatings and murders of civil rights protesters in the American south; the Bay of Pigs incident; the assassinations of John and Robert Kennedy, Malcolm X, and Martin Luther King; the Soviet invasion of Czechoslovakia; political terrorism in West Germany, Italy, and Quebec;

and, above all, American military involvement in Vietnam. In cities and on campuses throughout North America and Europe protests erupted. Loosely organized in the New Left movement, students challenged the institutions of bourgeois society, from university administrations to the materialistic values of capitalism; they promoted critical theory, participatory democracy, and personal expression, in contrast to the authoritarian and doctrinaire Old Left communism of the 1930s. Out of women's experiences in the New Left came radical feminism, which spoke of oppression rather than discrimination, liberation rather than equality or rights, and revolution rather than reform.

The founders of the women's liberation movement were younger than liberal feminists but otherwise similar: most were educated, white, and middle class, products of postwar affluence, the consumer culture, and 1960s counterculture. Many had mothers in paid employment. By late in the decade they were in their early to mid-twenties, either finishing or having recently finished their education, ready to face life choices and the likelihood of sex discrimination. Ann Popkin describes the American women attracted to women's liberation: "For the most part, we were not yet tied down to marriage, family, or career. We were at a crucial age when, having finished college, we had to face life decisions about these very issues. Our education and training for careers had been (or seemed) nearly the same as men's. But the futures we had to face at home and at work were quite different."[51] Testimony from British and German sources indicates that many participants in those countries were young housewives, often with small children.

The American women, who have been those most studied, enjoyed a background of privilege but not necessarily of complacency. They belonged to the first generation to know affluence fully, and they grew up with daily evidence of technological possibilities ranging from television to photocopying, from transistor radios to jet travel. Almost assured of postsecondary education, they shared family backgrounds of political idealism. Some were "red diaper" babies, whose parents had been communists or socialists; many more came from liberal families; and all had been raised on the platitudes of the Cold War, which seemed wanting and hypocritical when examined in the light of such realities as anticolonialism abroad and poverty at home. The civil rights movement provided them with the opportunity to act on their ideals.

The summer of 1964 saw volunteers heading south to help register voters. Along with white women from the South and from religious backgrounds, they found the experience catalytic in giving them the self-confidence they needed to face hostility, brutality, perhaps death. They looked up to the older black women, pillars of their communities, who predominated in the civil rights movement, and, like their nineteenth-century predecessors in social reform, these young white women gained organizing skills. They appreciated the flexibility and lack of hierarchy that they found in the Student Nonviolent Coordinating Committee (SNCC), which made up the radical student wing of the movement and which gave them the unique opportunity to develop their talents and self-respect.

Student radicals in the North joined Students for a Democratic Society (SDS), which, like SNCC, was non-hierarchical. Fired with idealism, they turned to community organizing in inner-city neighbourhoods. Regardless of whether they registered voters in the South or helped organize protests in the North, women had remarkably similar experiences. While the positive aspects were undeniable, they began to chaff at the sexism they encountered, frustrated at being assigned office work or housekeeping tasks, excluded from key decision making and seeing attention continually focused on the men and their activities. As early as 1963, black women in SNCC led a half-comic sit-in; in 1964 two white women drafted a position paper, circulated anonymously, in which they claimed that "the woman in SNCC is often in the same position as that token Negro hired in a corporation." It prompted the purportedly joking response of SNCC leader Stokeley Carmichel: "The only position for women in SNCC is prone."[52]

Although some black women were unhappy with male chauvinism in the civil rights movement, most found racism more important than sexism. As well, many women in SNCC apparently did share in the instrumental decisions, although Dorothy Coton, the highest-ranking female member, was consigned to getting coffee and taking notes until a male colleague protested on her behalf. To black women involved in often violent civil rights confrontations, white women's worry over gender discrimination seemed at times somewhat trivial. Advocacy of Black Power in the middle of the decade increased machismo in the movement and, in reaction, black feminism. White participants, now unwanted, returned north, the women among them meshing their new self-assurance and sensitivity with the similar experiences of their sisters in SDS.

It was only a matter of time before these women voiced their discontent publicly. In the mid-1960s, however, the New Left was experiencing a major change as the Vietnam War became the focus of attention and, with it, men, who were the heroes of the draft resistance movement. The enormous growth of the antiwar movement meant that the concerns of the older members with civil rights backgrounds became sidetracked. As the government became more intransigent, the movement took on more and more a macho flavour that made it even less open to discussion of women's grievances.

Nevertheless, sporadic debate on women's issues continued and by 1967 could no longer be ignored. In September at a national conference of the New Left, women secured a place on the agenda with difficulty. When the time came, the chair refused to call on them and patted Shulamith Firestone on the head, saying, "Move on little girl; we have more important issues to talk about here than women's liberation." In the words of the founder of the first autonomous women's group, formed one week later, "That was the genesis." For other women who were more reluctant to turn their backs on men in the left, the break came the following January, when Marilyn Webb rose to speak at a demonstration. Her speech was intended to enlist men as allies in women's liberation, but she was greeted with blatant hostility and shouts of "Take her off the stage and fuck her!"[53] Shulamith Firestone, scheduled to speak next, went up to the stage, grabbed the mike, and told the men that this "was the end."[54] In a subsequent letter to the leftist journal the *Guardian*, Firestone wrote,

We say to the left: in this past decade you have failed to live up to your rhetoric of revolution. You have not reached the people. And we won't hitch ourselves to your poor donkey. There are millions of women out there desperate enough to rise. Women's liberation is dynamite. And we have more important things to do than to try to get you to come around. You will come around when you have to, because you need us more than we need you. . . . The message being: Fuck off, left. You can examine your navel by yourself from now on. We're starting our own movement.[55]

The pattern of radical feminism originating within the context of the New Left was repeated in many European countries. Two French women, Anne Zelensky and Jacqueline Feldman, who had been members of the non-communist Mouvement democratique féminin (MDF) but wanted something more radical, formed a small, mixed discussion group, Féminin–Masculin–Avenir (Feminine–Masculine–Future), in 1967. The impetus to form autonomous women's groups came in the immediate aftermath of the May 1968 movement, an uprising of French workers and students against the authoritarian Gaullist state, the universities, and bourgeois society. Within a few weeks women were distributing leaflets, organizing a meeting to discuss "Women and Revolution," and forming their own all-women's group. Like their American counterparts, these women were young, better educated than their parents, often from leftist backgrounds, perhaps with some previous experience in student politics or in protests against French colonialism in the Algerian war. Like American women, they concluded that the rhetoric of personal expression and democratic participation fostered by the New Left movement rang hollow. They began to analyze critically the supporting roles they had played and became disillusioned. As one woman wrote later, "It takes just as long to cook a steak for a revolutionary man as it does for a bourgeois."[56]

That same spring, West Berlin women who were members of the Socialist German Student Federation met to discuss their problems, in particular their responsibility for child care, which often meant that they had to curtail their studies. The following September at a national student conference, Helke Sander attempted to persuade male colleagues that women's issues should be taken seriously and that the politics of sexual domination extended into private life. The men were dismissive, inspiring one woman to pelt them with tomatoes. At another conference in November, where, ironically, the fiftieth anniversary of German women's suffrage was celebrated, women were physically prevented from reading out loud a pamphlet they had written.

In the United States, France, and Germany, there was little perceived continuity with earlier feminism. In Germany in particular, the Nazi years discouraged a close look at the past. The exile and deaths of earlier radicals forced feminists to begin anew. In France, women were aware of the intellectual and cultural roots of feminism stretching back to the Renaissance, but more influential were the generation gap perceived by young women and the low participation of women in parliamentary politics. Young radicals had no illusions about working within traditional channels.

In countries such as Canada and Sweden, with social democratic parties that were part of mainstream politics, young women were not as alienated from politics and leftist traditions. Within Canadian feminism, the Quebec suffrage movement and the peace movement (through the Voice of Women) helped bridge the generation gap, as did enclaves of feminism within the social democratic left. Radical feminism began in 1967 when women in the Student Union for Peace Activism in Toronto concluded that "they were oppressed as women within an organization that was attacking oppression."[57] By the end of 1968, there were autonomous women's groups in most large cities, and most Canadian feminists from then through the early 1970s would probably have identified themselves as radical. Yet familiarity with leftist parties and politics that had been relatively receptive to feminism blunted women's sense of disaffection and encouraged anglophone feminists to work for change in co-operation with the state. The idea of co-operation with the federal state was more problematic for Quebec feminists, however, who would split over the question of whether Quebec should separate from Canada.

The British example was similar to that of English-speaking Canada. Second-wave feminism was nourished in ongoing pacifist, labour, and socialist traditions. British women's peace groups organized the 1968 commemoration of the fiftieth anniversary of women's suffrage. Also in the late 1960s the militancy of union women intensified; strikes in 1968 over the issue of equal pay inspired many young feminists. One of the earliest and most important theoretical works written from a Marxist perspective was Juliet Mitchell's 1966 article, "The Longest Revolution," which explored the relevance of Marxist analysis to women's production, reproduction, socialization, and sexuality. The vitality of socialism became obvious in the disinclination of British feminists to break with the male left. Leftist men were not necessarily sympathetic to feminists, however; when Sheila Rowbotham asked at a history workshop at Ruskin College in 1970 if anyone else was interested in working on women's history, she was greeted with general laughter from the floor.

Two further examples of intergenerational continuity, although from opposite ends of the feminist political spectrum, come from Italy and Switzerland respectively. When high unemployment hit Italy in the late 1960s, organizations such as the Italian Women's Union helped to mobilize women and connected past feminist action with what was to become "the biggest and most important social movement in Italy in the 1970s."[58] In particular, the Italian women's movement was able to reach across class lines and mobilize broad working-class support. No other Western European country was able to duplicate its ability to mobilize such large numbers of women to national action.

The situation was very different in Switzerland, where women still could not vote. When women in other countries were celebrating fiftieth anniversaries of women's suffrage, the Swiss were celebrating the anniversaries of still-active suffrage organizations. Switzerland had refused to sign the Declaration of Human Rights in the United Nations Charter of 1948, objecting to its provision for freedom irrespective of sex, and in 1968 was proposing to sign with "reservations," a step that suffragists feared would institutionalize the status quo. The major problem was that any proposed change to the constitution had to be submitted to all male voters in a national referendum. The first referendum, in 1959, was defeated by a two-thirds majority. Apparently antisuffragists were persuasive when they claimed that Swiss women had more rights without the vote than other women had with it, or that because rural women would have to walk one or more hours to the polls men would have to take care of the house and children in the interval. They refused to be cowed by the fact that they were the last European country outside of Liechtenstein to give women the vote.

What turned the tide apparently was the activism of young women, inspired by the 1966 translation of Betty Friedan's *Feminine Mystique* into German and the 1968 student demonstrations in France and Germany. Understandably impatient, they rejected the older strategy of polite requests and lobbying in favour of a march on the government in 1969. The older suffragists held back, preferring to show their support by meeting simultaneously but more decorously indoors. Whether the time was right or the public march tipped the balance, the government promised four days later to hold another referendum. Finally, between 1971 and 1975, female suffrage was established throughout most of Switzerland.

Swedish feminism did not have much of a second wave, probably because of the high participation of women in politics and the attention given women's issues by a long-serving social democratic government. Spain, under Franco's dictatorship from 1939 to 1975, represents the other extreme. Remarkably, leftist and feminist groups that either dated from the republic of the 1930s or sprouted underground during the 1960s and 1970s managed to meet clandestinely, resurfacing in 1975 to herald the "second epoch" of feminism. They joined others that had originated in university or professional circles and had operated legally but quietly. By December 1975 Spanish feminists held the First Conference on Women's Liberation.

Feminist Theory and Practice

The level of hostility towards the male left that marked American radical feminism was not universal. NOW women, as represented by Betty Friedan, never ceased to regard men as legitimate and welcome allies in the feminist movement. Friedan had little patience with what she described as "a new, abstract ideology of man hatred, sex warfare," fearing that it would put off "the women from the cities and suburbs of Middle America who were beginning to identify with the women's movement."[59] In Britain, feminists were at first divided over the issue of working with men. "We met with the husbands at first," recalled Hazel Galbraith, "but they took over, so we had to stop."[60] In France, the men in the mixed group, Feminine–Masculine–Future, dropped out within a few months. In the Netherlands, two major groups were mixed, but one feminist later thought that including men "was one of the many mistakes we made."[61]

Radical feminism meant breaking not only with leftist men but with Marxist ideology, which insisted on economic class as the main form of oppression. As Robin Morgan explained, "It became harder every day to put other oppressions first when my brain was barraged with objective facts, figures, statistics, and analyses—and subjective anguish—all on and of women."[62] Radical feminists prioritized the fight against patriarchy over the struggle against capitalism. The Redstockings Manifesto, issued by a New York group in 1969 (not to be confused with the Redstockings in Denmark or Iceland), exemplified this philosophy:

> We identify the agents of our oppression as men. Male supremacy is the oldest, most basic form of domination. All other forms of exploitation and oppression (racism, capitalism, imperialism, etc.) are extensions of male supremacy. Men dominate women, a few men dominate the rest. All power structures throughout history have been male-dominated and male-oriented. Men have controlled all political, economic and cultural institutions and backed up this control with physical force. They have used their power to keep women in an inferior position. *All men* receive economic, sexual, and psychological benefits from male supremacy. *All men* have oppressed women.[63]

While the manifesto was not directed at individual men, its language was uncompromising, as was the decision of another New York group, The Feminists, to allow only one-third of its members at any one time to live with men. Highly publicized actions, such as the disruption of the Madison Square Garden bridal fair in February 1969, by the Women's International Conspiracy from Hell (WITCH), did little to endear the movement to the prospective brides or to the wider public; the WITCH protesters had chanted, "Here come the slaves, off to their graves."[64] But these actions did give the media ammunition to create an image of feminists as man haters that has persisted. In France, the first major public action took place in 1970, when demonstrators unfurled two banners at the Tomb of the Unknown Soldier, one reading, "One man in two is a woman," and the other, "There is only one person more unknown than the soldier, his wife." They then presented a wreath to the "wife." The action sparked a furore since it amounted to desecration of a national shrine.

Robin Morgan pointed out that the word "radical" derived from going "to the root," meaning that sexism was the root oppression.[65] This was the theme of two early books of radical feminist theory published in the United States, Kate Millett's *Sexual Politics* (1969) and Shulamith Firestone's *The Dialectic of Sex* (1970). Kate Millett has been credited with the discovery of patriarchy: the insight that patriarchy, not capitalism, is the cause of women's oppression. Following the example of Simone de Beauvoir, Millett illustrated her argument with passages documenting the arrogant, domineering, and sadistic sexual hostility of writers such as Henry Miller and Norman Mailer. She concluded that all historical societies have been patriarchies. What Betty Friedan had called "the problem that has no name," was now named: it was "patriarchy." This made it difficult for women experiencing other oppressions, such as class or race, to identify with the unfolding women's movement. Shulamith Firestone's intention, revealed in the title of her book, was to adapt Marxist language and categories to a feminist analysis by replacing emphasis on economic class as the basic division in history with a radical feminist emphasis on gender, or sex class. Her goal was to develop a new materialist theory of history, which would replace productive forces with reproductive forces. Whereas a socialist revolution would socialize the forces of production, a feminist revolution would have to socialize the forces of reproduction, which, Firestone suggested, could be done through reliance on reproductive technology.

An important early text in France was Monique Wittig's novel, *Les Guérilleres* (1969), which exposed history as the record of great men. French feminists would eventually take the lead in creating feminist theory, a not surprising development since many of them were university students in literature, for whom philosophy was a required subject. They focused on criticizing language and through it the structures of male power.

The influence of the American style of radical feminism was felt in structures as well as theory. Consciousness-raising, or c-r, groups, where women began to talk to each other about their personal lives and understand their common experiences, spread like wildfire. As Ann Popkin describes,

> We told each other our life stories, poured out our feelings as women. . . . We shared the hurt, confusion, and anger that each of us had harbored inside, and the excitement and relief that came with the act of sharing. . . . This sharing of painful experiences had models in the Chinese notions of "speaking bitterness.". . . We began by venting our fury at men, our most immediate oppressors. . . . And we began to explore our relationships with women—to trust and value women more.[66]

A British feminist reported her experience: "Fifteen minutes after my arrival I was aware I would not miss another of these meetings if I could help it. So many of the women in that small sitting-room, despite their surface differences, seemed to share what for so long I believed to be my own, idiosyncratic suffering."[67] On the other hand, other British feminists condemned consciousness raising as wasteful navel gazing compared to undertaking practical efforts to improve women's lives.

By 1969 there were women's groups in most urban centres throughout North America and in major European cities. Journalists who were prepared to give flippant coverage became converted instead. Sophy Burnham, for example,

> laughed when she received an assignment from *Redbook* to do a story on the women's movement. "A lunatic fringe," she thought. But "within a week I was so upset, I could hardly focus my ideas.". . . By the end she was a convert: "I am now offended by things that would never have bothered me before. I am now a feminist. I am infused with pride—in my sisters, in myself, in my womanhood."[68]

Determined to be more consistent than the male left had been in practising internal democracy, second-wave feminists were ultrasensitive to charges of elitism or hierarchy. The Feminists, in New York, initiated a disc system to prevent discussions from being dominated by certain members.

Kate Millett's Sexual Politics (1969) was one of the key texts of the recent women's movement in the United States.

In America, recent events have forced us to acknowledge at last that the relationship between the races is indeed a political one which involves the general control of one collectivity, defined by birth, over another collectivity, also defined by birth. Groups who rule by birthright are fast disappearing, yet there remains one ancient and universal scheme for the domination of one birth group by another—the scheme that prevails in the area of sex. The study of racism has convinced us that a truly political state of affairs operates between the races to perpetuate a series of oppressive circumstances. The subordinated group has inadequate redress through existing political institutions, and is deterred thereby from organizing into conventional political struggle and opposition.

Quite in the same manner, a disinterested examination of our system of sexual relationship must point out that the situation between the sexes now, and throughout history, is a case of that phenomenon Max Weber defined as *herrschaft*, a relationship of dominance and subordinance. What goes largely unexamined, often even unacknowledged (yet is institutionalized nonetheless) in our social order, is the birthright priority whereby males rule females. Through this system a most ingenious form of "interior colonization" has been achieved. It is one which tends moreover to be sturdier than any form of segregation, and more rigorous than class stratification, more uniform, certainly more enduring. However muted its present appearance may be, sexual dominion obtains nevertheless as perhaps the most pervasive ideology of our culture and provides its most fundamental concept of power.

This is so because our society, like all other historical civilizations, is a patriarchy. The fact is evident at once if one recalls that the military, industry, technology, universities, science, political office, and finance—in short, every avenue of power within the society, including the coercive force of the police, is entirely in male hands. As the essence of politics is power, such realization cannot fail to carry impact. What lingers of supernatural authority, the Deity, "His" ministry, together with the ethics and values, the philosophy and art of our culture—its very civilization—as T.S. Eliot once observed, is of male manufacture.

Source: Kate Millet, *Sexual Politics* (New York: Avon, 1969, 1970). Reprinted with permission.

Each member received the same number of discs and had to return one each time she spoke. If she ran out before the others, she had to wait. They also designed a lot system to distribute tasks in order to avoid a monopoly by women of more privileged backgrounds. The requirement of unanimity for group decisions, or decision making by exhaustion, as it has been dubbed, was common. Antipathy towards elitism in American radical feminism some-times took bizarre forms. Naomi Weisstein, a charismatic speaker, was appar-ently forced to turn down an invitation to speak because her women's group feared she would become a "star."

The history of the early movement in most countries reveals deep splits over these and other issues, such as strategy. The Feminists thought of them-selves as a tightly organized military vanguard, whereas New York Radical Women hoped to create a mass movement through extensive reading and political education. The different currents were not always distinct. NOW, for example, which had originated as a liberal feminist organization, rapidly but not without controversy adopted most of the goals of the radical femi-nists, who swelled the organization's membership to 40,000 by 1974. In France, the movement was split into countless mini-groups. The Féministes Révolutionaires (Revolutionary Feminists) went for spectacular actions, American style. The maverick group, Psychanalyse et Politique, or Psych et Po (Psychoanalysis and Politics), wanted to work anonymously, "under-ground, like moles."[69] The major split in British feminism was a bitter one between socialist and radical feminists. Betty Friedan's description of American feminism as a "messy, paradoxical, impossible to pin down, ever changing complexity"[70] holds for other countries as well.

One source of conflict was the issue of sexual preference. Second-wave feminists prided themselves on their analysis of personal life, taking seriously the slogan "the personal is political," but lesbians in the movement did not initially feel comfortable enough to reveal their orientation. In the United States, women both in NOW and in the radical wing were hostile to les-bianism. Betty Friedan, who wanted a broad-based mass movement that would include churchwomen along with welfare mothers, described the les-bian issue as a "sexual red herring" that would sidetrack the movement and turn off "those 8,000,000 woman's magazine readers."[71] Radical feminists objected that lesbianism was a sexual rather than a political issue; the point of feminism, one said, was to get women out of bed rather than to change the gender of their partners. But, encouraged by the sexual permissiveness of the 1960s, many more women had already begun to explore the possibility of lesbian sex.

To those who styled themselves lesbian-feminists, lesbianism had the potential to demolish sexual stereotypes and even patriarchy. Lesbian-femi-nists understood lesbianism as profoundly *political,* a choice that any woman could make. To choose lesbianism was to choose to identify with women, to support women rather than men. Heterosexuality, in contrast, was imposed by men in their interests. Women could resist male domination by dispens-ing with men; hence, the logo emblazoned on T-shirts and posters, "A

Woman Without a Man is Like a Fish Without a Bicycle."[72] The split was smoothed over in the United States by 1970 but continued to be an issue in both Britain and France.

The debate on sexual preference prefigured a tendency towards cultural feminism, which was to become dominant in the United States, France, and Germany by the mid-1970s. Woman-centred values had been emphasized in second-wave feminism at the outset and had resulted in the mushrooming of alternative institutions, such as rape crisis centres, battered women's shelters, health clinics, feminist publishers, coffee houses, bookstores, and women's studies programs at colleges and universities. Reminiscent of first-wave social or maternal feminism, cultural feminism celebrated the validity and strength of specific characteristics attributed to women. With cultural feminism, lifestyle became the primary issue rather than one's political commitment.

One issue often absent from discussion in the early years was that of race. In their eagerness to establish the legitimacy of the notion of sexual oppression, radical feminists insisted on the shared experiences of women, blind to the extent to which their notion of shared experience reflected merely their own. Chicana feminists, for example, were more likely to value family solidarity and treasure children than to insist on sexual separatism and abortion rights. They, like black women, faced the dilemma of criticizing male sexism while being sensitive to the racist oppression their male co-workers experienced. Women of colour would eventually demand a new definition of feminism, as reflective of their experiences as of white women's. African-American Barbara Smith would write in 1982, "Feminism is the political theory and practice that struggles to free *all* women: women of color, working-class women, poor women, disabled women, lesbians, old women— as well as white, economically privileged, heterosexual women. Anything less than this vision of total freedom is not feminism, but merely female self-aggrandizement."[73] Smith was building on a tradition, established in the nineteenth century by Anna Julia Cooper and Ellen Watkins Harper among others, which acknowledged the intricate and reinforcing connections between sexism and racism.

Early on minority women established their own groups, such as Indian Rights for Indian Women, founded in 1964 in Canada, or joined mixed groups promoting ethnic identity, as did American-Asian or Chicana women. The involvement of a few black women leaders, such as Pauli Murray, who helped found NOW, and Aileen Hernandez, who became its president in 1970, did little to eliminate racism within the women's movement. Not until the 1980s would white feminists seriously analyze their racist assumptions.

In spite of these conflicts, women's groups united on the issue of reproductive rights. Demonstrations for legal abortion were held in Montreal and New York State in 1969. In 1970, Canadian feminists organized an Abortion Caravan, which proceeded from Vancouver to Ottawa, carrying a coffin symbolizing women who had died from illegal abortions and filled with petitions demanding repeal of abortion laws. When they reached Ottawa, protesters chained themselves to seats in the visitors' gallery in the House of Commons, forcing its closure for the first time in history. In the same year, Dutch feminists parading in front of a conference of gynaecologists pulled up their shirts to reveal the words "mistress of our own bodies"—literally, "boss of one's belly"—written on their stomachs. By 1974 Dutch women's groups united in a coalition, We Women Demand, as did women's groups in Norway. Abortion also became the unifying issue of the Austrian and British women's movements. In 1975 in Britain, the National Abortion Campaign organized the largest demonstration around a women's issue since the suffrage activity in the early part of the century.

Abortion was the decisive issue in both the French and German women's movements. Although in both countries abortion was still a punishable offence, 343 women in France and 374 in West Germany signed statements, published in the press, declaring that they had had abortions. Among the French signers was Simone de Beauvoir, who in fact had never had an abortion but who felt that she could better afford the legal risk than lesser known women. Feminists in West Germany had first marched for abortion rights on International Women's Day in 1970; in 1971 and again in 1972, tens of thousands of women demonstrated, and in mid-decade five thousand women marched on the government in Bonn, demanding reform. But the most impressive campaign was waged by Italian feminists, who collected an amazing 900,000 signatures for abortion reform. By 1974 it had become a national movement. The Italian Women's Union supported the abortion struggle in open disagreement with the Communist Party, which wanted to placate conservative politicians and voters.

The early 1970s represent the peak of second-wave feminism. Although internal divisions would continue to plague movements and would be joined by the external problems of hostile governments and economic downturn, the numbers of women mobilized and the wide publicity generated guaranteed that feminist issues would not fade away. More change in women's position had been accomplished, arguably, in the previous ten years than in the previous two hundred.

The 1950s and early 1960s were years of quiet but persistent and diverse women's activity. Above all, steady growth in the numbers of middle-class married women in paid employment created personal tensions that were perceived as social issues in the climate of the 1960s. Out of the frustrations of professional women came pressure on governments to address these issues. By the late 1960s many countries experienced a resurgence of liberal feminist activity.

The additional input of younger women created women's liberation movements in the late 1960s and early 1970s. Dismayed by the sexism of the progressive movements with which they were associated, these women formed autonomous groups, often in open hostility to their former male colleagues. They prioritized women's experiences under patriarchy, as they understood them, and created discussion groups and alternative institutions that mushroomed into broad but loose networks. Although beset by conflicts over strategy and sexual preference, among other issues, women's groups attained near unanimity on the issue of reproduction rights, staging mass demonstrations, and ensuring that feminism was in the public eye.

NOTES

1 Quoted in Jill Liddington, *The Long Road to Greenham: Feminism and Anti-Militarism in Britain since 1820* (London: Virago Press, 1989), 173.

2 Monique Remy, *De l'Utopie a l'intégration: Histoire des mouvements de femmes* (Paris: Éditions l'Harmattan, 1990), 36 (my translation).

3 Lucia Chiavola Birnbaum, *Liberazione della donna: Feminism in Italy* (Middletown, CT: Wesleyan University Press, 1986), 41.

4 Quoted in Nancy Gabin, *Feminism in the Labor Movement: Women and the United Auto Workers, 1935–1975* (Ithaca, NY: Cornell University Press, 1990), 41.

5 Ruth Milkman, "American Women and Industrial Unionism During World War II," in *Behind the Lines: Gender and the Two World Wars,* ed. Margaret Randolph Higgonet, Jane Jenson, Sonya Michel, and Margaret Collins Weitz (New Haven, CT: Yale University Press, 1987), 178.

6 Quoted in Gabin, *Feminism in the Labor Movement,* 47.

7 Quoted in ibid., 70.

8 Milkman, "American Women and Industrial Unionism," 180.

9 Roy Harrod, quoted in Denise Riley, "Some Peculiarities of Social Policy Concerning Women in Wartime and Postwar Britain," in *Behind the Lines: Gender and the Two World Wars,* ed. Higgonet, et al., 265.

10 Quoted in Sherna B. Gluck, *Rosie the Riveter Revisited: Women, the War, and Social Change* (Boston: Twayne Publishers, 1987), 36–37.

11 Elizabeth Wilson, *Only Halfway to Paradise: Women in Postwar Britain 1945–1968* (London: Tavistock Publications, 1980), 88.

12 Susan M. Hartmann, *American Women in the 1940s: The Home Front and Beyond* (Boston: Twayne Publishers, 1982), 157.

13 Quoted in Gary Kinsman, *The Regulation of Desire: Sexuality in Canada* (Montreal: Black Rose Books, 1987), 123.

14 Quoted in Claire Duchen, *Women's Rights and Women's Lives in France, 1944–1968* (London and New York: Routledge, 1994), 53.

15 Ute Gerhard, "Women's Rights and Family Law since the Nineteenth Century," in *The German Women's Movement: The Social Role of Women in the 19th Century and the Emancipation Movement in Germany,* ed. Ingeborg Drewitz (Bonn: Hohwacht, 1983), 121, 132.

16 Quoted in Rosalyn Terborg-Penn, "Discontented Black Feminists: Prelude and Postscript to the Passage of the Nineteenth Amendment," in *Decades of Discontent: The Women's Movement, 1920–1940,* ed. Lois Scharf and Joan M. Jensen (Westport, CT: Greenwood Press, 1983), 275.

17 Quoted in Wilson, *Only Halfway to Paradise,* 185.

18 Quoted in Leila J. Rupp and Verta Taylor, *Survival in the Doldrums: The American Women's Rights Movement, 1945 to the 1960s* (New York: Oxford University Press, 1987), 53.

19 Wilson, *Only Halfway to Paradise,* 187.

20 Quoted in Gertrude Bussey and Margaret Tims, *Pioneers for Peace: Women's International League for Peace and Freedom 1915–1965* (London: George Allen and Unwin, 1965), 188.

21 Naomi Black, *Social Feminism* (Ithaca, NY: Cornell University Press, 1989), 274.

22 Michael Wilson, *Salt of the Earth,* Screenplay (1953), and Deborah Silverton Rosenfelt, Commentary (New York: Feminist Press, 1978), 94, 62–63, 80.

23 Ibid., 142.

24 Quoted in Duchen, *Women's Rights and Women's Lives,* 181.

25 Rosa Parks with Jim Haskins, *Rosa Parks: My Story* (New York: Dial Books, 1992), 116.

26 Quoted in Duchen, *Women's Rights and Women's Lives,* 188.

27 Simone de Beauvoir, *The Second Sex,* trans. H.M. Parshley (New York: Alfred A. Knopf, 1952), xv.

28 Quoted in Deirdre Bair, *Simone de Beauvoir: A Biography* (New York: Simon and Schuster, 1990), 104, 626 n. 7.

29 Duchen, *Women's Rights and Women's Lives,* 188.

30 De Beauvoir, *The Second Sex,* 70, 36, 301, 315.

31 Quoted in Bair, *Simone de Beauvoir,* 478.

32 Quoted in Margaret A. Simons and Jessica Benjamin, "Simone de Beauvoir: An Interview," *Feminist Studies* 5, 2 (1979): 332.

33 Ferdinand Lundberg and Marynia Farnham, *Modern Woman: The Lost Sex* (New York and London: Harper and Brothers, 1947), 141, 143, 159.

34 Quoted in Duchen, *Women's Rights and Women's Lives,* 101, 106.

35 Quoted in Wini Breines, *Young, White, and Miserable: Growing up Female in the Fifties* (Boston: Beacon Press, 1992), 197, 138.

36 Betty Friedan, *The Feminine Mystique* (New York: Dell Publishing, 1963), 6.

37 Quoted in Duchen, *Women's Rights and Women's Lives,* 91.

38 Susan Ware, "American Women in the 1950s: Nonpartisan Politics and Women's Politicization," in *Women, Politics, and Change,* ed. Louise A. Tilly and Patricia Gurin (New York: Russell Sage Foundation, 1990), 294.

39 Quoted in Myrna Kostash, *Long Way from Home: The Story of the Sixties Generation in Canada* (Toronto: James Lorimer and Company, 1980), xv.

40 Quoted in Cynthia Harrison, *On Account of Sex: The Politics of Women's Issues, 1945–1968* (Berkeley: University of California Press, 1988), 154, 140.

41 Quoted in ibid., 189.

42 Friedan, *The Feminine Mystique,* 361.

43 Betty Friedan, *"It Changed My Life": Writings on the Women's Movement* (New York: Dell Publishing, 1991), 100, 94.

44 Ibid., 109.

45 Quoted in Monique Bégin, "The Royal Commission on the Status of Women in Canada: Twenty Years Later," in *Challenging Times: The Women's Movement in Canada and the United States*, ed. Constance Backhouse and David H. Flaherty (Montreal: McGill-Queen's University Press, 1992), 22.

46 "Manifesto *DEMAU*, 1966," in *Italian Feminist Thought: A Reader*, ed. Paola Bono and Sandra Kemp (Oxford: Basil Blackwell, 1991), 34–35.

47 Quoted in Donald Meyer, *Sex and Power: The Rise of Women in America, Russia, Sweden, and Italy* (Middletown, CT: Wesleyan University Press, 1987), 199.

48 Quoted in Paula Giddings, *When and Where I Enter: The Impact of Black Women on Race and Sex in America* (Bantam Books: Toronto, 1984), 326, 328.

49 William H. Chafe, *The Paradox of Change: American Women in the 20th Century* (New York: Oxford University Press, 1991), 170.

50 Gisela Kaplan, *Contemporary Western European Feminism* (New York: New York University Press, 1992), 29.

51 Ann Popkin, "The Personal is Political: The Women's Liberation Movement," in *They Should Have Served That Cup of Coffee: 7 Radicals Remember the 60s*, ed. D. Custer (Boston: South End Press, 1979), 189.

52 Quoted in Sara Evans, *Personal Politics: The Roots of Women's Liberation in the Civil Rights Movement and the New Left* (New York: Random House, 1979), 86–87.

53 Quoted in Alice Echols, *Daring to Be Bad: Radical Feminism in America 1967–1975* (Minneapolis: University of Minnesota Press, 1989), 49, 117.

54 Quoted in Maren Lockwood Carden, *The New Feminist Movement* (New York: Russell Sage Foundation, 1974), 62.

55 Quoted in Echols, *Daring to Be Bad*, 118–19.

56 Quoted in Duchen, *Women's Rights and Women's Lives*, 203.

57 *Women Unite! An Anthology of the Canadian Women's Movement* (Canadian Women's Educational Press, Toronto, 1972), 9.

58 Eleonore Eckmann Pisciotta, "The Strength and the Powerlessness of the New Italian Women's Movement: The Case of Abortion," in *The New Women's Movement: Feminism and Political Power in Europe and the USA*, ed. Drude Dahlerup (London: SAGE Publications, 1986), 26.

59 Friedan, *"It Changed My Life,"* 138–39.

60 Quoted in A. Coote and B. Campbell, *Sweet Freedom: The Struggle for Women's Liberation* (Oxford: Basil Blackwell, 1982), 34.

61 Petra De Vries, "Feminism in the Netherlands," *Women's Studies International Quarterly* 4, 4 (1981): 392.

62 Robin Morgan, *Going Too Far: The Personal Chronicle of a Feminist* (New York: Vintage Books, 1968), 117.

63 "Redstockings Manifesto," in *sisterhood is powerful: An Anthology of Writings from the Women's Liberation Movement*, ed. Robin Morgan (New York: Vintage Books, 1970), 534.

64 Morgan, *Going Too Far*, 74.

[65] Ibid., 9.

[66] Popkin, "The Personal is Political," 192–93.

[67] Quoted in Coote and Campbell, *Sweet Freedom,* 25.

[68] Sarah M. Evans, *Born for Liberty: A History of Women in America* (New York: Free Press, 1989), 288–89.

[69] Quoted in Claire Duchen, *Feminism in France: From May '68 to Mitterand* (London: Routledge and Kegan Paul, 1986), 17.

[70] Friedan, *"It Changed My Life,"* xx.

[71] Ibid., 202, 236.

[72] Quoted in Lillian Faderman, *Odd Girls and Twilight Lovers: A History of Lesbian Life in Twentieth-Century America* (New York: Columbia University Press, 1991), 208.

[73] Barbara Smith, "Racism and Women's Studies," in *All the Women Are White, All the Blacks Are Men, But Some of Us Are Brave: Black Women's Studies,* ed. Gloria T. Hull, Patricia Bell Scott, and Barbara Smith (New York: Feminist Press, 1982), 49.

Conclusion

"*W*hat is *your* message?" asked a reader, responding to an early draft of the middle chapters of this book. There was more than a trace of exasperation in her question as she absorbed my generally sombre assessment of feminism in the past. "If it is that historical feminism is flawed, and a minority concern, this certainly comes across," she concluded. "Do you *want* this to be your message?"

Yes and no. Feminism in the past *was* a minority concern. It could not have been anything but, given its revolutionary potential. If feminists themselves became despondent over their slow progress, antifeminists never wavered from their belief that feminism would destroy the family and society. One may also judge that, from our perspective, early feminism was "flawed"—that is, few feminists today would uncritically adopt the perspectives and strategies of their forerunners. But assessment does not exclude appreciation. We can and should appreciate early feminist achievements while recognizing the limitations. The historical context makes both understandable.

Take, for example, the difficulties of acquiring a feminist consciousness before the eighteenth century. We have seen how resourceful women were during the Middle Ages and Reformation in exploiting religious and cultural symbols, such as chastity, prophecy, or unruliness. Their strategy widened their practical options, enabling them to escape the restrictions of the patriarchal family, challenge authority, or find avenues of self-expression. Were these strategies, as has been claimed, a *feminism of action*? To identify them as such underestimates both the ability of patriarchy to accommodate dissent and the ingenuity of individuals to mould their environment. The lives of Hildegard of Bingen and Margery Kempe reflect the degree to which traditional society could accommodate resistance without challenging the sexual hierarchy that was so fundamental to it. When a twelfth-century contemporary observed that Hildegard "has transcended female subjection by a lofty height,"[1] he confirmed that female subjection was the destiny of women in general. Hildegard's use of female or androgynous symbolism and her celebration of the Virgin Mary may have been indirect protests against the devaluation of women in her culture, but she made no criticism of women's subordination. Although she celebrated the martyred virgins of the early church, she did not seek female role models. Margery Kempe, in contrast, looked to contemporary and past women, comparing herself to Birgetta of Sweden and seeking counsel with Julian of Norwich. But Margery was essentially alone in the world, whereas Hildegard had the support of a female community. More important, neither woman identified with women per se; they made no claims on behalf of all women. Their identification and appreciation of what was female contributed to or expressed a *female* culture but, as we have seen in Chapter 2, it was not a *feminist* culture. Scholar Naomi Black has defined feminism broadly as "the record of women's assertion of their autonomy and of the impact of their wishes on society,"[2] but women can and did assert their autonomy in many different and often subtle ways, not necessarily in the form of a direct challenge to gender hierarchy. When they did engage in direct confrontation with patriarchy, as did Joan of Arc or the seventeenth-century Puritan Anne Hutchinson, the authorities acted quickly and decisively to silence them.

Feminism begins with the recognition that all women, because of their gender, suffer injustice and with the refusal to accept that situation. The first women to leave written records of their awareness of and protest against women's subjection were those who entered the public sphere as scholars or writers. Studying, writing, or other forms of creative expression could be considered feminist acts as long as those activities were proscribed for women. From Christine de Pizan in the fifteenth century to Simone de Beauvoir in the twentieth, intellectual or creative women had to cope with the fact that contemporaries often found such "masculine" activity inappropriate. Painfully conscious of their uniqueness, women artists tried to disarm their critics by adopting or subtly subverting such genres as lyric poetry, the novel, or portrait painting. Some used such forms to comment unfavourably on female passivity and heterosexual relations, especially in marriage, and to affirm female friendships, initiative, or sexuality.

The bolder writers were explicit in their defence of women's intellectual, social, or sexual potential. They joined a feminism of action to a feminism of content, what one might call a *literary*, or *intellectual*, *feminism*—that is, a "tradition of women thinking about women and sexual politics."[3] Our first records of such feminism date from the fifteenth century: the well-known protest of Christine de Pizan against misogyny in literature, or the brief but ardent defence of the Italian humanist Cassandra Fedele of woman's right to study. Christine de Pizan and Cassandra Fedele were feminists not so much because they wrote but because of what they wrote. When we compare them to Bathsua Makin, for example, the seventeenth-century educator who signed a man's name to her defence of women's education, or to the Italian humanists who retreated without protest from public view, we can appreciate the courage it took to name the problem.

In naming the problem, however, these early feminists pointed to individuals rather than institutions. At most, they appealed for a change in attitudes. Inasmuch as social institutions were thought to mirror the divine order, these institutions, and the gender hierarchy they supported, were assumed unalterable. Nonetheless, early feminists believed that such institutions should not prevent individuals from using the potential that God had given them. In this sense, these literary feminists were, like the medieval mystics, appreciative of their own exceptionality. Christine de Pizan, Cassandra Fedele, and the other learned women who argued on behalf of women were really arguing on behalf of the exceptional woman who alone had the means to become educated. Class was as fundamental as gender to their perspective, and such an approach inhibited them from recognizing the wider structural barriers to women's equality. Although Christine de Pizan claimed to welcome women from all classes in her allegorical city, she never identified with poor women struggling to feed their families on one-third the wages of men. Learned women and those in a variety of nontraditional roles, from poets to queens, challenged sexual inequity by demanding that gender barriers not apply to themselves and other "woman worthies." They hoped for the relaxation, not the overthrow, of gender hierarchy. Although it was a momentous step when Christine de Pizan and others began writing about the injustices that they perceived, they still understood all women in their own image. Social privilege was an inherent component of early feminism and would continue to be for most manifestations of feminism throughout the nineteenth and twentieth centuries.

To summarize, then, even when women writers or painters identified with other women, they stressed the exceptional rather than the ordinary, looked to individuals rather than institutions, and at most reflected the values of a female culture. Pro-woman participants in the querelle des femmes, like François Poullain de la Barre in the seventeenth century, could suggest that women be allowed to pursue careers in science, theology, or law, but in the literary context of the querelle these suggestions had no concrete application. The first practical proposal for changing women's lives, which introduces a second stage of feminism, came from the early-eighteenth-century Englishwoman, Mary Astell, who linked a critique of marriage to a plan for a women's retreat or college that would allow women to choose husbands more carefully, or perhaps not at all. Although Astell was a social conservative, her thought reflected the new possibilities that Cartesianism and political liberalism opened up in the seventeenth century. These possibilities dimmed as masculine values came to dominate the Scientific Revolution and the eighteenth-century Enlightenment, but bold critics like Madame de Beaumer and the Marquis de Condorcet embraced an outspoken feminism in the stimulating atmosphere of prerevolutionary France. In championing nontraditional role models for working women as well as women worthies, Beaumer realized what had been hinted at in Christine de Pizan's city—that is, a cross-class awareness of gender injustice. At the end of the eighteenth century, during the French Revolution, women from the working class, such as Olympe de Gouges, developed specific political proposals as their contribution to feminism. For the most part, they, like Condorcet and Mary Wollstonecraft, favoured a *liberal feminism*, which would advance women's legal and political rights in keeping with the liberal goals and language of the American and French revolutions. They demanded the same rights and opportunities for women as most revolutionaries were demanding for men.

While liberal feminism affirmed the similarities between women and men, the political and economic changes of the late eighteenth and early nineteenth centuries helped to define women as different from men. The

ideology of domesticity and of separate spheres, the identification of religion
and prescriptive morality with women, and the idea of gender difference in
French romanticism and utopian socialism all encouraged an appreciation of
the "bonds" of womanhood, understood, as historian Nancy Cott has
pointed out, as connective as well as oppressive. The resulting sense of mission gave women the inspiration and courage to take a position on moral and
political issues.

The rapid changes of the early and mid-nineteenth century, the ideology
of liberalism, and the idea of progress encouraged women and men to organize to ameliorate all aspects of their society, from health care to the abolition
of slavery to the self-determination of oppressed nationalities. In the United
States and Britain, a third stage of feminism, *organized feminism*, or the
beginnings of the first wave, took the form of movements to improve the status of women by increasing their opportunities. The strategy was similar in
other Western countries, but the goals were often more modest: to make society more responsive to women's needs and abilities. That in fact was the goal
of American educator Catharine Beecher in the first half of the nineteenth
century. In Germany she would have been a radical figure, whereas in the
United States her aversion to women's public role compares unfavourably to
the stand taken by women in the antislavery movement.

The core of feminism was always its revolutionary challenge to gender
hierarchy, but the form this took and its repercussions varied enormously in
different political contexts. Making society more responsive to women's needs
could as easily mean organizing to perpetuate the status quo as to challenge
it; in other words, women could organize to combat as well as to promote
feminism. French women organized against secular education for girls,
German women organized against socialism, American women organized
against women's suffrage. The ideology of *maternal feminism*, based upon
gender difference, was inherently neither radical nor conservative but could
be either depending upon the context. It was radical when used by the French
femmes nouvelles or the German League for Protection of Motherhood and
Sexual Reform but reassuring in the hands of French Christian feminists or
most moderate suffragists. Liberals or socialists would argue that women's
values be used to transform politics; liberals or conservatives that women's
higher morality be used to reconcile political differences, or even restore family and religious values. Maternal feminism could bridge differences of class,
race, or marital status, or could reinforce them.

What I have stressed as most positive in first-wave feminism was the
attempt by women to form their own autonomous groups, but it is fair to
note that their contemporaries, male or female, did not always agree that
independent organizations were the answer. The radical Unitarians in Britain
in the 1830s and 1840s believed it insufficient for women to organize separately for their rights rather than to pursue a program of more far-reaching
reform in tandem with men. In Owenite and Saint-Simonian socialism, as
well, women's emancipation had been part of a broader reform program. In
the late nineteenth and early twentieth centuries, many women found the

emphasis in middle-class feminist organizations too narrow and preferred to join mixed-sex groups with more radical agendas. Whether working for German, French, or Canadian socialism, Spanish anarchism, or Irish nationalism, their experiences were remarkably similar. The problem was the difficulty both men and women had in recognizing and confronting the gender discrimination that seems to have been inevitable in mixed organizations. This remained true of radical and reform movements throughout the nineteenth and twentieth centuries. On the other hand, women organizing on their own found it difficult to summon the resources necessary to make an impact. They looked for allies and, in the process, often modified their agendas to incorporate more conservative goals.

The unifying factor of first-wave feminist movements was the desire of women to take control of their lives. In reflecting the interests of relatively privileged women, these movements represent a turn toward conservatism when compared to the radicalism of the early nineteenth century. This conservatism was exemplified in the tendency to prioritize gender over class and race. The conservatism of first-wave feminism has perplexed feminist historians, but it is reflective of the greater stake that all social groups came to have in the status quo as materialism and mass politics evolved in the second half of the century. Feminists were no better or worse than their contemporaries. Because they believed that, as women, they were uniquely placed to sympathize with other oppressed groups does not mean that they were right. What is impressive is the degree to which many acted on that belief and genuinely tried to assist other women in achieving their goals.

The concern of later first-wave feminists to court respectability becomes more understandable when we appreciate the hostility evoked by women acting in their own self-interest. The immediate result was usually a counter-reaction that attempted to put women back in their place. The tone of moral righteousness women reformers adopted gave them the courage they needed for public confrontations, and their appeal to motherhood was as much a tactic as a conviction. Did it work? It may be, as historian Carolyn Johnston has noted, that American feminists had more success when they appeared to support the family than when they appeared to threaten it,[4] but there were many instances, from married women's property laws to state support for maternity, where feminist arguments may have been irrelevant to politicians, or even harmful. At times, it seems that the only effect organized feminism had was to inflame the opposition.

Consider the case of British suffragism. The militancy of the suffragettes challenged the norms of proper feminine behaviour, but it also reinforced the old notion of woman as hysterical and irrational. Did it delay the grant of women's suffrage in Britain? Or did it aid it by making the moderate suffragist demands seem reasonable? Or did the First World War make both strategies irrelevant? Was the suffrage gain the fruit of fifty years of patient work? Supporting the last argument is the observation of English historian Martin Pugh that other democratic reforms commonly took a half century or more to implement.[5]

Even if we deem suffrage a feminist victory, it is hard to be enthusiastic about its aftermath. The gains of the war years—during both the First and Second World Wars—were swamped by the reassertion of normality at their end. Action, reaction—this is the pattern stretching back throughout the centuries, perhaps back to early Christianity: the radicalism of Jesus offset by the reaction of Paul, or the bishops; the opportunities enjoyed both by secular and religious women in the early Middle Ages checked by the eleventh-century Gregorian reform movement; the extremism of women's religious practices and claims in the late Middle Ages and Reformation period curbed by the consolidation of church and state; the opportunities offered by Newtonian science and the Enlightenment countered by the eighteenth-century cult of womanhood; late-eighteenth-century revolutionary activism checked by the idea of republican motherhood; the radicalism of the early and mid-nineteenth century measured against the conservatism of the later decades; and, neither last nor least, the two world wars and the postwar backlash to each. It becomes a familiar litany.

What, then, is the moral or, rather, the message? First, we must not minimize the obstacles to feminism. Setbacks have been, and can be expected to be, the norm. The apparent contraction of feminism in the 1980s and 1990s after the heady seventies does not mean its end. It is a cause for reflection, not for depression. As bell hooks has written, it is "commitment to protracted struggle that makes revolution possible."[6]

Secondly, the lack of an obvious cause-and-effect relationship between tactics and gains is liberating; it frees feminists from any single-minded "strategy for success." Moderation or militancy, radicalism or respectability, equal rights or social reform—all have to be evaluated within a particular context. It may seem, as many have maintained, that feminism will never have any chance of success unless it becomes a mass movement, unless feminists find common ground with women who represent the mainstream. But that is precisely when feminism ceases to be feminism, when it fails to offer a radical alternative to the status quo. And it is the status quo that feminists have consistently targeted, whether in the form of demanding that women have the right to study, write, or speak; the right or duty to take responsibility for private and public life; or the obligation to act to end the oppression of all women. In times of backlash, women have adapted as they believed necessary, whether consciously or not; but in weighing the reaction, we should not lose sight of the action that set the terms of the debate.

Ultimately, what makes activism worthwhile is not the chance of success but the process of struggle. It is the self-determination individuals achieve over their own lives and the supportive culture they create in league with other women or with men in a common fight. It is empowering, therefore, to recognize the efforts of activists over so many centuries while appreciating the obstacles that still exist.

NOTES

1   Quoted in Barbara Newman, *Sister of Wisdom: St. Hildegard's Theology of the Feminine* (Berkeley: University of California Press, 1987), 2.

2   Naomi Black, *Social Feminism* (Ithaca, NY: Cornell University Press, 1989), 3.

3   Joan Kelly, "Early Feminist Theory and the *Querelle des Femmes*, 1400–1789," *Signs: Journal of Women in Culture and Society* 8, 1 (1982): 5.

4   Carolyn Johnston, *Sexual Power: Feminism and the Family in America* (Tuscaloosa: University of Alabama Press, 1992), x.

5   Martin Pugh, *Women and the Women's Movement in Britain, 1914–59* (London: Macmillan, 1992), 312.

6   bell hooks, *Feminist Theory: From Margin to Center* (Boston: South End Press, 1984), 159.

Suggestions for Further Reading

GENERAL INTRODUCTIONS

Women's History

Anderson, Bonnie S., and Judith P. Zinsser. *A History of Their Own: Women in Europe from Prehistory to the Present.* 2 vols. New York: Harper & Row, 1988.

Bridenthal, Renate, Claudia Koonz, and Susan Stuard, eds. *Becoming Visible: Women in European History.* 2nd ed. Boston: Houghton Mifflin, 1987.

Faderman, Lillian. *Surpassing the Love of Men: Romantic Friendship and Love Between Women from the Renaissance to the Present.* New York: William Morrow, 1981.

Gilbert, Sandra M., and Susan Gubar. *The Madwoman in the Attic: The Woman Writer and the Nineteenth-Century Literary Imagination.* New Haven, CT: Yale University Press, 1979.

Jones, Jacqueline. *Labor of Love, Labor of Sorrow: Black Women, Work and the Family from Slavery to the Present.* New York: Basic Books, 1985.

Matthews, Glenna. *The Rise of Public Woman: Woman's Power and Woman's Place in the United States, 1630–1970.* New York: Oxford University Press, 1992.

Prentice, Alison, Paula Bourne, Gail Cuthbert Brandt, Beth Light, Wendy Mitchinson, and Naomi Black. *Canadian Women: A History.* Toronto: Harcourt Brace Jovanovich, 1988.

Shepherd, Naomi. *A Price Below Rubies: Jewish Women as Rebels and Radicals.* London: Weidenfeld & Nicolson, 1993.

Smith, Bonnie G. *Changing Lives: Women in European History since 1700.* Lexington, MA: D.C. Heath, 1989.

Woloch, Nancy. *Women and the American Experience: A Concise History.* New York: Alfred A. Knopf, 1984.

Modern Feminist Theory

Eisenstein, Hester. *Contemporary Feminist Thought.* London: Unwin, 1984.

Donovan, Josephine. *Feminist Theory: The Intellectual Traditions of American Feminism.* 2nd ed. New York: Continuum, 1992.

hooks, bell. *Feminist Theory: From Margin to Center.* Boston: South End Press, 1984.

Tong, Rosemarie. *Feminist Thought: A Comprehensive Introduction.* Boulder, CA: Westview Press, 1989.

General Histories of Feminism

Banks, Olive. *Faces of Feminism: A Study of Feminism as a Social Movement.* 2nd ed. Oxford: Basil Blackwell, 1986.

Cott, Nancy F. "What's in a Name? The Limits of 'Social Feminism': or, Expanding the Vocabulary of Women's History." *Journal of American History* 76 (1988): 809–29.

Eisenstein, Zillah R. *The Radical Future of Liberal Feminism.* Boston: Northeastern University Press, 1981.

Evans, Richard J. "The Concept of Feminism: Notes for Practicing Historians." In *German Women in the Eighteenth and Nineteenth Centuries: A Social and Literary History.* Ed. Ruth-Ellen B. Joeres and Mary Jo Maynes, 247–58. Bloomington: Indiana University Press, 1986.

Johnston, Carolyn. *Sexual Power: Feminism and the Family in America.* Tuscaloosa: University of Alabama Press, 1992.

Lerner, Gerda. *The Creation of Feminist Consciousness: From the Middle Ages to 1870.* New York: Oxford University Press, 1993.

Offen, Karen. "Defining Feminism: A Comparative Historical Approach." *Signs: Journal of Women in Culture and Society* 14 (Autumn 1988): 119–57.

Rendall, Jane. *The Origins of Modern Feminism: Women in Britain, France, and the United States 1780–1860.* Basingstoke: Macmillan, 1985.

Riley, Denise. *"Am I That Name?" Feminism and the Category of "Women" in History.* Minneapolis: University of Minnesota Press, 1988.

Rowbotham, Sheila. *Women in Movement: Feminism and Social Action.* New York: Routledge, 1992.

Anthologies of Primary Sources

Allen, Beverly, Muriel Kittel, and Keala Jane Jewell, eds. *The Defiant Muse: Italian Feminist Poems from the Middle Ages to the Present.* New York: Feminist Press, 1986.

Bell, Susan Groag, and Karen M. Offen, eds. *Women, the Family, and Freedom: The Debate in Documents.* Vol. 1. *1750–1880.* Vol. 2. *1880–1950.* Stanford: Stanford University Press, 1983.

Cocalis, Susan L., ed. *The Defiant Muse: German Feminist Poems from the Middle Ages to the Present.* New York: Feminist Press, 1986.

Flores, Angel, and Kate Flores, eds. *The Defiant Muse: Hispanic Feminist Poems from the Middle Ages to the Present.* New York: Feminist Press, 1986.

Langley, Winston E., and Vivian C. Fox, eds. *Women's Rights in the United States: A Documentary History.* Westport, CT: Greenwood Press, 1994.

McDonald, Lynn. *The Women Founders of the Social Sciences.* Ottawa: Carleton University Press, 1994.

O'Faolain, Julia, and Lauro Martines, eds. *Not in God's Image: Women in History from the Greeks to the Victorians.* New York: Harper & Row, 1973.

Rossi, Alice, ed. *The Feminist Papers: From Adams to de Beauvoir.* New York: Columbia University Press, 1973.

Spender, Dale, ed. *Feminist Theorists: Three Centuries of Key Women Thinkers.* New York: Pantheon Books, 1983.

Stanton, Domna, ed. *The Defiant Muse: French Feminist Poems from the Middle Ages to the Present.* New York: Feminist Press, 1986.

Waithe, Mary Ellen, ed. *A History of Women Philosophers.* Vol. 2. *Medieval, Renaissance and Enlightenment Women Philosophers, A.D. 500–1600.* Dordrecht: Kluwer, 1989.

EARLY CHRISTIAN ERA AND THE MIDDLE AGES

General Studies

Atkinson, Clarissa W. *The Oldest Vocation: Christian Motherhood in the Middle Ages.* Ithaca, NY: Cornell University Press, 1991.

Bennett, Judith M., Elizabeth A. Clark, Jean F. O'Barr, B. Anne Vilen, and Sarah Westphal-Wihl, eds. *Sisters and Workers in the Middle Ages.* Chicago: University of Chicago Press, 1989.

Bloch, R. Howard. *Medieval Misogyny and the Invention of Western Romantic Love.* Chicago: University of Chicago Press, 1991.

Brown, Peter. *The Body and Society: Men, Women, and Sexual Renunciation in Early Christianity.* New York: Columbia University Press, 1988.

Bynum, Carolyn Walker. *Holy Feast and Holy Fast: The Religious Significance of Food to Medieval Women.* Berkeley: University of California Press, 1987.

Bynum, Carolyn Walker, Stevan Harrell, and Paula Richman, eds. *Gender and Religion: On the Complexity of Symbols.* Boston: Beacon Press, 1986.

Davies, Stevan L. *The Revolt of the Widows: The Social World of the Apocryphal Acts.* Carbondale: Southern Illinois University Press, 1980.

Dronke, Peter. *Women Writers of the Middle Ages: A Critical Study of Texts from Perpetua (+202) to Marguerite Porète (+1310).* Cambridge: Cambridge University Press, 1991.

Fiorenza, Elisabeth Schussler. *In Memory of Her: A Feminist Theological Reconstruction of Christian Origins.* New York: Crossroad, 1986.

Herlihy, David. *Opera Muliebria: Women and Work in Medieval Europe.* New York: McGraw-Hill, 1990.

Labarge, Margaret Wade. *A Small Sound of the Trumpet: Women in Medieval Life.* Boston: Beacon Press, 1986.

McDonnell, Ernest W. *The Beguines and Beghards in Medieval Culture.* 2nd ed. New Brunswick, NJ: Rutgers University Press, 1969.

McNamara, Jo Ann. *A New Song: Celibate Women in the First Three Christian Centuries.* New York: Harrington Park Press, 1985.

Pagels, Elaine. *Adam, Eve, and the Serpent.* New York: Random House, 1988.

———. *The Gnostic Gospels.* New York: Vintage Books, 1979.

Petroff, Elizabeth Alvilda. *Body and Soul: Essays on Medieval Women and Mysticism.* New York: Oxford University Press, 1994.

Ruether, Rosemary, and Eleanor McLaughlin, eds. *Women of Spirit: Female Leadership in the Jewish and Christian Traditions.* New York: Simon & Schuster, 1979.

Shahar, Shulamith. *The Fourth Estate: A History of Women in the Middle Ages.* London: Routledge, 1983.

Warner, Marina. *Alone of All Her Sex: The Myth and the Cult of the Virgin Mary.* New York: Vintage Books, 1983.

Wemple, Suzanne Fonay. *Women in Frankish Society: Marriage and the Cloister 500 to 900.* Philadelphia: University of Pennsylvania Press, 1981.

Wiesner, Merry E. "Women's Defense of Their Public Role." In *Women in the Middle Ages and the Renaissance: Literary and Historical Perspectives.* Ed. Mary Beth Rose, 1–27. Syracuse, NY: Syracuse University Press, 1986.

Anthologies of Primary Sources

Blamires, Alcuin, ed. *Woman Defamed and Woman Defended: An Anthology of Medieval Texts.* Oxford: Clarendon Press, 1992.

Petroff, Elizabeth Alvilda, ed. *Medieval Women's Visionary Literature.* New York: Oxford University Press, 1986.

Wilson, Katharina M., ed. *Medieval Women Writers.* Athens: University of Georgia Press, 1984.

Zum Brunn, Emilie, and Georgette Epiney-Burgard, eds. *Women Mystics in Medieval Europe.* New York: Paragon House, 1989.

Individuals Mentioned in the Text

Atkinson, Clarissa W. *Mystic and Pilgrim: The Book and the World of Margery Kempe.* Ithaca, NY: Cornell University Press, 1983.

Barstow, Anne Llewellyn. *Joan of Arc: Heretic, Mystic, Shaman.* Lewiston, NY: Edwin Mellen Press, 1986.

Christina of Markyate. *The Life of Christina of Markyate: A Twelfth Century Recluse.* Ed. and trans. Charles H. Talbot. Oxford: Clarendon Press, 1959.

Flanagan, Sabina. *Hildegard of Bingen, 1098–1179: A Visionary Life.* London: Routledge, 1989.

Heloise and Peter Abelard. *The Letters of Heloise and Abelard.* Trans. Betty Radice. Harmondsworth: Penguin Books, 1974.

Hildegard of Bingen. *Hildegard of Bingen: Mystical Writings.* Ed. Fiona Bowie and Oliver Davies. New York: Crossroad, 1990.

Margery Kempe. *The Book of Margery Kempe.* Trans. B.A. Windeatt. London: Penguin Books, 1985.

McEntire, Sandra J., ed. *Margery Kempe: A Book of Essays.* New York: Garland, 1992.

Mechthild von Magdeburg. *Flowing Light of the Divinity.* Ed. Susan Clark. Trans. Christiane Mesch Galvani. New York: Garland Publishing, 1991.

Newman, Barbara. *Sister of Wisdom: St. Hildegard's Theology of the Feminine.* Berkeley: University of California Press, 1987.

Raymond of Capua. *The Life of Catherine of Siena.* Trans. Conleth Kearns. Wilmington, DE: Michael Glazier, 1980.

TRADITIONAL SOCIETY (FIFTEENTH THROUGH EIGHTEENTH CENTURIES)

Anthologies of Primary Sources

Ferguson, Moira, ed. *First Feminists: British Women Writers 1578–1799.* Bloomington: Indiana University Press, 1985.

Goreau, Angeline, ed. *The Whole Duty of a Woman: Female Writers in Seventeenth-Century England.* Garden City, NY: Dial Press, 1985.

Henderson, Katherine Usher, and Barbara F. McManus, eds. *Half Humankind: Contexts and Texts of the Controversy about Women in England, 1540–1640.* Urbana: University of Illinois Press, 1985.

King, Margaret L., and Albert Rabil, Jr., eds. *Her Immaculate Hand: Selected Works by and about the Women Humanists of Quattrocento Italy.* Binghamton, NY: Medieval and Renaissance Texts and Studies, 1983.

Levy, Darline Gay, Harriet Branson Applewhite, and Mary Durham Johnson, eds. *Women in Revolutionary Paris, 1789–1795: Selected Documents Translated with Notes and Commentary.* Urbana: University of Illinois Press, 1979.

Travitsky, Betty, ed. *The Paradise of Women: Writings by Englishwomen of the Renaissance.* Westport, CT: Greenwood Press, 1981.

Wilson, Katharina M., ed. *Women Writers of the Renaissance and Reformation.* Athens: University of Georgia Press, 1987.

Wilson, Katharina M., and Frank J. Warnke, eds. *Women Writers of the Seventeenth Century.* Athens: University of Georgia Press, 1989.

Comparative Studies

Benson, Pamela Joseph. *The Invention of Renaissance Woman: The Challenge of Female Independence in the Literature and Thought of Italy and England.* University Park: University of Pennsylvania Press, 1992.

Brink, J.R., ed. *Female Scholars: A Tradition of Learned Women Before 1800.* Montreal: Eden Press, 1980.

Burke, Janet M., "Freemasonry, Friendship and Noblewomen: The Role of the Secret Society in Bringing Enlightenment Thought to Pre-Revolutionary Women Elites." *History of European Ideas* 10, 3 (1989): 283–93.

Davis, Natalie Zemon. "Women on Top." In *Society and Culture in Early Modern France.* Stanford: Stanford University Press, 1975.

Fritz, Paul, and Richard Morton, eds. *Woman in the 18th Century and Other Essays.* Toronto: Samuel Stevens Hakkert, 1976.

Greaves, Richard L., ed. *Triumph over Silence: Women in Protestant History.* Westport, CT: Greenwood Press, 1985.

Hopkins, Lisa. *Women Who Would be Kings: Female Rulers of the Sixteenth Century.* London: Vision Press, 1991.

Hunt, Margaret, Margaret Jacobs, Phyllis Mack, and Ruth Perry. *Women and the Enlightenment.* New York: Haworth, 1984.

Jones, Ann Rosalind. *The Currency of Eros: Women's Love Lyric in Europe, 1540–1620.* Bloomington: Indiana University Press, 1990.

Jordan, Constance. *Renaissance Feminism: Literary Texts and Political Models.* Ithaca, NY: Cornell University Press, 1990.

Kelly, Joan. "Early Feminist Theory and the Querelle des Femmes, 1400–1789." In *Women, History and Theory: The Essays of Joan Kelly.* Chicago: University of Chicago Press, 1984.

Kelso, Ruth. *Doctrine for the Lady of the Renaissance.* Urbana: University of Illinois Press, 1956.

Labalme, Patricia, ed. *Beyond Their Sex: Learned Women of the European Past.* New York: New York University Press, 1980.

Marshall, Sherrin, ed. *Women in Reformation and Counter-Reformation Europe: Private and Public Worlds.* Bloomington: Indiana University Press, 1989.

Schiebinger, Londa. *The Mind Has No Sex? Women in the Origins of Modern Science.* Cambridge: Harvard University Press, 1989.

Sommerville, Margaret. *Sex and Subjection: Attitudes to Women in Early-Modern Society.* London: Arnold, 1995.

Wiesner, Merry E. *Women and Gender in Early Modern Europe.* Cambridge: Cambridge University Press, 1992.

Wiltenburg, Joy. *Disorderly Women and Female Power in the Street Literature of Early Modern England and Germany.* Charlottesville: University Press of Virginia, 1992.

England

Astell, Mary. *The First English Feminist: Reflections Upon Marriage and Other Writings by Mary Astell.* Ed. Bridget Hill. Aldershot: Gower Publishing, 1986.

Bassnett, Susan. *Elizabeth I: A Feminist Perspective.* Berg: Oxford, 1988.

Beilin, Elaine V. *Redeeming Eve: Women Writers of the English Renaissance.* Princeton, NJ: Princeton University Press, 1987.

Browne, Alice. *The Eighteenth Century Feminist Mind.* Brighton: Harvester Press, 1987.

Charke, Charlotte, with Fidelis Morgan. *The Well-Known Troublemaker: A Life of Charlotte Charke/Fidelis Morgan with Charlotte Charke.* London: Faber and Faber, 1988.

Flexner, Eleanor. *Mary Wollstonecraft: A Biography.* Baltimore: Penguin Books, 1972.

Fraser, Antonia. *The Weaker Vessel: Woman's Lot in Seventeenth-Century England.* London: Methuen, 1984.

Goreau, Angeline. *Reconstructing Aphra: A Social Biography of Aphra Behn.* New York: Dial Press, 1980.

Hannay, Margaret, ed. *Silent but for the Word: Tudor Women as Patrons, Translators, and Writers of Religious Works.* Kent, OH: Kent State University Press, 1985.

Heisch, A. "Queen Elizabeth and the Persistence of Patriarchy." *Feminist Review* 4 (1980): 45–78.

Hobby, Elaine. "Katherine Philips: Seventeenth-Century Lesbian Poet." In *What Lesbians Do in Books.* Ed. Elaine Hobby and Chris White, 183–204. London: Women's Press, 1991.

———. *Virtue of Necessity: English Women's Writing 1649–88.* London: Virago, 1988.

Howe, Elizabeth. *The First English Actresses: Women and Drama, 1660–1700.* Cambridge: Cambridge University Press 1992.

Hull, Suzanne. *Chaste, Silent and Obedient: English Books for Women, 1475–1640.* San Marino, CA: Huntington Library, 1982.

James, Regina. "Mary, Mary, Quite Contrary, Or, Mary Astell and Mary Wollstonecraft Compared." In *Studies in Eighteenth-Century Culture.* Vol. 5. Ed. Ronald C. Rosbottom, 121–39. Madison: University of Wisconsin Press, 1976.

Jardine, Lisa. *Still Harping on Daughters: Women and Drama in the Age of Shakespeare.* 2nd ed. New York: Columbia University Press, 1989.

Kinnaird, Joan K. "Mary Astell and the Conservative Contribution to English Feminism." *Journal of British Studies* 19, 1 (1979): 53–75.

Krontiris, Tina. *Oppositional Voices: Women as Writers and Translators of Literature in the English Renaissance.* London: Routledge, 1992.

Mack, Phyllis. *Visionary Women: Ecstatic Prophecy in Seventeenth-Century England.* Berkeley: University of California Press, 1992.

Mendelson, Sara Heller. *The Mental World of Stuart Women: Three Studies.* Brighton: Harvester, 1987.

Myers, Sylvia Harcstark. *The Bluestocking Circle: Women, Friendship, and the Life of the Mind in Eighteenth-Century England.* Oxford: Clarendon Press, 1990.

Offen, Karen. "Was Mary Wollstonecraft a Feminist? A Contextual Re-reading of a Vindication of the Rights of Woman, 1792–1992." In *Quilting a New Canon: Feminist and Gender Studies.* Ed. Uma Parameswaran. Toronto: Sister Vision, 1995.

Pearson, Jacqueline. *The Prostituted Muse: Images of Women and Women Dramatists 1642–1737.* New York: Harvester-Wheatsheaf, 1988.

Perry, Ruth. *The Celebrated Mary Astell: An Early English Feminist.* Chicago: University of Chicago Press, 1986.

Poovey, Mary. *The Proper Lady and the Woman Writer: Ideology as Style in the Works of Mary Wollstonecraft, Mary Shelley, and Jane Austen.* Chicago: University of Chicago Press, 1984.

Prior, Mary, ed. *Women in English Society 1500–1800.* London: Methuen, 1985.

Rogers, Katharine M. *Feminism in Eighteenth-Century England.* Urbana: University of Illinois Press, 1982.

Shapiro, Susan C. "Amazons, Hermaphrodites, and Plain Monsters: The 'Masculine' Woman in English Satire and Social Criticism from 1580–1640." *Atlantis* 13, 1 (1987): 65–76.

Shepherd, Simon. *Amazons and Warrior Women: Varieties of Feminism in Seventeenth-Century Drama.* Brighton: Harvester Press, 1981.

Smith, Hilda L. *Reason's Disciples: Seventeenth-Century English Feminists.* Urbana: University of Illinois Press, 1982.

Spencer, Jane. *The Rise of the Woman Novelist: From Aphra Behn to Jane Austen.* Oxford: Basil Blackwell, 1986.

Thomas, Keith. "Women and the Civil War Sects." In *Crisis in Europe: 1560–1660.* Ed. Trevor Aston. New York: Basic Books, 1965.

Turner, Cheryl. *Living By the Pen: Women Writers in the Eighteenth Century.* London: Routledge, 1992.

Ty, Eleanor. *Unsex–d Revolutionaries: Five Women Novelists of the 1790s.* Toronto: University of Toronto Press, 1993.

Wollstonecraft, Mary. *Maria or the Wrongs of Woman.* 1789. Reprint. New York: W.W. Norton, 1975.

———. *A Vindication of the Rights of Woman.* 1792. Reprint. New York: W.W. Norton, 1967.

Woodbridge, Linda. *Women and the English Renaissance: Literature and the Nature of Womankind, 1540–1620.* Urbana: University of Illinois Press, 1984.

France

Brookes, Barbara. "The Feminism of Condorcet and Sophie de Grouchy." *Studies on Voltaire and the Eighteenth Century.* Vol. 189. Oxford: Voltaire Foundation, 1980.

Cameron, Keith. *Louise Labé: Renaissance Poet and Feminist.* New York: Berg, 1990.

Condorcet, Jean-Antoine Nicolas de Caritat, marquis de. *Condorcet: Selected Writings.* Ed. Keith Michael Baker. Indianapolis: Library of Liberal Arts, 1976.

DeJean, Joan. *Tender Geographics: Women and the Origins of the Novel in France.* New York: Columbia University Press, 1991.

Delany, Sheila. "'Mothers to Think Back Through': Who Are They? The Ambiguous Example of Christine de Pizan." In *Medieval Literary Politics: Shapes of Ideology.* Manchester: Manchester University Press, 1990.

Fauré, Christine. *Democracy without Women: Feminism and the Rise of Liberal Individualism in France.* Trans. Claudia Gorbman and John Berks. Bloomington: Indiana University Press, 1991.

Gottlieb, Beatrice. "The Problem of Feminism in the Fifteenth Century." In *Women of the Medieval World: Essays in Honor of John H. Mundy.* Ed. Julius Kirshner and Suzanne F. Wemple, 335–64. Oxford: Basil Blackwell, 1985.

Gelbart, Nina Rattner. *Feminine and Opposition Journalism in Old Regime France: le Journal des Dames.* Berkeley: University of California Press, 1987.

Gibson, Wendy. *Women in Seventeenth-Century France.* New York: St Martin's Press, 1989.

Goodman, Dena. "Enlightenment Salons: The Convergence of Female and Philosophic Ambitions." *Eighteenth-Century Studies* 22, 3 (1989): 329–50.

Gutwirth, Madelyn. *The Twilight of the Goddesses: Women and Representation in the French Revolutionary Era.* New Brunswick, NJ: Rutgers University Press, 1992.

Hufton, Olwen H. *Women and the Limits of Citizenship in the French Revolution. The Donald G. Creighton Lectures 1989.* Toronto: University of Toronto Press, 1992.

Ilsley, Marjorie Henry. *A Daughter of the Renaissance: Marie le Jars de Gournay Her Life and Works.* The Hague: Mouton, 1963.

Jacobs, Eva, W.H. Barber, Jean H. Bloch, F.W. Leakey, and Eileen Le Breton, eds. *Woman and Society in Eighteenth-Century France: Essays in Honour of John Stephenson Spink.* London: Athlone Press, 1979.

Kelly, Linda. *Women of the French Revolution.* London: Hamish Hamilton, 1897.

Landes, Joan B. *Women and the Public Sphere in the Age of the French Revolution.* Ithaca, NY: Cornell University Press, 1988.

Lougee, Carolyn C. *Le Paradis des femmes: Women, Salons and Social Stratification in Seventeenth-Century France.* Princeton, NJ: Princeton University Press, 1976.

Maclean, Ian. *Woman Triumphant: Feminism in French Literature 1610–1652.* Oxford: Clarendon Press, 1977.

Melzer, Sara E., and Leslie W. Rabine, eds. *Rebel Daughters: Women and the French Revolution.* New York: Oxford University Press, 1989.

Pizan, Christine de. *The Book of the City of Ladies.* Trans. Earl Jeffrey Richards. New York: Persea Books, 1982.

———. *The Writings of Christine de Pizan.* Ed. Charity Cannon Willard. New York: Persea Books, 1993.

Poullain de La Barre, François. *The Equality of the Two Sexes.* Trans. A. Daniel Frankforter and Paul J. Morman. Lewiston, NY: Edwin Mellen Press, 1989.

Proctor, Candice E. *Women, Equality, and the French Revolution.* New York: Greenwood Press, 1990.

Qulligan, Maureen. *The Allegory of Female Authority: Christine de Pizan's Cité des Dames.* Ithaca, NY: Cornell University Press, 1991.

Rapley, Elizabeth. *The Dévotes: Women and Church in Seventeenth-Century France.* Montreal: McGill-Queen's University Press, 1990.

Rowan, Mary M. "Seventeenth-Century French Feminism: Two Opposing Attitudes." *International Journal of Women Studies* 3, 3 (1980): 273–91.

Scott, Joan Wallach. "French Feminists and the Rights of 'Man': Olympe de Gouges's Declarations." *History Workshop* 28 (Autumn 1989): 1–21.

Spencer, Samia L., ed. *French Women and the Age of Enlightenment.* Bloomington: Indiana University Press, 1984.

Stewart, Joan Hinde. *Gynographes: French Novels by Women of the Late Eighteenth Century.* Lincoln: University of Nebraska Press, 1993.

Willard, Charity Cannon. *Christine de Pizan, Her Life and Works: A Biography.* New York: Persea, 1984.

Germany and the Netherlands

Dekker, Rudolf M. "Women in Revolt: Popular Protest and Its Social Basis in Holland in the Seventeenth and Eighteenth Centuries." *Theory and Society* 16 (1987): 337–62.

Dekker, Rudolf M., and Lotte C. van de Pol. *The Tradition of Female Transvestism in Early Modern Europe.* New York: St Martin's Press, 1989.

Hertz, Deborah. "Salonieres and Literary Women in Late Eighteenth-Century Berlin." *New German Critique* 14 (Spring 1978): 97–108.

Spain, Italy, and Mexico

Armas, Frederick De. *The Invisible Mistress: Aspects of Feminism and Fantasy in the Golden Age.* Charlottesville, VA: Biblioteca Siglo de Oro, 1976.

Brown, Judith C. *Immodest Acts: The Life of a Lesbian Nun in Renaissance Italy.* New York: Oxford University Press, 1986.

Garrard, Mary D. *Artemisia Gentileschi: The Image of the Female Hero in Italian Baroque Art*. Princeton, NJ: Princeton University Press, 1989.

McKendrick, Melveena. *Woman and Society in the Spanish Drama of the Golden Age: A Study of the Mujer Varonil*. London: Cambridge University Press, 1974.

[Sor Juana de la Cruz]. *A Woman of Genius: The Intellectual Autobiography of Sor Juana Inés de la Cruz*. Ed. and trans. Margaret Sayers Peden. Salisbury, CT: Little Rock Press, 1987.

Perlingieri, Ilya Sandra. *Sofonisba Anguissola: The First Great Woman Artist of the Renaissance*. New York: Rizzoli, 1992.

Rosenthal, Margaret. *The Honest Courtesan: Veronica Franco, Citizen and Writer in Sixteenth-Century Venice*. Chicago: University of Chicago Press, 1993.

Scott, Nina M. "'If You Are not Pleased to Favour Me, Put Me out of Your Mind . . .': Gender and Authority in Sor Juana Inés de la Cruz and the Translation of her Letter to the Reverend Father Maestro Antonio Núñez of the Society of Jesus." *Women's Studies International Forum* 2, 5 (1988): 429–38.

Ward, Marilynn I. "The Feminist Crisis of Sor Juana Ines de la Cruz." *International Journal of Women's Studies* 1, 5 (1978): 475–81.

Zayas, Maria de. *The Enchantments of Love: Amorous and Exemplary Novels*. Trans. H. Patsy Boyer. Berkeley: University of California Press, 1990.

North America

Bacon, Margaret Hope. *Mothers of Feminism: The Story of Quaker Women in America*. San Francisco: Harper & Row, 1986.

Bradstreet, Anne. *The Works of Anne Bradstreet*. Ed. Jeannine Hensley. Cambridge: Belknap Press of Harvard University Press, 1967.

Fox-Genovese, Elizabeth. "Strategies and Forms of Resistance: Focus on Slave Women in the United States." In *Resistance: Studies in African, Caribbean, and Afro-American History*. Ed. Gary Okihiro, 143–65. Amherst: University of Massachusetts Press, 1986.

Kerber, Linda K. *Women of the Republic: Intellect and Ideology in Revolutionary America*. Chapel Hill: University of North Carolina Press, 1980.

Koehler, Lyle. *A Search for Power: The 'Weaker Sex' in Seventeenth-Century New England*. Urbana: University of Illinois Press, 1980.

Martin, Wendy. "Anne Bradstreet's Poetry: A Study of Subversive Piety." In *Shakespeare's Sisters: Feminist Essays on Women Poets*. Ed. Sandra M. Gilbert and Susan Gubar, 19–31. Bloomington: Indiana University Press, 1979.

Norton, Mary Beth. *Liberty's Daughters: The Revolutionary Experience of American Women, 1750–1800*. Boston: Little, Brown, 1980.

Rosenmeier, Rosamond. *Anne Bradstreet Revisited*. Boston: Twayne, 1991.

NINETEENTH AND TWENTIETH CENTURIES

Anthologies of Primary Sources

Bauer, Carol, and Lawrence Ritt, eds. *Free and Ennobled: Source Readings in the Development of Victorian Feminism.* Oxford: Pergamon Press, 1979.

Buhle, Mari Jo, and Paul Buhle, eds. *The Concise History of Woman Suffrage: Selections from the Classic Work of Stanton, Anthony, Gage, and Harper.* Urbana: University of Illinois Press, 1978.

Campbell, Karlyn Kohrs, ed. *Man Cannot Speak for Her.* Vol. 2. *Key Texts of the Early Feminists.* New York: Greenwood Press, 1989.

Hollis, Patricia, ed. *Women in Public: The Women's Movement 1850–1900: Documents of the Victorian Women's Movement.* London: George Allen & Unwin, 1979.

Kraditor, Aileen S., ed. *Up From the Pedestal: Selected Writings in the History of American Feminism.* Chicago: Quadrangle Books, 1968.

Lewis, Jane, ed. *Before the Vote Was Won: Arguments for and Against Women's Suffrage.* New York: Routledge & Kegan Paul, 1987.

Loewenberg, Bert James, and Ruth Bogin, eds. *Black Women in Nineteenth-Century American Life: Their Words, Their Thoughts, Their Feelings.* University Park: Pennsylvania State University Press, 1976.

Moses, Claire Goldberg, and Leslie Wahl Rabine, eds. *Feminism, Socialism, and French Romanticism.* Bloomington: Indiana University Press, 1993.

Waelti–Walters, Jennifer, and Steven C. Hause, eds. *Feminisms of the Belle Epoque: A Historical and Literary Anthology.* Lincoln: University of Nebraska Press, 1994.

Comparative Studies

Bacchi, Carol. "First-Wave Feminism: History's Judgment." In *Australian Women: Feminist Perspectives.* Ed. Norma Grieve and Patricia Grimshaw, 156–67. Melbourne: Oxford University Press, 1981.

Backhouse, Constance, and David H. Flaherty, eds. *Challenging Times: The Women's Movement in Canada and the United States.* Montreal: McGill-Queen's University Press, 1992.

Bammer, Angelika. *Partial Visions: Feminism and Utopianism in the 1970s.* New York: Routledge, 1991.

Black, Naomi. *Social Feminism.* Ithaca, NY: Cornell University Press, 1989.

Bock, Gisela, and Pat Thane, eds. *Maternity and Gender Policies: Women and the Rise of the European Welfare States, 1880s–1950s.* London: Routledge, 1991.

Bolt, Christine. *The Women's Movements in the United States and Britain from the 1790s to the 1920s.* Amherst: University of Massachusetts Press, 1993.

Boxer, Marilyn J., and Jean H. Quataert, eds. *Socialist Women: European Socialism Feminism in the Nineteenth and Early Twentieth Centuries.* New York: Elsevier, 1978.

Bradshaw, Jan, ed. "The Women's Liberation Movement—Europe and North America." *Women's Studies International Quarterly* 4, 4 (1981).

Bussey, Gertrude, and Margaret Tims. *Pioneers for Peace: Women's International League for Peace and Freedom 1915–1965.* London: George Allen & Unwin, 1965, 1980.

Dahlerup, Drude, ed. *The New Women's Movement: Feminism and Political Power in Europe and the USA.* London: Sage Publications, 1986.

Daley, Caroline, and Melanie Nolan, eds. *Suffrage and Beyond: International Feminist Perspectives.* New York: New York University Press, 1994.

DuBois, Ellen, Mari Jo Buhle, Temma Kaplan, Gerda Lerner, and Carroll Smith-Rosenberg. "Politics and Culture in Women's History: A Symposium." *Feminist Studies* 6 (Spring 1980): 26–64.

Evans, Richard J. *Comrades and Sisters: Feminism, Socialism and Pacifism in Europe, 1870–1945.* Sussex: Wheatsheaf Books, 1987.

———. *The Feminists: Women's Emancipation Movements in Europe, America and Australia, 1840–1920.* New York: Barnes & Noble, 1977.

Friedlander, Judith, Blanche Wiesen Cook, Alice Kessler-Harris, and Carroll Smith-Rosenberg, eds. *Women in Culture and Politics: A Century of Changes.* Bloomington: Indiana University Press, 1986.

Higgonet, Margaret Randolph, Jane Jenson, Sonya Michel, and Margaret Collins Weitz, eds. *Behind the Lines: Gender and the Two World Wars.* New Haven, CT: Yale University Press, 1987.

Jacoby, Robin Miller. *The British and American Women's Trade Union Leagues, 1890–1925: A Case Study of Feminism and Class.* Brooklyn: Carlson Publishing, 1994.

Kaplan, Gisela. *Contemporary Western European Feminism.* New York: New York University Press, 1992.

Koven, Seth, and Sonya Michel, eds. *Mothers of a New World: Maternalist Politics and the Origins of Welfare States.* New York: Routledge, 1993.

Meyer, Donald. *Sex and Power: The Rise of Women in America, Russia, Sweden, and Italy.* Middletown, CT: Wesleyan University Press, 1987.

Mies, Maria, and Kumari Jaywardena. *Feminism in Europe: Liberal and Socialist Strategies, 1789–1919.* The Hague: Institute of Social Studies, 1983.

Morgan, Robin, ed. *Sisterhood is Global: The International Women's Movement Anthology.* New York: Doubleday, 1984.

Pedersen, Susan. *Family, Dependence, and the Origins of the Welfare State: Britain and France, 1914–1945.* Cambridge: Cambridge University Press, 1993.

Pierson, Ruth Roach, ed. *Women and Peace: Theoretical, Historical and Practical Perspectives.* London: Croom Helm, 1987.

Sarah, Elizabeth, ed. "Special Issue: Reassessments of 'First-Wave' Feminism." *Women's Studies International Forum* 5, 6 (1982).

Slaughter, Jane, and Robert Kern, eds. *European Women on the Left: Socialism, Feminism, and the Problems Faced by Political Women, 1880 to the Present.* Westport, CT: Greenwood Press, 1981.

Wiltsher, Anne. *Most Dangerous Women: Feminist Peace Campaigners of the Great War.* London: Pandora, 1985.

Canada

Adamson, Nancy, Linda Briskin, and Margaret McPhail. *Feminist Organizing for Change: The Contemporary Women's Movement in Canada.* Toronto: Oxford University Press, 1988.

Bacchi, Carol. *Liberation Deferred? The Ideas of the English-Canadian Suffragists 1877–1918.* Toronto: University of Toronto Press, 1983.

Casgrain, Thérèse F. *A Woman in a Man's World.* Trans. Joyce Marshall. Toronto: McClelland & Stewart, 1972.

Cleverdon, Catherine L. *The Woman Suffrage Movement in Canada.* 2nd ed. Toronto: University of Toronto Press, 1974.

Clio Collective (Micheline Dumont, Michèle Jean, Marie Lavigne, and Jennifer Stoddart). *Quebec Women: A History.* Trans. Roger Gannon and Rosalind Gill. Toronto: Women's Press, 1987.

Crowley, Terry. *Agnes Macphail and the Politics of Equality.* Toronto: Lorimer, 1990.

Danylewycz, Marta. *Taking the Veil: An Alternative to Marriage, Motherhood, and Spinsterhood in Quebec, 1840–1920.* Toronto: McClelland & Stewart, 1987.

Duley, Margot. *Where Once Our Mothers Stood We Stand: Women's Suffrage in Newfoundland 1890–1925.* Charlottetown: Gynergy Books, 1993.

Hallett, Mary, and Marilyn Davis. *Firing the Heather: The Life and Times of Nellie McClung.* Saskatoon: Fifth House, 1993.

Kealey, Linda, ed. *A Not Unreasonable Claim: Women and Reform in Canada, 1880s–1920s.* Toronto: Women's Press, 1979.

Kealey, Linda, and Joan Sangster, eds. *Beyond the Vote: Canadian Women and Politics.* Toronto: University of Toronto Press, 1989.

Morris, Cerise. "'Determination and Thoroughness': The Movement for a Royal Commission on the Status of Women in Canada." *Atlantis* 5 (Spring 1980): 1–21.

Newton, Janice. *The Feminist Challenge to the Canadian Left, 1900–1918.* Montreal: McGill-Queen's University Press, 1995.

Sangster, Joan. *Dreams of Equality: Women On the Canadian Left, 1920–1950.* Toronto: McClelland & Stewart, 1989.

Strong-Boag, Veronica. "Pulling in Double Harness or Hauling a Double Load: Women, Work and Feminism on the Canadian Prairie." *Journal of Canadian Studies* 21 (Fall 1986): 32–52.

Strong-Boag, Veronica, and Anita Clair Fellman, eds. *Rethinking Canada: The Promise of Women's History.* 2nd ed. Toronto: Copp Clark Pitman, 1991.

Valverde, Mariana. "'When the Mother of the Race Is Free': Race, Reproduction, and Sexuality in First-Wave Feminism." In *Gender Conflicts: New Essays in Women's History.* Ed. Franca Iacovetta and Mariana Valverde, 3–26. Toronto: University of Toronto Press, 1992.

Williamson, Janice, and Deborah Gorham, eds. *Up and Doing: Canadian Women and Peace.* Toronto: Women's Press, 1989.

Women Unite! An Anthology of the Canadian Women's Movement. Toronto: Canadian Women's Educational Press, 1972.

France

Bair, Deirdre. *Simone de Beauvoir: A Biography.* New York: Simon & Schuster, 1990.

Beauvoir, Simone de. *The Second Sex.* Trans. H.M. Parshley. New York: Random House, 1952.

Beecher, Jonathan. *Charles Fourier: The Visionary and His World.* Berkeley: University of California Press, 1986.

Bidelman, Patrick Kay. *Pariahs Stand Up! The Founding of the Liberal Feminist Movement in France, 1858–1889.* Westport, CT: Greenwood Press, 1982.

Cross, Máire, and Tim Gray. *The Feminism of Flora Tristan.* Oxford: Berg, 1992.

Duchen, Claire. *Feminism in France: From May '68 to Mitterrand.* London: Routledge & Kegan Paul, 1986.

———. *Women's Rights and Women's Lives in France 1944–1968.* London: Routledge, 1994.

Gordon, Felicia. *The Integral Feminist: Madeleine Pelletier, 1874–1939: Feminism, Socialism and Medicine.* Cambridge: Polity Press, 1990.

Hause, Steven C. *Hubertine Auclert: The French Suffragette.* New Haven, CT: Yale University Press, 1987.

Hause, Steven C., and Anne R. Kenney. *Women's Suffrage and Social Politics in the French Third Republic.* Princeton, NJ: Princeton University Press, 1984.

Klejman, Laurence, and Florence Rochefort. *L'Égalité en Marche: Le féminisme sous la Trosième République.* Paris: des femmes, 1989.

McMillan, James F. *Housewife or Harlot: The Place of Women in French Society 1870–1940.* Brighton: Harvester Press, 1981.

Marks, Elaine, and Isabelle de Courtivron, eds. *New French Feminisms: An Anthology.* Amherst: University of Massachusetts Press, 1980.

Moses, Claire Goldberg. *French Feminism in the Nineteenth Century.* Albany: State University of New York Press, 1984.

Offen, Karen. "Depopulation, Nationalism, and Feminism in Fin-de-siècle France." *American Historical Review* 89, 3 (1984): 648–76.

Sowerwine, Charles. *Sisters or Citizens? Women and Socialism in France Since 1876.* Cambridge: Cambridge University Press, 1982.

Stetson, Dorothy McBride. *Women's Rights in France.* Westport, CT: Greenwood Press, 1987.

Tristan, Flora. *Flora Tristan, Utopian Feminist: Her Travel Diaries and Personal Crusade.* Ed. and trans. Doris Beik and Paul Bcik. Bloomington: Indiana University Press, 1993.

Germany, Austria, Switzerland, and the Netherlands

Allen, Ann Taylor. *Feminism and Motherhood in Germany, 1800–1914.* New Brunswick, NJ: Rutgers University Press, 1991.

Anderson, Harriet. *Utopian Feminism: Women's Movements in fin-de-siècle Vienna.* New Haven, CT: Yale University Press, 1992.

Bridenthal, Renate, Atina Grossmann, and Marion Kaplan, eds. *When Biology Became Destiny: Women in Weimar and Nazi Germany.* New York: Monthly Review Press, 1984.

Drewitz, Ingeborg, ed. *The German Women's Movement: The Social Role of Women in the 19th Century and the Emancipation Movement in Germany.* Bonn: Hohwacht, 1983.

Evans, Richard. *The Feminist Movement in Germany 1894–1933.* London: Sage Publications, 1976.

Fout, John C., ed. *German Women in the Nineteenth Century: A Social History.* New York: Holmes & Meier, 1984.

Frevert, Ute. *Women in German History: From Bourgeois Emancipation to Sexual Liberation.* Trans. Stuart McKinnon-Evans. Oxford: Berg, 1988.

Hogeweg-de Haart, H.P. "The History of the Women's Movement in the Netherlands." *Netherlands' Journal of Sociology* 14 (July 1978): 19–40.

Kaplan, Marion. *The Jewish Feminist Movement in Germany: The Campaigns of the Jüdischer Frauenbund, 1904–1938.* Westport, CT: Greenwood Press, 1979.

Koonz, Claudia. *Mothers in the Fatherland: Women, The Family, and Nazi Politics.* New York: St Martin's Press, 1987.

Moeller, Robert G. *Protecting Motherhood: Women and the Family in the Politics of Postwar West Germany.* Berkeley: University of California Press, 1993.

Prelinger, Catherine M. *Charity, Challenge and Change: Religious Dimensions of the Mid-Nineteenth-Century Women's Movement in Germany.* New York: Greenwood Press, 1987.

Quataert, Jean H. *Reluctant Feminists in German Social Democracy, 1885–1917.* Princeton, NJ: Princeton University Press, 1979.

Reagin, Nancy. *A German Women's Movement: Class and Gender in Hanover, 1880–1933*. Chapel Hill: University of North Carolina Press, 1995.

Vansant, Jacqueline. *Against the Horizon: Feminism and Postwar Austrian Women Writers*. New York: Greenwood Press, 1988.

Zetkin, Clara. *Clara Zetkin: Selected Writings*. Ed. Philip S. Foner. New York: International Publishers, 1984.

Great Britain

Alberti, Johanna. *Beyond Suffrage: Feminists in War and Peace, 1914–28*. New York: St Martin's Press, 1989.

Banks, Olive. *Becoming a Feminist: The Social Origins of "First Wave" Feminism*. Brighton: Wheatsheaf Books, 1986.

Bland, Lucy. *Banishing the Beast: Sexuality and the Early Feminists, 1885–1914*. New York: New Press, 1995.

Brittain, Vera. *Testament of Youth: An Autobiographical Study of the Years 1900–1925*. New York: Macmillan, 1937.

Caine, Barbara. "John Stuart Mill and the English Women's Movement." *Historical Studies* 18 (April 1978): 52–67.

———. *Victorian Feminists*. Oxford: Oxford University Press, 1992.

Coote, A., and B. Campbell. *Sweet Freedom: The Struggle for Women's Liberation*. Oxford: Basil Blackwell, 1982.

Delamont, Sara, and Lorna Duffin, eds. *The Nineteenth Century Woman: Her Cultural and Physical World*. London: Croom Helm, 1978.

Dyhouse, Carol. *Feminism and the Family in England, 1880–1939*. Oxford: Basil Blackwell, 1989.

Eoff, Shirley M. *Viscountess Rhondda, Equalitarian Feminist*. Columbus: Ohio State University Press, 1991.

Garner, Les. *Stepping Stones to Women's Liberty: Feminist Ideas in the Women's Suffrage Movement 1900–1918*. London: Heinemann, 1984.

Gleadle, Kathryn. *The Early Feminists: Radical Unitarians and the Emergence of the Women's Rights Movement, 1831–51*. Houndmills: Macmillan, 1995.

Harrison, Brian. *Prudent Revolutionaries: Portraits of British Feminists Between the Wars*. Oxford: Clarendon Press, 1987.

———. *Separate Spheres: The Opposition to Women's Suffrage in Britain*. London: Croom Helm, 1978.

Herstein, Sheila R. *A Mid-Victorian Feminist: Barbara Leigh Smith Bodichon*. New Haven, CT: Yale University Press, 1986.

Holcombe, Lee. *Wives and Property: Reform of the Married Women's Property Law in Nineteenth-Century England*. Toronto: University of Toronto Press, 1983.

Holton, Sandra. *Feminism and Democracy: Women's Suffrage and Reform Politics in Britain 1900–1918*. Cambridge: Cambridge University Press, 1986.

Hume, Leslie Parker. *The National Union of Women's Suffrage Societies, 1897–1914.* New York: Garland Publishing, 1982.

Jackson, Margaret. *The Real Facts of Life: Feminism and The Politics of Sexuality c 1850–1940.* London: Taylor & Francis, 1994.

Jeffreys, Sheila. *The Spinster and Her Enemies: Feminism and Sexuality 1880–1930.* London: Pandora, 1985.

Kent, Susan Kingsley. "The Politics of Sexual Difference: World War I and the Demise of British Feminism." *Journal of British Studies* 27 (1988): 232–53.

———. *Sex and Suffrage in Britain, 1860–1914.* Princeton, NJ: Princeton University Press, 1987.

Leneman, Leah. *A Guid Cause: The Women's Suffrage Movement in Scotland.* Aberdeen: Aberdeen University Press, 1991.

Levine, Philippa. *Feminist Lives in Victorian England: Private Roles and Public Commitment.* Oxford: Basil Blackwell, 1990.

———. *Victorian Feminism 1850–1900.* London: Hutchinson, 1987.

Liddington, Jill, and Jill Norris. *One Hand Tied Behind Us: The Rise of the Women's Suffrage Movement.* London: Virago, 1978.

McCrone, Kathleen E. "The National Association for the Promotion of Social Science and the Advancement of Victorian Women." *Atlantis* 8, 1 (1982): 44–66.

———. *Playing the Game: Sport and the Physical Emancipation of English Women, 1870–1914.* Lexington: University Press of Kentucky, 1988.

Mill, John Stuart, and Harriet Taylor Mill. *Essays on Sex Equality: John Stuart Mill and Harriet Taylor Mill.* Ed. Alice Rossi. Chicago: University of Chicago Press, 1970.

Mitchell, Hannah. *The Hard Way Up: The Autobiography of Hannah Mitchell, Suffragette and Rebel.* Ed. Geoffrey Mitchell. London: Faber and Faber, 1968.

Morgan, David. *Suffragists and Liberals: The Politics of the Woman's Movement in Britain.* Oxford: Basil Blackwell, 1975.

Murphy, Cliona. *The Women's Suffrage Movement and Irish Society in the Early Twentieth Century.* Philadelphia: Temple University Press, 1989.

Owens, Rosemary Cullen. *Smashing Times: A History of the Irish Suffrage Movement 1889–1922.* Dublin: Attic Press, 1984.

Pedersen, Susan. "The Failure of Feminism in the Making of the British Welfare State." *Radical History Review* 43 (1989): 86–110.

Pugh, Milton. *Women and the Women's Movement in Britain, 1914–59.* London: Macmillan, 1992.

Randall, Vicky. *Women and Politics.* London: Macmillan, 1982.

Rendall, Jane, ed. *Equal or Different: Women's Politics 1800–1914.* Oxford: Basil Blackwell, 1987.

Rosen, Andrew. *Rise Up, Women! The Militant Campaign of the Women's Social and Political Union, 1903–1914.* London: Routledge & Kegan, 1974.

Rubinstein, David. *Before the Suffragettes: Women's Emancipation in the 1890s.* Brighton: Harvester Press, 1986.

Rover, Constance. *Love, Morals and the Feminists.* London: Routledge & Kegan Paul, 1970.

———. *Women's Suffrage and Party Politics in Britain, 1866–1914.* London: Routledge & Kegan Paul, 1967.

Schwarzkopf, Jutta. *Women in the Chartist Movement.* London: Macmillan, 1991.

Shanley, Mary Lyndon. *Feminism, Marriage, and the Law in Victorian England, 1850–1895.* Princeton, NJ: Princeton University Press, 1989.

Smith, Harold L., ed. *British Feminism in the Twentieth Century.* Aldershot: Edward Elgar, 1990.

Spender, Dale. *There's Always Been a Women's Movement this Century.* London: Routledge & Kegan Paul, 1983.

———, ed. *Time and Tide Wait for No Man.* London: Pandora Press, 1984.

Strachey, Ray. *"The Cause": A Short History of the Women's Movement in Great Britain.* 1928. Port Washington, NY: Kennikat Press, 1969.

Stubbs, Patricia. *Women and Fiction: Feminism and the Novel, 1880–1920.* Sussex: Harvester Press, 1981.

Taylor, Barbara. *Eve and the New Jerusalem: Socialism and Feminism in the Nineteenth Century.* London: Virago Press, 1991.

Thomis, Malcolm L., and Jennifer Grimmett. *Women in Protest, 1800–1850.* London: Croom Helm, 1982.

Vicinus, Martha. *Independent Women: Work and Community for Single Women, 1850–1920.* Chicago: University of Chicago Press, 1986.

Walkowitz, Judith R. *Prostitution and Victorian Society: Women, Class and the State.* Cambridge: Cambridge University Press, 1980.

Wandor, Michelene. *Once a Feminist: Stories of a Generation.* London: Virago, 1990.

Ward, Margaret. *Unmanageable Revolutionaries: Women and Irish Nationalism.* London: Pluto Press, 1983.

Woolf, Virginia. *A Room of One's Own.* New York: Harcourt Brace Jovanovich, 1929.

———. *Three Guineas.* San Diego: Harcourt Brace Jovanovich, 1938.

Italy, Spain, and Mexico

Ackelsberg, Martha A. *Free Women of Spain: Anarchism and the Struggle for the Emancipation of Women.* Bloomington: Indiana University Press, 1991.

Birnbaum, Lucia Chiavola. *Liberazione della donna: Feminism in Italy.* Middletown, CT: Wesleyan University Press, 1986.

de Grazia, Victoria. *How Fascism Ruled Women: Italy, 1922–1945.* Berkeley: University of California Press, 1992.

Macias, Anna. *Against All Odds: The Feminist Movement in Mexico to 1940.* Westport, CT: Greenwood Press, 1982.

United States

Andolsen, Barbara Hilkert. *"Daughters of Jefferson, Daughters of Bootblacks": Racism and American Feminism.* Macon, GA: Mercer University Press, 1986.

Baker, Paula. "The Domestication of Politics: Women and American Political Society, 1780–1920." *American Historical Review* 89 (June 1984): 620–47.

Barry, Kathleen. *Susan B. Anthony: A Biography of a Singular Feminist.* New York: New York University Press, 1988.

Basch, Norma. *In the Eyes of the Law: Women, Marriage and Property in Nineteenth-Century New York.* Ithaca, NY: Cornell University Press, 1982.

Becker, Susan D. *The Origins of the Equal Rights Amendment: American Feminism Between the Wars.* Westport, CT: Greenwood Press, 1981.

Berg, Barbara J. *The Remembered Gate: Origins of American Feminism: The Woman and the City, 1800–1860.* New York: Oxford University Press, 1978.

Blair, Karen J. *The Clubwoman as Feminist: True Womanhood Redefined, 1868–1914.* New York: Holmes and Meier, 1980.

Braude, Ann. *Radical Spirits: Spiritualism and Women's Rights in Nineteenth-Century America.* Boston: Beacon Press, 1989.

Buechler, Steven N. *The Transformation of the Woman Suffrage Movement: The Case of Illinois, 1850–1920.* New Brunswick, NJ: Rutgers University Press, 1986.

Buhle, Mari Jo. *Women and American Socialism, 1870–1920.* Urbana: University of Illinois Press, 1981.

Caraway, Nancie. *Segregated Sisterhood: Racism and the Politics of American Feminism.* Knoxville: University of Tennessee Press, 1991.

Cassell, Joan. *A Group Called Women: Sisterhood & Symbolism in the Feminist Movement.* New York: Donald McKay Company, 1977.

Chafe, William H. *The Paradox of Change: American Women in the 20th Century.* New York: Oxford University Press, 1991.

Chmielewski, Wendy E., Louis J. Kern, and Marlyn Klee-Hartzell, eds. *Women in Spiritual and Communitarian Societies in the United States.* Syracuse, NY: Syracuse University Press, 1993.

Eastman, Crystal. *Crystal Eastman on Women and Revolution.* Ed. Blanche Wiesen Cook. New York: Oxford University Press, 1978.

Cott, Nancy F. *The Bonds of Womanhood: "Woman's Sphere" in New England, 1780–1835.* New Haven, CT: Yale University Press, 1977.

———. *The Grounding of Modern Feminism.* New Haven, CT: Yale University Press, 1987.

Davis, Flora. *Moving the Mountain: The Women's Movement in America Since 1960.* New York: Simon & Schuster, 1991.

DuBois, Ellen Carol, ed. *Elizabeth Cady Stanton, Susan B. Anthony: Correspondence, Writings, Speeches.* New York: Schocken, 1981.

———. *Feminism and Suffrage: The Emergence of an Independent Women's Movement in America, 1848–1869.* Ithaca, NY: Cornell University Press, 1978.

———. "The Radicalism of the Woman Suffrage Movement: Notes Toward the Reconstruction of Nineteenth-Century Feminism." *Feminist Studies* 3 (Fall 1975): 63–71.

Dye, Nancy Schrom. *As Equals and as Sisters: Feminism, the Labor Movement, and the Women's Trade Union League of New York.* Columbia: University of Missouri Press, 1980.

Echols, Alice. *Daring to Be Bad: Radical Feminism in America, 1967–1975.* Minneapolis: University of Minnesota Press, 1989.

Eckhardt, Celia Morris. *Fanny Wright: Rebel in America.* Cambridge, MA: Harvard University Press, 1984.

Epstein, Barbara Leslie. *The Politics of Domesticity: Women, Evangelism, and Temperance in Nineteenth-Century America.* Middletown, CT: Wesleyan University Press, 1981.

Evans, Sara. *Personal Politics: The Roots of Women's Liberation in the Civil Rights Movement and the New Left.* New York: Knopf, 1979.

Faderman, Lillian. *Odd Girls and Twilight Lovers: A History of Lesbian Life in Twentieth-Century America.* New York: Columbia University Press, 1991.

Feree, Myra Marx, and Beth B. Hess. *Controversy and Coalition: The New Feminist Movement across Three Decades of Change.* New York: Twayne Publishers, 1994.

Fitzgerald, Tracey. *The National Council of Negro Women and the Feminist Movement, 1935–1975.* Washington: Georgetown University Press, 1985.

Flexner, Eleanor. *Century of Struggle: The Woman's Rights Movement in the United States.* 1959. New York: Atheneum, 1972.

Frankel, Noralee, and Nancy S. Dye, eds. *Gender, Class, Race, and Reform in the Progressive Era.* Lexington: University Press of Kentucky, 1991.

Freedman, Estelle. "Separatism as Strategy: Female Institution-Building and American Feminism, 1870–1930." *Feminist Studies* 5, 3 (Fall 1979): 512–29.

Freeman, Jo. *The Politics of Women's Liberation: A Case Study of an Emerging Social Movement and its Relation to the Policy Process.* New York: David McKay, 1975.

Friedan, Betty. *The Feminine Mystique.* New York: Dell Publishing, 1963.

———. *It Changed My Life.* New York: Dell Publishing, 1991.

Gabin, Nancy. *Feminism in the Labor Movement; Women and the United Auto Workers, 1935–1975.* Ithaca, NY: Cornell University Press, 1990.

Giele, Janet Zollinger. *Two Paths to Women's Equality: Temperance, Suffrage, and the Origins of Modern Feminism.* New York: Twayne Publishers, 1995.

Ginzberg, Lori D. "'Moral Suasion Is Moral Balderdash': Women, Politics, and Social Activism in the 1850s." *Journal of American History* 73, 3 (1986): 601–22.

Griffith, Elisabeth. *In Her Own Right: The Life of Elizabeth Cady Stanton.* New York: Oxford University Press, 1984.

Guarneri, Carl. *The Utopian Alternative: Fourierism in Nineteenth-Century America.* Ithaca, NY: Cornell University Press, 1991.

Hall, Jacquelyn Dowd. *Revolt Against Chivalry: Jessie Daniel Ames and the Women's Campaign Against Lynching.* New York: Columbia University Press, 1979.

Harley, Sharon, and Rosalyn Terborg-Penn, eds. *The Afro-American Woman: Struggles and Images.* Port Washington, NY: Kennikat Press, 1978.

Harrison, Cynthia. *On Account of Sex: The Politics of Women's Issues, 1945–1968.* Berkeley: University of California Press, 1988.

Hayden, Dolores. *The Grand Domestic Revolution: A History of Feminist Designs for American Homes, Neighborhoods, and Cities.* Cambridge, MA: MIT Press, 1981.

Hersh, Blanche. *The Slavery of Sex: Feminist-Abolitionists in America.* Urbana: University of Illinois Press, 1978.

Hewitt, Nancy A. *Women's Activism and Social Change: Rochester, New York, 1822–1872.* Ithaca, NY: Cornell University Press, 1984.

Hoffert, Sylvia D. *When Hens Crow: The Woman's Rights Movement in Antebellum America.* Bloomington: Indiana University Press, 1995.

Kennedy, Elizabeth Lapovsky, and Madeline D. Davis. *Boots of Leather, Slippers of Gold: The History of a Lesbian Community.* New York: Routledge, 1993.

Klein, Ethel. *Gender Politics: From Consciousness to Mass Politics.* Cambridge: Harvard University Press, 1984.

Kolmerten, Carol A. *Women in Utopia: The Ideology of Gender in the American Owenite Communities.* Bloomington: Indiana University Press, 1990.

Kraditor, Aileen. *The Ideas of the Woman Suffrage Movement, 1890–1920.* New York: W.W. Norton, 1965.

Leach, William. *True Love and Perfect Union: The Feminist Reforms of Sex and Society.* New York: Basic Books, 1980.

Lemons, J. Stanley. *The Woman Citizen: Social Feminism in the 1920s.* Urbana: University of Illinois Press, 1973.

Lerner, Gerda. *The Grimké Sisters from South Carolina: Pioneers for Woman's Rights and Abolition.* New York: Schocken Books, 1967.

Mabee, Carleton, with Susan Mabee Newhouse. *Sojourner Truth: Slave, Prophet, Legend.* New York: New York University Press, 1993.

Meyerowitz, Joanne. "Beyond the Feminine Mystique: A Reassessment of Postwar Mass Culture, 1946–1958." In *Not June Cleaver: Women and Gender in Postwar America, 1945–1960.* Ed. Joanne Meyerowitz, 229–62. Philadelphia: Temple University Press, 1994.

Milkman, Ruth, ed. *Women, Work and Protest: A Century of Women's Labor History*. Boston: Routledge & Kegan Paul, 1985.

Morgan, Robin. *Going Too Far: The Personal Chronicle of a Feminist*. New York: Vintage Books, 1968.

———, ed. *Sisterhood is Powerful: An Anthology of Writings from the Women's Liberation Movement*. New York: Vintage Books, 1970.

Muncy, Robyn. *Creating a Female Dominion in American Reform 1890–1935*. New York: Oxford University Press, 1991.

O'Neill, William L. *Feminism in America: A History*. 2nd ed. New Brunswick, NJ: Transaction Publishers, 1989.

Parks, Rosa, with Jim Haskins. *Rosa Parks: My Story*. New York: Dial Books, 1992.

Rabkin, Peggy A. *Fathers to Daughters: The Legal Foundations of Female Emancipation*. Westport, CT: Greenwood Press, 1980.

Robinson, Jo Ann Gibson. *The Montgomery Bus Boycott and the Women Who Started It*. Ed. David J. Garrow. Knoxville: University of Tennessee Press, 1987.

Rosenberg, Rosalind. *Beyond Separate Spheres: Intellectual Roots of Modern Feminism*. New Haven, CT: Yale University Press, 1982.

Rupp, Leila J., and Verta Taylor. *Survival in the Doldrums: The American Women's Rights Movement, 1945 to the 1960s*. New York: Oxford University Press, 1987.

Scharf, Lois. *To Work and To Wed: Female Employment, Feminism, and the Great Depression*. Westport, CT: Greenwood Press, 1980.

Scharf, Lois, and Joan M. Jensen, eds. *Decades of Discontent: The Women's Movement, 1920–1940*. Westport, CT: Greenwood Press, 1983.

Schwarz, Judith. *Radical Feminists of Heterodoxy: Greenwich Village, 1912–1940*. 2nd ed. Norwich, VT: New Victoria Publishers, 1986.

Scott, Anne Firor. *Natural Allies: Women's Associations in American History*. Urbana: University of Illinois Press, 1991.

Sklar, Kathryn Kish. *Catharine Beecher: A Study in American Domesticity*. New Haven, CT: Yale University Press, 1973.

———. "Hull House in the 1890s: A Community of Women Reformers." *Signs: Journal of Women in Culture and Society* 10, 4 (1985): 658–77.

Skocpol, Theda. *Protecting Soldiers and Mothers: The Political Origins of Social Policy in the United States*. Cambridge, MA: Belknap Press, 1992.

Swerdlow, Amy. *Women Strike for Peace: Traditional Motherhood and Radical Politics in the 1960s*. Chicago: University of Chicago Press, 1993.

Tilly, Louise A., and Patricia Gurin, eds. *Women, Politics, and Change*. New York: Russell Sage Foundation, 1990.

Venet, Wendy Hamand. *Neither Ballots nor Bullets: Women Abolitionists and the Civil War.* Charlottesville: University Press of Virginia, 1991.

Walsh, Mary Roth. *Doctors Wanted, No Women Need Apply: Sexual Barriers in the Medical Profession, 1835–1975.* New Haven, CT: Yale University Press, 1977.

Wandersee, Winifred. *On the Move: American Women in the 1970s.* Boston: Twayne Publishers, 1988.

Ware, Susan. *Beyond Suffrage: Women in the New Deal.* Cambridge, MA: Harvard University Press, 1981.

———. *Still Missing: Amelia Earhart and the Search for Modern Feminism.* New York: W.W. Norton, 1993.

Yee, Shirley J. *Black Women Abolitionists: A Study in Activism, 1828–1860.* Knoxville: University of Tennessee Press, 1992.

Yellin, Jean Fagan. *Women and Sisters: Antislavery Feminists in American Culture.* New Haven, CT: Yale University Press, 1990.

Yellin, Jean Fagan, and John C. Van Horne, eds. *The Abolitionist Sisterhood: Women's Political Culture in Antebellum America.* Ithaca, NY: Cornell University Press, 1994.

Index

Flappers, 286
Forten, Charlotte, 178
Fourier, Charles, 156, 158
Fournel, Cécile, 164
Fox, George, 82
France
 and family planning movement, 323
 feminism and Industrial Revolution, 155
 feminist activities in 19th century, 192,
  218, 219
 French Revolution, 117, 134–40
 and maternal feminism, 236, 239
 post World War II feminism, 320–21
 pro-abortion movement, 344
 radical feminism, 336
 revolts by women, 139
 revolution of 1848, 168
 second-wave feminism, 332, 342
 suppression of feminism, in 19th century,
  170, 190, 213
 and women's rights, 317
 and women's suffrage, 213–14, 274, 317
 working-class women and feminism,
  250–51
Franco, Veronica, 69–70
Free love, 204–5
Freeman, Elizabeth, 133
Freemasons, 127
The Freewoman, 242, 244
French League for Women's Rights, 218
French Revolution. *See* France
Freud, Sigmund, 287
Friedan, Betty, 276, 328–29, 331, 338, 342
Froebel, Friedrich, 131, 200
Fronde, 93–94, 96
La Fronde, 196, 251
Fuller, Margaret, 65–66

Gage, Frances, 216
Gage, Matilda Joslyn, 192
Galbraith, Hazel, 338
Gallichan, Walter, 246
Gambara, Veronica, 55
Garrison, William Lloyd, 177
La Gazette des femmes, 168
Gender roles. *See also* Division of labour;
 "Separate spheres"
 challenge to assumptions of, by social sci-
  entists, 247
 education of women, as challenge to, 56
 reversion to, after World War I, 275
 and social conditioning, 108–9
 strengthened by scientific opinion, in 19th
  century, 239–40

General Austrian Women's Association, 257
General Federation of Women's Clubs, 252
General German Women's Association, 192,
 218
Gentileschi, Artemisia, 75–76, 93
German Catholicism, 175, 176
Germany
 and equal rights for women, 318–19
 feminism, after 1848, 152, 192
 feminism, and fascism, 302–4
 feminism, and socialism, 256, 257–58
 and maternal feminism, 200, 236, 239,
  302, 303
 post World War II feminism, 320
 pro-abortion movement, 344
 Prussian Law of Association, effect on feminism, 175–76
 and radical feminism, 336
 reaction against married women in workforce, 294
 reform movement, 175–76, 254
 revolution of 1848, 152, 168
 social climate after 1871, 190
 suppression of feminist and suffrage movements during
 World War I, 270
 during Weimar Republic, 277, 278
 women in politics, 282
 women's movement and social reform, 241
 and women's suffrage, 210–11, 228, 271
Gerson, Jean, 83
Gertrude the Great, 42
Gilbert, Sandra M., 72, 274
Gilman, Charlotte Perkins, 195, 202, 231,
 243, 286
Girton College, 193, 210
Gnostics, 29
Godwin, William, 142, 153
Golders Green Guildswomen, 321
Goldman, Emma, 245
Goldschmidt, Henriette, 239
Gordon, Linda, 48
Gore-Booth, Eva, 249
Gouges, Olympe de, 117, 126, 136, 137–39,
 178, 351
Gournay, Marie de, 59, 60–61, 63, 66, 108,
 127
Grassi, Angela, 196
Great Awakening, 151
Great Depression
 and backlash against feminism, 277
 and politics, 297–302
 and reaction to married women in labour
  force, 294–95

Wolstenholme, Elizabeth, 242
Woman and Socialism (Bebel), 201, 231
"Woman question." *See* "Querelle des femmes"
The Woman's Bible (Stanton), 246, 247
Woman's Christian Temperance Union (WCTU), 207, 208, 214, 277
Woman's Journal, 181
The Woman's Prize (Fletcher), 97
Women and Labor (Schreiner), 237
Women in the Nineteenth Century (Fuller), 65
Women of colour. *See also* Black women
  multiple oppressions of, 3
  and second-wave feminism, 343
Women Strike for Peace (WSP), 321, 322
Women's Charter of Rights and Liberties (McLaren), 243
Women's Club, of Hamburg, 175
Women's Educational and Industrial Union, 208
Women's Emancipation Union, 242
Women's International Conspiracy from Hell (WITCH), 339
Women's International League for Peace and Freedom (WILPF), 271, 288, 321
Women's National Loyal League, 216
Women's peace conference, 1915, 270
Women's Political Council, 324
Women's Protective and Provident League, 210
Women's rights conventions, 190, 192, 195, 198, 199. *See also* Seneca Falls meeting, 1848
The Women's Sharpe Revenge, 111
Women's Social and Political Union (WSPU), 227–28, 244, 249–50, 269, 272
Women's Speaking Justified (Fell), 89
Women's Trade Union League (WTUL), 251
Woodbridge, Linda, 96, 97, 100, 105
Woodhull, Victoria, 204, 205
Woodward, Charlotte, 7
Woolf, Virginia, 11, 14, 72, 193, 304
Work, household. *See also* Division of labour
  assumed as women's role, 243–44
  changes in, as result of Industrial Revolution, 153–55
  and feminism, 293–97
  increase in housekeeping standards, 291
  and labour-saving devices, 202

as legal responsibility of women in Germany until 1977, 319
as task of women, 200–3
value of, in 17th century, 100–1
and "wages for housework" proposal, 202, 243
Workers' Union (Tristan), 167, 168
Working-class
  conditions of, in 19th century, 189
  political movements, in 19th century, 160–62
Working class women. *See also* Socialism
  benefits from World War I, 274–75
  and feminism, 136–37, 208–9, 249–54, 296
  "Les femmes nouvelles," 163–66
  ignored by 19th century US feminists, 181
  lesbian culture, 323–24
  and marriage, 198, 291
  and public space, 13
  and right to stay at home, 253
  and socialism, 247
  strikes, 162
  and suffrage, 252, 285
  and unions, 161–62, 209–10, 251–52
World War I
  and backlash against feminism, 274–76
  effect on feminist movement, 269
  and women's suffrage, 226–27
World War II
  and end of unemployment, 295
  and feminism, 313–19
Wright, Fanny, 148, 170–72, 171
Writers, women
  15th century, 102
  between 1500–1650, 66, 68–74
  and "anxiety of authorship," 72
  effect of Protestant Reformation on, 85
  self-deprecation, 68
Wroth, Mary Sidney, 56

Youmans, Letitia, 238

Zahn-Harnack, Agnes von, 320
Zayas, Maria de, 67, 124
Zelensky, Anne, 336
Zell, Katharina, 90
Zetkin, Clara, 231, 244, 255, 256, 258, 270